Learning and Memory

This thoroughly updated edition provides a balanced review of the core methods and the latest research on animal learning and human memory. The relevance of basic principles is highlighted throughout via everyday examples to ignite student interest, along with more traditional examples from human and animal laboratory studies. Individual differences in age, gender, learning style, cultural background, or special abilities (such as the math gifted) are highlighted within each chapter to help students see how the principles may be generalized to other subject populations.

The basic processes of learning – such as classical and instrumental conditioning and encoding and storage in long-term memory in addition to implicit memory, spatial learning, and remembering in the world outside the laboratory – are reviewed. The general rules of learning are described along with the exceptions, limitations, and best applications of these rules. The relationship between the fields of neuropsychology and learning and memory is stressed throughout.

The relevance of this research to other disciplines is reflected in the tone of the writing and is demonstrated through a variety of examples from education, neuropsychology, rehabilitation, psychiatry, nursing and medicine, I/O and consumer psychology, and animal behavior.

Each chapter begins with an outline and concludes with a detailed summary. A website for instructors and students accompanies the book.

Updated throughout with new research findings and examples the new edition features:

- A streamlined presentation for today's busy students. As in the past, the author supports each concept with a research example and real-life application, but the duplicate example or application now appears on the website so instructors can use the additional material to illustrate the concepts in class.
- Expanded coverage of neuroscience that reflects the current research of the field including aversive conditioning (Ch. 5) and animal working memory (Ch. 8).
- More examples of research on student learning that use the same variables discussed in the chapter, but applies them in a classroom or student's study environment. This includes research that applies encoding techniques to student learning, for example: studying: recommendations from experts (Ch. 1); the benefits of testing (Ch. 9); and Joshua Foer's *Moonwalking with Einstein*, on his quest to become a memory expert (Ch. 6).
- More coverage of unconscious learning and knowledge (Ch. 11).
- Increased coverage of reinforcement and addiction (Ch. 4); causal and language learning (Ch. 6); working memory (WM) and the effects of training on WM, and the comparative evolution of WM in different species (Ch. 8); and genetics and learning (Ch. 12).

W. Scott Terry is Professor of Psychology at the University of North Carolina at Charlotte where he teaches psychology of learning to undergraduate and graduate students in I/O, clinical psychology, and education.

Learning and Memory

Basic Principles, Processes, and Procedures

Fifth Edition

W. Scott Terry

Routledge
Taylor & Francis Group

NEW YORK AND LONDON

Fifth edition published 2018
by Routledge
711 Third Avenue, New York, NY 10017

and by Routledge
2 Park Square, Milton Park, Abingdon, Oxon, OX14 4RN

Routledge is an imprint of the Taylor & Francis Group, an informa business

© 2018 Taylor & Francis

First edition published by Pearson Education, Inc. 2000
Fourth edition published by Pearson Education, Inc. 2009

Library of Congress Cataloging-in-Publication Data
A catalog record for this book has been requested

ISBN: 978-1-138-64591-2 (hbk)
ISBN: 978-1-315-62278-1 (ebk)

Typeset in Times New Roman
by Apex CoVantage, LLC
Printed and bound by CPI Group (UK) Ltd, Croydon, CR 4YY

Visit the companion website: www.routledge.com/cw/Terry

To Lorraine Piersanti Terry

Brief Contents

Contents

6 Verbal Learning   129

Preface

Learning and remembering what we have learned are fundamental psychological processes. The scientific study of learning and memory over the last 100 years has produced a sizable body of principles, laws, and sometimes only heuristic rules. During this same 100-year period, researchers who study learning have been asked to provide instruction in these principles. What do we know about learning, and how can this knowledge be usefully applied? My approach to writing a book on learning and memory is to present the basic methods and results of our research and to emphasize the relevance of our research to other disciplines.

I had several goals in mind in writing this book. The topical coverage is restricted to basic and central processes, such as classical and instrumental conditioning and encoding and storage in long-term memory. Yet today these basic processes should also include implicit memory, spatial learning, and remembering in the world outside the laboratory. In addition to presenting some general rules for learning, it is just as important to specify the exceptions and limitations to those rules. When is spaced practice or immediate reinforcement better, and when might massed practice or delayed reward be better?

I have tried to write a book that will appeal to a broad audience by including a range of research examples from education, neuropsychology, psychiatry, nursing, advertising, and ecological (or everyday) memory. I value basic research on learning and memory. This includes laboratory studies, often of animals, as fundamental means of determining the principles by which learning occurs and memory persists. Yet in my own teaching, I have found that the relevance of these basic principles needs to be made clear consistently. Lecturers often use everyday examples to maintain student interest. I believe that a more important purpose is to illustrate how basic principles can be translated into applications. It is simply not sufficient to be skilled and knowledgeable in the basics. Experts in animal conditioning are not necessarily good dog trainers. We also need to consider the extent to which our laboratory results will generalize to other subject populations that differ in age, personality, learning style, or cultural background.

A book on learning should also include aids to facilitate learning. Each chapter begins with an outline and concludes with a detailed summary. Review and recapitulation paragraphs are interspersed in the chapters. Some topics and terms are repeated across chapters. Important terms are in boldface, and these also appear in the glossary at the end of the book. An instructor's website is available, which includes lecture outlines, additional material for use in class, suggested readings, student activities, and links to online videos. A separate set of test questions is also available.

Acknowledgments

A number of people have influenced me, either directly or indirectly, in writing this book. I had the good fortune to have had mentors both in college and graduate school. At Fairfield University, the example set by Ron Salafia determined my choice of a career as a teacher and researcher in the field of learning. At Yale, Allan Wagner, in his classroom and in his laboratory, became a lasting role model and mentor. Both Ron and Allan, and their respective universities, offered exciting environments in which to learn. (A note to students: My guess is that many of your professors and instructors had similar relationships that led to their own decisions to become teachers. Ask them about it.)

I would also like to thank my extended Terry family for encouragement, and patience in living with an absent-minded professor; and a new generation of Terry children who have renewed my wonder in the potential for learning.

In addition, a number of people were directly involved. My editors—Becky Pascal, Carolyn Merrill, Susan Hartman, Stephen Frail at Allyn & Bacon, and now Paul Dukes at Taylor and Francis—have given me encouragement and support, not to mention their professional expertise. They each have worked to meld my interests with those of other instructors. Renata Corbani and the team at Apex CoVantage provided invaluable editing and production expertise.

Several university and college instructors commented on chapters and successive drafts of the several editions of this book, providing extensive commentary and their own insights into this field. For their efforts, I am both grateful and respectful. Any errors and mistakes that remain are mine, and the reviewers can safely reply, "I told you so."

Finally, I would like to thank my students, both undergraduate and graduate, from the last too-many years, for letting me try out ideas on them. I have found that if you present things in a good-natured manner, students will respond similarly. They have been a valuable source of feedback.

1 Introduction

Students who take a course in the psychology of learning are usually pretty knowledgeable about learning by the time they have reached this point. Through instruction and on-the-job training, they have already picked up numerous everyday, commonsense principles about how to learn. Students can readily tell their instructors that it is better to spread studying over several days rather than to cram it all into one day (what psychologists call *the spaced versus massed practice effect*), and that temporary forgetting for otherwise well-known information occurs, especially on exam days (what we otherwise call *retrieval failure*). Students are aware of what psychologists call *context-dependent learning*, that it is better to study in the place in which you will take the test. These practical principles are accurate as broad generalities, but they are also only partially true. They are half-truths. This is a book full of half-truths.

Let me quickly explain what I mean. There are numerous facts, laws, and principles of learning that have been uncovered over the past 120 years that psychology has formally been in existence. However, these principles are more complex than the simple statements we popularly use to describe them (e.g., spaced practice is better than massed practice). Statements of these principles almost always require qualifiers; they are true under certain conditions. In this book, I will attempt to tell both halves, and thus in the end something closer to the truth as we know it now.

Take some well-known popular generalizations. Spaced practice produces better learning than does massed practice. Well, yes, usually. But much depends on what we are attempting to learn and how long we will have to retain it, just two of several possible qualifiers we might add here. Actually, one line of research on remembering people's names suggests that it is better to mass repetitions of a given name at first, and then gradually lengthen the interval between successive presentations (Landauer & Bjork, 1978).[1] Repeat the new name immediately; repeat it again after a little while; and keep increasing the interval to the next repetition. As a second example, common sense seems to say that feedback is more effective when it is given immediately and consistently after each performance of a behavior. Yet, this is not always so. Skilled movements are sometimes learned better with delayed or only occasional feedback (see Chapter 11).

Other forms of learning pose questions that have alternative correct answers. Do subliminal audio messages, such as suggestions to induce self-control or weight loss, work? Both yes and no answers can be defended. Some data indicate they are effective, but more probably due to a placebo effect. Does this mean that there is no such thing as subliminal learning? No, learning can occur at many levels of awareness or consciousness. Does sleep learning occur? Instead of buying the hard-copy version of this text, should you get the audio version to listen to throughout the night? The answer depends on what you mean by *learning*. Research conducted in sleep labs indicates that factual information is probably not being learned, but possibly some other forms of learning (such as conditioning of the Pavlov variety) might occur.

The point of these examples is to give a sample of what real principles of learning look like. The goal of this book is to present a scientifically accurate and sophisticated view of the principles of learning. And this includes the qualifying statements: when a given principle holds and when exceptions occur. We can simplify a description to aid comprehension, but it can be simplified only so much before it becomes inaccurate.

The Origins of the Study of Learning

The field of research broadly described as learning has its origins in philosophy and science. In particular, the philosophical movements of empiricism and rationalism in the seventeenth and eighteenth centuries, and the development of evolution theory within biology in the nineteenth century, fostered an interest in the scientific investigation of learning. These movements are active influences in contemporary psychology.

Philosophy of Epistemology

The nature–nurture question, which asks how we are affected by biology on the one hand (i.e., nature) and by environment on the other (i.e., nurture), has long been a source of literary, political, and scientific speculation. If a child were raised in isolation from others, what would that child know? Would the child grow to be kind and just, or cruel and selfish? The philosopher Rousseau thought that "noble" peoples would be discovered living beyond the reach of the degrading influences of civilization. However, the discovery feral children, living apart from other humans, were intellectually and emotionally disabled (Candland, 1993).

The area of philosophy known as **epistemology** studies how we come to have knowledge. This is also the central question for the field of learning. The philosopher Descartes, while not denying that we learn, said that some knowledge is innately given, for example, our ideas of God, infinity, or perfection. This belief is known as **nativism**. Other knowledge is derived by reason, logic, and intuition, as illustrated by the derivation of geometric axioms and algebraic logic. This source of knowledge is known as rationalism. In each case, knowledge is present independent of particular experiences with the world (Descartes, 1641/1960).

By contrast, the British philosopher John Locke (1690/1956) said that the origin of knowledge is in experience, as provided to the mind through the senses. This is the notion of **empiricism**. For instance, our notion of cause and effect derives from our frequent experiences in which one event in the world is regularly followed by another event. What are the origins of our mental associations, such as from STOP to GO or TABLE to CHAIR? Locke said they derive from frequent contiguity: They occur close together in time or space. Therefore, their ideas are also contiguous in our minds.

The influence from empiricism led psychologists to investigate how we acquire knowledge through environmental experiences, and also made them receptive to the study of association learning. For example, how could a dog come to associate two stimuli? By using Pavlov's method of conditioning, experimenters could pair a tone with food several times, and then look for changes in the dog's reactions to the tone. Here we see the associative principles of contiguity and frequency.

Evolution

Nineteenth-century advances in the sciences also influenced the field of learning. One of the most significant influences was Charles Darwin's *On the Origin of Species*, published in 1859. Darwin's theory of **evolution** described how organisms change over generations in order to better adapt to the environment to which they are exposed. Darwin first noted that there were differences among members of a species; not all individuals were identical. Some of these differences increased the likelihood of survival and reproduction. If these differences were inherited, then the evolution of adaptive specializations would occur across generations.

The capacity to learn evolved as an adaptive specialization. Whereas evolution theory at first stressed anatomical changes over generations as a means of adapting to the environment, psychologists emphasized learning as a means of adapting within the organism's lifetime. In addition, the belief that different species were related through a common evolutionary history suggested that animals other than humans could be studied, with generalizations proceeding in either direction along the phylogenetic scale.

Contemporary Influences

This discussion of philosophy and biology may seem to be of historical interest at best, but each has had a continuous influence on the field of learning. In one contemporary example, the ideas of nativism, empiricism, and evolution are represented in a theory of *biological preparedness* for learning. For example, language is thought to be a biologically prepared form of learning in humans, something we learn quickly and readily due to our evolutionary history. This is shown by several aspects of human language: its universality; its common developmental progression in children across cultures; the fact that it is readily acquired even in language-poor environments; the possibility that there is a critical period for learning language; and that certain areas of the brain seem dedicated to language (Pinker, 1994). Environment is also essential to language development, determining the particular language we learn and the specific rules of our native language. But the fact that we even learn a language, as complex as this is and as intellectually immature as we are as infants, suggests the existence of a biological predisposition.

Another example of nature–nurture interaction is the theory that evolution has produced several memory systems through which organisms can learn. There may be specialized systems, such as one for song learning in birds or face memory by primates. Other systems might accommodate incremental learning of habits versus the memory for individual moments that so characterizes human memory (Sherry & Schacter, 1987). The point I am making here is that contemporary theory reflects the nativism of Descartes, the empiricism of Locke, and the evolution theory of Darwin.

The Definition of Learning

Learning is the acquisition of knowledge. Just as the philosophers of epistemology are interested in the nature and origin of knowledge, so also are psychologists. However, psychologists have defined learning both broadly and in a manner amenable to scientific study. Knowledge must be broadly defined to include not just verbal knowledge, but also skills, attitudes, and knowledge or behavior outside conscious awareness. (See Table 1.1.) So in addition to an intuitive definition of learning, scientific study requires a precise, operational definition of what can be observed as indicators that learning has occurred. Thus, the study of learning is guided formally by an objective definition, as well as informally by the actual practices and interests of the researchers.

Learning may be defined as a relatively permanent change in behavior or behavioral repertoire that occurs as a result of experience. This formal definition specifies what is included under the rubric of learning, and, just as important, what is to be excluded. This definition has several components.

First, learning involves an observed *change in behavior.* The point here is that the detection of learning requires some objective evidence. Learning and memory themselves are not observed directly; they are processes that occur in the nervous system. As much as we may be interested in the inner workings of the brain or mind, we often need to observe the organism's behavior in order see what is going on inside.

Certainly, researchers are coming closer to detecting the neural basis of learning. For instance, PET scans show which brain regions are active when we remember (Raichle, 1994). But each instance of learning and remembering involves nervous processes that are as yet undetectable. Learning and memory are therefore treated as hypothesized theoretical processes that intervene between the environment (which we can manipulate) and behavior (which we can measure).

What kinds of behaviors can we use to measure learning? Learning outcomes are multidimensional. Consider an experience you may have had as a child: a sibling jumping out of a darkened

Table 1.1 The Breadth of Learning

The everyday use of the term learning does not describe all of the diverse phenomena that psychologists study in the field of learning. Hillner (1978, pp. 1–2) presented a list of some of what is included by the term:

1. Learning encompasses both animal and human behavior. It is applicable to the behavior of intact or whole organisms, and even to the adaptive behavior of inanimate model systems such as computer simulations.
2. Learning involves events as diverse as the acquisition of an isolated muscle twitch, a prejudice, a symbolic concept, or a neurotic symptom.
3. Learning includes both the external responses of the organism and internal physiological responses.
4. Learning is concerned with the original acquisition of a response or knowledge, with its later disappearance (extinction), its retention over time (memory), and its possible value in the acquisition of new responses (transfer of training).
5. Learning is related to such nonlearning phenomena as motivation, perception, development, personality, and social and cultural factors.
6. Learning deals with the behavior of the average subject and with individual differences among people.
7. The study of learning is associated with a long academic and scholarly tradition but also serves as a source of practical application and technology.
8. The learning process is continuous with the more general linguistic, cognitive, information-processing, and decision-making activities of the organism.

room or closet in order to scare you. The fear learned from such an episode could be expressed *verbally* in your recollections of the event years later; *physiologically* by increased heart rate in fearful anticipation of a repeat of the episode; and *behaviorally* by the avoidance of entering dark hallways or rooms in the house.

The measurement of learning is nicely illustrated by an example from personnel psychology. For instance, say a psychologist has conducted a training workshop in an employment setting. How do we know what the workshop participants learned? Kraiger, Ford, and Salas (1993) suggested using three types of assessments. One outcome of training is the factual knowledge that the participants can recall. Another outcome is skill learning, represented by some behavior that the participants can now do more quickly or accurately. A final outcome would be affective (or attitude) changes. Do the employees now feel more competent, confident, or committed after training?

Learning involves changes in *behavioral repertoire*, or the stock of behaviors that might be performed. Not all learning is immediately evidenced by overt behaviors. What you have just learned from this text is probably not affecting your behavior now. Thus, the definition of learning includes the potential for a change in behavior to be demonstrated when testing conditions prompt the display of this new knowledge.

The distinction between potential and actual changes in behavior is demonstrated nicely by a classic study of socially learned aggression. Albert Bandura and his students conducted a series of studies showing that children imitate aggressive behaviors that they see adult models perform (e.g., Bandura, 1965). Children watched a videotape in which the models punched an inflated clown doll, or BoBo doll, by kicking it, throwing it, and so on. The children were later allowed to play with the BoBo doll. In one condition of the experiment, the model in the tape had been praised for playing aggressively, and the children later imitated many of the specific aggressive behaviors. In another condition, the model had been scolded for misbehaving, and the children who had seen this version of the tape now performed many fewer aggressive responses (see Figure 1.1). So far, we have a difference in the observed behavior between the two experimental conditions: Children imitated the praised model and less so the scolded model. Then the

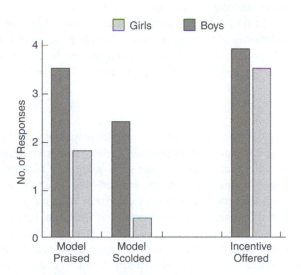

Figure 1.1 Mean number of different aggressive responses imitated by children during the first phase of testing as a function of the consequences to the model they had observed and the number of responses imitated when an incentive was offered to perform.

Source: Bandura (1965).

experimenter offered a reward for each aggressive response the child could reproduce. For the children who had seen the scolded model, the incentives increased imitation of the aggressive behaviors. For these children, the aggressive behaviors were part of the behavioral repertoire, even though they were not immediately displayed.

The Bandura study is also important for showing that the gender difference in aggressive behavior disappeared when incentives were offered to demonstrate what the model had done. The girls remembered the aggressive behaviors they had observed, but they inhibited imitating these responses until it was acceptable to do so.

Learning occurs *as a result of experience.* This book attempts to describe what some of these learning-producing experiences are. They may be as varied as a conditioning experiment conducted in the lab, a lecture heard, a skill practiced, or an attitude developed due to some now unrecalled event. The definition of learning excludes those changes in behavior that are not due to experience. One such nonlearning source of behavioral change is maturation. Organisms show some behavioral changes because of the physical, neural, or cognitive maturation that takes place over time. For example, when sparrows reach a certain age and at a certain time of year, they begin to sing. In some species, singing is not dependent on particular learning experiences of having heard other birds sing. Singing, and even the particular song, is innate. In human infants, walking is also dependent on maturation. Physical maturation in the muscles and the bones and cognitive maturation of coordination allow walking to occur. When we casually talk about children learning to walk, we are wrong in thinking that these skills are dependent only on learning. As we will see in what follows, however, the line between biological maturation and learning is often blurred. The point of the *experience* phrase in the definition is to ask us to consider what is the source of a behavior change.

Finally, learning is said to be *relatively permanent.* This may seem contrary to everyday experiences in which we all too frequently forget facts, names, appointments, and so on. But we may in fact remember more than we realize. After 40 years, people still recognized 70 percent of their high school classmates' names and pictures, although at first, only 20 percent of their graduating class could be named (Bahrick, Bahrick, & Wittlinger, 1975). Thus, much more was learned than was apparent on tests of the ability to recall names.

The purpose of the "relatively permanent" phrase is to exclude transient changes in behavior, changes that are not due to learning. Responding could temporarily fluctuate due to increases or decreases in, as examples, arousal, fatigue, or motivation. For example, rats run faster in a maze if they are hungrier, and slower if they are satiated. This does not mean they suddenly "know more" (or know less) about the maze's route. We have to separate the transient effects of variables such as arousal and motivation from their permanent effects on learning (Kimble, 1967).

Some Caveats

The study of learning includes phenomena that do not fit precisely within the formal definition. There are gray areas. One is the distinction between biology and environment.

The attribution of behavioral changes to either environment or biology is sometimes a false dichotomy. There is an inseparable interplay between the two, and the line between learning and other experientially based changes is not always clear. For instance, we say learning is based on experience. Yet experience affects the development of the brain, too. Exposing immature rat pups to an enriched environment, one with toys and other rats, enhances development of one area of the brain important for learning, the hippocampus. Both the number of nerve cells and the number of connections among them are increased (Rampon et al., 2000). These rats will be better at learning certain tasks (such as recognizing new objects or smells) than rats from more standard environments (Kemperman, Kuhn, & Gage, 1997). So, there can be a permanent change as a result of experience that we would not attribute to learning, even though some phrases of the definition of learning certainly fit.

Another gray area with respect to our definition is the separation between learning and maturation. The problem here is that the two interact with one another. How can we tell where one leaves off and the other begins?

At one extreme, there are some human behaviors that are substantially influenced by maturation. Infant development of sitting upright, standing, and eventually walking are primary examples. Gesell and Thompson (1929) conducted a classic experiment in which one infant twin of a pair received several weeks of practice at stair climbing. The other twin, denied this explicit practice, later took only a week to equal the proficiency the practiced sibling had achieved in four weeks. Similarly, Lenneberg (1967) describes a child who had been prevented from practicing language sounds for several months by a tracheal tube. When the tube was removed the child showed age-appropriate prelanguage development, progressing through the stages of cooing, babbling, and so on. In Gesell's case, early practice gave little benefit, and in Lenneberg's case, the absence of practice produced little decrement.

Other behaviors clearly illustrate the interaction of experience and maturation. Marler's (1970) study of white-crowned sparrows is especially instructive here. The male's song during breeding season shows variability across geographic regions. Marler raised some birds in isolation from others of their type. When singing began several months after hatching, the birds sang a song that was, in outline, the appropriate song for the white-crowned sparrows. However, in detail, the song was significantly different or abnormal. Exposing the birds to a song of their own type during the period from 10 to 50 days after hatching leads to normal song development. Thus, song is determined by the interaction of maturation (an innate predisposition) and learning (experience with specific songs). (See Ball & Hulse, 1998, for a review of research on the development of birdsong.)

The continued development of the brain after birth allows certain learning and memory abilities to appear. For instance, the hippocampus continues to develop over the first six months of life. During this time period the ability to remember specific experiences for short periods of time (such as a toy just seen) appears in children. During the second year of life, the connecting fibers between the two sides of the brain develop further. Children during their second year begin to attach emotional feelings, primarily processed in the right side of the brain, to knowledge of objects or situations, processed in the left side (Kagan, 2011). So, the ability to remember in infants is dependent on the maturational level of the brain.

The Learning/Performance Distinction

Earlier, we noted that learning itself is not directly observed. This process occurs in the mind or the brain, which is beyond direct observation. Instead, we infer that learning has occurred based on some behavior of the organism. **Performance** refers to the measures of behavior or memory used to indicate whether learning has occurred. However, these behavioral measures are sometimes imperfect and indirect. There is not always a one-to-one correspondence between what the organism knows and what the organism does.

Sometimes no behavioral change is observed even though (we realize later) learning has occurred. The classic example of this is Tolman and Honzik's (1930) study of **latent learning**. Rats were placed in a maze but were not given food or any other explicit reward in the goal box. Not surprisingly, the rats persisted in entering the blind alleys (that is, dead-ends) day after day. (Other rats which were fed in the goal box learned to run directly to the goal box.) When food was suddenly offered in the goal box, there was an immediate improvement in performance. The animals now made few wrong turns on their way to the goal box. The rats had indeed learned the layout of the maze in those previous trials without food reward, but this knowledge remained hidden until the subjects were motivated to complete the maze quickly. Latent learning is knowledge that is not displayed in performance. Similarly, your knowledge of this chapter may remain latent until an exam is given. The absence of performance has been aptly referred to as the "problem of behavioral silence" (Dickinson, 1980). If there is no change in behavior, we really do not know whether learning has not occurred or learning has occurred and is hidden.

Test anxiety may be one too-familiar illustration of the learning–performance distinction. Students who truly know the material can perform poorly on the exam because of excessive anxiety. Their performance does not accurately assess their underlying learning. (To cite one extreme case, Capretta and Berkun [1962] noted that soldiers crossing an unstable rope bridge over a deep ravine performed worse on a memory task than when tested under nonstress conditions.) The phenomenon of stereotype threat similarly shows that performance does not always match underlying ability. There are negative stereotypes about the abilities of certain groups, for example that women have trouble with math or that the elderly are forgetful. Reminding someone who is a member of that group of the stereotype can negatively affect their performance. Thus, instructions to a senior citizen that state "we are going to test your memory" and "we are interested in how good your memory is" can prime aging-forgetfulness worries. Older adults might then perform more poorly than younger adults. If neutral instructions had been given, the age difference could have been smaller or absent altogether (Rahhal, Hasher, & Colcombe, 2001).

Learning: A Recapitulation

Let's review the key ideas of the previous sections. Research on learning is guided by a formal definition that makes our study more objective: Learning is a relatively permanent change in behavior, or behavioral repertoire, that is due to experience. This definition excludes changes in behavior that are transient, and are thus likely to reflect behavioral changes due to fluctuations in attention, motivation, or arousal level. The study of learning intersects with studies of innate or maturationally determined behaviors. Although our formal definition emphasizes changed behavior as an indicant of learning, we also acknowledge that behavioral performance can be a misleading indicator of what has been learned.

The Relationship Between the Terms *Learning* and *Memory*

The words *learning* and *memory* in everyday language have related but distinct uses. The same holds for the technical meanings within psychology. The distinctions psychologists make are both ones of denotation (or exact meanings) and of connotation (suggested or implied meanings). Thus, in the past learning was used to refer to conditioning and reinforcement, to (nonhuman) animal subjects, or to skills requiring repeated practice. Memory was used in reference to verbal recall tasks, to studies of human subjects, and to material presented for study just once. These represent the connotative meanings of learning and memory: what the terms have usually implied. There are exceptions to each of these rules, such that each distinction (e.g., animal versus human) does not perfectly correspond with the difference between learning versus memory.

A more exact distinction is to say that learning refers to acquiring knowledge or behavior, whereas **memory** refers to retaining and recalling the knowledge or behavior. As a researcher or student, one could primarily be interested in the *acquisition*, or encoding, of new information: learning associations among stimuli, learning skills, or learning facts. Or, after these things have been learned, one could be interested in the *retention*, or retrieval, of the associations, skills, or facts. Essentially, we make a distinction between two phases and attempt to study each separately.

For instance, in studying learning, one might consider those factors that affect acquisition, such as the amount of reinforcement, the spacing of study trials, or the presence of individuals who model certain behaviors. We would illustrate the development or progression of learning by a learning curve. The **learning curve** is a graphic plot of some measure of behavior on the *Y*, or vertical, axis (e.g., number or size of the correct responses) as a function of the number of trials given shown on the *X*, or horizontal, axis (see Box 1.1). Such a study might make minimal demands on memory by testing learning after short intervals of time. On the other hand, in studying memory, one might consider those factors that affect the retention or retrieval of the previously learned material, such as the length of the retention interval, or the presence of distracting activities during that interval. We could measure the course of memory by a forgetting curve. This would be a plot of the measure of behavior (again, the number or size of the correct responses) as a function of time or events since learning was completed. Sometimes minimal demands are made on the learning portion of the study by presenting easily acquired material that can be immediately remembered.

Box 1.1   The Learning Curve

The phrase *learning curve* has entered everyday language, often used as a metaphor in comparing individuals. One person is said to be farther along the learning curve than another, for instance. An advertisement for computer software claims it will put you farther ahead of your competitors on the learning curve. What exactly is the learning curve?

The phrase refers to a particular shape of the curve that develops over training trials, particularly as described by Clark Hull, a prominent Yale learning theorist of the 1940s (Hull, 1943). He said the basic learning curve is a negatively accelerated curve. This means that learning (or rather performance, which is what is actually measured) starts off with a period of very rapid growth, in which each trial produces large increments in performance. These increments get smaller and smaller on later trials, which is what negative acceleration means. There is a point of diminishing returns, such that continued practice has smaller benefits. Figure 1.2 shows the hypothetical increments across successive trials as Hull depicted them.

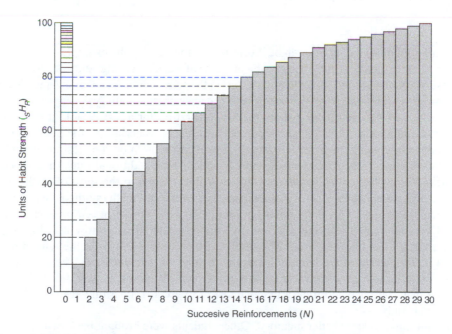

Figure 1.2 **Hull's Theoretical Learning Curve.** Notice that the increases in height in the curve are smaller and smaller across trials. This is a negatively accelerated learning curve.

Source: From *Principles of Behavior* (pp. 108, 116, 117), by C. L. Hull, 1943, New York: Appleton-Century-Crofts. Adapted with permission.

We could make an analogy to learning how to play tennis. At first, the improvements with each lesson may be fairly large. With yet more practice, improvements seem smaller. Performance may eventually reach an asymptote, or plateau, after which little or no further improvement is seen.

Learning curves are not always negatively accelerated. Sometimes performance improves very slowly at first, and then the negatively accelerated process kicks in. This produces an S-shaped curve: small increments at the start of training, large increments in the middle, and a return to slow growth at the end. So, to say that you are farther along the learning curve may mean that you are in the phase of rapid acceleration or have passed through it, whereas someone else is still stuck in that early phase of slow growth.

This prototypical learning curve has been documented in many situations, and is incorporated in contemporary theories of learning (e.g., the Rescorla-Wagner theory; see Chapter 3). Although the learning curve may be an accurate description of what we do observe, its interpretation can be challenged. By averaging over subjects whose individual performances vary, we produce a curve that may not accurately represent any one subject (Gallistel, Fairhurst, & Balsam, 2004).

Other theorists suggest that the rate of growth is better described by a power curve (e.g., Newell & Rosenbloom, 1981). This means that the *trials* units are expressed in log numbers. That is, the first point is trial 1, the next point is trial 10, then trial 100, etc. This compresses the larger numbers and produces a straight line rather than a curve.

The opposite of the learning curve is the *forgetting curve*. Here we would plot the amount remembered at different intervals of time after learning has been completed. Over time there is a decline in what can be recalled, the opposite of the learning curve. Is forgetting rapid or gradual? Is the rate of loss constant or does it vary? Forgetting curves can also take different forms. (A forgetting curve is shown in Figure 6.1, Chapter 6.)

The learning-memory distinction can be illustrated by considering the example of taking a test on learning and memory. We often measure the progress of learning during study or shortly thereafter. Certain variables lead to faster learning. But do the same conditions that enhance learning also produce better retention days or weeks later? The answer is, not always.

For example, say that you have just studied in preparation for a test. Would it be better to study the material another time, or take a practice test on the material? A first guess might be that additional study would be a better strategy. However, research on the "testing effect" (see Chapter 9) shows that a practice test can be more beneficial than additional study time. Roediger and Karpicke (2006) had college students study new information in the form of textbook-like paragraphs. One group of subjects (or *participants*, as we now call them) studied the paragraphs twice. A second group read the paragraphs once and then took a practice test on what they had just read. Everyone took a test, the real test, five minutes later. This is how learning is often measured, shortly after the study trial. The results of this test are shown in the left set of bars in Figure 1.3. The height of the bars indicates the number of facts recalled. The students who studied the material twice remembered slightly more facts (81 percent) than did students who had read the material once and took a practice test (75 percent). Learning seems to be better with additional study.

Which condition produces better memory? Other students were brought back two days or one week later to take the final test. The middle and right sets of bars in Figure 1.3 show that, at these times, the study-and-practice test groups remembered more facts than did the study-twice groups. For instance, the students who took the practice test recalled more a week later (56 percent correct) than did those who studied twice (42 percent). That is, although studying twice may have

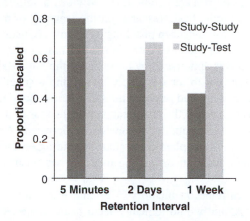

Figure 1.3 **Subjects Studied Twice or Studied Once and Took a Practice Test.** Learning was tested with different groups 5 minutes later, 2 days later, or one week later.

Source: From "Test-enhanced learning," by H. L. Roediger, III, and J. D. Karpicke, 2006, *Psychological Science, 17*, p.250. Copyright the Authors, 2006.

produced better recall in the short term, replacing additional study with a practice test produced more correct answers in the long-term.

In this example, we might say that learning is being studied during the initial session, whereas memory is studied in the second session. You might argue (validly) that the learning phase also tested memory by requiring recall even after five minutes. Indeed, some psychologists assert that any test of learning also involves a test of memory (e.g., Spear & Riccio, 1994).

So how do we decide whether any variable is better or worse if different results are found in acquisition versus retention studies, as shown in Roediger and Karpicke's (2006) experiment? Such discrepancies extend beyond individual experiments. Schmidt and Bjork (1992) made the important point that "Rather than viewing learning and posttraining retention as separable . . . we argue that the effectiveness of learning is revealed by . . . the level of retention shown" (p. 209). Their preference is to emphasize longer-term retention and transfer to new situations as the best measures of learning.

Basic and Applied Research

One might expect a textbook on learning to include detailed information on how to learn the material in the book. Instead, the processes of learning are illustrated by preparations such as eyeblink conditioning or word-list memorizing, sometimes with participants other than humans. This discrepancy reflects the different purposes of research.

Basic research is an interest in understanding the fundamental processes of learning and memory. It seeks to demonstrate cause-and-effect relationships between key variables. To demonstrate the probable causality of one variable, we must control or eliminate other contaminating variables that could affect behavior. This often can be accomplished using a simple task, a simpler organism, and a highly controllable setting such as the laboratory. For instance, if you want to discover whether synaptic changes occur in learning, you might begin your study on organisms that have few and large neurons, such as worms or snails.

The questions asked by basic researchers do not always have obvious and immediate applicability to everyday learning outside of the lab. Basic science researchers believe in the potential usefulness of their research, even if the applications are not known until the research is conducted.

As one physicist put it, basic research sometimes provides a solution in search of a problem (Lemonick, 1995). For example, basic research on the learning of aversions to new tastes by rats has been applied to controlling sheep poaching by coyotes (Gustavson & Garcia, 1974), and to blocking the development of food aversions in people undergoing chemotherapy (Bernstein, 1991). Neither application was anticipated by those doing the initial laboratory research.

Applied research is relevant to, or will apply to, solving a specific practical problem. The distinction between basic and applied research might be better thought of as a continuum rather than a dichotomy. (As with many of the terms encountered so far in this chapter, we first set out a dichotomy and then suggest the truth lies somewhere in between.) Any given piece of research falls somewhere along the basic–applied continuum depending on the relevance of the study to a specific target population, task, and/or setting to which we wish to apply our results. Some examples may illustrate.

What is the effect of caffeine on memory? Caffeine is a known stimulant, often used by students to boost alertness, and would logically seem to facilitate learning. Research on maze learning by rats has shown varied results: Caffeine sometimes facilitates performance, but also can inhibit performance (Lashley, 1917; Terry & Anthony, 1980). These studies are obviously examples of basic research. In other experiments, college students are asked to remember word lists. These subjects and this task have greater relevance if we are trying to generalize to humans. Yet this study still retains aspects of basic research, in that the caffeine is given under controlled conditions in the lab, using blind-run and placebo conditions, and so on. The results of one such experiment were that caffeine impaired the immediate retention of the lists (Erikson et al., 1985). One final study to consider is possibly the most relevant to student learning: What is the relationship of caffeine intake to grade point average? Now we are getting to the important question. Gilliland and Andress (1981) surveyed University of Oklahoma students to determine the amount of caffeine consumed and correlated consumption with the students' GPAs. The results showed a negative correlation: Higher caffeine consumption was associated with lower overall grades, and, conversely, lower caffeine went along with higher grades. This example would seem to present the most applicable and the most ecologically valid of the caffeine findings presented so far. Yet one can imagine reasons other than caffeine for these results. Do procrastinating students drink lots of coffee while cramming for exams and papers? Does self-reported caffeine consumption accurately reflect actual consumption? By leaving the lab for the actual world, we lose control over certain variables in our attempt to simulate naturalistic conditions. There can be a trade-off between experimental rigor and ecological validity in research, as occurs in the study of everyday remembering (see Box 1.2).

Box 1.2   Studying Everyday Memory

In 1978, Ulric Neisser, recipient of an American Psychological Association award for distinguished scientific contributions, criticized experimental psychology for its failure to study memory and cognition as they are used in our lives. "If X is an interesting or socially significant aspect of memory, then psychologists have hardly ever studied X" (Neisser, 1978, p. 4). Neisser criticized psychologists for too much basic research conducted in the laboratory and too little research on how memory works outside the lab. Neisser's remarks were soon followed by a proliferation of research on memory in the everyday world.

Ten years later, Banaji and Crowder (1989) chastised researchers for failing to produce a body of new scientifically valid principles of memory. Their article was titled "The Bankruptcy of Everyday Memory," words equally provocative to Neisser's earlier remarks. Banaji and Crowder argued that the ecological realism obtained by studying memory in naturalistic settings does not automatically ensure that general principles of memory will be found. These authors pointed to an analogy in chemistry. No one criticizes chemists for doing controlled lab studies in order to isolate key variables, instead of studying everyday compounds found in the kitchen or bathroom. Banaji and Crowder note that because so many variables are uncontrolled in the everyday world, research cannot always produce valid findings about cause and effect.

For example, Banaji and Crowder present one scenario in which eyewitnesses to a traffic accident are questioned. But who can say which witness is more accurate, or what conditions increase accuracy, when so many variables are uncontrolled? Witnesses may have observed from different perspectives or seen different things; the first story given to the police could contaminate that given the researcher later; and the delay until the researcher questions witnesses varies. How can valid results be obtained under such poor experimental conditions?

Somewhere between the two extremes of Neisser and of Banaji and Crowder probably lies the truth. Several commentators pointed out that the research setting, laboratory versus field, does itself determine the scientific validity of the results; that real-world research can produce generalizable principles; and that the study of everyday memory can provide a setting for testing the theories derived in the laboratory. The study of everyday memory has since flourished. There has been an increase in scientific rigor (see Cohen & Conway, 2008). Controlled experiments are frequently used to study ecological memory, in addition to methods of naturalistic observation and self-reports. Ecological research generates new questions to ask, a criterion sometimes used to judge the usefulness of psychological theories. Importantly, the study of everyday memory may provide practical remedies for real problems, such as determining the veracity of eyewitness testimony, the validity of recovered memories, or the remediation of memory loss produced by injury, illness, or aging.

Common Sense and Common Knowledge

As noted at the start of this chapter, many readers already possess sophisticated knowledge about how to learn. After all, students are professional learners. Is much of what psychologists teach about learning already common knowledge?

Indeed, Houston (1983) presented UCLA undergraduates brief descriptions of real-life situations in which a principle of learning applied. For example, if a child has been feeding pigeons at her window sill for several weeks, what happens if the feedings stop? Answering in a multiple-choice format, most students realized that the pigeons would stop coming (what we learning psychologists refer to as *experimental extinction*). The students also correctly predicted the outcome in 15 of 20 other situations. Houston then tested the same questions with people he found in a park on a Sunday afternoon. They were able to identify the expected outcomes corresponding to psychological phenomena, answering about 75 percent of the questions correctly. Does this show that we are teaching the obvious?

Although the general public does have some accurate knowledge about memory, there are also some particularly false conceptions. Klatzky (1984) refers to these as *memory myths*. These include distorted beliefs about amnesia, hypnosis, aging, and forgetting in general. For example, the common conception of amnesia is that it involves extensive forgetting of the past, particularly of personal identity, and that it occurs frequently (judging by its frequency in films). Do amnesic people forget their own names and personal identify? A survey of Americans found that nearly 48 percent strongly agreed that amnesics forget who they are, yet none of the experts agreed with this statement (Simons & Chabris, 2011). **Amnesia** typically does not involve loss of personal identity; and it is more likely to involve an inability to form new memories rather than a loss of old memories (see Chapter 7).

Can memory be improved by training? If physical exercise makes the body stronger, would mental exercise make memory stronger? A Scandinavian survey asked this question, and found that over 90 percent of the respondents believed that memory exercises would improve overall memory ability (Magnussen et al., 2006). However, the research evidence shows only that people can improve their ability to remember specific types of information through practice. Thus, people can improve memory for names, random sequences of the digits 0 and 1, or restaurant orders, if this is what they practice remembering. Someone who can memorize pi to one hundred decimal places does not remember names and faces any better than the rest of us.

One other too-common belief is that hypnosis can uncover hidden memories that are otherwise inaccessible. The older studies of hypnosis usually contrasted two groups: hypnotized and nonhypnotized subjects. What these simple studies failed to equate is the suggestibility of the subjects, their motivation to try to recall, and, importantly, the elaborate instructions to reexperience the remembered event given the hypnosis group. In fact, such instructions alone in nonhypnotized individuals can increase recall to that of hypnotized levels (see Chapter 10).

A final myth worth dispelling is the belief that forgetting is a weakness. Certainly, some of our memory failings are problematic, worrisome, embarrassing, even dangerous. Yet total recall could pose its own problems. If every event of the same type was remembered equally, how would you discriminate current from outdated information? Some mundane examples include remembering my current phone number versus my old number, and where I parked this morning and not where I left the car yesterday. Some forgetting is necessary for the survival of an organism. Psychologists have suggested the radical idea that forgetting may have evolved as a positive characteristic of memory, not a flaw.

Why Animals?

The reasons for using nonhuman animals in experiments on learning can be simply stated. First, the experiences of animal subjects often can be more highly controlled, obviously within the experiment itself, but also prior to the experiment in terms of the genetic and life history of the organism. Second, given our shared evolutionary history, there is a presumed similarity between animals and humans, and therefore an assumed generality in the basic principles of learning. Granted, there may be exceptions to these generalities.

A third, and controversial, reason for using animals is that procedures can be used on animals that cannot be applied ethically to humans. This justification is controversial because some would question why animals are not given similar protection from painful or dangerous procedures. How prevalent is dissatisfaction with animal use in psychological research? One survey of 1,200 psychology majors at 42 colleges found fairly strong support for the continued use of animals (Plous, 1996). About 70 percent supported the use of animals in psychological research and believed such research was necessary. A greater number (85 percent) believed that before a proposed study is approved, the investigators should be required to assess the degree of pain the animals will experience. (Incidentally, the survey found that fewer faculty in psychology departments are using animals than in previous years, and fewer psychology students take lab courses using animals.)

Neal Miller, in accepting the Distinguished Professional Contribution Award from the American Psychological Association, listed some contributions of behavioral research on animals (1985). These include the development of behavioral therapies for psychological disorders; applications to behavioral medicine, such as in the control of cardiovascular and asthmatic responses; research on the effects of early experience on neural development; the psychoactive effects of drugs; and benefits to animals themselves, both for those under our care and for wildlife. The contribution of animal research in psychology is not always acknowledged. Some introductory psychology textbooks reference certain findings to later studies of human participants, when in fact the phenomena first emerged from animal laboratories (Domjan & Purdy, 1995).[2]

Conceptual Approaches to the Study of Learning

When rats (who, along with college students, are psychologists' favorite research subjects) learn a maze, what exactly do they learn? Is it a list of specific turns, like a memorized set of directions? Do they acquire a sort of cognitive map of the layout of the maze? Or should we describe the neural changes that underlie the learning of routes or maps? Does an animal's natural history determine which form of learning will lead to the greatest likelihood of survival? These questions illustrate four broad approaches to studying learning and memory. A behavioral approach focuses on the acquisition of specific behaviors. A cognitive approach emphasizes the learning of knowledge and expectancies. A neuroscience approach studies the changes that learning produces in the brain. And finally, a functional approach emphasizes the necessity of learning for adaptation to changing environments.

These approaches, along with others, have played a major role in our understanding of learning and memory. The several approaches are not mutually exclusive, and in contemporary research questions are commonly being asked from a combination of perspectives.

The Functional Approach

Animals (people included) are adapted to their environments (e.g., the freezing tundra versus the steaming desert). In addition to the obvious physical adaptations, the capacity to learn and remember is another adaptation. Learning evolved as a way for organisms to adapt more quickly to the changes and inconstancies in their environment. The **functional approach** studies how learning and remembering aid survival.

One focus of the functional approach is the evolution of learning across species. Animals with a common evolutionary history would likely share certain kinds of learning or memory abilities. For instance, all animal species have the capacity to acquire associations: to link one stimulus to another or link behaviors and consequences. A second focus is on the unique adaptations that differentiate species. Thus, face recognition, language learning, and personal or autobiographical memories (what we'll call episodic memory in Chapter 7) may be specialized adaptations for certain species.

The Behavioral Approach

The **behavioral approach** emphasizes the relationship among, first, observable behaviors, second, the antecedent stimuli that precede behavior, and, third, the consequences that follow behavior. What are the environmental stimuli and conditions that come to evoke behavior? What are the consequences or outcomes that affect the likelihood of behavior? And what are the behaviors themselves that are learned? The goal of behavioral psychology is to predict and control behavior on the basis of knowledge of the antecedents, the behavior, and its consequences.

One version of this approach, known historically as radical behaviorism, shuns theorizing about inferred (and therefore speculative) processes within the organism's mind. Instead, behaviorism attempts to describe the lawful relationships among stimuli, responses, and consequences. An example of a behavioral law is "the likelihood that a certain behavior will occur increases if the response has been followed by a reinforcing stimulus in the past." "If a child's aggressive behavior is rewarded, the likelihood of aggression in the future will increase." If these empirical relationships correctly and accurately describe behavior, there is no need to postulate unobserved thought processes to explain the behavior (i.e., the child has a bullying personality, or aggression is cathartic).

The Cognitive Approach

The **cognitive approach** derives from information-processing approaches to the mind. Information, or knowledge, is encoded, transformed, stored, and retrieved. The influence from computer science is obvious: These are analogous to processes within a computer. The basic tenet of the cognitive approach is the postulation of an *internal representation*. That is, the organism is said to form an internal representation that is used as the basis for further processing or for guiding behavior (Pearce, 1997). (Cognitive researchers will often talk about this representation being in the mind, but this does not necessarily refer to a mental mind apart from the physical representation in the brain.) This internal representation, as well as the cognitive processes of storing it, transforming it, retrieving it, and so forth, are all inferred on the basis of behavior, much as in the approach of the behaviorists.

Although cognitive psychology obviously applies to humans, the generality of the cognitive approach can be illustrated in research on animals. Here we have to depend on behavior and not verbal report in order to infer cognitive processes. How can a researcher determine whether a rat has acquired a cognitive map of a familiar maze? If the animal is confronted with a blocked alley, does the rat readily select an alternate route to the goal box? We use these sorts of tests to infer the presence of an internal representation of the maze. Does the animal act as if it has learned a map of the maze, or instead as if it has memorized a series of turns?

The Neuroscience Approach

The *neuroscience approach* has existed in parallel with both the earlier behavioral and the newer cognitive perspectives. The **neuroscience approach** seeks to determine the underlying biological basis for learning and memory. What are the changes that occur in the nervous system during learning?

Neuroscience is often combined with the other approaches. Beginning in the 1920s, the eminent psychologist Karl Lashley attempted to find the areas of the rat's brain necessary for learning and memory (e.g., Lashley, 1929). He did this by systematically removing various regions of the brain. Twenty years later, the neurosurgeon Wilder Penfield studied memory localization by stimulating the brain of his human patients with weak electric current (Penfield & Rasmussen, 1950). The patients, who were conscious during this portion of the operation, reported sights and sounds that felt like memories. A few years later, the Swedish biochemist Holger Hydén sought to find a biochemical change that occurred in the rat's brain when a new behavior was learned, a sort of memory molecule (e.g., Hydén & Egyhazi, 1963). These classic experiments illustrate the strategy of combining approaches: behavioral (maze learning), cognitive (memory recall), and physiological (lesioning, brain stimulation, and chemical assays).

Contemporary neuroscience uses methods such as brain scans and case studies of brain-injured individuals. For example, positron emission tomography (or PET) and functional magnetic resonance imagery (or fMRI) scans measure the relative levels of activity in the brain. You have probably seen photographs of scans in which the brain is color-coded to show which areas are most active. We can ask an experimental subject to perform different memory activities, and then scan the brain. For instance, I could first ask you to remember a list of simple words, such as DOG, TABLE, GLASS, and so on. This is a memory *encoding* task: It involves putting a list of words into memory. Later I could ask you to recall that list. This test is a memory **retrieval** task: It involves recalling what is (maybe) in memory. The scans made during these two tasks are compared. Some areas are more active while encoding the list, and other areas are more

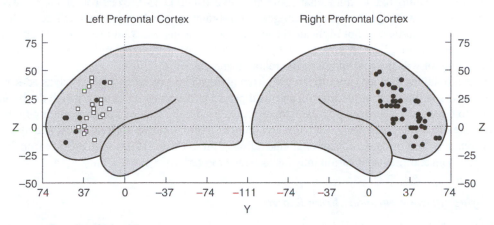

Figure 1.4 **Peak Activation Areas in the Left and Right Hemispheres of the Brain During Two Memory Tasks.** The left half of the brain shows more encoding peaks, whereas the right half shows more retrieval peaks.

Source: From "PET Studies of Encoding and Retrieval: The HERA Model," by L. Nyberg, R. Cabeza, and E. Tulving, 1996, *Psychonomic Bulletin & Review, 3,* p. 143. Copyright © 1996 by the Psychonomic Society. Reprinted with permission.

active during retrieval of the list. Figure 1.4 shows drawings of the left and right halves of the brain, with markers showing points that were particularly active during encoding versus during retrieval (Nyberg, Cabeza, & Tulving, 1996). As can be seen, when learning the list, many more points in the left-front part of the brain are active; when recalling the list, there are more points active in the right-front part.

Historically, there has been tension between the behavioral and cognitive approaches. In the example that began this section, we posed the question of whether maze learning could be best described in terms of learning a series of turns versus acquiring a cognitive map of the maze. Research from a neural sciences approach may offer a reconciliation between behavioral and cognitive psychologies, by showing that there are both habit learning and cognitive learning systems in the brain (Petri & Mishkin, 1994). For example, learning that food is always found in one particular location in the maze, day after day, is habit learning, and this learning is impaired by damage to an area of the brain called the hippocampus. If the food location is varied from day to day, remembering where it is today is cognitive learning, and performance is impaired by damage to another part of the brain, the amygdala (McDonald & White, 1993).

Applications

Earlier, we distinguished between basic and applied research and suggested that each can inform the other. Educators are keenly interested in applications of neuroscience to instruction. Research on the Mozart effect illustrates one extrapolation of neuroscience to education. In a well-publicized study, college students who listened to 15 minutes of music by Wolfgang Amadeus Mozart showed an increase of several points in their spatial intelligence test scores in comparison to days they did not hear Mozart or listened to a different type of music (Rauscher, Shaw, & Ky, 1993). (*Note:* Finish reading this paragraph. Do not stop to download Mozart in preparation for tomorrow's math exam.) The publicity surrounding this finding led some to advocate Mozart's music as an IQ booster.

All of us would like to think that something like listening to Mozart (or playing chess or learning a new language) somehow reprograms our brains and make us more intelligent. Unfortunately, other studies did not replicate the Mozart effect or instead found less interesting explanations (e.g., Steele, Bass, & Crook, 1999). Was the Mozart selection simply more exciting and stimulating, or was the control music too relaxing and calming?

Educational implications are often drawn from neuroscience research. Ideas such as educating both halves of the brain or identifying a critical period in development during which the brain is ready to learn have also been popular. However, we need to be cautious in generalizing findings from one discipline to another. Brain research may be a bridge to memory research, and memory research may be a bridge to educational innovations. But as Bruer (1997) said, the link from brain science to educational application may be "a bridge too far" (p. 4).

Studying: Recommendations From Experts

Most psychologists who study learning and memory also teach learning and memory. So we are interested in applying what we have learned in our research to aid academic learning. Several study groups have reported on the advice these teacher-scientists offer (e.g., Dunlosky, Rawson, March, Nathan, & Willingham, 2013). Below are a few of their recommended principles. I start with the one that may be most fundamental.

1. *Elaboration.* Effective learning requires an active mind, and not passive exposure to the material. Learning has less to do with the intention to learn ("I really need to learn this for the test") and more about how you think about the information. Elaboration includes strategies such as: Can you restate the ideas in your words? Can you think of an example? Can you connect it to something else you know? Does this idea make sense? Elaboration also involves choosing to use strategies, such as those listed as numbers 2 and 3 below.
2. *Spaced repetition.* Spreading out or spacing exposures to material leads to better learning than does massing exposures. Sometimes a second presentation that occurs too close to the first (massed repetition) adds nothing at all to memorability. The repetitions can be in the form of a review of the material, a summary, or a practice test, but in general, spaced is better.
3. *Interleaving.* Intermix the study of different materials. In a sense, this promotes some spacing. If you have a few topics to learn, intermix studying of them rather than focusing just on the first, then the second, etc.
4. *Testing.* As noted in the earlier discussion of the testing effect, taking a practice test or self-testing your knowledge can convey more benefit than simply studying the material a second (third, or even a fourth) time.
5. *Beware of self-judgments about learning.* Your intuition about whether you know something can be wrong. When we review just-studied material, a feeling of familiarity falsely suggests that we know it. Students are often wrong in their judgments about whether, and how well, they have learned.

For example, if the material is easily learned, we assume it will also be easily remembered. Given a list of word pairs to memorize, the pair TABLE-TREE will be learned quicker than the pair TABLE-AARDVARK. Surely the easily-learned pair will be remembered better. Unfortunately, if something is too easily learned, it may be too readily forgotten. Remember that password you made up on the spur of the moment, the one that seemed so obvious? The one you can no longer remember? A more difficult learning task can engage more mental resources (rehearsal, imagery, meaningfulness, *elaboration*) to help us learn the connection.

Summary

The point of this book is to present a scientifically accurate and sophisticated view of the principles of learning. This includes adding qualifying statements to general principles: specifying when a given principle holds and when exceptions occur.

The Origins of the Study of Learning

The philosopher Descartes suggested that some knowledge was independent of experience. Some knowledge is innate, which is the idea of nativism. Other knowledge is derived by reason and logic; this is rationalism. In contrast, the philosopher John Locke suggested that the origin of all knowledge comes from experience. This is empiricism.

Darwin's theory of evolution suggested to psychologists that learning evolved as an adaptive specialization. Learning is a means of adapting to the environment within the organism's lifetime. That different species are related through a common evolutionary history suggests that learning by animals can offer insights into how humans learn.

The Definition of Learning

Learning is defined as a relatively permanent change in behavior, or behavioral repertoire, that occurs as a result of experience. Each phrase of the definition is significant. Because learning itself, in the mind or in the brain, is not directly observable, behavior change is necessary to provide objective evidence that learning has occurred. Measures of learning can be physiological, behavioral, or verbal.

The phrase *behavioral repertoire* acknowledges that not all learning is immediately evidenced in behavior. Learning includes the potential for a change in behavior, to be demonstrated when conditions prompt the display of this new knowledge. Learning is said to produce relatively permanent changes in behavior, which excludes transient changes in arousal, fatigue, or motivation.

Biologically determined maturation illustrates gray areas around the edge of our definition of learning.

The Learning/Performance Distinction

There is not always a one-to-one correspondence between what an organism knows (i.e., learning) and what an organism does (performance). Tolman and Honzik's study of latent learning showed that rats learned the layout of the maze without reward, but this knowledge remained hidden until the subjects were motivated with food to complete the maze quickly. In an exam situation, students who have truly learned the material can still perform poorly on the exam (maybe due to excessive anxiety, for instance).

The Relationship Between Learning and Memory

Learning refers to the acquisition, or encoding, of knowledge or behavior. We could illustrate its development with a learning curve, a graphic plot of a measure of behavior on the vertical axis (e.g., number or size of the correct responses) as a function of the number of trials given, shown on the horizontal axis. Memory refers to the retention of knowledge or behavior that has been learned. We could illustrate the course of memory by a forgetting curve, plotting a measure of behavior on the vertical axis, as a function of time or events since learning was completed on the horizontal axis.

Basic and Applied Research

Basic research is an interest in understanding the fundamental processes of learning and memory, by demonstrating cause-and-effect relationships between key variables. We must often use artificial situations or tasks in order to control, eliminate, or hold constant contaminating variables that could affect behavior. Applied research, the other end of the continuum, is designed to be relevant to, or will apply to, answering a specific practical problem. Each type of research is appropriate for answering certain kinds of questions.

Are most principles of learning already common knowledge? In fact, there are discrepancies between what professionals and laypeople believe about memory. These memory myths include distorted beliefs about amnesia, hypnosis, and forgetting in the aged.

Nonhuman animals are used in experiments on learning because their experiences can be highly controlled and because there is a presumed similarity in learning processes between animals and humans. Research on animals has made numerous contributions to the welfare of both animals and people.

Conceptual Approaches to the Study of Learning

There are several broad approaches to the study of learning. The functional approach proposes that learning and remembering evolved as means for organisms to adapt to the changes and inconstancies in their environment and thus to aid survival. A behavioral approach focuses on the acquisition of specific responses or behaviors. It emphasizes the relationship between these observable behaviors to the stimuli that precede behavior, and to the consequences that follow behavior. A cognitive approach emphasizes internal (mental or neural) cognitions and expectancies. It derives from information-processing approaches to the mind, in which information is encoded, transformed, stored, and retrieved. A neuroscience approach studies the changes that learning produces in the brain. It seeks to determine the underlying biological basis of learning and memory within the nervous system.

Applications

Those psychologists who study learning and memory can draw on basic research conducted by neuroscientists, and learning psychologists can offer applications to educators. However, research on topics such as the Mozart effect, critical periods in neural development, and environmental enrichment, may not yet be applicable to education. Advice on how to study, such as self-testing, using spaced repetitions, and being cautious of our own estimates of what we know, do have empirical support.

Notes

1. The standard format for noting sources in psychology is to list the authors' last names and the year of publication. Complete source information is provided in the References at the end of the book.
2. In this text, I will typically refer to humans or animals, which only means a distinction between human animals and other animals. See Dess & Chapman, 1998.

2   Habituation and Other Forms of Stimulus Learning

Researchers often start with a simple model, system, or paradigm with which to derive some first principles, and progress to more complex phenomena and laws. Learning about single stimuli, uncomplicated by associations or rules relating them to other events, would seem to offer such a simple learning situation.

As a starting point, suppose an innocuous stimulus is presented some number of times. Your behavior at first indicates that you notice the stimulus, but since it has no apparent significance, your reaction to the repetitions of the stimulus decreases. This effect is called *habituation*, a simple form of learning. A noise in the house at night awakens you, but you realize it is just the house settling or the furnace humming, and so you come to ignore these house sounds. However, you can probably think of times when you became more reactive to a stimulus after a first exposure. A noise in the house awakens you; and as you worry about what it might be, the behavioral and physiological reactions increase each time the noise recurs. Rather than habituating, you are more responsive to the noise.

Exposure to a stimulus can affect our behavior in other ways also, even if we are not aware of the previous exposure. For instance, a stimulus could be flashed on a screen so briefly (only a fraction of a second) that it cannot be consciously recognized. Yet this unawares presentation can affect reactions to a repetition of the stimulus later, such as increasing our liking of the previously seen stimulus. Repetition increases our preference for particular songs, for works of art, and for particular foods.

The starting point for this chapter is that stimulus repetitions reduce one form of responsiveness to a stimulus. However, we will see that stimulus exposure potentially can produce a number of other reactions: greater responsiveness, preference and liking, and speeded reactions. "The main lesson to be learned from the study of habituation—and this makes it an even more appropriate subject to start with—is that habituation is almost never as simple as it first seems" (Walker, 1987, p. 34).

The Orienting Response

The occurrence of a novel or an unexpected stimulus elicits an **orienting response** (**OR**, also called an *orienting reflex* or *orienting reaction*). Pavlov aptly described the OR as an investigatory reflex. The organism reacts to identify the nature and source of the stimulation, which may be important to the survival of the organism. The OR is actually not a single response, but is a composite of several physiological and behavioral reactions. First, a stimulus may evoke a startle response. This may involve whole body startle to extremely loud noises, or simply head movements or an eye blink to milder stimuli. In addition, the novel stimulus produces sense receptor orienting. We turn to look in the direction of a sight or sound; dogs perk up their ears to hear better. There is also a readiness for a fight or flight response. Orienting reactions are a preparation for danger, and so defensive behaviors are primed. Finally, there is increased arousal. This arousal could be described physiologically, as measured by heart rate or breathing changes, and also psychologically, as measured by degree of attention and alertness (Siddle, Kuiack, & Kroese, 1983).

Not all of these components occur to every new stimulus. A starter's pistol that goes off unexpectedly can elicit a head-jerking startle, whereas a tone stimulus presented in a lab experiment may simply elicit an eye blink. Thus, the OR depends on stimulus intensity, the situation, the potential for danger, and other factors.

The novelty of a stimulus is just one factor determining whether an OR is made, but it is not a necessary factor. A familiar but meaningful stimulus can also elicit an OR. Hearing one's name mentioned unexpectedly is a potent elicitor of an OR, although this is hardly a novel stimulus. A predatory animal will orient to the sound of its usual prey, a familiar stimulus.

Habituation

Habituation is the decrease in orienting (and other) reactions to a stimulus that is repeatedly presented. An often-used phrase describes habituation as "the waning of responsiveness" to repetitive stimulation. An initially new stimulus becomes familiar with repeated presentations, and thus becomes less likely to elicit an OR. The word *habituation* is used in the research literature both to refer to the procedure (repetitive presentation of a stimulus) and to the effect or outcome (a decrease in responding).

Habituation is a simple form of learning in which the organism learns something about a single stimulus. Unlike most other indications or measures of learning that we will consider in later chapters, learning is indicated by less responding over trials. This is just the opposite of the learning curve described earlier, which increases over trials.

If the stimulus turns out to have some significance to the organism, because it is followed by other events or consequences, orienting may be replaced by learned adaptive responses. For example, in Pavlov's experiment, the tone stimulus is followed by food. Orienting to the first several tone presentations is gradually replaced by conditioned responses, such as salivating to the tone, as the dog learns that the tone is followed by food. In most habituation experiments, only the to-be-habituated stimulus is presented so that the addition of other acquired responses does not complicate interpretation.

Habituation also occurs to intense and/or painful stimuli. The responses to noxious (or aversive) stimuli are called defensive responses or unconditioned responses. These defensive reactions to noxious stimuli habituate: Reflex responses to potent stimuli may decrease across repeated presentations of the stimulus (Wetherington, 1982). Although some researchers differentiate orienting responses from defensive responses, other researchers treat both sorts of reactions as being on a continuum, with the strength or kind of response being more a function of stimulus intensity.

Habituation is ubiquitous: It is seemingly found everywhere. Habituation occurs across the phylogenetic scale, from snails to humans. It occurs in various segments of nervous systems, including isolated spinal neurons and at synapses. The study of habituation has brought together diverse groups of basic researchers, from those interested in the physiology of habituation to those studying attention and memory in children. These investigators share a common terminology, have uncovered similar principles of learning, and sometimes even use the same theoretical explanations. Such cross-fertilization between different levels of research is desirable for the scientific advancement of learning.

Methods of Studying Habituation

A variety of tasks and measures may be used to investigate habituation. In animals, the whole-body *startle* reaction to loud tones can be studied using rats (e.g., Davis, 1974). In the *novelty recognition task*, mice or rats are allowed to explore some objects, such as blocks, in a test environment. New objects are then added before the next test is conducted. The animals explore the objects that are not recognized, touching, sniffing, and even climbing on them. This active exploration indicates *orienting*. Objects that are remembered as familiar are explored less. The reduced attention given to the old objects indicates *habituation*. The novelty recognition task is widely used among neuroscience researchers to assess how brain lesions, genetic alterations, new drugs, and environmental manipulations might affect memory (e.g., Tang et al., 1999).

In humans, physiological responses are often used to monitor reactions to new stimuli. The **skin conductance response** (or **SCR**) measures subtle changes in electrical conductivity in the skin that are associated with arousal or emotionality. The SCR is probably familiar to you as a component of the lie detector test, in which electrodes are placed on the body (e.g., the hand or arm). Illustrative data from a habituation experiment measuring SCR are shown in Figure 2.1.

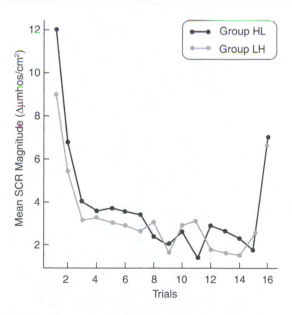

Figure 2.1 **Habituation of the Skin Conductance Response to a Simple Tone Stimulus.** One group received high-pitch (H) tones; the other group received low-pitch (L) tones. After 15 presentations, the opposite tone was presented to each group.

Source: From "The Orienting Reflex," by D. A. T. Siddle, M. Kuiack, and B. S. Kroese, in *Physiological Correlates of Human Behavior* (p. 161), edited by A. Gale and J. A. Edwards, 1983, London: Academic Press. Copyright 1983 by Academic Press. Reprinted with permission.

Siddle et al. (1983) presented 15 brief tones, one every minute or so, to college student participants tested individually in a laboratory setting. Some students were presented with a high-pitched tone, and the others heard a low-pitched tone. As can be seen in the graph, the skin conductance response decreased across stimulus presentations for each group of subjects. After 15 stimulus presentations, the experimenters switched tones. The final tone in the series was the one habituated for the other group, so the high-pitched tone was replaced by a low-pitched tone, and vice versa. Orienting returned when the tones were changed.

One widely used measure of orienting is that of eye fixations to novel visual stimuli. We visually explore new stimuli, and gradually shift our gaze away from these stimuli once they become familiar. Measuring the change in duration or number of eye fixations to a stimulus is a good indicator of habituation. In a sense, the eyes become the windows of the mind. Measuring eye movements is especially useful for studying learning by infants. A novel object or image is shown repeatedly, and habituation is shown by a decrease in fixations across trials. We could interpret this as an indication that the child comes to recognize the stimulus as familiar. Following habituation to one stimulus, a second experimental phase is sometimes given in which two stimuli are presented for a comparison, one old and one new stimulus. The child may then show more inspection of the new stimulus than of the old one (see Box 2.1).

Box 2.1   Dishabituation as a Measure of Infant Perception and Cognition

Habituation tasks have been used to study perception, learning, and even reasoning in infants. The cognitive capabilities of preverbal children are difficult to measure. The absence of a response does not mean an absence of knowledge. Measuring the decrease in eye fixations to familiar stimuli, and increase in fixations to novel stimuli, provides a valuable tool for investigating learning in infants. In this method, one stimulus is presented repeatedly producing habituation, that is, a decrease in the eye fixations to the stimulus. Then a test stimulus can be presented to see whether dishabituation occurs, indicating the test stimulus is noticed as different from the familiar stimulus. This technique can be used to address several intriguing questions about what infants are capable of perceiving, remembering, or thinking.

Adults typically divide the light spectrum into several distinct primary colors. Intermediate hues can be reliably assigned to one or another of these categories. For example, between those colors labeled as blue or green are intermediate hues, what we might call greenish blue and bluish green, which adults consistently categorize (if forced to) as either blue or green. How would preverbal infants, who have not learned these divisions of the color spectrum yet, classify intermediate hues? Bornstein, Kessen, and Weiskopf (1976) used the dishabituation procedure, first presenting 4-month old infants with 15 repetitions of a 15-second light. Different groups of infants were shown lights of different colors, for example, greenish BLUE for one group and bluish GREEN for another group (the color in capital letters is the adult category label). Fixation times declined from 8 to 9 seconds on the first presentations to 2 to 3 seconds over the last few. Thus, habituation occurred. The infants were then given test presentations of the habituated color, and one color on either side of the color spectrum (see Table 2.1). In each case, less eye fixating occurred to the hue within the same adult color category, even though each tested hue was equidistant from the habituated color. For example, after habituating to bluish GREEN, the infants spent even less time looking at GREEN, and spent more time fixating to greenish BLUE.

Similar results were shown with the other color boundaries. By 4 months of age, colors are seen categorically. Wide ranges of reds, yellows, greens, and blues are categorized as equivalent, whereas there are sharper boundaries between these color categories.

Table 2.1 Design and Results of One Color Condition in a Study of Infant Dishabituation to Novel Colors

Colorwavelength (nm)	**Blue** 450	480	510	**Green** 540
Group 1 fixation time (sec)	Blue 5.8	*greenish Blue* 5.9	bluish Green 7.0	
Group 2 fixation time (sec)		greenish Blue 7.0	*bluish Green* 4.9	Green 4.0

Note: Mean eye fixation times during testing. The colors that were first habituated are in italics. The other colors were first introduced during testing.

Source: Bornstein et al. (1976).

This same technique is used to study infants' perception of number (Wynn, 1992). If the infant is shown a fixed number of objects on several trials (e.g., one puppet or two puppets), there is an increase in eye fixations when a puppet is added or subtracted on test trials. In another study, 6-month-old infants were shown a puppet that jumped either two times or three times on each habituation trial. A change in the number of jumps on the test trial elicited dishabituation and increased looking (Wynn, 1995).

The starting point for research like this is, indirectly, the philosophical question of nativism versus empiricism: Do we innately perceive colors, do we learn the concept of number? Curiously, a technique used to study learning (habituation) can be used to show evidence for native perceptual abilities.

Parametric Features of Habituation

Thompson and Spencer (1966) derived a list of parametric features of habituation. *Parametric* refers to taking one dimension of an independent variable and systematically varying it to see the effect on the response. For example, one can vary the spacing of stimulus presentations across a range of values and measure the amount of response at each interval. The Thompson and Spencer features have become a standard or benchmark for evaluating whether response changes that occur in other species, preparations, or response systems are really habituation. A consideration of several of these features illustrates the process of habituation.

Frequency of Repetition

Habituation is a function of the number of repetitions of a stimulus. The exact number of repetitions necessary to produce a substantial response decrement varies considerably. As shown in Figure 2.1 earlier, human habituation occurs after a few presentations of a mild tone stimulus. Rat startle response to loud tones continues to decline across hundreds of presentations.

Spontaneous Recovery

If the stimulus is withheld for a period of time, the response tends to recover. The next time the stimulus is presented, the response will be larger than before the delay interval. The phrase **spontaneous recovery** refers to the reinstatement of the response after an interval of time without stimulations. Indeed, if the delay interval is sufficiently long (e.g., overnight in an animal experiment), the reaction to the previously habituated stimulus may completely recover. (Spontaneous recovery is illustrated in Figure 2.3 in experiments that will be described later.) Actually, for many years, this feature was used to argue that habituation was not an example of learning. If habituation produced only a temporary change in responding, then habituation did not fit the *relatively permanent* clause in the definition of learning. Why would we later come to believe that habituation is learning? The answer is in the next feature.

Effects of Repeated Habituations

If the stimulus is habituated a second time, and after another delay, a third time, a fourth, and so on, habituation occurs more quickly on each successive occasion, and the amount of recovery (or loss of habituation) is less after each delay. Fewer stimulus presentations are required to re-habituate the stimulus as compared to the initial course of habituation. Habituation accumulates across trials and sessions.

Spacing of Stimulations

The shorter the interval between successive stimulus presentations, the more quickly responding declines. Basically, closely spaced stimulus repetitions produce more habituation than do widely spaced repetitions.

The massed-spaced effect is more complicated than Thompson and Spencer (1966) originally stated. Massed repetitions may produce less responding than spaced repetitions during the habituation phase, but not when tested again afterwards. This can be shown in a study by Gatchel (1975) in which college student participants heard a series of tones, one tone presented every 20 seconds for one group or every 100 seconds for the second group. Across 15 tone presentations, there were smaller responses to stimuli spaced 20 seconds apart than to stimuli 100 seconds apart, which is a massed-presentation effect.

The complication here goes back to the earlier distinction between learning and memory. Do massed presentations produce better learning, or do they simply suppress performance? The interesting test observation is to see whether massed and spaced stimulations differ in the amount of recovery after a delay. Gatchel (1975) gave his subjects a 15-minute rest interval and then presented the tones again. Both groups showed spontaneous recovery: a larger response after the delay than before. The massed group showed more recovery to the tone presentations following the delay than did the spaced group. The spaced group made smaller responses (i.e., more habituation) on the delayed test.

The lesson here may be that to suppress responding immediately, use massed presentations. Spaced presentations can be less efficient in the short run, but more effective in producing durable habituation.

Dishabituation

Another means of reinstating responding to a habituated stimulus is through the procedure of dis-habituation. Orienting to a habituated stimulus can be temporarily returned by presenting another novel stimulus. Even after a stimulus has been habituated, the presentation of a new stimulus increases orienting to the first stimulus. **Dishabituation** is the reinstatement of orienting to a habituated stimulus by presentation of a different stimulus.

For example, in one study, college student participants heard 15 presentations of the same 4-second tone. The size of the OR decreased, which is simply habituation. Then a new stimulus, say, a patch of red light was projected on a computer screen. The light itself should elicit an OR.

When the tone is next presented, its sixteenth presentation, there is a larger response to it than to the previous (fifteenth) occurrence. The light stimulus was the dishabituator; the enhanced response to the sixteenth tone shows dishabituation. Dishabituation is a transient aftereffect of the dishabituating stimulus. Presenting the tone again (the seventeenth presentation) should lead to a reappearance of the smaller, habituated response (Siddle, 1985).

Dishabituation is a sensible reaction to changed conditions of stimulation. The dishabituator reinstates arousal, investigatory reflexes, sense receptor orienting, and so on, in preparation for potential changed environmental conditions. (Dishabituation is shown in Figure 2.3, described in a later section.)

Generalization of Habituation to Other Stimuli

The habituation to a specific stimulus, so that it no longer elicits the OR, may spread to other like stimuli. That is, after habituating one stimulus there can be generalization of habituation to other stimuli that are similar. The degree of generalization depends on the similarity of the test stimuli to the habituated stimulus. For example, in the Siddle et al. (1983) study noted earlier in this chapter, habituation to a high- or low-pitched tone did not generalize to the opposite tone (see Figure 2.1). The different tone elicited a large OR. However, if a tone of medium pitch had been presented, likely a smaller or weaker OR would have occurred. Test stimuli that are similar to the originally habituated stimulus should elicit smaller responses; test stimuli that are different stimuli should elicit more orienting.

Summary of the Parametric Features of Habituation

The response to a novel stimulus decreases as a function of the number of repetitions of the stimulus. The habituated response spontaneously recovers over time without stimulus presentations and can dishabituate following the occurrence of some other novel stimulus. Habituation cumulates across repeated series of stimulus presentations. Habituation generalizes from the habituated stimulus to other similar stimuli. Although closely spaced presentations may suppress the orienting response quickly, there is evidence that more widely spaced presentations produce more long-term habituation.

Explanations of Habituation

Why does responding decrease after a certain number of stimulus presentations? One possibility is that habituation is not learning at all but instead is due to changes in either the sense receptors or the muscle effectors. Theories that do assert that habituation is learning fall into two broad categories of explanation: cognitive and neuroscience.

Nonlearning Explanations

One nonlearning explanation suggests that habituation is due to sensory adaptation. Possibly, the sense receptors simply become less sensitive as a function of repeated stimulus presentations. An example of adaptation is when you detect a distinct odor or smell on entering a room, but, later, the smell is no longer noticed. Here, the olfactory receptors lose their sensitivity to detect a constant odor.

A second nonlearning alternative is fatigue in the response system. After so many responses to the stimuli the response system is too depleted to continue. Either sensory adaptation or motor fatigue will build up over trials, and both will recover with rest, thus producing effects that look like habituation and spontaneous recovery.

Neither of these alternatives seems likely when only 10 to 20 mild tones have been presented, but sensory adaptation or response fatigue becomes plausible with the large number of stimulations and more intense stimuli often used in other studies. Control procedures are necessary to determine the contribution of either factor to any response decrement we observe. One such control procedure is changing the stimulus, as in the Siddle and colleagues' study shown earlier in Figure 2.1. If responding occurs to the changed stimulus then, obviously, the sense receptors detected the stimulus and the effectors are capable of responding.

Neuroscience Theories

Dual Process Theory

Although habituation, a decrease in the magnitude of the response, is a robust and general phenomenon, there are exceptions. Sometimes the size of the response increases across repetitions. **Sensitization** is an increase in orienting responses that occurs with repeated stimulation. That tingle you noticed on your arm may habituate when you realize it is just your sleeve rubbing. If the tingle was caused by a spider walking on your arm, sensitization will occur, and you will overreact to the next tingle.

Research by Thompson (e.g., Groves & Thompson, 1970) showed that the stimuli used in habituation experiments can elicit two separate reactions. Habituation is one reaction. But if the stimulus is intense, painful, or fearful, sensitization also occurs. Sensitization produced by electric shocks or loud tones increases the level of arousal in the nervous system. Groves and Thompson found two types of neurons in their studies of spinal cord reflexes. Those neurons most directly involved in the reflex response (sensory nerves that detect the stimulus, and motor neurons that control the response) showed habituation. Other neurons reflected the general level of arousal of the nervous system and could produce sensitization. This sensitization-produced arousal increases the excitability of the motor neurons involved in the response. The **dual-process theory** of habituation states that the overall behavioral response to stimulus repetition depends on the balance between two factors: habituation and sensitization.

When mild and innocuous stimuli are presented, habituation alone occurs. When strong or intense stimuli are presented, sensitization can increase responsiveness and overshadow any habituation.

The separation of habituation and sensitization is shown in a study of the effect of background noise level on the startle response (Davis, 1974). Two groups of rats received the same series of startle-eliciting tones. The difference was that one group heard these against a background noise level of 60 decibels; the second group had a background level of 80 decibels. Those with the quieter background showed habituation (i.e., a decrease in startle) over 100 trials; those with the louder background showed sensitization (i.e., an increase in startle) across trials. The loud background noise increased the arousal to a degree that counteracted habituation. Sensitization is believed to affect the performance of responses rather than learning. Thus, the effect of sensitization seems to be a transient aftereffect of intense stimulation that dissipates over time.

Aplysia: A Model System

A second example of the physiological approach, like Thompson's, also seeks to discover the underlying synaptic events involved in learning. Eric Kandel, a psychiatrist who decided to go into basic research, studies habituation in a giant marine snail, *Aplysia californica*. This particular snail is used because it has a simple nervous system with few neurons. Many of these nerve cells are relatively large, and their functions are known. But what behaviors can *Aplysia* perform that we can study? *Aplysia* uses a siphon to take in seawater from which food is filtered, and

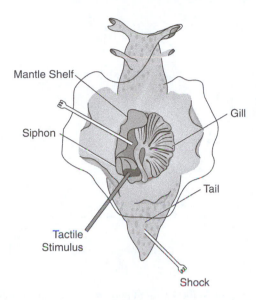

Figure 2.2 **Aplysia, an Ocean-Dwelling Slug Studied by Eric Kandel.** This view looks down at the *Aplysia* from above. The mantle and other structures are spread apart to show the gill and siphon. Touch by the tactile stimulus causes withdrawal of these parts; repeated tactile stimulation produces habituation; a shock stimulus produces sensitization.

Source: From "Relationships between Dishabituation, Sensitization, and Inhibition of the Gill- and Siphon-Withdrawal Reflex in *Aplysia Californica:* Effects of Response Measure, Test Time, and Training Stimulus," by R. D. Hawkins, T. E. Cohen, W. Greene, and E. R. Kandel, 1998, *Behavioral Neuroscience, 112,* p. 25. Copyright © 1998 by the American Psychological Association and reprinted with permission.

that can be withdrawn back into the body cavity in times of danger. Stimulation of the siphon, either by touch or by a squirt from a water jet, elicits this withdrawal (see Figure 2.2). Siphon withdrawal, controlled by a few identifiable neurons, shows habituation and many of the features listed by Thompson and Spencer (1966).

Both dishabituation and spontaneous recovery of siphon withdrawal to a tactile stimulus are illustrated in Figure 2.3. After six touch stimulations, responding has nearly ceased. This indicates habituation. A light is then flashed as a dishabituator (indicated by L on the abscissa), which reinstates responding to the next presentation of the tactile stimulus. The light stimulus is repeated again later, but it has a smaller dishabituating influence when given after the ninth tactile stimulus presentation. A 60-minute rest interval leads to spontaneous recovery of response to the touch stimulus: Presentation of the tactile stimulus produces a large response, which then rehabituates. Once again, the light stimulus produces dishabituation to the tactile stimulus.

By measuring nerve potentials on the stimulus and the response sides of the siphon circuit, Kandel and his colleagues have isolated the change that occurs in habituation to a decrease in the sensitivity of the motor neuron to stimulation by the sensory neuron. Basically, habituation occurs at the synapse (or junction) between two cells. The sensory neuron, which detects the touch, retains its sensitivity; the motor neuron controlling withdrawal retains its responsivity. The learned change is in the flow of synaptic chemicals between the two nerve cells, so that the sensory neuron does not activate the motor neuron.

Biological psychologists have long sought an *engram,* a word used to refer to the change that occurs in the nervous system to encode new learning. The work of Thompson and Kandel and their students illustrates how contemporary researchers are closing in on the engram. This is

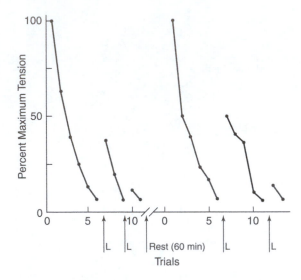

Figure 2.3 **Habituation of Siphon Withdrawal of *aplysia* to a Tactile Stimulus.** The response measured is the tension of the siphon withdrawal to tactile stimulation. Dishabituation to the tactile stimulus occurs following presentation of a light stimulus.

Source: Adapted from Lukowiak and Jacklet (1972).

obviously basic research, not applied, and it has contributed substantially to our understanding of the neural basis of learning. In fact, Eric Kandel was awarded the Nobel Prize in Medicine or Physiology in 2000. His life and work are described in his autobiography *In Search of Memory* (Kandel, 2006).

Cognitive Theories

The cognitive approach to habituation suggests that orienting responses are elicited by stimuli that are not recognized, that is, by stimuli that are not already represented in memory. Repeated presentations of a stimulus lead to the formation of a memory of the stimulus. Habituation of orienting indicates the acquisition of that memory.

The Russian psychologist Sokolov introduced many Western researchers to the study of orienting reflexes (e.g., Sokolov, 1963). Sokolov hypothesized that there is a comparator mechanism, which compares the current sensory input to the image of the stimulus stored in memory. An OR is made if the comparator does not find a match to the stimulus in memory, whereas the OR is inhibited if the comparator finds a match. This idea of comparing a stimulus in the environment to one in memory is a characteristic of the cognitive theories.

The theories of Wagner (1976; Whitlow & Wagner, 1984) and Olson (1976), developed from experiments on animals and human infants, respectively, elaborate on the memory system. They state that a stimulus could be remembered in short-term memory, long-term memory, or both. The more permanent, durable habituation seen across sessions or over long intervals reflects the long-term memory for the stimulus. This is the learning we have been talking of when we say that the stimulus becomes known or familiar. However, a stimulus may also be recognized if it has occurred very recently and is still remembered in short-term memory. Thus, a current stimulus can be recognized by the comparator if it matches a representation in either short-term memory or long-term memory (see Figure 2.4).

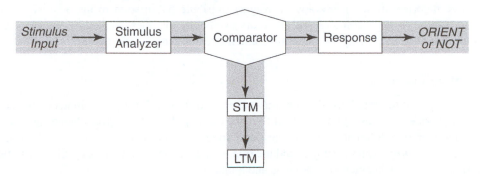

Figure 2.4 **A Generalized Cognitive Model of Habituation.** Stimulus input is compared to representations in short-term memory and in long-term memory. A match between input and what is stored in memory will lead to inhibition of responding. A mismatch will lead to an orienting response.

This dual-memory theory describes why massed stimulus presentations can produce more habituation than spaced presentations. When the stimuli are repeated closely together, a given stimulus can be recognized as familiar either from short-term or long-term memory. When stimuli are spaced apart, the short-term representation will have been forgotten, and so recognition can only occur if the stimulus is represented in long-term memory (Whitlow & Wagner, 1984).

Memory also stores knowledge that the stimulus occurred in a particular setting or at a particular time. Cognitive theories incorporate the notion of *expectancy*, or an active prediction, for what stimulus will occur, where it will occur, and when. You have probably habituated to the bell that rings in the school halls to signal class changes. If the bell now rings off schedule, or if the bell rang in your home, it would no doubt elicit a startle reaction. This notion is incorporated in Sokolov's (1963) and Wagner's (1976) ideas that the surprising occurrence of a stimulus elicits orienting. An expected occurrence of that same stimulus does not elicit orienting, even though the stimulus is objectively the same in both cases.

An example of this expectancy effect is the study of the *missing stimulus* (e.g., Siddle, 1985; Siddle & Lipp, 1997). After exposure to a fixed sequence of stimuli, such as Tone-Light (T-L), on test trials the second stimulus is omitted, so just T—occurs. The absence of an expected light stimulus in this case provokes an OR, just after the time when the light should have occurred. What is interesting here is that an OR is triggered by—nothing. The absence of an expected something elicits orienting. Cognitive theory says that, based on our experiences, we learn an expectancy for a particular pattern of stimulation. When events violate the expectancy, orienting occurs.

The missing stimulus effect occurs in daily life with the sudden realization that what was expected did not happen: The alarm clock didn't go off! The missing stimulus effect is vividly illustrated by my own experiences with opposite ends of the child-rearing spectrum: suddenly awakening at night because the baby *did not* cry for a late feeding; and 17 years later awakening because I *did not* hear him come home yet.

Explanations of Habituation: Summary

A response may decrease because the stimulus is not detected (sensory adaptation) or because the response apparatus is temporarily inhibited (effector fatigue). These are two nonlearning explanations that are alternatives to learning-based habituation. Physiological theories of habituation, such as Thompson's, derived from the study of spinal neurons, and Kandel's, from the study of

Aplysia, seek the physiological and biochemical basis for the changes that underlie habituation. Cognitive theories, those of Sokolov or Wagner, attribute habituation to the acquisition of a memory for the repeated stimulus. This memory eventually includes detailed information about the stimulus, such as its temporal patterning, and the relationship to other stimuli.

Perceptual Learning

If we are exposed to variations of a stimulus—such as different font styles, brands of coffee, or varieties of wines—we usually learn the differences among them. **Perceptual learning** refers to learning to perceive differences and similarities among stimuli based on exposure to the stimuli. *Perceptual Learning*, both the subject and the title of an award-winning book by Eleanor Gibson (1969), is a robust phenomenon in animals and humans.

In a classic study of perceptual learning, human subjects, both children and adults, were given a deck of "scribble" cards (Gibson & Gibson, 1955). The scribbles differed in dimensions, such as the tightness of the coils and left–right orientation (see Figure 2.5). One coil was labeled the standard. After viewing it for 5 seconds, the participants then decided whether the other scribbles in the deck matched the standard. The subjects were not informed whether their choices were correct. Over successive sortings of the deck of cards, subjects became more accurate in identifying matching versus different scribbles. On the basis of such experience, the participants had learned to perceptually differentiate among the scribbles.

Exposure to a stimulus can affect later learning about the stimulus. For example, it should be easier to learn someone's name if the name is a familiar word rather than an unfamiliar name. Once we have learned to perceive, recognize, or identify a stimulus, it is easier to learn other things about this stimulus, such as its name or its use. In a perceptual learning experiment by Gibson and Walk (1956), young rats were continuously exposed in their home cages to cutouts

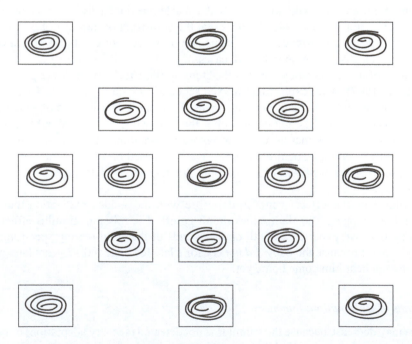

Figure 2.5 Scribbles Used to Assess Perceptual Learning.

Source: From "Perceptual Learning: Differentiation or Enrichment?" by J. J. Gibson and E. J. Gibson, 1955, *Psychological Review*, 62, p. 36. Copyright © 1955 by the American Psychological Association and reprinted with permission.

of a triangle and a circle for 90 days. Subsequently, these same stimuli were used as cues in a discrimination experiment. One of the shapes was used to mark the correct turn in a maze that led to the food-rewarded goal box. The other shape marked the incorrect choice that led to the nonrewarded goal. Gibson and Walk found that subjects given preexposures learned the maze faster. These subjects had already learned to distinguish between the two shapes. The control subjects without prior exposure to the shapes first had to master this discrimination between circle and triangle.

Researchers have studied perceptual learning using numerous classes of stimuli, from colors and faces to reading X-ray negatives. Simple exposure to different stimuli does not ensure learning to differentiate among them. When asked to select the picture of a penny from among eight versions shown, few people could identify the real one (Nickerson & Adams, 1979). (Does Lincoln face right or left?) Perceptual differentiation among stimuli seems to require attentional weighting: increasing our attention to features that distinguish among stimuli (Goldstone, 1998). In the penny example, we assign a higher weight to the color "copper" to differentiate a penny from a dime, than to which direction Lincoln is facing. (He is facing to our right.)

Perceptual learning occurs in learning to discriminate language sounds, such as "ba" and "da," or the *r/l* difference that is present in English (but not in Japanese). Adult English language users differentiate these sounds. However, the language Hindi has a pair of *t* sounds, which adult speakers of Hindi differentiate but which English-speaking adults do not. Do we learn to differentiate sounds in our language through exposure? Or is the capacity to discriminate there to begin with, and we lose those differences that are not present in the language we are hearing? Werker (1989) studied infant perceptual categorization, and found that infants in English-speaking environments can discriminate the two Hindi *t*s at 6 months of age, but lose this ability between ages 8 and 12 months. Experience may both promote new categories of knowledge and may also prevent the loss of existing categories.

Factors Affecting Perceptual Learning

Presenting Contrasting Stimuli

Stimuli differ along a number of dimensions, and perceptual learning requires identification of which dimensions are relevant for discrimination. Thus, presentation of both positive and negative instances seems to be necessary. Simply repeating a single standard stimulus should not lead to efficient learning to distinguish that stimulus from others.

In the Gibson and Gibson (1955) scribbles experiment mentioned earlier, the different scribble cards were presented in an unsystematic order. Does the sequence of presentation of correct and incorrect exemplars affect ease of learning? This question was addressed in a study in which subjects learned to differentiate similar looking faces (Dwyer, Mundy, & Honey, 2011). The face pictures were sequenced to alternate pairs of similar faces (say face A and then face A'), or a block of face A pictures was shown followed by a block of A' faces. Because the two pictures were not presented simultaneously, the comparison had to be made between the memory of the previous face with the presently viewed face. Stimulus learning was faster when similar items were contrasted more often in the alternation sequence.

Transfer from Easy to Difficult Stimuli

Initial experience with an easy discrimination can facilitate learning of a more difficult discrimination. For instance, one perceptual-learning task requires the detection of a line that has a different vertical orientation than the remaining lines—for example, the last upright line in the following:// /// /// \. An easy differentiation occurs when the test line is rotated 45 degrees from the orientation of the remaining lines, such as// / \. In a page full of lines, a more difficult detection is finding a test line that is only 30 degrees different, such as// //|. Practice with the more obvious differentiation facilitates later learning of the more difficult differentiation.

Attention and Feedback

Does the subject need to be actively attempting to distinguish among the stimuli, as in sorting them into same–different categories? Is feedback about the correctness of the categorizing necessary? Research on other types of learning, such as the mere exposure effect (later in this chapter), shows convincingly that learning about stimuli occurs in the absence of intention to learn. However, learning to differentiate among similar stimuli seems to require some intention to focus on differences among the stimuli. Gibson (1969) said that perceptual learning is an active process of exploring stimuli in an attempt to obtain information about them. Perceptual learning does occur in the absence of experimenter feedback about performance. Yet the demands of the tasks we impose on our subjects suggest there are dimensions that separate specific stimuli. The experimenter's instructions "Are these scribbles the same or different?" suggests we should look for differences.

Other Effects of Stimulus Exposure

Simple exposure to a stimulus produces learning that can be revealed by a variety of other behavioral outcomes. Habituation is just one outcome. Learning from exposure to a stimulus can be manifested in several other phenomena.

Preference for Familiar Stimuli

Exposure to a stimulus sometimes leads to an affective, or emotional, increase in the preference for the stimulus. This is known as the **mere exposure effect** (Zajonc, 1968), so-called because the stimulus has merely been presented in the absence of rewards, problems, or other tasks that might actively evoke stimulus processing. Both animals and humans show this increased liking of familiar stimuli. Abraham Maslow (1937), later known for his contributions to humanistic psychology, conducted a study in which his experimental participants performed a number of tasks across several evenings in a laboratory setting. Some tasks were repeated, for example, copying sentences or reading lists of foreign names. Other tasks were used as distractors to mask the true purpose of the study, for example, completing personality inventories. When subsequently asked to judge their preferences, subjects liked familiar tasks, the familiar lab, and even the familiar pictures that were on the wall!

Animals also develop a preference for the familiar, especially places or foods (Hill, 1978). Rats are at first wary of a new food, taste, or odor. This **neophobia**, or literally "fear of the new," declines with continued (safe) exposure to the food. Rats exposed to a saccharine solution will at first drink very little, but eventually come to prefer it over less familiar tastes. (See Box 2.2 for a further discussion of food neophobia.) Apparently, here familiarity breeds liking and not contempt.

Box 2.2 Avoidance and Preference for New Food Tastes

Many animals are reluctant at first to consume new foods. *Taste neophobia* makes good evolutionary sense, to be cautious about new foods whose effects on the body are unknown. Some phenomena we have considered in this chapter, habituation and mere exposure, suggest that taste neophobia could be overcome by simple exposure to the new food. Indeed, animal researchers often must incorporate this as a preliminary stage in a research study. We realize the animal subjects will need to adapt, or get used to, the various food reinforcers to be employed.

The reduction of neophobia via exposure has been experimentally demonstrated. Domjan (1976) gave rats 30 minutes daily access to a solution of saccharin in water, a new taste for the rats. Saccharin consumption was weak at first but increased across the 20 days of the study.

Is the reduction of taste neophobia purely a habituation effect? Taste learning might involve something more, specifically learning that the food is safe to eat. This is referred to as the *learned safety* hypothesis. Learning that a food is not poisonous is different from learning to ignore a stimulus that is without consequence, as a habituation explanation might suggest. Rats given a single exposure to a distinctive flavor later had difficulty in learning an aversion to this taste when it did cause illness (Siegel, 1974).

Getting children to eat new foods is often a challenge. Can exposure to a new food increase liking? Most of us have heard the line "I tried it once; I didn't like it." The problem is, once is not enough. Studies of adults (Pliner, 1982) and children (Birch & Marlin, 1982) have shown that many exposures, 10 or more, may be necessary to induce acceptance of new cheeses or juices.

By contrast, a single exposure to a taste in 4- to 7-month-olds sufficed to make a new food acceptable, with some generalization to another food within the same category (i.e., between baby food peaches to pears or from carrots to corn; Birch, Gunder, Grimm-Thomas, & Laing, 1998). Infants have had less experience with tastes than children have had, so one exposure may have a greater impact than does a single taste for a 4-year-old child. So, new foods may be accepted more readily at an earlier age.

Habituation can play a role in regulating meal duration and meal termination. Repeated or extended exposure to a taste over short time periods decreases preference. Thus, habituation can occur to the taste of a single food sampled several times within a taste testing session, leading to a decrease in preference or consumption (Booth, 1990; Rolls, 1990). Sometimes that first bite of your favorite food is the best tasting. For example, after consuming one meal of crackers and cheese, subjects will eat less of a second meal of the same food, but will eat more if a different food is offered. This taste habituation is transient, and the overall liking will return after a period of abstinence from the taste.

The implication of this finding is that meals with few different tastes will produce more taste habituation, leading to less overall consumption and less likelihood of meal resumption. Your cafeteria's strategy of making everything taste the same might actually promote healthier eating.

In one demonstration of the mere exposure effect, college-aged and elderly subjects were shown a list of Japanese ideograms (Wiggs, 1993). These are complex symbols representing words and are unfamiliar to U.S. subjects. Each stimulus was presented for 2 seconds. Later, these ideograms and some new ones were presented and the subjects were asked to rate their "liking" of each stimulus on a 7-point scale. The results, shown in Figure 2.6, show average liking of stimuli by the two age groups as a function of how often the stimuli had been presented during the mere exposure phase. Stimuli seen three times previously were more liked than stimuli seen once or never before. These liking effects were found with both age groups.

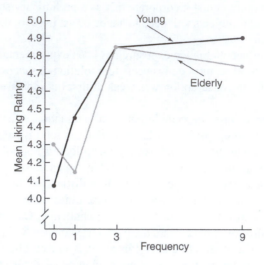

Figure 2.6 **Liking for Japanese Ideogram Stimuli.** Graph plots mean liking rating by elderly and young
adult subjects who had previously seen each stimulus 1, 3, or 9 times, or had never seen it.

Source: From "Aging and Memory for Frequency of Occurrence of Novel, Visual Stimuli: Direct and Indirect Measures,"
by C. L. Wiggs, 1993, *Psychology and Aging, 8,* p. 406. Copyright © 1993 by the American Psychological Association.
Reprinted with permission.

According to the cognitive theories of stimulus learning, exposure leads to the formation of a
memory for the stimulus. We could have tested memory by simply asking subjects if they remembered the stimulus (e.g., have them choose the familiar one from an array of distractors). But what if
the subjects did not remember the stimulus that had been presented? Would they still prefer it? The
intriguing possibility is that the affect, expressed as a liking or preference, is a separable judgment
from conscious memory for the stimulus. Kunst-Wilson and Zajonc (1980) tested this hypothesis by
flashing pictures of irregularly shaped nonsense objects at a speed faster than their subjects could
consciously perceive them. Later, the subjects were shown pairs of shapes and were asked one of two
questions: Which shapes had they seen before and which shapes did they like better? Performance on
the memory test for the previously seen shapes was at chance level: The subjects could not correctly
distinguish between the old shapes and new ones presented for the first time during testing. This
finding seems perfectly reasonable, because the images had initially been presented for such a short
duration that they could not be consciously perceived, much less remembered. However, when asked
which objects they liked, there was a consistent preference for the preexposed shape. The subjects
seemed to prefer these objects even though they did not recognize the shapes as familiar.

The study by Kunst-Wilson and Zajonc (1980) is an important demonstration of the fact that
experience can have a variety of effects, not all of which are available to conscious recall.

Why does mere exposure make a stimulus more pleasing? The perceptual fluency hypothesis
states that we affectively prefer stimuli that are easily perceived. That is, images, sounds, tastes,
and so on that are more readily perceived because of previous experience are more preferred.
Several exposures to a difficult-to-read word increases our fluency in reading that word, and also
increases preference (Reber, Winkielmanm, & Schwartz, 1998).

Potentiated Startle

As noted earlier in this chapter, one component of the orienting reaction is the startle response.
For instance, a 90-decibel noise burst, lasting 40 milliseconds, will cause a startle reaction. This
startle response can be magnified if the stimulus occurs in the presence of other, background

sources of arousal. In **potentiated startle**, the arousal elicited by the startle noise can combine with arousal due to nervousness or fear, leading to a larger startle reaction. The potentiated response procedure is useful for detecting the presence of fear: the more fear, the greater the enhancement of the startle.

The sources of fear that would potentiate a startle response include a steady state of fear, as when someone is generally nervous, and a specific moment of fear, as when I suddenly announce a pop quiz to the class. Both general and specific sources of fear enhance startle (Grillon, 2002). For instance, startle is enhanced in individuals with some types of anxiety, such as panic disorder or posttraumatic stress disorder (PTSD). In the context of the laboratory setting, people who are anxious produce a larger startle to the noise burst than do less-anxious subjects. In addition, we can present specific stimuli that signal the threat of an electric shock. If the startle noise is presented during the threat signal, the startle response is larger than that elicited by the noise burst without the threat signal.

The two sources of anxiety, general and specific, can be combined if we study individuals with PTSD. Such individuals are generally anxious, and respond with larger and more persistent startle responses during the experimental sessions. In addition, they may show potentiated startle during a threatening stimulus. The point of such research is to learn something about anxiety, both general and specific; about the cues that that trigger fear, such as the laboratory or the threat; and about the underlying brain circuitry involved.

Recapitulation: The Effects of Repeated Stimulus Presentation

Exposure to a given stimulus produces varied, and sometimes conflicting, results. A series of repetitions of a meaningless stimulus can lead to habituation, or a decrease in orienting to the stimulus. Exposure can also increase the liking or preference for the now-familiar stimulus, what we called the *mere exposure effect*. Familiarization with a stimulus can facilitate new learning, what Gibson called *perceptual learning*. Presentation of a fear-associated stimulus can produce *sensitization*, or an increase in the orienting response to the stimulus; or *potentiated startle*, an enhanced response to another stimulus. This pattern of effects from ostensibly the same manipulation, stimulus presentation, is disconcerting. However, there are rules making the outcome of a particular manipulation more predictable.

Applications

Habituation certainly occurs outside the laboratory, often in some fairly mundane ways. The reminders you posted on the refrigerator, too far in advance, are unnoticed by the time you need to act on them. You decide to study in a new place thinking there will be less distraction, but in fact there is more distraction as you orient to this new environment.

In a laboratory simulation, students attempted to study while office noises and speech sounds were played in the background (Banbury & Berry, 1997). The noise initially disrupted learning, but after 20 minutes of exposure the noise was less disruptive. As with other forms of habituation, a brief interval without stimulation restored the disruptive effect of the noise, that is, there was spontaneous recovery.

Other instances of habituation have considerably more significance.

Warning labels have been on cigarette packages for decades, yet the warnings on U.S. packages may not work well. Heavy smokers may be exposed to 7,000 warnings per year, and have probably habituated to the messages. Thus, new graphic warnings have been mandated in the United States. The warnings would be larger, and include color and pictures (e.g., diseased lungs). The changed warnings are noticed—at least at first. But whether the new warnings will habituate over time is not yet known. A cross-national study found that in countries with graphic warnings, such as Canada and the United Kingdom, more people noticed the warnings, even several years after introduction, than noticed the blander warnings in the United States (Hammond et al., 2007).

Exposure Therapy for Fears

An application of considerable importance is the use of stimulus exposures in treating anxiety and phobias. The method of exposure therapy, sometimes called emotional flooding or implosion, uses controlled exposure to feared stimuli or situations. **Exposure therapy** is the use of repeated or prolonged exposure to fear stimuli in order to reduce fear. If you have a fear of flying, your therapist might at some point prescribe a long plane flight. If you fear snakes, attendance at the Indiana Jones Film Festival may be suggested.

(Some therapies go a step further by pairing the phobic object with pleasant consequences such as relaxation. These counterconditioning therapies are discussed in the next chapter.)

Exposure therapy often starts off with presentation of a milder version of the phobic object and gradually increases its intensity or proximity across presentations. An example from animal behavioral therapy is a report of a large dog named Goliath who was fearful during thunderstorms. The dog ran around the room, jumping on furniture, knocking things over, and generally causing mayhem. Treatment consisted of playing a thunderstorm recording, starting at a low volume that did not elicit fear. The volume was gradually increased as the dog came to tolerate the noise without adverse reaction, until the recording could be played at high volume. The researchers said the dog did not react to real thunder sounds afterwards (Tuber, Hothersall, & Voith, 1974).

One proponent of exposure therapy is David Barlow (e.g., Barlow, 2000). Rather than trying to minimize the fear that the situation provokes, Barlow advocates exposure with maximal arousal and contact with the feared stimulus or situation. For example, for a young man who feared closed places, the advice was to shut himself in a small space for as long as he could take it. The man repeatedly locked himself in the trunk of his car until the last such experience simply left him bored (Slater, 2003). Patients are sometimes encouraged to "juice up" on coffee to increase their feelings of anxiety during exposure treatment—for example, just before giving a public speech. (This could be the basis for a new reality TV show.)

A novel modification of exposure therapy is *virtual reality* exposure therapy. For example, to treat the fear of flying, an individual is presented with flying-related stimuli while wearing a virtual reality helmet. Computer-generated visual images are displayed on the inside of the helmet's visor, and airplane sounds are presented over headphones or from large bass speakers (which also produce vibrations that mimic an actual plane). Takeoffs and landings can be simulated, as well as different flying conditions. In one study, four sessions of virtual reality therapy were as effective as a control therapy conducted in actual (nonflying) airplanes. The treated subjects in both conditions reported less fear and anxiety about flying, and 76 percent actually took a post-treatment air flight to prove the point (Rothbaum et al., 2006).

Do exposure therapies work? They have proved difficult to evaluate because of the many variations across clinical research studies: different versions of exposure therapy; exposure to actual phobic stimuli or exposure to imagined stimuli; students who volunteer as subjects versus clinic patients who seek therapy; and the criteria for evaluating success of the therapy. However, a recent review concluded that exposure treatments for specific phobias (heights, animals, flying, etc.) are effective by several measures of fear: self-reported distress; decreased arousal in skin-conductance or heart rate; and greater willingness to approach feared stimuli (such as allowing proximity to a snake, or actually flying in a plane; Choy, Fyer, & Lipsitz, 2007). Exposure is also effective in treating post-traumatic stress disorder (PTSD). In these days of evidence-based medicine, exposure therapies have strong scientific support for their efficacy. However, there is reluctance by some people to expose themselves to the thing they most fear, and by therapists to employ exposure (Foa, Gillihan, & Bryant, 2013).

Summary

Habituation is a simple form of learning. Yet, however simple, the fact is that exposures to a stimulus have complex effects on the organism's subsequent reactions to that stimulus.

The Orienting Response

A novel stimulus elicits an orienting response, a composite of physiological and behavioral reactions that includes startle, sense-receptor focusing, increased arousal, and a readiness for fight or flight. A familiar stimulus can also elicit orienting if the stimulus is meaningful or unexpected.

Habituation

Habituation is the decrease in size or frequency of the orienting reaction to a stimulus that is repeatedly presented. Habituation is a simple form of learning. Habituation of orienting applies to neutral or innocuous stimuli, although defensive reactions to painful and noxious stimuli also show habituation.

Habituation is studied via responses such as startle, eyeblink, or the skin conductance response. A widely used measure with infants is the decrease in duration of eye fixations to visual stimuli.

Thompson and Spencer described several parametric features of habituation. These features represent a standard set of criteria for evaluating habituation across different species, tasks, or responses. More frequent repetitions of a stimulus produce a greater decrement in the size or frequency of the response. If the stimulus is withheld for a period of time, the response tends to recover. Habituation is affected by the spacing between successive stimulus presentations. Massed stimulations produce more habituation in the short term; spaced repetitions sometimes produce more long-term habituation as assessed hours or days later. The presentation of a different stimulus will temporarily restore orienting to the first stimulus, a phenomenon called dishabituation. Habituation is stimulus-specific. Responding diminishes specifically to the repeated stimulus, not to all novel stimuli. Habituation may generalize to similar stimuli.

Explanations of Habituation

A response decrement could occur for reasons other than learning. Sensory adaptation or effector fatigue are two such nonlearning possibilities.

Dual-process theory states that the response to repetitive stimulation reflects the combination of habituation and sensitization. Some neurons show habituation, whereas other neurons react to intense levels of stimulation and increase responsiveness. For example, the startle response actually increases across stimulations if tested against a sensitizing loud background noise level.

Another biological approach is to study habituation in *Aplysia*. Siphon withdrawal, controlled by a few identifiable neurons, shows many of the parametric features of habituation. By measuring nerve potentials on the stimulus and the response sides of the siphon circuit, Kandel has found that habituation is a decrease in the sensitivity of the motor neuron to stimulation by the sensory neuron.

Cognitive theories hypothesize that a memory of the repeated stimulus is formed. Subsequent sensory input is compared to this memory. Orienting occurs when a new stimulus differs from memory, and habituation occurs when there is a match. Cognitive theory also says that a stimulus can be remembered in either short-term or long-term memory. Short-term habituation occurs when there is a smaller response after a short interval between stimulus repetitions than after a longer interval. Long-term memory generates an expectancy for which stimuli will occur when. Dishabituation occurs in the absence of an expected stimulus (the missing stimulus effect).

Perceptual Learning

Exposure to variations in a stimulus leads to learning about differentiating features of that stimulus. After experience with a number of similar stimuli, such as the scribbles in Gibson's research, we can learn to perceptually differentiate one scribble from a different one. Perceptual learning is enhanced by attention to the features that distinguish among stimuli, exposure to contrasting stimuli, and prior practice with stimuli that are easier to distinguish before practicing more difficult discriminations.

Other Effects of Stimulus Exposure

Stimulus repetition does not always lead to a decrement in responding as in habituation. Exposure to a stimulus sometimes leads to a preference or liking of the stimulus. This is known as the mere exposure effect, because the stimulus has merely been presented. In potentiated startle the usual orienting reaction to a stimulus is increased when the stimulus occurs in the presence of high background levels of arousal, as occurs when the participant is nervous or anxious.

Applications

Stimulus exposure is used in treating anxiety and phobias. Exposure therapy uses controlled exposure to feared stimuli or situations. Exposure begins with a milder version of the phobic object and gradually increases in intensity or proximity across presentations. Exposure may be to the actual phobic object itself, or the subjects can be asked to imagine the phobic objects or situation.

Do exposure therapies work? They have proved difficult to evaluate because of many variations in subject populations, procedures, and assessment criteria used across clinical research studies. Extensive research has shown that exposure therapy is effective in reducing specific phobias and in the treatment of posttraumatic stress disorder.

3   Classical Conditioning

Most students have some general familiarity with Pavlov's experiments. In a typical salivary conditioning experiment on dogs, the sound of the bell was followed a few seconds later by the presentation of some food. Several of these bell–food trials were administered and salivation to the bell was monitored. After several pairings, the dog began to salivate during the bell (Pavlov, 1927/1960, which is the standard reference to G. V. Anrep's translation). Pavlovian conditioning, as this procedure is also known, suffers from something of a multiple-personality problem. On the one hand, it is considered to be a simple, almost reflexive form of learning that does not require sophisticated nervous system involvement. Conditioning simply transfers a response from one stimulus to another. These beliefs underlie popular culture references to someone who responds like "Pavlov's dog," a caricature promoted by writers such as Aldous Huxley (in his *Brave New World*) to the Rolling Stones.

On the other hand, researchers have long known that conditioning is more complex than any popular stereotype suggests. Osgood, in the standard textbook of experimental psychology from the 1950s, wrote, "Naivete with regard to conditioning is due . . . more to the fond hope that the process would prove as simple as conventional diagrams imply. The phenomena of conditioning are actually very complicated" (1953, p. 316). Contemporary theories have a distinctly cognitive flavor in describing conditioning. "Pavlovian conditioning is not a stupid process by which the organism willy-nilly forms associations between any two stimuli that happen to co-occur. Rather, the organism is better seen as an information seeker using logical and perceptual relations among events . . . to form a sophisticated representation of the world" (Rescorla, 1988, p. 154). By using the knowledge learned in conditioning, organisms can flexibly respond in an adaptive fashion.

Research on **classical conditioning** has gone through cycles in its 100-year history. At first eagerly grasped as a tool to study learning, Pavlovian conditioning was replaced by reward conditioning with its emphasis on the modification of voluntary behavior. However, research into Pavlovian conditioning once again became popular. What factors contributed to this renewed dominance of Pavlovian conditioning? Some researchers view conditioning from an ecological or evolutionary perspective and consider its role in ensuring survival (Hollis, 1997). The application of conditioning to areas such as drug tolerance and immune system regulation has connected conditioning to the field of health psychology. And classical conditioning offers model systems for neuroscientists to study the biology of learning.

Possibly foremost among our reasons for studying classical conditioning is to conduct basic research on associative learning. *Associative learning* refers to the hypothesized connections that are formed between the internal representations of events, such as stimuli and responses. A simple illustration is word associations, for example, the stimulus word TABLE often evokes CHAIR as a response. But when and how are associations formed? Classical conditioning is one tool we can use to study the conditions under which associative learning occurs.

The Definition of Classical Conditioning

Simply put, *classical conditioning* can be defined as the presentation of two (or more) events in an experimentally determined temporal relationship. A change in responding to one of those events is measured as an indication of whether an association has been learned between them. The learning that occurs in classical conditioning can be described on several levels: behavioral, as the learning of a new response; cognitive, as the acquisition of knowledge about the relationship between stimuli; or neural, as the pattern of synaptic changes that underlie conditioning.

Say we are to perform an experiment in which mild but aversive electric shocks are to be presented randomly in time. Because of our ethical discomfort with shocking animals or college students, let us suppose the participants are all faculty in the Economics Department. The shocks, delivered to the participants' forearm, are unavoidable, but our participants would desperately like to know when each is about to occur. We sound a tone for a few seconds before each shock. What will the participants learn? After several pairings of tone followed by shock, the tone will probably come to elicit a behavioral reaction of hand flexion; physiological reactions such as muscular tensing or bracing; and knowledge of the tone–shock relationship that can be verbalized.

Classical conditioning is a procedure that incorporates several features illustrated in the preceding example. First, two stimuli are presented. One stimulus, labeled the **unconditioned stimulus** (or **US**), is significant to the subject at the start of the experiment; for example, food or shock. The unconditioned stimulus elicits an **unconditioned response** (or **UR**), often reflexively

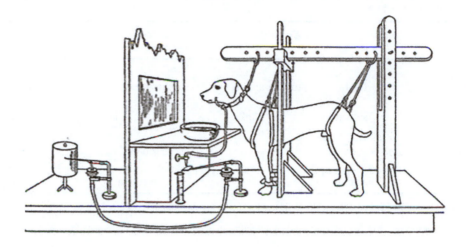

Figure 3.1 Pavlov's Salivary Conditioning Apparatus.

Source: From "The Method of Pavlov in Animal Psychology," by R. M. Yerkes and S. Morgulis, 1909, Psychological Bulletin, 6, p. 257–273. Copyright © 1909 by the American Psychological Association. Reprinted by permission.

without prior training. For example, in Pavlov's experiments, food served as the US to elicit salivation as the UR. The second stimulus, the **conditioned stimulus** (or **CS**) is a neutral stimulus such as a tone, light, or bell. This stimulus is actually a to-be-conditioned stimulus at the onset of the experiment. The CS is neutral in the sense that it does not at first elicit the same response as does the US. For example, the tone at first does not evoke flexion or salivation. Certainly, if the tone is novel, it will evoke orienting reactions (as described in Chapter 2).

The CS and the US are presented in a specified sequence, usually the CS first followed by the US. In Pavlov's experiments, a tone sounded for a few seconds and then food powder was blown via a tube into the dog's mouth (see Figure 3.1). After a sufficient number of pairings, the CS elicited some of the responses originally elicited by the US. Thus, salivation occurred during the tone. This response during the CS (tone) is called the **conditioned response** (or **CR**). The development of a conditioned response to the CS is an indication that conditioning has occurred.

(More appropriate translations of Pavlov's terms would be unconditio*nal* and conditio*nal*. A response is unconditionally elicited by the US at the start of the experiment, but a response to the CS is conditional on the pairing operation. However, psychologists' habit of using the *-ed* ending is hard to break.)

Because the conditioned—and unconditioned—responses are both salivation, how do we determine which stimulus is eliciting the salivation? *Conditioned* responding usually occurs during the CS, before the onset of the US. That is, the dog salivates during the several seconds the tone is on before food is presented on that trial. The CR is sometimes referred to as an anticipatory response. We can also intersperse CS-alone test trials, omitting the US, among the conditioning trials. In this manner we can see response to the CS in the absence of any response elicited by the US.

Methods of Studying Classical Conditioning

Pavlov's procedure of salivary conditioning is rarely used today. The tendency is to use smaller animals or to use humans, both of which are more economical, or to use preparations that are relevant to a specific application. A few exemplar methods referred to often in this chapter are described below (see Table 3.1).

Table 3.1 Examples of the Stimuli Used and Responses Measured in Sample Conditioning Tasks Described in This Chapter

TASK:	Salivary Conditioning	Eyeblink Conditioning	Taste-Aversion Learning	Fear Learning
A				
CS → US:	tone → food	tone → airpuff	saccharin → poison	tone → shock
	\	\	\	\
UR:	salivation	blink	illness	fear[a]
B				
CS → US:	tone →	tone →	saccharin →	tone →
	\	\	\	\
CR:	salivation	blink	aversion	fear[a]

A: on CS–US conditioning trials; **B:** on CS-alone test trials after conditioning has occurred.

[a] "Fear" is a nonspecific term that refers to startle, immobility, or attempts to escape the source of the fear.

Representative Procedures

Eyeblink Conditioning

In *eyeblink conditioning* the US is a puff of air directed toward the eye, which elicits an eyeblink as the UR (and other responses as well, such as heart rate changes, but typically only one response is measured at a time). A CS, such as a tone, can be presented just before the airpuff US. The CR would be an eyeblink that occurs to the CS. The eyeblink can be detected by monitoring electrical activity in the eye muscles and recorded from surface electrodes on the skin around the eye. Alternatively, movement of the lid can be detected when the blink breaks a light beam reflected off the eye. In either case, a signal is fed into a computer. From this record, the size of the blink can be measured.

Eyeblink conditioning with human subjects is convenient in that participants are often available, the apparatus is portable, and an experiment can be completed within a single session. The eyeblink response has also been used with dogs, cats, and even rabbits (Gormezano, 1966; Osgood, 1953). Rabbits are especially accommodating (well, maybe passive) and have been the source of much of our recent data. The human and rabbit preparations has been useful in mapping out the neural circuitry involved in eyeblink conditioning.

SCR

Another measure of conditioning is the change in the amplitude of the **skin conductance response**, or **SCR**. This measure of the electrical conductivity of the skin varies with changes in the level of emotionality of the subject. The SCR is measured via electrodes usually placed on the arm or palm. A US such as a loud noise or a mild shock will cause an increase in the SCR as the unconditioned response. On conditioning trials, a CS such as a soft tone or a light is followed with the US, and after several pairings, a conditioned SCR elevation occurs during the CS.

Eyeblink and SCR conditioning fit the traditional definition of classical conditioning, one that closely follows Pavlov's original method by using well-defined stimuli and responses (Gormezano & Kehoe, 1975). In modern research, however, the label of "classical conditioning" is often applied to situations that deviate from the traditional in any of several ways. In some procedures the CR is not the same as the UR, or conditioning is indirectly assessed by the effects that the conditioned stimulus has on other behaviors. These characteristics are illustrated in the following preparations.

Taste Aversion Learning

At one time or another, most of us have developed a food aversion after becoming ill, even if the food itself did not cause the illness. One researcher referred to this as the "sauce Bernaise" effect (Seligman, 1972). Experimental studies of taste aversion typically employ rats as participants. In **taste aversion learning**, a novel taste, saccharin-flavored water for instance, is presented as the CS, which is followed by the administration of an illness-inducing drug as the US. The UR is politely referred to as "gastrointestinal distress," although typically no direct measurements are made of the extent or magnitude of the rat's illness. After the animal has recovered, the taste CS is re-presented to assess the degree of conditioning. Learning is indicated by a decrease in the amount of saccharin-flavored water consumed or by avoidance of the saccharin flavor, as compared to consumption prior to conditioning. Note that gastrointestinal distress to the taste CS is not directly measured as a CR. Instead, conditioning is indirectly assessed by the tendency to avoid the taste, hence the label "taste aversion learning." A variety of other behaviors have been observed as indications of an aversion to the food. Cats shake it off their paws, coyotes bury it, and rats will tip over the food cup (Gustavson, 1977).

Learning which foods are poisonous has obvious survival value. Unlike more traditional responses, such as salivation or the eyeblink, taste aversions are acquired after only a single taste–illness pairing, and are learned with wide temporal separation between the taste and the illness. For these reasons taste aversions can be learned inadvertently. Patients receiving chemotherapy for cancer will sometimes develop an aversion to those foods consumed shortly prior to treatment (Bernstein & Webster, 1980; Carey & Burish, 1988).

Evaluative Conditioning

In **evaluative conditioning** an affectively neutral stimulus, one that is neither particularly liked nor disliked, is presented along with another stimulus that already evokes a strong affective evaluation. We then see if the emotional tone of the neutral stimulus changes as a function of this conditioning experience. The stimuli, both neutral and affective, are often words, names, faces, or pictures. In evaluative conditioning, measurement of the CR and UR are determined by the participants' ratings (or evaluations) of the stimuli (Martin & Levey, 1987).

In one example (Hammerl, Bloch, & Silverthorne, 1997), the USs were scenic photographs of city, park, and public locations that were rated very high or very low on a scale of "liking." Other pictures that had neutral ratings were used as the CSs. Each neutral picture was presented for 2 seconds, followed by a liked or disliked picture for 2 seconds. Five of these pairing trials were given. What the participants actually see is a long series of slides arranged in a particular sequence in which a neutral slide is immediately followed by one of the liked (or disliked) slides. A cover story is used to try to mask the true purpose of the experiment. The participants are later asked to rate the individual pictures for liking. The neutral pictures that had been paired with liked stimuli received more positive ratings than they had before; the neutral slides paired with disliked pictures now received more negative ratings.

Gorn (1982) used evaluative conditioning to demonstrate how advertising could affect product preferences. He showed slide images of a product, a ballpoint pen, during music that was familiar and liked by U.S. college students (music from the film *Grease*) or was unfamiliar (classical Indian music). Evaluative conditioning was measured by allowing the students to choose from among pens of various colors. The color paired with the preferred music was chosen more often.

Evaluative conditioning is not without its skeptics. Some theorists question whether, in the absence of traditional CRs and URs, evaluative conditioning is really classical conditioning. Others question whether the preferences are based on conscious knowledge (DeHouwere, Baeyens, & Field, 2005). As we will see, some of these same concerns are raised about other classical conditioning procedures.

Summary of the Methods of Conditioning

The traditional definition of classical conditioning is exemplified in salivary or eyeblink conditioning: Reflex-eliciting stimuli are used as USs, the food or the airpuff, and the conditioned response is similar in form to the unconditioned response, salivation or an eyeblink. Broadening the domain of conditioning has demonstrated that the laws and regularities of conditioning apply to a wide range of naturalistic behaviors. In addition to the taste aversions described here, conditioning has also been shown to play a role in aggressive, territorial, and mating behaviors in animals (Hollis, 1997). Some methods represent mixtures of several forms of learning. For instance, the initial acquisition of a taste aversion could be due to classical conditioning. The subsequent avoidance of that taste is an instance of reinforcement learning (see avoidance learning in Chapter 5). Classical conditioning has also become a synonym for *associative learning*, when in fact it is one of several methods for studying associative memory.

What Stimuli can Serve as CSs?

The usual textbook examples of to-be-conditioned stimuli are discrete signals such as lights and tones. However, the sudden *offset* of an already present stimulus can serve as an effective CS (e.g., Logan & Wagner, 1962). In a film, the forest suddenly becoming quiet is a sure signal that something dramatic is about to happen. Stimuli including touch, smells, and tastes have also been successfully conditioned.

Diffuse stimuli of time or place can act as conditioned stimuli. *Contextual stimuli*, the place or environment in which training occurs, are readily conditioned (e.g., Dweck & Wagner, 1970; Siegel, Hinson, Krank, & McCully, 1982). Thus, we may fear the dentist's office, just as our pets fear the veterinarian's.

What Stimuli can Serve as USs?

Unconditioned stimuli are typically events that have some biological significance to the organism such as food and shock (Gunther, Miller, & Matute, 1997). The USs in the evaluative conditioning procedure, such as photos, music, or words, have acquired significance. In other cases, we can ask the participant to imagine receiving an aversive US rather than actually presenting an aversive US. That is, "imagine you have been shocked" (Dadds, Bovbjerg, Redd, & Cutmore, 1997). The use of mental imagery and imagination form the basis of some behavioral therapies such as systematic desensitization to reduce phobias (described later in this chapter) or aversion therapy to reduce smoking or drinking. Alternatively, the subject in a conditioning experiment might only observe some other participant receiving it. In a taste-aversion procedure, rats learned an aversion when they saw another rat become ill after eating a certain food (the "poisoned partner" effect, Revusky, Coombes, & Pohl, 1982).

It is important to remember that USs are complex events. They have specific sensory components, for example, taste, touch, sound, as well as general emotional components, for example, fear. Thus, we should expect conditioned responses to be multidimensional also.

Basic Phenomena of Conditioning

Acquisition

Acquisition refers to the development of a conditioned response as a result of CS–US trials. Some procedures, such as eyeblink conditioning, require many pairings to produce CRs and are ideal for plotting learning curves. Other procedures produce such rapid conditioning that a single pairing is sufficient. Not surprisingly, taste-aversion learning is one of these. In some cases, multiple CS–US pairings are given, but measurement of conditioning is made only once at the end of the sequence, as in the evaluative conditioning procedures mentioned earlier. (An example of conditioning is shown in Box 3.1)

Box 3.1   Anxiety and Conditioning

This chapter presents many experimental variables that influence classical conditioning. One variable not considered elsewhere is that of individual differences: Different individuals show different amounts of conditioning. Pavlov described temperamental differences among his dogs that he believed affected ease of conditioning. Surely people differ from one another also.

One personality variable that has been well studied is that of anxiety. The British psychologist Hans Eysenck (1981) believed that anxious individuals have a higher level of arousal in certain brain areas that should facilitate conditioning. Measures of autonomic nervous system activity are elevated in anxious people (e.g., heart rate or sweating). Anxious individuals experience higher levels of emotional responsiveness, which would add to the mild fear produced by an aversive US, such as an airpuff or shock.

Individuals with posttraumatic stress disorder (or PTSD) are also characterized by heightened responsiveness to emotional stimuli. Do these individuals classically condition more rapidly than non-PTSD individuals? Orr et al. (2000) compared aversive conditioning in PTSD and non-PTSD individuals. One important matching variable was the fact that the members of the non-PTSD group had also experienced traumas, such as combat experiences or motor vehicle accidents, but had not developed PTSD in reaction. The CSs were colored circles projected on a computer monitor. A certain color was consistently paired with an electric shock to the fingers as the US (described by the investigators as "highly annoying"). A measure of conditioning was the size of the skin-conductance response during the CS. During a habituation phase, only the color CSs were presented. Yet the PTSD group gave a larger skin-conductance response, indicating greater reactivity to stimuli in an emotional situation (see Figure 3.2). During the conditioning phase, the PTSD group

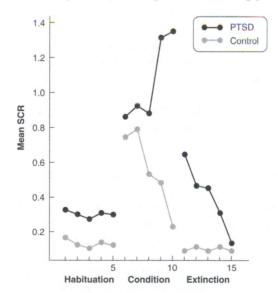

Figure 3.2 Mean size of the SCR (skin conductance response) during the CS-only habituation trials; CS-shock conditioning trials; and CS-only extinction trials.

Source: From "De Novo Conditioning in Trauma-Exposed Individuals with and without Posttraumatic Stress Disorder," by S. P. Orr, L. I. Metzger, N. B. Lasko, M. L. Macklin, T. Peri, and R. K. Pitman, 2000, *Journal of Abnormal Psychology, 109*, p. 294. Copyright 2000 by the American Psychological Association. Adapted with permission.

showed larger reactions during the color CSs. The responses of the non-PTSD participants actually became smaller across conditioning trials, probably reflecting some adaptation to the shock. Finally, during an extinction phase, the PTSD subjects were more persistent in responding to the CS, even though the shock was no longer given.

A cognitive explanation of the effects of anxiety assumes that anxious individuals are more likely to rehearse aversive experiences, such as the unpleasant US (Davey & Matchett, 1994). To test this idea, subjects were first given conditioning involving a loud noise US. Following this, an explicit "rehearsal" stage was added in which the participants were encouraged to imagine, as vividly as possible, the noise US. Subsequent testing showed that the anxious individuals became more fearful of the CS. The conditioned response had increased without further direct experience with the conditioning stimuli, but through rumination about them.

This enhancing effect of anxiety may sound paradoxical at first. We usually assume that anxiety inhibits learning. However anxiety may retard performance in a more complex task. For example, in discrimination training a CS+ is paired with the US, but a CS− is not. High anxiety participants respond more to CS+, but they also respond more to CS− than do low anxiety participants. There is a smaller difference in responding between the two CSs than among the low anxiety participants, or less discrimination (Orr et al., 2000).

According to Eysenck (1981), high anxiety individuals who are exposed to aversive life experiences (just like the low anxiety individuals) unfortunately may acquire more conditioned fear reactions from those experiences. The high anxiety individuals may also discriminate less between stimuli that do or do not predict dangers, and thus they may generalize these fears to more stimuli. The result is more generalized anxiety, provoked by more stimuli in the world.

Control Procedures

Although a conditioned response to the CS may indicate that conditioning has occurred, the response could occur for other reasons. A rat that has been given poison as the US may then shy away from all new foods and not only the conditioned taste. Eyeblinks and SCRs occur as orienting and startle responses to the novel stimuli used as the CSs. Therefore, control conditions are needed to demonstrate that the response we observe is due to conditioning. The amount of responding to the CS in a control condition can serve as a baseline with which to compare responding by the conditioning group.

In the usual procedure, both the CS and the US are presented during the experimental sessions, but the two stimuli are not presented together. Experimental participants receive CS–US pairs and control participants receive unpaired CSs and USs. This equates the overall exposure to the stimuli. In the *random control* procedure (Rescorla, 1967) the CS and the US are each separately programmed to occur at random times during the experimental sessions. The idea is that the occurrences of the CS and US are not correlated; they have a zero correlation.

What is the appropriate control condition to use? The answer may be to determine for each preparation (eyeblink, SCR, etc.) whether the different controls produce different baseline levels of responding. For instance, Schneiderman, Fuentes, and Gormezano (1962) studied eyeblink conditioning in the rabbit and included a number of control conditions: presentations of the CS only, the US only, unpaired CSs and USs, and randomly scheduled CSs and USs. The results showed that none of the controls produced many eyeblinks during the CS.

Extinction

Extinction is the presentation of an already conditioned CS alone, but without the US. The result is a decrease and maybe the eventual disappearance of the CR, which we call extinction of the response.

One might think that extinction is the opposite of acquisition: If pairing the CS and US leads to conditioning, then it seems logical that the process could be reversed to remove conditioning. However, extinction does not eliminate the CS–US association, but only suppresses it. We see this when the supposedly extinguished response reappears after the CS has been withheld for a while. Then, re-presentation of the CS leads to a recurrence of the conditioned response. This **spontaneous recovery** shows that responding to the CS was only inhibited by extinction.

Extinction and spontaneous recovery are illustrated in Figure 3.3 using data from salivary conditioning in dogs (Wagner, Siegel, Thomas, & Ellison, 1964). Within each session, the response to the CS alone extinguishes. From the end of one session to the start of the next, spontaneous recovery occurs. Extinction proceeds more rapidly day by day, and less spontaneous recovery occurs, so eventually the CR nearly disappears.

The pattern just illustrated has a practical implication for what to expect if you try to extinguish an unwanted conditioned response. Repeated extinctions likely will be necessary. For example, after a single session in which snake or spider fears were extinguished by exposure to the phobic stimuli, there was significant "relapse" when participants were retested after four weeks (Rachman & Lopatka, 1988). This is spontaneous recovery. Additional sessions of exposure are needed to more permanently reduce the fear.

Generalization

Stimuli that are similar to the CS will often also trigger a conditioned response, even though the stimuli have never been paired with the US. New tones similar in pitch to the tone CS will elicit

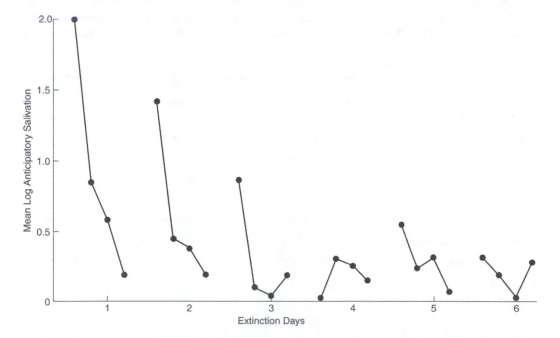

Figure 3.3 Extinction of a Conditioned Salivary Response, Showing Spontaneous Recovery Each Day.
Source: Adapted from Wagner et al. (1964, p. 356).

a CR, although maybe not as large as that to the original tone CS. This is known as **generaliza-tion**: the conditioned response to a trained CS will be elicited by similar stimuli. To test for generalization, a novel CS, which has not been paired with the US, is presented to see whether a CR occurs to it. Care needs to be taken in conducting a generalization test and in interpreting the results. Extinction or learning that the test stimuli are not paired with the US could counteract any generalization that occurs.

Generalization may occur along many different dimensions of similarity, for example, size, shape, color, and meaning. A story in the local newspaper described an alligator that had become accustomed to eating marshmallows offered by residents in a golf course community. The alliga-tor soon took to eating golf balls, too.

Discrimination

Not all of the stimuli in the environment are paired with unconditioned stimuli. So, we need to discriminate among stimuli that are, or are not, paired with USs. In **discrimination** training, one CS (sometimes labeled the CS+) is followed by the US and another CS (labeled the CS−) is not. For example, a tone is paired with food, but a light occurs alone. CS+ US trials and CS− trials are usually intermixed within conditioning sessions. We would conclude a discrimination has been learned when the subject makes a conditioned response to the CS+ but not to the CS−.

During the first trials of discrimination training, some responding to the CS− will occur due to generalization from the CS+. Discrimination (i.e., respond only to the CS+) counteracts the ten-dency to generalize (i.e., respond to something like the CS+). Discrimination is used to explicitly differentiate among CSs.

Second-Order Conditioning

In **second-order conditioning**, a CS that has already been conditioned is now used to condi-tion another CS. For example, in the first phase a tone is paired with food. In the second phase, a light is then paired with the tone. Test trials with the light alone are used to detect the transfer of conditioning to it (see Table 3.2). Second-order conditioning is demonstrated if there is now a

Table 3.2 Procedure for Second-Order Conditioning

	Phase I	*Phase II*	*Phase III*
Second-Order Conditioning			
Stimuli presented	CS1 → US	CS2 → CS1	Test CS2
CRs made	CR to CS1	CR to CS1	CR to CS2?
Example	tone → food	light → tone	light
	\	\	\
	salivation	salivation	salivation?
First-Order Conditioning			
Stimuli presented	CS1 → US		Test CS2
CRs made	CR to CS1		CR to CS2?
Example	tone → food		light
	\		\
	salivation?		salivation?

Note: First order conditioning is included as a comparison.

conditioned response (such as salivation) to the light CS, even though the light was never directly paired with the food US. Second-order conditioning is interesting as an example of a behavioral syllogism: If light equals tone, and tone equals food, then does light equal food?

It may be possible to use the light to condition some third CS, which would be third-order conditioning. The more general label "higher-order conditioning" is used to encompass all orders of distance from the original US.

The Role of Contiguity

We have repeatedly referred to CS–US pairings in classical conditioning, but so far without precisely defining what a *pairing* means. The idea is that the two events need to be **contiguous**, or close together in time, in order to become associated. The role of contiguity raises two important questions: Does the sequence of stimuli matter? How close is close enough?

When we talk of pairing the CS and US, we usually mean that the CS begins a short time before the US. In *forward conditioning*, the onset of the CS precedes the onset of the US, for example, tone and then food, or tone and then airpuff (see Figure 3.4). Earlier experimenters searched for the optimal interval between CS onset and US onset for conditioning. However, the effective length of the CS-to-US interval depends on the response being used. As examples, eyeblink conditioning occurs rapidly when tone precedes the airpuff by half a second. Salivary and SCR conditioning are obtained with intervals of 5 to 10 seconds between the CS and the US. Taste-aversion learning occurs effectively with intervals of hours separating taste from the illness. Although there are specific CS-to-US intervals that produce the faster learning, conditioning can usually be obtained across a range of intervals.

Does contiguity demand this forward sequence? In *simultaneous conditioning*, the CS and US have onset at exactly the same time: They are simultaneous. The typical finding is that there is a poor conditioning to this CS. (Test trials in which the CS is presented alone are needed to assess any conditioned

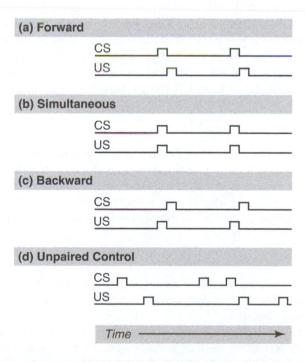

Figure 3.4 Sequential Arrangements of CS and US in Classical Conditioning: Forward, Simultaneous, Backward, and Explicitly Unpaired (Control).

responding that would otherwise be masked by the unconditioned response.) In *backward conditioning*, the US occurs first and then the CS is presented. Backward pairings can produce conditioned responses under certain circumstances (Heth, 1976; Wagner & Terry, 1975). However, conditioned responding in the backward procedure is not as strong or enduring as is forward conditioning.

Why is there such a difference between forward versus simultaneous and backward pairings? One explanation is that the purpose of conditioning is to produce an adaptive response. A CS that precedes the US allows opportunity for a response to be made in anticipation of the US. Second, maybe simultaneous and backward pairings do produce some associative learning, but these arrangements are simply not conducive to producing conditioned responses. This is the learning–performance distinction. To phrase it casually, the organism may know the tone follows the shock, but it does no good to prepare for a shock that has already come and gone.

Summary of the Basic Phenomena

Already we have seen how classical conditioning is sensitive to many procedural variables. Conditioning occurs rapidly in taste-aversion learning procedures, and more slowly in the eyeblink preparation. The strength of conditioning is affected by the sequence of the CS and US and the interval of separation between the two stimuli. Many events can serve as CSs or USs, both discrete stimuli (such as tone or food) and diffuse stimuli (such as place). Conditioning generalizes from the trained CS to similar stimuli, but a discrimination can be learned among stimuli that are or are not paired with the US.

Other Factors Affecting Conditioning

In the real world, a significant stimulus occurs in the presence of many stimuli, but not all available stimuli become conditioned. There is a process of *stimulus selection* by which only certain of the stimuli become associated with the US. For instance, if you become ill after eating, you develop an aversion to one of the foods, but not to the plate and fork you used, the music that played in the background, or the other foods you ate. Each of these stimuli is contiguous with the US, but only certain stimuli become conditioned. Several factors determine which stimuli acquire conditioning: previous experience with the CSs, the presence of competing CSs, how predictive each CS is of the US, and the relevance of the CS to the US. Each of these factors are described in what follows.

Prior Exposure

One factor seems obvious in the preceding illness example: previous safe experience with a particular food reduces the likelihood of a taste aversion developing when that food is later paired with illness. In general, exposures to a potential conditioned stimulus by itself, before pairing it with the US, inhibits conditioning when the CS is later paired with the US (Lubow, 1973). Prior exposure habituates attention to the CS and thus makes it difficult to condition.

Compound CSs

When two or more conditioned stimuli occur together before the US, each may become conditioned but to varying degrees. In a **compound CS** procedure, two CSs, a tone and a light as examples, are presented together and followed by the US. After a sufficient number of pairings, the tone + light compound elicits a conditioned response. Conditioning to each stimulus is then assessed by separately presenting the tone and the light. There is sometimes a weaker conditioned response to each stimulus alone than to the compound (see Figure 3.5). There would be less salivation, for example, to the tone or the light separately than to the tone + light compound.

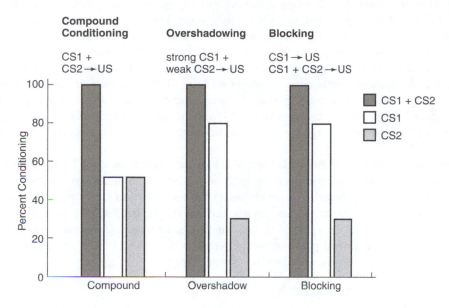

Figure 3.5 **Conditioning to Three Compound CS Conditioning Procedures.** Hypothetical outcomes of amount of responding to the compound (CS1 + CS2 presented simultaneously) and to each element (CS1 or CS2) alone.

The amount of conditioning that occurs to each CS can be dramatically altered in several ways, most of which make intuitive sense. One CS that is more salient than another, because it is louder, brighter, or otherwise more attention-getting, would *overshadow* the less-salient stimulus. After conditioning to a compound made up of CSs of unequal intensities, the more salient stimulus will produce a greater reaction than the less salient one.

The amount of conditioning to each element of a compound could also vary if the two CSs begin at different times. If the first CS comes on too far in advance of the food the second CS may convey more immediate information. This idea has been employed by Bernstein (1991) to minimize taste-aversion learning by pediatric cancer patients who were undergoing treatment. Between a meal and a chemotherapy session, she gave the children a novel taste, a new flavor of Lifesavers. Because the candy was closer to the subsequent illness, it became the "scapegoat" and protected the prior meal's food from becoming aversive. This study is a nice combination of a basic laboratory finding with a real-world application.

Surprise

At the beginning of this chapter, I said that interest in classical conditioning goes through cycles. One of the "up" cycles was stimulated by an experimental finding known as the **blocking effect** (Kamin, 1969) and a theory that describes the course of conditioning, the Rescorla-Wagner model (1972; Wagner & Rescorla, 1972).

The Blocking Effect

Leon Kamin (e.g., 1969) observed that under certain conditions, a CS paired with the US failed to condition. *Blocking* of conditioning to one CS occurs when the CS is presented in compound with another CS that has already been trained with the US. The already trained CS blocks conditioning to the new CS. Blocking is demonstrated by using a multiphase experiment. During the first phase of the experiment, one CS is conditioned. For example, a tone is paired with the food. In the second phase of the experiment, the tone and a new stimulus, a light, for example, are presented simultaneously and followed by food. This phase resembles the compound CS procedure. Our real interest is in the amount of conditioning to the added cue, the light. When it is tested alone, there is little if any conditioning to it. The tone apparently blocked conditioning to the light. (A control condition would be used to demonstrate that conditioning to the light would occur if the first phase had been skipped.) Even though the light and food were contiguous, and frequent light–food pairings are given, conditioning to the light was severely inhibited (see Figure 3.5).

Why was conditioning to the added stimulus blocked? The answer has been phrased in several ways. Kamin suggested that what normally occurs on a conditioning trial is that the sudden occurrence of the US is surprising, which causes the participant to "retrospectively review" in memory what recent events might have caused this US. (If you got a static electricity shock, you might think back: "What did I just do to cause that?") In the blocking procedure, the occurrence of the US during the second phase was expected: It was signaled by the already trained tone. Maybe a US has to be surprising to produce conditioning.

Rescorla-Wagner Model

The idea that conditioning depends on the surprisingness of the US has been captured, both conceptually and mathematically, in a formula by Robert Rescorla and Allan Wagner (Rescorla & Wagner, 1972; Wagner & Rescorla, 1972). The **Rescorla-Wagner model** (or the Wagner-Rescorla model, as it is known to Wagner's students) provides a trial-by-trial description of the learning that accrues to each CS that is present. The theory particularly focuses on those cases in which multiple CSs are presented, as in the compound CS and blocking experiments.

The starting point is the learning curve (first discussed in Chapter 1). According to this particular curve, the increments in the CS-to-US conditioning on each trial become smaller as learning progresses. Early pairings produce large gains in conditioning, whereas later pairings produce smaller increases. According to the Rescorla-Wagner model, the increase in new conditioning on any trial is a function of the difference between (a) the amount of conditioning possible with a given US and (b) the strength of conditioning already accrued to the CSs. If the discrepancy between the maximal and existing conditioning is great, then we could say that the US is surprising and so additional conditioning to the CSs occurs.

The amount of conditioning that a given US will support, the end point of the learning curve, is represented by lambda (λ) in the Rescorla-Wagner model. On a given trial, one or more CSs may be present. The associative strength of the several CSs is summed and is represented by V. The increment in new conditioning in that trial is determined by the difference between λ and V. If the difference is large, because the CSs have little strength to begin with, there will be large increases in conditioning to those CSs present. This would correspond to the large increases seen early in the learning curve. If the difference is small, because one or all of the CSs already have a great deal of strength, the increment will be small. This corresponds to the later sections of the learning curve, in which the increases per trial become smaller.

The mathematical formula is written $\Delta V = f(\lambda - V)$, which reads in English as delta V (or the change in V) is a function of lambda minus V. (There are a few constants in the equation that are omitted here.)

An illustration of the course of conditioning to a tone–light compound is shown in Figure 3.6. In the left panel, in each trial, the amount of conditioning is set at 50 percent of the difference from the last trial to the maximal amount of conditioning. Thus, in the first trial when conditioning is assumed to be zero, the increment is 50 percent, or halfway to 100 percent. In the

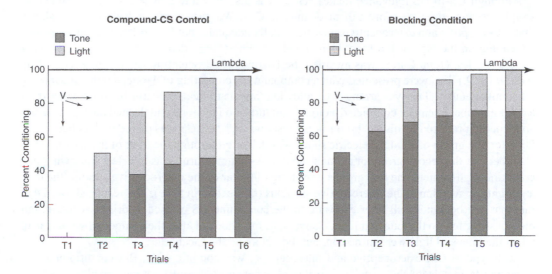

Figure 3.6 **Hypothetical Growth of Conditioning to Each Element of a Compound CS and Their Summed Strengths (*V*), According to the Rescorla-Wagner Model.** The left panel shows conditioning when *V* starts at zero. The right panel shows the blocking effect when *V* has a positive value because of preconditioning to the tone.

next trial, conditioning increases to 75 percent, half the distance between 50 and 100. What is important to notice is that conditioning is divided between the tone and the light equally in this example.

How does the Rescorla-Wagner model explain the blocking effect? As a result of the first phase, the tone has acquired some associative strength. The right panel of Figure 3.6 shows the hypothetical course of conditioning during the second phase, when both tone and light are presented. *V* starts with a high positive value because of preconditioning to the tone. During the second phase, the difference between the amount of conditioning possible (lambda) and the amount present (summing tone and light, even though the latter has no strength to start with) is smaller. The result is that the trial-by-trial increments in conditioning are small, and what little there is is divided between the tone and light. The net result is little conditioning to the light.

The Rescorla-Wagner model has been successful in describing a variety of conditioning phenomena. The model has also generated a good deal of research that challenges it (e.g., Miller, Barnet, & Grahame, 1995). The Rescorla-Wagner formula has been applied to other phenomena, including human learning of cause-and-effect relationships and the "delta rule" used in connectionist models of learning and memory (see Chapter 7).

CS–US Relevance

Another factor that affects conditioning is the relevance of the CS to the US. Referring back to our taste-illness example, how likely is it that the illness was caused by the food versus by the plates? In learning about cause-and-effect relationships in the world, organisms may have a bias toward perceiving that something eaten is more likely to cause illness than something seen or heard. A symmetrical property of relevance asserts that sights or sounds in the environment are relevant signals for external stimuli such as shocks or airpuffs.

Although CS-to-US relevance makes sense, it is also possible that tastes readily condition simply because they are more salient or intense CSs. We need a research design that shows that interoceptive and exteroceptive cues are equally adequate, but they differ in their relevance depending on the type of US used. Garcia and Koelling (1966) demonstrated this in their now classic studies. (John Garcia was awarded the Distinguished Scientific Contribution Award by APA in 1979.) Rats were presented with a compound CS consisting of a tone, a light, and a taste, all simultaneously. This was arranged by allowing the rats to lick saccharin-flavored water from a drinking tube. Each lick completed a circuit that turned on the tone and flashed the light. Garcia and Koelling referred to this as "bright-noisy-tasty water." This CS was paired with either of two USs: for one group of animals, electric shock was delivered through the floor of the conditioning chamber; for the second group of animals, an illness-inducing drug was injected. Following this conditioning treatment, the two groups were tested for fear of the exteroceptive stimuli (the tone and light) or aversion to the interoceptive stimulus (the saccharin taste). The results showed that rats that had been made ill after exposure to the compound CS refused to drink saccharin, but did not show fear to the tone and light. Conversely, rats shocked after the compound were fearful when the tone and light were turned on, but did not avoid the saccharin.

Each type of CS, exteroceptive and interoceptive, was conditionable. But conditioning was selective: taste selectively associated to illness, whereas tone and light selectively associated with shock. The Garcia and Koelling study nicely illustrates the advantages of basic research in a laboratory setting. In this situation, the conditioned stimuli could be highly controlled, ensuring equal exposure and contiguity of each with the US.

What determines CS-to-US relevance? The theory of **prepared learning** asserts that the evolutionary history of different species has prepared them to form certain associations (Rozin & Kalat, 1971; Seligman, 1970). Taste-aversion learning may be one of several instances of prepared learning, which also include the human capacity to learn language and biases toward acquiring certain types of phobias (discussed in the Applications section of this chapter).

An alternative explanation of relevance is that the bias toward associating certain classes of stimuli is learned (Davey, 1995). Selective associating occurs because an individual's prior experience with taste stimuli has shown them to be related to illness, and other types of cues were not.

We should note that conditioning does occur between nonrelevant CSs and USs, although maybe not as readily as with prepared CSs. Animals do condition to color, feeding containers, places, and other exteroceptive cues (see Mackintosh, 1983). Even among foods, not all foods are equally conditionable as a result of an illness experience. Midkiff and Bernstein (1985) surveyed 1,500 introductory psychology students about their experiences with food aversions. More than half reported at least one aversion, and many had more than one. Foods in certain categories, particularly proteins, were more likely to become aversive. A sample of the most- and least-likely targets for aversions are shown in Table 3.3.

Table 3.3 Targets of Learned Food Aversions in Humans

Category	Percent of All Aversions
Meat; poultry; fish	21
Vegetables	14
Alcohol	14
Eggs or egg dishes	4
Bread, crackers, or flour products	3
Rice; potatoes	3

Conditioned Inhibition

The capacity to anticipate the presence of food or danger is important for an organism's survival. Knowing when food is not available or danger is not present is just as important. Our references to conditioning so far have actually been to excitatory conditioning. Simply put, in *excitatory conditioning*, a CS becomes associated with the occurrence of the US. By contrast, in *inhibitory conditioning*, a CS becomes associated with the absence of the US. Imagine a situation relevant to student life: predicting the dreaded pop quiz. Unfortunately, cues are rarely available to signal on what days the quiz (the US) will occur, hence the name "pop quiz." Inhibitory conditioning would occur if a cue reliably signals when the quiz *will not* occur. If the teacher arrives empty-handed, then a quiz is not imminent. Instead of remaining tense and anxious, the students can relax!

How is an inhibitor produced? Inhibitors must be actively trained by arranging what is essentially a negative correlation between the CS and a specific US. This means this CS occurs without the US; and the US occurs without this CS. The standard procedure is to present the potential inhibitor, call it CS*x* (where *x* is the mystery stimulus), simultaneously with a conditioned excitor, but leave out the US. That is, the training sequence would alternate CS+US trials and CS+/CS*x*–no US trials. To describe this procedure casually, at those times when the US fails to appear after CS+, its absence is attributed to the CS*x*.

Conditioned inhibitors often do not evoke a measurable response: no eyeblinks, no salivation. So how can the presence of inhibition be detected? One method is based on the idea that inhibitory stimuli inhibit responding to excitatory stimuli. The suspected inhibitor (CS*x*) is presented at the same time as an excitatory CS, to see if it will reduce responding otherwise seen to the excitor (e.g., Neumann, Lipp, & Siddle, 1997). The rationale is like adding a negative number to a positive number: The net result will be less than the positive number was to begin with, for example, the sum of −3 and +5 is +2. So adding an inhibitor to an excitor reduces the size of the response to the excitor.

What is Learned in Classical Conditioning?

Classical conditioning is an example of associative learning. Given the presence of four elements in a traditional Pavlovian trial, the CS, the US, the UR, and eventually the CR, we can ask what is associated with what? There are several theories of what is learned in classical conditioning.

According to the *stimulus–response* (S–R) theory, the CS becomes associated with the UR. That is, the CS comes to elicit the unconditioned response, or some portion of the UR. The presence of a US ensures that a UR will occur contiguous with the CS. This response-learning theory seemingly fits a simple description of what happens during Pavlovian conditioning: a tone now elicits an eyeblink, salivation, or leg flexion, and so on. It even applies to subtle aspects of the response. In one preparation, pigeons were conditioned to make a pecking response as the CR by using either food or water as the US. Interestingly, the pecks took the form of biting movements when the US was food (and eating is the UR), but sucking movements when the US was water (and drinking is the UR). The pigeons were making the same response that had originally been elicited by the particular US used (Jenkins & Moore, 1973). The appeal of S–R theory is that it provides a simple and direct account of what is conditioned in classical conditioning.

Although the S–R theory adequately describes some forms of the conditioned response, there are several problems with it. One difficulty is that the CR is not always the same as the UR. In heart rate conditioning, a shock will often elicit acceleration as the UR, but the CR will sometimes be deceleration. (Actually, the response in cardiac conditioning is complex, but this does illustrate a deviation from the S–R theory.) If the drug morphine is used as a US, heart rate, general activity, and sensitivity to pain all decrease. The CR, however, is the opposite in each case: Heart rate, pain sensitivity, and activity all increase (Siegel, 1991; these studies are described later in this chapter).

An alternative theory states that conditioning produces an association between the CS and the US. This is the *stimulus–stimulus* (S–S) theory. The modern version of the S–S theory is decidedly cognitive in orientation. The first step in learning is the formation of memory representations of the CS and the US. Conditioning further involves the formation of an association between the two representations, just as you have acquired an association between the representations of TABLE and CHAIR.

An advantage, as well as a disadvantage, of the S–S theory is that it does not specify what the conditioned response will be or what form it will take. Instead, knowledge is acquired, with some flexibility as to how that knowledge is applied. The CR is not a rigid, reflexive reaction that becomes attached to the CS.

The contrast between the S–R and S–S approaches is illustrated by the question of whether two CSs can become associated in the absence of a US. What if we paired two CSs, say, a tone and a light? There is no unconditioned stimulus. Do the tone and light become associated? In the absence of an obvious conditioned response after numerous pairings, S–R theory says no. S–S theory says that CS-to-CS associations can be learned. In the second phase, the tone is paired with food, until conditioned responses are observed. In the final phase, the *light* is tested for CRs. A CR to the light indicates there is an association of the light to the tone, which S–S theory expects. It is as if the participant is chaining through associations: light to tone and tone to food.

Additional support for the S–S theory comes from studies of US devaluation. If the US is altered after conditioning has occurred, will responding to the CS change to match the new value of the US? For example, a tone is first paired with an electric shock US. (This is psychology; you knew there would be shock eventually.) Then, in a second phase, milder shocks are given. This manipulation should devalue the US, and its representation in memory. When we go back and retest the tone CS, will there be as much fear as occurred during the first phase? Or will the fear be weaker, reflecting the less-intense US experienced in the second phase? The results suggest that there is often a weaker CR to the tone after as compared to before devaluation (Rescorla, 1987). According to the cognitive version of the S–S theory, a CR of a specific size and shape was not acquired. Rather, a response is available that can be flexibly altered depending on the current status of the organism's knowledge.

A third theory of what is learned states that a different form of conditioning, instrumental conditioning, controls the acquisition and performance of conditioned responses. This is a reinforcement theory (discussed further in Chapter 4). Conditioned responses are acquired, reinforced, or more colloquially "rewarded," because they make the US more palatable or less aversive (Perkins, 1968). This *preparatory response* theory might be labeled an R–S theory, in that the CR prepares for receipt of the US. An eyeblink CR is reinforced because the airpuff US strikes your eyelid rather than your eyeball. If the mouth is moistened by a salivary CR, the dry food powder US is made more palatable. Preparatory response theory essentially says that CRs are shaped over trials to better anticipate and coincide with the onset of the US.

Unfortunately, behavior is not always as sensible as preparatory response theory predicts. In a pigeon study, the CS was a panel that illuminated at one end of the conditioning chamber, which was followed by the food tray opening for a few seconds (the US) at the other end (Hearst & Jenkins, 1974). The counterintuitive outcome in this "long box" was that the pigeon approached and pecked at the lighted panel at one end, but could not get back to the food tray in time before it closed! This behavior does not sound very reinforcing. Other studies that have also explicitly introduced an instrumental reinforcement arrangement have actually found it reduces conditioned responses (Coleman, 1975).

So, What is Learned in Pavlovian Conditioning?

The three theories of what is learned in Pavlovian conditioning are summarized in Table 3.4. Which explanation is correct? Although each is fine in some cases, none of the theories appears to be sufficient for all situations. Part of any resolution to this question goes back to the learning-versus-performance distinction: What has the participant learned versus what does the participant do? Stimulus–stimulus theory describes the knowledge about stimulus relationships that is learned, but the stimulus–response and preparatory response theories describe how that knowledge is translated into behavior.

Other research suggests that conditioning produces multiple conditioned responses. For instance, Wagner and Brandon (1989) say that conditioning leads to both a general, emotional response and a specific, localized response. When using a shock US, there is a general or diffuse emotional conditioned reaction to the CS, such as fear; and a specific motoric reaction, such as an eyeblink. As another example, we can point to the varied roles of conditioning in advertising. One claim has always been that conditioning associates an affective feeling with a product: By pairing the right images and sounds with the product name in a commercial, the viewer will associate the product with pleasure, action, or fun. However, the conditioning procedure may also associate the product with factual information, for example, that the product is fast, effective, or long-lasting (Kim, Allen, & Kardes, 1996).

Learning in the Brain

A different approach to answering the question "what is learned" is to attempt to map out the changes in the brain that correspond to conditioning.

The brain circuit involved in eyeblink conditioning has been mapped by Richard Thompson and his colleagues and students (e.g., Thompson, 2005). Although the tone CS and the airpuff US produce activity in several regions of the brain, it appears that a final common destination for the association is in the cerebellum. The cerebellum, literally the "little cerebrum," is in the lower back portion of the brain. An experimentally produced lesion in the cerebellum of an animal prevents tone-to-eyeblink conditioning. The tone CS is heard and registered in the brain. The airpuff US produces an eyeblink UR. However, the tone–airpuff pairings do not give the tone the capacity to produce an eyeblink CR. Similar results are found in case studies of people who have sustained damage to their cerebellums. Normal eyeblinks occur; reflexive eyeblinks occur; but there is impaired eyeblink conditioning (Daum et al., 1993).

Do Thompson's results show that the cerebellum is where classical conditioning is localized in the brain? Yes and no. Eyeblink conditioning may operate through the cerebellum, but conditioning of other reactions undoubtedly involves different areas. For instance, conditioned fear produced by pairing a tone CS with a painful US involves the amygdala. (This is described more in Chapter 5.) If we measure skin conductance responses, individuals with cerebellum damage will make conditioned responses to the tone, reactions that are mediated through other areas of

Table 3.4 Comparison Among Several Theories of What Is Learned in Classical Conditioning

Theory	*S–R*	*S–S*	*Preparatory Response*
Associated elements	CS–UR	CS–US	CR–US
Example	Tone–salivation	Tone–expectancy for food	Salivation–food
Evidence for	CR often same as UR	US devaluation	CR reduces impact of US
Criticisms	CR often different from UR	Does not specify what response will be made	Reinforcement can reduce conditioning

the brain (Daum & Schugens, 1996). Even learning as simple as classical conditioning is represented in multiple areas of the brain.

The Role of Awareness in Conditioning

If classical conditioning is considered to be a simple, possibly even primitive form of learning, then conscious cognitive factors are not necessary for conditioning to occur. If conditioning is considered to involve cognitive processes, then awareness may be a factor. What is the role of awareness in conditioning? Evidence from several different sources can be considered.

It is certainly the case that college student participants can often verbally report the CS–US contingency that they have experienced. This has been shown in eyeblink and SCR conditioning, and in some cases of evaluative conditioning (e.g., Shimp, Stuart, & Engle, 1991). But is awareness of the CS–US contingency necessary for conditioning? The data from unaware participants are contradictory. In some cases, experimental participants who cannot report the CS–US arrangement did not make conditioned responses (see review by Dawson & Schell, 1987), but in another study, unaware and aware participants responded comparably (Papka, Ivy, & Woodruff-Pak, 1997). Interestingly, participants who can report that the tone was followed by the airpuff are not always aware that they were making eyeblinks during the tone (Papka et al., 1997).

Conscious awareness of the conditioning procedure can be minimized or excluded by using distracting secondary tasks or response systems beyond awareness. As examples, eyeblink conditioning occurs even when a second task is being performed simultaneously, such as reacting to words presented visually or watching a video (Papka et al., 1997). We can also cite the case of a man with spinal cord injury who showed conditioned control over his bladder, even though neither the stimuli nor the responses involved could be detected by the patient (Ince, Brucker, & Alba, 1978). Together, these sorts of observations suggest that Pavlovian conditioning does not require conscious awareness.

In some instances, awareness of the CS–US relationship will affect responding to the conditioned stimulus. In a conditioning preparation such as the eyeblink or SCR, simply telling our human participants that extinction is about to begin, and reinforcing this belief by disconnecting some of the wires, leads to an immediate cessation of the CR. There is no reaction to the very next CS presentation. However, awareness that an aversive US will no longer occur does not always override all conditioned responses. The fear of phobic-type stimuli, such as pictures of spiders or snakes that were paired with a shock US, are persistent in spite of awareness (Dawson, Schell, & Banis, 1986; Ohman, Fredrikson, Hugdahl, & Rimmo, 1976).

Extensions of Conditioning

Conditioning With Drug USs and the Development of Tolerance

Pavlov noted that after repeated injections of morphine, the dog became nauseous simply at the sight of the hypodermic needle. Contemporary work on conditioned drug reactions has broadened our conception of classical conditioning in several ways: Drugs can act as unconditioned stimuli; contextual stimuli can function as CSs; and the conditioned response is sometimes opposite to the UR.

These factors are illustrated in the development of drug tolerance. Repeated administrations of a drug can lead to a reduction in the drug's effectiveness. Rats given a series of injections of opiate drugs such as morphine or heroin develop a tolerance, as measured by respiration, body temperature, and pain threshold. What role might classical conditioning play here? Is tolerance a CR?

One way to test for classical conditioning after drug exposure is to replace the drug in the injection with an inert saline solution. This is a placebo injection. The idea is to monitor the body's conditioned response to the injection procedure (the CS) in the absence of the drug (the US). For some drugs, the physiological reaction is *opposite* of that initially elicited by the drug. For example, morphine raises body temperature, but the saline injection lowers temperature. Morphine has analgesic effects, in reducing pain; the placebo increases pain sensitivity (see Siegel, 1991, for a review).

Why is the reaction to a saline injection opposite to that of the morphine? One theory proposes that conditioning can lead to the development of conditioned responses that are the opposite of the unconditioned responses. The UR to a stimulus stays the same over presentations. But a second response, the CR, gradually develops over trials, and is opposite in direction from the UR. Siegel (1991) refers to this conditioned response as a **compensatory response**, one that counteracts the effects of the drug itself to maintain bodily homeostasis.

Another feature of the drug conditioning experiments is the recognition that the context in which the drug occurs is a CS. This means that the original reaction to the drug can be reinstated by giving the drug in a different context where the compensating response (or CR) is not evoked. An illustrative pattern of results is shown in Table 3.5. After animals had been given frequent morphine injections, they had the same threshold for pain as animals given saline injections. This demonstrates tolerance to morphine. Giving the morphine in a different room reinstated morphine's usual pain-suppressing property. The effectiveness of the drug returned simply by testing the rat in the "nondrug" room.

In one particularly dramatic demonstration of room-specific tolerance, rats were given heroin or saline in different rooms. Rats that had a tolerance to an otherwise lethal dose of heroin in the heroin room showed a 50 percent increase in the death rate when injected in the nondrug room (Siegel et al., 1982). This may explain why some drug users overdose when taking amounts they previously tolerated. If the drug is taken in a different environment from usual, the compensating responses may not be evoked, and so the drug has its full effect. In a retrospective interview study of overdose victims who lived to tell about their experience, 7 out of 10 reported changed environmental conditions associated with the overdose reaction (Siegel, 1984).

By extension, the compensatory-response model also addresses withdrawal symptoms. Say that an addicted individual is confronted with cues associated with drug taking: the place where opiates have frequently been used, at the time of day in which the drug was usually taken, or after the usual number of hours since the last administration. These characteristics define context, circadian, and temporal CSs, respectively. If the drug is not taken, then the compensating CRs are seen in unadulterated form. The responses may be a drop in body temperature, speeded respiration, cramping and nausea, and hyperactivity. These symptoms of withdrawal, evoked in the absence of the drug, are opposite to the reactions elicited by opiate drugs. The conditioning theory also suggests that detoxification that takes place in a very different environment from the drug-taking environment does not extinguish the context–drug association. Relapse occurs

Table 3.5 Illustrative Pattern of Results in Testing the Effects of Morphine Tolerance

Several days of morphine exposure are first given to develop a tolerance then testing occurs in the same room that morphine had been given in or in a different room.

Test Situation	Hypothesized Elements Present	Pain Threshold
Saline control condition	No CR, no UR	Normal pain threshold
Morphine given in test room	CR and UR	Normal pain threshold
Saline given in test room	CR only	Lower pain threshold
Morphine given in different room	UR only	Higher pain threshold

because on returning to the original living environment associated with drugs, withdrawal and craving are elicited (Siegel, 1982).

The theory of compensating responses has its share of criticisms. In particular, only some drugs show CRs that oppose the UR. Eikelboom and Stewart (1982) suggested that some drugs have different effects on the central nervous system than on other parts of the body. Only the central nervous system effects would be conditioned.

Research on drug conditioning illustrates three important points: first, that drugs can act as USs; second, that contextual stimuli can act as CSs; and third, that the conditioned response does not have to mimic the unconditioned response.

Modification of Immune System Response

The immune system is the body's defense against foreign substances and microorganisms, such as viruses and bacteria. The central nervous system (CNS) plays a role in coordinating immune functions, which opens the way for the possibility of conditioning immune reactions. For example, we have long known that asthmatic reactions can be conditioned. Human studies have shown that the pairing of neutral stimuli with allergens (used as USs) can lead to conditioned allergic responses (e.g., Dekker, Pelser, & Groen, 1957).

A discovery during a taste-aversion learning experiment led to even more surprising findings. Ader and Cohen (1975) paired a saccharin taste with the drug cyclophosphamide, which was being used as the US to induce illness. A side effect of the drug (from Ader's perspective) is that it is an immunosuppressant. Incidental to conditioning an aversion to the taste, the saccharin CS also developed the capacity to suppress immune functioning as a CR. Conditioning of the immune system is now an accepted phenomenon (see Ader & Cohen, 1993).

Observations in humans suggest similar results. Bovjberg et al. (1990) found that women who had received a number of chemotherapy treatments (which can include drugs such as cyclophosphamide) displayed an immune suppression after being brought to the hospital, but before the next round of chemotherapy actually began. Their immune suppression may have been a conditioned response evoked by the conditioned stimulus of the context of the hospital.

Unlike morphine conditioning discussed in the preceding section, the conditioned and unconditioned responses in immune conditioning are alike. Could a placebo in this case have a practical application by mimicking the effects of the actual drug? In certain disorders, an overactive immune system attacks the body and so suppression becomes a desirable treatment. Ader and Cohen (1982) found that occasionally substituting the conditioned saccharine solution for the drug was as effective as giving the drug each time in treating an immune system disorder in mice. That is, the placebo reaction was sufficient to delay onset of the disease.

One other extension of classical conditioning is *modeling causality learning*, or the learning of cause and effect relationships. This application is described in Box 3.2.

Box 3.2   Detecting Causality

Pavlovian conditioning has sometimes been described as an example of causal learning: When an organism is being conditioned, it is learning cause-and-effect relationships among events (Hall, 1994; Young, 1995). Whatever stimulus regularly precedes the US could logically be thought of as having causal properties.

Interest in cause-and-effect relationships has a long history in philosophy and psychology. Some philosophers in the rationalist and nativist traditions said that we are programmed to perceive these sorts of patterns, just as with other innate categories of knowledge and perception. David Hume, a British empiricist philosopher, instead argued that our belief that one event causes another derives completely from our past experience with those stimuli, which is the frequent repetition of one event following another. "When we look about us toward external objects, and consider the operation of causes, we are never able . . . to discover any power of necessary connection. . . . We find only that the one does actually follow the other" (Hume quoted in Jones, 1952). Hume argues that, logically, there need not be any connection between one event and another; and that our expectation and anticipation that the "cause" will be followed by an "effect" is simply an inference and not necessarily a fact.

Hume further listed the conditions for judging causes and effects. They must be contiguous in time and space, the cause must be prior to the effect, and the effect arises only from the same cause. These features well describe the ideal contingencies for producing classical conditioning: The CS and US are paired, the CS closely precedes the US, and the US does not occur in the absence of the CS (Hall, 1994).

Researchers of human cognition have noted the parallel between classical conditioning and learning about other kinds of contingencies between stimuli. For example, in medical diagnoses, one may look for symptom–disease correlations. What kinds of information do you need to conclude that a particular symptom is diagnostic of the disease? First, look for the conjunction of the two stimuli. For example, a fever must be present in order to diagnose the flu. But, logically, we would need to tally the other possible contingencies between the two events. Does a fever occur without the flu? Can the flu be present without fever? If any of these were the case, then fever would be an unreliable indicator of the flu. This sort of contingency analysis can be set up in a 2×2 table: presence or absence of the symptom and presence or absence of the illness (see Table 3.6). In evaluating the information from these sorts of contingencies, we humans do a rather poor job. We seem to have a bias to attribute cause based on the conjunction of two events and neglect the information obtained from the other cells of the table. Wasserman, Dorner, and Kao (1990) asked subjects about the relative importance of these four cells in making inferences about hypothetical problems, such as the relationship of a symptom to an illness. For example, the cell in which the symptom and illness are both present was judged to be the most important fact in making a judgment (by nearly 100 percent of the subjects). The other cells, in which the symptom occurs alone or the illness occurs alone, were judged less important, and the cell in which neither occurs was rated least important (by 50 percent of the subjects).

Studies of human contingency learning, using paradigms like symptom–disease learning, have found parallels to animal conditioning, such as the blocking effect. For instance, first learning that a fever is associated with the flu may block subsequent learning that a second symptom, stomach distress, is also a predictor (Chapman, 1991). Similarly, a stimulus will come to be ignored if it is not a reliable predictor. Public security alerts or storm warnings that (thankfully) turn out to be false alarms nevertheless reduce future attention to such warnings. The result of all this research has been a fertile cross-pollination of ideas between animal and human learning theories.

Table 3.6 2×2 Tables to Assess Causality

	Effect Present	*Effect Absent*
Cause Present	Cause, effect	Cause, no effect
Cause Absent	No cause, effect	No cause, no effect

Applications of Conditioning

Behavioral Medicine

Classical conditioning has applications in the field of behavioral medicine. Innovations in medical devices that treat disease also present new adverse psychological reactions. The implantable cardiac defibrillator (ICD) detects and corrects heart arrhythmias. Over 50,000 of these devices are implanted yearly (Jauhar, 2002). The device delivers an electric shock to restore the heart's beat to a normal rhythm. The occurrence of these shocks, which are painful and unpredictable, causes anxiety and depression, and leads to the restriction of social activities in some patients. Imagine someone going about their normal life when BAM! The heart is given a jump start. In conditioning terminology, you have the pairing of potential CSs (place, context, ongoing activities) with the defibrillating shock US. Although some people are less affected by the shocks, other patients report frequent or intense shocks. These latter individuals can learn to fear the places or situations in which defibrillation occurred, and subsequently avoid those situations. Although the ICD solves one problem, it presents a different set of distresses to be treated by psychologists (Sears, Kovacs, Azzarello, Larsen, & Conti, 2004).

Another application in behavioral medicine is that knowledge of classical conditioning can offer a better understanding of learned taste aversions as persistent aftereffects of chemotherapy. We know that the pairings of foods with the illness induced by cancer-treating drugs can produce an aversion to those foods. These aversions might not be simply passing symptoms. Patients who had received chemotherapy up to 20 years prior reported distress and nausea to sights, smells, or tastes that reminded them of the cancer treatment (Cameron et al., 2001).

The Conditioning Theory of Phobias

A **phobia** is an excessive and intense fear, usually of a specific object or situation, such as a fear of snakes and spiders, of heights, or of speaking in public. Where do phobias come from? Psychologists can offer a variety of explanations. Maybe phobias are instinctive or innate reactions to certain stimuli, just like our reactions to sudden loud noises; maybe fear is unconsciously displaced from the true cause to some innocent or symbolic object; or possibly a phobia reflects an unremembered trauma. There is one other explanation that psychologists point to whenever they want to demonstrate the significance of Pavlovian conditioning. Maybe fears and phobias originate through classical conditioning: An initially neutral stimulus becomes phobic because it has been paired with an aversive stimulus: something traumatic, painful, or frightening.

The initial statement of the conditioning theory of fear learning is embarrassingly simple. John Watson and Rosalie Rayner (1920) set out to condition an 11-month-old child named Albert to fear a laboratory rat. The first exposures to the rat showed that fear was not innate; Albert readily attempted to touch and grasp the rat. However, when exposure to the rat (used here as the CS) was followed by the banging of a steel bar with a steel hammer (the US), a change in Albert's reactions took place. Over the course of a few pairings, Albert became more tentative in his reaching for the rat, his lip began to quiver, and finally he would cry. This fear of the rat was conditioned fear, the CR.

Watson and Rayner's demonstration of fear conditioning was both powerful and influential. Where do phobias come from? No longer would we need to explain fears on the basis of instincts or unconscious forces. According to Watson and Rayner, they originate in conditioning experiences. This study has served as the basis for speculations in literature on the applications, mostly evil, of Watson and Rayner's theory to future societies. In *Brave New World*, for example, Aldous Huxley describes children who are conditioned to fear books by electrically shocking them when books are touched. The idea was to produce a working class that would not be distracted by ideas and education.

Although widely cited, Watson and Rayner's study leaves much to be desired as a valid scientific experiment. The story has been distorted over the years, like a rumor that becomes exaggerated with each retelling (Harris, 1979). Watson and Rayner's conditioning theory has been rightly criticized for being far too simple. Its exclusive reliance on pairings omits other factors known to affect conditioning. (Recent historical research has attempted to ascertain the identity and fate of Little Albert. See Beck, Levinson, & Irons, 2009).

Current knowledge about classical conditioning offers a better fit than the Watson model as an explanation for the development of phobias. Mineka and Zinbarg (2006) applied contemporary learning principles to phobia learning (and other anxiety disorders). For instance, not everyone who becomes phobic has had a traumatic experience associated with the phobic event (that is, a Little Albert experience). In this case, the phobia might have been learned vicariously, based on the observation of phobic behavior in someone else (see, e.g., Cook & Mineka, 1990). It is also the case that some people have had a traumatic experience but they did not become phobic. This absence of conditioning might be attributed to prior safe experience with the potentially phobic object. A child with a history of safe experiences with dogs will be less likely to develop a dog phobia than the child with less prior experience.

Finally, individual differences in personality or temperament could predispose some people towards acquiring a phobia. For instance, research was cited earlier in the chapter that anxious subjects conditioned more readily in laboratory experiments, as did individuals with PTSD (see the earlier Box 3.1).

One significant revision to the conditioning model is the addition of the notion of **prepared learning** (Seligman, 1972). *Preparedness* suggests that evolution has predisposed us to acquire certain fears that have high survival value. Earlier, we saw that taste-aversion learning might be an instance of prepared learning. Similarly, phobias do not develop to any arbitrary object that happens to occur in proximity to trauma. Instead, people become fearful of the dark, heights, and enclosed spaces; of snakes and spiders; or of other people. These are stimuli that have represented dangers during human and primate evolution. There are other classes of stimuli with which we surely have more unpleasant contact but which do not become the object of phobias. Children fall off bicycles daily, but they do not develop bike phobias.

Ohman and Mineka (2001) suggest that there is an evolved neural system or "module" that is dedicated to learning prepared fears. (A learning module is a hypothesized specialization in certain areas of the brain that has evolved for a particular type of learning. For example, birds may have a song module.) The prepared fear module has several characteristics.

1. It responds selectively to certain stimuli, particularly those that evolution has determined to be potential threats or dangers.
2. Responding is automatic and involuntary, much like a reflex reaction.
3. The fear response is relatively unaffected by other modules, in particular by cognitive operations. Thus, consciously realizing that this snake is not harmful does not reduce your fear.
4. There are specialized neural circuits. For fear conditioning, the amygdala of the brain seems to be centrally involved in fear conditioning.

Preparedness can be supported by evidence for selective conditioning of fear-relevant CSs. The rationale for these studies is the same as for demonstrating selective conditioning of tastes and illness. Marks (1977) anecdotally describes an incredible (but unfortunate) coincidence in which a young woman passenger was in a car crash while browsing through a book on snakes. Did the woman develop a fear of cars or driving? No, she became snake phobic. In laboratory studies of preparedness, we compare learning about fear-relevant CSs, such as pictures of snakes, to fear-irrelevant CSs, such as pictures of flowers. When the pictures are paired with an aversive US, we learn fears to snakes quicker than fears to flowers (Ohman et al., 1976).

Another example of this research strategy comes from studies of fear in monkeys. Cook and Mineka (1990) studied monkeys that had never been exposed to snakes. These monkeys were not fearful of snakes at first exposure, indicating that the fears were not instinctive. Young rhesus monkeys watched a video in which footage of phobia-relevant stimuli (snakes) or unprepared stimuli (flowers) were spliced together with footage of other monkeys showing fear and fright. That is, the participant monkeys saw another animal apparently exhibiting fear to a snake or to some daisies. In conditioning terminology, the snake and flowers are the CSs, and seeing the fearful monkey on film is the US. The participant animals were later tested for fear of snakes by requiring them to reach over or go around a toy snake in order to get a food treat. Those monkeys who saw the snake film were more fearful of the snakes than those who saw flowers. Those who saw flowers did not acquire a fear of the flowers.

Alternative explanations of preparedness have been offered. Are we predisposed to fear snakes (and other potential phobic stimuli) because of exposure to negative information about snakes during our lives? This is a *learned* associative bias. When college students show up to participate in a psychology experiment, they probably already have some fear or trepidation about snakes but not flowers. These preexisting biases can then be magnified through aversive conditioning. In one experiment, human participants are told they would receive shocks. From this moment on, these participants have a higher expectation that shocks will follow the prepared CSs than the unprepared CSs, even if no shocks are actually given (see Davey, 1995).

The preparedness hypothesis has received other criticisms as well (see McNally, 1987). People do develop fears of nonevolutionarily prepared stimuli, such as dental anxiety. Many people become afraid to drive after having a car accident. Some categories of human fears tend to be more age-related than evolutionarily determined; for example, 3- and 4-year-old children develop animal fears, whereas 13- to 18-year-old adolescents have social fears (Miller, Barrett, & Hampe, 1974).

Overview of the Conditioning Theory of Phobias

A conditioning theory suggests that an initially neutral stimulus becomes phobic when it has been paired with a traumatic or aversive event. Mineka's research on monkeys, as well as other research on what is known as observational learning, shows that phobias can be learned through observation of others' traumatic experiences with the phobic stimulus. However, not everyone develops a phobia from adverse experiences: Many of us have been bitten by a dog, but fewer of us develop a phobia of dogs (some fear or trepidation maybe, but not a phobia). Some phobic learning may occur readily because it is biologically prepared. On the other hand, maybe cultural and social influences determine the readiness of learning to fear bugs and snakes.

Extinction as Therapy

If fears can be conditioned, it is reasonable to suppose that they could be unlearned. Extinction, which is the presentation of the CS alone, should reduce conditioned responding. For example, if you have a phobia of snakes, spiders, or heights, we might expose you to pictures or videos of snake-, spider-, or height-related stimuli. Your fear should decline as the exposures continue and nothing unpleasant happens (that is, the phobic CS occurs without an aversive US). Extinction occurs.

Extinction does not eliminate the CS-to-US association. (Thus, the appropriately titled "Pavlovian associations are forever," Baeyens, Eelen, & Crombez, 1995). And in fact, conditioned responding can recover even after extinction has occurred. This return of the extinguished response has important implications for the efficacy of extinction as psychotherapy (Bouton, Westbrook, Corcoran, & Maren, 2006; Hermans, Craske, Mineka, & Lovibond, 2006).

Recovery of the Extinguished Response

There are at least three ways by which the fear can be revived. First, through spontaneous recovery. By simply waiting some period of time before presenting the phobic stimulus again, the next occurrence of the stimulus will likely elicit a CR. The extinction that occurs during one session with the therapist could be followed by spontaneous recovery at the start of the next session.

Second, if the aversive US happens to occur alone without the original CS, **reinstatement** occurs. Maybe something else happens to you that gives you a scare. The phobic stimulus itself is not present, yet the next occurrence of the phobic CS could provoke a return of the CR.

Third, the original phobia conditioning occurred in one context (someplace in the real world), but the extinction likely occurs in a different context (maybe a therapist's office). Upon return to the initial (conditioning) context, there can be a **renewal**, or return of the extinguished CR. A fear of spiders learned in your house is then extinguished in the counseling center's office. However, an encounter with a spider in your house renews the extinguished fear.

Each of these procedures can restore the extinguished fear CR. In each case fear returns without pairing the phobic stimulus (spiders, heights, etc.) with a traumatic US. Nevertheless the fear returns. Table 3.7 summarizes these three procedures that produce a return of the once-extinguished response. A simple mnemonic is to remember the three Rs: (spontaneous) Recovery, (US) Reinstatement, and (context) Renewal. (Now to remember which R is which, you're on your own.)

Extinction is the basis for some behavioral psychotherapies. Yet, even after extinction, the conditioned (fear) response can be reinstated. How can exposure therapy be made more effective if extinction is so impermanent?

One way to think of this is to consider that two associations are learned: first a CS-to-US connection during acquisition, and then a CS-to-absence of US association during extinction. Afterwards, the CS might retrieve either of these two associations. The goal of extinction is therefore to make the US-absent association dominant. An analogy is the need to learn a new password. At first there are two memories: the old and the new passwords. You will slip and use the old password by mistake for a while, until the new one becomes dominant. Similarly, in exposure therapy, you want the new response to become dominant over the previous response.

This can be facilitated by using a large-enough number of extinction exposures. In *extinction overtraining*, a large number of extinction trial are given. Not just enough trials so the condition response ceases; but then continued extinction trials after the response ceased. This reduces the return of conditioned responses. Also, extinction could be conducted in multiple contexts (for instance, in the presence of different contextual stimuli). This would reduce the phenomenon of renewal.

Systematic Desensitization

If extinction does not readily eliminate a phobia, maybe a more forceful approach is necessary. Systematic desensitization, developed by Joseph Wolpe (1969), is one such method. In **systematic desensitization**, the phobic stimulus is treated as a CS, and it is paired with a US

Table 3.7 Three Procedures That Lead to Return of an Extinguished Conditioned Response

Conditioning	Extinction	Other Event	Test CS for CR
CS → US	CS alone	time	CS → CR spontaneous recovery
CS → US	CS alone	US alone	CS → CR reinstatement
CS → US in context A	CS alone in context B	return to context A	CS → CR renewal

or a response that is incompatible with fear. The idea is to *countercondition* the phobic CS. In an early instance of counterconditioning, Mary Cover Jones (1924) removed a fear of rabbits in a young child (Peter this time, not Albert) by pairing ice cream with presentations of the rabbit.

Wolpe's method of systematic desensitization has several distinctive features. He most often uses muscle *relaxation* as the response to pair with the phobic CS. His patients are first taught how to relax their muscles. Also, Wolpe does not present actual phobic stimuli, but instead has his clients imagine the feared stimuli, which is frightening enough for phobic individuals.

Counterconditioning involves pairing phobic images (the CS) with the instruction to relax (the US). Less fearful scenes are imagined first and paired with relaxation, followed by progressively more fearful images as they become tolerated. Tension (anxiety) and relaxation are incompatible responses. Wolpe seeks to have relaxation dominate over the tension.

Systematic desensitization is a mix of conditioning theories. The basis is behavioral, by trying to attach the relaxation response to the phobic stimulus. But the method is also cognitive, by having the participant imagine the fearful stimuli.

Is desensitization effective? Some now classic studies found it was more effective than "insight" or psychoanalytic therapy (Paul, 1967). However, the effectiveness may due more to extinction (nonthreatening exposure to phobic stimuli) rather than to counterconditioning (pairing the stimuli with relaxation.) Reviews of the research literature suggest have that the essential component of desensitization is "repeated exposure to anxiety-evoking situations without the client actually experiencing any negative consequences" (Spiegler & Guevremont, 1993, p. 205). Contemporary treatments for phobias seem to regularly include exposure as part of the therapy. This is supplemented with cognitive therapies that attempt to give the patient a sense of control, self-confidence, and self-competence, and some understanding into the disorder.

Summary

Classical conditioning, also called Pavlovian conditioning, is not the simple form of reflex learning portrayed in popular stereotypes. It is a flexible and adaptive form of associative learning.

The Definition of Classical Conditioning

In classical conditioning, an initially neutral conditioned stimulus, or CS, is presented with a biologically significant unconditioned stimulus, or US. The US elicits an unconditioned response, the UR. After a number of pairings, the CS comes to elicit a conditioned response, the CR. Contemporary examples of conditioning allow for indirect measures of learning other than the traditional CR.

Methods of Studying Classical Conditioning

A variety of specific procedures are used in studying conditioning, including salivary conditioning, eyeblink conditioning, and skin conductance responses (SCR). Tones and lights serve as CSs, and the USs are significant stimuli such as food, airpuff, or shock. The learned CR often resembles the UR, such as salivation or an eyeblink. Some other methods of conditioning include taste-aversion learning and evaluative conditioning. The CR in these cases is indirectly assessed, through aversion or avoidance of the CS, for example.

Various kinds of stimuli can serve as CSs, including external and interoceptive stimuli, and contextual and temporal stimuli. The unconditioned stimuli are often reflex-eliciting, but stimuli with acquired values are sometimes used.

Basic Phenomena of Conditioning

Acquisition refers to the development of a CR across pairings of the CS and US. Control procedures, such as unpaired CS and US presentations and randomly scheduled CS and US presentations, are needed to evaluate nonconditioning sources of responding.

Extinction refers to the presentation of the CS alone after conditioning, and to the decline in responding to the CS that then occurs. The CR spontaneously recovers after a period of time without stimulation, indicating the CS–US association has been suppressed but is still present. Conditioned responding generalizes to stimuli that are similar to the CS. A discrimination can be trained by presenting one CS with the US and another CS without the US.

The Role of Contiguity

Conditioning is affected by the temporal contiguity, or spacing, between the CS and US. Forward pairings, in the sequence CS then US, produce more conditioning than do the simultaneous presentations of CS and US, or backward pairings of US followed by CS. There are optimal CS-to-US intervals, but the exact time interval varies, and conditioning effectively occurs within a range around this optimal interval.

Other Factors Affecting Conditioning

Usually, a number of potential CSs are available on any trial. Through stimulus selection, only certain of these stimuli become associated with the US. In a compound made up of two or more CSs, the amount of conditioning is divided among stimuli and a more intense CS will overshadow a weaker CS.

Conditioning to a CS can be blocked by presenting it simultaneously with another CS that has already been trained with the US. Blocking shows that the occurrence of the US must be surprising for conditioning to occur.

The Rescorla-Wagner model describes the trial-by-trial acquisition of conditioning with multiple stimuli. The increase in conditioning on each trial is a function of the associative strengths of whatever CSs are present at the start of a trial. In the blocking procedure, previous training with one CS blocks conditioning to an added CS, because there is less room left for new learning due to the high associative strength after pre-training.

Conditioning is affected by the relevance of the CS to the US, also referred to as CS and US belongingness. CSs such as taste and odor readily condition with certain types of USs, such as poison and illness, but condition slowly if at all with other USs, such as electric shock. Correspondingly, exteroceptive CSs such as tones and lights quickly condition with shock USs, and poorly if at all with the illness US. This was shown in Garcia and Koelling's experiment using a bright-noisy-tasty CS. Taste-aversion learning may occur readily because organisms are biologically prepared to form associations between certain classes of stimuli. Alternatively, there may be a learned bias, acquired during the organism's lifetime, to form these associations.

Conditioned inhibition occurs when there is a negative correlation between the CS and the US: The US is more likely to occur without the CS than with it. Inhibition can be conditioned by pairing a potential inhibitory CS with an excitatory (CS+/CSx-no US). Inhibition is assessed by summation tests.

What is Learned in Classical Conditioning?

Stimulus–response (S–R) theory states that the CS comes to elicit the unconditioned response, or some portion of the UR. However, an overt UR is not necessary for conditioning to occur, and sometimes the CR is not the same as the UR.

The stimulus–stimulus (S–S) theory states that conditioning produces an association between the learned, internal representations of the CS and the US. This theory specifies that knowledge of the US is learned, not a specific conditioned response. S–S theory is supported by studies in which an association is sometimes demonstrated between two neutral CSs that have been paired. The size of the CR after conditioning also changes in reaction to devaluation of the US.

The preparatory response (R–S) theory states that the conditioned response is reinforced because it makes the US more palatable or less aversive. However, counterproductive CRs are sometimes acquired.

Contemporary research shows that conditioning produces multiple forms of learning: both general reactions (emotion or motivation) and specific responses (eyeblink, salivation). Neuroscience research indicates that one form of conditioning, the eyeblink, occurs through a circuit in the cerebellum of the brain, but that other brain areas are involved with other forms of conditioning.

What is the role of awareness in conditioning? Participants can often verbally report the CS–US contingency that they have experienced. However conditioning still occurs if conscious awareness is minimized by using distractor tasks, simpler organisms, or response systems beyond awareness.

Extensions of Conditioning

Repeated exposure to a drug can lead to the development of tolerance: The drug seemingly loses its effectiveness. Research on drug conditioning shows that drugs can act as USs, that contextual stimuli can act as CSs, and that the conditioned response may be opposite to the UR. Thus, tolerance may develop due to compensating CRs that counteract the UR.

Immune system reactions may become conditioned. A taste (the CS) paired with an immune-suppressing drug (the US) may itself acquire immune system-suppressing properties. Unlike tolerance with morphine, the immune CRs mimic the URs.

Applications of Conditioning

How do fears and phobias originate? A classical conditioning theory says that an initially neutral stimulus becomes conditioned (phobic) because it has been paired with fear, pain, or trauma. In Watson and Rayner's study, a child became fearful of a rat (used as the CS) that was paired with a loud noise (the US). The conditioning model has been updated by the addition of vicarious learning (learning fears through observation of other's fears) and preparedness (evolution has prepared us to readily acquire certain fears that have high survival value, such as fear of darkness, heights, or snakes). However, previous learning may bias our expectancies that certain stimuli (such as snakes) are dangerous.

If fears can be conditioned, they could be unlearned also. Simple extinction of fear, or the safe exposure to a phobic stimulus, should weaken the phobia, but the extinguished response returns under a number of conditions: through spontaneous recovery, reinstatement, and renewal. The counterconditioning technique of systematic desensitization, developed by Joseph Wolpe, is another method. The phobic stimulus is treated as a CS, and is paired with a response that is incompatible with fear, usually relaxation. Desensitization is effective in treating phobias, possibly due to extinction of fear to the phobic object or situation.

4   Instrumental Conditioning

Reward

Many of us engage in various behaviors we wish we didn't: vices such as smoking or drinking too much, dangerous actions such as speeding, and so-called nervous habits of nail biting, hair pulling, and teeth grinding. These bad habits are seemingly automatic, pervasive, and beyond remediation. Why do we do these things? There are other behaviors we wish we did perform habitually: studying, exercising, and controlling our diets. Why are they so difficult to start and maintain?

As a starting point, our bad behaviors are usually rewarded by some positive outcome. Maybe nail biting is calming. Speeding certainly gets you where you are going faster, and beyond that there may be the thrill of fast driving. Smoking is rewarded with peer approval and maybe a little rush from the nicotine. Habitual behaviors are also associated with stimuli in the environment that trigger, signal, or set the occasion for the habitual behavior. Smoking becomes attached to too many eliciting stimuli: after eating, after class, after a meeting, while socializing. Nail biting or hair pulling are triggered by ever more nervous situations: scary movies, talking to instructors or bosses, working out conflicts with roommates, and ruminating about tomorrow's assignment.

On the other hand, desirable behaviors are not often immediately reinforced. Studying is daily, but the opportunity to earn a good exam grade happens only occasionally in the semester. Exercising has long-term consequences, but little in the way of immediate gratification for all that expenditure of energy.

The remedies are, first, change the consequences of the behavior. Penalize yourself for smoking, speeding, or cursing. Schedule positive rewards for studying or exercising. Next, establish set stimulus conditions to be associated with the desired behaviors: a time and place exclusively devoted to exercise or study. Such prescriptions sound like exercises in self-control, which is what we believe we are lacking to begin with. After all, if you had the willpower, you would stop snacking and start exercising. The learning perspective shies away from explanations based on personal weaknesses, and instead replaces them with eliciting stimuli and reinforcing consequences, objective conditions that can be manipulated and that do influence behavior.

The topic of this chapter is instrumental learning. **Instrumental learning** is learning the connection between a behavior and its consequence. The behaviors of individual organisms are instrumental in producing various outcomes, some positive and some unwanted. This chapter deals more broadly with behavior than just our bad habits. Our intention is to derive some systematic principles that apply to eliciting stimuli, instrumental behaviors, and the consequences arranged.

Definition and History

Thorndike and Trial-and-Error Learning

Learning evolved as a means for organisms to adapt to changing environments. The underlying mechanisms need to be universal and applicable across the phylogenetic scale. Edward Lee Thorndike sought to observe the development of an adaptive behavior in order to systematize the principles involved (Thorndike, 1898, 1911).

Thorndike is best known for training "cats in a puzzle box." Cats are placed in a wooden crate having a hinged door in the front and a trip mechanism somewhere in the box. For example, pushing a pole that sticks up through the floor or pulling a loop of wire hanging in the back of the box would open the door, allowing the cat to escape. Thorndike chose responses that were not already in the cats' repertoire to study how the response developed with practice. Learning was measured by the time required to escape the box across trials.

Thorndike observed and named a number of characteristics of what we now call instrumental learning. First, he described the animal's efforts to escape as *trial and error*. **Trial-and-error learning** involves attempting to solve a problem by trying various responses, sometimes at random, until one produces the desired outcome. The cat tries different behaviors at first, such as clawing and scratching at the door. Gradually, over trials, ineffective responses drop out. Another response becomes more frequent, the one that immediately precedes the door opening. If the cat was brushing against the pole, the animal comes to do this more frequently.

Thorndike explained the learning by his *law of effect*: "Of several responses made to the same situation, those which are accompanied or closely followed by satisfaction to the animal will, other things being equal, be more firmly connected with the situation, so that, when it recurs, they will be more likely to recur; those that are accompanied or closely followed by discomfort to the animal will, other things being equal, have their connections to the situation weakened" (Thorndike, 1911, p. 244). The law of effect is a statement of the *principle of reinforcement*: Behavior is modified by the consequences of the behavior.

The escape response comes to be controlled by the environmental stimuli present at the time the response occurs, in this case, the stimuli of the puzzle box. These stimuli are now called *discriminative stimuli.* They signal when (or where) reinforcement is available. The response is called the **instrumental response**; it is instrumental in producing reinforcement. Learning, according to Thorndike, is the formation of a *stimulus–response* (or S–R) connection, from discriminative stimulus to the instrumental response, and reinforcement is what conditions or strengthens this S–R connection.

Thorndike's conception of learning was that reward exerted its effect automatically and without conscious thought or reasoning. In opposition to this was the view that learning occurred through intelligent problem solving, or insight. Insight implies that the animal suddenly comprehends the door-opening mechanics. The light bulb flashes overhead, the cat slaps its forehead and says to itself, "Oh, now I get it! The pole is connected to the door." As intelligent as many animals (including humans) are, much of their learning is nevertheless governed by trial and error. In one example of what should have been easy learning, food was placed beyond a gorilla's reach outside of the cage. A stick was nearby. Would the gorilla insightfully realize that the stick could be used to pull in the food? In fact, learning by the gorilla showed many similarities to that of Thorndike's cats. Sometimes the gorilla would bump the stick while reaching for the food. Other times, the gorilla would pick up the stick and slap the ground in frustration. Learning to use the stick to retrieve the food was a gradual process (Peckstein & Brown, 1939).

Skinner and Operant Learning

Beginning in the 1930s, B. F. Skinner began to develop techniques, terminology, and principles of learning by reinforcement. Skinner's entire system of conditioning is called **operant learning**. Skinner first developed a small experimental chamber in which to condition animals such as rats or pigeons (Skinner, 1938). This "operant conditioning chamber" allows precise experimental control over the presentation of discriminative stimuli and reinforcers, and the recording of responses. (The term **Skinner box** is generally used today; see Figure 4.1.) A contingency is arranged between an operant response, for instance, pressing a handle or bar, and a reinforcer, usually a small round food pellet delivered through a chute. Skinner coined the label *operant response* to indicate that the subject's response operates on the environment to produce a certain outcome. The bar-press-to-food contingency should lead to an increase in bar pressing, known technically as *positive reinforcement* (and informally as *reward training*). Once conditioned, operant responses can be extinguished. In *extinction*, the reinforcer is withheld, which should lead to a decrease in the frequency of responding.

(Skinner [1956] later recounted how he came to invent the operant bar-press task. He was running rats in a straight alley, in which rats ran from the start end to the goal end for food reward. Skinner soon tired of retrieving them and wondered, why bother having the rat go somewhere to obtain the reinforcer? Why not let the rat stay in one place and do something else? And so the bar-press response was invented.)

Figure 4.1 B. F. Skinner and a Rat in an Operant Conditioning Chamber (a.k.a. the "Skinner box").

Source: From *A History of Modern Psychology*, 6th ed. (p. 299), by D. P. Schultz and S. E. Schultz, 1996, Fort Worth, TX: Harcourt Brace. Reprinted courtesy of B. F. Skinner Foundation.

The distinction between *instrumental conditioning* and *operant learning* is significant among researchers of each, but may be less obvious to outsiders. One difference is that in instrumental learning, the subject is given discrete trials during which the response may be performed, for example, a trial in a maze or puzzle box. In operant studies, the subject is allowed more-or-less continuous availability to the response. The rat is placed in the Skinner box for a 50-minute hour and can perform the response whenever.

A more important distinction is that the instrumental approach tends to adopt a particular form of theorizing to explain learning. For instance, Edward Tolman said that rats develop "cognitive maps" of mazes. These hypothesized maps cannot be observed directly, and can be inferred only from behavior. Skinner eschewed this form of theorizing and opted instead for a strictly functional approach: The frequency of responding is a function of the amount of reinforcement, or its delay, or its schedule, and so on. These functions sometimes take the form of mathematical formulas.

Methods of Study

Instrumental learning is studied through a variety of methods. Rats and pigeons are frequently trained in Skinner boxes. With pigeons, a round Plexiglas disk placed at eye level can be pecked. This response is called key pecking and is reinforced with pieces of grain or seeds.

Mazes are once again popular now that spatial learning and memory are topics of renewed interest. The simplest mazes are T-shaped, with a start alley leading to a choice point and left and right goal boxes. Entry into the correct goal leads to food or some other reinforcer. (Maze learning is discussed in detail in Chapter 11.) Another instrumental task is the straight alley, or runway. It is simply a long alley, with a start compartment at one end and a goal compartment where reward is available at the other end. Learning is measured by the speed of running, which increases across rewarded trials.

Several interesting methods have been developed to study instrumental learning in human infants. Turning the head to the left or right can be reinforced by sucking milk or juice from a bottle. Trials can be initiated by a discriminative stimulus, such as a tone, which signals the availability of milk if the baby turns to the right (or left, whichever is selected as the target response). Somewhat older infants learn to move their legs in order to shake an overhead mobile tied to the limb via a ribbon, as illustrated in Figure 4.2. During acquisition training, leg movements increase when they are rewarded. After untying the ribbon, extinction occurs: The flexions decrease when no longer rewarded by movement of the mobile (Rovee-Collier, Sullivan, Enright, Lucas, & Fagan, 1980).

With older children or college students, instrumental learning can be embedded in a computer game. For instance, students may be told that they are playing an investment game; each press of the space bar invests some of their money; the computer occasionally displays the profit or

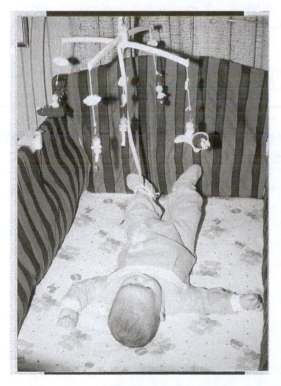
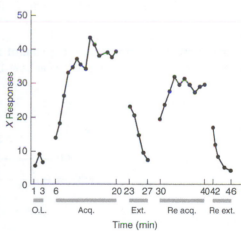

Figure 4.2 The left panel shows the experimental arrangement for infant conditioning of leg movements to elicit movement of the mobile as the reinforcer. The right panel shows acquisition and extinction of leg movements.

Sources: (*left panel*) From "Organization of infant memory," by C. K. Rovee-Collier and M. W. Sullivan, 1980, *Journal of Experimental Psychology: Human Learning and Memory, 6*, p. 801. Copyright American Psychological Association. Reprinted with permission. (*right panel*) From "Conjugate Reinforcement of Infant Exploratory Behavior," by C. K. Rovee and D. T. Rovee, 1969, *Journal of Experimental Child Psychology, 8*, p. 36. Copyright Elsevier, reprinted with permission.

interest earned as the "reward" (Reed, 2001). Students learn which scenarios (stimuli) are associated with a profit, and which responses to choose.

Positive Reinforcement

What we call reward in everyday language is a somewhat imprecise description of positive reinforcement. Reinforcement is defined by the presence of a response-to-reinforcer contingency. (A contingency is essentially a rule.) In **positive reinforcement**, the reinforcer is delivered contingent on performance of the instrumental response. The response should increase in frequency because it leads to a reinforcing consequence. Who establishes and maintains the contingency? It may be the experimenter, but it could also be a parent or teacher, or even society.

The notion of **contingency** is important to defining instrumental conditioning: The reinforcer is contingent on, or dependent on, the occurrence of a response. Control conditions are required in an experiment to assure that the responding we observe is due to the contingency and is not incidental to some other aspect of the experiment. If I attempt to "reward" my dog's tail wagging with a food treat, tail wagging will surely increase. But this is not due to wagging-leading-to-food, and in fact it is probably the reverse (giving food causes wagging!). A noncontingent control condition is sometimes used, in which the rewards are programmed to occur randomly, independent of the subjects' behavior. That is, the control reinforcers do not require a bar press or keystroke. The control can tell us how much more responding occurs when the instrumental contingency is in effect. Figure 4.3 diagrams response-contingent and -noncontingent reinforcement.

When college students play the investment game, an instrumental condition arranges for a profit to occur after every so many presses of the space bar. A noncontingent control group receives the same profits, but they are dispensed randomly by a computer program and are not dependent (are not contingent) on bar presses. The rewarded group makes many more presses than does the noncontingent group. If you question the students, the reward subjects will believe their responses lead to reward; the control subjects will not perceive a connection between response and reward (Reed, 2001; Shanks & Dickinson, 1991).

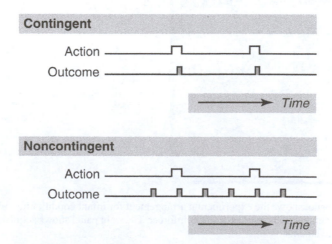

Figure 4.3 **The Contingent Relationship Between Action and Outcome.** In the contingent relationship, each instance of the action is followed by the outcome. In the noncontingent relationship, outcomes occur independently of the actions.

Reinforcement Variables Affecting Acquisition

Positive reinforcers can be manipulated along several dimensions, each of which affects how quickly a response is acquired and the level of performance that is attained. These variables include the amount and delay of reinforcement and the consistency with which reinforcement is administered.

Amount of Reinforcement

As a general principle, larger rewards produce better, faster learning and better performance than do smaller rewards. For instance, rats will run faster in a straight alley for larger rewards than for smaller rewards. Illustrative data are shown in the top left panel of Figure 4.4. The reinforcer was

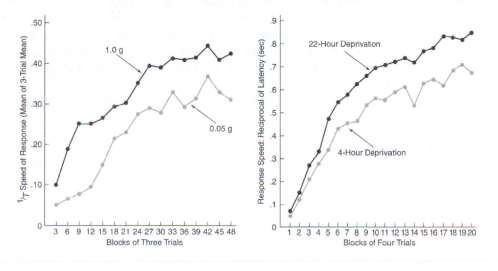

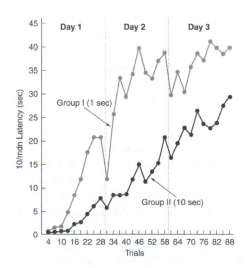

Figure 4.4 **Effects of Three Reward Variables on Running Speed by Rats.** (*top left*) Amount of food reward, 1 gram versus 0.05 gram; (*top right*) number of hours of food deprivation, 4 hours versus 22 hours; and (*bottom*) delay between response and reinforcer, 1 second or 10 seconds.

Sources: (*top left*) and (*bottom*) from *Behavior Theory and Conditioning* (pp. 131 and 157), by K. Spence, 1956, New Haven, CT: Yale University Press. Copyright © 1956 by Yale University Press. Reprinted with permission. (*top right*) from "Performance in Selective Learning as a Function of Hunger," by C. K. Ramond, 1954, *Journal of Experimental Psychology, 48*, pp. 265–270. Copyright American Psychological Association. Reprinted with permission.

either 1 gram of food or 0.05 gram. The large-reward animals ran faster than did the small-reward animals (Spence, 1956). Children offered points for completing school work accomplished more when more points were offered (e.g., Wolf, Giles, & Hall, 1968). The points are later exchanged for a toy, stickers, play time, and so on.

Similarly, reinforcers that are more highly preferred will produce better performance. Rats will respond more for water having a higher concentration of sucrose than a lower concentration.

Contrast Effects

A reinforcer **contrast effect** occurs when reward value of a current reward is influenced by experience with previous rewards that differed in amount or quality. Crespi (1942) demonstrated contrast in rats running a straight alley for food pellets. After switching from a larger to a smaller reward, the rats ran more slowly than animals trained with the small reward throughout. It is as if the small reward is perceived as really meager in contrast to the previous larger amount. Conversely, after switching from a small to a large reward, the rats ran even faster than animals given the large reward from the beginning.

Contrast in human instrumental learning is also readily shown. In one study, infants made instrumental sucking movements, recorded through an artificial nipple, which were reinforced with either water or sucrose. There was more sucking for sucrose, indicating that it was a qualitatively more effective reinforcer than was water. When water was substituted for sucrose, sucking decreased dramatically, to a level even less than that obtained by using water as the reward throughout (Kobre & Lipsitt, 1972).

Drive

Drive can be described as a motivational need or desire for a given reinforcer. The level of an appetitive drive is usually manipulated by depriving the subject of access to the reinforcer for some period of time. For example, depriving a rat of food or water overnight increases the hunger and thirst drives, respectively. Drive increases responding to reinforcers that are relevant to the drive. The data from the top right panel of Figure 4.4 are from a study of rats that were food deprived for 4 hours or 22 hours before training sessions. The rats trained under a state of longer deprivation ran faster during the acquisition trials.

Social interaction can be used as an effective reinforcer in a school setting. To build up a drive for this reinforcer, socializing could be blocked for a while. "Isolation," often called time-out, increases the effectiveness of a teacher's attention as a reinforcer. The longer the period of social deprivation, the greater the effectiveness of attention.

Do drive and reward amount affect learning, or do they instead affect the motivation to respond? Contrast effects are rapid shifts in performance that are consistent with a motivational interpretation. When a rat runs more slowly for a smaller reward than for a larger reward, does that mean the rat knows less than on the previous trial? No, smaller rewards are less motivating and so performance declines. This illustrates the learning-versus-performance distinction made earlier in this text (Chapter 1).

Clark Hull (1949) acknowledged the roles of learning and motivation in his theory. Learning was represented by the factor of Habit Strength (H), which was determined by the number of reinforced training trials (and other variables). Motivation was separately represented by the theoretical variables of Drive (e.g., the number of hours of food deprivation) and Incentive (e.g., reinforcer amount). The actual degree of responding was determined by the combination of Habit Strength (H), Drive (D), and Incentive (I), as

Response strength $= H \times D \times I$

Put informally, the rat runs quickly in the straight alley because these three factors take on high values. The rat has received prior reinforced training to run (H). The rat is hungry now (D). The reinforcer is really appealing (I). (Hull actually used another letter for incentive because I was already used for inhibition.)

Schedules of Reinforcement

In his early research, Skinner discovered that reinforcement need not be given for each response, but instead could be given after some number of responses according to various schedules of reinforcement (Ferster & Skinner, 1957). A **schedule of reinforcement** refers to the specific rule that relates the timing or frequency of responding on the one hand and the delivery of reward on the other. In general terms, reinforcement can be given for each occurrence of the instrumental response or for only some. Reinforcing each instance of the response would be *continuous reinforcement*. In a **partial reinforcement** schedule, some percentage of the responses are reinforced.

During the initial training of a behavior, a continuous schedule of reward generally produces more rapid conditioning or a higher level of responding than does a partial reinforcement schedule. A continuous schedule provides more accurate information about the contingency between response and outcome. If one considers instrumental learning to be a form of trial-and-error learning, then the occasional nonrewards of the partial schedule may lead the subject to try other responses in an attempt to be more successful. Stevenson and Zigler (1958) compared children in a button-pushing task. Only one of the three buttons produced reward (a light flashed and points accumulated), and for different groups that button was reinforced 100, 66, or 33 percent of the time. The other two buttons had no effect whatsoever. The optimal strategy is to discover which button produces reward, and then push only that button. The results nicely showed a schedule effect: There was a higher frequency of pushing the correct button when reinforcement was given on a continuous rather than on a partial schedule.

The rule that continuous schedules are better than partial schedules is not absolute. As we will see later, partial schedules during *acquisition* produce more persistent performance during *extinction* (see Chapter 5).

Given that a partial reinforcement schedule is used, there are various ways of arranging the response–reward contingencies. In a *fixed-ratio* schedule, reinforcement occurs after a fixed number of responses (e.g., every fifth or seventh response). Fixed-ratio schedules lead to very high response rates. By contrast, on a *fixed-interval* schedule, reinforcement is given for the first response that occurs after a set interval of time. For instance, during a 30-second fixed-interval schedule, 30 seconds must have passed since the last reward before a response will be reinforced. On this schedule, there is often a pause in responding after each reward, and then responding gradually increases as the time for the next available reinforcement approaches.

Reinforcement can be made less predictable by varying the number of responses required for a reinforcer, a *variable-ratio* schedule, or varying the time interval between rewards, a *variable-interval* schedule. Thus, reinforcement on a variable-ratio 5 schedule occurs after different numbers of responses that averages to 5 over trials. On a variable-interval, 30-second schedule, reinforcement occurs following the first response after intervals that average 30 seconds. Variable schedules produce relatively constant rates of responding because the occurrence of reinforcement is less predictable. Some everyday examples of schedules are described in Table 4.1.

The common textbook example for intermittent reinforcement is the slot machine. The designers of slot machines use several behavioral principles to induce high rates of responding and persistence in playing (Rivlin, 2004). Reward is given on a variable schedule. It occurs only

Table 4.1 Examples of Schedules of Reinforcement

Fixed ratio: Being paid for each piece manufactured, each envelope stuffed, or each assignment completed.
Fixed interval: Making the response of checking to see if the coffee is ready. No reward is provided until a certain amount of perk time has passed.
Variable ratio: Sales associates' attempts to help customers are sometimes rewarded with sales. Which customer will buy may be unpredictable, but more attempts should produce more sales.
Variable interval: Checking e-mail or texts when the annoying "ding" is in silent mode. The messages arrive unpredictably, but the recipient won't know unless he or she checks.

intermittently and unpredictably and thus induces persistence in responding. Frequent small rewards maintain playing between the rare big payouts. The cycle could be paced more quickly, but designers have determined that about 6 seconds is short enough. If the player needs to frequently reach for more money, he or she might walk away. The lights and sounds act as secondary reinforcers (stimuli associated with reinforcement and thus rewards themselves). Even though some machines now issue winnings as paper tickets or credits, the machines' speakers make the sound of coins dropping down the chute when players win, again acting as a secondary reinforcer.

Schedules are interesting because they demonstrate that the rate and patterning of responding is sensitive to the specific reinforcement contingencies. Skinner challenged the critics who argued that behavior is too complex to be predictable (Skinner, 1953). Instead, some behaviors can be precisely predicted and controlled.

Delay of Reinforcement

Reinforcement that occurs immediately after the correct response is generally more effective than reinforcement that is delayed for some interval of time. The lower panel of Figure 4.4 shows the results of an experiment with rats trained to run a straight alley and given a food reward 1 second after reaching the goal box, or the reward was delayed for 10 seconds after entering the goal box. The short-delay group ran faster.

Delaying reward can impede learning in several ways. If reinforcement does not immediately follow the instrumental response, other behaviors may occur during the delay interval, and they might inadvertently become conditioned. For instance, a rat presses a bar but reward does not occur, so the animal starts turning around and the food pellet suddenly drops in after the delay times out. From the rat's perspective, the reinforcer occurs after turning, not after bar pressing!

Another explanation for delayed-reward effects is that the response has been forgotten by the time reinforcement occurs. Now what was it that I did that worked? Delay effects should be reduced if memory for the response could be made to persist across the delay interval. Lieberman, McIntosh, and Thomas (1979) presented a distinctive stimulus after the response, a "marking stimulus," to make the response more memorable. In their experiments, rats ran a T-shaped maze but were held in a delay box before reward was given for a correct turn or withheld for an incorrect turn. In the marking condition, when the rat made a turn in the maze a tone sounded. The tone marked the response in memory, making the response memory more distinctive, so it could be connected later with the outcome.

Self-Control

Instrumental tasks can be expanded to allow several responses. For instance, two levers could be available in the Skinner box, each having a different reinforcement contingency. One response (say, the right lever) produces an immediate small reward and the other lever produces a delayed but larger reward. On a given trial, the subject can only press one of the levers. This sort of choice defines **self-control**: the capacity to inhibit immediate gratification in preference for a larger reward after a delay. Impulsiveness, then, would be choosing the small but immediate reward. Whether self-control or impulsiveness occurs depends on the exact combinations of amount and delay. Self-control decreases if the delay is too long or the reinforcer at the end of the delay is not large enough.

The initial experiments on self-control were conducted with children. Self-control shows a developmental trend. For example, 3-year-olds choose the immediate small reward, whereas 5-year-olds display more self-control (Logue, Forzano, & Ackerman, 1996). Adolescents and adults are quite capable of exercising control and make the choice associated with a delayed large reward, as long as the reinforcers are points or tokens. When food is the reinforcer, even adults sometimes break down and choose immediate reinforcement.

Self-control, or learning to tolerate a delay, can be increased. By beginning with a relatively brief delay for the larger reward, and then gradually lengthening the interval, the more preferred reward after a longer delay will be chosen.

Secondary Reinforcement

So far in this chapter we have cited a variety of different reinforcers, such as food, accumulating points, or the opportunity to socialize. Some of these can be labeled as primary reinforcers, or events that are inherently reinforcing. *Primary reinforcers* reduce biological needs of the organism, such as food does for a hungry subject. Other primary reinforcers include water, or relief from excessive heat or cold, or from pain.

Other stimuli that function as reinforcers are derived from primary reinforcers. **Secondary reinforcers** are neutral stimuli that have been paired with primary reinforcers and acquire the capacity to reinforce on their own. For example, a tone that has been paired with food can function as a reinforcer for the instrumental response of bar pressing. Animal trainers often develop secondary reinforcers, such as whistles or clickers, to reinforce from a distance or to reward correct performance without having to interrupt the animal's routine.

This procedure of pairing a neutral stimulus with a primary reinforcer sounds like classical conditioning, and indeed the goal is the same in both: to develop an association between the neutral and unconditioned stimuli (e.g., between tone and food). The classical conditioning comparison also suggests other similarities. For instance, the secondary reinforcer will extinguish if it is not regularly paired with the primary reinforcer. Thus, some periodic reconditioning of the secondary reinforcer is necessary.

Social Reinforcement

An especially powerful class of reinforcers for human behavior is **social reinforcement**. Praise, attention, physical contact, and facial expressions given by parents, teachers, or peers can exert considerable control over our behavior. In one example, a young student remained apart from the other children during recess. This withdrawn behavior received inadvertent social reinforcement by attention from the teacher, who would spend time with the student. (Attention is not always rewarding; on some occasions, we might actually seek not to be noticed.) Rearranging the reinforcement contingencies to provide attention when the student interacted with others, and ignoring the other behavior, led to a change in the student's socialization (Kirby & Shields, 1972).

Why do social reinforcers have such power? One theory is that social reinforcers are primary reinforcers, based upon social drives inherent in humans and other animal species (Harlow, 1959). Another theory treats social reinforcement as secondary reinforcement. Approval has been paired with primary reinforcers such as food or protection from danger (Miller & Dollard, 1941; Skinner, 1953).

Social reinforcers have several advantages in behavior modification over natural reinforcers such as food. Praise can be immediately given, and does not usually disrupt ongoing behavior. Classroom social reinforcers not only improve academic behavior, but often generally improve attentiveness to possible social reinforcement for other behaviors, and decrease disruptiveness that leads to social disapproval (Kazdin, 1994).

Summary of Reinforcement Variables

Positive reinforcers can be primary reinforcers, such as food or water; secondary reinforcers, or stimuli associated with primary reinforcers, such as a tone, token, or gold star; and social reinforcers, such as praise. A positive reinforcer is more effective in conditioning and maintaining instrumental responding when the reinforcer is large; when the organism has a drive or need for the reinforcer; when the reinforcement is given immediately; and when given after each response. There are exceptions to these general rules. Contrast effects show that a given reinforcer may be more or less effective, depending on the comparison to previously given reinforcers. In self-control procedures, the characteristics of delay, amount, or quality of the reinforcers can be opposed. For example, one response produces a large but delayed reinforcer, whereas another response produces a small immediate reinforcer.

Theories of Reinforcement

What makes reinforcers reinforce? A variety of things function as reinforcers: food or water for animals, moving a mobile for infants, tokens and stickers for young children, and accumulating points for button pushing by college students. Do these events have something in common that makes them act as reinforcers? Thorndike defined a reinforcer as that which produces a satisfying state of affairs, but this is a vague and subjective description, and does not offer much guidance. Skinner adopted a very pragmatic definition: A reinforcer is whatever works to increase the frequency of the operant response. We still do not know why a reinforcer reinforces. Over the years, the explanation of reinforcement has been a central concern of learning theorists.

A number of theories have been offered to explain reinforcement. The major categories describe reinforcers as stimuli (things such as food, tokens, and points); reinforcers as activities (e.g., consuming, exploring); and reinforcers as information (the response was correct versus incorrect). To anticipate the conclusion derived from the following discussion, reinforcers work because of several different reasons. A single explanation may not subsume all instances of reinforcement.

Reinforcers as Stimuli

Drive Reduction

One characteristic of primary reinforcers is that they reduce biological drives. Thus, food reduces hunger, water reduces thirst, and so on. Clark Hull (1943) postulated that, at the most basic level, **drive reduction** was the basis for primary reinforcement. Drive-reduction is consistent with the effect of reinforcement variables mentioned earlier. Thus, larger (rather than smaller) rewards should reduce the hunger drive more; immediate reward reduces drive sooner than delayed reward; etc.

But what about reinforcement that has no obvious relationship to drive reduction, such as tokens, points, or even money? Here, secondary reinforcement enters in. Stimuli acquire secondary reinforcing properties through association with primary, or biological, reinforcers. The many stimuli that reinforce human behavior may be said to have acquired reinforcing properties.

Hull's drive-reduction theory was an enormous influence on learning theory for many years. It nicely tied psychological explanations of learning to biological ones. Unfortunately, numerous instances of learning without apparent drive reduction began to accumulate. As examples, rats would learn a variety of instrumental responses for saccharin reinforcers perfectly well (Sheffield & Roby, 1950). Saccharin, a nonnutritive substance, does not satisfy hunger but is still highly reinforcing. When juvenile monkeys were made fearful, they sought out a soft and comfortable manikin to cling to, rather than one that had previously provided food reinforcement (Harlow, 1959). In the face of these contrary results, alternative theories of reinforcement were devised.

Incentive Motivation

Instead of reducing drive, maybe reinforcers actually increase drive. Saccharin is reinforcing because it arouses and stimulates the organism. The ideas of Sheffield (the saccharin study), Crespi (contrast effects), and Tolman (latent learning) evolved into the theory of **incentive motivation**: Reinforcers are incentives that elicit responding. This corresponds to the way we talk of rewards in everyday language: We perform in order to get the reward. The difference between drive reduction and incentive is the difference between push and pull: Drives (such as hunger) push us into action, whereas incentives (such as chocolate) pull us on to obtain them.

Incentive motivation is illustrated by a manipulation known as *reinforcer priming*. Simply giving a free reinforcer, one that need not be earned, can enhance instrumental responding to obtain more of the reinforcer. Imagine giving a rat a small portion of the food reward before it enters the maze. What would drive-reduction theory predict? There should be slower maze running because hunger had been lessened. Actually, a priming reinforcer increases running speed (Terry, 1983). This is the "salted peanuts" effect (Hebb, 1949). You had no thought or desire for eating peanuts until someone offers you one; then, you have to have more!

One difficulty with an incentive theory of reinforcement is that instrumental responding will sometimes persist even after the incentive value is gone. As will be noted later, satiated rats will persist in responding even though they no longer consume the accumulating food pellets.

Brain Stimulation

A third approach to defining reinforcers as stimuli seeks the underlying physiological basis of reinforcement. Possibly there is a common area of the brain that is activated by those stimuli that work as reinforcers. James Olds and Peter Milner (1954) discovered that stimulation of the reticular formation in the rat's brain was reinforcing. Rats were trained to make bar-press responses in which brief bursts of electrical stimulation were given as the reinforcing stimulus. Stimulation worked well as reinforcement. This result suggested the possibility that a final common path had been discovered for all reinforcers. Subsequent research has discovered brain areas involved with other reinforcers, such as those for the opiate drugs or alcohol.

Reinforcement by brain stimulation has several properties that differentiates it from conventional reinforcers. Satiation does not occur. Also, responding maintained by brain stimulation dissipates rapidly once reward ceases, whereas behavior reinforced with conventional rewards typically persists longer before extinguishing.

Reinforcers as Behaviors

As an alternative to characterizing reinforcers as stimuli, we could think about reinforcers as activities or behaviors. That is, it is not food that is a reward, but rather the activity of eating that is reinforcing. This at first seems just a matter of semantics, but the altered perspective expands the category of positive reinforcers to include all sorts of other activities that we know function as such.

The major proponent of the reinforcement-as-activity approach is David Premack (1962, 1965). His notion, generally speaking, is that behaviors can be ranked in terms of their preference or value to an individual. Some activities are highly preferred by many of us, such as going to the movies or eating ice cream, and other activities are less preferred, such as studying or mowing the lawn. These preferences can be established by observing the relative probability with which the various behaviors occur. According to what we now call the **Premack principle**, a higher-probability activity will reinforce a lower-probability activity. Thus, going to the movies will reinforce studying, but not vice versa.

A simple statement of the Premack principle glosses over some important technical details. Preferences have to be determined individually, ideally under conditions allowing unrestricted opportunity to engage in all of the relevant activities in order to determine their baseline frequency of occurrence. The probabilities of different behaviors vary over time because the activities are subject to deprivation or satiation (Timberlake & Allison, 1974). Thus, after watching all of *The Lord of the Rings*, watching videos temporarily lose their reinforcing property.

The Premack principle was neatly demonstrated in a study of two behaviors of children who were allowed access to candy and a pinball machine to first assess individual preferences for each. In the next phase of the study, each behavior was used either as an instrumental response or a reinforcer for different subsets of children. The children who had originally preferred pinball now increased their eating of candy (used here as the response) in order to get access to pinball (used here as the reinforcer). Children who initially preferred eating candy now played pinball (the response) to gain more candy (the reinforcer) (Premack, 1965).

Reinforcers as Strengtheners

We speak casually of reinforcers as rewards or incentives, but there is an alternative sense of the word *reinforce*: to strengthen. This is the original sense used by stimulus–response theorists such as Thorndike and Hull. The reinforcer strengthens the association between a discriminative stimulus and an instrumental response. For instance, when a stimulus light is followed by a bar-press response, the food reinforcer strengthens the association between the light and the bar press. Contemporary research has validated this strengthening role.

The potential strengthening effects of a reinforcer are usually confounded with its reward or incentive effects, both of which lead to improved performance. One way to distinguish the two roles that a reinforcer can take is to oppose them. Huston, Mondadori, and Waser (1974) conditioned mice to remain on a platform in a Skinner box. Stepping down off the platform, which is in fact the first thing mice do, results in a foot shock. When returned to the chamber the next day, the control mice remained on the platform for some time, the latency to step down being a measure of fear learned on the previous day. The experimental animals were given food reinforcers in their home cages immediately after stepping down and being shocked. What effect would food have on learning to stay on the platform? If the food did have a "rewarding" effect, this would be to reward stepping down, the last response made, so the mice should step down more quickly the next day. However, if food took on the role of a strengthener, it could enhance the association between stepping down and receiving shock, leading to longer latencies to step down. And, in fact, the mice given food after the training trial stayed put on the platform longer than animals not fed.

According to the theory of memory consolidation (e.g., Hebb, 1949), a learning experience produces transient activation within certain areas of the nervous system. Reinforcers may reexcite those neural units, allowing additional opportunity for permanent changes to occur in the nerve cells to encode the learning experience (Landauer, 1969). Reinforcers do not have to be rewards like food, water, or gold stars in order to strengthen learning. The critical feature is that the reinforcer enhances excitation of those neural units involved in the learning experience and in memory consolidation. This means that strengthening effects can be produced by other means than simply presenting a reinforcing stimulus. Administering, as examples, stimulant drugs or hormones shortly after a learning experience, or electrically stimulating certain areas of the brain (White & Milner, 1992), also seem to facilitate learning, and by implication, consolidation.

Reinforcers as Information

Whether a reinforcer reduces drive, is an incentive, or strengthens memory, all reinforcers provide information. Was this the correct response? Was the response performed accurately, efficiently, timely? The reinforcer provides information in the form of feedback: "yes, I did it right" or "no I didn't." Reinforcement conveys information as to whether the response was correct.

Biofeedback is an example of the informational role of reinforcement. A subtle, usually undetectable bodily reaction is monitored by an electrode attached to the body, such as muscle tension in the forehead. In *biofeedback*, this bodily response can be converted into an external signal, such as a tone. Changes in muscle tension are converted into increases or decreases in the volume or pitch of the tone. The goal is to learn to control the tone, thereby also controlling the muscle tension. The tone provides information about muscle tension, information that we otherwise did not recognize.

So, What is Reinforcement?

Several theories of reinforcement have been reviewed. Although one or another explanation can be adopted exclusively, many theorists accept that reinforcement plays multiple roles. In some cases, a reinforcer is a significant stimulus that the organism needs to learn about for survival. In other cases a reinforcer can be well described as an incentive for certain behaviors. In still other cases, reinforcement is information about whether a response is correct. Reinforcers are events that elicit affective reactions of pleasure or displeasure, provide information about the world, and stimulate certain forms of neural activity. Thus, there may be no one answer to our question.

Is Reinforcement Necessary for Learning?

Much of human learning goes on without explicit reward. Memory occurs without a deliberate intention to remember. Although animal studies routinely use reinforcement, such as food, water, or relief from shock, is reinforcement even necessary for learning by animals?

The classic test of this question was Tolman and Honzik's study of latent learning (1930). Three groups of rats were trained in a maze. One group received food in the goal box on each daily trial. Across 11 days of training, these animals learned to run faster and to enter fewer blind alleys. A second group never received food in the goal box. Their performance improved only slightly over days. So far, this looks like a fairly standard study showing that reinforcement affects learning. But is it likely that the nonrewarded rats learned nothing about the layout of the maze in 11 days? Maybe they did learn the route, but had no reason to run promptly into the goal box. After all, it really wasn't a "goal" box for the nonrewarded animals. Tolman and Honzik included a third group that was first trained without reward. On day 11, food was placed in the goal box for the rats to discover when they eventually got there. On the next opportunity, day 12, the rats in this third group quickly traversed the maze, entering few wrong alleys en route to the goal box (see Figure 4.5, upper panel). Tolman said that these rats had learned the maze during those first days without reinforcement but that this knowledge was *latent* (or hidden) until a reason to display the learning was present.

In a second experiment, Tolman and Honzik employed a symmetrically opposite manipulation: After training with reward, on the eleventh day, food was omitted in the goal box. On day 12, the rats, which obviously knew their way through the maze, suddenly started taking wrong turns (see the lower panel of Figure 4.5).

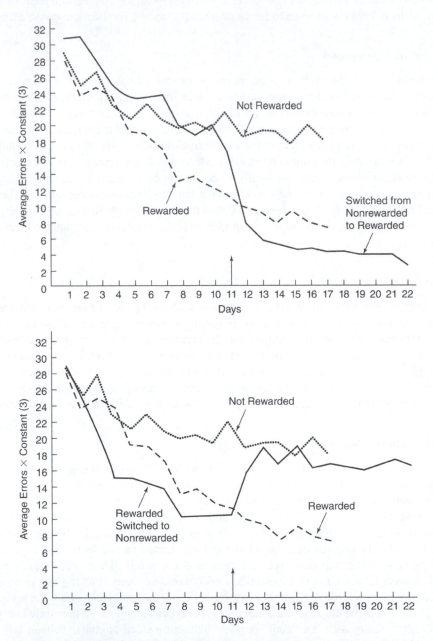

Figure 4.5 **Results of the Tolman and Honzik Latent Learning Experiments.** Both graphs show the number of maze errors made over days. The upper panel shows the effect of switching from nonreward to reward on day 11; the lower panel shows the effect of switching from reward to nonreward on day 11.

Source: From "Introduction and Removal of Reward, and Maze Performance in Rats," by E. C. Tolman and C. H. Honzik, 1930, *University of California Publications in Psychology, 4,* pp. 257–275. Copyright © 1930, The Regents of the University of California.

Traditional reinforcement theorists at first disputed Tolman's interpretation of latent learning. Maybe actually there was reinforcement on the no-food days: Removal from the goal box reduced the fear of this unknown place in which the rats had been placed. Possibly 10 days of acclimation and adaptation to the experimental procedure eliminated irrelevant behaviors and motives, and so the single reinforcement on day 11 was sufficient to condition the correct maze choices. However, even granting the contribution of these other factors, the now-accepted conclusion is that learning can occur without explicit rewards.

Awareness in Human Instrumental Learning

In the 1950s and 1960s, claims were made that subliminal perception and learning occurred: Sub-threshold stimuli would command us what to do and we would unconsciously respond. This possibility raised the specter of manipulation of human behavior by unscrupulous individuals. In reaction to such fears, the U.S. Congress passed legislation forbidding embedded subliminal commercial messages in films (Moore, 1982). For a decade afterwards, the scientific claims and data went back and forth over the possibility of learning without awareness. What role does conscious awareness of the response–outcome contingency play in learning?

In one of the first demonstrations of unawares conditioning, Greenspoon (1955) simply told his subjects to say out loud each word that came to mind. Greenspoon would mutter "umm humm" whenever a plural noun was emitted and make no response to other words. The students began to use more plural nouns during the course of the session. This is *verbal conditioning*: An instrumental response (here, plural nouns) is followed by a reinforcer ("umm humm") that affects the frequency of the response. In postexperimental interviews, the college student participants said they were not aware of the contingency between the words they spoke and the experimenter's mumbling. These results were taken to suggest that unconscious conditioning had occurred. Such claims were readily accepted at first, given also that animals, infants, and psychotic mental patients were already assumed to learn without conscious awareness.

Our contemporary reaction to the claim for unconscious learning is both "yes" and "no." Other research discussed throughout this text shows that learning occurs without our awareness or recollection. You may recall Zajonc's demonstration of the acquisition of a preference for familiar stimuli, even though those stimuli had been initially presented subliminally (Chapter 2). So, yes, learning can occur without our awareness that we have learned.

But does unawares learning occur in verbal conditioning studies? Self-reports are too often inaccurate measures of awareness. The subjects may be reluctant to report an awareness of which they are not quite certain or they give the answer for which they think the experimenter is looking. More detailed interviewing revealed that many participants were indeed aware of the response–outcome contingency (Dulany, 1968). In general, the participants who were aware showed conditioning. Participants who were unaware of the contingency did not increase their use of the target words. Interestingly, an occasional aware participant decreased using the selected words as a reaction to awareness ("No psychologist is going to mess with my brain!").

It is also clear that normal instrumental performance can be enhanced through verbal instruction of the contingencies. We tell children the "rules" relating behavior to consequences. Systems of reward for appropriate behaviors are more effective even with psychiatric patient groups, when the contingencies are first described verbally (Ayllon & Azrin, 1964).

Criticisms of the Use of Reinforcement

The application of reinforcement principles to everyday behavior has been a spectacular success for psychology. Behavior modification is applied in schools, institutions, workplaces, and the clinic. However, behavioral technology has been criticized both for its underlying philosophy and its long-term effectiveness. One objection is a moral one: that the use of reinforcement is manipulative. Granting and withholding reward is a form of control. Appropriate behavior should be expected, and should not depend on bribery or rewards. Proponents of behavioral psychology, such as B. F. Skinner, reply in return that our behavior is already controlled by its consequences (Skinner, 1971). Parents, peers, schools, churches, employers, and governments all use rewards or sanctions to control human behavior.

Another objection is that reinforcement undermines intrinsic motivation, or a desire to perform a given behavior for its own sake. With *intrinsic motivation* the incentive to perform comes from the activity itself, in contrast to the extrinsic motivation by rewards. In one study, nursery school children were first observed while they drew with colored markers, something kids like to do anyway. Drawing is intrinsically motivated. Then, in one condition, the children were offered reinforcement for doing more drawing, and in another condition there was no reinforcement. Later, the children were again allowed to play with the markers. Those who had been reinforced now colored less than did those not previously reinforced. Reward had provided an explicit reinforcer for the behavior, replacing intrinsic reasons for using the markers, such as doing it for fun (Lepper, Greene, & Nisbett, 1973).

The belief that rewards undermine intrinsic motivation is widely accepted (Kohn, 1993). However, the detrimental effects of external rewards may be explained by mechanisms already discussed in this chapter. For example, the decline in drawing after reward might be due to negative contrast. The intrinsic rewards of the activity are less appealing in contrast to the explicit rewards the children had recently received (Eisenberger & Cameron, 1996).

Finally, some critics challenge the effectiveness of reinforcement, saying that all too often, reinforcement produces transient changes in responding, which disappear when reinforcement ceases or becomes infrequent. In one sense, this should be anticipated, given our knowledge of the importance of incentive to performance as shown by Tolman and Honzik's latent learning experiment. On the other hand, learning is supposed to produce relatively permanent changes in behavior, as noted in the definition of learning given in the first chapter. We could expect more durability to learned habits.

The counterargument by behavior modifiers is that the use of explicit reinforcers is often intended to be temporary. Once behavior starts to occur with some regularity, other reinforcers in the individual's environment may take over. A person will be praised for good behavior or feel satisfaction in accomplishing a task. And some behaviors simply have little intrinsic motivation to begin with. Not many of us find real satisfaction in cutting the grass or doing calculus homework. External motivation in the form of rewards may be better than not doing the work at all (Chance, 1992). (The literature on the disadvantages of reward is summarized in a book titled *Punished by Rewards* [Kohn, 1993].)

Response Learning

Some of the instrumental responses described so far were chosen by researchers for their experimental convenience. However, a significant use of instrumental conditioning is in shaping a particular form of the response. The contingencies we arrange between the exact response desired and presentation of reinforcement can be used to create new behaviors and modify existing behaviors precisely.

Shaping

Say we want to train a behavior that is not presently in the organism's repertoire. How can we reinforce something that does not occur? Skinner offered the method of response **shaping**: a behavior that is not currently in the organism's repertoire could be gradually shaped by reinforcing a series of successive approximations to the desired response. Skinner used the analogy of a potter molding clay. We start by selecting a response that approximates the desired behavior, and reinforce it. Then step by step, we only reinforce responses closer to the target behavior. To teach a rat to bar-press, the rat is first reinforced for standing near the bar, then touching the bar, then pawing the bar, then bearing weight on the bar, etc. By the process of *successive approximations*, reinforcement is used to create a new response.

Some remarkable examples of shaping are evident in the work of Mary Joan Willard, a former research assistant to Skinner. She founded an organization called Helping Hands: Simian Aids for the Disabled, which trains capuchin monkeys to assist quadriplegics. The monkeys are trained to open and shut doors, turn lights on or off, change books in a reading stand, or get and hold beverages for their owners (MacFadyen, 1986). Shaping was used to train novel behaviors that certainly were not present in the animals' repertoires to begin with.

Chaining

Instrumental conditioning can be used to construct a sequence of behaviors, with reinforcement occurring only after the final response in the sequence. This process is called response **chaining**, the notion being that each response is like a link in the chain. Some explanations of chaining attribute dual roles to each link in the chain. One hypothesis is that each response also acts as a discriminative stimulus for the next response in the series. Another description is that each response also acts as a secondary reinforcer for the previous response (Grant & Evans, 1994; Williams, 1994).

In the classic demonstration of chaining, a laboratory rat named Barnabas learned to perform a sequence of eight behaviors before receiving a reward. He had to climb a stairway, lower a bridge, go through a tunnel, and eventually enter a little elevator to take him to the bar-press lever. The terminal response of bar pressing produced the food reinforcer. Other examples of chaining range from teaching a sequence of steps in manufacturing assembly (Walls, Zane, & Ellis, 1981) to learning to play notes in sequence on a keyboard (Ash & Holding, 1990).

Chains can be trained in the forward direction, that is, by practicing the first response in the chain and then adding successively the next elements; backwards, beginning with the last element; or by training the entire chain simultaneously. No one method is clearly better than another in all situations. Starting from either of the ends will lead to overtraining of that response, whereas the opposite end will receive less practice. If either the first or last response is more difficult than the other links in the chain, then starting with that end may be the best strategy. For example, pilot trainees who were practicing landings in a flight simulator were trained with backward chaining, by practicing the landing first, then adding the runway approach, and so on (Wightman & Sistrunk, 1987). The landing itself is the most important element in the chain and one that benefits from overtraining.

Limitations of Response Learning

As powerful as reinforcement is for conditioning behavior, not all responses can be modified through reinforcement. Skinner himself noted that some reflex responses could be modified only through classical conditioning.

There are also species-specific limitations on what can be modified. Not any arbitrarily selected behavior can be shaped using reward in any given species. As Shettleworth (1975) demonstrated using golden hamsters, behaviors such as digging and standing were readily conditioned with food reinforcement. Other behaviors, such as face washing and scratching, did not increase when rewarded with food.

Species limitations on instrumental learning were nicely shown in the field of animal training by two of Skinner's students, Keller and Marion Breland (Breland & Breland, 1961). They titled their paper "The Misbehavior of Organisms," a play on Skinner's book title *The Behavior of Organisms*. The Brelands found that certain behaviors were resistant to modification with food rewards. For example, they tried to teach a pig to put wooden coins in a piggy bank. (This is just too cute!) If the pig did this, it received food. Instead, the pig persisted in rooting the coins, rubbing the coins on the ground with its snout as if digging them up. Rooting delayed and even prevented reward. Yet, as training continued, rooting became even more frequent.

One explanation for some limitations on response learning is that of evolutionary prepared-ness. Animals may have evolved a readiness to learn certain categories of response-to-outcome associations, such as which behaviors might lead to food or which behaviors escape from danger. Alternatively, once the coins became associated with food, maybe as conditioned stimuli, the rooting behavior might have been a classically conditioned response that competed with the instrumental response of dropping the coins in the bank.

The principles of response learning would seem to be obviously applicable to the field of animal training. However, the scientist's study of learning by animals is an entirely different field from animal training, roughly corresponding to the basic-versus-applied distinction. Nevertheless, science may offer some unique insights into animal training. Some instances are described in Box 4.1.

Box 4.1   Animal Training

In Chapter 1 I offered some reasons for using animals in research, reasons which primarily benefit the science of learning and memory. Here I want to suggest that research on animals can benefit the animals themselves. Zoo animals and endangered species are examples of animals whose well-being is our responsibility. Behavioral learning principles are used to reduce the risk of injury to the animal and increase safety of those humans who work with them (Young and Cipreste, 2004).

Sutherland (2006) wonderfully describes the Exotic Animal Training and Management program at Morelock Community College in California. "Animal training" in this context does not mean teaching animals to perform cute tricks. Caretaking often requires that the animals be compliant in medical procedures to monitor health or treat illness. But how do you get an untamed monkey to consent to a blood draw, or a tiger to a dental inspection? Instrumental learning principles are used to train the animals to acquiesce in these proce-dures. An integral part of the academic program is the study of learning through course work, labs, and practical training. Habituation (discussed in Chapter 2) would be used to adapt animals to the presence of the human technicians. The presentation or omission of reward is used to teach an animal to allow the techs to touch it, or put apparatus nearby. An example of a secondary reinforcer is training an animal to maintain head contact with the end of a stick held by the technician (who would usually remain safely outside the cage). The stick can be used to lead the animal to a desired location or position. By the end of the program, students will have trained several categories of animals, such as primates, birds, and reptiles. These would include the range of species in zoos, entertainment parks, wildlife sanctuaries, etc.

Another example of training animals for their own benefit is to train dogs in animal shelters. These pets are often in shelters because of behavioral problems: The dog is uncon-trollable or aggressive, or has destructive misbehaviors when left alone. Such behavioral problems discourage adoption or, even sadder, lead to the return of an adopted dog to the shelter. David Tuber has for many years maintained a program using volunteers (often, his

own college students) to train shelter dogs (Tuber et al., 1999). Using positive reinforcement, shaping, and discriminative stimuli, dogs learn to sit, enter a crate, or bark less. Shy
dogs can be rewarded for seeking contact with people. A "living room" is simulated in the
shelter so the dog can be trained in a home-like environment. Animals that acquire some
basic skills and a few commands are more readily adopted. Incidentally, this training seems
to lower stress in the shelter animals. This in itself seems to me to justify the training.

Discriminative Stimulus Control

We have discussed two of the elements of instrumental learning, the response and the reinforcer. The third critical element is the discriminative stimulus. Learning involves not only what
response to make, but also when to make it. A **discriminative stimulus** signals the availability
of reinforcement. In the bar-press situation, a tone or a light can be used as the discriminative
stimulus, or S^D, signaling that the reinforcement contingency is in effect. Responses during S^D
(pronounced "S-dee") are reinforced. Responses in the absence of the S^D are not reinforced. So,
bar presses would only produce food when the S^D tone was present.

Stimulus control refers to conditioning a response to occur in the presence of the discriminative stimulus. A response is brought under control of a stimulus. For us, many of these stimuli
are contextual stimuli of time and place. Behaviors that are acceptable at a frat party are not
appropriate in the classroom. A student may have difficulty studying because sitting at their desk
is also associated with listening to music, talking on the phone, or mind-wandering. Cigarette
smoking is cued by a variety of situations, places, and people, thus making elimination of smoking difficult.

An interesting example of discriminative control is that of the remote-control rat (Talwar et al.,
2002). Electrodes were implanted in the rat's brain, in sensory and reinforcement areas, that
could be stimulated wirelessly from a distance. Left or right turns could be rewarded by stimulation of the reward area (actually, the medial forebrain bundle). The cue for when to make a turn
was stimulation of the area of the brain that simulated touch to the left or right whisker (sort of
like tapping the rat on the snout). After activation of the left whisker area (the discriminative
stimulus), if the rat turned left (the instrumental response), the experimenter gave a burst of
rewarding brain stimulation (the instrumental reward). After first being trained on the basic routine in an enclosed maze, the rats were tested in open areas outside. For instance, a rat could be
guided via remote control up a ladder, across a narrow ledge, through a pipe, and across a brightly
lit area at a distance, according to a news report, of up to 1,600 feet. (Okay, why would anyone
want remote-control rats? The researchers suggest that with the addition of a miniature camera,
rats could be used in searching dangerous locations.)

Generalization and Discrimination

In Chapter 3 we introduced the idea of generalization of the conditioned response to stimuli that
were similar to the CS. Instrumental learning can also show the effects of **generalization**: A
response initially trained to a particular discriminative stimulus will be made during stimuli that
are similar to the trained S^D. Figure 4.6 shows responding by pigeons and humans to a discriminative stimulus, in this case a particular color, and generalized responding to test stimuli of colors
of different wavelengths (Kalish, 1958). In each case, the subjects were first trained to make a
response in the presence of one stimulus. Testing involves presenting other stimuli and recording
the number of responses to each. For example, a pigeon trained to peck in the presence of yellow
(580 nm) pecked less to orange (600 nm), and not at all to green (530 nm). Stimuli that are similar

but not identical to the S^D typically elicit fewer responses than does the trained stimulus. Figure 4.6 shows that the pigeons showed generalization to similar colors whereas the human subjects had very sharp generalization gradients, with very little responding to different colors.

Generalization may be one reason why learned behaviors do not always transfer from one situation to another. The stimuli are different (or perceived as different) and therefore exert less stimulus control.

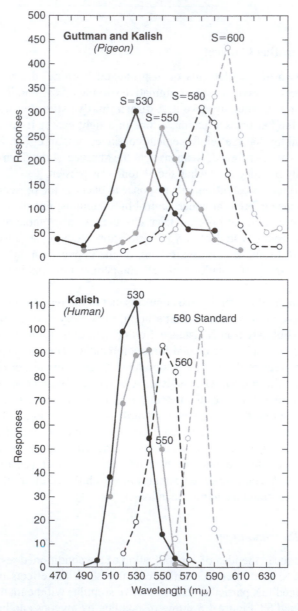

Figure 4.6 **Gradients of Generalization to Color Discriminative Stimuli.** Frequency of response by four pigeons (*upper panel*) and four humans (*lower panel*) who were reinforced for responding in the presence of colored lights of 530 nanometers (basically green), 550 nm, 560, 580 nm (yellow), or 600 nm (orange), and then tested with colors above and below the trained stimulus.

Source: From "The relationship between discriminability and generalization: a re-evaluation," by H. I. Kalish, 1958, Journal of Experimental Psychology, 55, p. 637. Copyright American Psychological Association. Reprinted with permission.

The complementary process to generalization is discrimination. In **discrimination** training, responses are reinforced in the presence of S^D. These responses are not reinforced in the presence of S^Δ (pronounced "S-delta"), a stimulus signaling that reinforcement is not available. For example, a pigeon's key pecks will be rewarded while a red light is present, but not during a blue light. A child may be reinforced by praise or attention for doing homework in the presence of one parent, but is not reinforced in the presence of the other parent.

Responding sometimes occurs during S^Δ, especially if there is generalization from S^D. Non-reinforced responses can produce emotional reactions, such as frustration. Imagine teaching a child a difficult discrimination. The child becomes upset over the large number of mistakes, making the task aversive and something to be avoided in the future. Herbert Terrace introduced a conditioning method that produces less emotional reaction to S^Δ, called *errorless discrimination training* (e.g., Terrace, 1974). The idea is to minimize responding to the S^Δ (i.e., errors), and thus reduce the negative emotional reactions that accompany nonreinforced responding. S^Δ is introduced in such a way that the subject is not likely to respond to it: the stimulus is so weak, or so different at first. The S^Δ then is gradually changed, a process called stimulus fading, making it more like the S^D.

In one demonstration study, the subjects were children who had difficulty discriminating consonants in speech, such as "ba" and "da." Via an animated computer game, syllables were presented that had certain components exaggerated by making them longer and louder (e.g., "bbbaa" and "dddaa"). The syllables were gradually normalized over trials as the children were able to identify them correctly, leading to nearly errorless learning (Merzenich et al., 1996).

Summary of Response Learning and Stimulus Learning

Instrumental learning involves three elements: a discriminative stimulus, a response, and a reinforcer. By specifying the form of the response that will be followed with reinforcement, the response can be shaped. In addition, a series of behaviors can be linked together by a process of response chaining, so that only the terminal behavior is itself followed by a reinforcer. As powerful as shaping and chaining are for producing novel behaviors, not all behaviors can be modified through reinforcement. There may be species-specific limitations on which response–consequence sequences can be learned, such as digging for food rewards and running when shock is administered.

A response can be brought under stimulus control, such that a stimulus controls when the response is to be made. Stimulus control is subject to limitations such generalization and discrimination.

What is Learned in Instrumental Conditioning?

In the previous chapter on classical conditioning, we asked which elements from among the CS, US, CR, and UR became associated. We can ask a similar question with respect to instrumental conditioning. Given the three elements of discriminative stimulus, instrumental response, and reinforcer, what are the associations that are acquired? All combinations have been seriously considered.

Response–Reinforcer Learning

The obvious answer to "what is learned?" is that the response becomes connected to the reinforcer. Speaking casually, we say that the organism performs the response in order to get the reward. Rats bar-press for food, schoolchildren read books for stickers, and so on. The **response–reinforcer** theory says that learning is the formation of a connection between the instrumental response and the reinforcer.

Responding often seems to be under exquisite control of the reinforcement conditions: Larger and tastier rewards provoke more vigorous response, delayed rewards weaken responding, and satiation of drive leads to a reduction in responding.

The theory of *response–reinforcer* association predicts that changes in the reinforcement conditions should lead immediately to changes in the response. This has been studied by changing reinforcement expectancies. An example is the earlier-cited latent learning experiment of Tolman and Honzik. Rats would run faster or slower, corresponding to their changed expectations of what would be found in the goal box. Introducing food in the maze led to immediate improvement in performance; omitting food led to an immediate decrement.

Unfortunately, behavior is not always so sensitive to the changes in outcome. In an early study, Tolman (1933) first trained rats to run a maze for food. Then he placed the rats in the goal box and gave them a strong foot shock. What did the rats do the next time they were in the maze? Tolman reported that the rats "dashed off . . . just as usual . . . and bang whack into the very food compartment in which they had just been shocked."

Stimulus–Response Learning

Stimulus–response theory says that instrumental learning is the formation of a connection between the discriminative stimulus and the instrumental response. Theorists such as Thorndike and Hull were S–R theorists. Reinforcement acts to condition (consolidate, strengthen) this association, but is not itself part of the learned sequence.

Evidence for stimulus–response conditioning would be the case in which the response seems to have become separated from its reinforcing consequence, and has become an automatic reaction to the stimulus. For example, the instrumental response sometimes persists even though reinforcement is freely available and the response is no longer needed to obtain reward. Singh (1970) demonstrated the effects of "free rewards" in a pair of experiments using rats and children. He first trained rats to bar-press for food on one side of the apparatus, and then, in the next phase, food pellets were simply delivered on the other side. In a parallel study, 6-year-old children first learned to button-press for marbles while standing along one side of a large box (in which the experimenter was concealed, dispensing marbles), and later free marbles were dispensed from the other side of the box. Both rats and children still choose to make the response. Rats would press the bar, go over and eat some from the dish, and then go back and bar-press some more.

Other evidence for the disconnection of response and outcome comes from studies of habitual behavior in mazes. Well-trained rats will run through a pile of food pellets placed in the middle of a maze alley on their way to the goal box. The rats go through food, slipping and sliding, pellets flying everywhere, on their way to get food (Stoltz & Lott, 1964).

In a contemporary example, rats first trained to bar-press for sucrose solution were then given sucrose–poison pairings in a taste-aversion learning procedure. The result of this second treatment was that the rats would no longer drink sucrose. Still, the rats continued to bar-press even though they did not drink the sucrose they earned (Adams, 1982).

What's wrong here? These outcomes appear contrary to common sense. Behavior should change in response to changed reinforcement. However, persistence in the old mode of behavior is comprehensible in light of the habits acquired over many (sometimes hundreds of) trials. S–R theory predicts that the discriminative stimuli come to elicit the previously reinforced instrumental responses.

Clearly, however, behavior is not always so inflexible and habit-like as S–R theory predicts. The point is that organisms, both rats and humans, do sometimes act out of habit and in accordance with S–R theory (see Habit Slips in the Applications section).

Stimulus–Reinforcer Learning

A typical sequence of events in an instrumental trial is discriminative stimulus, response, and reinforcement. Because of this, the S^D is paired with reward. Thus, classical conditioning can occur between the stimulus and the reinforcer, or relabeling these in Pavlovian terminology, between the CS and the US. The S^D then elicits conditioned responses in anticipation of the reinforcer (such as conditioned excitement or fear), which increase performance of the instrumental response.

An example of stimulus–reinforcer learning occurs in the pigeon key-pecking task. Illumination of the Plexiglas key is followed with grain presentation. If the pigeon simply observes the light being followed by the grain tray opening, the pigeon will key-peck when given the opportunity. Conditioning occurred in the absence of response–reinforcer training, but which followed stimulus–reinforcer experience.

What is Learned? Stimulus–Response–Reinforcer

Rather than concluding that any one of the preceding explanations is exclusively correct, we might instead suggest that each may make a contribution to instrumental learning. Combining the several associative relationships is possibly the best descriptor of what can be learned in instrumental learning (Rescorla, 1987). As Skinner noted, the discriminative stimulus sets the occasion for when a response will be reinforced, but the stimulus does not elicit the response. And as Tolman noted, the subject may learn a set of expectancies, some being means-to-ends sequences (e.g., bar pressing to obtain food), others being stimulus–reward expectancies (the goal box signals food or shock).

Applications

Habit Slips

Persistence in habitual behaviors is not restricted to animals in laboratory experiments. Humans are creatures of habit also, and often enough, we perform a habitual response instead of an intended response. James Reason (1990) describes numerous errors due to habits that intrude when a new response had been intended: putting sugar in your cereal when you meant to cut back; driving past the intended stop only to realize you don't have dinner when you arrive home; and, nearly tragically, a military pilot flying in an air show who momentarily forgot he had live missiles that day and shot down another jet (the other pilot bailed out safely). Sometimes we act no differently than our rats who ran through food pellets on the way to the goal box to get food.

These sorts of errors are called **habit slips**: the intrusion of a habit when an alternative behavior had been intended. Reason suggests that habit takes over when we are in familiar situations, and we are distracted or preoccupied. While driving a familiar route, your mind wanders elsewhere and so habit takes you past the intended stop or turn on your way home. For the fighter pilot, the momentary distraction to a warning gauge allowed the habitual response, practiced in hundreds of hours of training, to occur.

Other errors are what D. A. Norman (1981) categorizes as capture errors: If two behavior sequences have identical starting elements, the more habitual behavior may capture the less frequent behavior. William James (1890) described a gentleman who intended to change for dinner, but instead changed into pajamas and got into bed. Reason reported the same slip nearly 100 years later. Both behaviors, changing for dinner and changing for bed, have identical discriminative stimuli and starting sequences: It is evening, you go to your bedroom, start to undress, and so on. As Reason notes, if your thoughts are elsewhere, your habits put you to bed.

Breaking Habits

Habits are behaviors that can be performed with minimal conscious awareness, and are capable of being elicited by various discriminative stimuli, such as environment cues, moods, feelings, or other behaviors. Breaking a habit requires forceful measures. So-called informational interventions, such as public health warnings against smoking, or personal intentions, such as to change one's diet, are relatively uninfluential at the moment the habitual behavior is triggered (Verplanken & Wood, 2006). The cookie is already in your mouth before you remember you're cutting back on sweets.

One suggestion to correct a habit is to take advantage of the absence or disruption of eliciting stimuli. For example, after we move to a new place to live some of the habit-triggering stimuli may have changed. A new dorm, apartment, or house is accompanied by new contextual stimuli or different daily routines. A change in jobs can involve different commuting patterns or friends. The old cues might not be present in the new locations to trigger the old habits. Wood, Tam, and Witt (2005) conducted a survey of students who were transferring from one university to another. The researchers quantified the strength of good and bad habits, such as exercising or watching too much television. The researchers also noted how much the context had changed. For instance, was the TV in the same room of the old and new houses? Did the student exercise in the same or a different place? Did roommates change? The researchers found that the more the surroundings had changed from before to after the move, the more the habit (good or bad) was disrupted. One lesson is that a move may be a good time to change your routine and add better habits. At the same time, you have to be vigilant against the disruption of existing good habits.

Behavior Modification

In this chapter, we have frequently cited examples of reinforcement in everyday behavior. The field of **behavior modification** (or simply behavior mod) applies the principles of operant learning to changing behaviors in a variety of settings. In an early demonstration project, Ayllon (1963) was asked to assist with problem patients in a psychiatric setting. For example, one 44-year-old schizophrenic resident engaged in a number of disruptive behaviors. Ayllon first assessed the frequency of each and then applied a behavioral remedy. One problem was stealing food from other patients in the cafeteria. Ayllon used a reward-omission procedure. Each time the woman took food she was removed from the cafeteria and that meal was forfeited. (This would not be allowed today because it violates the patient's rights.) The effects of this procedure are shown in Figure 4.7. Within a week she ceased stealing food, and (with only an occasional lapse) did not regress during the year-long follow-up. Her weight also dropped to a healthier level.

Another problem was towel hoarding. The psychiatrically trained staff attributed this to childhood deprivation, and the towels were substitute satisfiers for some other inner need. Ayllon treated the unwanted behavior directly. He suggested a novel procedure of "stimulus satiation": If towels are reinforcing, then a larger number of towels should produce satiation (analogous to satiating the hunger drive by giving a large amount of food). He instructed the staff to give the patient towels every day, which the patient at first appreciated, until 600 towels had accumulated in the patient's room. At that point, she no longer wanted any more; she asked the staff to remove them and, in fact, she began to take them out herself. She eventually reduced the number to just a few towels, a level that remained stable thereafter.

Ayllon's methods were considered radical. Schizophrenics were not considered to be reasonable enough to show learning. Their symptoms were thought to be due to childhood problems that had to be resolved before any improvement could occur. Ayllon suggested that if people are institutionalized because of behavioral difficulties, these problems could be treated and the individual could return, or remain, in the community.

An application of secondary reinforcement in institution-wide systems is known as a *token economy.* For example, the staff of a residential facility (such as a half-way house or group home)

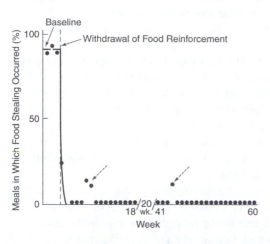
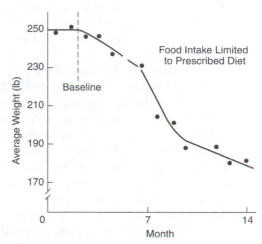

Figure 4.7 (left panel) The response of food stealing decreases when it results in the withdrawal of food reinforcement. Occasional regression to food stealing is marked by arrows. Weeks 20–40 are omitted, as no stealing occurred then. (*right panel*) Reduction in body weight that paralleled the suppression of food stealing.

Source: Reprinted from *Behavior Research and Therapy, 1,* T. Ayllon, "Intensive Treatment of Psychotic Behavior by Stimulus Satiation and Food Reinforcement," pp. 53–61. Copyright © 1963 Elsevier. Reprinted with permission.

is faced with the problem of motivating residents to perform a number of daily living behaviors: dress and groom in the morning, arrive for meals on time, clean their rooms, and so on. The residents can be given tokens for each desired behavior, or for completion of several behaviors if a partial reinforcement schedule is used. The tokens can then be exchanged for various reinforcers such as candy, movie tickets, outdoor activities, and so on (Ayllon & Azrin, 1968).

The methods of instrumental learning are not only useful in changing the behaviors of other individuals. The procedures can be used to change our own behaviors. Some examples of self behavior modification are presented in Box 4.2.

Box 4.2   Self Behavior Modification

We all have bad habits we wish we didn't, and there are some worthwhile habits we wish we did. Self behavior modification uses instrumental learning to change our own behaviors. One approach labels the components of behavior modification the ABCs, referring to Antecedents (those stimuli that control behavior); Behaviors (the habits we want to modify); and Consequences (reward, extinction, or punishment). We can illustrate the ABCs by application to several habits: cigarette smoking, swearing, and exercising regularly.

The starting point is to specify the behavior we want to change. Well-defined behaviors, such as the number of cigarettes smoked daily or the number of swear words used, are readily measured and improvements can be monitored. "Studying more" is too vague and needs to be redefined in terms of specific tasks, such as reviewing class notes or doing homework. "Exercising more" needs to be measurable in terms such as number of reps or workout time.

A baseline measure of the frequency of the behavior should be compiled. How much time do you spend exercising or studying now? How much do you swear or smoke? Just tracking the behavior day by day can reduce bad behaviors. Because they are habitual, we are often unaware we are doing them. Nail biting, hair pulling, and smoking can be performed unconsciously. You might recruit a friend to alert you when you are acting habitually.

Try to determine the antecedent circumstances that elicit or contribute to the target behavior (the A of the ABCs). Are there stimuli or situations that seem to trigger the behavior? Do you mainly smoke when you are with your friends, at work, or at school? One strategy to decrease the bad habit is to avoid or eliminate the eliciting stimuli. Maybe stay away from those friends who lead you to smoke. (Okay, I sound like your mother. Sorry.) Are there distractions that compete with studying? Can you shut off the phone for a while? Continue to monitor the frequency of the habitual behavior as the change is implemented.

Another strategy is to substitute a different behavior in place of the unwanted behavior (the B of the ABCs). In *response substitution*, a different behavior is used to replace the unwanted response. When you want to cut back on drinking soda, stock your fridge with bottled juices or carry water with you to drink as a substitute. Chewing gum would substitute for cigarette smoking, or interfere with nail biting.

Another strategy is to arrange new rewarding or punishing consequences (the C of the ABCs). For instance, impose a fine for swearing or smoking: You must put money away for each transgression. (One particularly effective fining procedure is to give the money to your friend or roommate.) To punish nail-biting you could paint your fingernails with a bitter tasting substance (actually sold in pharmacies). This gives immediate punishment, and gets around the problem of lack of awareness that you are biting.

A self-modification plan can be illustrated by an attempt to reduce swearing. A baseline measure of the daily frequency of the use of certain predetermined words was established, as shown in Figure 4.8 (Powers & Osborne, 1976). A treatment phase followed, in which

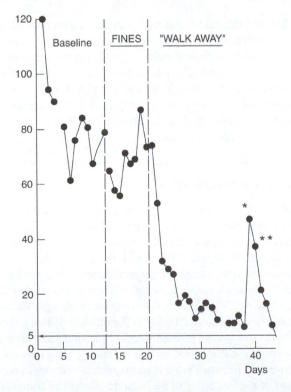

Figure 4.8 Number of swear words used per day during baseline, and two treatment phases: the student paid a fine for swearing, or her roommates walked away from her when she swore. * and ** indicate days when she had arguments with boyfriend.

Source: Adapted from Powers, R. B. & J. G. Osborne, *Fundamentals of Behavior*, 1976, St. Paul, MN: West Publishing.

the subject tried self-fining: putting a certain amount of money in a jar each time she swore. As can be seen, this had little effect, partially because the subject simply would not pay the fine. The next treatment phase was more successful. The student worked out an arrangement with her suite mates that they would immediately turn their backs on her and ignore her whenever she swore in their presence. As can be seen in the results of this phase, the strategy resulted in an immediate and sustained decline in swearing. Oh, there were occasional regressions, like the time she had an argument with her @#/*%& boyfriend.

Some unwanted behaviors are more than simply bad habits. Smoking has an addictive component. Nevertheless, self-modification can be used in combination with other treatments to produce desired changes in behavior.

Behavioral Economics

An expanding area of research and theory is the field of behavioral economics. One can think of much of everyday human behavior in economic terms, regulated by the profits and losses (rewards and nonrewards) that accrue. The economic law of supply and demand has its parallel in instrumental learning: As the demand for a pellet of food rises (due to hunger, for example), the cost can be raised by increasing the number of bar presses necessary to obtain food. This way of thinking has led psychologists and economists to consider new ways of integrating the two fields (DiClemente & Hantula, 2003). Two examples follow.

Loss Aversion

Traditional economics is based on the idea of rational behavior. However consumers are not always rational in their behavior. One example is loss aversion: We are more sensitive to potential losses of a given magnitude than to potential gains of an equivalent size. The risk of losing $20 is perceived as much worse than is the possibility of gaining $20. Traditional economics views $20 as $20. Period.

In one study of loss aversion, monkeys were trained to trade a token for apple slices offered to them by different human experimenters. One person would show two slices, but then after the monkey handed over the token the human would sometimes give the animal just one. The other human would show one apple slice, but then after accepting the token that person would sometimes give the monkey two slices. Over all trials, each person gave the monkey the same number of apple slices, the same mix of one slice and two slice trials. Yet the monkeys learned to avoid exchanging with the person who gave them less than offered. This is loss aversion: avoiding a potential loss (Chen, Lakshminarayanan, & Santos, 2006).

The Goal Gradient Hypothesis

The learning theorist Clark Hull (1943) provided a corollary to his principle of reinforcement. (Hull was mentioned earlier in the chapter in the discussion on drive and motivation.) The effect of a reward becomes stronger as you come closer to receiving the reward. In maze running, rats ran faster the closer they got to the goal box. This is the goal gradient hypothesis.

Marketing researchers applied the goal gradient hypothesis to a consumer rewards program (Kivetz, Urminsky, & Zheng, 2006). Students were given a reward program card at a campus coffee bar. Each purchase was punched on the card, and 10 purchases led to a free coffee. According to the goal gradient hypothesis, the first few purchases had little motivational influence because they were so far away from the freebee. However, the nearer one got to 10 purchases, the more reinforcing was the possibility of a free coffee. As coffee punches accumulated, the students began purchasing their next coffees sooner.

In a second experiment, the researchers created "illusory" progress toward the goal. The program still required 10 stamps for a free coffee. However, one group of students received cards with 12 stamp positions, but two were punched as a "bonus" to new participants in the reward program. This group that believed they were closer to the goal completed their purchases quicker.

Summary

Edward Lee Thorndike sought to systematize the principles involved in the development of adaptive behavior. Acquisition was governed by the law of effect: Responses that produced a satisfying consequence became connected to the situation. Thorndike's learning by trial and error, or instrumental conditioning, consists of three elements: the discriminative stimulus, the response, and the consequence.

B. F. Skinner used the label operant learning to indicate that the response operates on the environment to produce a certain outcome. Skinner described extinction of the operant response and patterned behavior by providing reinforcement according to certain schedules.

Positive Reinforcement

Reinforcement is defined by the experimental contingency, or rule, stating that performance of a target behavior leads to a particular consequence. A positive reinforcer is one whose occurrence increases the frequency or vigor of the behavior.

Instrumental-response learning is influenced by several reinforcement variables. Reinforcement is usually more effective if it occurs immediately after the response than if it is delayed for some time; if reinforcement is administered for each response than if only given after some of the correct responses; and if larger or more preferred reinforcers are used rather than smaller or less preferred rewards. (There are important exceptions to these principles if responding is assessed during extinction instead of during acquisition.) Response-contrast effects, or changes in the level of responding, can occur when the reinforcer is changed from what was previously used.

Drive level, often manipulated through reinforcer deprivation, also affects responding. Given the learning-versus-performance distinction, variables such as drive and amount reinforcement determine the motivation to respond, but they may also affect learning.

A schedule of reinforcement refers to the specific timing or frequency of responding required for the delivery of reinforcement. A partial reinforcement schedule reinforces the response only some of the time. The basic schedules involve reinforcing a certain number of responses (ratio schedules) or reinforcing responses after certain amounts of time have passed (interval schedules); these ratios and intervals may be fixed or varying.

A neutral stimulus, such as a tone, can become a secondary reinforcer by pairing it with a primary reinforcer, such as food. For example, token reinforcers are used to reinforce human behaviors in a variety of situations.

A powerful class of reinforcers for human behavior is social reinforcement, in the form of praise, attention, physical contact, or facial expressions. Alternative theories say that social stimuli are primary reinforcers or learned secondary reinforcers.

Theories of Reinforcement

Skinner pragmatically defined a reinforcer as being whatever works to increase the frequency of the operant (or instrumental) response. But what makes reinforcers reinforce?

Reinforcers can be described as stimuli. Hull said that reinforcers were stimuli that reduce biological needs, such as hunger. However, some reinforcers, such as saccharin, do not reduce any bodily need. According to incentive motivation theory, reinforcers are stimuli that elicit responding through appetitive sensory or affective properties. Another stimulus approach shows that electrical and chemical brain stimulation can serve to reinforce instrumental responding. This suggests that certain neural processes are the final common denominator for all reinforcers.

An alternative approach defines reinforcers as activities or behaviors. According to the Premack principle, an activity that has a higher probability of occurrence will reinforce a lower-probability activity. Preferences for activities are not fixed, but can vary across individuals, and can vary within individuals due to deprivation and satiation.

A third approach suggests that reinforcers strengthen the association between a stimulus and a response, in the sense of cementing the connection. Reinforcers are significant stimuli that produce neural arousal that aids memory consolidation.

Finally, reinforcers convey information about correct performance of a behavior. Biofeedback, for example, uses an external signal to provide information concerning the performance of otherwise unobservable bodily responses.

Is reinforcement necessary for learning? Tolman and Honzik's classic study demonstrated that maze learning by rats occurred in the absence of reward. The learning was latent until motivated by reward.

What role does conscious awareness of the response–reinforcer contingency play in human instrumental learning? In the verbal conditioning paradigm, an experimenter "reinforces" ("umm humm") the use of a target word, causing an increase in the frequency of the target word. However, conditioning seems to be limited to those participants who are aware of and can report the contingency.

The real-world application of reinforcement procedures has been criticized on several grounds. Reinforcement can be characterized as manipulative and controlling. It may supplant intrinsic motivation with an external, material motivation for performance. And, the effects of reinforcement are said to dissipate when it is discontinued.

Response Learning

A significant use of instrumental conditioning is to shape particular forms of the response. By the use of differential reinforcement and successive approximations, new behaviors are created. In response chaining, a sequence of behaviors is constructed and reinforcement is given after the final response.

As powerful as reinforcement is in modifying behavior, not all responses can be altered through reinforcement. For example, there are species-specific limitations. Hamsters can be reinforced with food for standing but not for washing. These limitations may be due to an evolutionarily determined preparedness to learn certain response–reinforcer associations.

Discriminative Stimulus Control

Learning involves not only what response to make but also when to make it. A discriminative stimulus, or S^D, signals the availability of reinforcement if a response is made. Responding initially trained in the presence of a particular S^D will generalize to similar stimuli. Through discrimination training, S^Δ comes to signal that reinforcement is not available, and so responding may then be inhibited. In errorless discrimination training, errors (i.e., responding to the S^Δ) are minimized, reducing the negative emotional reactions that otherwise accompany nonreinforced responding.

What is Learned in Instrumental Conditioning?

One possibility is that the response and the reinforcer become associated. The response is seemingly sensitive to variations in reinforcement, and sometimes changes immediately in reaction to altered conditions of reinforcement, as shown in the latent learning experiments.

Thorndike and Hull instead said a connection was learned between the discriminative stimulus and the response, with the reinforcer serving to strengthen this bond. Behavior sometimes persists in the face of altered reinforcement conditions, taking on the character of habitual responding in the presence of certain stimuli.

Because the S^D is frequently followed by reinforcement, classical conditioning can occur between this stimulus and the reinforcer.

In conclusion, we acknowledge that associations among any of the three elements of an instrumental trial are possible, with one dyad or another predominating in a given situation.

Applications

Environmental stimuli elicit well-practiced habits. Habit slips are unconscious intrusions of a habit when an alternative behavior had been consciously intended. Slips occur when we are in familiar places, and we are distracted. If two behavior sequences have identical starting elements, the more frequent behavior may capture the less frequent behavior.

Habits are difficult to change because they occur unconsciously and are attached to many eliciting stimuli. It may be easier to break a habit when your environment changes, as in when you move, or change jobs or schools, which take you away from the old stimuli.

Behavior modification is a field that applies the principles of operant learning to changing behavior in a variety of settings, such as schools, institutions, workplaces, and everyday life. For example, Ayllon used reward omission to eliminate food stealing by a patient in a psychiatric institution. He then used satiation to decrease towel hoarding.

Another instance of behavior modification is the use of token economies in institutional settings. Tokens are given for certain behaviors or for completion of several behaviors, and the tokens then can be exchanged for other reinforcers.

The field of behavioral economics merges two disciplines, drawing on psychology to explain irrational economic behavior. Two examples are loss aversion (the disproportionate aversion to potential loss versus an equivalent gain) and a test of the goal-gradient hypothesis in a campus coffee bar rewards program.

5 Instrumental Conditioning
Nonreward, Punishment, and Avoidance

The previous chapter described how rewarding consequences could be used to change behavior. This chapter will concentrate on the use of aversive consequences. The outcomes of nonreward and punishment seem obvious: You simply stop doing whatever it is that is not rewarded or is punished. Do we need a whole chapter on this?

The effects of aversive consequences are not always so obvious. Imagine we visit a research lab and see a cat lever pressing and then receiving unpleasant blasts of air to its face each time. Bar press. Air blast. Where did this masochistic behavior come from? Is punishment paradoxically sustaining lever pressing instead of suppressing it?

At one time there was a popular saying that parents would speak as they were about to spank a child: "This will hurt me more than it will hurt you." There may be some truth to this phrase. The one who administers punishment may do so even though there is a cost for doing so. For instance, in laboratory studies of group cooperation each individual contributes and shares in the rewards. A member of the team who does not share in the risks might be fined by other members, even if there is a cost to them for doing so (Seymour, Singer, & Dolan, 2007).

Inventors are known for being persistent. They try something new, but it does not work as well as expected. What do the inventors do then? They try new versions, continuing until the product is right. The Wright Brothers tested 200 different curvatures of a wing; Edison said he was not exaggerating that he had tested 3,000 theories for the electric light. In these cases (and in literally thousands of cases) the lack of initial success, what we would call nonreinforcement, did not lead to extinction. How do we reconcile the persistence of nonrewarded behavior with extinction, which is the expected outcome of nonreward?

These oddities appear to be contrary to the laws of learning and so we might try to attribute them to quirky personality traits. Some people are just born masochists or persistent. An alternative explanation is that the principles of learning can account for these paradoxical behaviors.

Defining the Contingencies: Nonreward, Punishment, and Avoidance

Instrumental conditioning is defined as the contingency between a particular response and an outcome. In the case of positive reinforcement, the instrumental response leads to a rewarding outcome and an increase in instrumental responding. Response–outcome contingencies also define the three aversive-outcome learning procedures that are the topics of the current chapter.

In two *nonreward* contingencies, the target response is not followed by a positive reinforcer. In **extinction**, reward is omitted after those responses that once produced positive reinforcement. Another nonreinforcement procedure is **omission**, in which a selected response prevents a positive reinforcer from occurring. An omission contingency usually implies that doing something else will lead to positive reinforcement. The intention with the nonreward contingencies is to decrease the frequency of the response.

In **punishment**, a response is followed by an aversive stimulus, which should act to decrease the frequency of this response. Punishment is more than just withholding reward, but is instead the application of an aversive event. If you misbehave and your allowance is withheld, that is omission. If you misbehave and you are spanked, that is punishment. (The term punishment is sometimes broadly used to include the nonreward procedures described in the preceding paragraph. Here, we are restricting the meaning to the active application of an aversive consequence.)

In **avoidance learning**, an instrumental response prevents the aversive stimulus. The intention is to increase the frequency of the response. Avoidance is also called *negative reinforcement*: reinforcement because the instrumental response increases in frequency, just as in positive reinforcement; negative because the response removes or prevents the (aversive) reinforcer. Negative reinforcement is often misused, frequently being misapplied to punishment. Learning psychologists themselves often use the more descriptive phrase, *avoidance learning*, as a synonym.

The basic instrumental contingencies of reward, omission, punishment, and avoidance learning are summarized in Figure 5.1.

Reward and omission are often used together. Among several potential behaviors in a situation, one response is rewarded (positive reinforcement) but another response is not (omission). In the behavior modification technique of "praise and ignore," a teacher praises certain appropriate classroom responses and ignores (or at least tries to ignore) inappropriate responses.

Punishment and avoidance sometimes also pair up. A certain behavior leads to punishment, and so this response should decrease. Some alternative behavior prevents the punishment, and so that response should increase.

Sometimes the same response could be described by either of two contingencies. Do you study to get high grades (positive reinforcement) or to prevent low grades (avoidance learning)?

Reinforcing Consequence

	Pleasant, Appetitive	Unpleasant, Aversive
The response *produces* the reinforcing outcome	**Reward Training** (*positive reinforcement*) (response increases)	**Punishment** (response decreases)
The response *prevents* the reinforcing outcome	**Omission, Extinction, Time-Out** (response decreases)	**Escape, Avoidance** (*negative reinforcement*) (response increases)

Figure 5.1 **The Four Basic Instrumental Conditioning Contingencies.** The columns list the outcome, or reinforcing event, as appetitive or aversive. The rows designate the response–reinforcer contingency: The response is or is not followed by the reinforcer.

Nonreward

Extinction

If a behavior is maintained by reward, then the elimination of reward should lead to a decrease in the response. In *extinction*, positive reinforcement is withheld following each occurrence of the instrumental behavior, with the expectation that the response will extinguish. In a study of infants, leg-movements that once shook the mobile extinguish when the mobile stops moving. (Those results were shown in the previous chapter's Figure 4.2). In a study using rats, extinction of running for food is illustrated in Figure 5.3 (right panel): the rats run slower, and some even stop running, when they are no longer rewarded.

Practitioners of behavior modification advocate extinction as an alternative to punishment. In practice, however, extinction produces certain side effects that discourage its use. First, extinction can produce unpleasant emotional effects, primarily frustration. The subject becomes frustrated because the expected reinforcer does not occur. This is evidenced by increased activity or aggression. Second, to make matters worse, extinction can temporarily increase the nonreinforced behavior. This is called an *extinction burst*. An example is shown in Figure 5.2 for infants conditioned to make arm movements that activated an overhead mobile (Alessandri, Sullivan, & Lewis, 1990). Movements increased during extinction instead of decreasing, probably due to frustration. If you put your money in the soda machine and no soda comes out, what do you do? You push the button several more times, an example of an extinction burst. (Kicking the machine is frustration-elicited aggression.) Eventually, however, the extinction procedure should cause the response to cease. Then comes the third side effect, **spontaneous recovery**. After a delay interval, the response recovers. This is the same phenomenon that occurs in classical conditioning. Repeated extinctions are often necessary to thoroughly suppress a response. Extinction really does work. But given extinction bursts, frustration behavior, and spontaneous recovery, you can see why some practitioners might be put off.

There are beneficial effects of extinction-elicited behavior, as a means of adapting to changed circumstances. When the old response no longer works, the organism engages in new behaviors to try to restore reward. In one demonstration, Neuringer, Kornell, and Olafs (2001) first trained rats

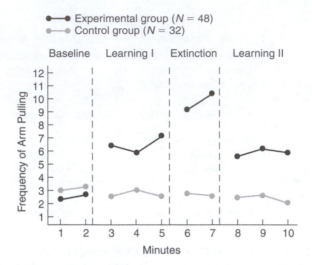

Figure 5.2 **Mean Rate of Arm Movements.** During the learning phase, arm pulling activated the mobile, producing an increase in movements from the baseline phase. During the extinction phase, when arm movements no longer affected the mobile, responding paradoxically increased, illustrating an extinction burst of responding.

Source: From "Violation of Expectancy and Frustration in Early Infancy," by S. M. Alessandri, M. W. Sullivan, and M. Lewis, 1990, *Developmental Psychology, 26*, p. 740. Copyright © 1990 by the American Psychological Association. Reprinted with permission.

to press three levers (of five levers present) in a particular sequence. Pressing the three in correct sequence was rewarded with a food pellet. Then food was withheld during the extinction phase. The animals tried the old three-lever sequence, but also tried other sequences and included the other two levers. This makes obvious sense in terms of real-world adaptation: If food (or safety) is not obtained with the old behavior, the organism must select a new behavior. Whereas one might think of instrumental conditioning as inducing repetitive, stereotyped responding (which is one interpretation of Thorndike's cats in the puzzle box), in some cases it leads to new behaviors.

The Partial Reinforcement Extinction Effect

Even though the response is not rewarded during extinction, the response may persist. **Resistance to extinction** refers to how persistent a response is during extinction (or in the face of extinction.) The specific conditions of reinforcement used during acquisition determine the ease or difficulty of extinguishing a response. Many of the reward variables that slow or retard acquisition of an instrumental response actually lead to sustained responding during extinction.

The **partial reinforcement extinction effect** (the PREE) is the most studied of these factors that affect extinction. After instrumental training with a partial reinforcement schedule, say, reinforcement for a random half of the correct responses instead of reinforcing all of them, extinction is slower. The data in Figure 5.3 show data on running speeds by rats in a runway (Weinstock, 1954). During acquisition, the continuously reinforced animals ran faster. During extinction, when the rats were no longer rewarded, the (previously) partially reinforced animals ran faster. This is the PREE. Similar effects are found in human tasks in which button pressing is only sometimes rewarded. We can ask our human participants to estimate their perceived likelihood of being "correct" (i.e., reinforced) on the next trial. During extinction the partially reinforced groups maintained higher expectations than do continuously rewarded groups (Lewis & Duncan, 1958).

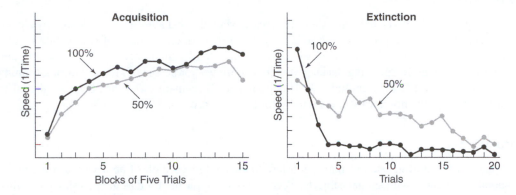

Figure 5.3 **Speed of Running by Rats in a Straight Alley.** During the acquisition phase, reinforcement occurred either every trial (100 percent) or on half of the trials (50 percent). No reward occurred during extinction, yet the previously partially reinforced group ran faster.

Source: From "Resistance to Extinction of a Running Response Following Partial Reinforcement under Widely Spaced Trials," by S. Weinstock, 1954, *Journal of Comparative and Physiological Psychology, 48,* p. 319 (*left*) and p. 320 (*right*). Copyright © 1954 by the American Psychological Association. Reprinted with permission.

(Students are often confused by the PREE phrasing. The PR—for partial reinforcement—refers to what happened during the acquisition phase. This is the left panel of Figure 5.3. The EE—for extinction effect—refers to what happens during the extinction phase. The 100 percent and 50 percent labels there refer to the reward schedule during the acquisition phase. There are no rewards for anybody during the extinction phase.)

The PREE at first seemed paradoxical to learning researchers. Conditioning should have been stronger after 100 percent reinforcement and therefore should be more persistent. There are several explanations for why a partial schedule produces more resistance. According to the *discrimination hypothesis*, the onset of extinction is not readily discriminated from the partial reinforcement of the acquisition phase. Only after several nonrewarded trials can the participant notice that conditions have changed from before.

Two other theories focus on the sequence of rewarded and nonrewarded trials during acquisition training as determiners of persistence during extinction. According to the *frustration hypothesis* (Amsel, 1962), the frustration experienced after nonreward on one trial is followed by reward on some subsequent trial. Frustration thus becomes a discriminative stimulus for reward. The subject who is reinforced on every trial during training does not experience frustration and so does not come to associate it with eventual reward.

A related theory suggests that the PREE occurs because the memory of nonreward on one trial becomes associated with the occurrence of reward on a later trial. According to the *sequential hypothesis* (Capaldi, 1971), at the start of a new trial the participant remembers the outcome of the previous trial and associates it with the outcome of the current trial. The sequential theory, though similar to frustration theory, makes some different assumptions. Fewer acquisition trials are required: the memory of a single nonrewarded (N) trial followed by a rewarded (R) trial is sufficient to produce the PREE. Another difference from frustration theory is that trials can be spaced farther apart because the memory of nonreward persists longer than the frustration produced by nonreward. The frustration from the soda machine failure lasts a few minutes. The memory will be recalled the next day when you think twice about trying that machine again.

The frustration and sequential hypotheses for the PREE say something interesting about the effects of nonreward. Whereas our initial reaction to being nonrewarded might be to give up, the absence of reward can instead become a cue for continued effort in the hope that it eventually will be reinforced.

Extinction: An Overview

The frequency of a given behavior should decrease when that behavior is not followed by a positive reinforcer. This expected decrease is interrupted by extinction bursts of responding and by spontaneous recovery. The course of extinction is affected by the history of reinforcement and nonreinforcement. Responding during extinction continues, or persists, if reward during training is intermittent rather than continuous. This partial reinforcement effect has been attributed to initial learning that nonreward is eventually followed by reward.

Punishment

In punishment, a designated response is followed by the presentation of an aversive stimulus. In laboratory research with animal subjects, electric shock is typically used as the punishing stimulus, mainly because the timing and intensity of shock are readily controllable. With human subjects, mild shocks are sometimes used, but more often loud noises are used, or penalties or fines are applied.

In our everyday language, punishment refers either to the application of a noxious outcome, such as spanking, or to withholding a positive outcome, such as your allowance. These two uses are similar in intended outcome, which is to decrease the frequency of the punished behavior. In our usage here, punishment is being distinguished from extinction or omission.

There are claims that punishment does not work, or at least does not work as well as extinction. The evidence goes back to some early experiments from Skinner. Estes (1944), in his Ph.D. dissertation under Skinner, attempted to suppress bar pressing in rats by extinction or by punishing the response with electric shock. Notice the distinction between nonreward and punishment. The rats were first trained to bar-press for food reward. Then, bar pressing was no longer rewarded (i.e., extinction), or bar pressing was followed by shock (i.e., punishment). During the single treatment session, the shocked rats did indeed bar-press less than did the nonrewarded rats. This is shown as the first point in Figure 5.4. But on succeeding test days, when shock was no longer given, bar pressing gradually returned. In the short run, punishment suppressed responding more

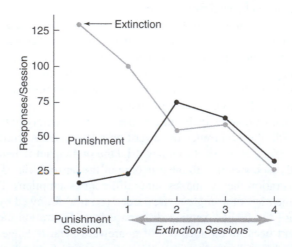

Figure 5.4 **A Comparison of Two Means of Suppressing Bar Pressing by Rats.** On day 1, the animals in one condition were punished with shock for each bar press. Extinction was used with both conditions in the next 4 days.

Source: Adapted from "An Experimental Study of Punishment," by W. K. Estes, 1944, *Psychological Monographs, 57 (3)*, Figure 1 p. 4. Copyright American Psychological Association. Reprinted with permission.

than did extinction; in the long run, it was no more effective than extinction. This finding led to the conclusion that the same end result can be accomplished by simply withholding reward.

Staddon (1995), another of Skinner's students, notes that contemporary research discounts this conclusion. Punishment is indeed quite effective in altering behavior, if it is applied correctly (see what follows). In fact, in laboratory studies, the most persistent responding is motivated by punishing consequences.

When Does Punishment Work?

Response-Contingent Punishment

Punishment is defined by a response-to-consequence rule. An effective punishment is one that is administered contingent upon the response. A specific response is punished.

It is important to demonstrate that the response suppression we observe is truly due to the punishment contingency and not to nonspecific effects of punishment. Once again, a control group is needed to assess the effect of presenting punishment in no particular relationship to the response, versus the effect of punishment that is delivered contingent on a specific response.

Intensity

An intense punisher is more effective than a mild punisher. Numerous studies have shown that a stronger shock will suppress bar pressing more quickly and more permanently than will weaker shocks.

This immediately poses an ethical quandary, because our tendency is to start with mild punishment and gradually increase the intensity if the weaker punishment doesn't work. Unfortunately, this actually decreases the effectiveness of the intense punishment. J. S. Brown (1969) introduced shock in a short segment of a maze that the rats ran through on their way to the goal box. By gradually increasing the shock level from 0 to 40 volts across days, running was essentially unaffected. Beginning with the intense shock would have immediately stopped running. Adaptation occurs when punishment gradually increases in intensity.

Delay of Punishment

Punishment is more effective if it is applied immediately after the target behavior, and decreases in effectiveness the longer it is delayed. Solomon, Turner, and Lessac (1968) punished dogs by hitting them with a rolled newspaper for eating food placed next to the experimenter. Punishment was given immediately after the dog began to eat, after 5 seconds, or after 15 seconds. The dogs all learned not to eat under these conditions. The challenging test of delayed punishment was a series of trials in which the dogs were returned to the room, with the experimenter absent, to see how long they would resist eating. The 15-second-delay animals lasted about 3 minutes before eating. The 5-second-delay dogs avoided the food for 7 test days before breaking down. The immediately punished dogs resisted eating for the whole 2 weeks of the test.

In many circumstances, punishment is necessarily delayed. Corporal punishment in schools, trials in the legal system, and waiting in your room until your parent comes home all involve delayed punishment. There are means of reinstating the inappropriate behavior at the time of punishment. With pets, we show them the shoe they chewed or drag them back to the room they trashed earlier. With children, we verbally remind them why they are being punished.

Schedule of Punishment

Punishing each instance of a behavior is generally more effective in suppressing the behavior than punishing only some instances of the behavior.

However, once punishment ceases, the response may recover, much like spontaneous recovery during extinction. We saw an example of recovery earlier when Estes's rats resumed bar pressing when the shocks stopped (Figure 5.4). A punished response may recover more after a continuous schedule, whereas a partial schedule of punishment produces more persistent response suppression.

Incompatible Responses

The punishing stimulus can elicit behaviors that are incompatible with the desired outcome. Have you ever seen a harried parent trying to quiet a crying child by yelling at the child? There is a folksy example about trying to punish a dog's leaving the house by the window. (Apparently, this was a problem in the old days. Lassie did this all the time.) As the dog is about to jump, swatting its tail only facilitates the jumping.

Concurrent Reinforcement

The effects of punishment can be neutralized if positive reinforcement of the inappropriate behavior occurs along with punishment. In one sense, this occurred in Solomon's study cited earlier. Dogs that received delayed punishment also received more food before being hit. The opposing outcomes, reward and punishment, may arouse conflicting motives.

Anyone who uses punishment should assess the alternative sources of reinforcement in a situation. For instance, punishment administered by a teacher in a classroom may be counteracted by the positive social reinforcement of attention from the student's peers.

Providing a Verbal Rationale

With children, we can provide verbal instructions to supplement punishment. But will punishment be made more effective by explaining the behavior–punishment contingency? In one case, less severe punishment was made more potent by adding instructions. Cheyne, Goyeche, and Walters (1969) arranged a situation in which children were tempted to reach over and touch a desirable toy. This behavior was punished by an unexpected sudden loud blast of noise. In the absence of any other instructions, a loud buzzer was much more effective than a softer buzzer (75 decibels) in suppressing future attempts to touch the toy. However, when an admonition *not* to play with the toy followed the buzzer, the lower-intensity noise was most effective. As shown in Figure 5.5, without instruction, the kids attempted another reach within 20 to 30 seconds, although they waited the longest after the loud noise. When a verbal admonition was added, the latency to reach was literally off the graph, approaching 300 seconds. The kids did not reach for the toy, and the experimenters basically quit waiting.

This experiment demonstrates the benefit of using verbal instructions to supplement punishment. It also shows that a strong punisher may actually *inhibit* learning. Cheyne et al. (1969) ask us to consider the distracting and disruptive effects that punishment may have on learning. The severely punished child may be too upset to attend to and remember the verbal admonition.

Individual Differences

Finally, we should mention the possibility that there are individual differences in susceptibility to punishment's effects. Individual differences have been demonstrated in comparing breeds of dogs. Freedman (1958) used the Soloman procedure in which dogs were slapped with a newspaper and told "no" when offered a bowl of food in the laboratory room. Shetland sheepdogs refused to eat during subsequent tests, whereas basenjis and beagles ate in spite of punishment.

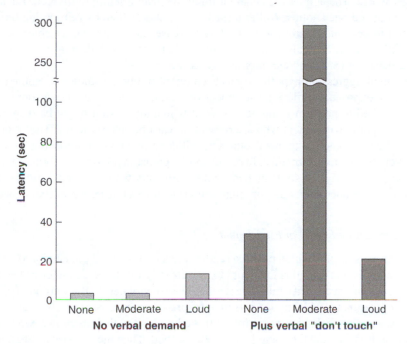

Figure 5.5 **Mean Number of Seconds Before Children Reached Toward a Desirable Toy Following a Moderate or Loud Noise Punishment or No Punishment.** The first three groups received no verbal reprimand. The other three groups received a verbal admonition following the noise.

Source: Based on Cheyne, Goyeche, & Walters, 1969.

Unwanted Side Effects of Punishment

Whatever desired benefit punishment holds for changing behavior, it also produces unwanted side effects. These include fear, aggression, and avoidance of situations associated with punishment.

Conditioned Fear and Avoidance

The punishment situation is exactly that used to condition fear through classical conditioning: A neutral CS is paired with an aversive US. The place in which punishment occurs or the person doing the punishing becomes a conditioned stimulus that evokes fear as a conditioned response. For example, if a child is punished in school, the school or the teacher could come to elicit fear. The child's fear would likely interfere with academic performance, and the child may avoid school altogether.

Aggression

Punishment can elicit aggression. In some early studies of the "punishment–aggression" hypothesis (Miller, 1948), pairs of rats confined within a conditioning chamber were given electric shocks. The rats began to nip at one another, what is called shock-elicited aggression. The parallel to the human case is obvious: Physically punishing someone may provoke aggression. If the punishment is for aggression in the first place, then we have perversely designed a method to increase, rather than decrease, the undesired behavior.

Matters get worse. The aggressive behavior might be inadvertently reinforced. Each time the shocked rats attacked one another, Miller turned off the shock, thereby reinforcing biting. (This is negative reinforcement. The response of biting increases because it causes shock to be terminated.) A child's aggression against siblings could be reinforced by a decrease in their annoying or disturbing behavior (Snyder, Schrepferman, & St. Peter, 1997).

The punishment-aggression hypothesis has been tested in human studies. In some cases, college students are exposed to mild electric shocks or loud noise as the aversive stimuli. The students are then asked to perform some other task in which aggression might be displayed, such as a cooperative game with others who are present, to earn points or money. The prior aversive conditions evoke a tendency to "punish" others by withholding points or imposing loud noises on the other players for poor performance. In one example, punishment took the form of highly critical comments on an essay the students had written. Students who received critical evaluations chose to administer louder noises and or longer-duration noises (Bushman & Baumeister, 1998).

Paradoxical Rewarding Effects of Punishment

Pairing a punishing stimulus with a positive reinforcer can convert the punisher into a secondary reinforcer. The punishing stimulus then could inadvertently reinforce behavior rather than suppress it. The work of psychiatrist Jules Masserman was mentioned in the introductory pages of this chapter. Masserman (1943) trained cats to lever press for unpleasant blasts of air to the face. Where did this perverse behavior come from? If we had visited the lab earlier, we would have seen Masserman first training the cat to lever-press for food. Then the air blasts were added, only occasionally and mild enough so as not to disrupt lever-pressing. By gradually increasing exposure to the air blasts, and tapering off the food rewards, he eventually had the cat bar pressing for punishment. Here, the air blast became a conditioned reinforcer by virtue of pairing with a positive reinforcer (food). Gradually increasing the intensity of punishment minimized its power to suppress behavior. Thus, knowing the learning history of an organism can sometimes explain behavior that appears irrational.

Punishment or Nonreward?

The preceding research could suggest that an alternative to punishment (again, here defined as the application of an aversive stimulus) would be to withhold reward as a means of suppressing unwanted behavior. Extinction or omission are each alternatives to punishment. But are nonreward and punishment all that different in their side effects? Both function similarly in several ways. The frustration provoked by nonreward can elicit aggression, just as punishment does. Animals seek to escape from stimuli associated with nonreward, just as they attempt to escape from stimuli that have been paired with punishment (Wagner, 1969). Maybe the deciding difference between the two is that withholding reward is categorically different from the application of aversive stimuli as used in punishment.

Does punishment work in everyday practice? Many studies have been conducted, but definitional and methodological limitations abound (Benjet & Kazdin, 2003; Hicks-Pass, 2009). For instance, does punishment mean getting a spanking, or receiving a vocal reprimand? These are different forms of punishment. Also, who decides whether a child's behavior is changed after punishment—the same person who administers the punishment or an impartial observer? Reviews of the research literature have shown that corporal punishment is sometimes associated with *more* problems in children, such as poor parent–child relationships and continued misbehavior. Other studies have found neither benefits nor deficits associated with mild punishment. A survey of dog owners seems to point to the same conclusion that can be drawn from the human studies: Namely, there is a correlation between the more frequent use of rewards and more obedience in certain tasks; and a parallel correlation between the greater use of punishment and an increased number of problem behaviors (Hiby, Rooney, & Bradshaw, 2004). Do problem dogs (or children) simply misbehave more often than nonproblem dogs and thus need more punishment? Or does punishment actually produce more misbehavior? This problem of the direction of cause and effect shows the difficulty in assessing the effects of punishment in the real world.

Should Punishment Be Used?

The answer requires a consideration of both efficacy (i.e., does punishment work?) and ethics (should it be used?). In the first case, we can ask whether punishment in a particular case will be applied according to parameters that are effective. Punishment is effective when it is intense, immediate, and consistently applied.

The answer in the second case is that punishment involves moral and ethical issues as much as it involves scientific ones. As a behavior modifier, you could decide not to use punishment as a moral decision, no matter how well it works. Or you might abstain from punishment on scientific grounds if you conclude that the conditions under which it is being administered are known to be ineffective. The practical and ethical issues are especially contrasted in the case of using electric shock on a child who engages in self-injurious behavior (see Box 5.1).

Box 5.1   Punishing Self-Injurious Behavior

Self-injurious behavior (*SIB*) occurs occasionally among developmentally disabled, autistic, or brain-damaged children. The children will bite themselves, scratch their skin, or bang their heads, in some cases with incredible frequencies. One case study reported extrapolated counts of hundreds of hits per minute (extrapolated because someone intervened and stopped the child before a full minute of such self-injury passed). Therapists have tried to control SIB with drugs, restraints, or the behavioral methods of reward, extinction, and omission. These methods have limited value.

One controversial treatment is the use of electric shock as punishment for head banging. The apparatus for this, called the *Self-Injurious Behavior Inhibiting System* (SIBIS), was developed collaboratively by parents, physicians, psychologists, and engineers. SIBIS consists of a lightweight headgear that senses sudden movements typical of head banging and triggers an electric shock, and an arm or leg band, powered by a 9-volt battery, to deliver the shock. The shock is response-contingent, immediate, consistently delivered, and can be intense, all of which are conditions conducive to effective punishment.

Taken out of context, the SIBIS procedure sounds pretty immoral: shocking defenseless, disabled children. A number of advocacy groups have protested the device, its use was legally banned in some states, and government officials questioned "whether society can sanction for use with disabled citizens forms of punishment, such as electroshock, that would never be tolerated for use with nonhandicapped children and adults" (Landers, 1988, p. 22). In addition, many behavior modification specialists cited Skinner's research as expert testimony on the ineffectiveness of punishment.

The issue of whether to use shock is not so clearly one-sided. Proponents argue that the effects of a small number of shocks more than outweigh the potential physical injury that results from SIB. Linscheid, Iwata, Ricketts, Williams, and Griffin (1990) report several single-case experiments in which SIBIS virtually eliminated SIB. Skinner felt compelled to enter the debate to clarify his own position on punishment. "Punishment is usually used to the advantage of the punisher." But Skinner also said: "If brief and harmless aversive stimuli, made precisely contingent on self-destructive behavior, suppress the behavior and leave the child free to develop in other ways, I believe it can be justified. When taken out of context, such stimuli may seem less than humane" (Skinner, 1988, p. 22).

Why does the pain from shock suppress SIB, when the pain from the self-inflicted injuries does not? Some have suggested that SIB is a form of compulsive behavior. Once engaged, there is no end point and so it continues. The shock is intense enough to break the cycle temporarily. Further research is needed on the causes of SIB and why SIBIS works.

Persistence

So far in this chapter we have presented extinction and punishment as ways to eliminate behaviors. However, there are certain behaviors we wish would persist, even in the face of unrewarding consequences. **Persistence** is the continued performance of an instrumental response even though the outcome is aversive (such as no reward, reduced reward, or even punishment).

We admire the inventors, artists, scientists, or entrepreneurs who work persistently with little reward. As noted in the introduction to this chapter, Thomas Edison claimed to have tried 3,000 different materials for the element (the part that glows and produces the light) of his electric light bulb (Evans, 2004). Wouldn't anyone else have given up at, oh say, a thousand, maybe two thousand, failures? The question here is why do some individuals persist in the face of failure? Principles of learning might explain such counterintuitive behavior.

We already know that the use of partial reinforcement during acquisition can make a response more resistant to extinction. The partial reinforcement extinction effect (the PREE) is an instance of a more general principle: Experience with any of a variety of what we might call "trying" experiences can induce persistence. Experience during the acquisition phase with delayed rather than immediate rewards, or with small rather than larger rewards, also increases the resistance of the response to extinction. Notice that these are opposite of the effects of these same variables during acquisition: Initially learning a response proceeds faster with continuous, immediate, and larger rewards (Mackintosh, 1974).

The similar effects induced by punishment, delayed reward, or nonreward suggest a common underlying factor. Possibly transfer occurs across aversive consequences that share similar negative emotional effects. (The expected outcomes in generalized persistence are illustrated in Table 5.1.)

Persistence may also generalize from one situation to another. A nice demonstration of generalized persistence is a pair of parallel studies that tested persistence in performing chores and school

Table 5.1 Generalized Persistence: The Relationship Between Acquisition Conditions and Subsequent Persistence During Extinction

Partial Reinforcement

Phase I: Acquisition	*Phase II: Extinction*
100%: Rewarded for each response	The 50% group is more persistent
50%: Rewarded for some responses	

Partial Punishment

Phase I: Acquisition	*Phase II: Extinction*
Food: Food given after each response	Food + shock is more persistent
Food + shock: Food after each response, and shock after half the responses	

Delayed Reinforcement

Phase I: Acquisition	*Phase II: Extinction*
Immediate: Reward immediately after each response	Delayed reward is more persistent
Delay: Reward given after a delay	

work (Eisenberger, Heerdt, Hamdin, Zimet, & Bruckmeir, 1979). In the first experiment, adult, institutionalized, depressed patients were asked to perform some ward chores (picking up, putting things away, making coffee, etc.). In the continuous-reward condition, a single chore was requested, for which the patient was thanked. In the partial-reward condition, three or four chores were performed before the patient was thanked. Later, a different person asked for some help in sorting computer punch cards. Persistence was measured by the number of cards sorted and the amount of time spent sorting. On both measures, patients in the partial-reward group were more persistent. Persistence generalized beyond the initial task of doing ward chores, and extended to requests by another person. In a second study, similar procedures were used to reward learning-disabled children. Those who were first reinforced for doing several math or several spelling problems were more persistent on the alternate task than were the children first rewarded for every problem.

Why is the study of generalized persistence important? For two obvious reasons: bad habits are often persistent, even in the face of unpleasant consequences, and good habits are ones we would like to persist in spite of unpleasant consequences.

Avoidance Learning

In avoidance learning, an instrumental response prevents an aversive outcome. That response should then increase in frequency or strength. You click your seat belt before the reminded buzzer, to prevent its sounding. Studying can be an avoidance response to prevent a bad grade. A familiar example of avoidance is the scene in every horror movie in which someone is confronted with a door. We all know, "Don't open the door!" Not opening it would be avoidance, although avoidance seems to occur rarely in films.

A typical avoidance learning task begins with a warning signal (WS), which is followed a few seconds later by an aversive stimulus. On succeeding trials, the performance of a selected instrumental response during the WS prevents the aversive stimulus and terminates trial. A standard task in animal experiments uses a two-compartment, or shuttle-box, apparatus. When the WS sounds, the animal has to move from one compartment to the other to avoid being shocked by the electrified metal bars that form the floor of the apparatus. Another trial begins shortly; the WS sounds and the animal hops back to the first compartment to avoid shock.

Animal subjects often figure out ways to prevent being shocked, showing that they are at least as clever as their experimenters. The walls of conditioning chambers are smooth sheet metal or Plexiglas. Otherwise, rats and mice would jump off the shocked floor and cling to a seam, ledge, or even a screw head until the WS went off. Some rats discovered that by standing with just their hind legs on the floor they could interrupt the electrical circuit (Broadhurst, 1963). One rat rolled over on the grid floor and used its fur as an insulator while it continued to bar-press for food rewards (Schwartz, 1978)!

Avoidance learning may play a role in the development and maintenance of social aggression in children. Children sometimes become aggressive as a way of avoiding conflict or arguments with their parents. If the child's aggression forces the parent to back down in an attempt to keep the peace, then aggression is reinforced. Field observations of families of children referred for conduct disorders show a strong relationship between reinforcement of aggression and subsequent behavioral problems two years later (Snyder et al., 1997).

Theories of Avoidance Learning

Conditioning Theory

A seminal and influential theory of avoidance learning is the **two-process**, or Watson-Mowrer, **theory** (Mowrer, 1947). The pairing of the WS with shock conditions fear to the signal via classical conditioning. This is exactly the mode of fear and phobia learning we discussed in Chapter 3. Little Albert learned to fear the white rat after it was paired with a loud noise, and this is the Watson part of the two-process theory. Once the WS is conditioned, escape from the signal is reinforced by fear reduction. Albert would get away from the rat, and doing so reduced the child's level of fear. Escape from the WS is instrumental conditioning, the second process, which was added by Hobart Mowrer. Note that according to the two-process theory, the subject is motivated to escape the WS, rather than avoid what the signal signals. That is, Albert is said to escape from the rat rather than avoid the loud noise that had been paired with the rat.

The two-process theory suggests that termination of the WS after a correct response is critical for avoidance learning. After all, escape from the WS is what is important. Albert is trying to get away from the rat and not the noise. The data are consistent with this prediction. If WS termination does not occur promptly, avoidance conditioning is markedly impaired (Kamin, 1956).

There are aspects of avoidance that a conditioning theory does not explain. One of the remarkable features of avoidance behavior is its persistence. Well-trained animal subjects will make the avoidance response for hundreds of trials. Phobic individuals will avoid their feared target for years. On all these successful avoidance occasions, the aversive outcome does not occur. Why doesn't fear of the WS extinguish? The WS occurs repeatedly and is not followed by an aversive outcome.

Cognitive Theory

It seems obvious to us that avoidance persists because you have acquired a pair of expectations: Responding prevents an aversive outcome, and if you do not respond, you can expect to be punished. The first expectation is continuously verified: If I respond, I don't get shocked. The second expectation is never subjected to a reality check: not responding to see what happens now. This explanation is the basis of a *cognitive theory* of avoidance learning (Bolles, 1972; Seligman & Johnson, 1973). Eliminating avoidance behavior therefore requires modifying both expectations. That is, the subject must learn that the warning stimulus no longer signals danger, and that not responding will not lead to punishment. This is the goal of some behavioral therapies for certain anxiety disorders that include avoidance responses (see Box 5.2).

Box 5.2   Repression and Avoidance

Our thoughts and memories sometimes provoke anxiety. Think of your most embarrassing moment or an instance of danger in your life. To prevent distress, we could simply try not to think about these things. Repression is a more extreme version of "not thinking" about something. Although initially developed within Freud's theory of the unconscious, learning theorists suggested that repression might be an instance of avoidance. Avoiding certain thoughts is reinforced by a reduction in fear (Dollard & Miller, 1950).

Avoidance learning could be a means of suppressing word-associations. Anderson and Green (2001) first taught their subjects 40 pairs of words. They then had their subjects practice some of the associations, by showing the first item and requesting recall of the second. For other word pairs, the subjects were instructed not to reply with, or even think about, the response to the cue word. That is, the subjects practiced not-remembering those associations. After 16 practice suppression trials, the subjects were asked to recall the associated items. The subjects were less able to recall the suppressed associations, even though the word pairs were well known after preliminary training. Anderson and Green say that we can learn to keep memories from entering consciousness. When people encounter a cue to an unwanted memory, repression keeps the unwanted associate from being retrieved.

"Not thinking" the response word is analogous to not making a habitual movement: When a stimulus occurs you begin to do something but then stop yourself (e.g., I start to dip my spoon in the sugar bowl . . . but then stop). Anderson and Levy (2009) refer to this as response override. With repetition, you can learn not to make that response. Similarly, you can learn to not think of the word response. The same neural mechanisms may be involved in suppressing memory retrieval as in suppressing physical responses.

Everyday memory lapses are sometimes attributed to a motivated desire to forget. You forget an appointment that you didn't want to keep. But do we really forget appointments or do we remember and simply decide not to keep them? After all, when asked why an appointment was missed, the all-too-ready reply is "I forgot," which may not be the real reason. In fact, one researcher concluded that "People are not likely to forget unpleasant intentions; they may, in fact, think about them obsessively . . . but they may very well not carry them out when the time comes" (Kvavilashvili, 1992, p. 514).

Extreme cases of repression fall under the category of **amnesia** (discussed in Chapter 7). The memory for a traumatic experience, such as an accident or a physical assault, may be seemingly forgotten. They are not forgotten in the sense of being lost from memory; instead, they remain unrecalled or repressed. Remembering such traumas would provoke considerable distress and psychological pain. A traumatic memory becomes inaccessible as a coping reaction of avoidance. Although the notion of repressed memories often raises skepticism among research psychologists, clinical observations document cases of amnesia for wartime experiences, crimes, natural disasters, and abuse (van der Kolk & Fisler, 1995).

If you cannot avoid remembering, you might be able to psychologically distance yourself when you do remember. View the unpleasant experience from the vantage point of an observer, someone watching the event unfold, rather than from point of view of yourself looking out. Self-distancing arouses less negative emotion, and produces a smaller rise in blood pressure (Ayduk & Kross, 2008). The self-distancing perspective spontaneously occurs in some cases of posttraumatic stress disorder (PTSD; Kenny et al., 2009; McIsaac & Eich, 2004). This perspective avoids some of the negative emotion of re-experiencing the traumatic event, but in the long run may lead to less recovery from the trauma.

Studies of PTSD in Vietnam War veterans have documented gaps in memory lasting from minutes to hours to days. For instance, some soldiers have no explicit recollection at all of a battle they were in. At the same time, too much remembering is a central problem with PTSD. Vivid memories return as flashbacks in nightmares, or during periods of intense emotional arousal (Bremner, Krystal, Southwick, & Charney, 1995). Why are some traumas repeatedly remembered, and others simply repressed? Why do some people experience posttraumatic stress and others do not? These are some of the challenging questions awaiting research answers.

Functional Approach

In our laboratory studies, some avoidance responses prove difficult to train. Rats will readily learn to bar-press for food but not so quickly to bar-press to avoid shock. A functional approach to avoidance learning studies the natural behavior of the organism's reaction to threats in the wild. These reactions contribute to the ease or difficulty of learning certain avoidance responses.

Robert Bolles labelled these natural behaviors *species-specific defense responses* (SSDRs; Bolles, 1970). SSDRs are innate responses that are primed in a fearful or threatening situation, and so could readily be "learned" in a laboratory study. (To say we have conditioned the response is not really accurate; we have simply increased the frequency of what a scared animal does anyway.) As one example of an SSDR, mice in a fearful situation readily learn to remain immobile (or freeze). It makes sense for a mouse in the wild to remain motionless to avoid detection. A threatened rat may stand up on its hind legs to defend itself with both paws and mouth. In parallel, the lab rat learns to stand on its hind legs and rotate a wheel with its front paws to avoid shock. It is more difficult to teach rats to bar-press than to wheel-turn to avoid shock.

The functional approach says that avoidance learning is affected by principles of learning and by principles of natural behavior.

Summary of Avoidance Learning

In avoidance learning, a response is acquired that prevents an aversive outcome. This is also called negative reinforcement: An instrumental response escapes or prevents an aversive outcome ("negative") and that response should then increase in frequency ("reinforcement"). According to the two-process theory, the warning signal first becomes associated with the aversive outcome. Thereafter, termination of this signal is reinforced by fear reduction. The cognitive theory of avoidance learning states that pairs of expectancies are learned: the belief that nonresponding leads to the aversive stimulus, whereas responding prevents the aversive stimulus. A functional approach studies the contribution of species-specific defense responses, the natural responses that are primed in a fearful situation, to learning.

Approach–Avoidance Conflict

Why would anyone persist in behavior that is punished? The sensible thing to do is to cease and desist. However, a punished behavior might persist because it has other sources of motivation. Perhaps it was previously reinforced, as in the case of Masserman's cats, and reinforcement may still be available. Children misbehave because the misbehavior is fun.

When a behavior has opposing outcomes, positive and aversive, conflict results. A child is drawn to a parent who often provides nurturance and security, but the child also fears outbreaks of anger. A dog that has been punished is simultaneously drawn by anticipation of food or petting, and repelled by the threat of further punishment. Although either approach or avoidance may predominate, there can be a point where the strength of the approach tendency is about equivalent to the strength of the avoidance tendency. Vacillation of behavior occurs between the competing motives, a pattern of called **approach–avoidance conflict** (Miller, 1959)

Given that a behavior has been both rewarded and punished, what determines whether approach or avoidance occurs? One factor is the relative intensities of the outcomes: the magnitude of the reward versus the severity of the punishment. A second factor is the proximity to the consequence, physically or temporally. The tendency to avoid is stronger the closer you get to the previously rewarded/punished goal.

Approach or Avoidance as a Coping Response

The distinction between approach and avoidance has been extended to characterize individual styles of coping with stressful situations. In dealing with traumatic stressors, such as the aftereffects of a natural disaster or an accident, some people avoid thinking about the situation, whereas others confront the stressor. The avoidant coping style has been variously labeled as blunting, selective inattention, and denial (see Roth & Cohen, 1986). For example, when confronted with a frightening medical diagnosis, one could avoid talking about the illness, deny its severity, or engage in distracting activities to block thinking about the illness. The approach-coping style has been labeled as monitoring, selective attention, and sensitization. The approach orientation might lead one to seek out more information about the illness, talk about it, or join a support group.

Approach and avoidance styles of coping were demonstrated in college students who participated in a shock-avoidance experiment (Averill & Rosenn, 1972). The students listened to an audiotape that had two tracks: One track played music and the other track would sound a tone warning of an upcoming shock. The subjects could switch between tracks. Whereas some students switched back and forth between the music and the warning, other subjects actually chose to listen to the music exclusively and ignore the warning signal. Sometimes the anticipation of unpleasantness is worse than the actual aversive stimulus.

Is one coping style better than another? The answer partially depends on whether the aversive outcome is controllable or not. In one study, students who were anticipating midterm exams used "problem-focused" coping, which was an active preparation for the exams. After the exams, but before grades were posted, the students used distancing and avoidance coping strategies. At that point, the stressor was beyond their control and the outcome was unknown (Folkman & Lazarus, 1985).

Imagine having to return to the scene of an accident or an assault. To approach a stressor provokes more immediate fear, whereas avoidance reduces fear. However, approach allows habituation, counterconditioning of the fear, and the acquisition of instrumental behaviors that control the stressor, and so may lead to more long-term reduction of anxiety. Assault victims who had more postassault exposure to the location had significantly less distress after 6 months (Wirtz & Harrell, 1987).

Learned Helplessness

Punishment and avoidance represent symmetrical and opposite rules that relate instrumental responses and an aversive outcome. In a given situation, there is one response that leads to punishment and another that avoids it. But what if the aversive stimulus is not controllable? What if there is no response that either produces or prevents the punishing stimulus? **Learned helplessness** is learning that there is an explicit lack of contingency between responses and an aversive outcome. Experience with uncontrollable stressors can lead to passivity in the face of subsequent stressors, even though they might be controllable.

Learned helplessness is demonstrated using a two-phase experimental design: one phase to induce helplessness and a second phase to assess the effects of helplessness training. Table 5.2 shows the design of a study to condition helplessness in rats. During the first phase some rats are given tail shocks. The escapable-shock group is given shocks that can be escaped by performing an instrumental response, such as turning the wheel to terminate shock. The helplessness group is given unavoidable and uncontrollable shocks. These two groups receive the same duration and sequence of shocks, the only difference being whether there is a response that could terminate the shocks. A third control group is left untreated in this phase of the study. In the next phase of the experiment, all three groups are trained on a new avoidance response. Typically, animals are

Table 5.2 Design of the Learned-Helplessness Experiment

	Phase I	*Phase II*
Control group	No training	Avoidance training
Escapable group	Escapable shock training	Avoidance training
Inescapable group	Inescapable shock	Avoidance training

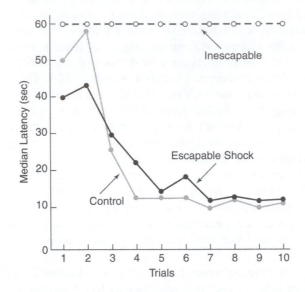

Figure 5.6 **Average Latency to Escape Shock During the Second Phase, After a Previous Experience With Escapable Shock, No Shock, or Inescapable Shock.** The maximum allowed latency of 60 seconds was reached by the helpless animals.

Source: From "Learned Helplessness: Theory and evidence," by S. F. Maier and M. E. P. Seligman (1976), *Journal of Experimental Psychology: General, 105*, Figure 2 p. 6, Copyright American Psychological Association. Reprinted by permission.

conditioned to shuttle between two compartments in reaction to a warning signal of impending shock.

The results of one study of learned helplessness are shown in Figure 5.6. The animals that were not shocked and those that received escapable shock during Phase 1 rapidly learned the avoidance response in Phase 2. That is, they responded more quickly over successive trials. The animals given helplessness training in the first phase showed no learning, and their latencies remained at the ceiling, the 60 seconds maximum allowed in each trial (Maier, Seligman, & Solomon, 1969).

Helplessness-like phenomena occur in humans in simple laboratory tasks. For example, college student participants are exposed to loud tone pulses that are "unpleasant but not harmful." The students are seated in front of a small box with a push button on it. The students are told "when the tone comes on, there is something you can do to stop it." Actually, only those in the escapable-noise group could turn off the tone with a button press. For the inescapable-noise participants, the button did not work. After 30 tones, the subjects are escorted to a different apparatus, a version of a shuttle box. This is a box with a knob on top that obviously slides from side to side. The participants are again told there is something they can do to terminate the tones. This is the crucial task, the one used to measure the effects of helplessness training. Prior exposure to inescapable tones in the push-button phase of the study lead to slower reactions in the second phase when the tones were now avoidable (Hiroto, 1974). Students exposed to escapable loud tones or not exposed to the tones (the control group) both responded more quickly in Phase 2.

What causes learned helplessness? Seligman (1975) suggests that the experience with uncontrollable stressors produces emotional, motivational, and cognitive deficits. Emotional deficits are shown by various psychosomatic illnesses, such as ulcers (e.g., Weiss, 1977). Motivational deficits are shown by a lack of initiative to respond, thus producing the maximal response latencies shown in Figure 5.6.

Cognitive deficits are beliefs that no matter what responses are attempted, they will be unsuccessful. With our college students, we can ask them to estimate their expectation for success on their next attempt at a task. Each successful solution should increase the expectation that more success will follow. However, the expectations of students exposed to helplessness conditions are unchanged by success. They do not believe they will do any better.

The cognitive belief in uncontrollability may be more important than the actual experience with uncontrollable stressors. That is, helplessness might be induced through altering the subject's beliefs about controllability, regardless of the actual experience with the aversive stimuli. This was nicely demonstrated in a study of the effects of uncontrollable noise on psychological performance (Glass & Singer, 1972). College students were exposed to aversive noise presented via headphones. The sound was a 100-decibel mix of office machine noises and people speaking in several languages. One group was told there was a panic button they could hit to briefly turn off the noise, but were asked to resist using it. Thus, these participants believed they had some control over the noise, although in fact they did not exercise this control. (We might call them the "potentially" escapable-noise group.) The inescapable-noise participants were not told about a panic button. After termination of the noise-exposure phase of the study, both groups were given puzzles to solve. The panic-button students were more persistent in working at puzzles, whereas the inescapable-noise group gave up more quickly. This study shows that it is the perception of control, acquired in the first phase, that is important.

Evans and Johnson (2000) studied further the potential debilitating effects of office noise. Clerical workers were assigned to a condition in which they heard low-intensity office noise for 3 hours. The noise-stress group had an elevated level of stress hormones relative to the non-noise control, and was less persistent in working at cognitive puzzles. One other interesting finding was that the noise subjects made fewer ergonomic or postural adjustments to the work station. Could it be that a feeling of lack of control extends to attempting to make workplace accommodations that increase comfort and ease during work?

Extensions of the Learned-Helplessness Concept

Learned helplessness is one of several important psychological conceptions that had its roots in the animal lab (Domjan & Purdy, 1995) and has since entered the vocabulary of everyday discourse. Several extensions of helplessness have particular relevance to human learning, in applications to psychopathology, classroom education, and health.

Depression

In laboratory studies with human participants, depressed and helplessness-induced individuals in the same experiments perform in a similar fashion (e.g., Klein & Seligman, 1976). Seligman (1975) noted the similarities between helplessness and depression in their symptoms, cause, and treatment. (After completing his degree in animal conditioning, Seligman moved on to clinical psychology. We could define his field of work as experimental psychopathology.) The symptoms of both helplessness and depression include reductions in activity, aggression, and motivation; and disruptions in eating, sleeping, and sexual behavior. Helplessness and some depressions have similar etiologies: They can be caused by traumatic experiences that are uncontrollable.

One remedy for helplessness is to force exposure to the fact that escape is possible. In one study, dogs that acted helpless in the presence of shock were physically dragged from one side to the other in the shuttle box, as shock terminated coincident with each shift (Seligman, Maier, & Geer, 1968). This procedure of forced exposure to shock escape was successful in teaching the avoidance response. One parallel therapy for depression is assertiveness training. Depressed individuals are forced into action, both to demonstrate that responding leads to reinforcing outcomes (the behavioral component) and to alter the belief that all efforts are useless (the cognitive component).

Classroom Education

Helplessness is ultimately determined by the belief that our behavior is ineffectual in determining what happens to us. This hypothesis has been used to explain why some school children lack motivation, persistence, or self-confidence. Dweck and Reppucci (1973) categorized school-aged children as helpless or persistent on the basis of the children's beliefs. Helpless children blamed their failure on lack of ability. These fifth graders with reading difficulties had little expectation for future success at reading. Retraining them to attribute their poor school performance to lack of effort offered a remedy: Work harder, rather than giving up.

What kind of experiences should reverse helplessness? Insuring success would seem the obvious answer: Provide the child with a series of solvable problems to virtually guarantee successful completion. But children realize when the problems are too easy, and attribute their success to this and not their own efforts. Dweck (1975) instead used a training procedure that ensured some problems were not solved, mixed in with a number the child could solve. This procedure was better at reversing helplessness beliefs than giving the child only problems that could be solved correctly. We earlier saw a related idea of using partial reinforcement schedules as a way of inducing persistence (e.g., Eisenberger et al., 1979).

Physical Health

Helplessness is associated with emotional reactions of the body to stress. Correlational findings from human research indicate that a cluster of negative attitudes, which includes pessimism, cynicism, helplessness, and depression, has been linked to a variety of physical health problems, from the common cold to cancer (Scheier & Carver, 1993). It seems logical to assume that an opposite, positive set of traits would lead to better health. Indeed, an optimistic orientation does seem to convey psychological and physical health advantages. Aspinwall and Taylor (1992) studied the adjustment of new freshmen to college. At the beginning of their first semester, the students completed an optimism inventory. Three months later, the more optimistic students were experiencing less distress, even after equating academic performance.

How else do optimists and pessimists differ? The optimistic individuals are more likely to confront and deal with stressful situations, which is the approach mode of coping discussed earlier. Pessimists tend to deny stressors or try to avoid them, which is the avoidance mode of coping (Scheier & Carver, 1993).

Correlations between traits of optimism or helplessness and health have to be interpreted cautiously. Does optimism lead to better health or does good health promote optimism? Do illness and disease lead to pessimism about the outcome of future illness?

Summary of Learned Helplessness

An older psychiatric literature refers to the notion of hopelessness, or of psychologically giving up in the face of stress or adversity. The experimental work on learned helplessness gave a firm scientific basis to this idea. Helplessness is learning that there is a lack of contingency between responding and an aversive outcome. Helplessness produces behavioral, motivational, and cognitive deficits. A behavioral approach to learning emphasizes the first two categories, such as acquisition of passive behaviors or reduced motivation as the sources of helplessness. A cognitive approach emphasizes the beliefs and expectancies that are acquired, such as a belief that aversive stimuli are uncontrollable or the expectation that responding is useless. Learned helplessness has merged with other ideas in the areas of health, educational, and clinical psychology to help explain the origins of illnesses, school failure, and depression. In one sense, helplessness has come full circle, from clinical observations through the laboratory and back to the applied areas.

Neuroscience and Aversive Learning

Aversive learning is not a singular trait, and so neuroscientists will not be announcing the discovery of the "aversive learning" area of the brain. Aversive stimuli occur in both classical and instrumental learning, and undoubtedly a number of neural circuits will be found to underlie aversive learning.

The Amygdala and Aversive Learning

One step in our understanding of aversive learning is to map the brain circuits involved in fear conditioning. Several researchers, using a variety of methods and species, have documented the role of the amygdala in the classical conditioning of fear (LeDoux, 2000; Davis, 2006). For example, the amygdala of rats can be injected with a chemical that temporarily suppresses its action. The subjects are then given tone-shock pairings in a standard conditioning protocol, but the infused rats do not learn to become fearful during the tone. The amygdala must be functioning for this form of learning to occur.

In addition, normal activity in the amygdala is important *after* the conditioning training in order to consolidate the newly formed knowledge. In this type of study, rats are first given tone-shock training, and testing shows they have conditioned and express fear during the tone. The amygdala is then inhibited chemically, as in the first study, but now the suppression occurs shortly after the conditioning trials have been completed. When the rats are tested later, the fear to the tone is absent. Thus, normal activity in the amygdala is necessary for the initial registration of the fear conditioning, and for the consolidation of the fear learning (Wilensky, Schafe, Kristensen, & LeDoux, 2006).

The neurologist Antonio Damasio and his students have studied individuals who have a damaged amygdala (Bechara et al., 1995). The patients are tested in a classical fear-conditioning procedure. When a certain color of light is flashed on the computer monitor (say, blue), an extremely loud noise burst is presented through the subject's earphones. Other colors are not followed by anything. Those of us with normal amygdalas would learn a fear response to the blue light: skin conductance would jump, as would heart rate. The amygdala-damaged individuals do not show a conditioned fear reaction. They show a normal spike in the skin-conductance response to the loud noise, so they perceive the noise as aversive. However, without a functioning amygdala, they do not learn the fear response. Interestingly, the amygdala-damaged patients can verbally report the blue light–noise connection, so they "know" these two go together.

Avoidance Conditioning

In a classical conditioning arrangement, a signal (the CS) is followed by an unavoidable shock (the US). In an instrumental avoidance task, there is a warning signal and a response that can prevent shock. The comparison of amygdala activity in both forms of conditioning was investigated within the same study (Delgado, Jou, LeDoux, & Phelps, 2009). The participants, students this time rather than rats, were exposed to both classical conditioning and avoidance learning, with trials intermixed. The participants were classically conditioned to discriminate between colored squares that were presented on the computer screen. For instance, a blue square was paired with a shock to the wrist (defining a CS+), and a green square was not followed with shock (CS−). In addition, a yellow square was also followed by shock but a button response would prevent shock. So, the yellow square was a warning signal (WS) for avoidance responding.

The researchers were particularly interested in which brain areas became more active during the CS+ and the WS trials. We know the amygdala is involved during classical conditioning with aversive USs; and an area known as the striatum is involved in instrumental conditioning. For the two stimuli paired with shock, the CS+ and the WS, there was more amygdala activity than on nonshock trials. There were also slightly different patterns of activity. There was more amygdala activity during CS+ trials (the classical conditioning task) than during WS trials; but there was more striatal activity during WS trials (an instrumental task) than during the CS+. So, for two stimuli paired with shock, classical and instrumental conditioning produced slightly different patterns of activity.

Social Learning

In most studies of conditioning, there is direct experience with aversive outcomes. Fear can also be learned indirectly, through observation of another's experiences or through verbal communications. Does indirect fear conditioning also involve the amygdala?

In one series of experiments (Olsson & Phelps, 2004, 2007), participants received one of three different versions of classical conditioning. In the direct experience group, subjects were shown faces on the computer screen. One face (the CS+) was paired with shock and another face was not. The observational experience group watched a video of someone receiving the direct-experience conditioning. These subjects watched someone else receive the face-shocks pairings. In the instructed experience condition, subjects were told about the direct experience procedure of the first group. These subjects were shown and told which face was paired with shock and which face was not.

The direct experience subjects showed conditioned fear to the CS+ face (as measured by skin conductance responses). No surprise here. The observational experience subjects also conditioned to the CS+ face. We could imagine that watching someone get shocked would arouse fear, even if we did not experience any pain. Interestingly, the instructed experience group showed elevated fear to the CS+ face. Explicit conditioning, social learning, and instructional learning: each produced fear learning.

The amount of activity varies in different brain regions when someone receives a shock versus watching someone getting shocked. Yet in all three conditions there was increased activation in the amygdala in the presence of the CS+. The amygdala that is essential to direct (experienced) fear conditioning is also involved in learning fears through indirect experiences. The only real difference among the groups was that the instructed fear group had elevated activity mainly in the left side of the brain. This would correspond to verbal or aware learning.

Applications of Aversive-Learning Contingencies

Pet Containment Systems

Electronic fences are available to confine dogs to the yard around the home. A wire is buried around the perimeter of the yard. The dog wears a collar that tracks the location of the dog, sounds a tone, and if necessary, delivers a shock. When the dog gets close to the perimeter, the tone turns on; if the dog continues approaching the wire, a shock is triggered. (The shocks are said to be not painful; comparable to that generated by a 9-volt battery.) The idea is the dog will learn to avoid triggering the tone. This is a direct application of the Watson-Mowrer theory of conditioning. Do experimental psychologists know anything else about avoidance learning that might apply to these perimeter systems?

Maybe we should be concerned about shock-elicited aggression. It is possible that when the dog is shocked the animal will become aggressive. Polsky (2000) found several legal cases which alleged that dogs crossed the barrier and attacked someone. Did the shocks intensify the attacks? The instances cited are anecdotal; there may have been other circumstances that contributed to the attacks. Yet, we have some expectation based on laboratory research that electric shock can elicit aggression.

The warning tone could also elicit aggression through conditioning. In laboratory research, stimuli paired with shock can themselves become elicitors of aggression (Miller, 1948). Could the dog-collar tone elicit aggression? The tone might cause the dog to become aggressive while still within the yard, and bite someone inside the perimeter.

Treatment of Obsessive-Compulsive Disorder

Contemporary psychotherapy employs both cognitive and behavioral approaches. Each offers fruitful application to certain disorders. In obsessive-compulsive disorder, an individual has an excessive fear of something and/or compulsive behaviors that need to be performed. An obsessive fear of germs on objects that others have handled leads to compulsive behavior such as hand washing, wearing gloves, or disinfecting objects. Cognitive therapy might examine the irrationality of the thoughts and beliefs behind the obsession. Behavioral therapy would try to recondition the compulsive behavior.

The cognitive approach to avoidance learning suggests there should be two steps in eliminating obsessive-compulsive behavior: (1) provide safe exposure to the feared object to extinguish the fear and (2) prevent the compulsive behavior to prove that no adverse consequences occur when the response is blocked. A parallel is seen in the laboratory experiments on eliminating an avoidance response: (1) extinguish the fear to the warning signal or (2) prevent the avoidance response. Studies that have assessed the separate contributions of *stimulus extinction* versus *response prevention* have sometimes shown a desynchronization between the two. That is, fear to the warning signal can be extinguished by prolonged exposure to it. The stimulus seemingly no longer provokes any fear. When given the opportunity, however, the subject will still perform the avoidance response during the warning signal. On the other hand, repeated experience with response prevention, by blocking the avoidance response, reduces the need to perform the avoidance response. Yet the warning signal is still feared (see Mineka, 1979).

The same thing happens in humans, so we may need to use two methods to reduce obsessive-compulsive behavior. For example, individuals who have an intense fear of dirt and germs use excessive hand washing as a means of decontamination. Foa, Steketee, Grayson, Turner, and Latimer (1984) found that therapy involving just exposure (i.e., extinction) to contaminants indeed reduced fear to dirt, garbage, or public telephones. Alternatively, preventing hand washing (response prevention) reduced fear if the response was not made, and it decreased the need to engage in this obsessive behavior. However, neither alone was as effective as the combination of treating both the obsessive fear of contaminants *and* the compulsive hand washing behavior (i.e., extinguish fear to contaminants *and* prevent hand washing).

Summary

Instrumental conditioning is defined by the contingency arranged between a particular response and an outcome. In addition to positive reinforcement, instrumental learning includes three aversive-outcome procedures, which are the content of this chapter: nonreinforcement, punishment, and avoidance.

Nonreward

Instrumental learning includes contingencies that use nonreinforcement: A target response is not followed by a positive reinforcer. In extinction, the reinforcer is omitted after those responses that once produced positive reinforcement. In omission, a selected response prevents a positive reinforcer from occurring.

Extinction produces side effects that sometimes discourage its use: unpleasant emotions such as frustration; an extinction burst of responding; and spontaneous recovery of the extinguished response after a delay interval.

The specific conditions of positive reinforcement present during acquisition affect the persistence of responding during extinction. The *partial reinforcement extinction effect* (PREE) is the most prominent of these factors. Extinction is slower following training with a partial reinforcement schedule rather than a continuous schedule. The PREE may develop because of what is learned during partial reinforcement: during acquisition, frustration becomes associated with reward on a later trial, or the memory of nonreward is followed by reward. Other reward variables that slow or retard acquisition, such as small or delayed reinforcers, can also lead to persistent responding during extinction.

Punishment

In punishment, a response is followed by an aversive consequence, which acts to decrease responding. There have been claims that punishment does not work (Thorndike) or it only temporarily suppresses responding (Estes and Skinner). However, punishment is effective when it is given contingent on a particular response, and is intense, immediate, and consistently applied. The punishing stimuli should not elicit responses that are incompatible with the desired outcome.

Punishment can produce side effects of learned (or conditioned) fear, and avoidance of the punisher or the punished situation. Punishment can also provoke aggression, which may be inadvertently reinforced and thus strengthened. The punishment (or the punished behavior) may become a secondary reinforcer through association with a positive reinforcer.

Nonreward and punishment share some common features: They both produce negative emotional reactions, and behavior may transfer between these two types of outcomes.

Persistence

Persistence refers to continued responding during extinction or punishment. Response persistence can be enhanced by previous exposure to partial reinforcement, small and delayed rewards, or even mild and occasional shock during acquisition. Persistence can generalize from one set of adverse consequences (e.g., nonreward, punishment, shock, etc.) to another set of adverse consequences. The study of response persistence is significant because bad habits are often so persistent and because good habits are not persistent enough.

Avoidance Learning

In avoidance learning a response prevents the occurrence of the aversive stimulus. Avoidance learning is an example of negative reinforcement. The increase in the frequency of the response (i.e., "reinforcement") leads to a decrease in the frequency of punishment (i.e., "negative").

How do we explain the fact that avoidance responding increases even when it is reinforced by the occurrence of "nothing" as the consequence? Mowrer said the pairing of a warning signal with shock conditions fear to the signal via classical conditioning. Escape from the warning signal is reinforced by fear reduction, which is instrumental conditioning. One difficulty for the two-process theory is the fact that the warning signal does not seem to extinguish (lose its fear-motivating property) even though it is not followed by shock on successful avoidance trials.

A cognitive theory of avoidance states two sorts of expectancies are acquired: a stimulus–outcome expectancy (e.g., tone is followed by shock) and a response–outcome sequence (e.g., the avoidance response is not followed by shock). Successful avoidance responding requires the acquisition of two expectancies: Tone means shock, and a response will prevent the shock. Eliminating avoidance behavior requires modifying both expectations.

A functional approach to avoidance studies the contribution of an organism's natural, evolved response to fear and pain to the acquisition of protective behavior. Some responses may be easier to learn than others, such as behavioral freezing by a mouse and or a rat standing and rotating a wheel.

When a given behavior has two opposing outcomes, one pleasant and one aversive, approach–avoidance conflict may result. Approach or avoidance can also characterize styles of coping in stressful situations. Some people try to avoid thinking about a stressful situation, whereas others confront the stressors. Avoidance coping leads to reinforcement through immediate fear reduction. Approach coping provokes more immediate fear, but may lead to more adaptive learning in the long run for controllable stressors.

Learned Helplessness

Learned helplessness is learning that there is an explicit lack of contingency between response and an aversive outcome: There is no response that is causing punishment, nor is there one that prevents it. Helplessness is demonstrated using a three-group design. During the first phase of an experiment, one condition is exposed to escapable shocks, a second condition is exposed to inescapable shocks, and the third condition receives no shocks. In the second phase of a study, the inescapable-shock subjects fail to learn an avoidance response.

Uncontrollable stressors produce emotional, motivational, and cognitive deficits. Emotional deficits are shown by various psychosomatic illnesses, such as ulcers. Motivational deficits are shown by a lack of initiative to respond. Cognitive deficits are shown by beliefs that whatever response made will be unsuccessful. Helplessness is ultimately determined by the belief that behavior is ineffectual in affecting what happens to us.

Learned helplessness has been extended and applied to explaining depression, failure in classroom learning, proneness to stress-related illnesses; and to an opposite disposition, learned optimism.

Neuroscience and Aversive Learning

The amygdala of the brain is important for learning fear. In classical conditioning, suppression of this area before or shortly after conditioning blocks the appearance of conditioned fear.

Activity in the amygdala was studied during a CS in classical conditioning, and during a warning signal in instrumental avoidance learning. Both stimuli showed more amygdala activity than during stimuli that signaled no shock.

Amygdala activation is also found during observational learning of fear (watching someone else go through a classical fear conditioning procedure); and after instructed conditioning (listening to the description of the fear conditioning procedure).

Applications

Pet containment systems employ principles that correspond to the Watson-Mowrer theory of avoidance learning. A warning tone sounds as the dog approaches the perimeter of the yard, and shock occurs if approach continues. Backing away from the area turns off the tone and prevents shock. Shock-elicited aggression is a potential side effect.

In obsessive-compulsive disorders, individuals often have an excessive fear or phobia, and compulsive behaviors that need to be performed. Research on avoidance learning suggests that eliminating obsessive-compulsive behavior requires (1) safe exposure to the feared object to extinguish the fear and (2) prevention of the compulsive behavior to prove that no adverse consequences follow. An effective behavioral treatment uses both stimulus-extinction and response-prevention components of the two-process theory.

6 Verbal Learning

The previous chapters described the methods of classical and instrumental conditioning, areas of learning that were heavily influenced by the behavioral approach to psychology. Later chapters will focus on the area of memory, which is more influenced by the cognitive approach. The current chapter is transitional between behavioral psychology, with its emphasis on association learning; and cognitive psychology, with its emphasis on mental strategies. **Verbal learning** refers to the study of factors that affect acquisition, retention, and recall of verbal items (usually words.) Work on verbal learning follows in a tradition begun by Herman Ebbinghaus, a German psychologist working in the 1880s, who introduced some of the methods. Early verbal-learning researchers studied the effects of such variables as the number and spacing of the repetitions, or the transfer of learning from one list to another. Although verbal learning as a term now sounds old-fashioned and not as contemporary as *cognitive psychology*, the topics studied are still very much in vogue and have a decidedly applied nature.

Two caveats are in order. First, *verbal* learning is a misnomer because often we study learning of nonword materials: faces, pictures and objects, places and locations, odors, and action sequences are just a few examples. Second, *rote* learning implies a passive, uninvolved subject (*S*) who is attempting to memorize information. Our subjects are rarely passive. "The image of the subject in a verbal-learning experiment as being a tabula rasa upon which the investigator simply chisels associations, and quite against the *S*'s wishes, is archaic. The *S* is far from passive and the tablet has already impressed upon it an immense network of verbal habits. A more accurate description of the verbal-learning experiment is one in which the subject actively 'calls upon' all the repertoire of habits and skills to outwit the investigator" (Underwood, 1964, p. 52). Therefore, cognitive variables are considered in our studies: the effects of rehearsal, imagery, and organization. In verbal-learning experiments, we may not be dealing with "raw" learning; we study the formation of associations influenced by associations the subject already possesses.

The Ebbinghaus Legacy

In 1879, a twenty-something German scholar named Herman Ebbinghaus began a remarkable series of experiments on himself. Ebbinghaus had still not yet decided on his life's work. Although six years beyond his Ph.D., he worked as a tutor for a wealthy family. There was a long history of the memory arts, but until this time memory was not thought to be amenable to the methods of science. Ebbinghaus became convinced that a quantitative approach to learning was also possible. Ebbinghaus's research was summarized in his classic (and brief) book *On Memory*, published in 1885 (reprint edition, 1964).

Ebbinghaus's procedure involved *serial learning*, or memorizing lists in sequence until they could be recalled perfectly. The learning materials were three-letter syllables, each composed of a consonant, vowel, and a consonant, referred to in English as *nonsense syllables*. Most of the syllables were not words, but some were. Ebbinghaus used this material to produce sequences of syllables that would not be meaningful prose. Ebbinghaus's greater contributions were his methods for objectively measuring learning and retention. Learning (or acquisition) could be measured by the number of study trials that were necessary to repeat the list back without error. For instance, a list of 10 syllables might be memorized after 4 study and test trials, whereas a list of 15 syllables might require 8 study trials.

Ebbinghaus would later attempt to recall the list. Failing perfect recall after a delay interval, he would relearn the list. His measure of memory (or retention) was the number of trials needed to relearn the list to a perfect recitation. By comparing the number of trials initially needed to learn a list with the number of trials needed to relearn the list, Ebbinghaus derived a measure of *savings*: how many trials were saved in relearning. If a list originally took 10 repetitions to learn, but could be relearned in 4 repetitions the next day, there was a savings of 6 repetitions. This could be converted to a percentage or a 60 percent savings.

Suppose you are studying for finals, and you run across some material that is unfamiliar. You have no recollection of it, even though you must have studied it for an earlier exam. Savings would be evidenced if you can now learn it faster than you had originally learned it. The significance of the savings measure is that it allows the detection and measurement of memory even in the absence of the ability to recall or recollect an experience.

An example of a savings measure was used in a study of the effects of **electroconvulsive therapy** (or ECT) on forgetting. ECT is administered by psychiatrists in a hospital setting as a treatment for depression. Individuals who receive ECT later cannot remember events that immediately preceded ECT. Is the memory really gone, or is there some residual memory that cannot

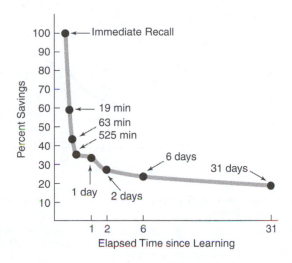

Figure 6.1 **The Curve of Forgetting Across an Interval of 31 Days.** Derived from Ebbinghaus's own recall data, retention is plotted in terms of the percentage savings in relearning.

Source: Adapted from *Memory: A Contribution to Experimental Psychology*, by H. Ebbinghaus, 1885/1964, New York: Dover; tabled data p. 76.

now be recalled? Talland (1968) had patients learn narrative paragraphs before ECT and then relearn the passages after treatment. After ECT the patients said they had never read these passages before, yet they relearned them more quickly than they learned new control passages. ECT did not eliminate memory, but did affect the retrieval of memory.

Another of Ebbinghaus's contributions to quantification was his description of the **curve of forgetting**. After learning a list, Ebbinghaus would relearn the list after various intervals: immediately, hours later, days later, a month later. In the first minutes and hours after learning, the amount retained dropped dramatically. After longer retention intervals, the rate of loss of the remaining memory decreased and eventually leveled off. Figure 6.1 shows Ebbinghaus's data. The Ebbinghaus curve of forgetting shows that most forgetting occurs shortly after the initial learning. Whatever persists past this early phase is better retained and is forgotten at a slower rate.

Ebbinghaus studied how acquisition and retention were affected by variables such as the length of the lists, the number of practice trials, and the spacing of trials. In summary, Ebbinghaus's contributions included methods for performing controlled learning experiments; means of quantifying the results; and a description of the effects of several variables on learning.

This chapter will consider three basic verbal-learning methods. Serial learning requires recall of a list in the same sequence in which the items were presented. Free recall also refers to remembering lists, but the items can be recalled in any order. The method of paired associates refers to learning lists of pairs of items, in which the first item is used as a stimulus for recall of the second.

Serial Learning

In **serial learning**, a list of items is learned and reproduced in the same sequence in which the items were presented. Serial learning occurs frequently outside the laboratory. Everyday examples include learning the alphabet by young children, poetry by middle schoolers, and statistical formulas by college students ("Sum and then square, or square and then sum?"). There are many alpha-numeric codes we need to memorize, such as those for the ATM or computer passwords.

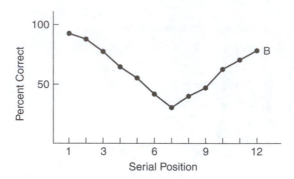

Figure 6.2 **The Serial Position Curve in Serial Learning**. Number of correct responses in memorizing a list of 12 nonsense syllables.

Sources: Derived from "Experimental studies in rote learning theory. III. Distribution of practice with varying speeds of syllable presentation," by C. I. Hovland, 1938, *Journal of Experimental Psychology, 23*, Figure 2, p. 178. Copyright American Psychological Association. Reprinted with permission.

In a serial-learning task, study trials in which the list is presented are alternated with test trials in which the subject attempts to recall the list. Learning can be quantified by counting the number of correctly recalled items at each serial position. Another measure of learning is the speed with which a list can be recalled or performed.

Serial Position

One of the most prominent factors affecting serial learning is the position of each item within the list. The beginning and end portions of the list are typically learned faster and with fewer errors, whereas middle items are learned with more difficulty. Figure 6.2 shows a typical serial-position curve. In this study, a list of nonsense syllables was presented and tested until it could be reproduced in sequence without error (Hovland, 1938). The figure shows the average number of correct syllables recalled at each position during learning. There is a U-shaped curve: More correct responses were made in learning the starting or ending serial positions than in learning the middle positions.

Serial-position curves are found in many situations, both in laboratory and naturalistic research. For instance, in testing memory for spatial locations a series of pictures or objects are pointed to in sequence, and the subject must reproduce that sequence. A serial position curve occurs in both animals and humans (Jensen, 1962; Swartz, Chen, & Terrace, 1991). Several other serial position phenomena are described in Box 6.1.

Box 6.1   The Ubiquitous Serial-Position Curve

The classic U-shaped curve in the recall of serial information is seemingly ubiquitous: It can be found in many different situations. Like Ebbinghaus's Curve of Forgetting, it is a general principle of learning to which we can point. This chapter illustrates the curve with data from nonsense syllables and word recall. Some other examples of the U-shaped curve are the following.

Long-Term Personal Memory

Sehulster (1989) attended the New York Metropolitan Opera for 25 years. He tested his own recollection of over 260 performances he had attended. In attempting to date given performances, and in remembering who sang which role, he obtained U-shaped curves, with more accurate recall (e.g., month, week, day, and matinee versus evening performance) for the first and last 5-year blocks.

Long-Term Factual Memory

Crowder (1993) asked college students to name all of the U.S. presidents. The first few and the most recent presidents were better recalled than the presidents in the middle. There were several jogs in the curve, where some presidents were especially well remembered (e.g., Lincoln, FDR).

Long-Term Skill Retention

Gymnasts were asked to reproduce a 12-step floor routine, either immediately or after a delay of up to a week. U-shaped reproduction curves were seen, subject to several modifiers. Expert and older gymnasts recalled more elements of the routine than did novices and younger participants. Also, the experts could recall much further into the list before forgetting a step; that is, they could recall the first 6, 7, or 8 steps before making an error (Tenenbaum, Tehan, Stewart, & Christensen, 1999).

Infant Memory

Six-month-olds learned to kick their legs to shake each of three mobiles that were suspended overhead. (This method was described in Chapter 4.) Testing a week later showed a U-shaped curve: The infants reacted more to the first and the last mobiles than to the one in the middle. The infants even remembered the sequence the mobiles came in: The middle mobile was better recognized when it was preceded in testing by the first mobile (Gulya, Galluccio, Wilk, & Rovee-Collier, 2001).

Spatial Memory

Eight- and 12-year-old children were taken for a stroll across a university campus, in the company of their parents and/or the researchers. The children were then asked to lead the way back to the starting point. At each choice point the child decided which direction to turn. The children more accurately remembered directions near the end of the walk, which demonstrates a clear recency effect. There was only a hint of primacy for the early choices in the path (Cornell, Heth, Kneubuhler, & Sehgal, 1996)

Sometimes either primacy or recency occurs. Pillemer, Goldsmith, Panter, and White (1988) asked alumni to recall five events from their freshman year of college, 5 to 20 years earlier. More events were recalled from early in the academic year (a primacy effect) than later. On the other hand, when college students attempted to name all of their teachers since first grade, a recency effect was seen: The more recent teachers were recalled better (Whitten & Leonard, 1981). Recency effects also appear in many subject populations in which primacy is impaired, such as individuals with amnesic syndrome, children, and the elderly.

The serial-position curve poses a theoretical challenge, both to explain why the same phenomenon occurs under so many different conditions and to explain those exceptions that do occur.

Several hypotheses have been proposed for position effects in a serial task. The anchoring hypothesis says that subjects latch onto the end items in the list to serve as anchors from which the rest of the list is attached. Middle items in the list are too distant to be firmly attached to either end, and more likely to become associated to one another (Bower & Hilgard, 1981).

An analogous finding is our tendency to organize personal memories around various temporal anchors. Students, not surprisingly, anchor their memories with respect to the start and finish of the academic year. Their recall of personal experiences will sometimes produce a serial-position curve, with more recollections from early and late in the school year and fewer from the middle of the year (Kurbat, Shevell, & Rips, 1998).

An interference hypothesis argues that learning some list items can interfere with learning others. **Proactive interference** occurs when learning the items at the beginning of the list interferes with learning items in the middle and end of the list. **Retroactive interference** occurs when learning the end of the list interferes with learning the beginning and middle of the list. The middle items suffer maximal interference, both proactive from learning the early list items and retroactive from learning the end items.

Zhao (1997) contrasted proactive and retroactive interference effects in the recall of commercials broadcast during several Super Bowl football games. Zhao compared recall of commercials that were preceded by different numbers of commercials, thus varying the potential amount of proactive interference; or that were followed by different numbers of commercials, thus varying the potential amount of retroactive interference. The first commercials in a string were typically well recalled, and were relatively uninfluenced by how many commercials followed (that is, there was little retroactive interference). However, the last commercials in a block were poorly recalled, and recall of these was worse the more commercials had preceded (that is, there was proactive interference).

Remote Associations

One description of list learning is that item-to-item associations are formed. Each item in the list serves as a cue for the next. In learning the alphabet, A triggers B, which in turn triggers C, and so on.

Ebbinghaus contrasted item-by-item associations with an alternative hypothesis that **remote associations** are learned among nonadjacent items. The letter A can be associated with C and D, although with less strength than A's association to B. Ebbinghaus tested this notion of "connections at a distance" by first learning one list and then deriving new lists in which successive items had been two, three, or more positions away in the original lists. For example, the list A–B–C–D–E could be transformed to A–C–E–B–D, in which every other item from the first list now follows in the transformed list. This defines a second-degree transformation. A third-degree list would have every third item now follow one another. Ebbinghaus found savings in learning the derived list as compared to original learning, and the amount of savings was a function of the number of steps removed from the original lists.

In remembering material such as prose, poetry, or speeches, lines and phrases in the middle are sometimes forgotten, yet we can recall portions that come later and continue to the end (Rubin, 1977). Remote associations may account for our ability to continue later in the sequence even though some previous sections are forgotten.

Karl Lashley (1951) pointed out that a theory of item-to-item associations would be much too slow to accommodate quick, skilled, and unified behaviors. Lashley argued that there must be earlier anticipation of responses than would occur from the immediately preceding items. He also criticized item-to-item association theory by noting that well-learned items are seemingly grouped, or unitized. An accomplished pianist does not play one note at a time; rather, whole groups of notes are played as if they were a single unit. Listen to children recite the alphabet and hear the groupings: the letters H–I–J–K form one group, and L–M–N–O–P form another.

This grouping notion is captured in Estes's theory of hierarchical associations: Lists or sequences are divided into sections, and those into subsections, and so on (Estes, 1972; Lee & Estes, 1977). For example, at the top of the hierarchy might be the code for "alphabet," the next level codes for segments within the list (e.g., "beginning," "middle," "end"), and the lowest level contains the items within the segment ("A, B, C"). Carrying out a sequential activity involves activating the higher-order code, which then activates the lower-order segments in sequence. The idea is that each single item is not activated via association from the immediately preceding item, but instead all the items contained within a segment are activated. Items within a unit are primed and run off relatively quickly (ABCD), whereas there may be pauses between units (between D and the next segment, EFG).

Serial Learning: A Summary

Serial tasks include learning and recalling items in sequence. Serial-learning phenomena have generated considerable interest, both empirically, for example, in describing the shape of the serial position curve, and theoretically, in terms of explanations of serial position effects, such as interference theory. In addition, the starting point for other research on items that occur in sequence, from television commercials to memory for personal events distributed in time, has been to plot serial memory.

Paired-Associate Learning

The method of paired associates was described in the 1890s by Mary Whiton Calkins, a student of William James, and subsequently president of the American Psychological Association (Madigan & O'Hara, 1992). In **paired-associate learning**, two items are presented for study, labeled stimulus and response (abbreviated S and R). Study trials in which both S and R are presented alternate with test trials in which the stimulus alone is presented and the subject attempts to recall the response. For example, I could pair the stimulus word TABLE with the response AARDVARK; when you next hear TABLE, you should respond with what? AARDVARK, of course. This description of paired-associate learning resembles that of classical conditioning, each having an emphasis on stimulus–response pairings and association learning.

Examples of paired-associate learning abound in our everyday lives. Learning the vocabulary in another language is heavily dependent at first on paired-associate learning: Spanish to English, English to Russian, and so on. So is learning the names of people (see Box 6.2). And don't forget those many hours of your youth spent memorizing multiplication tables.

Box 6.2   Name Learning

Surveys of everyday memory problems always find that forgetting names is a common complaint (e.g., Crook & Larabee, 1990). Why are names so difficult? As with many such questions asked in this book, there is no single answer. To begin with, there is a sort of cognitive helplessness when it comes to remembering names. Because we expect to forget them, we just don't try. Also, names may not receive the kind of attention that other aspects of people receive. A name is spoken, it fades quickly from memory, and it is gone. A face can be continuously inspected while we converse with someone.

Are names in fact unusually difficult to learn? They are in comparison to learning other things about people, such as their occupations or interests. Cohen and Faulkner (1986) presented lists of sentences about fictitious individuals to a sample of older adult subjects (e.g., "In Glasgow a policeman named James Gibson recently won a prize for ballroom dancing"). These sentences list names, places, hobbies, and occupations. On later testing, the names were the least recalled facts. Names and occupations differ along several dimensions. Many names are less familiar, meaningful, or imageable. Interestingly, even if we equate the words used as names and occupations, the names are still poorly learned. In what has been called the Baker/baker paradox, we remember that a person *is* a baker but not that his *name* is Baker (McWeeney, Young, Hay, & Ellis, 1987). In a similar fashion, nurses could recall that a person had Hodgkin's disease or Bell's palsy, but could not remember a person was named Mr. Hodgkin or Ms. Bell (Terry, 1995).

Various mnemonics have been promoted to overcome our name-learning weakness. Names can be made meaningful by trying to relate the names to already known words, or by activating our existing knowledge the way we do to remember other things (e.g., the next time you meet someone named George, think of five things you know about Georges).

Memory-improvement books advocate a technique that is a version of the keyword mnemonic. The trick is to find a verbal link between the person's name and some distinctive facial feature. For example, a dimple in Mr. Wellman's chin could be pictured (in an exaggerated fashion) as a "well." Seeing the well on his chin would then remind us that his name is Wellman. Abstract names could be associated with concrete words that sound like the name: silver for Silber or garden for Gorden. In one study that compared this method to various controls, name recall was maintained better after a 1-week delay (Groninger, Groninger, & Stiens, 1995). Wilson (1987) successfully had her amnesic patients use images to connect names and faces, such as imagining Sue eating soup or Mike speaking into a microphone.

As important as encoding strategies are for name learning, name *retrieval* also needs to be practiced. One mnemonic method, the "name game," encourages frequent retrieval of newly learned names. Given a small group of people, each person gives his or her name. However, the person must also repeat the name of each person who went before him or her in the introductions. Thus, the third person repeats the name of the first two. After the final introduction, the cycle repeats, but now the first person must repeat the names of everyone else. This name game method uses practice at retrieving names from memory. An experimental test of the name game using several hundred students found significant retention even after 11 months (Morris & Fritz, 2000).

In the typical paired-associate learning experiment, several S–R pairs are presented. Calkins herself often used lists of 7 to 12 pairs. The sequence of pairs is varied over trials to prevent serial learning of the responses. Many kinds of materials have been used as stimuli and responses: nonsense syllables, letter or number strings words, pictures, movements, odors, and so on.

Analysis of Paired-Associate Learning

One useful approach to understanding paired-associate learning is to partition it into a series of stages or tasks: stimulus discrimination, response learning, and S–R associating (McGuire, 1961). The stage approach attempts to determine the contribution of certain variables to paired-associate learning.

Stimulus Discrimination

The stimuli used in a paired-associate learning task can vary in their similarity to one another. High similarity can impair paired-associate learning. How can you give the correct response if you can't tell the stimuli apart? In learning a new language, for example, some words may be alike in spelling and pronunciation. The Latin phrases *in vitro* ("in glass") and *in vivo* ("in life") are confusable. In art class, there is the discrimination between the French painters Manet and Monet.

Stimulus discrimination can be facilitated by finding ways to differentiate among the items. When young children are first learning to read, they have a difficult time with similar looking letters: the pairs *b* and *d*, *p* and *q*, and *m* and *n*. Lockhead and Crist's (1980) starting point was that certain typefaces are easier to read than others. Some styles of type are especially elaborated with serifs: a line or a bar at the end of the main strokes of a letter. Serifs contribute to readability by making the letters distinctive. Lockhead and Crist translated this notion into a test of children's ability to discriminate between pairs of similar stimuli. They gave 5-year-olds sets of cards to sort into piles of *b*'s and *d*'s, or *p*'s and *q*'s. In some decks, a distinctive element was added to the letters—for example, a line might pass through the descending arm of the *q*, or a dot might be placed within the *b*'s lower loop (see Figure 6.3). The children were able to sort these letters more quickly and more accurately than those without distinctive markings (i.e., sans serif). Adding distinctive elements might facilitate learning the names of letters, and once learned, the serifs could be gradually faded out.

Response Learning

The ease or difficulty in learning the paired-associate response items can also vary. Again, using our example of learning a new language vocabulary, responding in your native language to foreign word stimuli is easier than learning the foreign language words as the responses. When definitions are to be learned, it is easier to learn the word as a response than to memorize the (usually longer) definition as a response.

Response learning is affected by several factors. Meaningful response items are learned more easily, that is, responses that already have many associations, that are familiar, or that are encountered frequently in language.

Stimulus–Response Associating

The third stage in paired-associate learning is connecting the stimuli and responses (the term most often used is *associated*). The ease of S–R associating is affected by the variables of prior knowledge and cognitive elaboration.

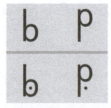

Figure 6.3 Example of Letters Given Distinctive Features

Source: From "Making Letters Distinctive," by G. R. Lockhead and W. B. Crist, 1980, *Journal of Educational Psychology*, *72*, p. 485. Copyright © 1980 by the American Psychological Association. Reprinted with permission.

Prior knowledge could take the form of already existing associations. For example, learning a list of paired associates that contained the pairs TABLE–KITCHEN and WHISTLE–TRAIN would be facilitated by the associations that already exist between these words. (Prior knowledge could inhibit learning if the pairings were TABLE–TRAIN and WHISTLE–KITCHEN.)

S–R associating can also be facilitated by *cognitive elaboration*. Additional information, or elaboration, can help link the stimulus and response terms. In a study by Pressley, McDaniel, Turnure, Wood, and Ahmad (1987), stimulus–response pairs were presented in the form of sentences, such as "the short man bought the broom." The to-be-learned associations are between the actions (e.g., bought a broom or read the sign) and the different men (e.g., the short man or the poor man). For the cognitive elaboration group, an additional phrase was given to suggest a reason why a particular man and action are related. Thus, the short man bought the broom "to sweep out the crawl space." Or, the large man read the sign "warning about thin ice." When tested later with a series of "who" questions (Who read the sign? Who bought the broom?), more person–action sequences were recalled by participants who studied sentences with the elaborations. Cognitive elaboration is a case in which added information is beneficial to remembering.

There are individual differences in paired-associate learning. A learner with a large body of knowledge will be able to retrieve more potential mediators and possibly select the best from among them. This was nicely demonstrated in a study of individual learner's vocabulary and paired-associate learning (Kyllonen, Tirre, & Christal, 1991). The participants were U.S. Air Force recruits in basic training. (The military is interested in the study of learning, and so they sponsor much research.) The researchers found that a good vocabulary predicted ease of learning across a range of study conditions.

Direction of Associations

In the clinical psychological method of free association, a person responds to a stimulus with the first word that comes to mind. Given the stimulus word BUTTER, many people would respond FLY. However, when tested in the reverse sequence, FLY will rarely elicit BUTTER.

Does paired-associate learning also produce a connection in one direction, from stimulus to response? Typically, if subjects are given the response items, recall of the stimulus is much weaker than the forward association that was practiced. The possibility of unidirectional association learning has important implications for academic learning. Studying language vocabulary in one direction, for example, from Spanish to English, does not guarantee recall in the opposite direction, from English to Spanish. Practicing multiplication tables, for example, 8 x 6 = 48, does not ensure that reverse sequences will be available during a division drill, for example, 8 goes into 48 how many times?

Paired-Associate Learning: Putting it all Together

The paired-associate method is an important component in learning vocabulary in a new language. Schneider, Healy, and Bourne (2002) studied the relative contributions of several variables to learning a list of French vocabulary items and their English language translations. One variable was the direction of initial learning: from the French words as stimuli (e.g., BOUCHE and DOIGHT) to their English equivalents (MOUTH and FINGER), or the reverse, from English to French. Examples are shown in the upper sections of Table 6.1. You can probably already guess that the French-to-English direction is easier to learn. The English response words are already known and just need to become connected to the French words. The student needs only to recognize BOUCHE and DOIGHT, not actually produce these words. Unfortunately, there was poor transfer when the students tried to recall in the unstudied direction, from English to French

Table 6.1 Examples of French Vocabulary to Be Learned in Different Directions (French-to-English, or vice versa); and With Blocking or Intermixing of Words From a Common Category

Easier to Learn	Better Retained
French stimuli-to-English responses	*English stimuli-to-French responses*
bouche? (mouth)	mouth? (bouche)
doigt? (finger)	boat? (bateau)
camion? (truck)	truck? (camion)
Blocked Condition	*Intermixed Condition*
bouche – mouth	bouche – mouth
doigt – finger	bateau – boat
camion – truck	doigt – finger
bateau – boat	camion – truck

Source: Adapted from "What Is Learned under Difficult Conditions Is Hard to Forget: Contextual Interference Effects in Foreign Vocabulary Acquisition, Retention, and Transfer," by V. I. Schneider, A. F. Healy, and L. E. Bourne, Jr., 2002, *Journal of Memory and Language*, *46*, 419–440.

(what is French for MOUTH? FINGER?). Schneider et al. (2002) found that initial learning in the English-to-French direction produced better backward recall of the English equivalents.

Vocabulary needs to be remembered over long intervals—longer than the convenient one-hour sessions available with our college student participants. The students who had studied the more difficult English-to-French response pairings also remembered better when tested one week later. The easier task during initial study, learning to say the English translations, did not produce the most enduring knowledge.

Another variable Schneider et al. (2002) studied was whether the vocabulary words were grouped by theme (body parts, foods, clothing items), or were intermixed. Examples of the grouping and intermixing conditions are shown in the lower sections of Table 6.1. Learning was faster when the items are grouped. Students had more difficulty learning the pairings when the categories of BOUCHES and CAMIONS were intermixed. Again, however, ease of learning does not mean better learning. These students were also tested for long-term retention. The more difficult-to-learn intermixed theme pairs produced better retention of the pairs a week later. The general idea from this research is nicely captured by the title of another of this research group's papers: "What is learned under difficult conditions is hard to forget."

Factors Affecting Paired-Associate Learning: A Summary

Paired-associate learning has been described here as a series of steps: learning the responses, discriminating among the stimuli, and associating the responses to the stimuli. Learning is facilitated by creating meaningful S–R relationships and by cognitive elaboration. Recall of the stimulus, given the response, is sometimes poor, but backward associations benefit greatly from practice in recalling the stimulus items.

Free Recall

In **free recall** a list of items is presented and the subject attempts to recall as many of them as possible. Unlike serial learning, ordered recall is not necessary, which is why recall is called *free* (meaning unconstrained). Retention can be tested after a single presentation of a list; or repeated

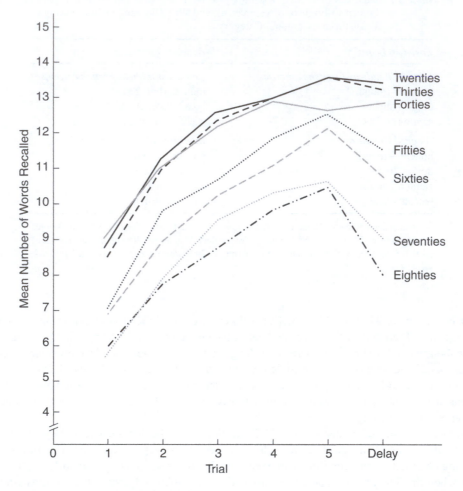

Figure 6.4 Age Effects on Free (unordered) Recall of 15 Word Lists Across Five Presentation and Test Tri-
    als and on a Final Test After a Brief Delay

Source: From "Lexical priming deficits as a function of age," by H. P. Davis et al., (1990), *Behavioral Neuroscience, 104,*
p. 295. Copyright © 1990 by the American Psychological Association. Reprinted with permission.

presentations and tests can be given to assess learning across trials. Multitrial free recall is used
in some standardized tests of learning ability, such as the California Verbal Learning Test (Delis,
Kramer, Kaplan, & Ober, 1987). In this test, a 15-word list is presented, and recall tested, 5 times
in succession. The average number of words recalled can be derived for various groups, by age,
gender, educational level, or medical status. Figure 6.4 shows the average numbers of words
recalled in multitrial free recall as a function of age groupings (Davis & Bernstein, 1992). A
delayed test of memory for the list was given 30 minutes later. College students recalled nearly
9 words on the first trial, and over 13 on the fifth, whereas the oldest participants recalled fewer
than 6 words after the first presentation and only 10 after 5 trials.

   Free recall is one of the most widely used research tasks because it is affected by many variables and many processes that occur during learning. By way of illustration, we can describe
three widely studied factors: serial position, rehearsal, and organization.

Serial-Position Effects

Even though the participants are free to recall the words in any order, we can tabulate recall as a function of each word's position in the list during presentation. Just as with serial-learning tasks, a **serial-position effect** is sometimes found. That is, more words are recalled from the beginning and the end of the list, and fewer words are recalled from the middle. The enhanced recall of the first items in the list is called the **primacy effect**. The enhanced recall of the last items in the list is called the **recency effect**. So, the serial-position effect actually can encompass two subeffects, primacy and recency.

This serial-position effect in free recall is one of the most investigated phenomena in the field of learning. Much of this research has endeavored to dissociate the two end points. Generally different variables affect primacy and recency (see Glanzer, 1972). For instance, recall of the first items (primacy) is increased by a slower rate of presentation of the list items or by using familiar rather than unusual words. Recall of the final items (recency) is enhanced when testing occurs immediately after the list presentation and may be entirely absent if a delay or distraction occurs before recall is tested.

Some of the theoretical explanations offered for the serial-position curve in free recall are similar to those given for serial learning discussed earlier, in particular the roles of position stimuli and interference. Thus, the first and last items may be more accessible to recall because they are associated with their distinctive positions in the lists. Alternatively, both end positions are exposed to less interference from other items (Greene, 1986).

A third explanation actually says that serial-position effects result from the influence of two separate memory systems, long-term memory and short-term memory (Atkinson & Shiffrin, 1968). Primacy is due to the additional rehearsal that the first items receive, thus increasing the likelihood that they have been stored in long-term memory. Recency occurs because the final items are still in short-term memory when testing begins. They are recalled first during output, before forgetting has had a chance to occur. (This dual-memory interpretation of the serial-position effect is discussed further in Chapter 7.)

Rehearsal

As children grow older, they are able to recall more items. The increased recall by older children is especially evident for items at the beginning of a list (Ornstein, Naus, & Liberty, 1975). If primacy is due to the extra rehearsals some items receive, possibly age differences between younger and older children, and between children and adults, are due to differences in the amount or pattern of rehearsal.

In an early study of rehearsal, Keeney, Cannizzo, and Flavell (1967) monitored self-talk of 6- and 7-year-old children. The subjects were shown six photographs of objects. The experimenter pointed to three of the pictures, and after a 15-second delay, the child had to reproduce the sequence. During the experiment the child wore a toy space helmet. The visor would be lowered to prevent the child from seeing the pictures during the delay, and allowed the experimenters to watch unobtrusively for mouth movements indicative of rehearsal. Children who were observed to rehearse also recalled more. In a follow-up phase, the nonrehearsers were instructed to rehearse, and then they also recalled more.

Another study compared recall of 18-word lists by third, sixth, and eighth graders. The left panel of Figure 6.5 shows that most of the age superiority occurred in recall of the first three words of a list—the primacy portion of the curves. Eighth graders recalled more here than did sixth graders, who in turn recalled more than third graders (Ornstein et al., 1975). These children had been instructed to rehearse out loud. (The researchers insightfully realized that the space helmet procedure was not going to work with eighth graders.) The right panel of Figure 6.5

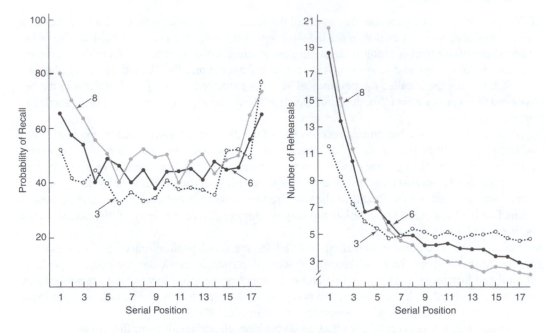

Figure 6.5 Free recall and rehearsal by third, sixth, and eighth graders who were instructed to rehearse out loud. The left bars show the mean number of words recalled; the middle bars show the total number of rehearsals each word received; the right bars show the mean number of distributed rehearsals.

Source: Adapted from "Rehearsal and Organizational Process in Children's Memory," by P. A. Ornstein, M. J. Naus, and C. Liberty, 1975, *Child Development, 46*, pp. 818–830.

shows the number of rehearsals recorded for words at each serial position of the list. Older children rehearsed the first words of the lists more often than did the younger children. In addition, rehearsal patterns differed by age. The younger students simply rehearsed each word as presented, whereas the older students would alternate rehearsal across several items. For example, given the partial list APPLE, HAT, STORY, the younger children would rehearse "apple, apple, hat, hat, hat . . . ," whereas the older kids would rehearse "apple, hat, story, hat. . . ." The latter form of rehearsal, sometimes called *distributed rehearsals* (Modigliani & Hedges, 1987), is more beneficial to learning, possibly because it better interassociates the list items.

Organization

Memory for longer word lists is far from perfect after a single presentation. For example, high school students listened to lists of 12, 24, and 48 words, and remembered about 8, 11, and 15 words, respectively (Tulving & Pearlstone, 1966). The number of words that can be recalled increases dramatically if the words can be organized in some fashion. **Organization** refers to using existing knowledge to group together items that are similar or are related. For example, lists can be constructed so that there are several words from the same semantic category, such as words that name tools, animals, or foods (Mandler, 1967). Organization might also be based on associations (Jenkins & Russell, 1952). If BLACK, TABLE, WHITE, and CHAIR are presented sequentially in a list, the words will likely be recalled in a sequence that pairs the already associated word, such as BLACK–WHITE, TABLE–CHAIR.

Organization increases the number of words recalled. Instead of remembering 15 unrelated words, it is easier to remember 5 categories, each containing 3 related words. Organization might better be labeled reorganization, because the subject changes the organization from that provided by the experimenter to one that the subject imposes. Organization has several effects: It seems to reduce memory load, it influences the sequence in which items are recalled, and it directs memory search during recall.

The power of organization was shown in a study by Bower, Clark, Lesgold, and Winzenz (1969). They employed a multilevel organizational scheme. There were 112 total words from four basic categories (PLANTS, MINERALS, etc.), each of which was further subdivided. For example, MINERALS included STONES and METALS; STONES was further subdivided into MASONRY and PRECIOUS STONES. The students who were shown the hierarchical organization learned and correctly recalled all 112 words after only four study trials. A control group not given the organizational scheme remembered about 70. These results also make the point that it helps to know what the organization is. The control subjects likely perceived that the 112 words were related by some categories, but they had not been shown the complete outline.

What if the lists do not have an organizational scheme? People will tend to impose their own organization on the lists. This *subjective organization* (Tulving, 1962) will vary from person to person, but we can see the unique organization by inspecting output across successive trials. Certain words are recalled together from trial to trial. For example, a list may include the words APPLE, BELL, COFFEE, and SCHOOL. One person might recall BELL and SCHOOL together across several test trials, even though these words are separated in the list. This is that person's subjective organization. Others might recall COFFEE and SCHOOL together.

Organization in Animal Memory

Animals remember related or organized information better, and will even cluster similar items at output. Menzel (1973) tested young chimpanzees in an outdoor enclosure, in which he first showed them the hidden locations of nine pieces of fruit and nine vegetables. Shortly after, he released an animal to retrieve the food. The chimps clustered by food type: They first retrieved the fruit pieces and then went back for the vegetables. Dallal and Meck (1990) tested rats in a maze in which food was placed in different locations, with three different types of foods instead of just one. The rats organized their choices by reward: First, they retrieved the cereal pieces, then the seeds, and so on.

Free Recall: A Summary

The variables that affect free recall of lists show that human learners are not passive participants in our experiments. Serial-position curves can indicate the use of strategies in learning: rehearsing the first items to increase learning, and quickly reporting the last items before they fade from memory. Rehearsal, which develops during childhood, enhances recall and indicates a conscious attempt to remember. Finally, participants attempt to organize to-be-recalled lists, grouping items on the basis of associations or meaning to facilitate retention.

Available Memories Versus Accessible Memories

As noted earlier, the significant contribution of Ebbinghaus's savings test is that it can show the presence of memory that cannot be recalled. Tulving and Pearlstone (1966) elaborated on Ebbinghaus's idea with their distinction between available and accessible memories. **Available memories** are those present in the memory. As we well know, not everything in memory can be recalled. **Accessible memories** are those that can actually be recalled or retrieved. This distinction should be readily appreciated by students: It is the difference between knowing the material for the exam (it is available) and being able to recall it during the exam (it is accessible). Too often, it seems, learned information is not accessible during the exam, but is recalled after the test has been turned in. The distinction also applies to the *tip-of-the-tongue* experience (Brown & McNeil, 1966). You are searching for a name or a word, and you know that you know it, but you just can't recall it right then. The item is temporarily inaccessible. The lost word will come to mind later, showing that the word was available in memory all along.

How can we probe memory to retrieve those currently inaccessible items? Alternative means of testing may offer more sensitive measures of what has been learned, methods such as cued recall, recognition testing, or relearning.

Cued Recall

A direct method to facilitate access to unrecalled information is to provide additional retrieval cues to prompt memory. In **cued recall** a cue or prompt is presented to aid recall of a specific item from memory. For example, in assessing memory for a categorized list of words, category names can be given to cue recall. In Tulving and Pearlstone's (1966) study, participants first recalled as many of the 48 words from a categorized list as possible. During a second recall attempt, the category names were given, and these helped to retrieve additional unrecalled categories of words. (A student might be given the cue CITIES and then recalls a few cities from the list.) The effect of category name prompting indicates that more was available in memory than was accessed by free recall.

Given the advantage of cued recall, one might assume that the more cues the better, right? If either TABLE or SOFA helps to retrieve the target word CHAIR, both cues should help even more. Unfortunately, there can be such a thing as too many cues. In one study, participants studied lists of categorized words. During testing, the category names and some of the list items from that category were given. All that the participants had to do was recall the remaining words from that category! But the participants actually recalled fewer remaining items than if the extra cues had not been provided (Roediger, 1973). As memory is searched during testing, the cue words, which are currently the strongest traces in memory, compete with retrieval of the remaining words, and bottle up the retrieval process. A cue word comes to mind, but then the more you search, the more that cue word keeps popping up, blocking retrieval of the sought-after word.

Recall Versus Recognition Versus Relearning

A **recall test** requires the subject to reproduce, or recall, the studied information. A **recognition test** assesses memory by presenting studied items, along with unstudied or distractor items, to see if the previously studied item can be identified. Does the subject recognize which items were presented earlier? In a **relearning test**, the initially studied material is relearned and the amount of savings is assessed. Do these different testing formats differ in their sensitivity to detect learning? We need to be careful in comparing these methods, because each produces a different type of measurement. Simply put, recalling 50 percent of the items is not the same as a 50 percent savings (i.e., taking half as many trials to relearn the list).

These several measures were used in a study in which college professors tried to remember their former students' names (Bahrick, 1984b). Faculty members were given tests of name recall to students' pictures, name recognition, and savings in relearning names-to-faces, in comparison to new names and faces as controls. The students were from classes from different semesters, ranging from courses just completed to some 8 years earlier. Bahrick's results are shown in Figure 6.6. Professors were pretty poor at recalling students' names from their photos. Faculty members were much better at recognizing names and pictures of former students, and in matching

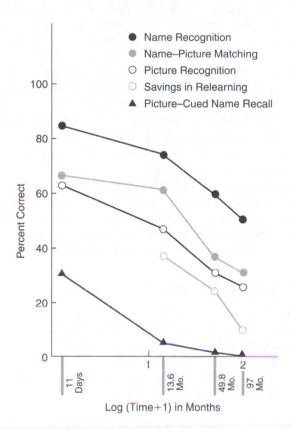

Figure 6.6 **College Professors' Memory for Their Students.** Name recognition, picture recognition, recall of names to student's photos, name and photo matching, and relearning of names to student photos.

Source: From "Memory for People," by H. P. Bahrick, in *Everyday Memory, Actions, and Absentmindedness* (p. 27), edited by J. E. Harris and P. E. Morris, 1984, New York: Academic Press. Copyright © 1984 by Academic Press. Reprinted with permission.

names to pictures. In this case, recognition and savings were superior to recall. Bahrick says that more is available in memory than is accessible with certain forms of testing. It is also of interest that forgetting apparently occurred within 11 days of the end of the semester!

Nelson (1978) used a different procedure to compare the several methods of assessing retention. College students learned lists of number–word pairs and were tested 4 weeks later. During the test session, first the stimuli were presented to see which responses could be recalled. Many were unrecalled, as expected after a month-long delay. Responses that could not be recalled were then tested by matching recognition: The participants attempted to match each response with the correct stimulus. Responses that were matched incorrectly were then relearned and compared to learning of new pairs. Nelson found that items that could not be recalled were sometimes recognized; and items that were neither recalled nor recognized showed savings during relearning. This suggests that the several tests could be ranked: The relearning test was more sensitive than the recognition test, which in turn detected more than the recall test.

The difference between recall and recognition is illustrated by a comparison of the two methods in a study of Alzheimer's and age-matched control subjects (Shimamura, Salmon, Squire, & Butters, 1987). Alzheimer's disease produces ongoing memory problems, as exemplified by the forgetting of daily events seemingly as they occur. Lists of 15 words were presented and tested. One list was tested by the method of free recall, the other by recognition. After a single presentation, the Alzheimer's subjects recalled about 15 percent of the words, whereas age-matched control subjects recalled 40 percent. On testing recognition, the Alzheimer's subjects were over 60 percent correct and the controls about 85 percent. Thus, this study demonstrates two major effects: Both control and Alzheimer's participants recognized more words than could be freely recalled, and control subjects did better than the Alzheimer's subjects on both sorts of tasks.

One interpretation of the recall–recognition difference is that recognition is a more sensitive test: recognition can detect weak learning that a recall test does not. This may be why students commonly believe that multiple-choice tests are easier than essay exams. Recognizing the correct answer is thought to be easier than recalling it.

An alternative interpretation is that the effectiveness of any type of test depends on its ability to reinstate the original context in which the material was learned (Tulving & Thompson, 1973). Maybe recognition testing is better at reinstating the original context and meaning. However, even recognition may fail if the item does not retrieve the original context. The idea is analogous to being unable to identify a familiar actor who plays a different role in a new setting.

Recognition: Remembering Versus Knowing

Recognition is rooted in judgment. We decide that something is familiar on the basis of several types of memory evidence. When shown a list of students' names, the college professors tested in Bahrick's (1984b) study could have specifically remembered certain students. Maybe details about the students' level of class participation and other personal facts were recalled. On the other hand, a name might have looked or sounded familiar, without having any specific memory or image to back up that feeling. This example illustrates a judgment based on **remembering** versus just **knowing**.

To conduct an experiment on remembering versus knowing, we would first present a list of words for our subjects to study. Then we would give them a recognition test: studied items are intermixed with plausible distractors. In a standard recognition test, we would ask the participants to check off which items they had seen earlier. Here we would also ask the participants why they checked off each item: Did they remember something about it from studying it, or did they just know it was among the studied items?

What is the basis for a "know" judgment? An item might simply engender a feeling of familiarity. Or we make a judgment because we recall the answer quickly or effortlessly. Unfortunately, that may not provide enough justification for remembering. This is illustrated by studies of the *false fame* effect (Jacoby, Woloshyn, & Kelley, 1989). Fabricated names (PETER TERRY, for instance) were presented without instructions to remember them. Later the subjects saw a list of names and were asked to identify which were names of famous people. The participants sometimes misidentified names encountered earlier as those of famous people. "Peter Terry? Sounds familiar, but I can't place him. Must be famous." This is a "know" judgment, not a "remember" judgment.

In academic learning, we can have both remember and know types of memories. We might remember a lecture or class discussion of a topic or idea. There are also words and phrases in our major disciplines that we just seem to know, without recalling specifically how, when, or where we learned them. Conway, Gardiner, Perfect, Anderson, and Cohen (1997) found that among their better college students (i.e., those who scored well on an end-of-year exam), there was a high frequency of remembering-type responses shortly after learning. The students could remember the context in which a term had been encountered. When tested months later, more items from the remember category had shifted to the know category. These good students now just knew this information.

Implicit Learning

Implicit tests can present evidence for memory that explicit testing, such as instructions to recall or recognize previously studied items, do not. **Implicit learning** refers to learning that seemingly occurs without awareness or intention to learn. Often the knowledge cannot be verbally described. Even if you cannot remember your credit card number, notice how quickly you can type it after all that practice. Instead of requesting explicit verbal recall from our subjects, implicit learning might be shown by their faster or more skilled performance of a task.

Paired-associate learning can be demonstrated implicitly using a word-fragment completion task. The subjects are shown a series of word pairs, such as BOOK–FOREST. The subjects are not instructed that this is a learning or memory task. Sometime later, the subjects are given a string of letters and blanks and asked to complete each with the first word that comes to mind. The instructions make no reference to the previously seen words. Some of the word fragments are presented with the same words they were previously paired with, e.g., BOOK–FOR_ _ _, whereas other fragments now appear with different words, for example, WINDOW–FOR_ _ _. Implicit learning of the new association is shown when the fragments are more often completed with the studied response word in the same-cue condition than in the different-cue condition. The idea is that the previously seen cue word primes the response word that had been paired with it.

Because college students are likely to notice that the study and fragment lists are the same, this procedure may not be a pure test of implicit learning (Bowers & Schacter, 1990; Graf & Schacter, 1989). A stronger case for implicit associations can be made by testing amnesic individuals who do not consciously remember the study list. Nevertheless the amnesics complete the fragments with words from the study list (Graf, Squire, & Mandler, 1984).

Is an implicit test of learning simply a more sensitive test of knowledge? The indication instead is that implicit learning represents a different form of learning from the deliberate forms of learning we have otherwise been discussing in this chapter. The evidence for a distinction between implicit learning and explicit learning is presented in detail in Chapters 7 and 11.

Relationships Among the Verbal-Learning Tasks

Do serial learning, paired-associate learning, and free recall all tap the same underlying processes? Does proficiency at one ensure ability in the others? Underwood, Boruch, and Malmi (1978) tested 200 undergraduates on 28 different memory tasks, which were spread across 10 sessions. Several versions of each verbal-learning procedure were included. For example, free recall was tested with lists of imageable words, abstract words, associatively related words, and categorically organized words. The statistical procedure of factor analysis was used to determine which tests were correlated. Underwood and colleagues found that paired-associate learning and serial-learning tests were positively correlated: Individuals tended to do well on both types of tests, poorly on both, or average on both. This suggests that paired-associate and serial learning are similar. One possibility is association learning, between stimulus and response or among items in a list. Free-recall performance was statistically separate. That is, performance on serial learning or paired associates was unrelated to free recall. Unlike paired-associate and serial learning, which are typically multitrial learning tasks, free recall is usually single-trial. This suggests that the capacity to remember once-presented information may be separable from multitrial learning.

The correlational approach is used to determine whether verbal learning is a single ability or process, or involves multiple processes. The evidence suggests that, even among these simple learning tasks, different abilities or strategies are being tapped.

Do these laboratory tests predict the ability to remember in the real world? Kurtz-Costes, Schneider, and Rupp (1995) tested 5- to 9-year-olds with tasks meant to simulate everyday remembering, school-related memory, or traditional laboratory tests of memory. For example, list recall could be measured in the "shopping game," in which the children had to remember a list of items to get in the "store" across the room. Recall could also be measured by the more standard task of presenting and testing recall of a list of words. "Geography" was a school-related paired-associate task, requiring remembering facts about different countries. Learning names and faces was considered an everyday paired-associates task. The researchers found that there were low correlations among the several tasks; good performance on an everyday simulation was unrelated to performance on a school-related or laboratory task. There was little evidence of consistency across tasks within individuals. That is, a child's remembering would vary from one paired-associate test (remembering names/faces) to a second (remembering countries and products) to a third (remembering arbitrarily chosen stimulus and response words in the laboratory task). Kurtz-Costes et al. suggest that the child's use of strategies, such as whether to rehearse or not, can vary with the familiarity of the material and the child's knowledge base. Any one test might not be representative of what the child could potentially remember.

Statistical Learning

The world is full of uncertainties. Any given stimulus might lead to several outcomes; and any given outcome might be due to many potential causes. However, the world is also full of regularities. Through experience we abstract the probability that X leads to Y, or X never occurs with Y. In **statistical learning** associations, rules, or algorithms are acquired through experience that reflects actual consistent patterns experienced in the world. Statistical learning is a factor in several forms of learning, such as causal learning (discussed in Chapter 3), propositional learning, and language learning.

Propositional Learning

By the end of a conditioning experiment, our human subjects can often describe the relationships among the stimuli, responses and outcomes that they have experienced. These relationships can be stated in the form of propositions, or facts: a tone signals reward; a key press leads to points. Psychologists have developed several verbal learning paradigms with which to study conditioning-like phenomena. These methods are labeled **propositional learning** here.

The general procedure for investigating propositional learning is to present a number of different stimuli and outcomes. These occur in the form of a game or set of problems for the subject to discover what leads to what. For instance, in a food allergy scenario sentences are presented in which a food item (such as strawberry) is paired with an allergic reaction (such as hives) or no reaction. Across trials, the subjects learn which allergic reaction occurs with each food. There is an obvious parallel here to classical conditioning, in which a CS (the tone) is followed by a US (the food). And indeed, some propositional research questions have parallels in conditioning experiments.

The purpose of studying propositional learning studies is not just to avoid running rats. It is used to answer questions about learning from experience with various combinations of stimuli and outcomes. In particular, we can compare an associative theory of learning to a cognitive theory. The traditional associative theory says that pairings of the stimuli (foods and allergies) lead to the formation of associations between the two stimuli. Across trials there is growth in the strength of the association. Associative theory does not require conscious awareness of these associations.

The cognitive theory asserts that learning is the acquisition of propositions or beliefs about the relationship among events. These propositions can be combined to make inferences, in a form of logic, to derive new beliefs. For instance, if strawberries and cream are eaten and hives occur as a

Table 6.2 Example of Propositional Learning Experiment to Demonstrate Integration of Knowledge Across Phases

Condition	Phase 1	Phase 2	Subject's Belief
Control	(A+B) → reaction		Either A or B is cause
Blocking	A → reaction	(A+B) → reaction	A causes reaction
Retrospective Evaluation	(A + B) → reaction	B → reaction	B causes reaction

reaction, we might think either of the foods is the cause. However, when cream alone is presented without a reaction, the inferred proposition is that it was the strawberries that caused hives.

An influential finding in classical conditioning is the **blocking effect** (Chapter 3). In a control condition, when two foods (A and B) are followed by an allergic reaction, the subject believes that each is a possible cause of the allergic reaction (see Table 6.2). The subjects are asked to rate, maybe on a 100-point scale, how likely each stimulus is the cause of the reaction. In this case, foods A and B receive the same ratings. Either could be the cause. In the blocking condition, food A by itself is paired with the allergic reaction during Phase 1 of training. In Phase 2, A and B are presented simultaneously and the allergic reaction occurs. In this case, the Phase 1 association of A with the allergic reaction blocks learning an association between B and the allergy. In Phase 2, food A is rated as a stronger cause.

Propositional logic is shown by a third condition. In retrospective evaluation, A+B trials occur in the first phase. The subject believes that either could cause an allergic reaction, just as in the control condition. Then during Phase 2, trials with B and the reaction occur. Now the subject reevaluates and concludes that B alone must be the cause of the allergies, and that A had nothing to do with it (Shanks, 2010).

Statistical Language Learning

Language is determined by both nature and nurture. The specific language each of us uses is learned, and there are biological adaptations of brain and voice that allow speech. Previous generations of learning psychologists tried to explain language as simply an instrumental response: certain sounds made by the infant were reinforced, and eventually speech develops.

Contemporary research focuses on a statistical approach to language development in pre-verbal infants. Regularities occur in language at several levels. On the phonological level, certain sounds follow one another in the formation of words. In English the sound of the letters CH is often followed by an O or U, but not by an S or F. On a grammatical level, certain categories of words regularly precede other categories. Adjectives such as LARGE precede nouns such as DOG but not verbs such as CHASE.

Analysis of the sound spectrum shows that words often run together in speech. From (what sounds like) a continuous stream of speech, infants learn to identify individual sounds. Although there are spaces between written words, there are not silent-spaces between spoken words. In fact, silences often occur within words. In the spoken word SILENCE there is a gap in the sounds between the *si-* and the *-lence*. How do infants learn the individual words from this sort of input?

The regularities of spoken language can be simulated by exposing infants to an artificial language. In one study, eight-month-old infants were exposed to fabricated three-syllable words such as DAROPI and GOLATU. The words occurred in a continuous stream lasting several minutes. There were no pauses or gaps between words, and no stress or intonation in the syllables. To determine whether the infants had learned the sequences of syllables, individual words were played and the listening time was measured. Old words, such as DAROPI, were compared to new nonwords, such as PIGOLA (the PI from DAROPI and the GOLA from GOLATU), which had not occurred together as a word. The infants listened longer to the novel sound combinations, indicating that the nonwords were recognized as different from the familiar words. Similarly, the children listened longer to new syllable pairs that spanned words, such as TUDA, than pairs that had been within words, such as GOLA (Saffran, Aslin, & Newport, 1996).

Similar methods are used to study the learning of regularities at the grammatical level. In English, the words THE or A are likely to be followed by a noun (DOG) and not by a verb (WENT). Infants more easily learned nonsense languages in which these grammatical regularities were present than when the absent (Saffran, 2009).

Fast Mapping

There are other factors that affect language learning. How do we learn what individual words refer to? The notion of association formation suggests that people learn to associate the names of things with the objects themselves. Infants hear "dog" at the same time that they see a dog. Word learning is slow at first, but with experience learning becomes faster. Children develop the capacity to learn the names of objects after a single pairing. The idea of *fast mapping* takes learning a step further: if a new word and a new object occur together, by inference the new word must be the name of the new object. This is fast mapping: quickly inferring new words as labels to new objects, action, or events.

Although we could cite examples of fast mapping in human infants, there are impressive demonstrations in dogs. Border collies have been taught name-object associations by having the dogs retrieve the named objects. Learning at first was gradual, spread out over several years of daily practice. Rico had by then learned 200 object names, and Chaser knew 1,000 names (Kaminski, Call, & Fischer, 2004; Pilley & Reid, 2011). The dogs were then tested with the presentation of one new object among a number of already-named objects. The experimenters asked the dogs to retrieve the unfamiliar object, using a new word ("bring me the PIGOLA"). This required the dogs to infer that the new word must refer to the new object. Both dogs were able to do this on multiple tests using novel words and objects. After a single presentation and test, the new names were usually forgotten within a day. As with the previously learned words, practice was necessary for the dog to permanently retain the new names.

Application: Mnemonics

Mnemonics are various techniques or strategies that aid encoding and retrieval. Students are familiar with first-letter and *acronym* mnemonics: remembering a list of things by their first letters. For example, the first letter of each of the Great Lakes makes the acronym HOMES. First-letter mnemonics can encode both items and their order. In the past, we had a sentence that helped us to remember the planets: "My very earnest mother just served us nine. . ." but then astronomers dropped Pluto (or "pizzas" as the final word in the mnemonic). Prior to the invention of the printing press, epic tales such as the Iliad were transmitted orally for hundreds of years. In the European Middle Ages, elaborate schemes, often based on imagery, were devised to organize, store, and retrieve whole books of information. "Memory was needed by the entertainer, the poet, the singer, the physician, the lawyer, and the priest" says the historian Daniel J. Boorstin (1983, p. 482).

Verbal Mnemonics

The *keyword method* was developed by Atkinson and Raugh (1975) to aid foreign-language acquisition. The idea is to find a mediating word to link to-be-associated words. In learning Russian–English vocabulary, for example, a mediating word is chosen that sounds like the

Russian word, but that can also be visualized interacting with the English translation. The Russian word for "bell" is *zvonok*, pronounced "zuahn-oak," which sounds like the English word "oak," and so oak can be the mediating word. One can imagine an oak tree containing "bells" instead of acorns.

College student subjects using the keyword method learned nearly twice as many Russian vocabulary words as did control subjects on the first study day. The keyword subjects were still superior after 3 days of practice (Atkinson & Raugh, 1975). Similarly, school-aged children who were studying Spanish as a second language learned twice as many vocabulary words as did controls (Pressley & Dennis-Rounds, 1980). However, keyword-trained participants were poor in backward recall from English back to the Spanish words.

Other school-related materials can be adapted to the paired-associate format, such as linking the names of famous people with their accomplishments (Jones & Hall, 1982) and cities with their products (Pressley & Dennis-Rounds, 1980).

A mnemonic for remembering lists of words is the *narrative story method* (Bower & Clark, 1969). The idea is to make up a story that includes each word in sequence. For example, the following student-generated sentence includes six to-be-remembered words (capitalized): a LUMBERJACK DARTed out of a forest, SKATEd around a HEDGE past a COLONY of DUCKs. College student participants studied 12 lists of 10 words each. One group was instructed in the narrative procedure, and the other group was simply told to memorize the list. When each list was studied and tested immediately, both groups did equally well, which is no surprise given the level of ability of the participants (Stanford undergraduates). The interesting results occurred at the end of the session, when the students were given only the first word of each list and were asked to recall the rest in the correct order. The narrative subjects remembered about 93 percent of the words, whereas the control subjects recalled only 13 percent.

Imagery Mnemonics

Most mnemonic systems are based on visual imagery. The *method of loci*, or *locations*, is an ancient mnemonic based on imagery. It is sometimes described as taking a mental walk. In the method of locations, you first learn a fixed series of places. You must be able to readily form an image of each, and mentally go through the locations in the same sequence each time. Later, when you have a list of things to remember, you mentally follow the route, imagining a to-be-recalled item at each location. When you want to recall the list, you rewalk the route and look to see what is stored at each location. In medieval times, scholars were said to recall thousands of facts by locations spread through churches, theaters, or even cities (Yates, 1966).

Another imagery technique is the *peg word* system. As with the method of locations, the first step is to memorize a series of images. In this case, the numbers 1 to 10 and their rhymes are the pegs on which to-be-recalled items will be imagined. Thus, "one is a bun, two is a shoe, three is a tree," and so on. Later, the to-be-remembered items are imagined interacting with the pegs. As with the method of locations, the peg-word system allows recall of the list starting from either end, or for individual items. What was the sixth item in the list? Well, six is sticks, so what image is stored with sticks?

Our everyday theories about distinctiveness suggest that bizarre or unusual images would be well remembered. Generally, this is true with the imagery mnemonics. However, bizarre images might not be effective in paired-associate learning (Einstein, McDaniel, & Lackey, 1989). It can be difficult to reinstate what you had associated with the bizarre stimulus. A similar rule applies to storing objects in unusual places: The association of objects and their locations is worse when unusual locations are chosen (see Box 6.3).

Box 6.3   Forgetting the Location of Stored Objects

One particularly annoying lapse of everyday memory is forgetting where you put something. Items that have some value to us, such as keys, jewelry, or important documents are likely to be put in special places to ensure future access or to hide the objects from others. A certain logic prevails at the time that makes us think this location will be readily remembered. But, of course, weeks or months later, this logic cannot be reconstructed and the object remains lost. Winograd and Soloway (1986) cited a friend who put his passport in a suitcase pouch. This seemed to make eminent sense, except that their friend could not remember this and only stumbled on the lost passport long after it had been replaced.

Based on their survey of people's actual experiences with hiding objects, Brown and Rahhal (1994) characterized the typical situation as one in which the person hid a valuable object, began searching a month afterwards, searched four times over a two-week period, and eventually found the object accidentally. Half of the time the object's hiding place had been searched; obviously not very effectively.

Winograd and Soloway (1986) asked their participants to imagine in what locations they would hide a series of items. In paired-associate terminology, the objects were the stimuli (e.g., a camera) and the locations were the responses (in the closet). Both likely and unlikely hiding places were used (e.g., hide the camera in the closet or under the couch). When the subjects were tested a few minutes later, there was already significant forgetting for the unusual locations of objects. Even people who strongly believed that the unusual locations were more memorable still recalled only half as many objects in unusual as in usual locations.

Why do we forget unusual locations for objects? Winograd and Soloway say we mistakenly apply a "distinctiveness" principle of memory. We believe that distinctive is better remembered than plain and common. But distinctiveness applies to memory for individual items, such as objects *or* locations, but not necessarily to the connection between the object *and* its location. Thinking of either item alone (the camera or the couch) may not be sufficient to retrieve an atypical association to the other item. (Your association between TABLE and CHAIR will be much stronger than the unusual association between TABLE and AARDVARK that I gave earlier in this chapter. Although AARDVARK is a bizarre and distinctive item, fat chance you will remember it 6 months later as an associate to TABLE.) Putting objects in unusual places is an instance where everyday beliefs about memory prove to be incorrect.

Object locations are forgotten for other reasons. Absentmindedness occurs when we put something down while our attention is directed elsewhere. Objects are also lost because we make *updating* errors. Where did I leave something last, as opposed to the location before that? The changing nature of knowledge sets up ideal conditions for interference.

A contemporary parallel to misplacing objects is misplacing electronic files (e-files). Where did I save that picture, document, or password? One survey of college students found that most had misplaced e-files (Mammes & Terry, 2013). Typically, the file had been placed in a location that the student thought would be remembered, although 24 percent forgot they had stored the file on another device. The file was often found in a location previously searched, as occurs with misplacing physical objects. Misplacing was often caused by not placing the e-file in its usual location, or giving the file a name that was not recognized later.

Although men out-perform women on certain tests of spatial memory, Silverman and Eals (1992) reported an exception in which women were better at recalling the locations of objects. In their study, individual subjects were left in a waiting room for several minutes. The subjects were then ushered into the experiment room and told the real purpose of the study, which was to recall everything they had seen in the waiting room. The women recalled more of the objects than the men, and they were more accurate about where the objects had been located.

Analysis of Imagery Mnemonics

What are the essential components of a mnemonic system such as the peg-word or location method? Bower (1970) reviewed the research findings with respect to these two, and noted the following features:

1. There is a known list of cues that need to be present at encoding and at retrieval.
2. Imagery that is unusual, bizarre, or striking is better.
3. The cues used at recall must be the same as those thought of while studying.
4. Multiple items can be stored at each location or with each peg.
5. Surprisingly, the systems are reusable with little interference from trial to trial.

Do mnemonic systems really work? A simple answer is "yes"; they can be quite effective. In one experimental comparison, three imagery techniques (location, peg-word, and linking items in an image) were used to memorize 20-word lists. The college students recalled more one day later than did control subjects who were told to simply rehearse each word, or form a mental image of each (Roediger, 1980). The results of one test are shown in Figure 6.7. The data here are words recalled in the correct serial position. These results show that the method of location and the peg-word system produced better recall of items in sequence.

A more complex answer is that different mnemonic systems may work better for different memory tasks. Herrmann (1987) found that for paired-associate learning, linking images (as is used in the keyword method) was the most effective. For free-recall tasks, in which order of recall is not important, the narrative story method was superior. For serial recall of items in sequence, the narrative method and the method of locations were best.

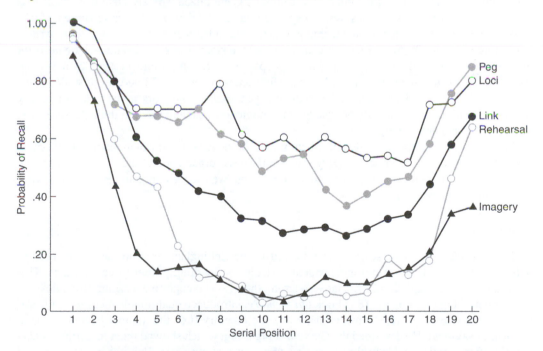

Figure 6.7 **Serial Recall of 20-Word Lists as a Function of Several Mnemonic Strategies.** Strategies are rehearsal (repeat each word), imagery (vividly picture each word), a linking story, the peg-word system, and the method of loci (locations).

Source: From "The Effectiveness of Four Mnemonics in Ordering Recall," by H. L. Roediger, 1980, *Journal of Experimental Psychology: Human Learning and Memory, 6*, p. 565. Copyright 1980 by the American Psychological Association. Reprinted with permission.

Joshua Foer was a recent college graduate, working as a journalist, and living in his parents' basement. He had written an article about memory competitions, informally referred to as Memory Olympics. Each participant competes in tasks such as memorizing poetry, the first and last names of 100 faces, or random strings of digits (the winner learned 148 numbers in five minutes.)

Foer decided to enter himself. He spent a year in full-time training, and consulted with experts in psychology and mnemonics. The mnemonics systems used by the mental athletes are far more sophisticated than the first-letter or narrative chaining techniques described earlier in this section. The methods mostly use imagery, which can encode letters or numbers; and locations, which will guide the rememberer correctly through the sequence. Foer's major "event" in the Olympics was memorizing the sequence of a deck of cards. He used a version of the method of locations, combined with a multi-level imagery system that encoded three cards at a time. Thus, the title of his book, *Moonwalking with Einstein* (Foer, 2011), was one of the images. Foer did in fact win the USA Championships with his record score of learning the card deck in 1 minute and 40 seconds.

One of the important lessons from this demonstration is that almost anyone can develop an exceptional memory skill. The capacity is not genetic, not IQ, and not pharmacologically aided. Another lesson is that the ability is task specific. Foer says he is no better at remembering everyday things than he as before training.

So, who really uses mnemonics? Generations of college and professional students have used first-letter mnemonics to remember lists of facts, from memorizing the 12 cranial nerves (On Old Olympia's Towering Tops, A Finn and German Vault and Hop) to ROY G BIV (the colors of the visible spectrum). Nursing students use acronyms such as RICE for the treatment for a sprain (rest, ice, compress, and elevate; Beitz, 1997). Psychology majors have mnemonics for the symptoms of various mental disorders. For example, Generalized Anxiety Disorder is coded as FIRST: fatigue, irritability, restlessness, sleep disturbance, and tension (Reeves & Bullen, 1995).

Whatever their value, mnemonic techniques take time to learn and use. It is simpler to write a list before going to the store. Electronic aids such as the smartphone have replaced the need for mnemonic systems. Surveys show that most people use external reminders, such as notes and lists. The only true mnemonic reported was the first-letter mnemonic: 73 percent of students had used it recently (e.g., Harris, 1980). A survey of psychologists who work in the field of memory research found that even they do not use the mnemonic devices they teach in their classes (Park, Smith, & Cavanaugh, 1990).

Perhaps the contemporary value of mnemonic techniques is in their demonstration of which variables most affect learning: imagery, meaningfulness, organization, and retrieval cues. We may not use formal mnemonic systems to remember, but we use the components in smaller ways in everyday remembering.

Summary

Verbal learning refers to research that followed in the Ebbinghaus tradition and that seeks to determine the effects of certain independent variables on learning primarily verbal items. This research uses both behavioral associative learning theories and cognitive learning strategies.

Herman Ebbinghaus, in his 1885 book *On Memory*, introduced quantifiable measures of learning (i.e., the number of repetitions to criterion) and memory (i.e., the number of repetitions to relearn, or savings). He described the Curve of Forgetting, which showed most forgetting occurs shortly after learning, with further losses occurring at a slower rate. Ebbinghaus also devised new learning materials (the nonsense syllable) and introduced methods of experimental control in his research.

Three basic tasks have been developed to study verbal learning: serial learning, paired-associate learning, and free recall.

Serial Learning

In serial learning, a list of items is presented in a fixed order on each trial, and the subject is required to reproduce items in order. The serial-position of items within the list influences learning, as the first and last items in the sequence are learned more quickly than are the middle items.

Item-to-item associations in a list are learned, and remote associations are acquired between separated items. The theory of hierarchical associations says that serial lists are divided into sections, and those into subsections, and so on. Rather than each single item being activated via association from the immediately preceding item, all the items contained within a segment are activated.

Paired-Associate Learning

In paired-associate learning, two items are presented for study, labeled stimulus and response (abbreviated S and R). The task is to recall the response when presented with the stimulus alone. Paired-associate learning can be analyzed into the components of stimulus discrimination, response learning, and S–R associating.

The stimuli used in a paired-associate learning task may be similar, causing interference. Learning will be faster if the stimuli are made more discriminable from one another, for example, by adding distinctive features.

Response learning is affected by the difficulty in learning the response items. Meaningfulness, familiarity, and prior knowledge will facilitate response learning.

Associating the stimulus with the response is affected by preexisting associations among items in the to-be-learned set and by cognitive elaboration. For example, generating a mediator to relate stimulus and response will facilitate association.

Paired-associate connections are typically stronger in the studied stimulus-to-response direction, and are weaker in the backward direction of recalling the stimulus when given the response.

Free Recall

In free recall, a list of items is presented and the subject attempts to recall as many of them as possible. Unlike serial-learning procedures, ordered recall is not necessary.

One of the most-studied features of free recall is the serial-position effect. Enhanced recall of the first items in a list, or primacy, is often attributed to the additional rehearsal that the first items receive. Enhanced recall of the last items in a list, or recency, occurs because these items are often recalled first before forgetting has had a chance to occur.

Free recall is influenced by rehearsal or repeating the items until they are tested. Rehearsal shows a developmental progression in children. Rote repetition is not as effective as some sort of elaborative rehearsal, which seeks meaning or associations among the to-be-remembered items.

Free recall improves if the material can be organized, that is, if items can be grouped. Categorical organization occurs when items from the same semantic category are grouped together at output. Subjective organization occurs when subjects devise their own grouping of items and is detected by analyzing the sequence of recalled items across successive tests.

Do serial learning, paired-associate learning, and free recall tap the same underlying learning processes? Correlational studies suggest that there are different abilities or strategies involved instead of a single verbal-learning ability. Do these laboratory tests predict everyday remembering? The correlations are generally low, but this may be because laboratory and everyday memory tasks differ in kind, interest levels, and ecological relevance.

Available Versus Accessible Memories

Ebbinghaus showed that something could be present in memory even if it could not be recalled. This is the distinction between availability and accessibility. Available memories are those present in the memory store, whereas accessible memories are those that can actually be recalled or retrieved. This distinction is illustrated by the tip-of-the-tongue phenomenon, in which you know that you know a word or name but you can't recall it right now. Presenting additional memory prompts during cued recall makes more information accessible. Cue overload occurs when too many prompts actually block recall of an item that otherwise would have been remembered.

How do tests of recall, recognition, and relearning differ in their sensitivity to available memories? Items that are not recalled are sometimes recognized, and savings occurs for items that are neither recalled nor recognized correctly. Tests of implicit memory, such as word-fragment completion, detect memory in amnesic individuals who otherwise do poorly on recall and recognition tests of explicit memory. Recall, recognition, and implicit memory may differ in sensitivity to detecting memory, or they may be assessing different aspects of what is remembered.

Statistical Learning

Statistical learning describes the strength of individual relationships among stimuli, responses, and outcomes that have been experienced. The relationships can be stated in the form of *propositions* or factual statements. Statistical learning applies to causal, propositional, and language learning. One theoretical use is to compare associative and cognitive explanations of learning. For instance, in a blocking design, the (hypothetical) pairing of food A with an allergic reaction blocks later learning that an added food B might also be a cause of the allergy. In retrospective evaluation, presenting A and the allergic reaction after the AB pairing will lead to the inference that A, and not B, is the cause of the allergy.

The statistical approach to language acquisition in preverbal infants focuses on the regularities that occur in language at several levels: phonological, word, and grammatical. Studies of learning artificial languages show that regularities at each level are detected and learned.

Mnemonics

Mnemonic techniques or strategies aid encoding and retrieval, such as using the first letters to form an acronym for the to-be-remembered items. In the keyword mnemonic, first developed to assist learning foreign-language vocabulary, a mediating word is chosen to link the to-be-associated words. In the narrative chaining method, a string of unrelated words are connected through a made-up story. In the method of loci, or locations, items are imaged in certain locations along a fixed mental route. Mnemonics work because there is a list of cues that the to-be-recalled items are associated with during study and that can be used to guide retrieval.

The various mnemonic systems do indeed work, although some are better for serial-learning tasks (such as the method of loci) than for paired-associate learning (linking images) or free recall (narrative chaining). However, mnemonic techniques are time-consuming to learn and to use. Few students use more than acronyms. Most people instead use external cues such as lists and sticky notes, or electronic devices such as smartphones. However, mnemonics are important in demonstrating the principles of acquisition and retrieval.

7　Human Memory Conceptual Approaches

Forgetting is the bane of every student's existence. It is bad enough to forget course material, but forgetting continues beyond the classroom. Students who kept a diary of memory lapses reported all too frequently forgetting meal cards and keys, appointments, classes, and even exams (Terry, 1987). In another survey, students actually reported more instances of forgetting than did an elderly sample, even though the popular stereotype is that the latter are the forgetful ones (Reason, 1993). There is the story of one student who worked all night to complete a history paper, only to realize the next morning that his English paper was due that day.

We are all subject to memory lapses. One news clipping describes someone who took a break while moving into his new apartment in the city. After lunch, he couldn't remember his new address, and was still looking days later. The alumni notes of a 90-year-old reports that not only does he forget what he was going upstairs to get, but while pausing to consider, he forgets whether he was going up or coming down.

When students ask why they have trouble remembering, I have to respond that this is too broad a question for a simple answer. Memory is better explained when partitioned into separate components. A more helpful answer is the realization that forgetting is due to a failure of one type of memory or another, or of one stage or another.

This chapter considers several theoretical approaches to memory, each of which partitions memory along different dimensions. One approach postulates different types of memory, such as short-term and long-term memories. Another approach divides memory into a series of stages:

Table 7.1 Three Approaches to Memory

Memory Components	Stages of Memory	Processes of Memory
Short-term memory	Encoding into memory	Depth of processing
Long-term memory	Storage in memory	Passive (shallow)
Episodic	Retrieval from memory	Elaborative (deep)
Semantic		
Procedural		
Priming		

forming, retaining, and retrieving memory. A third approach emphasizes differences in how memories are processed. These approaches are outlined in Table 7.1. A final approach attempts to model memory in the nervous system by describing the formation and activation of neural connections.

This chapter's theories generally derive from cognitive psychology, but other fields also offer insights into the nature of memory. The field of neuropsychology, with its emphasis on brain and behavior, seeks to distinguish those areas of the brain associated with the different components of memories. Case studies of individuals with brain injuries provide important means of testing our theories and for generating new conceptions of memory. In addition, connectionist models merge the physiological psychology of the neuron with cognitive theories of memory.

Partitioning Memory

Why do we hypothesize multiple memory systems instead of a single memory? Tulving (1985) considered several reasons. One reason is that we cannot make many generalizations about memory as a whole, although statements about particular forms of memory are valid. Thus, there may be general principles for long-term memory and for short-term memory, or for personal memories versus knowledge, but just not the same principles.

Another reason is the heuristic value in postulating multiple memory systems. A heuristic is a sort of rule of thumb. It is a guideline that often works, although it may not be perfectly accurate and it does not explain what is going on. The hypothesis of multiple memory systems has heuristic value in simplifying our theories. The several components, each with different characteristics, may be a simpler model to construct and to use.

A third reason for postulating multiple memory systems is that the results of our studies suggest multiple processes are involved. This is part of the research strategy of uncovering dissociations. **Dissociation** occurs when an experimental variable has different effects on different tasks or measures. For example, are verbal learning and spatial learning encompassed by a single memory system, or are they separate? Injury to the left hemisphere of the brain can impair learning of verbal items, such as free recall of word lists. Spatial learning of a maze or a new route is unaffected. Because only verbal learning is affected by left-brain injury, this could suggest these two types of materials are learned by different brain areas.

A simple difference between verbal and spatial learning could occur for reasons other than a specialized learning capacity in the left hemisphere. A more convincing demonstration would be a *double dissociation*, in which the experimental variable differentially affects performance on two tasks. If we can also show that right-hemisphere lesions impair spatial memory but not verbal learning, then we would have a double dissociation.

Figure 7.1 shows the results of one such study. The subjects had to remember, in one case, whether a test word had been recently presented on the video screen, and in the other case,

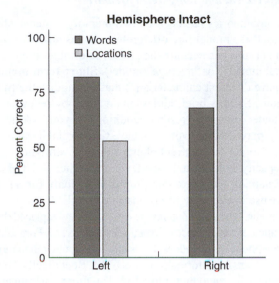

Figure 7.1 Example of the Effects of Lesions to One Side of the Brain on Recognition Memory for Words or Spatial Locations.

Source: Adapted from Kesner, R. P., Hopkins, R. O., & Chiba, A. A. (1992). Learning and memory in humans, with an emphasis on the role of the hippocampus. In L. R. Squire and N. Butters (Eds.), *Neuropsychology of memory* (p. 109). New York: Guilford Press. Adapted with permission from Guilford Press.

whether an X had been presented at a certain location on the screen. The subjects were individuals who had surgical lesions of one hemisphere of the brain to control epilepsy. Those with lesions to the left hemisphere (usually the language side of the brain) did worse on the word-recognition test than did subjects with right lesions; those subjects with lesions to the right hemisphere (usually the nonlanguage side) were more impaired on the spatial location test than were people with left lesions (Kesner, Hopkins, & Chiba, 1992). This finding suggests that the two cerebral hemispheres play different roles in verbal and spatial learning.

Dissociations may be produced in several ways: experimental manipulations (e.g., the length of the retention interval before testing); memory tasks (such as recalling words or completing words when some letters are missing); neurological differences (as in comparing people with injuries to the left or right hemisphere); and subject populations (such as children versus older adults).

Each uncovered dissociation needs to be cautiously interpreted. A dissociation does not automatically imply that there are separate underlying memory systems. Two tasks could vary in their procedures, difficulty, or familiarity (Hintzman, 1990). For example, Hanley-Dunn and McIntosh (1984) gave college students and elderly adults lists of names to remember. The students did better when the to-be-remembered names were rock music performers; the elderly did better when the names were of Big Band musicians. This pattern of results does not show that there are separate memory systems for different categories of musicians. In this case the meaningfulness of the to-be-learned materials varied between the two age groups.

Components of Memory Approach

One approach to partitioning memory divides memory into different stores or types. The primary divisions are short-term memory and long-term memory.

Dual-Store Theory: Short-Term and Long-Term Memories

The emphasis within many theories has been on two memory systems, short-term memory and long-term memory. Thus, these models are often referred to as dual-storage theories. The theory of Atkinson and Shiffrin (1968) has become the prototype of other theories and so is sometimes referred to as the "modal model" (or "average" model). **Short-term memory** (STM) and **long-term memory** (LTM) have different characteristics that distinguish the two systems.

First, and most obvious, STM is brief. Unless maintained by rehearsal, information in STM lasts 15 to 30 seconds under laboratory testing conditions. If you look up a new phone number, you will forget it quickly, maybe before you even have time to dial it. Memories in LTM are more durable. You won't likely forget your current phone number overnight.

STM has a limited capacity, holding at most a few items, whereas LTM is assumed to be virtually limitless in size. Retaining one seven-digit number is plenty for STM; retaining the many numerical sequences we use in everyday life is possible with LTM.

Forgetting from STM occurs when the contents are displaced (and replaced) by later-occurring items. Reading a second phone number can displace a first number from STM. Forgetting does not easily occur from LTM. Forgetting your phone number does not usually occur, other than momentary lapses.

Finally, STM serves to transfer information into LTM. Specifically, rehearsal in STM keeps information available longer for encoding into LTM. The more you rehearse a phone number in STM, the better you should remember it in LTM.

(The preceding listing includes the modal properties of short- and long-term stores. The next chapter contains an elaboration of STM and developments since Atkinson and Shiffrin's original theory.)

What sorts of evidence suggest that there are two memory systems? Short-term and long-term memories are dissociated in several ways. The **serial-position** curve that is obtained in free-recall tasks is differently affected by several independent variables. In remembering a list of words presented a single time, recall of the first words, also called the **primacy** effect, is enhanced if the list is presented at a slower pace (Glanzer & Cunitz, 1966). The slower pace allows more opportunity for rehearsal in STM, allowing more encoding into LTM. The results from one study are shown in the left panel of Figure 7.2. As can be seen, there was better recall after the 9 second-per-item

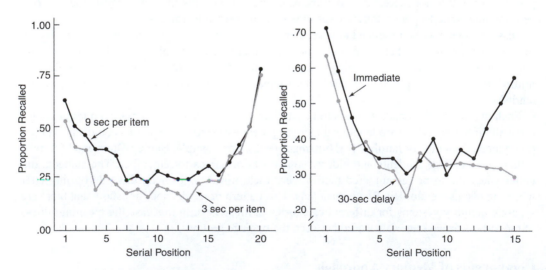

Figure 7.2 Serial Position Curves, as Affected (*left*) by Rate of Presentation of the Items, Fast or Slow, and (*right*) Immediate or Delayed Testing.

Source: From *Experimental Psychology: Contemporary Methods and Applications* (p. 214), by I. P. Levin and J. V. Hinrichs, 1995, New York: McGraw-Hill. Copyright 1995. Reprinted with permission of The McGraw-Hill Companies.

rate (slow presentation) that after the 3-second rate (fast presentation). Fast or slow presentation did not affect recall of the last items of the list.

Recall of the final list items, called the **recency** effect, is enhanced if testing occurs immediately after list presentation. Recall is impaired if testing is delayed (Glanzer & Cunitz, 1966). This is shown in the right panel of Figure 7.2. When testing was delayed for 30 seconds after list presentation, recency disappeared but the primacy effect was still there. Immediate recall of the last items is from STM. The delay is usually filled by distractor activity to prevent rehearsal.

Short-term and long-term memories are also dissociated by the patterns of memory loss by injuries to different areas of the brain. The amnesic subject H. M., now known to generations of students, had damage to the interior of his temporal lobes. Specifically, as a result of experimental surgery in 1953 for the relief of epilepsy, H. M. was unable to form new long-term memories. He could not learn new facts, vocabulary, places, faces, or mazes. However, his short-term memory was preserved. He could remember short strings of letters, digits, or words, and he could remember long enough to carry on a conversation. H. M.'s pattern of what was remembered and forgotten, and that of other amnesic individuals like him, suggests there is a dissociation between short-term memory, which was spared, and the ability to acquire long-term memories, which was lost to the brain lesions (Scoville & Milner, 1957).

The case of K. F. provides the opposite deficit. K. F. cannot repeat back even the shortest strings of words. If read two or three items, he would likely recall only one. However, K. F. can form long-term memories. Curiously, if read longer lists of 7 to 10 items, K. F. shows a serial recall curve with primacy; that is, he recalls more of the first items than middle items (Shallice & Warrington, 1970).

(These descriptions of H. M. and K. F. are overly broad. As will be shown later in other chapters, H. M. can learn conditioned responses and motor skills, or what will be called "procedural learning." Individuals like K. F. may have short-term memory in other sensory modalities.)

Finally, a dissociation between short-term and long-term memory is suggested by the effects of other types of brain trauma, such as electroconvulsive shock. This research is discussed in Box 7.1.

Divisions of Long-Term Memory: Episodic and Semantic

In contrast to STM, long-term memory is relatively permanent. There are several types of information retained in our permanent memory, such as autobiographical memories, factual knowledge, and various skills and habits, which suggest to theorists that LTM itself is made up of several separate memory components. One broad division of long-term memory is that between episodic memory and semantic memory, a difference that corresponds to what we might casually label "memory" and "knowledge" (Tulving, 1985). **Episodic memory** is our personal memory system. These are autobiographical memories. Episodic memories contain temporal and contextual information about when and where the events occurred. We can use time of occurrence to retrieve episodic memories, and recollected memories can be approximately dated. An example would be remembering moments from last summer's vacation. **Semantic memory** is our store of general knowledge. It is more like dictionary or encyclopedic knowledge. It includes facts, words, language, and grammar. It has sometimes been referred to as generic memory, or knowledge that most of us have in common, in distinction to the unique and personal episodic memories. Semantic memory includes knowledge, but not the memory of how or when it was learned. For example, you have a great deal of generic knowledge about dogs in semantic memory—they make good pets, they bark, they are related to wolves, and so on. You probably don't recall how or when you learned each fact. By contrast, a specific memory of an event in your life involving a dog at a particular time and place would be episodic recall. Our everyday phrases "I remember" versus "I know" parallel episodic and semantic memory.

Box 7.1   Electroconvulsive Shock and Amnesia

Electroconvulsive shock therapy (ECT) is sometimes used as a treatment for severe depression. Memory loss is one prominent side effect of ECT. Most people will report some retrograde amnesia for events that preceded ECT.

Retrograde amnesia for real-life memories was assessed in a seminal study by Janis and Astrachan (1951). During a pre-ECT interview, the patients were questioned in detail about their life histories: schools attended, jobs held, places lived, and so on. The purpose of the pretest was to determine what was recallable before treatment. A second interview occurred 1 month after the completion of ECT. Every one of the subjects forgot some facts that they could recall before ECT. For example, one patient had first reported being unemployed for several months prior to treatment. Afterwards, he was unable to recall this, and claimed to have worked right up until the time of hospitalization. Interestingly, some of the forgotten material was for events many years prior, things that certainly had been in long-term memory. Janis and Astrachan suggested that ECT affected retrieval, reducing access to certain memories.

Squire, Slater, and Miller (1981) also sought objective assessments of the loss of naturalistically acquired memories. Their subjects first answered questions about public events, or TV shows that had aired for a single season. Forgetting these facts would indicate the precise time periods encompassed by the amnesia. In the first week following ECT, the patients showed some retrograde amnesia that extended back 1 to 3 years for some personal events and a decade for public and political events. However, a second test given 7 months after ECT showed that much of what had been forgotten on the first post-ECT test could then be remembered.

One hypothesis for the retrograde-amnesic effects of electroconvulsive shock (ECS) was that it disrupts the consolidation of short-term memories into long-term memories (Hebb, 1949; McGaugh, 1974). Supporting evidence came from animal conditioning experiments in which the timing of a learning trial and ECS administration could be precisely controlled. For example, rats were first given minimal training in how to avoid a foot shock. They then received ECS at delays ranging from seconds to hours after the avoidance training. The results of one study are shown in Figure 7.3 (Chorover & Schiller, 1965).

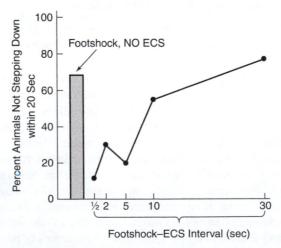

Figure 7.3 **Memory Disruption as a Function of the Delay Between Learning and Administration of ECS.** The graph plots the number of subjects who avoided the shocked floor when the single training trials had been followed by ECS after different intervals or no ECS.

Source: From "Short-Term Retrograde Amnesia in Rats," by S. L. Chorover and P. H. Schiller, 1965, *Journal of Comparative and Physiological Psychology, 59,* p. 76. Copyright © 1965 by the American Psychological Association. Reprinted by permission.

The closer the ECS was to training, the more forgetting occurred. Delaying ECS allowed more time for consolidation of the training experience into long-term memory.

Retrograde forgetting can also be produced by stimulating certain areas of the brain, those thought to be necessary for consolidation. Rats who received convulsive stimulation of the hippocampus following maze exposure forgot their maze choices when tested later (Knowlton, McGowan, Olton, & Gamzu, 1985).

If ECS produces retrograde amnesia, would forgetting occur through other sources of seizures? The study of epilepsy is relevant here. Individuals with frequent seizures, particularly those that involve memory areas of the brain, might show forgetting similar to that of those who had received ECT. Milton et al. (2010) found that individuals with temporal lobe epilepsy did show especially poor memory for their own past (episodic memory) and some impairment in memory for public events (semantic memory). This could be related to the disruptive effects of the seizures on memory consolidation.

Consolidation theory is challenged by some discordant findings. The presumably lost memories spontaneously return over time, or are reinstated by various cuing treatments (Miller & Springer, 1973). Neither could occur if consolidation had really been blocked.

Besides ECS, much milder experimental treatments can induce retrograde amnesic-like effects. Tulving (1969) found that placing an unusual word in the middle of a list of words interfered with subjects' recall of the preceding words. The unusual word was remembered, but not the one before it. In a study of rats, several mazes were presented, each with food in the goal box. Later, the sudden omission of the expected food in the second maze was enough to cause the rats to forget the first maze in the series (Terry, 1996). Finally, inducing frustration in infants, sufficient to cause crying, also caused retrograde forgetting: They forgot what made them cry (Fagan, Ohr, Flechenstein, & Ribner, 1985).

Many of the laboratory experiments on human memory presented in this text are tests of episodic memory: memory for words and pictures that occurred in a particular context (the lab) at a particular time (often just a few minutes ago). In a free-recall task, you might be asked to recall the most recent list of words but not the previous lists presented in the day's session. The unremembered words are forgotten from episodic memory, but they are not forgotten in the sense that the student is no longer able to use or comprehend those words. These word are retained in semantic memory.

The episodic–semantic distinction is evident in certain types of amnesias. Schacter (1983) reports a case of impaired episodic but spared semantic memory in an acquaintance with Alzheimer's. A person with Alzheimer's often has trouble with ongoing memory, or remembering events as they occur, and so are forgetful about the recent past. Rather than simply reporting data from laboratory tests, Schacter assessed memory during a couple of rounds of golf. Schacter's friend remembered the rules of the game and knew which club to use and when. For example, realizing he probably could not drive the ball over the water hazard, he selected a short iron to safely lay up before the pond. He correctly used an extensive vocabulary of technical terms, such as birdie, bogey, and divot. This is knowledge in semantic memory. Yet after a brief delay the man could not remember which direction his ball had gone, or which of two balls on the fairway was his. After moving on to the next tee, he could not recount any details of the previous hole. This is failure of episodic memory, an inability to form ongoing memories of personal life.

A dramatic case of episodic memory loss involved a man who received a head injury in a motorcycle accident (Tulving, 1989). The young man can remember all sorts of facts about his life. These generic facts, about where he lived and worked, where he went to school, or how to play chess are in semantic memory. Note that not all our knowledge about ourselves is episodic.

We can have personal semantic knowledge, just as we have generic knowledge of the world. However, this young man could not remember a specific episode involving himself in any of these known events. He could not remember a single episode of having vacationed in the family cabin, or having been at work, or having ever played chess. This is loss of episodic memory.

Attempts to functionally dissociate episodic and semantic memories in laboratory experiments have had mixed success. One difficulty is that testing the two hypothesized forms of memory requires different materials, procedures, or tasks. For example, a list of words might be presented to subjects in an experiment. Later, half of the subjects are given a recognition test of episodic memory: A long list is presented from which to select the words studied earlier. The remaining subjects are given a test of semantic memory. Strings of letters are briefly flashed on the screen, and the task is to decide which strings form real words (e.g., CAT) and which do not (e.g., ATC). The problem is we are confounding the type of test with type of memory. Maybe the difference is not episodic versus semantic, but recognition memory versus perceptual identification.

Some theorists downplay the episodic–semantic distinction. Others defend it for its heuristic value. The distinction between forms of long-term memory is useful in describing the development of semantic or generic memories. In children, for example, a child's first experience with a cow leads to an episodic memory. Repeated experiences lead to the formation of a generic memory of cow-related facts and lore. The same logic applies to our autobiographical memories. Your first college class meetings produce distinct episodic memories. The day-by-day episodic memories are eventually supplanted by generic memory of what a typical class is like, and rapid loss of memory for individual class meetings (Linton, 1982). This process could be described as the transition from episodic to semantic memory.

Divisions of Long-Term Memory: Procedural Learning and Priming

Explicit versus Implicit

Direct questioning about the contents of memory is an **explicit memory task**. Explicit tests tap the episodic and semantic knowledge that we can report on. An **implicit memory task** assesses the effects of prior experience indirectly, by measuring performance on some task that does not requires explicit recall. For example, a stimulus is reacted to more quickly the second time it occurs than during its first presentation. Performance improves regardless of whether you recall the previous experience. Implicit memory is performance that occurs independently of conscious attempts to recall.

The meaning of the terms explicit and implicit has evolved in their history in the psychology lexicon. Some of the contrasting terms used to distinguish between implicit and explicit memory are shown in Table 7.2. The terms are sometimes used to refer to separate types of memory, that

Table 7.2 Some of the Contrasting Terms Used to Distinguish Implicit and Explicit Memory

Explicit Memory	Implicit Memory
Fact memory	Skill memory
Declarative	Procedural
Knowing that	Knowing how
Conscious recollection	Perceptual identification
Memory	Habit

Source: Squire (1987, p. 169).

is, explicit memory systems such as episodic and semantic memory, and implicit memory systems as demonstrated by procedural learning and priming (described in the sections that follow). The implicit procedures are hypothesized to be mediated by different neural systems from the explicit memory systems of episodic and semantic memories.

Procedural Learning

Procedural learning is the acquisition of knowledge of how to do things and includes perceptual skills, motor skills, and cognitive skills. Procedural knowledge has been characterized as "knowing how" rather than episodic and semantic's "remembering that." I know *how* to skate versus I remember *that* I once fell (Squire & Cohen, 1984). Procedural learning is the acquisition of general rules for performing a task or procedure. This knowledge may not be accessible to conscious verbal recall.

The procedural learning tasks most commonly used in research have different combinations of perceptual, motor, and cognitive skills. For instance, mirror star tracing combines perceptual and motor skills. Subjects trace the outline of a printed star, but by watching their hand movements through a mirror reflection. This requires reversing the direction of hand movements from the direction seen in the mirror. Learning to read text that has been inverted or mirror-reversed is another procedural task, one that combines a cognitive skill and a perceptual skill. Another procedural task is serial spatial learning. Spatial locations are sequentially presented in a grid on a computer screen. As the sequence repeats, the subjects come to anticipate the next location and respond more quickly to the repeated sequence, even if the sequence cannot be described verbally.

Priming

Priming refers to the facilitated response to a stimulus that has been recently experienced, or has been "primed" in memory. For example, you readily perceive a word that was recently seen or heard. A typical word-priming experiment has two stages. First, participants are shown a list of words. The participants may be simply asked to read the words as they are presented. In the second phase, degraded versions of the words are presented again, along with other distractor words. For instance, the words are flashed briefly on the screen, or word stems (the first three letters of the word) are given for the subject to complete. Priming is demonstrated if identification is facilitated by the previous exposure. Note, the participants are not explicitly told in the second phase that the words were previously seen. The control comparison is to words that were not exposed during the first phase. These provide a baseline for word identification with which to compare the preexposed items.

Say, for example, the word EARTH had been presented in the first phase. In a word completion test, the first several letters of a word are given (EAR_ _) and the subject is asked to complete it with the first word that comes to mind. Priming occurs when the stem or fragment is completed with words studied during the first, priming phase, as opposed to other words that may fit (such as EARLY). For instance, in one study, the stem EAR_ _was completed with EARTH about 30 percent of the time in the unprimed control condition, whereas in the priming condition EARTH was the solution 49 percent of the time (Rajaram & Roediger, 1993).

Another test of priming is perceptual identification. In this task the subject attempts to read a target word flashed on a screen for a fraction of a second, a duration that makes conscious recognition difficult. Primed words are more likely to be identified than unprimed words. For example, in a study by Hamann, Squire, and Schacter (1995), a number of words were first

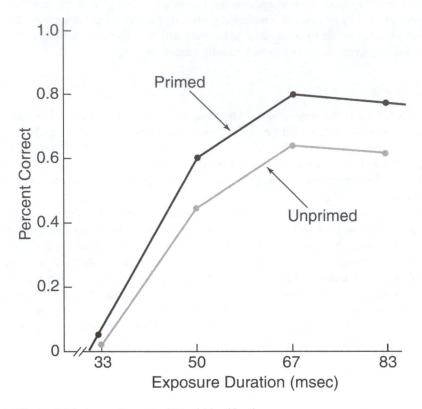

Figure 7.4 Effects of Priming on Perceptual Word Identification.

Words are presented for durations ranging from 33 to 83 milliseconds and the subjects attempted to identify the words. The "primed" words were identified more readily than were unprimed (new words).

Source: From "Perceptual thresholds and priming in amnesia," by S. B. Hamann, L. R. Squire, and D. L. Schacter, 1995, *Neuropsychology*, 9, p. 11. Copyright American Psychological Association. Reprinted with permission.

presented. The subjects were simply asked to rate the pleasantness of each word. In the next phase of the experiment, some of these words and some new words were flashed on a screen for durations ranging from 33 to 83 milliseconds. The task here was to identify each word, if possible. The results are shown in Figure 7.4. As can be seen, very few words could be identified from 33-millisecond exposures, but most could be read with the longer exposures. The primed words, those seen earlier in the session, were more likely to be identified from brief exposures. New words could not be perceived at these presentation durations. Priming facilitated word identification.

In some cases, implicit test performance is better than explicit testing. For example, college students attempted to explicitly recognize words they had studied 7 days previously or complete word fragments based on those words. In the latter condition, the students were not reminded that some of the words were presented a week earlier. Only 20 percent of the words were correctly recognized a week later, but 50 percent of fragment completions produced words that had been presented a week earlier (Tulving, Schacter, & Stark, 1982). In other research, amnesic subjects (those having amnesic syndrome like H. M.) simply cannot recall many of the words they have studied earlier. Yet amnesics do as well as nonamnesic individuals in completing word stems (Shimamura et al., 1987).

Visual Object Priming

Priming can occur with pictorial stimuli. For example, drawings of objects can be presented and then tested later through a method of fragmented pictures (see Figure 7.5). Subjects attempt to identify the object from the fragmented picture. On each trial, one drawing is shown at a time, from most fragmented to most complete, until the subject can identify the object or word. Across trials, identification can be made with ever more degraded images. The pictures become easier to identify from the fragments. This technique of fragmented pictures was actually one of the first used to show that amnesics could in fact learn and remember implicitly (Warrington & Weiskrantz, 1968a). Subjects like H. M., who could not recall the pictured

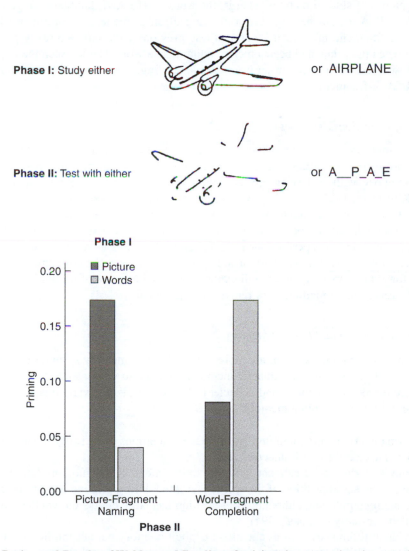

Figure 7.5 **Design and Results of Weldon and Roediger.** Studying pictures produced more priming than did words on the picture-fragment test; studying words produced more priming on the word-fragment test.

Source: From "Implicit Memory: Retention without Remembering," by H. L. Roediger, III, 1990, *American Psychologist*, *45*, p. 1051. Copyright © 1990 by the Psychonomic Society. Reprinted with permission.

objects when explicitly asked to do so, could nevertheless identify objects more quickly from fewer and fewer fragments.

Repetition priming tends to be modality specific. That is, a picture prime will not facilitate identification of the word that names the picture; and a word prime will not facilitate recognition of a picture that represents the word. In a study by Weldon and Roediger (1987), their college student participants studied lists of both pictures and words in Phase I. The pictures were simple line drawings like that shown in Figure 7.5 and had simple one-word names (e.g., airplane). In Phase II, either a picture fragment or a word-completion test was given. The task then was, given the fragment, could the subject name the picture or word? Is it possible that the picture would prime both the picture and word? The results instead showed limited priming effects. In the word-fragment completion test, previously studied words were more easily completed than were the names of studied pictures. That is, the word AIRPLANE facilitated fragment completion of A_ _P_A_E, but having seen a drawing of an airplane did not aid in filling in the A_ _P_A_E fragment. In a picture-fragment test, previously viewed pictures were more easily identified when the prime had been a picture rather than a word. Having seen the airplane drawing in Phase I facilitated recognition from the picture fragments, but did not aid completion of the A_ _P_A_E fragment.

The Role of Conscious Awareness

Implicit memory is recollection without awareness that one is remembering. "An increasingly large literature from both patient and nonpatient populations indicates that people can display implicit memory without having any conscious recollection of the experiential basis of the effect" (Kihlstrom, 1987, p. 1449). However the contribution of explicit memory to an implicit test cannot readily be discounted. With college students as participants, there is a likelihood they may notice the relationship between the words presented in the first phase and the test items in the second phase, and then perform the task explicitly. By testing amnesic subjects, awareness of a previous study trial is less of a factor in an implicit memory test. Yet most amnesics retain some capacity for explicit memory. They will explicitly remember some of the studied items. So, the role of awareness in implicit memory remains controversial.

Dissociating Priming and Explicit Memory

In order to argue that implicit priming represents a different memory system than that accessed by explicit tests of episodic or semantic memory, we need to demonstrate that the two classes of tasks are dissociable. Tulving and Schacter (1990) categorized several types of evidence that dissociate implicit and explicit memory.

1. Performance on explicit and implicit tests are sometimes statistically independent; that is, performance on the two is uncorrelated.
2. Certain experimental treatments affect explicit memory but not implicit memory. For instance, the serial position of the words presented during priming has little effect on later word-stem completion, although serial position has large effects on whether the words are recalled explicitly (Brooks, 1994).
3. Individual differences such as age affect explicit memory but not implicit memory. Parkin and Streete (1988) tested picture-fragment identification and explicit recognition of pictures in children aged 3 to 7. Explicit memory increased with age but implicit memory did not.
4. Neurological and psychopharmacological treatments affect explicit and implicit memory differently. For instance, amnesics recall poorly on explicit tests of memory, but do as well as nonmemory-impaired individuals on some priming tests.

The Organization of Long-Term Memory

What is the relationship among the several hypothesized components of long-term memory? Various organizations of memory have been proposed. Tulving (1985) suggests that three of the memory systems form a "monohierarchy" in descending order of inclusiveness: Procedural learning includes within it semantic memory as a subset, which in turn includes episodic memory as its subset. This memory system hierarchy would appear as follows:

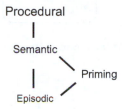

Priming effects are attributed to still another memory system (or set of systems associated with different sensory modalities) that overlaps both the procedural and semantic memory systems. This other memory Tulving calls the *perceptual representation system* (Tulving & Schacter, 1990).

In a different hypothesized organization of long-term memory, Squire (1987; Squire, Knowlton, & Musen, 1993) divides memory into two major categories, declarative and nondeclarative:

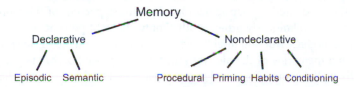

Declarative memory can be consciously recalled and reported. That is, we can "declare" these memories. Instructions that explicitly request recollection from memory are accessing declarative memory. Declarative memory includes episodic and semantic memory.

Nondeclarative memory is defined by exclusion. It is whatever types of memory that are not declarative. Nondeclarative memory includes procedural skill learning, priming effects due to recent exposure to a stimulus, habit learning, and classical conditioning. Nondeclarative knowledge, as is obvious from its label, is often assessed implicitly and not by direct or explicit verbal recall.

Stages of Memory

A second approach to memory separates it into a series of three stages. A memory must first be formed, then retained, and later retrieved. These stages are labeled **encoding**, **storage**, and **retrieval**. Forgetting could arise from problems at any one of these stages. For example, if you cannot remember the answer to an exam question, it may be because (1) you never really learned the material, (2) you learned it but it has since been lost from memory, or (3) you learned it, it's there, but you can't recall it right now (although you will probably remember shortly after turning in your exam). The stage approach is not so much a theory about memory, but rather a set of assumptions or "givens" about memory. The goal of the stage approach is to identify the effect of certain variables on one stage of memory or another.

Figure 7.6 shows the stages and some terms associated with each stage.

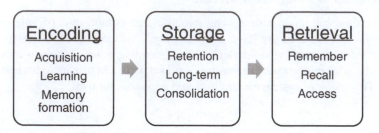

Figure 7.6 The stage approach to partitioning memory, showing some of the terms associated with each stage.

Dissociating Stages

Experimental Dissociations

Experimental dissociations of the stages occur when a manipulated variable primarily affects either encoding, storage, or retrieval. This can be illustrated by a study of the effects of alcohol on learning and retention (Miller, Adesso, Fleming, Gino, & Lauerman, 1978). Male participants, characterized as "heavy social drinkers," were given word lists to remember either while sober or after consuming alcohol. When these two conditions were compared the next day, after the drug had worn off, the sober-study group remembered about 25 percent of the words from the day before, whereas the alcohol-study group recalled only about 14 percent. This could suggest that alcohol impairs encoding. But you might object that the change in conditions from intoxication to sober made the memories of the alcohol group less retrievable. That is, maybe both groups encoded equally well, but the intoxicated group experienced retrieval failure when tested without alcohol. To test for changes in retrieval conditions, two additional groups could be run that are tested on Day 2 after consuming alcohol. Now we can see whether the group given alcohol at both study and test remembers as much as the group that was sober at study and test. The full results from this experiment are shown in Table 7.3. The data are the average percentage of words recalled on the second day. The participants who were sober on Day 1 recalled more the next day, whether they were sober or intoxicated during the test. Alcohol prior to retrieval had little effect on recall. We would conclude from these comparisons that alcohol impaired encoding.

A different pattern of results occurred when a physical stressor was applied prior to either learning or retrieval. Just as in the Miller et al. (1978) study described above, subjects were given lists of words to remember on Day 1 and were tested on Day 2. The encoding-stress subjects were asked to hold one hand in a bucket of ice water for as long as they could stand—up to three minutes. Then the word lists were presented. The retrieval-stress subjects were given the ice-water treatment on Day 2 just before they attempted to recall the word lists. Cold-stress before encoding had no effect on learning; however, the stress before testing impaired recall (Smeets, Otgaar, Candel, & Wolf, 2008).

The stages of encoding, storage, and retrieval cannot be completely isolated from one another. For instance, a study of retrieval failure presumes prior encoding, so that something can be (temporarily) forgotten. Also, an experimental treatment can influence more than one stage. The organization of to-be-remembered items into categories aids encoding, and this organization also facilitates retrieval.

Neuropsychological Dissociations

The neuropsychologist attempts to dissociate stages by finding individuals with impairment at one or another stage. H. M. had an encoding deficit: He could not form new memories. H. M.

Table 7.3 Effects of Alcohol Before Studying and/or Before Testing on Relearning Word Lists

		Testing State	
		Sober	*Alcohol*
Study	*Sober*	26.4	25.2
State	*Alcohol*	13.7	14.7

Note: Mean percentage of words recalled on Day 2 as a function of alcohol-state during Day 1 study and alcohol state during Day 2 testing.

Source: From "Effects of alcohol on the storage and retrieval processes of heavy social drinkers," by M. E. Miller, V. J. Adesso, J. P. Fleming, A. Gino, & R. Lauerman, 1978, *Journal of Experimental Psychology: Human Learning and Memory, 4*, pp. 246–255. Copyright © 1978 by the American Psychological Association. Reprinted by permission.

could still retrieve many of his older memories from before his operation: He recalled much of his early life history.

Other aspects of amnesics' performance suggest that their forgetting may be a retrieval rather than encoding problem. For example, in the typical experiment several lists are presented and tested in succession. Although few words are recalled from the just-heard list, amnesic individuals sometimes "misrecall" words from earlier lists. These intrusion errors show that there is some memory for the other lists (Warrington & Weiskrantz, 1968b).

Tests of implicit memory also suggest that amnesics encode information that is not explicitly recallable. For example, amnesic participants read a list of words and later are tested with word stems. If explicitly asked to complete the letter stems with words from the list, the subjects perform poorly. ("What lists?" they ask. After all, they are amnesic.) However, if the stem completion task is presented as a game ("Can you think of a word that begins with these letters?"), the amnesics complete the stems with previously studied words. Implicit recall here suggests that some form of encoding took place.

Another dissociation strategy is to compare individuals who have different brain pathologies. Some amnesic individuals are able to encode and retain new memories, although with great difficulty. N. A., who suffered damage to his thalamus (a structure near the hippocampus), at first appears to be just as amnesic as H. M. Both had difficulty retaining new memories. Yet N. A. can attain nearly normal levels of recall with sufficient practice. He must spend considerably more time studying than do nonamnesic subjects. Once learning has occurred, forgetting occurs at a normal rate (Squire, 1981). Thus, amnesia associated with the hippocampus (which characterizes H. M.) and amnesia associated with the thalamus (which characterizes N. A.) may dissociate the encoding stage (Squire, 1987).

Processing Approaches to Memory

Depth of Processing

A third approach to memory suggests that the kind or quality of processing determines memorability. *Depth of processing theory* (Craik & Lockhart, 1972) was initially offered as an alternative to the theory of separate short-term and long-term memories. In **depth of processing** theory, remembering depends on the amount of cognitive elaboration, or processing depth. Rapid forgetting is due, not to a loss from a transient short-term storage, but rather to shallow processing. Sustained retention is due to deeper or more elaborate processing. Remembering and forgetting reflect variations in the cognitive depth to which information is processed.

The idea of shallow versus deep processing is illustrated by two kinds of rehearsal. When we try to remember something, we are sometimes subjectively aware that we are rehearsing the to-be-remembered information. **Maintenance rehearsal** is the passive repetition of information, repeating something over and over. This is shallow processing. We use maintenance rehearsal to remember a phone number just long enough to dial it or to recall a message long enough to write it down. On the other hand, **elaborative rehearsal** is a more active form of processing. It involves meaningful analysis and comprehension of the material, and thus represents a deeper level of processing. Elaborative rehearsal of a phone number could include looking for a pattern among the numbers or the similarity to a familiar number (a date, your ID number, or pin number). Many learning strategies are instances of elaborative rehearsal: using mnemonic systems, forming mental images, and relating the to-be-recalled material to existing knowledge. Elaborative rehearsal should lead to better retention than does maintenance rehearsal.

According to depth of processing theory, remembering is due more to the quality of processing than a deliberate intention to learn. Craik and Tulving (1975) demonstrated this in experiments on *incidental learning*, in which college student participants were shown a list of words but without instructions to remember them. Instead, the students answered a question about each presented word, with different types of questions used to elicit different levels of processing. In one condition, the participant decided whether the word contained the letter *e* (this requires processing the surface form or appearance of the word); in a second condition, a rhyme for the word had to be generated (which requires processing the sound of the word); in the final condition, the participant could be asked whether the word fits a given category, such as "animal" (which requires processing the meaning of the word). Later, the subjects were given a surprise test of memory for the words. Words that had received deeper processing during presentation were better recalled. Interestingly, the incidental learning in the deep-processing condition led to memory as good as that found in an intentional learning condition, one in which participants were explicitly instructed to remember.

Neuropsychologists have considered whether amnesia is due to deficient processing. Individuals with anterograde amnesia like H. M. have been tested in the depth-of-processing procedure of Craik and Tulving (1975). Like normal-memoried people, amnesics show better retention after categorizing a word than after rhyming it (Graf et al., 1984). However, the amnesics are still severely impaired. Getting them to deeply process material does not eliminate their amnesia. Schacter (1983) reports some observations on his Alzheimer's golfing partner. While playing a particularly challenging hole, the man was asked to elaborate on his actions: why he chose the club he did, why this shot was difficult, how it turned out. These elaborations certainly exemplify deep processing. Still, after moving on to the next tee, the man could not recall any details of the just-elaborated hole.

Depth-of-processing theory has been challenged on several grounds (e.g., Baddeley, 1978). One criticism was that there were no independent measures of depth. Processing depth was instead inferred on the basis of manipulations that led to good or poor memory, the thing we were trying to account for. There are now independent measures of processing. In one procedure, participants attempt to perform two cognitive tasks at once, such as remembering words and adding numbers. If the primary task requires deeper processing, this leaves less capacity left over for the other task. Thus, deeper processing on the first task is shown by poor performance on the second task.

A second criticism was that the term "depth" is unclear, taking on different meanings. It was sometimes interpreted as elaboration of an item in memory, and other times it referred to a more distinctive representation in memory. We now acknowledge that deep processing can produce either elaboration or distinctiveness, and that both are beneficial to memory (see Chapter 9).

The notion of qualitative variations in processing at encoding has now been incorporated into the other approaches to memory. Thus, dual-store theorists distinguish between the two forms of rehearsal in STM, maintenance and elaborative. Elaborative processing is accepted as a significant factor that enhances encoding, and the distinctiveness of a memory is a significant factor that facilitates retrieval.

Summary

The processing approach, exemplified by depth of processing theory, emphasizes cognitive processing of information rather than separate memories systems. Remembering and forgetting depend on the nature of the processing an item receives rather than where it is stored or which stage is involved. However, the processing approach does not preclude the other approaches presented in this chapter. For instance, we can combine two approaches and study encoding, storage, and retrieval in short-term memory (or long-term memory). Or, one could study processing depth in episodic memory (or semantic, or procedural memory). The several approaches could be viewed as complementary rather than as exclusionary.

Connectionist Models

Research on learning has historically proceeded on several levels. On the behavioral level, researchers attempt to describe the relationships between environmental and behavioral variables. On a neural level, researchers search for the most basic changes in neurons and synapses that underlie memory. Connectionism attempts to unite these levels by modeling the neural changes that underlie learning and memory. The abbreviation CNS, which usually stands for the *central* nervous system, can be reinterpreted as the *conceptual* nervous system (Hebb, 1955; Skinner, 1938, earlier offered this interpretation tongue-in-cheek).

Connectionist models simulate various memory phenomena in a network of hypothetical neurons. These models are sometimes called neural network models. Researchers attempt to statistically model this conceptual nervous system through computer programs.

Older psychological theories offered simple models of neural connections in the brain. Classical conditioning occurred, for instance, when a tone stimulus activated auditory neurons at the same time that the movement neuron activated a leg flexion. From such a starting point, modern connectionist theories offer more sophisticated elaborations. To anticipate the following discussion, the connectionist approach makes certain assumptions. These include the following:

1. Each neural unit, or hypothetical neuron, can have connections to many other units, analogous to the way a given letter can be used in many words.
2. Connections strengthen with "pairings" of active neural units, and weaken when activation of one unit occurs without activation of the other. The increase or decrease in strengths over trials is described mathematically by a learning algorithm, or formula.
3. Activation of a neural unit may require stimulation from multiple input units. This is the concept of a threshold for activation.
4. Once activated, the activity of a neural unit gradually fades back to baseline or resting level over a brief period of time.
5. There are multiple layers of neural units. The outer layers correspond to input and output, and thus only they are observable. Inner layers, called hidden units, combine and summate activation from units in the previous layer.

Modeling Person Identification

Connectionism can be illustrated by modeling person knowledge: the connections between names and individual identities. In a connectionist model, each neural unit has multiple connections to other neural units. As an analogy, for many of us the name JOHN can apply to several individuals. JOHN specifies a particular person when it occurs in combination with certain other features (e.g., a classmate, a fellow worker, a relative). Thus, there is not a simple one-to-one connection between JOHN and a specific individual.

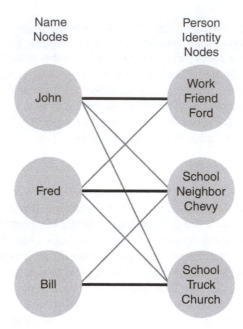

Figure 7.7 **Possible Connectionist Name–Person Identity Model.** The potential name–person connections are shown with the thinner lines. The heavier lines show the stronger connections eventually learned.

In connectionist models, the starting point is the rule that simultaneous activation of two units leads to a strengthening of the connection between them (e.g., TABLE— CHAIR), whereas the activation of one without the other leads to a weakening of this connection (e.g., TABLE but no CHAIR). This feature parallels synaptic changes in the nervous system, in which synaptic junctions are strengthened by repeated use.

To illustrate, we can have one set of "nodes" (or neural units) that represent names, for example, John, Fred, and Bill, as shown in Figure 7.7. The system needs to learn which name goes with which person. To begin with, each name could connect to any or several of the person identity nodes. The latter are representations of particular individuals. On each trial, one name and the corresponding person are presented. The strength of the connection between that name and that person is increased. (In some models, inhibition actually accrues between the activated name and the other *in*active person nodes.)

The Delta Rule

The increase or decrease in strength represents the effects of experience, or learning. One formula for computing the trial-by-trial increases in strength is the *delta rule*. (Delta, and its symbol Δ, often stands for "change" in mathematical formulas.) The increment from each trial is a proportion of the difference between the maximum possible activation and the current level of activation. Usually, delta is assigned a constant value, such as .10, representing 10 percent. At the start of training, the strength between any name and a particular person is low, and 0 will be arbitrarily assigned. The maximum amount of activation is set at the number 1 (or 100 percent). If delta is .10, then each pairing of the name with the person increases the connection by .1 (or 10 percent) of the distance remaining to 1. For example, at the start of training, the difference between the maximum activation and the current level of activation is 1 (or 1 minus 0, which

Table 7.4 Trial-by-Trial Learning of a Name–Person Connection with Delta Set at .1

Trial Number	Increment on That Trial	Strength at End of Trial
1	$(1 - 0) \times .1 = .10$	.10
2	$(1 - .1) \times .1 = .09$	.19
3	$(1 - .19) \times .1 = .081$	.271
4	$(1 - .271) \times .1 = .073$	.344
5	$(1 - .344) \times .1 = .066$	.410
6	$(1 - .410) \times .1 = .059$	.469
7	$(1 - .469) \times .1 = .053$	.522
8	$(1 - .522) \times .1 = .048$	.570
9	$(1 - .570) \times .1 = .043$	.613
10	$(1 - .613) \times .1 = .039$	.652

Note: Each increment is computed using the formula (maximum–existing) $\times$ delta. The maximum strength is set at 1.00, and the starting strength of the connection is 0. The increment in each trial is then added to the strength at the end of the previous trial, giving the strength in the last column.

is 1) times delta, or .1. Thus, after the first pairing, the strength of the connection between a name and the person nodes has increased from 0 to .1. On trial 2, the difference between maximal activation and the actual strength is $1-.10$, or .9. This difference is multiplied by delta, giving trial 2 an increase of .09 (i.e., $.9 \times .1 = .09$). The strength of the connection is then .19, or .09 added to the existing .10.

The delta rule, which specifies that increments are a constant proportion of the distance from the maximum, produces a classic learning curve. As described in Chapter 1, such curves are characterized by relatively large increases in learning on the early trials. On later trials, the increments become smaller and smaller in absolute size, although the delta proportion stays the same. This is illustrated with hypothetical numbers in Table 7.4, which continues the example started in the preceding paragraph. (For further detail on the delta rule, see Shanks, 1995.)

An alternative formula works backwards by comparing the predicted outcome with the actual output from the connectionist model. If the output is incorrect, it can be altered by assigning different weights to the connections leading up to the output. If a name leads to recollection of the wrong person, then the weighing of different facts needs to be altered so the connections lead to the correct person. As a rough analogy, in learning the names of a man and a woman, gender information is informative in narrowing the search set of possible names for each, so gender should be weighed more heavily. Gender is less helpful if the two people are both male, because both men will likely share the same name set to be searched.

In our name-person example, activation of the person identity node may require input from multiple sources. In addition to the name, nodes representing time and place can help push the person node above some threshold for activation. We have all had the experience in which a name by itself is not enough to trigger identification of the person. A reminder of where we know this person from helps trigger recollection. This connectionist feature also parallels activity in synaptic transmission among neurons in an actual nervous system. Multiple synaptic input pulses are often required to trigger the next neuron in the chain.

What other sorts of knowledge can be represented by connectionist networks? Neural models have been proposed for semantic memory, spatial learning in the hippocampus, instrumental response–outcome contingencies, and classically conditioned associations (see, e.g., McNaughton & Smolensky, 1991; Shanks, 1993).

Connectionism and the Other Approaches

How does connectionism relate to the other approaches described in this chapter? Items in short-term memory are, in connectionist models, those items that are currently active in the neural network. Asking you to briefly retain the words TABLE–DOG–GRASS results in the activation of their neural representations above threshold. These units are now "in" short-term memory. Activation will gradually decay back to resting or baseline levels, corresponding to forgetting from short-term memory.

Elaborative rehearsal in short-term memory could be described as the activation of other units concurrently with those already active. The name JOHN can be elaborated by activation of connected units, such as the image of John's face, other knowledge about John, and so on. In the stage model, encoding is the strengthening of connections between nodes, whereas retrieval is the activation of the retrieval cue's neural units, which in turn activate the units connected to them.

Applications

The approaches presented in this chapter are part of the general public's knowledge about memory. Popular media descriptions of memory regularly refer to short-term and long-term memory, or to retrieval failure. The finer details of the several approaches presented here have more precise implications for memory outside the laboratory.

The Study of Abnormal Memory: Amnesia

Cognitive neuropsychology has contributed substantially to testing theories developed in the lab. As we have noted by examples in this chapter (e.g., H. M. and N. A.), case studies of brain-injured individuals are used to dissociate components, stages, or processes of memory. The influence works in the opposite direction also. Our understanding of amnesic disorders has benefited from the laboratory-based theories of memory.

We all have some familiarity with the concept of amnesia. Yet most amnesias do not match the stereotype depicted in soap operas and films. Amnesia is actually too broad a term, as it can originate from several causes and can take many forms. To appreciate the give and take between the cognitive psychologists and the neuropsychologists, an understanding of the nature of amnesia is a useful starting point.

Classification of Amnesias

The amnesias can differ along two major dimensions, one of cause (organic or psychological) and the other time (loss of memory about events that preceded or followed trauma; Kopelman, 1987). *Organic* amnesia is caused by injury or damage to the brain. This might be head trauma; a brain infection such as encephalitis or meningitis; stroke or anoxia (the loss of oxygen); exposure to toxic substances and chemicals, such as lead or solvents; or prolonged alcohol abuse. The resulting amnesia can vary in severity depending on which areas of the brain are damaged and the extent of that damage.

Psychogenic amnesia is a result of psychological trauma. Someone experiences a psychological trauma but then becomes amnesic for the event. Psychogenic amnesias are the stuff of film fiction, yet they are real enough, although the cause is not as simple as popular media suggests.

The second dimension of amnesia is the dichotomy between forgetting the past versus an inability to form new memories. **Retrograde amnesia** is forgetting of events that occurred before

Figure 7.8 The Temporal Division of Retrograde and Anterograde Amnesia.

the onset of the disorder. This is our everyday conception of amnesia: forgetting of some portion of the past that was once recalled or should be recallable. Retrograde forgetting may be limited to the few minutes or hours preceding trauma, or it may extend back months or years. For example, after a head injury, retrograde amnesia can be extensive, but the time span of forgotten material gradually shrinks, leaving a residual permanent amnesia that is usually fairly limited. In other disorders, such as Korsakoff's and Alzheimer's diseases, the opposite pattern occurs. Retrograde amnesia increases over time as more and more of the past becomes unavailable.

Forgetting can proceed in the opposite direction, from the moment of trauma onward. **Anterograde amnesia** is the inability to form new memories or acquire new knowledge. Anterograde amnesia is less familiar to many of us, but it is a common and serious outcome of brain trauma. The anterograde amnesic individual cannot report the events of the previous hours or days because those memories have not been formed or are not accessible. The inability to keep a running memory of our lives can often be a more serious problem than that of retrograde amnesia.

Retrograde amnesia and anterograde amnesia can be thought of as forgetting that proceeds in different temporal directions from the trauma that provokes forgetting:

Retrograde amnesia ← TRAUMA → Anterograde amnesia

At the time of memory testing, amnesics cannot remember some portions of the past. (See Figure 7.8.) If they cannot now remember things from before the onset of the amnesia, this is retrograde amnesia. If they cannot now remember things since the onset, this is anterograde amnesia.

Retrograde and anterograde amnesias can occur separately, although commonly both are present. H. M. learned very little in his 50+ years after the operation (see Box 7.2). This is the result of anterograde amnesia. He also had some retrograde amnesia: He forgot things that happened in the few years that preceded the operation (Ogden & Corkin, 1991). Tulving's motorcycle accident patient has both retrograde and anterograde amnesia. He cannot recall episodic memories from before the accident and he cannot acquire new episodic memories since the time of the accident (Rosenbaum et al., 2005).

Box 7.2   H. M.

The study of memory has been significantly advanced through case studies of people with unique brain injuries. H. M. is one of the best-known cases in psychology, and his name (or his initials, at least) is more familiar than are the names of the 100 or so researchers who studied him over the years. The initial description of his case by Scoville and Milner (1957) is one of the most cited papers in the scientific literature on the brain and memory.

Henry Molaison, at the age of 28, had portions of the insides of the temporal lobes removed as a treatment of last resort for epilepsy. Remarkably, little about H. M. changed. His epilepsy was controlled; his IQ went up a bit; his personality was unchanged. But over time, his doctors realized that his postsurgery memory problems, which had been expected to resolve, instead became permanent. From the time of the operation in 1953 until his death in 2008, H. M. had been unable to acquire new episodic and semantic memories.

Some details of everyday living and a few major public events sifted into his memory. For instance, he could identify presidents Kennedy and Reagan, who came to fame after H. M. became amnesic. In the years following the deaths of his parents, he knew each had died but did not remember the details. He did not learn new vocabulary (semantic memory), even with explicit practice, and so did not know phrases like *rock 'n' roll* (never mind *hip-hop*). His deficits included both verbal and spatial anterograde amnesias, reflecting the hippocampal lesions in the left and right sides of his brain. However, he could draw the floor plan of the small house he lived in for many years after the operation. His short-term memory was spared; and he could learn through classical conditioning and acquired new motor skills (which together define procedural learning).

H. M. was never able to live on his own, which is characteristic of other severe amnesics. He could wander off and not remember how to get home. Similarly, he did not remember whether he has just eaten a meal and would eat another if offered. If he turned on the stove or another appliance, he forgot within a few minutes. He once went out to rake leaves and persisted for hours, not having a sense of how long he had been at it.

H. M. was a frequent research subject. Each new generation of neurological test or psychological theory (CAT scans, implicit and procedural learning) was tried out on him. Many of the studies were conducted at the Massachusetts Institute of Technology. He had been there often, for days at a time. Yet if he awakened at night he had no idea where he was. Suzanne Corkin (2013) studied H. M. for 20 years, but he did not recognize her. (Brenda Milner studied him for 20 years before that, and he never recognized her either.)

If H. M. could not update his knowledge, was he constantly startled by the new world he saw? What did he think when he looked in the mirror? When asked his age, he reported some number in the 30s when he was then actually 60 (Corkin, 2002). H. M. showed no reaction to seeing this now quite elderly man looking back at him from the mirror. (Remember, the rest of his knowledge basically stopped at age 28.) The absence of surprise here may have been because there was some updating of information over the years due to residual tissue left after the operation, or perhaps the constant repetition supports the learning of familiarity. By contrast, neurologist Oliver Sacks (1985) reported a Korsakoff's patient who panicked at the sight of his 70-year-old face in the mirror because the man thought he was still only 21.

The treatment of epilepsy has advanced considerably since the 1950s, and the devastating effects of temporal lobe resection on memory have been well documented. H. M. was probably the last individual to undergo this procedure.

Types of Amnesias

Amnesic syndrome and Korsakoff's disease are two examples of organic amnesias that are caused by identifiable injury or damage to the brain.

Amnesic syndrome is the label given to individuals like H. M. It is characterized by the inability to form and retrieve new long-term memories. Amnesic syndrome individuals have difficulty acquiring new general knowledge, or what we earlier called semantic memories, as well as impairment in forming episodic memories. These amnesics still have reasonably normal short-term memory. Significantly, these amnesics often can demonstrate new learning via procedural learning. For example, amnesic syndrome individuals can be classically conditioned (Daum, Channon, & Canavan, 1989). Amnesics can learn other perceptual, motor, and cognitive skills as well. The hippocampus is usually the damaged brain region in amnesic syndrome, although naturally occurring brain traumas rarely damage a single region of the brain.

Korsakoff's syndrome is an amnesic disorder named after the Russian psychiatrist who described it over 100 years ago. This syndrome is associated with prolonged alcohol abuse (literally, decades long) and the thiamine vitamin deficiency that accompanies such use. Damage to the diencephalon of the brain, which includes the thalamus and mammillary bodies, is evident, but not necessarily the hippocampus. The disease develops gradually over months and years. Korsakoff's is characterized by both anterograde and retrograde amnesia. Tests of general knowledge may show profound amnesia that extends back over decades. Some of this memory loss is retrograde (forgetting of information that was once known) and some is anterograde (forgetting of the period in which memory ceased to function).

Psychogenic Amnesia results from psychological trauma. Psychogenic amnesias (or "functional" amnesias, to use a medical term for disorders of unknown causes) are almost always retrograde: there is forgetting for the past, or some part of the past, that preceded the trauma. The degree of amnesia can be quite limited or very extensive.

Sometimes the forgetting is for a specific traumatic episode, as when a soldier forgets a terrifying battle. The early French psychiatrist Janet recounted the case of a woman who was told her husband had just died. The report turned out to be a malicious prank. Afterward, she became amnesic for the whole episode but forgot nothing else. Interestingly, memory of the event would recur in nightmares (described in Nemiah, 1979).

A more dramatic form of psychogenic amnesia is forgetting one's entire past life and identity. In a *fugue* reaction, the person literally does not remember who he or she is. For example, one young man developed fugue after the death of his grandfather, to whom he had been particularly close. For a week afterwards, the young man was unaware of who he was, and could not recollect any personal (episodic) memories (Schacter, Wang, Tulving, & Freedman, 1982). Note that the fugue individual retains language and other sorts of general knowledge. In this case, the fugue ended when a funeral scene in a television show reinstated the lost memory. The entire fugue period was itself no longer remembered. Fugue reactions generally resolve after a week or so, although some may persist for months. Sometimes the person wanders off and adopts a new identity, hence the derivation of the word *fugue* from the Latin *to take flight*.

In certain dissociative disorders, a person exhibits multiple personalities or identities. These different personalities can be unaware of, and so are amnesic for, each other. Nemiah (1979) recounts a Reverend Bourne, who alternated between being a preacher and a gambler, and each personality was unaware of the other and what the other did.

In the psychogenic amnesias, the memory is not lost from the brain as it may be with some organically caused amnesias. Instead, memory becomes inaccessible to conscious retrieval. In our stages of memory terminology, the amnesic is experiencing retrieval failure. The memory may return later under various conditions: sometimes spontaneously; possibly in a dream, as it did for Janet's patient; through hypnosis; after the administration of anxiety-relieving drugs; or in the alternate personality of dissociative identity disorder.

One interpretation of psychogenic amnesia is the repression hypothesis. This originally derived from a Freudian psychoanalytic theory, but does have some intuitive appeal. Traumatic memories are repressed into some unconscious part of the mind as a way of relieving anxiety and fear. Fugue is an extreme version of repression, which allows escape from a distressing life situation full of reminders.

Another explanation suggests the memory has become dissociated or separated from conscious awareness (Janet, 1907). Psychogenic amnesia may be an instance of state-dependent or mood-dependent forgetting (see Chapter 10). If the episode was one of intense arousal and fear, the memories could become difficult to retrieve during normal consciousness when the strong emotional states are absent. There are claims that reinstating the intense emotional arousal of an original experience under hypnosis can lead to memory recall. Diamond (1969) reports that

Sirhan Sirhan, who murdered Robert Kennedy (the brother of President John Kennedy), denied having committed the murder. However, with hypnosis, he gradually reexperienced the anger and emotion felt at the time and recalled the crime.

Another possibility is that psychogenic amnesia is an instance of implicit memory. As such, the memories are not available to conscious recollection, although they may be expressed in other ways. In one case of fugue, a woman could not recall any details about her life, but she did show skin-conductance changes (used to assess emotional reactions) to familiar stimuli. When presented with some true and some false statements about her life, such as her birth date, she showed stronger reactions to the correct facts than to incorrect ones (Gudjonsson, 1979). We have seen examples before of a separation between conscious memory and unconscious knowledge.

Everyday Forgetting and the Models of Memory

Surveys reveal that many people are concerned about everyday forgetting. A news poll showed that 46 percent of respondents worried more about failing memory than about failing health. The numerous memory-improvement self-help apps, websites, and herbal remedies that are available attest to a market for advice. British psychiatrists described "mnestic hypochondria," or an excessive concern about memory problems among middle-aged individuals who nevertheless test fine on memory (Berrios, Markova, & Girala, 2000). These "worried but well" individuals are characterized as bright, educated, ambitious, and perfectionistic. One could suppose that such people, working and living busy and stressful lives, might become anxious about perceived declining memory abilities.

Accurate data on everyday forgetting is difficult to obtain. Nevertheless, certain forms of everyday forgetting are more frequently mentioned than others. What follows are some items from the *Short Inventory of Minor Lapses* that were rated with the highest frequency of occurrence by two samples of participants in England: college students and other adult visitors to the Applied Psychology Unit (Reason, 1993). As noted at the start of this chapter, the several approaches presented in this chapter may explain why forgetting occurs, and offer means for remediation and prevention.

1. How often do you forget to say something you were going to mention?
2. How often do you have the "what-am-I-here-for?" feeling when you have forgotten what it is you came to do?
3. How often do you forget to do something that you were going to do after dealing with an unexpected interruption?

At first glance, each of these seems to be a failure of short-term memory. The intention to say or do something was displaced during a brief time interval by ongoing events and so was not remembered. Consciously repeating (via maintenance rehearsal) the intention to say or do something should keep it in mind until it can be acted on. Alternatively, the stage approach suggests that retrieval failure is the source of the forgetting here. At the moment of action, nothing reminded you of what you wanted to say, do, or get. You realize that it was retrieval failure when your intention is suddenly remembered sometime later.

4. How often do you find yourself searching for something that you've just put down?

This could be an example of absentmindedness: Your mind was occupied elsewhere and so you did not deeply or elaborately process where you placed the object. The interesting next question is: When you find the lost object, do you then recall having mislaid it? If you still have no recollection, then maybe you did have an encoding failure. If you do recall putting down the object, then you were earlier experiencing retrieval failure. (One final possibility is that this is not a memory failure at all, but instead you have kids who misplace things when you aren't looking.)

5. How often do you find you cannot recall the name of a familiar person or object?
6. How often do you find that you cannot recall a word or name at that moment? You know the word; it is on the tip of your tongue.

Remembering names is important and forgetting them has social and professional implications. Sometimes names are known but they cannot be recalled at will, an example of retrieval failure. In this case, additional retrieval cues may help prompt the memory. We incidentally do this anyway, running through an alphabetical listing of names to see if any seem to fit (Harris, 1978; Reason & Lucas, 1984).

When we see a familiar person, their name is often the most difficult thing about them to remember. Young, Hay, and Ellis (1985) proposed a model for associating names to people that places these steps in the reverse direction. First, we recognize someone's face. Then, we recall all the other things we know about the person, such as his or her occupation, where we know him or her from, and so on. This is person identification. Only after these steps are successfully completed do we recall the name. Ellis, Hay, and Young point to everyday memory studies that show we often remember everything except a person's name, but we never remember the name and nothing else.

In attempting to recall a name or word that is on the tip of your tongue, some other word or name may repeatedly come to mind. The problem is, once this wrong word is retrieved, it seems to block recall of the sought-after item. Connectionist theory offers an explanation here. These blockers are often more familiar or more frequently used, as compared to the less familiar word on the tip of your tongue (Reason & Lucas, 1984). Partial information places us near the target in memory, but then triggers items that are closer to threshold or that have stronger connections to the cues. The blocking name or word pops into consciousness. Each subsequent recall attempt finds the most active item, which happens to be the blocker. How can blocking be overcome? *Stop trying to remember.* Let the blocker fade back to its resting level. The sought-after word will come to you later. (Or, as most people reported doing: look up the word, or ask someone else.)

Certain other memory distortions fall between the amnesias and everyday forgetting. Some of these are described in Box 7.3.

Box 7.3   Anomalous Forgetting Phenomenon

The theoretical approaches we have covered in this chapter can also be applied to some unusual memory experiences, such as cryptomnesia, déjà vu, or altered perspective.

There are times when you think you have come up with an original idea, only to realize later it was actually suggested by someone else. This lack of awareness that the idea is a memory has been called *cryptomnesia*. Freud once thought he had an original insight into the origin of the neuroses, only to be reminded that his friend Wilhelm Fliess had suggested the idea to Freud a year earlier (Freud, 1901/1960, p. 143). Musicians have been sued because their songs resembled an earlier song. B. F. Skinner described the phenomenon well: "One of the most disheartening experiences is discovering a point you have just made—so significant, so beautifully expressed—was made by you in something you published a long time ago" (Hostetler, 1988).

One explanation is that cryptomnesia may be an example of *source amnesia*. You know something, but without the where and the when of the learning (Brown & Murphy, 1989).

Déjà vu, French for "never seen," is the sense of familiarity evoked by a present experience, even though you believe the experience is novel. For instance, you feel like you have been here before, but you have not. Penfield and Jasper (1954) called this an illusion of familiarity. If cryptomnesia is remembering without awareness, then déjà vu is awareness without a memory to validate the feeling.

A behavioral theorist might attribute déjà vu to generalization across stimuli: There may be sufficient resemblance between the new and a previous situation to remind you of the old. Similarly, as an older memory weakens, losing resolution and detail, it becomes easier to confuse with other memories. One could make an analogy to a badly faded photograph. Thus, a new experience may "match" the fuzzy image of an older memory, one that is not actually similar to the present. (See Brown, 2003, for a review of déjà vu.)

In addition to the factual elements of memory (the when and where; the sights and sounds), memories also have an emotional component. There is a feeling that accompanies the recognition of familiarity. In déjà vu, a person experiences the feeling that goes along with a memory but not the memory itself. On the other hand, in *misidentity* disorders, the affective feeling of familiarity or recognition is absent. In Capgras Syndrome, the affected individual recognizes familiar people but the emotion that should accompany recognition of someone you know is missing. The Capgras person infers these other familiar-looking people must be imposters, or believes they have been replaced by near-duplicates (Breen, Caine, Colthart, Hendy, & Roberts, 2000). (A fictionalized account of Capgras syndrome is presented in Powers, 2006.) Curiously, there was a report of a man who did not recognize himself in the mirror, and assumed the reflection was some other person there. These misidentity disorders probably involve dementia or other neurological problems, and are not just memory failures. They do illustrate, however, the contribution of memory to anomalous conditions.

A more common (and normal) experience is seeing yourself in memory. Nigro and Neisser (1983) asked college students to remember personal experiences, such as giving a speech or being in an accident. Most of the students recalled at least a few memories from the perspective of observing themselves. *Observer memories* were reported more often in older rather than recent memories, and in memories rated as emotional and self-conscious, such as giving a public presentation. How do observer memories originate? Nigro and Neisser suggest that some memories are rehearsed more often, as would occur for emotional events. This rumination leads to a change in orientation, from the self looking out to the self being looked on.

One reason for considering these anomalous memory experiences is to show they may not be so odd after all. Although multiple interpretations have been offered for several of these phenomena, the explanations all derive from principles of learning and memory otherwise discussed in this text. The usefulness of a science of memory is not just to explain basic research findings, but also to explain the unusual in everyday life.

Summary

Partitioning Memory

Memory may be better understood when partitioned into separate components, stages, or processes than when treated as a unitary trait. We hypothesize multiple memory systems because generalizations about memory as a whole are not always valid; and for the heuristic value in simplifying our theories of memory. The dissociations that are produced when a variable has different effects on different tasks also suggest separate systems. Dissociations may be produced by the use of experimental manipulations, different memory tasks, neurological disorders, or varied subject populations.

Components of Memory Approach

The dual-storage conception of short-term and long-term memory is referred to as the "modal" model. Short-term memory has a limited duration and capacity, stores items verbally, and is subject to disruption. Long-term memory retains indefinitely, has virtually unlimited capacity, and retains information in many forms. The distinction between two memory stores is suggested by the serial-position effect. Different experimental variables affect the primacy and recency portions of the curve. Short-term and long-term memories are also dissociated by the patterns of memory loss in amnesic individuals. H. M. cannot form new long-term memories, but his short-term span is normal. K. F. is impaired in short-term verbal span.

Long-term store can be further divided into episodic and semantic memories. Episodic memory is our personal or autobiographical memory system. Semantic memory is our store of general knowledge. It is more like dictionary or encyclopedic knowledge. Although not always separable in laboratory experiments, the distinction is useful in describing the development of memory from episodic to semantic or generic memories.

Two other hypothesized divisions of long-term memory are considered to be instances of implicit memory. Procedural learning is knowing how to do things: perceptual, motor, and cognitive skills. Procedural tasks include mirror star tracing, reading reversed or inverted text, or learning recurring sequences of numbers or locations. Priming refers to the facilitated response to a stimulus that has been recently experienced, or has been "primed" in memory. For example, the identification of a word from a few letters, or fragments, is facilitated by recent exposure to that word.

Explicit and implicit memory are terms used to refer to how we test memory. Direct questioning about the contents of memory is an *explicit* task, as in recall and recognition tests of episodic and semantic memory. Indirect assessment of the effects of prior experience by measuring performance rather than recall is an *implicit* task. Procedural learning and priming effects are both examples of implicit memory, although explicit recall may influence performance on these types of tasks.

Stages of Memory

Another approach to memory separates it into several stages: encoding, storage, and retrieval. The stages are experimentally dissociated when a variable primarily affects one stage or another. For example, alcohol primarily affects the encoding stage.

Neuropsychological dissociations are demonstrated by individuals with impairment at one or another stage. H. M. is believed to have an encoding deficit: He cannot form new memories. However, some amnesics misrecall words from previous, supposedly forgotten lists, which suggests that encoding occurred, but the amnesics have trouble directing retrieval.

Processing Approaches

Remembering and forgetting can be attributed to the type of processing information receives. Depth-of-processing theory hypothesizes only a single memory store, and variations in the degree of cognitive processing determines whether something is remembered. Rapid forgetting is due to shallow processing, whereas sustained retention is due to deep processing. The distinction between shallow and deep processing is illustrated by two kinds of rehearsal. Maintenance rehearsal, or the passive repetition of information, is shallow processing. Elaborative rehearsal involves meaningful analysis and comprehension of the material, and thus represents a deeper level of processing. According to depth-of-processing theory, robust incidental learning occurs due to the cognitive involvement and interest in the target material.

Connectionist Models

Connectionism attempts to combine cognitive and biological approaches by modeling the neural changes that underlie learning and memory. Each neural unit can have connections to many other units. The strength of connections increases when neural units are simultaneously active. Inner layers, or hidden units, may combine and summate activation from units in the previous layer. A neural unit can be activated much as a neuron is activated, and activation gradually fades back to the prestimulation baseline or resting level over a brief period of time.

The trial-by-trial increases in connection strength are described by the *delta rule*. The increment on each trial is a constant proportion of the difference between the maximum possible activation and the current level of activation. The application of the delta rule in simulations produces a classic learning curve characterized by relatively large increases in learning in the early trials and smaller increments in later trials.

Applications

The amnesias are described along two major dimensions, one of cause (physical or psychological) and the other time (loss of memory of events that preceded or that followed trauma). Most amnesias have a physical or organic cause due to injury or damage to the brain. Psychogenic, or functional, amnesias result from psychological trauma. Retrograde amnesia is forgetting of events that occurred before the onset of the disorder. Anterograde amnesia is the inability to form new memories or acquire new knowledge.

Amnesic syndrome, caused by damage to the hippocampus, is characterized by the inability to form and retrieve new long-term memories (anterograde amnesia), some retrograde amnesia, and a reasonably normal short-term memory. Amnesic syndrome individuals, like H. M., are impaired in acquiring semantic as well as episodic memories. However, new learning occurs via procedural learning.

Korsakoff's syndrome is an amnestic disorder associated with prolonged alcohol abuse and vitamin deficiency. It is characterized by both anterograde and retrograde amnesia. Tests of general knowledge may show profound amnesia that extends over decades. Damage to the thalamus and mammillary bodies in the brain is usually present.

Psychogenic amnesias are retrograde: forgetting the past, or some part of the past, that preceded the trauma. They fall into one of three categories: limited amnesia, fugue state, or dissociative disorder. In psychogenic amnesia, the memory is not lost, but it becomes inaccessible to conscious retrieval. The lost memories sometimes spontaneously return, are accessible through hypnosis, or are demonstrated by implicit memory testing. Psychogenic forgetting may be due to repression, avoidance, or dissociation in the form of state-dependent remembering.

Many forms of everyday forgetting can be described within the approaches covered in this chapter. Understanding where a breakdown occurs offers a better chance for prevention and remediation. Examples of forgetting from an inventory of memory lapses include momentary forgetting, prospective forgetting, absentmindedness, and temporary forgetting of common words and names.

8   Short-Term Memory

"When deeply absorbed, we do not hear the clock strike. But our attention may awake after the striking has ceased, and we may then count off the strokes" (Exner, quoted by William James, 1890, p. 646). This quote captures well the subjective feel of short-term memory. William James was making a distinction between primary memory and secondary memory. Something in *primary memory* has never left consciousness and is part of the psychological present. Something in *secondary memory* has been absent from consciousness and therefore belongs to the psychological past.

The idea that there are (at least) two memory systems has long been a part of psychology's history, both in cognitive and biological theory. In addition to William James, the German psychologist G. E. Muller hypothesized a transient "perseveratory activity" in the brain that could eventually consolidate into a permanent long-term memory (Muller & Pilzecker, 1900; see Lechner, Squire, & Byrne, 1999).

In the previous chapter we discussed the amnesias, which for the most part involve forgetting from long-term memory. In our everyday lives, forgetting over short time intervals is also troubling. Absentmindedness, a common label for everyday lapses, occurs when people forget what they were doing, were about to do, had intended to do, and so on. You go upstairs to get something but become distracted by something else. You wonder what you were looking for, wander around looking for something that needs getting, and likely return empty-handed. The fretting about age-related memory decline so often discussed in the media is often in reference to something forgotten from just a few minutes earlier.

This chapter is about remembering over brief intervals of time. *Short-term memory* (STM) refers to memory that is limited both in its duration and its capacity. As assessed in laboratory tests, STM retains on the order of five to seven items, for several seconds to less than a minute in the absence of rehearsal. Short-term memory is distinguished from *long-term memory* (LTM), which in the laboratory is typically any memory more than a few minutes old, and in the real world, our memories of a lifetime.

One difficulty that memory psychologists encounter is the mistaken use of the phrase "short-term memory." I often hear people refer to any forgetting of recent events as a short-term memory problem. What they are usually referring to, however, is forgetting that takes place over hours or even days. Technically this is not STM or working memory as discussed in this chapter. These forgettings could be described as problems with *recent memory*, which is a nontechnical term, but possibly should be added to describe everyday lapses than encompass recent events.

Remembering over short intervals has important implications for our everyday cognitive functioning. "Without it, you couldn't understand this sentence, add up a restaurant tab in your head, or even find your way home" (Wickelgren, 1997, p. 1580). (Now that I reread this sentence, I realize you'll probably use your smartphone to do these tasks.) Short-term memory, and its newer variation of working memory, have been referred to as our mental blackboard: a temporary, reusable workspace in the mind used for comprehension, reasoning, and planning.

Short-Term Memory

Some History

The concept of an "immediate" memory, or what can be recalled from the immediate past, lay dormant in psychology for many years before Waugh and Norman (1965) reintroduced the primary–secondary memory distinction. The next major step in theory development was the multistore system of memory of Atkinson and Shiffrin (see Figure 8.1). Atkinson and Shiffrin (1968) refer to two kinds of memory: short-term store and long-term store. As noted in the previous chapter, this developed into the "modal" model of memory, or the schematic that serves as the outline for other theories of memory.

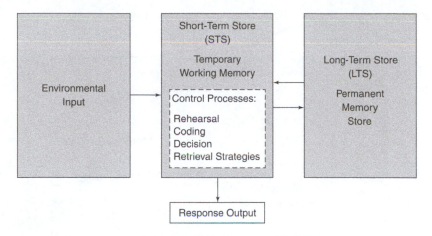

Figure 8.1 The Modal Model of Short-Term Store and Long-Term Store.

Source: Adapted from "The Control of Short-Term Memory," by R. C. Atkinson and R. M. Shiffrin, 1971, *Scientific American*, Figure 1 p. 82. Copyright © 1971 by Allen Beechel. Reprinted with permission.

Atkinson and Shiffrin's hypothesis that there are separate short-term and long-term memory stores provoked markedly different reactions from other psychologists. A few argued that postulating two kinds of memory was unparsimonious (i.e., complicated). The other reaction was that two memory stores was not enough! Baddeley and Hitch (1974) proposed the evolution of a single short-term memory into *working memory,* which has separate stores for verbal information and spatial information. Working memory also has a separate central executive that controls and deploys attention. Finally, there was a need to acknowledge the overlap between short-term and long-term memory. Information moves back-and-forth between the two. Baddeley (2000) added the episodic buffer to address this connection between the working memory and long-term memory.

Working memory is the focus of much current research, and the term "working memory" is used much more frequently in the current literature. However, working memory and short-term memory are sometimes used interchangeably. What follows in this chapter is first a consideration of the characteristics of short-term memory, second of working memory, and finally some applications of each.

Short-Term Memory Tasks

Short-term retention is often assessed by one of two tests. The *distractor task* attempts to quantify the duration of immediate memory over brief delay intervals when rehearsal is prevented. The *memory span* attempts to quantify the capacity of immediate memory.

The Brown–Peterson Distractor Task

The distractor task was described by British researcher John Brown in 1958, and the Americans Lloyd and Margaret Peterson in 1959 (but see Pillsbury & Sylvester, 1940). In the **Brown–Peterson task**, a few items are presented for retention, usually three letters or words. These items can be recalled accurately if the subject is tested immediately. However, the subject is instructed to perform a distractor task, such as counting backwards by threes, until told to recall the target items. Thus, the sequence of events in a trial might be a visual presentation of the

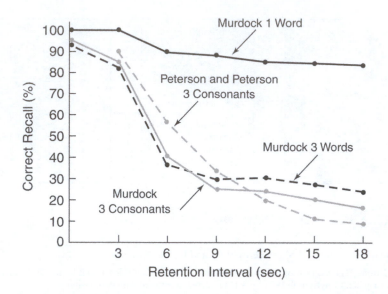

Figure 8.2 Mean Percent Recall of Words or Letters in the Brown–Peterson Distractor Task.

Source: From "Implications of Short-Term Memory for a General Theory of Memory," by A. W. Melton, 1963, *Journal of Verbal Learning and Verbal Behavior*, 2, p. 9. Copyright 1963 by Elsevier. Reprinted with permission.

to-be-remembered items (e.g., DOG–CAT–TREE), a number (e.g., 933), counting backwards ("... 933, 930, 927 ..."), and finally the instruction to recall the target items. Representative data from two studies are shown in Figure 8.2 for the retention of three consonants or three words. The amount recalled drops off dramatically after as little as 9 seconds of distractor activity.

The rapid forgetting found with the distractor technique was thought to be significant for it seemed to demonstrate how brief STM was in the absence of rehearsal. Memory for the to-be-remembered items faded quickly.

However, some of the forgetting in the Brown–Peterson task may be due to interference from earlier or preceding material. Imagine you are participating in one of these experiments. You are given list after list of three words to remember, for as many as 50 lists. Is it really the case that each list is forgotten, totally and completely, at the end of each trial? After all, the assumption is that this is an STM task. Or is it likely that there is confusion in memory, and that recall of the current list is affected by remembering items from the previous lists? This is called **proactive interference**: Items presented on earlier trials interfere with recall of the current list of to-be-remembered items.

Curiously, performance in the Brown–Peterson distractor task is often perfect on the very first trial: Subjects remember the word triplet or consonant triplet perfectly after delays of 15 seconds. Forgetting only develops as the number of trials increases, consistent with the notion that proactive interference occurs.

Interference from previous lists also increases with the similarity of the to-be-remembered items. If the words across adjacent trials come from the same category (e.g., names of fruits) rather than being unrelated words, forgetting occurs even more rapidly across trials. Proactive interference seems to build up. If after several trials the category of target words is shifted, say, to professions, recall of the changed triplet increases dramatically, a phenomenon labeled *release from proactive interference*. This buildup and then release from proactive interference is illustrated in the left panel of Figure 8.3 (Wickens, Dalezman, & Eggemeier, 1976). Recall of word

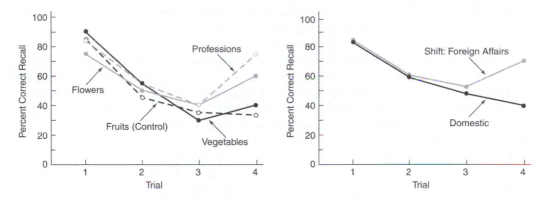

Figure 8.3 Buildup (across Trials 1 to 3) and Release (Trial 4) of Proactive Interference for Words (*left panel*) and News Stories (*right panel*).

Source: (*left panel*) From "Multiple encoding of word attributes in memory," 1976, by D. D. Wickens, R. E. Dalezman, & F. T Eggemeier, *Memory & Cognition, 4*. 307–310. Reprinted with permission. (*Right panel*) From "Proactive interference effects with television news items: Further evidence" by B. Gunter, C. Berry, C., & B. R. Clifford (1981), *Journal of Experimental Psychology: Human Learning and Memory, 7*, 480–487. Copyright © 1991 by the American Psychological Association. Reprinted with permission.

triplets that came from the same semantic category (names of fruits) declined across the first three trials. Changing word categories on the fourth trial from fruits to professions or flowers led to an increase in recall, as compared to maintaining the initial category. Switching from fruits to vegetables did not produce much release.

Another illustration of the buildup and release of proactive interference is in memory for television news stories (Gunter, Berry, & Clifford, 1981). A series of brief news reports from the same thematic category (e.g., domestic politics or foreign affairs) was presented as the to-be-remembered items. Recall of story triplets from within a category decreased over trials, consistent with the hypothesis of the buildup of proactive interference. If the category of stories then changed, release occurred and the final list of stories was recalled better. (See the right panel of Figure 8.3.)

Memory Span

A second measure of STM is its capacity, or how many items can be held in immediate memory. **Memory span** is defined as the longest sequence of items that can be recalled in correct order after a single presentation. Recall is attempted immediately, without a delay or a distractor. Memory span is tested by presenting lists of increasing lengths, often five to nine items, to assess the maximum length than can be recalled correctly. The to-be-recalled items are typically letters, numbers, or words. Our spans seem to be limited to about seven items (Miller, 1956).

Memory span is relevant to our remembering outside of the laboratory. Is it simply a coincidence that seven digits is the length of a standard telephone number? Conrad (1958) asked his participants to listen to and then dial eight-digit numbers. Only about 50 percent of the numbers were dialed correctly. When a constant prefix was added (such as the "9" often needed to get an outside line), recall dropped even further. Memory span is also included some intelligence tests. The Wechsler Intelligence scales have a digit span as one subtest. For more fun, there is the digits-backward portion, in which the numbers have to be recalled in reverse order.

Memory span seems to be a straightforward measure of short-term memory capacity. However, span is not fixed and invariant, but is affected by numerous variables. For example, non-rhyming items are recalled better than rhyming words; digits are remembered better than words;

and drawings of objects are remembered better than the names of the objects (Brooks & Watkins, 1990). Span also increases with practice. In one study, adolescents with severe learning disabilities were given 10 minutes of daily practice at recalling digit and word strings. After 2 weeks there was a significant increase in span length (Hulme & Mackenzie, 1992).

An important determinant of memory span is the *word-length effect*: More items can be remembered when shorter words are the to-be-remembered items. Baddeley, Thomson, and Buchanan (1975) found that college students' spans were dramatically shorter for sets of words that were each five syllables long (such as ASSOCIATION, CONSIDERABLE, or UNIVERSITY) than for lists of one-syllable words. Five one-syllable words could be remembered 75 percent of the time, yet barely 30 percent of five five-syllable word sequences could be recalled.

Baddeley et al. (1975) found that span correlated with articulation rate, which is a measure of how fast you can simply pronounce the target words. Longer words take longer to vocalize than shorter words, and so maybe longer words also take longer to mentally rehearse. Support for the articulation hypothesis comes from a study of Welsh bilingual speakers, who could recall more digits in English than in Welsh. English has shorter words for numbers (Ellis & Hennelly, 1980). Later work extended these findings across a range of different languages (Chinese, Hebrew, Arabic) and showed a consistent relationship between memory span and the amount of time it takes to articulate digits in that language (Naveh-Benjamin & Ayres, 1986; Stigler, Lee, & Stevenson, 1986).

Characteristics of Verbal Short-Term Memory

Short-term memories seem to have a different character from long-term memories. "This primary memory image is . . . an extremely lively one, but is subjectively quite distinct from every sort of after-image or hallucination. . . . It vanishes, if not caught by attention, in the course of a few seconds. Even when the original impression is attended to, the liveliness of its image fades fast" (Exner, cited by James, 1890, p. 646). Recent memories are rich in sensory quality, such as sound, color, and texture. In addition to these subjective impressions, certain objective features have been attributed to short-term memory:

    Acoustic encoding
    Limited capacity
    Limited duration
    Susceptibility to forgetting
    Transfer to long-term memory
    Control processes

As we will see, some of the features may not in fact uniquely discriminate short-term from long-term memory, thus blurring any ready distinctions between the two hypothesized memory systems.

Acoustic Encoding

In a typical laboratory task, words, letters, or digits are read or shown to the participant, and the items are recalled out loud. Not surprisingly, the words are remembered as they sound, as if they were being verbally rehearsed. Long-term memory, on the other hand, is usually characterized as involving semantic encoding. That is, we remember the meaning or interpretation of a word rather than the exact word or its sound. One way of demonstrating this difference is to attempt to remember words that sound similar but that have different meanings (e.g., MAN, CAN, MAD, CAP, MAP). If the words are encoded by sound, they are confusable and errors occur as sound-alike substitutions are remembered in STM tests (Baddeley, 1966; Conrad, 1964). If the words are encoded semantically in LTM, they are not confusable: A MAP is different from a MAN and a CAP. On a delayed test of recall, the errors in recall are synonyms of the presented words: HAT is remembered instead of CAP.

The verbal–semantic distinction helps explain why we can recall a just-heard sentence verbatim, but in recalling later from long-term memory we paraphrase the sentence into somewhat different words. Sachs (1967) demonstrated this idea in memory for sentences. The participants listened to short paragraphs, which were occasionally interrupted to test for a discrimination between verbatim and paraphrased versions of recently heard sentences. If the sentence was one just heard, the subjects could usually identify a verbatim copy. If the sentence had occurred about 30 seconds earlier (or two to three sentences back) in the passage, verbatim test sentences were often confused with paraphrased versions that had the same meaning.

There are exceptions to the acoustic-in-STM versus semantic-in-LTM distinction. Exact wording is sometimes remembered in long-term memory, not just the gist. Distinctive sentences heard in conversations can be discriminated from their paraphrases, even 2 days later (Keenan, McWhinney, & Mayhew, 1977).

The use of acoustic encoding may reflect the strategies people adopt to remember. When the task is to retain short lists of words or numbers for brief periods of time, one list after another, subjects may adopt a passive and repetitive rehearsal strategy, much like when we rehearse a phone number just long enough to dial it. When meaningful material is used and the task requires retention over a longer interval, the subjects may use an elaborative rehearsal strategy. Thus, the subject might try to form associations among list items, organize the items, or relate the items to existing knowledge.

Limited Capacity

Short-term memory has a limited capacity to hold information, in contrast with the virtually unlimited capacity of long-term memory. Most people probably could remember seven items in a memory span test, or "the magical number seven, plus-or-minus two," as George Miller titled it in a famous article in 1956. However, this does not mean that the actual capacity of STM is seven items. The immediate recall of a string of items reflects the simultaneous use of the short-term and long-term memories. Some of the items are stored temporarily in long-term memory while additional new items are processed in the short-term store (Waugh & Norman, 1965). Short-term capacity needs to be measured without the long-term component, and in the absence of rehearsal. Under these conditions, the current corrected estimates of the capacity of STM are on the order of three to five items, with an average of four (Cowan, 2001). "The magical number four" (Cowan, 2010)? This doesn't have the same ring to it.

But what exactly is an item? The data from the Brown–Peterson procedure shown in Figure 8.2 show equivalent retention of three letters or three words, even though the words contain more letters. So, is an item a letter, a word, an idea? One answer is that an item is a unit already existing in long-term memory. Letters, digits, and words are each represented in permanent memory; each is an already known item.

Miller (1956) suggested that span could be enlarged by increasing the amount of information contained within each item. For example, the apparent capacity of memory span can be increased by parsing and encoding the material in terms of meaningful units, called chunks. Remembering the string FBITSACIA is more difficult than remembering FBI–TSA–CIA. Nine letters become three chunks. This chunking strategy can allow remembering strings much longer than seven digits or words. Miller describes one subject, Sydney Smith, who could recall lists of 20 randomly sequenced 1's and 0's. Had Smith enlarged his short-term memory capacity to 20 items? Not at all. A code was created that translated three-digit strings into letters. Thus, 100 = A, 101 = B, 110 = C, and so on. As Smith listened to a list, he parsed it into triplets, converting each to a letter, and remembered the letter. Thus, he would actually remember something like A–D–F–C–C–B. In reproducing the "digit" string, he decoded the letters back into 1's and 0's.

There are two points to emphasize here. One is that STM capacity is indeed limited. Apparent enlargements of STM are often accomplished by recoding items into more encompassing units. The second point is that short-term memory uses long-term memory. We can remember items in STM that are already represented somewhere in long-term memory.

Limited Duration

Short-term memory is short, although the answer to "How short?" varies. Estimates of primary memory when rehearsal is limited are on the order of seconds (Waugh & Norman, 1965). As we saw earlier, forgetting occurred after 15 to 30 seconds of distraction in the Brown–Peterson task. Informal use of the term often refers to something on the order of one to several minutes in everyday life.

Forgetting: Short-Term Memory is Sensitive to Disruption

In the Atkinson and Shiffrin (1968) model, forgetting from short-term memory is due to the displacement of old items by new items. The capacity limit means that the addition of a new item requires dropping some item already in STM.

It does not take much to disrupt STM. You look up a phone number, someone asks you a question, and the number's gone. A laboratory example of this sort of distraction is the *suffix effect*. At the end of each list of to-be-remembered items a recurring item is added that need not be remembered. This suffix reduces recall of the last item, or sometimes the last few items. For instance, the word "zero" presented after a list of nine items caused more forgetting of the final item in the list than did presenting a buzzer after the list (Crowder, 1972). Similarly, when lists are presented via sign language to deaf subjects, a suffix effect occurs with an added sign (Shand & Klima, 1981).

Schilling and Weaver (1983) tested the effects of a phone company policy for directory assistance calls. In the suffix condition, each number was followed with the phrase, "Have a nice day!" The suffix phrase interfered with recall when unfamiliar prefixes (the first three digits) were used. Ironically, the phone company's attempt to be friendly could have the perverse effect of causing you to forget the number!

Short-term retention in the real world often takes place in the context of a divided-attention task. Instead of the quiet background conditions of the laboratory, other sounds occur simultaneously with the to-be-remembered list (e.g., you look up a phone number and then attempt to dial it while the television is on in the background). How loud the background noise is turns out to be less important that the pattern of background sound. There is more interference with memory span if the background sound is speech than if the background is white noise (Banbury, Macken, Tremblay, & Jones, 2001).

Transfer to Long-Term Memory

STM has a role in transferring information to LTM. This characteristic has commonsense appeal. When we decide we really need to remember something in permanent memory, we seem to process information in a certain way in STM. We rehearse a name or number, try to form an image, or devise a mnemonic to aid later recall. Maintenance in short-term memory allows the opportunity for information to be copied into long-term memory.

Several sorts of evidence seem to support this transfer function of STM. If subjects are asked to rehearse out loud when attempting to remember a list of words, we find that words receiving more rehearsals are generally recalled better (Rundus, 1971). That is, more rehearsals correlate with better long-term memory for those words. (This is illustrated in Figure 6.5 in Chapter 6.)

Verbal rehearsal may be necessary in learning some kinds of knowledge, such as the sound of new words. Blocking rehearsal might prevent learning. This process was simulated experimentally by asking subjects to remember nonwords. Adult subjects attempted to learn a simulated foreign language. Rehearsal was prevented by having the subjects repeat nonsense speech sounds, such as "da, da, da . . ." (Gathercole, 1994). The subjects had more difficulty learning the new words when articulation was suppressed.

There is other evidence, however, which shows that remembering in STM is not necessary for LTM formation. One telling observation comes from brain-injured participants like K. F., who are impaired in the immediate recall of auditory information. K. F. has a limited verbal short-term memory, often restricted to recalling a single item in the Brown–Peterson distractor task. Nevertheless, he can learn and retain long-term memories at normal rates (Shallice & Warrington, 1970). If a 10-word list was repeated until memorized perfectly, K. F. learned just as quickly as normal control participants. K. F. shows a dissociation between poor performance on a STM task and normal performance on LTM tasks.

It is also the case that maintenance of information in short-term memory does not guarantee entry into long-term memory. Football players who had just suffered a concussion could remember the events leading up to the head injury. These memories gradually became less available as time passed, and were essentially gone after 4 hours. Even though the information had been in STM, as shown by the players' reproductions of their stories during the first several posttraumatic minutes, eventually forgetting occurred (Lynch & Yarnell, 1973).

Overall, the evidence suggests that processing in short-term memory does aid long-term learning. Control processes employed within short-term memory, such as rehearsal and imagery, benefit long-term retention. However, simple passive residence in STM may not suffice to transfer information to LTM.

Control Processes

Atkinson and Shiffrin said that we can choose (to a degree) when and how we use STM. There are active control processes in STM. We can control where to direct attention, how to code new inputs, when to rehearse, and which retrieval cues to use. Control processes define STM as an active rather than passive store. (Control processes are discussed in more detail in the section on Working Memory.)

Summary of the Features of Short-Term Memory

The just-reviewed characteristics suggest that there are few absolute distinctions between verbal short-term memory and long-term memory. Acoustic or semantic encoding can occur in either memory. The capacity of STM, although indeed limited, is expandable by using coding schemes to draw on what is already stored in LTM. Finally, rehearsal in STM does not necessarily ensure entry into LTM. Thus, not all of the supposed characteristics of verbal STM neatly dichotomize it from LTM.

Other Modalities of Short-Term Memory

The research described so far has focused on memory for verbal material. This bias derives partly from the use of college students and word lists in our experiments, and partly from our tendency to equate short-term memory with rehearsal. However, short-term retention occurs in other sensory modalities and with other types of materials.

Visual Short-Term Memory

To study visual short-term memory, stimuli are presented as short lists of images, pictures, or even objects. The images may be meaningless, such as nonsense shapes, or the pictures may be meaningful, for example, scenic mountain views. Retention is tested by a recognition procedure: A test picture is presented and the subject decides whether it was in the previewed list.

The use of picture stimuli does not preclude verbal encoding of the images. Subjects could recode the pictures into words and then rehearse these descriptions. Verbal encoding can be reduced by using materials that are not readily described in words. Wright et al. (1990) compared memory for scenic and kaleidoscope pictures. Lists of 10 images were presented and the "off" time (or blank screen time) between images was varied between 0.5 and 6 seconds. Longer off times facilitated recall of the scenic pictures, as if subjects were verbally rehearsing between pictures ("tree, brook, snow . . .") during the longer intervals between pictures. Memory for the kaleidoscope images, on the other hand, did not improve with longer off times between images, suggesting they were not being verbally rehearsed. Remembering these images thus seemed to depend on a visual memory.

Spatial Short-Term Memory

Short-term memory for spatial positions can be illustrated using a grid on a computer screen, something like a tic-tac-toe board. An asterisk is presented in one square at a time, in a random sequence, to mark locations. After presentation of this list of positions, the participant attempts to point to the locations in the same order in which they had appeared.

Dark and Benbow (1991) tested spatial memory in the preceding manner using mathematically or verbally gifted seventh graders. Strings of three to nine items were presented, using lists of spatial positions, digits, or words. The mathematically gifted performed better than did the verbally gifted students on the spatial and digit spans. On the word span, the verbally gifted kids did better. These results are shown in Figure 8.4, which also includes data from children who were both mathematically and verbally gifted.

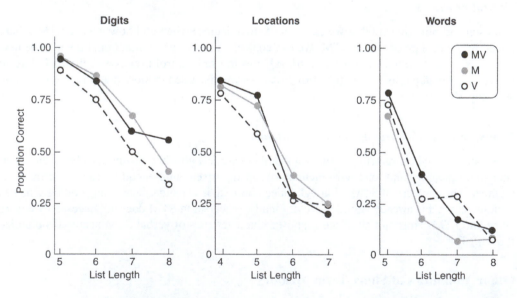

Figure 8.4 **Correct Recall in Three Span Tasks.** Graphs plot the number of digits, locations, and words recalled by the mathematically gifted (M), verbally gifted (V), and mathematically and verbally gifted 13-year-olds (MV).

Source: From "Differential Enhancement of Working Memory with Mathematical versus Verbal Precocity," by V. J. Dark and C. P. Benbow, 1991, *Journal of Educational Psychology, 83*, p. 52. Copyright © 1991 by the American Psychological Association. Reprinted with permission.

Short-Term Memory for Actions

STM for movements has been tested using short lists of hand and arm actions. In a version of the distractor technique, Kausler, Wiley, and Lieberwitz (1992) presented movement triplets to adult subjects. Example actions might include clapping, waving, or pressing a button, although not all of the movements were so readily described in words. After delays of 15 seconds, there was little forgetting if the participants did nothing or if they counted backwards. There was significant forgetting if the participants performed interfering actions or if they watched the experimenter perform distracting actions during the 15-second delay. Thus, just as in the Brown–Peterson task, forgetting occurs when the distracting material was in the same sensory modality as the target material.

Short-Term Memory for Odors

Olfactory memory is so robust that it is virtually a contradiction in terms to link "short-term memory" and "odor memory." Engen, Kuisma, and Eimas (1973) presented their participants either a single smell or a list of five odors. These were chosen from a pool of 100 odorants being used. After distractor intervals of from 3 to 30 seconds spent counting backwards, the participants were given a test odorant and asked whether it was the same as one just presented (or one of the five presented, in the list version). Overall accuracy averaged around 80 percent, with no significant forgetting between 3 and 30 seconds. Although a short-term memory procedure was used here, there was little evidence of short-term forgetting.

Other research has shown some forgetting across intervals of seconds to minutes, particularly if the odors are unfamiliar and not easily encoded verbally (de Wijk, Schab, & Cain, 1995). An odor can be encoded as a word (e.g., *talcum powder*) and then after the delay interval, the subject decides whether the test stimulus is talcum. However, recognition of unfamiliar odors, which depends more on memory for the sensory attributes, was still excellent after a delay of 100 seconds.

Short-Term Memory in the Hearing Impaired

Another way to study nonverbal STM is to use hearing-impaired individuals as subjects. What is the nature of their encoding in STM? Generalizations are complicated by a number of factors across participants: different levels of hearing impairment, training in oral speech, and alternative forms of sign language (signing versus spelling words). Hearing-impaired children who have learned some spoken English make phonological confusions, just as do hearing children. Deaf children without spoken language more often make confusions based on visual similarity of the printed words and similarity in the form of manually presented signs (Conrad, 1970).

Bellugi, Klima, and Siple (1974–1975) found something analogous to the word-length effect: Signed words may take longer to "rehearse" than spoken words. In a word span test, normal hearing participants recalled more of the words they heard; hearing impaired subjects recalled fewer of the words they saw signed.

The generality of STM is further extended by research on animal short-term memory. This work is reviewed in Box 8.1.

Box 8.1   Animal Short-Term Memory

The study of animal short-term memory has a long history, going back to Walter Hunter's studies in the 1920s. Some tests used today are variants of Hunter's delayed response. A cue is presented that tells where food is hidden, but the animal is not allowed to retrieve it until a delay interval has passed. For example, the animal watches as food is hidden in one of several dishes that have distinctive covers. After a delay, the animal is allowed to retrieve the food, to see if the location is recalled. The delayed response was even included in an intelligence test for dogs (Coren, 1994).

Delayed responding can tell us many things about animal memory. Rats and raccoons could remember where the food was hidden for several seconds, dogs and cats for 2 to 3 minutes, and monkeys and young children for a few minutes. Maier and Schneirla (1935) also report a gorilla that remembered the food location 2 days later. (I wouldn't want to be the research assistant who tells the gorilla "no, not now; later.") Clearly, the latter is long-term memory for the location, and some of the other retention intervals tested also seem long for "short-term memory."

(Control procedures are necessary to assure that correct choice after the delay is due to memory rather than some alternative strategies. For instance, odor cues from the food reward need to be neutralized or eliminated.)

We can also ask detailed questions about the animal's memory. In addition to remembering *where* food was hidden, do animals remember *what* was hidden? Tinklepaugh (1928) would sometimes hide lettuce and sometimes pieces of fruit. Monkeys performed well with either, retrieving the food at the end of the delay and immediately consuming it. What happened if the food type was switched during the delay? Monkeys, particularly chimps, quickly realized that Tinklepaugh had pulled a fast one on them. They sometimes refused to eat the changed food, and they would search the other containers. One chimp hurriedly stuffed the food into her mouth, but then spat it out, as if realizing this was not the expected taste!

Another task is the delayed matching-to-sample procedure, or DMTS. A to-be-remembered stimulus (called the "sample") is presented, and after a brief delay a pair of choice stimuli are given. When the subject chooses the one that "matches" the sample, reward is given. DMTS is often used with pigeons, which can remember various color, line, shape, and pattern stimuli over a period of a few seconds. However, in a study of dolphin STM, the animals matched objects (cylinders, balls) that could not be seen visually but were perceived through echolocation (Roitblat, Penner, & Nachtigall, 1990).

Parallels between human and animal STM have been noted. Serial-position curves for visual short-term memory by pigeons, monkeys, and humans are shown in Figure 8.5 (Wright, Santiago, Sands, Kendrick, & Cook, 1985). A common set of procedures was developed in which subjects were shown a sequence of four pictures on each trial. After a delay interval, and these intervals varied across species, a single picture was presented for subjects to identify as having been from the list or as being a different picture. The shape of the curves is remarkably similar across species. There is the U-shaped curve having both primacy and recency.

Animal research has produced other surprising findings. One was in the study of memory span in chimpanzees. In the chimp version, the numerals 1 through 9 were displayed simultaneously on a touch screen. The locations of the items varied randomly from trial to trial. The animals were taught to touch the digits in numerical sequence. The fact that the animals could learn to select the numbers 1, 2, 3 . . . through 9 in sequence is pretty neat in itself. However, in the next phase of the study, the animals had to *remember* the numerals. As soon as the chimp touched the first number, the remaining digits were replaced by white squares. So the chimp had to remember which number was at each spot, and still touch them in the correct sequence. Inoue and Matsuzawa (2007) report that one well-trained chimp (named Ai) could recall strings of five numbers correctly at far-above chance levels. Ai inspected each newly presented screen for less than one second, and then started punching off the locations. The animal was faster and more accurate than was a human performing the same task.

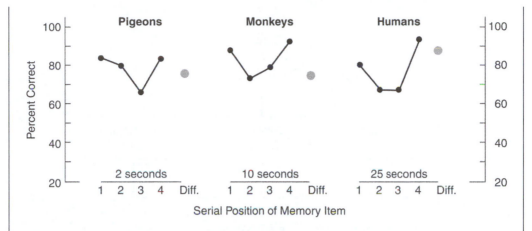

Figure 8.5 **Serial-Position Curves for Pigeons, Monkeys, and Humans.** Participants were shown sequences of four pictures on each trial. After a delay interval, a single picture was presented for participants to identify as having been from the list or as being a different picture (the points above "Diff." in the graphs).

Source: From A. A. Wright & M. J. Watkins, 1987, "Animal learning and memory and their relation to human learning and memory," *Learning and Motivation, 18,* 131–146. Copyright 1987 and reprinted with permission from Elsevier.

Studies of animal STM are important for several reasons. They are widely used in comparative cognition, a field that studies different species from an evolutionary perspective. Neuroscientists use animal STM to investigate the effects of brain lesions, neurotransmitter substances, and brain chemistry. Finally, pharmacologists use animal memory as a sensitive assay of potential cognitive side effects of new drugs and compounds.

Working Memory

Theoretical Overview of Working Memory

Although the concept of STM was an important theoretical advance, there are still some limitations to it. First, short-term memory is not simply verbal but includes other modalities as well. Second, STM is not only a place for the temporary storage of information. We plan, elaborate, compute, and imagine in STM. The concept of working memory (or WM) was devised as an advancement and elaboration of short-term memory. Specifically, the **working-memory** model (Baddeley & Hitch, 1974; see also Baddeley, 2001) proposes four components. The temporary storage of information occurs in either the *phonological loop* or the *visuospatial sketchpad*, each a storage buffer in a different sensory modality. The *central executive* allocates attention, and the *episodic memory buffer* connects working memory to long-term memory (see Figure 8.6).

One reason for advocating a multicomponent model is that people can indeed do two things at once little cross-interference, depending on certain factors. Performance in the Brown–Peterson distractor task shows that counting backward disrupts the memory for three target words. However, both counting and remembering are verbal. If two tasks involve different modalities, such

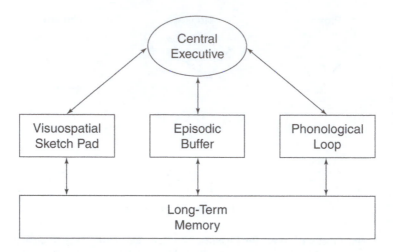

Figure 8.6 Working-Memory Model.

Source: Reprinted from "The Episodic Buffer," A. D. Baddeley et al., *Trends in Cognitive Sciences, 4,* pp. 417–423, copyright 2000, with permission from Elsevier.

as a verbal and a spatial activity, then interference is reduced. For example, we can drive and carry on a conversation simultaneously. (Sort of.)

Another feature of working memory is its emphasis on simultaneous processing and retention of information. For instance, in computing a tip in a restaurant, we are both manipulating the numbers and remembering subtotals along the way. To calculate a 20 percent tip, we might first figure 10 percent, then remember that number and multiply it by 2 to get 20 percent. To calculate a 15 percent tip, we might mentally average the 10 percent and 20 percent tips. In a similar manner, experimental tasks used to assess working memory are more challenging than the simple distractor and span tests of STM. The measures of working memory are also predictors of more complex cognitive capacities, such as general verbal and spatial ability, reasoning, academic achievement, and maybe even aspects of intelligence (e.g., Engle, Tuholski, Laughlin, & Conway, 1999).

Let's look at each component of the four-part model of working memory.

The Phonological Loop

The **phonological loop** is comparable to verbal short-term memory. It represents our brief storage of verbal material, which we use in rehearsal, verbal problem solving, arithmetic, and so on. The phonological store has most of the characteristics described earlier for the modal model of short-term memory (e.g., it is brief, has a limited capacity, and is easily disrupted). As noted before, verbal short-term memory is measured by a test of digit span or word span: the number of items that can be recalled after a single presentation. Working memory adds a second processing task to the span task. For instance, intermixed in the presentation of the to-be-remembered words are true–false arithmetic problems. For example, try to remember this string: DOG–CAT–is 6 + 3 = 7?–TREE . . . etc. Remembering DOG–CAT–TREE might be impaired by the arithmetic process.

The Visuospatial Sketchpad

As the name implies, the **visuospatial sketchpad** retains visual images (e.g., pictures, scenes, or imaged versions of words) and spatial information (e.g., the locations of squares on a checkerboard). In a simple spatial-span test, we might ask the subject to remember a sequence of up to eight red and black blocks on a checkerboard as we point to them. In a dual-task condition, we might also ask the subject to judge the symmetry of the blocks or whether a pattern exists.

(Note: Baddeley named this component the *visuo*spatial store. A more familiar version of the term is *visual*-spatial, as in visual-spatial intelligence or visual-spatial memory. However I believe either term may be used when talking about the WM component and the referent will be clear.)

Several lines of research support the independence of the phonological and visuospatial stores. Remembering a string of words is disrupted by simultaneously answering arithmetic questions. Similarly, remembering a picture or a nonsense shape is impaired by simultaneously having to perform a visual-tracking task, such as tracking a moving dot of light with your finger. In both of these cases, a single short-term store, either the verbal or the visual, is doing two things at once and so interference occurs. If the two tasks use different stores, however, interference is reduced. Remembering a word list is not severely affected by a visuospatial tracking task: Each can be performed at the same level alone as when done together (Shah & Miyake, 1996; see review by Gathercole, 1994).

The Central Executive

The **central executive** focuses, allocates, or distributes attention across multiple tasks. The difficulty we experience in attempting two things at once may be due to the inability to focus full attention on each.

Attention is a limited resource. How is it allocated across dual tasks? One possibility is that attention is divided so each task gets a portion. Alternatively, the central executive could be rapidly alternating (nearly) full attention from one task to another. So, as applied to an earlier example, does our subject allocate some attention to remembering DOG–CAT–TREE and some attention to solving the arithmetic? Or does the subject focus full attention on rehearsing DOG and CAT, then switch full attention to adding 6 + 3, and then quickly switch back to add TREE to memory?

An additional role of the central executive is to act as a sort of manager between the two memory stores, and this is the sense of *executive*. The executive manipulates and coordinates information stored in the buffers, directs attention, and engages in problem solving and planning.

Episodic Buffer

The **episodic buffer** integrates information across (a) the phonological and visual stores; (b) the operations of the central executive; and (c) information entry and retrieval from long-term memory (Baddeley, 2000).

The episodic buffer was a new addition to the theory. The several components of STM necessarily interact with LTM. For instance, earlier in this chapter, I mentioned that seven items is the usual capacity of STM, but the sizes of those items can vary, from digits to words to proverbs. These items are represented in LTM, and the episodic buffer acts as a bridge between the markers or tags retained in phonological store and LTM, from which the whole items (such as the proverbs) would be recalled at time of retrieval. Similarly, the arithmetic operations (i.e., addition, subtraction, division, and multiplication) must be retrieved from LTM to be applied to the contents of STM.

Measuring Working Memory

Working memory is typically measured by the capacity to do two things at once, what is referred to as *dual tasks*. For instance, one might ask participants to do some mental arithmetic problems

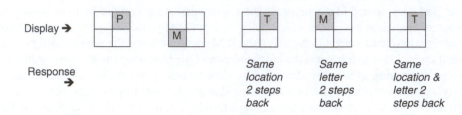

Figure 8.7 **Illustration of a Dual N-Back Task.** A new grid is shown every few seconds. For n = 2 the subject must make separate responses to note whether the current letter appeared two steps back, and whether the same location was occupied two steps back.

(e.g., 2 + 3 = ?; 4 × 2 = ?; 9–3 = ?), and then recall the answers. Alternatively, the task might use both the phonological and visuospatial stores, for instance by remembering a string of words and mentally counting the number of windows in your house.

The n-back task is frequently used to test working memory. As a starting point, in the simple **n-back** task the participant sees a continuous string of letters (B P M T M). As each letter is presented the subject must decide whether that letter occurred immediately before (when n = 1), or not. (See Figure 8.7.) N can take different values: if n= 1, does the this item match the previous letter? If n = 2 does it match the item two-steps back? In the example in Figure 8.7, if n = 2 the final letter T matches the T that occurred two steps before; M matched the M two steps before.

In a *dual n-back* task, two strings of items are presented simultaneously in different modalities. For example, in Figure 8.7 the letters are displayed in a 3 x 3 grid. The participant must make two responses, deciding whether each item matches a previous letter, and/or a previous location. In the dual 2-back level, the task is "Is this letter the same as the one 2 steps back? Is this location the same as 2 steps back?"

Working Memory and Consciousness?

The questions "what is mind?" and "what is consciousness?" are technically beyond the purview of this book. However, we cannot help but speculate on the relationship of working memory to consciousness. An essential property of the central executive is the control of attention. This suggests something (or someone) is inside the mind or the brain actively directing and choosing what to attend to. Unattended information is, by definition, outside of consciousness. Rehearsing words in the phonological store, essentially talking to one's self, is an attribute of consciousness. Images can be created and manipulated in the sketchpad. Who (or what) is doing this? Finally, human working memory is a highly evolved system. We find variants of working memory in animals, but the development has peaked in humans. Mind- and brain-scientists have not reached a consensus, yet many see the need to discuss consciousness and working memory together (Maia & Cleeremans, 2005).

A related and also unresolved issue is how the mind integrates information that is represented is so many different codes. This is called the consciousness binding problem. For instance, verbal and visual information originate in different sensory modalities and are coded differently in the brain. Yet the mind translates one to another, and combines both. The same sort of question can be asked about the many other codings the brain uses for the other senses, for emotions, etc. On the surface this may not seem like such a difficult problem to those of us now accustomed to having computers translate from one format to another, or from one software program to another.

Yet most of us do not know the underlying machine language by which this is done. A parallel understanding of the brain would seek to discover the mind's "machine language."

Individual Differences in Working Memory

Given the number of components of working memory, the possible dimensions along which individuals can differ is multiplied. Nor is working memory a fixed capacity, because individual performance varies with practice and training, and the scoring procedures, e.g., assigning partial credit when some items are recalled (Unsworth & Engle, 2007).

We have already described differences in simple span between math and verbally gifted students. We will consider a few other categories of differences among individuals in the following sections: working memory in aging, in dementia, and in the presence of anxiety.

Aging and Working Memory

Memory over short retention intervals, as assessed by the distractor or span tests, decreases with age. Is this decline due to a reduction in the capacity of short-term memory? There are other aging variables that adversely affect memory. One such factor is slower processing. For example, older participants encode into memory more slowly. On some tasks older adults need more study time to perform as well as younger adults. Once the stimuli are in memory, the rate of forgetting across delay intervals is the same in older and younger participants. In another example, participants performed a reading and an arithmetic task concurrently. The older participants took longer to respond to questions about what they had read, suggesting that they are slower at switching from one task to another (Salthouse, 1994).

A second factor associated with aging is the ability to inhibit distracting thoughts. Hasher and Zacks (1988) studied working memory in language processing: listening, reading, and comprehension. They believe that older participants have particular trouble inhibiting extraneous associations that are activated by the target material. These tangential thoughts can be triggered by the material itself (such as personal associations or reminiscences) or by the external environment (noticing the room, maybe the lecturer, but not the lecture). Working memory's capacity is taxed by this irrelevant content. One result may be a lack of focused attention: failure to keep up with the conversation or not being aware of what was just read. Another effect is that unrelated thoughts can foster weaker encodings of the target material and interference among target and irrelevant memories.

Dementia and Working Memory

Alzheimer's disease is a particularly devastating form of cognitive dementia. Although some studies show mildly impaired verbal and spatial memory in patients (Baddeley, 1992a), other reviewers conclude that genuine Alzheimer's victims show profound memory impairments across the board (Kopelman, 1994). One reason for this discrepancy may be whether a single task is being performed or two tasks. In one study, Alzheimer's patients were found to be impaired at doing two tasks at once, even though each alone could be performed competently (Baddeley, 1992a). The difficulty of each task alone, a visual tracking task and verbal memory span, was adjusted so that each could be performed well. However, when both tasks needed to be performed simultaneously (tracking a moving light while remembering a string of words), performance dropped off dramatically. Unimpaired control participants were able to perform both tasks simultaneously with little cross-interference. The Alzheimer's patients had difficulty in alternating between the two tasks. This may reflect impairment in the coordination of attentional resources by the central executive.

Anxiety and Working Memory

Working memory capacity can be compromised by worry. Attention is diverted to preoccupation over performance, self-criticism, and other forms of negative thinking. Negative self-talk engages the phonological store.

Worry can impair working memory in several areas related to academic performance. Individuals with mathematics anxiety do more poorly than less-anxious students on mathematics problems. No surprise there. The math-anxious also have difficulty on working memory tasks that involve numbers and computation, but the deficit is not all related to math ability. There also seems to be some preoccupation with anxious feelings and negative thoughts that co-opt resources. Working memory impairment is especially evident on more difficult problems, for example, those that require mentally adding two-column numbers in which there is a carry operation (Ashcraft & Krause, 2007).

The after-effects of worry and rumination carryover onto subsequent academic tasks. For instance, students with elevated depression scores (not clinically depressed, just higher-than average scores from a college student sample) were asked to think about their feelings, physical sensations, and reactions to emotional cue words. What the experimenter was doing here was eliciting some controlled worry. In the next phase of the study, these students were given reading comprehension passages to work on. The students required more time to read, and had lower comprehension scores on those passages. In a parallel study, elicited worry led to poorer memory of a class lecture (Lyubomirsky, Kasri, & Zehm, 2003).

Worry also contributes to *stereotype threat*. One stereotypical belief is that women perform poorly at math. When a negative stereotype is activated in the mind of a member of that group, performance can be inhibited. Reminding women of the stereotype before a math test, or emphasizing that the test is a math test, leads to worse performance than they otherwise would have achieved. Note that the comparison in this case is not between women and men. The comparison is between college women who are reminded, or not, of the stereotype.

Does stereotype threat elicit negative thinking, and does the threat impair working memory? Beilock, Rydell, and McConnell (2007) found affirmative answers to both questions. In a challenging task requiring number manipulation and problem solving, the activation of a stereotype threat in women led to more errors. Also, women in the stereotype condition reported more worry about their performance. The researchers suggest that the phonological loop is especially taxed in these tasks: both the arithmetic and the worrying occupy the verbal store.

Multitasking

Multitasking is a perfect example of the complexity of working memory. In many everyday situations, there are several tasks being conducted simultaneously, each of which has several steps. Paul Burgess (2000) provided a nice summary of the components of everyday multitasking situations.

1. (Obviously) there are several separate tasks being attempted.
2. At any one moment only one task (or one step in a task) can be performed at a time due to physical or cognitive limitations.
3. The steps involved across tasks are therefore interleaved (start one task, put it on hold and start a second task, then back to the first task . . . etc).
4. Interruptions and unexpected outcomes lead to delays and re-planning. These increase the demands placed on short-term memory and the central executive.
5. Remember to return to a task that has not yet been completed.

In many occupations that require multitasking, the correct performance of each step of each task is essential. In a medical setting, for example, a nurse has several required steps in administering a drug. First ensure aseptic conditions (washing hands, wearing gloves); then matching the prescription or order with the drug's label and with the patient's ID. The nurse may be alternating these steps with those for a second drug, and maybe a second patient. This activity defines a working memory task: executive function in organizing the steps; short-term memory to retain steps completed; and dual-tasking with multiple drugs or patients. As if this is not difficult enough, there are invariably interruptions, such as requests made by the patient or someone else. In one study in which the nurses were observed at work, an interruption increased errors by 12 percent. These errors occurred even though the nurses knew they were being observed. (In this study, the observers could intervene if they anticipated that a serious error was about to occur.) The point of this example is that even well-trained professionals are subject to working memory failures under stressful, time limited, or distracting conditions (Westbrook, Woods, Rob, Dunsmuir, & Day, 2010).

Supertaskers? One area of special concern is the danger of multitasking while driving a car (or plane, train, or even walking.) We may all agree that texting while driving is dangerous. However too many of us believe that talking on the phone is not distracting. Studies of healthy, intelligent college students in driving simulators show driving impairment even during hands-free phone conversation (Strayer & Drews, 2007).

Any statistic we cite suggesting that most people are adversely affected is countered by the belief that you (or I) are the exceptions. Well, how exceptional are you? Students were tested in a driving simulator while simultaneously performing a difficult WM task (interspersing words to remember and arithmetic questions). The WM task was presented over a hands-free phone while the students were driving. Among 200 participants, the researchers found only five, that is, less than 3 percent (of bright, motivated, college students), who could multitask without impairment on the driving simulator in the dual task condition. For 97 percent of the participants, the WM task produced a significant decline in driving measures such as braking reaction time when performing the WM task (Watson & Strayer, 2010). (It is also the case that the driving adversely affected WM performance.) So, you may think the averages do not apply to you. But are you really among the top 3 percent?

Can working memory be improved? There is a large literature on the effects of training on so-called "executive functions," and frequent reports in the media of treatments that will supposedly increase cognitive performance. Some of these questions are addressed in Box 8.2.

Box 8.2 Training Working Memory

Working memory is important for functioning in everyday life. It is associated with intelligence, language, and problem solving. Is it possible to improve WM? The buzz on the internet these days is that brain training can improve memory, thinking, and attention.

There are many brain-training programs available. The phrase "use it or lose it" seems to be the rationale for programs that use repetition as the basis of improvement. However, repetition alone is not likely to produce substantial improvements in WM. The psychologist Klingberg (2009) elaborated the memory-as-muscle analogy to dispute the logic of repetition: It is not just passive activation of a muscle that increases strength. After all, we are constantly picking up small objects all day long; our arm muscles are not strengthened from these minor exertions. Strength training requires pushing muscles to their limit, and then increasing that limit. Similarly, WM training must be challenging. If there is little mental effort, there will be little mental gain.

Morrison and Chein (2011) noted characteristics of challenging WM training programs. They include multiple modalities (verbal, visual, and spatial); use a variety of materials; require maintenance of information in short-term memory in the face of distraction; and they minimize the possibility of automatizing subcomponents. For example, an ineffective program would be repetitive practice on digit span: items are presented in one modality (verbal); only one type of material is practiced (numbers); there is no simultaneous distractor or second task; and the task can be accomplished by memorizing certain combinations (e.g., the digits in a familiar area code).

Morrison and Chein (2011) also suggest that effective WM training should improve core skills that will generalize beyond the trained task. It is not enough that you are better just in digit span. Variations in the n-back task, such as the dual n-back, and increasing the length of n (2-back, 3-back) are examples of such challenging tests. (The n-back was discussed earlier, and illustrated in Figure 8.7).

There are numerous training programs available on the web, as apps or for personal computers. Some programs are marketed to special populations, such as for older adults, or children with ADHD. There are claims that "executive functions" improve, but this is a loose term in this context. Executive function can refer to memory, reasoning, and self-control. So if a given program is said to have positive benefits, it is unclear what exactly improves (Diamond & Lee, 2011).

The important question is whether such training benefits everyday functioning or other cognitive abilities such as general intelligence. In spite of an enormous number of studies to test working memory training, this is an as-yet unsettled issue. The discordant outcomes may be related to the use of different WM training regimes, transfer tasks, and subject populations. The programs do improve the specific skills trained. However, there is not often generalization to other cognitive abilities (e.g., Melby-Verlag & Hulme, 2013).

Working memory training may be of more benefit to those with specific deficits, such as ADHD, impulse control, learning disabilities, or brain injury, as a means to develop an alternative strategy to perform cognitive tasks. It is also clear that much more testing and development will be needed before we know the true benefits of cognitive training.

Is There Really a Separate Short-Term Memory?

Is there a really a separate short-term or working memory? It seems perfectly obvious that some things are forgotten quickly and others slowly, if at all. Some researchers seek the biological basis of STM and the neural areas involved with it (e.g., Desimone, 1996; Goldman-Rakic, 1996). Their view presumes the physical reality of STM. However, the existence, or even necessity, of hypothesizing an STM remains unproven to other theorists. Maybe STM could be considered as purely theoretical, a metaphor, or a heuristic.

Neuropsychological Dissociations of Two-Memory Systems

Neuropsychological studies of individuals with impairment of auditory-verbal short-term memory indicate that they have different sites of brain injury than do patients without STM losses. In the last chapter we described H. M., who had normal STM. His digit span had declined somewhat over the years to about 5—not bad for an older gentleman. K. F. is just the opposite, being grossly impaired on memory span and distractor tasks, particularly for verbally presented items (Shallice & Warrington, 1970). H. M. and other "amnesic syndrome" patients have damage to the hippocampus and related structures deep within the temporal lobe. K. F. suffers from injury to a different area, one roughly on the border between the temporal and the parietal lobes of the left hemisphere. The discovery of other patients like K. F. has led to the naming of a "short-term memory" syndrome, referring specifically to impaired auditory-verbal STM (Shallice, 1988).

Studies of animal memory also show dissociation between brain areas necessary for remembering over the short term versus the long term. In a nicely matched set of comparisons, Mishkin and Appenzeller (1987) showed that damage to the combined hippocampus and amygdala impaired short-term retention of objects recently shown to a monkey, but did not prevent long-term learning of objects. In both experimental tasks, food was given as a reward for choice of the correct object and withheld for choice of the incorrect object. In the short-term memory task, the lesioned animal could not remember which of two objects had been shown most recently. However, in the long-term memory task, the animal could learn which of two objects was consistently paired with food.

Counterpoint: A Single-Memory Approach?

Critics of two-store memory theories argue that many variables have the same effect on retention after short intervals and after long intervals (Crowder, 1993). For example, STM and LTM are each susceptible to proactive and retroactive interference. If STM and LTM are similarly affected by experimental variables, maybe a simpler explanation would be to hypothesize a single memory store.

Can the evidence that favors a separate STM be parsimoniously accommodated within a single memory system? One possibility is to suggest that there is a single set of memories, but memories can differ between those that are currently active and those that are inactive (Lewis, 1979). Suppose I ask you to recall the name of your third-grade teacher or your favorite pet's name. What you have just done is taken an inactive memory and made it active. The latent memory corresponds to what we have called long-term memory, and its activation is what we have called short-term memory. The fading or return of the active neural elements to their resting levels corresponds to forgetting from STM.

Another single-memory hypothesis reminds us of two facts: Memories are multidimensional, and each dimension could have a different rate of forgetting.

The memory for an item or an event may be encoded in multiple dimensions, such as sight, sound, touch, emotion, and so on. In a *memory-attribute* model, memories are complex representations containing several attributes (Tulving & Watkins, 1975; Underwood, 1983). When we are introduced to someone, we may later recollect attributes that are auditory (e.g., hearing a name or the sound of his or her voice), visual (appearance), olfactory (a fragrance), tactile (a handshake), and emotional (tension, e.g., if this is your new boss). The rate of forgetting of each attribute may differ. Thus, the forgetting curves for different memories can vary, such as acoustic versus semantic, but not because they were in different memory stores (Wickelgren, 1970). The several attributes may be forgotten from a single memory store, but forgotten at faster or slower rates relative to each other (see Figure 8.8).

What otherwise appears to be forgetting from short-term memory may instead be the rapid forgetting of certain stimulus modalities, such as sound. What appears to be more persistent long-term memory may be the slower forgetting of other stimulus modalities, such as image or emotion.

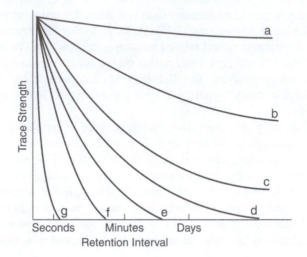

Figure 8.8 **Hypothetical Curves of Forgetting for the Different Attributes That Make Up a Memory.** Different dimensions (e.g., auditory, visual, tactile, emotional) may be forgotten at different rates, corresponding to what is otherwise described as short-term memory (e.g., attribute *f*) or long-term memory (e.g., attribute *a*).

One Memory or Several?

We have considered the hypothesis of a single memory system as an alternative to postulating two memory systems, STM and LTM. Which model is correct? The single-memory hypothesis has not been as accepted as the dual-store theory (Healy & McNamara, 1996). The modal model embodying STM and LTM is the basis of much physiological research (Zola-Morgan & Squire, 1993). Neuroscientists are delineating brain areas that are active during short-term retention, which are separate from those involved in LTM. Finally, the concept of STM has provided valuable insights into learning and memory in general. A familiar phrase attributed to the psychologist Kurt Lewin is, "There's nothing so practical as a good theory." Any single experiment or observation does not prove the existence of separate memory systems. The usefulness of the multiple-memory concept may be in how readily it allows us to think about, and advance, our knowledge of memory.

As noted elsewhere in this book, memory is not a single "thing." The alternative ways of partitioning memory often cause confusion in comparing one theory to another. Box 8.3 addresses some alternative senses of "short-term memory."

Box 8.3   Short-Term Memory, Working Memory, Executive Function: What's the Difference?

Short-term memory is the verbal rehearsal buffer. It is usually tested with the distractor task or the memory span task, to measure the retention of strings of 3–7 digits, letters, or words.

Working Memory is an expansion of STM. WM includes a verbal storage; a visuospatial storage; and control processes to select and allocate resources. WM is assessed with a dual-task that requires doing two things simultaneously, such as remembering visual and verbal items, or remembering and mental problem solving.

Executive function is an elaboration of Baddeley's central executive. The core functions of the central executive are: focusing attention on a relevant task; resisting distraction from irrelevant stimuli; retaining information in working memory; inhibiting responses (e.g., previously correct responses); and flexibly shifting strategies.

The phrase *executive functions* is used in a much broader sense in education and neuropsychology. Here the term may encompass aspects of self-control (self-discipline), self-regulation (monitoring goals and performance), emotional control (reactions to frustration), planning, and creativity.

Applications

What Is Short-Term Memory for?

What purpose does a primary, short-term, or working memory serve? Does it do or allow certain functions that are not easily accommodated by long-term memory? Two potential functions are language comprehension and problem solving (McCarthy &Warrington, 1990). A third, which we have already considered in one context, is as a gateway to long-term memory.

Comprehending and Using Language

Language comprehension, through reading or listening, or watching signed symbols, takes time. The first words and phrases of a sentence need to be remembered until the end of the sentence in order to comprehend the entire thought the speaker (or writer) is expressing. For example, given the sentence HE STRODE ACROSS THE COURT AND PROTESTED VIGOROUSLY TO THE JUDGE THAT HIS OPPONENT WAS INFRINGING ON THE RULES BY USING _____. What is the meaning of this sentence? You have probably formed some idea even without the missing last words, but that meaning could be different from your expectation. One ending is (*he protested*) AN ILLEGALLY STRUNG TENNIS RACKET. Another is (*he protested*) INADMISSIBLE EVIDENCE. Each ending gives a different meaning to the first part of the sentence. Comprehension of the meaning of either requires the memory for the lengthy early portion of the sentence. Maybe this is what short-term memory is for: to provide continuity in reading and listening.

Many studies have demonstrated the correlation between working memory and reading comprehension (e.g., Daneman & Merikle, 1996). In an early study, Daneman and Carpenter (1980) used a dual-task procedure in which students read a series of unrelated sentences out loud and also tried to remember the last word in each sentence. This is a dual-task procedure, in which both tasks (reading and remembering) use a single verbal memory store. For example, the following sentences might be read by the students:

THE POLICEMAN ATE THE APPLE.
THE GIRL SANG THE SONG.
THE RAIN BEAT ON THE WINDOW PANES.

After a few sentences (the exact number varies over trials), a question is asked about one of the sentences to ensure comprehension ("Who sang?"), and at other times, the experimenter requests recall of the final words. In this example, these are APPLE, SONG, and PANES. Good readers had a longer memory span (i.e., recalled the final words from more sentences) than did poor readers. Dual-task performance in older students also correlates with their verbal SAT scores and standardized reading scores (Daneman & Merikle, 1996). By contrast, simpler measures of STM capacity, such as the word span, correlate less well with reading comprehension. Daneman and Carpenter say that simple span assesses only the storage capacity of STM and not the combination of capacity and processing that occurs during reading. Consider an analogy of reading comprehension to a conveyor belt. As words come down the line, the meaning must be abstracted and transferred into long-term memory. Some students simply cannot keep up: Accessing the meaning of some words on the "conveyor" takes too long, causing some other words on the conveyor to be missed or forgotten (Perfetti & Lesgold, 1979).

Problem Solving

Mental problem solving requires attention, encoding, storage, and manipulation of information, all processes for which *working memory* is well designed. Dark and Benbow (1990) studied memory for arithmetic word problems in mathematically and verbally gifted seventh graders and correlated these scores with several measures of memory span. An example problem might read: "The entertainment portion of a 30-minute TV show on Tuesday night lasted 4 minutes longer than four times the portion devoted to commercials. How many minutes of commercials were there?" Solving such problems requires retention and manipulation of the numerical facts. The academically gifted children, who have longer word- and digit-memory spans than did average children, were better at remembering word problems. Gifted children seem to form what Dark and Benbow refer to as more "compact encodings," which is much like Miller's idea of chunking to pack more information into an item.

Problem solving requires translating relational statements into a mathematical proposition (the "4 minutes longer than 4 times the . . . commercials" portion). In the preceding example, commercial duration could be expressed as x, and the entertainment duration as $4x + 4$, and the sum of these two equals 30 minutes. Or $5x + 4 = 30$. Relational statements pose particular difficulties for students, including college students. Undergraduates who had longer memory spans accurately recalled more relational statements in math word problems (Cooney & Swanson, 1990).

Efficient use of working memory also means deciding what not to rehearse. Capacity can be freed by excluding irrelevant facts, such as the fact that the show in the problem aired on Tuesday evening. Students with longer memory spans were able to forget more of the irrelevant statements (Cooney & Swanson, 1990).

Working memory's central executive is accorded a prominent role in problem solving. The central executive allocates attention to the component-memory systems and is involved in planning and decision making. These traits appear to be disturbed in frontal-lobe-damaged and Alzheimer's individuals. Frontal-lobe injury produces a set of symptoms that has been labeled the "dysexecutive syndrome" (Shallice, 1988). Short-term memory is impaired because the individual is easily distracted. Perseveration, or persisting in one mode of behavior, is manifested by a difficulty in switching between tasks (e.g., from a verbal to a spatial task, or from sorting a deck of cards by color, then sorting by suit). Finally, planning, or following a plan, is disrupted.

Shallice and Burgess (1991) described a naturalistic example of executive dysfunction by frontal-lobe-injured patients. Their participants were given a list of errands in a shopping mall (actually, since the researchers are British, the location was a "pedestrian precinct"). These tasks required memory retention (e.g., what to buy), planning (sequence errands efficiently), retrieval (remembering when and where each task occurs), and information manipulation (there were limits on spending and on time to complete the errands). The patients made many more errors than did the control participants. Memory failures often occurred as a by-product of planning errors: failing to sequence activities efficiently or establish retrieval cues (e.g., remember to deposit a letter in the mailbox that is just outside the bakery).

The Role of Short-Term Memory in Theories of Long-Term Memory

Many theories of learning postulate a role for STM as a gateway into long-term memory. Both consolidation theory (Hebb, 1949) and dual-store theory (Atkinson & Shiffrin, 1968) state that interference with short-term processing will likewise interfere with the formation of long-term memory. For example, electroconvulsive shock (ECS) interferes with memory for events that just preceded ECS. This is an instance of retrograde amnesia (Chapter 7). According to consolidation theory, the electroshock "clears" a neural short-term memory and thus prevents sufficient opportunity for consolidation into long-term memory. A similar explanation is offered for the retrograde amnesia that head injuries cause: Events immediately preceding the trauma are displaced from a short-term memory before they can be transferred into long-term memory.

A similar effect is predicted from dual-store theory. Here, the occurrence of surprising events can cause a retrograde amnesic-like effect. For example, Ellis, Detterman, Runcie, McCarver, and Craig (1971) tested free recall of lists of line drawings. The surprising occurrence of a nude photograph in the middle of one list zapped memory for the picture that just preceded the photo, maybe by displacing that item from short-term memory.

Working Memory and Culture

The concept of working memory has been influential beyond psychology. What is it that defines what it is to be human? Tool use, language, consciousness? Wynn, an archaeologist and Coolidge, a psychologist, proposed that the major characteristics of working memory—the capacity to temporarily hold and manipulate information—led to the evolution of our present day cognitive abilities (Coolidge & Wynn, 2009). According to Wynn and Coolidge, the significant evolutionary leap from the other animals was the development of our working memory. This allowed humans to plan, develop symbolic language, and create art. The appearance of carved objects, burial rituals, cave art, and more developed tools are taken as evidence for this increase in cognitive ability. The idea that working memory led evolution is still untested. After all, working memory did not suddenly appear in humans; other animals have working memory to varying degrees. However, Wynn and Coolidge's theory illustrates the wide-ranging influence of a psychological theory (Balter, 2010).

Summary

Short-term memory (STM) refers to memory that is both brief and of limited capacity. STM is distinguished from long-term memory, which in the laboratory is typically any memory more than a few minutes old.

The distinction between these two memory systems has long been a part of psychology's history. William James distinguished between primary memory and secondary memory. The next step was the development of the multistore theory of Atkinson and Shiffrin. According to this model, STM has a limited capacity, old items can be displaced by new items, rehearsal facilitates transfer to LTM, and control processes are employed in STM. The next stage in the evolution of STM was Baddeley's working memory model, which has a phonological loop for the rehearsal of verbal information; a visuospatial sketchpad to manipulate visual information; a central executive to control the limited resource of attention over one or more tasks; and an episodic buffer to control interactions with LTM.

Short-Term Memory Tasks

Short-term memory is often studied through the distractor technique and the memory-span task. The Brown–Peterson distractor task is used to measure the duration of STM. To-be-remembered items are presented, the subject performs a distractor task such as counting, and then attempts to recall the target items. The amount recalled drops off dramatically after as little as 9–15 seconds of distraction. This rapid forgetting seemed to demonstrate how brief STM was in the absence of rehearsal. However, short-term retention is reduced by proactive interference, and so the distractor task may underestimate the duration of STM.

Memory span measures of the number of items that can be recalled after a single presentation. It is the capacity of short-term memory. Span is limited to about seven items (plus-or-minus two). This span is composed of probably four items actually in STM, and the others are in LTM. Span is increased by chunking, and by practice with the to-be-remembered material. An important determinant of span is word length: More short items can be remembered than long items. Memory span may be governed by articulation rate, as longer words take longer to speak than shorter words.

Characteristics of STM

The verbal short-term store of Atkinson and Shiffrin and the phonological store of Baddeley's working memory are characterized by acoustic encoding: Words are remembered as they sound. STM has a limited capacity, with estimates ranging from two to seven items. Capacity can be increased by chunking or coding to increase the amount of information contained within each item. STM is of limited duration in the absence of rehearsal, lasting from several seconds to less than a minute in the absence of rehearsal. Forgetting occurs due to displacement of an item from short-term memory.

Rehearsal of information in STM allows transfer to LTM. Verbal rehearsal may be necessary in forming some kinds of long-term knowledge, such as in vocabulary learning. However, residence in STM is neither necessary nor sufficient for LTM formation. Brain-injured subjects like K. F., who has a limited verbal short-term memory, can nevertheless learn and retain long-term memories at normal rates. Also, maintenance of information in short-term memory does not guarantee entry into long-term memory. Thus, in sum, there are few absolute distinctions between the features of verbal short-term memory and long-term memory.

Short-term retention can be demonstrated in nonverbal modalities: for visual and olfactory stimuli, for spatial locations, and for actions.

Working Memory

The working-memory model divides STM into phonological and visuospatial substores. A prominent feature of the working-memory approach is to assess dual-task performance. If two tasks use different STM stores, there will be less cross-interference than if two tasks involve the same store. The central executive acts as a sort of manager between the two memory stores and manipulates, organizes, and plans the routing of information. The final component of working memory, the episodic buffer, acts as a bridge between the short-term stores and long-term memory. For instance, knowledge in LTM (such as arithmetic rules) can be applied to the items in STM (add or subtract the numbers there).

Working-memory tasks have been employed to study aging and dementia, which in turn helps illuminate working memory. Aging is associated with slower processing, as shown by slower encoding of target items into memory or slower switching between tasks. Alzheimer's patients are impaired at doing two tasks at once, even if each can be performed competently alone. This finding illustrates the distinction between the single store of STM and the dual stores of working memory.

Anxiety impairs working memory by limiting the attention of the central executive, and by occupying space in the phonological store. Working memory deficits have been found in the performance of mathematics and reading comprehension.

Is There Really a Separate Short-Term Memory?

Can memory be parsimoniously accommodated by a single-memory system? The necessity of hypothesizing separate STM and LTM remains unproven to some theorists.

One alternative hypothesis is that there is a single set of memories, but memories can differ between those that are currently active (STM) and those that are inactive (LTM). Another hypothesis is that memories are multidimensional and that each dimension has a different rate of forgetting. What appears to be forgetting from short-term memory is rapid forgetting of certain stimulus modalities, such as sound. What appears to be long-term memory is the more enduring retention of other stimulus modalities, such as sight or smell.

Strong evidence in favor of an STM–LTM distinction comes from neuropsychological studies. Individuals with impairment of verbal short-term memory have damage to different areas of the brain than do patients without STM losses. Studies of animals also show a dissociation between brain areas necessary for remembering over the short term versus the long term.

Applications

What is the purpose of short-term memory? One possibility is that it is necessary for language comprehension. The span of working memory correlates with measures of reading comprehension. Dual-task performance, such as reading sentences and remembering the final words, correlates with verbal SAT scores and standardized reading scores.

Several distinct working-memory processes contribute to problem solving. Information must be encoded into working memory, other information must be retrieved from LTM, steps in problem solution must be sequenced, and irrelevant information must be excluded. Working memory's central executive seems to play a central role in organizing these types of activities necessary for problem solving. By contrast, injury to the frontal lobes produces a "dysexecutive syndrome," characterized by excessive distractibility, perseveration, and lack of planning.

Finally, numerous theories of long-term learning have hypothesized that STM is a sort of gateway into long-term memory. Both consolidation theory and dual-store theory state that interference with short-term processing would prevent long-term memory formation. Studies involving ECS, head trauma, and surprising stimuli as interfering events show impaired long-term learning.

9   Encoding

Encoding refers to the acquisition of information: the formation of a memory trace. A textbook such as the one that you are now reading can cite references to learning under ideal conditions: simple materials, minimal distractions, and students physically and mentally prepared to learn. Yet how often will such controlled learning conditions occur in the real world? Recall your first year of college, taking what seemed like too many courses, each requiring a different form of studying. Long hours and lots of stress. Or consider having to learn under particularly trying conditions: the U.S. Marine Corps boot camp at Parris Island, South Carolina. The physical training and emotional pressure the recruits experience are well known from film and television. What many of us are not aware of is the academic learning that occurs over 11 weeks of training. Each recruit attends classes and is issued a set of textbooks totaling over a thousand pages. Studying occurs at odd times of the day (or night)—whenever opportunity allows. The recruits are physically fatigued when they study. They are under intense emotional stress (read: FEAR). The recruits are motivated to learn, but some of the material might appear more like Ebbinghaus's nonsense syllables than meaningful prose. How do variables such as time of day, emotional arousal, incentive, and meaningfulness affect learning? This chapter will consider these and other more usual laboratory variables that affect encoding.

Separating Encoding From Retrieval

The division of information processing into stages of encoding, storage, and retrieval is in some ways arbitrary. One means of separating stages is to experimentally manipulate variables during encoding, while holding constant the conditions of storage and retrieval.

Neuroscience methods offer another means of separating encoding, storage, and retrieval. Brain activity at each stage of memory can be assessed with neuroimaging. The differences in activity between encoding (e.g., studying a list of words) versus retrieval (e.g., recognizing previously studied words) may indicate which brain regions are involved at each stage. In one such imaging study, the brain activity during study of each individual item was measured. This activity was then correlated with whether those items were recalled or forgotten. Certain areas in the left hemisphere were found to be more active during the study of verbal items that were recalled and were less active during study of items that were later unrecognized (Wagner et al., 1998). Similarly, certain areas of the right hemisphere were more active during encoding of photographs of scenes that were subsequently recognized than during the study of photographs that were not recognized (Brewer, Zhao, Desmond, Glover, & Gabri, 1998).

Some Basic Variables in Encoding

In the laboratory, encoding into episodic memory is most-often studied. Episodic memory is remembering information based on its occurrence at a particular time and place. The free recall of a list of words, sentences, or pictures are tests of episodic memory: recalling the items you just saw, here in the laboratory. A number of factors are reviewed in the several following sections: rehearsal, imagery, and arousal, just to name a few. Several of these factors are summarized for quick reference in Box 9.1.

Box 9.1   Summary of Some Factors Related to Encoding and Their Definitions

Characteristics of the To-Be-Learned Material

Word Meaningfulness

Meaningful words are ones having some combination of the following: a high frequency of occurrence in language and print, are easily pronounced, have many associations to other items, and are more imagable.

Concrete/Abstract Words

Words that refer to actual, physical things, and that tend to be imagable and have a number of associations versus words that refer to nonphysical abstract ideas.

Imagery

The degree to which items can be mentally imaged. Pictures or objects actually seen are better remembered than if their names are simply read.

Factors in the Presentation of To-Be-Remembered Materials

Testing Effect

Taking a practice test on recently studied material instead of additional study of the material. A criterion test given later assesses the effects of the additional study versus practice testing.

Spacing of Repetitions

Two presentations of an item can be massed, one immediately after another, or spaced, with some interval of time or some other items occurring between repetitions.

Isolation Effect

An unusual or distinctive item that stands apart from the other items in a series.

Cognitive Strategies

Maintenance Rehearsal

Somewhat passive, repetitive thinking about to-be-remembered material.

Elaborative Rehearsal

Thinking about the material in such a way as to require more cognitive effort, to activate more associations, or to produce a more distinctive memory representation.

Subject Factors

Arousal

Mental or physiological arousal, associated with circadian rhythms, stimulant and depressant drugs, or emotional arousal.

Incentives

The provision of explicit rewards for learning or remembering.

Incidental versus Intentional Learning

The participants are instructed to remember the material ("Please try to remember this") or the participants are simply asked to process the material in some other way ("Is the word a food or an animal?") without mention of a later test of retention.

Elaborative Rehearsal

The role that rehearsal plays in remembering has been described in several previous chapters. Generally, the number of words that are recalled from a list correlates with the number of rehearsals the words receive (Chapter 6). This is consistent with the notion that rehearsal promotes better representation in long-term memory (Chapters 7 and 8). However, all rehearsal is not the same; there are qualitative differences in rehearsal.

One important distinction is between elaborative rehearsal and maintenance rehearsal. The two terms derive from the levels-of-processing approach of Craik and Lockhart (1972), which posits that information can be processed to a greater or lesser extent, and thus by analogy to different "depths," along a continuum from shallow to deep processing. **Maintenance rehearsal** is a form of shallow processing, a recycling of information in order to keep it available in short-term memory or the phonological store. We use maintenance rehearsal to temporarily remember a phone number, simply repeating the number until it is no longer needed. Maintenance rehearsal can be effective for short-term retention, and our research participants will use maintenance rehearsal if they know they will be allowed uninterrupted rehearsal until the time of recall (Wixted, 1991).

Elaborative rehearsal is processing in which to-be-remembered material is related to other information. There is an active or deliberate attempt to cognitively interact with, reflect on, or use the to-be-remembered information. Elaborative rehearsal represents deep processing. We use elaborative rehearsal to memorize a phone number. Elaborative rehearsal produces more of an episodic memory, a recollection of having studied the material at a particular time and place. Maintenance rehearsal does not: The facts seem familiar, but you cannot remember how or where you learned them (Gardiner, Gawlik, & Richardson-Klavehn, 1994).

The idea of elaborative rehearsal is a central theme in this chapter: Many of the variables that affect encoding can be interpreted as instances of elaborative processing.

What Exactly is Elaborative Processing?

The standard procedure for manipulating processing depth is to present a list of words and have the subjects answer a question about each word as it occurs. Different types of questions require different levels of processing of the target items. For instance, given the target word BONE, the various questions asked might be, "Does it contain the letter *e*, does it rhyme with *train*, is it an *animal*?" These questions require different kinds of processing: the surface form or appearance of the word; the sound of the word; or the meaning of the word. Later, the subjects are tested for memory of the list. Items that received deeper processing during presentation are more likely to be recalled (Craik & Tulving, 1975).

The analogy of elaborative processing to deep processing may be a useful description, but this does not specifically define what elaboration is. At least three hypotheses have been offered: elaboration, distinctiveness, and effort (Horton & Mills, 1984).

Elaboration refers to expanding a newly formed memory trace. If you have to remember the word AARDVARK, you might try to think of any associations to the word or any facts you know about aardvarks. Figure 9.1 illustrates the sets of possible associates that could be activated by the target words CRAB, FACT, and LAMP (Nelson & Schreiber, 1992). The words CRAB and FACT have larger sets of associations that could be activated than does the word LAMP. CRAB and LAMP, however, could evoke specific mental pictures or images, whereas FACT does not. Imagery is a form of encoding also. Elaborated traces have more connections or associations to other memories. This increases the number of possible retrieval cues, and so elaboration affects both encoding and retrieval.

Alternatively, elaborative rehearsal may increase the *distinctiveness* of the memory. A distinctive memory is one that stands out from other memories, and will suffer less confusion with other memories during retrieval. Unlike elaboration, the distinctiveness hypothesis allows that shallow processing may sometimes lead to good retention, as long as the memory representation is distinctive. For instance, words that are unusual looking (such as LYMPH, KHAKI, or PHLEGM) are recalled better than are orthographically common words (such as LEAKY, KENNEL, or PRIMATE), even when the words are matched for meaningfulness and frequency of occurrence in language (Hunt & Elliot, 1980).

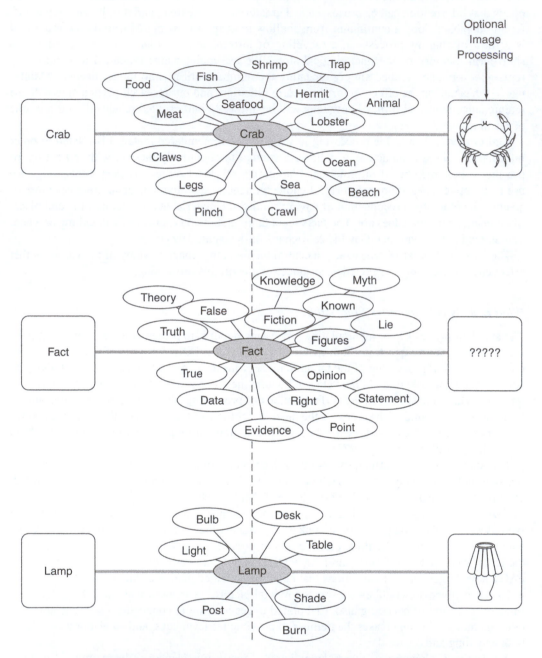

Figure 9.1 **Hypothetical Elaborative Encoding of Three To-Be-Remembered Words: CRAB, FACT, and LAMP.** Each word activates associated words and ideas, although the size of the associated sets vary. In addition, some words may evoke a mental image of the word's referent.

Source: From "Word Concreteness and Word Structure as Independent Determinants of Recall," by D. L. Nelson and T. A. Schreiber, 1992, *Journal of Memory and Language, 31*, p. 240. Copyright © 1992 by Elsevier. Reprinted with permission.

The third possibility is that elaborative processing requires more effort, and it is actually the amount of effort expended that determines retention. *Cognitive effort* can be measured by the impairment in performance on a second task done simultaneously with the memory task. For example, as a to-be-remembered list of words is presented, the subject must also push a button every time a tone stimulus sounds. An increase in the cognitive effort required in the memory task leads to slower reaction times to the tone (Eysenck & Eysenck, 1979). Elaborative rehearsal in the memory task leaves less capacity available for the tone-detection task. The results of a dual-task procedure are shown in Figure 9.2. More words were recalled when the participants had to make a deeper judgment about the word ("Does it name something you could eat?") rather than a shallow judgment ("Does it contain a letter *e*?"), but it took them longer to react to a tone or light stimulus that occurred during or near to the deep judgments. The slowed reaction times are an indicator of the cognitive effort being expended on the judgment task.

The various definitions of elaborative processing can be illustrated by considering several studies of memory for faces. Subjects in Bower and Karlin's (1974) study were shown high school yearbook photos. In one condition, the subjects made shallow judgments about the faces (e.g., identify gender). In the other condition, they were asked to make character judgments for each face (e.g., "Does this person look honest?"). The character judgments require deeper processing. When tested afterwards, the character judgment participants correctly recognized more faces than did the group that made shallow judgments. If you want to remember a face, ask yourself, "Would I buy a used car from this person?" Following on Bower and Karlin's study, Winograd (1981) had participants study faces for distinctive features. For instance, "Does he have a large nose? Is she wearing glasses?" The more features that were searched, the better memory for the faces was. A focus on facial features increased distinctiveness. What about the role of cognitive effort? Given deep-processing instructions, participants make more eye movements when inspecting the pictures, implying more processing effort (Bloom & Mudd, 1991). Deep-processing subjects also report more interest and involvement in the task, whereas the

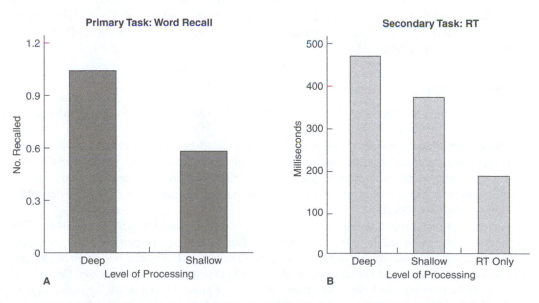

Figure 9.2 Dual-Task Performance Illustrating Trade-Off between Cognitive Effort and Reaction Time.

Source: From "Processing depth, elaboration of encoding, memory stores, and expended processing capacity," by M. W. Eysenck & M. C. Eysenck, 1979, *Journal of Experimental Psychology: Human Learning and Memory, 5*, p. 479, 481. Copyright American Psychological Association. Reprinted by permission.

shallow-processing groups find their task boring and undemanding (Sporer, 1991). So, why does elaborative processing enhance face memory? There is experimental support for all three hypotheses of elaboration, distinctiveness, and cognitive effort.

How Can Elaborative Processing Be Enhanced?

The techniques used in the various mnemonic devices discussed in Chapter 6 exemplify elaborative processing. In the keyword mnemonic, a mediating word is selected to connect two target items. How can you remember that Pittsburgh is a steel-producing town? Link Pittsburgh to the Steelers, and then to steel. In the narrative method, a story is fabricated to link together a series of target words. In the peg-word and location mnemonics, images are formed of the target and the mnemonic cue. These methods require meaningful analysis of the targets, the creation of distinctive representations in memory, and cognitive effort.

The method of elaborative interrogation increases cognitive processing. This technique involves asking "why" questions about to be remembered facts: Why is this so? Why would this be? Why are these connected? The intention is to integrate new facts with existing knowledge. An example of cognitive elaboration was cited in Chapter 6 as a mnemonic for learning to connect stimulus and response words in paired associate learning (Pressley, McDaniel, Turnure, Wood, & Ahmad, 1987). Given the target sentence "the large man read the sign," an elaborative question could be "why did he read the sign?" The answer "to see the warning about thin ice" elaborates and gives meaning to the target sentence. The general idea is that the learner should adopt a questioning attitude during study.

Conclusions about Elaboration

"People will probably learn more if we can find ways of making them work harder at encoding and if they are encouraged to deal with new information in terms of its meaning and semantic content. Getting students to simply repeat material or spend more time looking at it is not the most efficient way to ensure they will learn and remember the content" (Kulhavy, Schwartz, & Peterson, 1986, p. 122). This summary reminds us of several aspects of elaboration: effort, meaningfulness, and active rehearsal.

Imagery and Memory for Pictures

Visual encoding is another way of learning material. We can see this both through the use of imagery and in the recall of pictures versus words.

If words are presented for study, *concrete* words are typically better recalled than *abstract* words. Concrete words refer to things that can be readily imagined or pictured (such as the word CRAB), whereas abstract words refer more to ideas (such as the word FACT). Concrete words have a memory advantage over abstract words, as shown in a variety of learning situations (reviewed by Nelson & Schreiber, 1992).

Memory for pictures is often remarkably good. In one study, subjects were shown over 2,200 photographs presented in 2-hour sessions on 4 days. During testing, 280 pairs of slides were presented and the participants had to decide which picture in each pair they had been seen before and which one was new. Correct choices were made over 90 percent of the time (Standing, Conezio, & Haber, 1970). Photographs have much more detail than a printed word, allowing many cues to discriminate old from new photos. Still, the number remembered is impressive.

Objects are remembered even better than pictures. Given stimuli displayed in one of three ways, actual objects were better recognized than were photographs of the objects, which were in turn better remembered than the printed name of the objects. This is also one case in which younger students did as well as older ones: fourth graders were as good as college students in recalling objects (Bevan & Steger, 1971).

Instructing participants to visually image to-be-remembered items such as words often increases recall (e.g., Roediger, 1980). We saw further evidence for the beneficial effects of visual imagery with mnemonic techniques such as the peg-word system and the method of locations, described in Chapter 6.

Why is picture memory so much better than word memory? One reason is that pictures can be remembered with two encodings, one visual and the other a verbal translation of the picture. This is referred to as **dual coding** (Paivio, 1969). Another advantage for pictures is that the memory is more specific and distinctive than is the memory for an unelaborated word. As shown in Figure 9.1, the words CRAB and LAMP can take on specific images. For example, imagine remembering the word DOG versus a simple line drawing of a dog. The drawing cannot be too generic; it must show some kind of dog. (A large dog or small? Pointy or floppy ears?) This image may activate other knowledge of dogs, possibly unique facts that the word DOG does not retrieve, or it may remind us of a particular dog.

Pictures can be processed to different depths. Bransford, Nitsch, and Franks (1977) showed students a photograph of a living room, and gave orienting instructions to induce different forms of processing. Some subjects were told to try and find small hidden x's within the picture, a form of shallow processing. Another group was told to think about the kinds of actions they could perform with the objects. The students were then unexpectedly asked to recall as many objects from the picture as possible. The x group remembered only about 8 objects, but the action group remembered over 20. What is nice about this manipulation is that the x-searching subjects did closely attend to and scan the picture. Even so, their recall was poor.

Meaningfulness

Ebbinghaus compared his retention of poetry versus nonsense syllables. He found that the meaningful material was remembered better than the nonmeaningful, a conclusion that has stood for 130+ years now. Meaningful is remembered better than the nonmeaningful. Okay; no surprise there. But what exactly is meaningful? And how can we increase it?

The starting point for analyzing **meaningfulness** was to discover those variables that correlate with ease of learning. Meaningful words have more *associations* to other ideas and knowledge. One of the strongest predictors of memorability is the frequency with which a word is given as an association to other words (Rubin & Friendly, 1986). A meaningful item can be elaborated in memory by drawing on an extensive network of interassociations. This network involves semantic memory (general knowledge) and episodic memory (personal recollections).

Meaningful words are often more *imagable* (Rubin & Friendly, 1986). A mental image or a remembered picture can often be generated for meaningful words (DOG, LIBERTY). (In attempting to remember an abstract word such as LIBERTY, you remember it as the Statue of Liberty.)

Meaningful words are familiar. They have a high *frequency* of occurrence in the language: we hear them, read them, and use them often. Meaningful words are also rated high in ease of *pronounceability.* This may be related to familiarity and frequency.

Meaningful words are also rated as higher in emotionality than less-meaningful words (Rubin & Friendly, 1986). Meaningful knowledge is significant, interesting, relevant, pleasant, frightening, etc. (*insert your own adjective*).

This list of characteristics suggests that meaningfulness has to do with prior knowledge: Meaningful material is stuff you already know about. Generally, learners use knowledge they already possess to relate new items to this existing knowledge. The implication is that the more you know, the more you can learn. This truism has been substantiated in comparing people who are experts in certain domains and novices. For example, if shown various arrangements of chess pieces on a board, chess masters will remember them more accurately than less experienced players. This is particularly true if the pieces are in a meaningful arrangement (Gobet & Simon, 1996). When given 31 lines of a computer program to memorize, advanced student programmers learned them more readily than did students of intermediate ability. Again, the advantage for the experts was dependent on the program lines being in a logical sequence, and the advantage virtually disappeared when the program lines were scrambled (McKeithan, Reitman, Rueter, & Hirtle, 1981).

This expertise these individuals demonstrated occurred because the *domain-specific knowledge* was meaningful. There are certain subject areas (or domains) in which we are knowledgeable. We encode and remember new information easily from areas with which we are familiar. For instance, college students who are knowledgeable about baseball can remember fabricated baseball facts better than less knowledgeable students. Students knowledgeable about music remember more fabricated facts about music than about baseball (Kuhara-Kojima & Hatano, 1991).

How Can Meaningfulness Be Used to Increase Learning?

One suggestion is to use existing knowledge to make new information more meaningful. Learners themselves may attempt to create meaningfulness in otherwise unfamiliar material. Given a lengthy, random series of items, one strategy is to chunk them into more meaningful units. For example, one 38-year-old savant (otherwise described as having lower than average intelligence) had exceptional memory for numbers. He would memorize things like city populations, distances between cities, or the number of rooms in hotels. He could readily remember strings of numbers, such as 4836179621. How? "When I saw this number, I read it as 4, 836, 179, 621. I remembered 4 because of the fourth of July,. . .836 was the Chinese population of the State of Texas in 1910,. . .179 is the number of miles from New York to Harrisburg, and 621 is the number of a house I know in Denver" (Treffert, 1989, p. 74). Another mnemonist, fluent in several languages, readily picked up words in new languages by looking for similar-looking or -sounding words in other languages (Bernstein, 1993).

Meaningfulness can also be provided through the surrounding context. A list of vaguely worded instructions was more readily recalled when a label was given ("How to fly a kite" or "Washing clothes"). Without the label, the instructions are meaningless (Bransford & Johnson, 1973).

Presentation Variables

Testing Effects

Say you have a big test tomorrow and you are planning your study strategy. After you have studied the material once, should you study it a second time, or should you instead take a practice test on the material? Students would probably think that more studying is better. After all, it is called "studying" for a test. However, a significant finding from current research is that taking a test on the material is often more beneficial to remembering (on tomorrow's exam) than is additional study of the material. This finding is referred to as the **testing effect**: the greater benefit of taking a test over additional study on retention of the studied material.

In the prototypical design for a study of testing effects the research participant is exposed to the material two (or more) times, and then takes a final test on the material. In the standard condition, students might study the material, and then study it again. We can label this condition S–S. In the tested condition, the students would study the material, and then they would take a practice test on the information. Therefore, this is condition S–T. Later, a final test is given to both conditions to see which group remembers more: the one that studied twice, or the group that studied once and was tested once. We are interested in performance on the final test. Thus the design of such studies is as follows:

Standard condition, S–S: study once . . . study again . . . final test
Tested Condition, S–T: study once . . . practice test . . . final test

Roediger and Karpicke (2006) used this design to assess learning and retention of new information in the form of textbook-like paragraphs. Some college students studied the material twice; other students studied once and then wrote as much as they could remember. If the final test was given a few minutes later, the S–S group remembered slightly more. But when the final test was given two days, later, the S–T condition remembered more than did the study-twice condition. Specifically, Group S–T had 68 percent on the test whereas Group S–S only got 54 percent. (The results of this experiment were shown in Figure 1.3 of Chapter 1.)

Roediger and Karpicke (2006) extended the above design to compare a condition in which students studied four times (S–S–S–S) and a condition in which the students studied once and then made three practice attempts at recalling the information (S–T–T–T). The final test was given one week later to measure long-term learning of the material. Recall on this final test showed that more testing led to more remembering; and more studying led to less remembering. Testing your memory on what you have just studied may help you remember better in the long run than simply studying more. This may sound counterintuitive, and indeed the students in this experiment thought so also. Some students had studied the material four times, and they thought for sure they would remember more on the test than did those who had studied only once. However, a week later the S–T–T–T group recalled more.

Why is testing better than additional studying? Several explanations have been considered. (You should know by now that there is never just one explanation, the correct one.) One explanation is that taking a practice test is just another version of studying. After all, the material is presented a second time, although now in the form of questions and the students' answers. This re-exposure during testing may be a contributing factor to the testing effect, but it is not the whole explanation. Memory in the S–T condition is not simply as good as the S–S condition. The tested students perform better than the students who studied more. The testing manipulation does more than simply provide a second study exposure.

A more likely explanation is that the test provides a more challenging restudying of the material than passively reading it over a second time. Answering test questions requires more cognitive effort than rereading.

A third possibility is that the practice test mimics what students are required to do on the final test, that is, retrieve the information from memory. Retrieval is better when the mental operations being performed during the test match the operations that were performed during encoding. The cognitive activity on the practice test—retrieval—is a closer match to that on the final test—retrieval. (The testing effect is now often called *Retrieval Practice*, acknowledging the importance of retrieval in the practice test.)

The testing effect raises a number of procedural questions about its generality. What about the material that was not tested on the practice test? Does testing some of the information aid memory for items that were not tested initially? A practice test on some of the information even aids recall of the untested information, although not to the degree that the questions activate memory for related (untested) information (Chan, McDermott, & Roediger, 2006).

Testing usually implies feedback: Which questions did you get right or wrong? Is corrective feedback necessary for testing to have any benefit? The best learning occurred when the participants took a practice test *and* received feedback. This was better than studying a second time. The practice test alone, even without feedback, was still sometimes better than restudying a second time (Kang, McDermott, & Roediger, 2007). Does corrective feedback need to be immediate?

Apparently not. Delaying feedback until the end of the practice test produced better retention than did correction after each question (Butler & Roediger, 2008).

Another way to look at feedback is to consider that, on the practice test, you knew the correct answers to some questions but not others. Maybe all you really need is a refresher on the unremembered items. Karpicke and Roediger (2007) used a procedure in which study trials and tests alternated until the list was learned. Trial by trial, items that were remembered on a test were dropped from the next presentation of the list. Only the forgotten items were re-presented. Restudying the items you already remember does not help, but restudying the items you forgot does help.

There can be negative effects of testing. On the final test you might remember the wrong answer from the practice test. This is why feedback, in terms of which answers were correct and incorrect, is important. Or, some of the multiple-choice alternatives on the final test look familiar because, well, they are familiar. They were the wrong answers used on the practice test but are chosen on the final test because they look familiar. The negative effects of "misinformation" are discussed more in Chapter 11.

Isolation Effects

A commonly held belief about memory is that unusual or distinctive material is better remembered. Helena von Restorff, a Berlin Ph.D. of the 1930s, studied this phenomenon. In presenting a list of to-be-remembered items, one item in the list was made *distinctive*. For example, if the other words were printed in black, one word was printed in red. In a list of words, a number would be inserted as an item. The distinctive item, distinctive in the context of the list, was learned more quickly or remembered better. This finding was initially called the **von Restorff effect**, but the more recent literature refers to it as the **isolation effect**: In a series of items, an unusual item or an item presented in a distinctive manner is especially remembered. A nice example of the isolation effect is a television commercial that contains no sound whatsoever; the message is signed by an actor, and printed at the bottom of the screen. The sudden silence in the midst of the other attention-seeking ads certainly stands out.

The isolation effect could be attributed to enhanced encoding. The isolated item is simply processed differently from other items in the list. The isolated item receives more attention, more rehearsal, or more elaboration in memory (Waddill & McDaniel, 1998). Measures of brain waves indicate that subjects orient more to the isolated item (Fabiani & Donchin, 1995). However, the isolated item might be remembered better because it is more distinctive in memory during retrieval. The isolated item stands out against a blur of memories of many similar items (Hunt, 1995).

An isolation effect can occur in memory for people. If someone we know does something out of character, this might be especially remembered. In a study by Hastie and Kumar (1979), hypothetical individuals were described by a list of traits to induce a personality impression in the participants. For instance, someone would be described as intelligent, clever, quick, and smart. After this, a list of 20 to-be-remembered behaviors of this hypothetical person was presented. Most were congruent with the initial personality labels, for example, the person had won a chess tournament or liked reading history. But importantly, an incongruent behavior was also presented: failed math twice, or always getting lost. When the participants tried to recall the list of behaviors, the incongruent one was especially recalled. For example, whereas congruent behaviors were recalled about 50 percent of the time, incongruent behaviors were recalled 77 percent of the time.

Other research has shown a more complex and interesting pattern of results when memory for the whole list is considered. Whereas the isolated item is well recalled, this comes at the expense of memory for items before and after it in the list. For example, suppose the following partial list of words is presented: table, dog, tree, grass, COLUMBUS, school, coffee, and soup. The enhanced recall of the distinctive item (COLUMBUS) impairs recall of the words just before it (GRASS and TREE). Tulving (1969) called this a *retrograde amnesic effect*. In Tulving's experiment, the participants did not actually experience trauma from the word COLUMBUS, but the unusual word was surprising enough to have an amnesic-like effect.

In addition, the distinctive item may impair memory for the words that follow it. Detterman (1975) found an *anterograde amnesic effect*, in which the isolated item blocked memory for the words that followed the distinctive one. In the preceding example, SCHOOL and COFFEE might not be recalled. The results of one of Detterman's experiments are shown in Figure 9.3. A list of 15 words was presented auditorily. The distinctive item in the eighth position was much louder than the other words. The graph nicely illustrates the enhanced retention of the isolated item as compared to the control word (presented at normal volume) in the eighth position. The words before the loud item were less recalled, which is the retrograde amnesic effect (the shaded portion before the distinctive item). The words that followed the isolated word were also less well-remembered, which is the anterograde amnesic effect (the shaded portion after).

Similar effects have been shown with other forms of distinctiveness. For instance, if a taboo word (an obscenity) is presented as the isolated item, the obscenity is remembered but the words before and after it in the list are not (Mackay et al., 2004).

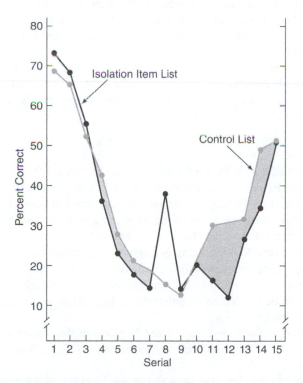

Figure 9.3 **The Isolation Effect in the Recall of a List of 15 Words.** A distinctive item occurs at the eighth position in the experimental list. The distinctive item is well recalled, but there is some forgetting of the items that preceded and followed it in the list.

Source: From "The von Restorff Effect and Induced Amnesia: Production by Manipulation of Sound Intensity," by D. K. Detterman, 1975, *Journal of Experimental Psychology: Human Learning and Memory, 1*, p. 626. Copyright © 1975 by the American Psychological Society. Reprinted by permission.

Seductive Details

Often, a lecturer or writer will cite an interesting but tangential fact to keep the audience's attention, hoping that the interesting tidbit will help them remember the main facts of the lecture or text. Students might find the topic of classical conditioning less than invigorating, but their interest increases upon learning that John Watson, who conditioned Little Albert to fear a lab rat (Chapter 3), reputedly had some fears of his own. He slept with a night-light and refused to drive a car.

Unfortunately, people remember the tangents but not the main facts. This is the **seductive detail effect**. Novel, concrete, or personally involving details are remembered, in contrast to the blander material the seductive details were meant to illustrate. Why do seductive details impair recall? One possibility is that they distract attention away from the main ideas of the text or lecture. Processing tangential facts comes at a cost to processing other information. But there can be a second effect, as well. Interesting tidbits may disrupt the flow of the text or lecture. The coherence of the material may be interrupted. Seductive details are less harmful when presented at the end of the passage, presumably after the readers have already formed an outline for the material (Harp & Mayer, 1998).

Spacing Effects

What student has not heard the admonition, "Study every night, don't wait and cram at the last minute." So, you are already familiar with the **spacing effect**: Spaced practice (or distributed practice, as it is sometimes called) leads to better retention than does massed practice. If something is to be studied two (or more) times, it is better to distribute the repetitions than to mass them close together. Like the serial-position curve, this is an amazingly general fact about learning (Dempster, 1996).

Why does spacing repetitions produce better retention? Several theories have been offered over the years. No single explanation seems to accommodate all of the available data. Yet each explanation has led to novel experimental tests that offer insights into the spacing effect.

Hypothesis 1

The two presentations of a to-be-remembered item can be labeled P1 and P2. The two occurrences can be massed (P1 is immediately followed by P2) or spaced (P1 is followed by some other items before P2 occurs). Participants attend less to a second presentation when it is repeated too soon. The idea here is that participants are attempting to remember a list of items, and so processing must be distributed across the items. A massed P2, seeming so familiar, is skipped through to devote more time to other items. Shaughnessy, Zimmerman, and Underwood (1972) actually let participants pace themselves through the list by giving them the remote control. They skipped through immediate repetitions, but spent more time on repetitions that occurred after longer delays. This can be labeled an *attention-deficit* hypothesis: the massed second presentation received less attention.

The attention-deficit explanation is supported in research that monitors eye movements to photographs. The number of fixations decreases to repeated pictures (Ryan, Althoff, Whitlow, & Cohen, 2000).

One way to assess whether learning from the first occurrence of an item (P1) or the second occurrence (P2) is reduced during massed trials is to tag the two occurrences so that they are somewhat different. For example, the target word can be presented in different modalities at P1 and P2. The first occurrence might be auditory and the second is visual. By then asking participants to recall not only the items but also whether they had been seen or heard, we find that it is the second presentation and not the first item that is less-well remembered with massed repetitions (Hintzman, Block, & Summers, 1973).

Hypothesis 2

Recall is enhanced when there are multiple retrieval cues, or routes, to the target. When the two study presentations are more widely spaced, they might be encoded somewhat differently into memory. For example, given the list TABLE, FORK, SCHOOL, BOOK, TABLE, the first TABLE may be encoded as a kitchen item and the second as a classroom item. Recalling either FORK or BOOK might aid retrieval of the target word TABLE. Thus there are two routes to TABLE. This explanation is known as the *encoding variability hypothesis*. Back-to-back TABLEs are likely to be encoded similarly, both as kitchen items, for example.

Encoding variability suggests that massed repetitions might not be so bad if P1 and P2 are encoded differently, just as they supposedly are when repetitions are spaced. Different encodings can be simulated by using homographs, or words that have two meanings. For example, the homograph FOOT is first presented in the context of "inch," and the second time in the context of "toe." Words presented in this fashion do not show a massed-practice decrement (e.g., Gartman & Johnson, 1972). That is, using our previous example, FOOT is well remembered even though the two presentations were massed. Okay, so this is a contrived manipulation, and the homographs are actually different words (Martin, 1975). However, it does illustrate that the general idea is that words may be encoded differently when they are encountered on separate occasions.

Short Retention Interval

As universal as the spacing effect is, there is one deviation to the spaced-is-better rule: If retention is tested immediately after the second presentation, massing is usually better. For example, Balota, Duchek, and Paullin (1989) used a paired-associate procedure with college-aged and elderly adult subjects. Spacing varied from having back-to-back presentations of the same pair of words (TABLE–DUCK, TABLE–DUCK) to presentations that were separated by 20 other pairs. Item pairs were sometimes tested immediately (TABLE–?) or after a delay of about 20 items. The results are shown in Figure 9.4. Both younger and older subjects recalled more massed items on the immediate test and recalled more spaced items on the delayed test.

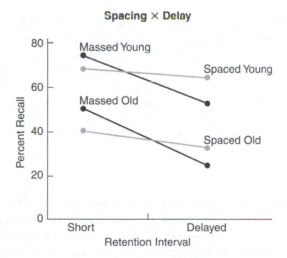

Figure 9.4 **Mean Percent Correct Recall in a Continuous Paired-Associate Procedure by Younger and Older Subject Groups.** Items were presented either massed (presented 1 pair apart) or spaced (presented 20 items apart) and tested shortly after (2 items later in the list) or after a longer delay (20 items later).

Source: From "Age-Related Differences in the Impact of Spacing, Lag, and Retention Interval," by D. A. Balota, J. M. Duchek, and R. Paullin, 1989, *Psychology and Aging, 4*, p. 7. Copyright © 1989 by the American Psychological Association. Reprinted by permission.

Is There an Optimal Spacing Interval?

How long must an interval be to be considered spaced, and therefore beneficial? The answer depends on how much time there is between the completion of studying and the test. In general, the longer the interval before the test occurs, the wider the spacing interval during study should be. As we move from retention intervals of minutes, characteristic of many laboratory experiments, to retention intervals of days, weeks, and months, characteristic of academic learning, the spacing between separate study sessions must increase dramatically. Spaced practice intervals of minutes are perfectly effective if the test will occur at the end of the hour-long experimental session. When the test is a week away, spacing the initial presentations a day or so apart is better.

The most effective spacing can best be described as a ratio of the length of the spacing interval to the length of the retention interval (Cepeda, Pashler, Vul, Wixted, & Rohrer, 2006). For instance, spacing study periods one day apart and testing seven days later, produces a ratio of 1/7, or about 14 percent. That same spacing of one day between study periods but testing 30 days later produces a ratio of 1/30, or about 3 percent (in round numbers). Optimal ratios are said to fall in the range of 10–20 percent. So, the longer the retention interval, the longer the spacing intervals should be to produce a ratio within this range. Further increases in the spacing interval seem to convey no additional benefit. For instance, spacing intervals of 1 day, 2 days, or 4 days were about equivalent when the test occurred 10 days after the final studying (Pashler, Rohrer, Cepeda, & Carpenter, 2007).

Conclusions about Spacing

One consensus idea that has emerged from all the research on distributed practice is that "a little forgetting may be good for learning" (Cuddy & Jacoby, 1982; Krug, Davis, & Glover, 1990). With a massed second presentation, there is a false feeling of knowing when in fact the material is not known well at all. After a longer spacing between the two presentations, the participant may recognize that the item has been temporarily forgotten, which should heighten processing of the repetition. In addition, longer spacing gives an opportunity to practice recalling the target material from long-term memory.

There is a significant implication from the results of spacing research. You can arrange a situation to make learning appear to be easy by using massed repetitions; or you could arrange to make learning lasting by spacing repetitions (Schmidt & Bjork, 1992).

Although the spacing effect is well known, some researchers note that it is not practiced enough in education (Dempster, 1988). For example, textbooks could be written that repeat certain ideas from chapter to chapter, thus ensuring repetition and spacing. Academic calendars could be revised to spread courses over longer intervals than quarter and semester systems to allow more widely spaced exposure to the topic's content (Bahrick, 1979).

Generation Effect

In most of the experiments presented so far in this book, the researcher presented the to-be-remembered material. The participant looks or listens and tries to remember. An alternative means of presentation is to have the participant involved in presenting the to-be-recalled items. Slamecka and Graf (1978) described a procedure in which their participants generated the target items in response to certain cues. For example, in the following word pairs, fill in the blanks with a word that is opposite in meaning: HOT: _ _ _ _; STOP: _ _. Participants who generated the words COLD and GO were more likely to recall these words later than did subjects who simply read the word pairs. The **generation effect** refers to increased memory for study material that is generated by the participant rather than being provided by the experimenter. The generation effect has been shown in a variety of testing formats: free recall of the generated words, cued recall in which the first word of each pair is presented as a cue for the second, and recognition in a multiple-choice format (Burns, 1990, who also notes some complications).

Having the participant generate the target material induces elaborative processing that the read-only condition does not. The participant must attend to the relationship between the cues and generated items. Generation also mimics what will be required during memory testing: Produce the to-be-remembered item in response to some cue. As noted elsewhere in this chapter, recall is improved when the encoding and retrieval (or testing) requirements are more nearly alike.

Limitations of Elaborative Processing

The general claim has been made here that elaborative processing leads to better encoding. Are there any limits to the benefits of elaborative processing? Are there tasks for which elaboration does not help?

One situation in which elaboration may be harmful is *verbal overshadowing*. The verbal description of nonverbal information such as pictures and faces can lead to less accurate retention. In essence, we remember the words we used to encode an item rather than the event itself. Verbal overshadowing can occur when we try to remember a face (Schooler, Ryan, & Reder, 1996). In describing the face, we name features that can be verbalized, such as eye color or the shape of the lips, and not on features that are difficult to articulate (such as the configural arrangement of facial features) but that may be more important for face recognition.

Verbal overshadowing occurs in other tasks, such as remembering the taste of specific wines. Novice and expert wine tasters were asked to describe several wines. Later, they were given a recognition test to distinguish the tasted from new wines. The untrained tasters did worse when they had verbally described the earlier wines. Not having a sophisticated vocabulary for describing wine, the participants tended to remember what they said rather than what they tasted. Expert tasters were not impaired by verbalization; presumably, their vocabulary matched their subtle taste discriminations (Melcher & Schooler, 1996).

Learner Variables

The learner brings a number of characteristics to the learning situation. Encoding is influenced by the intention to learn, the use of incentives, and the level of arousal. Other learner factors such as age, gender, and learning style are discussed in Chapter 12.

Incidental Versus Intentional Learning

A paradox involving everyday memory is that often we spontaneously remember things without any deliberate intention to remember. You can remember what you had for breakfast this morning and something you heard earlier in the day. This is **incidental learning**: learning occurs without intention to remember, but incidental to other processing of the information. At other times, in order to remember, we need to deliberately study, rehearse, and so on. This is *intentional learning*. How important is intention to remembering?

The general experimental method used to test incidental learning is to present a series of words with instructions to the subjects to process the words in different ways. They might be asked to state whether the word has an *e* in it; count how many letters are in the word; or categorize the word as pleasant or unpleasant (Hyde & Jenkins, 1969). Across this series of judgments, deeper levels of cognitive processing are required. You need to process the meaning of the word to rate its pleasantness, but not whether you see a letter *e*. In the incidental learning condition,

Table 9.1 Number of Words Recalled After Different Orienting Instructions, and Incidental or Intentional Learning Instructions

Instruction	Incidental (Unexpected memory test)	Intentional (Expected memory test)
Is there an e in the word?	9.4	10.4
How many letters are in the word?	9.9	12.4
Is the word pleasant or unpleasant?	16.3	16.6
No orienting task		16.1

Source: Adapted from "Differential effects of incidental tasks on the organization
of recall of a list of highly associated words," by T. S. Hyde & J. J. Jenkins, 1969,
Journal of Experimental Psychology, 82, p. 475.

the participants are not told there will be a memory test. In the intentional learning conditions,
the subjects are told there will be a memory test. When the participants are later asked to recall the
words, words that had received deeper processing were recalled better (see Table 9.1). The incidental learning participants who performed the deeper processing recalled as many words as
participants who were told in advance about the memory test. Incidental recall can be as good as
intentional.

Incidental learning is sometimes better than intentional. Medical students and faculty were
given patient protocols containing about 20 pieces of information, mostly laboratory test results.
The participants were asked to diagnose the patient or to try to memorize the case data. The
medical specialists who made a diagnosis recalled more specific facts than did the students who
diagnosed or memorized. Paradoxically, the physicians actually recalled less when they tried to
memorize (Norman, Brooks, & Allen, 1989). The diagnosis incidentally retrieves an organization or a schema (both discussed elsewhere in this chapter) that makes up for the absence of
intentional elaboration.

Incentives

Does offering a reward increase performance in a memory task? The research seems to suggest
that once a subject has committed to learn, reward has little additional effect. When college
students were offered different sums of money for each word remembered, 10 cents versus 1
cent, there was no difference in the number of words recalled (Nelson, 1976). Offering $10 to
participants if they were among the best in the experiment did not produce any better memory
than not offering an incentive (Nilsson, 1987). Given that the participants were motivated and
were trying to remember to begin with, as is typical of college students, the amounts offered had
no additional effect.

However, if greater incentives are offered for remembering specific items, students will devote
more processing to the high value items. The learner must be told of the differential values before
studying. For instance, if students were also told that recalling one set of items has a higher pay-
off than items from another set, then more of the high-value facts are remembered (Kassam, Gilbert, Swencionis, & Wilson, 2009). A rational strategy is employed: Given a limited processing
capacity, devote more effort to remembering the high value words than the low value words. This
is what students do in juggling their workload among courses: Devote more time to the important
courses (such as this one) and less to other classes.

What about offering the incentive after learning? Telling the participant after all the material
has been presented does not help memory for the high value facts. In the above Kassam et al.
(2009) study, informing the participants about the high-value targets after studying did not aid

recall. In another study a list of 75 words was studied. One week later, the students came back to the lab and attempted to recall as many words as possible. After this first test, some participants were offered $1 for each additional word they could recall. The average number recalled was five, the same as by the participants not offered the incentive but simply asked to try and remember some more (Nelson, 1976; see also Nilsson, 1987).

The point is that the promise of an incentive for remembering does not affect memory itself but rather behaviors that will lead to better retention, such as rehearsal or cognitive elaboration.

Arousal

We could expect arousal to facilitate learning, and generally it does. But the findings often must be qualified by interacting variables. One limitation is that the term *arousal* is ambiguous and has varied meanings in psychology. **Arousal** can refer to a psychological state of increased attention or alertness; or to physiological excitement as assessed by measures of heart rate, skin conductance response, or EEG; or to personality traits such as anxiety or impulsiveness.

Another important qualification is that the optimal level of arousal for any given task varies. Performance is usually better at some intermediate level of arousal and is less efficient at both lower and higher levels. A corollary to this is that different tasks have different optimal levels. These two statements together define the **Yerkes-Dodson law**: Performance follows an inverted U-shaped curve, with peak performance occurring at intermediate levels of arousal and decreased performance at higher or lower levels (Yerkes & Dodson, 1908). As a hypothetical example, remembering facts from a classroom lecture might be poor if you are either too fatigued or too hyper. It is also likely that taking an exam or demonstrating video game skills requires different optimal arousal levels than does classroom learning.

A real-world example of the Yerkes-Dodson law is the recall by 3- and 4-year olds of a hurricane they had experienced (Bahrick, Parker, Fivush, & Levitt, 1998). Arousal was defined by the amount of damage to the house produced by the storm: High arousal was assumed in cases where the house was penetrated, moderate arousal if there was extensive outside damage, and low arousal if the damage was minimal. The number of facts the children recalled is shown in

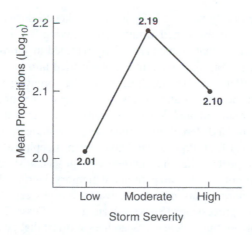

Figure 9.5 Mean number of facts recalled (the means are log-transformed) by 3- and 4-year olds as a function of hurricane damage.

Figure 9.5. The moderately stressed children recalled more than did those presumed to have experienced lower or higher levels of arousal.

The effects of arousal on memory have been studied in several ways. Arousal is manipulated directly through the administration of stimulant drugs and indirectly through correlations with circadian rhythms. We can also consider the effects of extremely low levels of arousal, such as sleep (see Box 9.2), and extremely high levels of arousal, such as that produced by strong emotions (discussed separately in a following section).

Box 9.2   Sleep Learning

Does learning occur while we sleep? An entire industry developed around the promotion of sleep-learning audio products. Simply listen through a pillow speaker during the night and wake up the next morning refreshed and fluent in Spanish! But if sleep is a state of low arousal, can anything really be learned then?

Early studies of sleep learning found conflicting outcomes (see Aarons, 1976). The discrepancy was due to whether the participants were actually asleep when the to-be-learned information was presented. No learning occurred if the participants were truly asleep, as verified by EEG and REM recordings (rapid eye movements, not REM the band). For example, Emmons and Simon (1956) presented a 10-word list *46 times* during the night. The list was played only when EEGs indicated the participant was in deep sleep. Otherwise the tape was stopped. When given multiple-choice tests the next day, the participants recognized a hardly encouraging 25 percent of the target words, as compared to a chance level of 20 percent. In other studies, researchers adopted a pragmatic philosophy about instruction, and simply played the audios from lights-out until wake-up the next morning. Learning did occur under these conditions, but most probably when the participants were awake (i.e., when drifting off to sleep, or during awakenings in the night).

Some forms of learning do occur during sleep. Simple classical conditioning and habituation have been demonstrated to occur in sleeping animals and humans (see Badia, 1990).

Why are dreams so poorly recalled? If you are awakened during REM sleep, often a dream is recalled. If you are awakened minutes after leaving REM the dream has already slipped away. One theory is that dreams are briefly retained in short-term memory, but in the absence of sufficient arousal, the dream is not encoded into long-term memory (Koulack & Goodenough, 1976). Of course, dreams may be forgotten for other reasons discussed in this chapter: the images and events in our dreams are not always meaningful; they are not logically organized; and they do not conform to our waking schemas.

Sleep *after* learning has a different effect than sleep during learning. A classic study by Jenkins and Dallenbach (1924) showed that 8 hours spent sleeping after learning was more beneficial than 8 hours spent awake. Current theory suggests that sleep is an important time for consolidation of memory traces into permanent memory. During sleep, those neural elements that were active during learning are reactivated during sleep. This has been referred to by analogy to "offline processing" (Stickgold, Hobson, & Fosse, 2001). In back-to-back articles published in the journal *Science*, researchers showed that postlearning REM sleep enhanced learning both of mazes by rats (Wilson & McNaughton, 1994) and motor skills in humans (Karni, Tanne, Rubenstein, Askenasy, & Sagi, 1994). If the experimenters disrupted the REM stage of sleep, later retention was impaired. So, in a sense, learning does occur during sleep—the learning that began before sleep commenced.

Remembering under Anesthesia?

Learning while anesthetized poses similar research problems to sleep learning, primarily knowing whether the subject is truly unconscious. There may be some consciousness even though pain and movement are blocked (Andrade, 1995). In experimental tests of the effects of low doses of inhaled anesthetic drugs, memory on verbal tasks such as the digit span and free recall was poorer (Adam, 1979). Interestingly, implicit memory was found after surgical anesthesia (Kihlstrom, Schacter, Cork, Hurt, & Behr, 1990). Pairs of moderately associated words (such as TABLE and KITCHEN) were repetitively read to patients during surgery, with the intention of strengthening the words' associations. Half of the participants heard one list of word pairs, and the other half heard a second list. Thus, the unheard lists provided baseline rates of free associations later. On two occasions after surgery, the participants were given free-association instructions. The first word in each pair was presented and the participants were asked to respond with the first word that came to mind. More of the words presented under anesthesia were recalled than nonpresented associates. Thus, implicit memory may be one form of learning that can occur under low levels of arousal.

Stimulant Drugs

Stimulant drugs that increase central nervous system arousal should increase learning. The stimulant strychnine, a poison when taken in higher doses, was an ingredient in tonics once prescribed for memory loss and forgetfulness (Essman, 1983). The behaviorist psychologist John Watson claimed the only reason he passed his final exam in Greek was that he drank a quart of cola syrup, which contains caffeine, while cramming overnight (Watson, 1936). However, it is unclear whether these stimulants actually increase learning (by facilitating encoding) or simply affect performance (reducing fatigue; Essman, 1983).

In a contemporary experiment, some participants received a dose of amphetamine one hour before lists of to-be-remembered words were presented. When the subjects were tested shortly after list presentations (immediately or within 30 minutes), there was no difference in recall between the stimulant and control groups. So the stimulant had no effect on recall over a short interval of time. However, the amphetamine group recalled more words one day later. The control subjects forget words over time, and so recalled fewer words a day later. The stimulant drug subjects recalled as much a day later as they had after the first half-hour (Zeeuws & Soetens, 2007).

Unfortunately, there are no simple effects of most stimulants on learning. Caffeine has produced complex interactions with other variables such as gender, age, and the type of memory task (e.g., Hogervorst, Riedel, Schmitt, & Jolles, 1998). For example, performance on a practice verbal SAT test (a measure of semantic knowledge) showed that caffeine sometimes aided and sometimes inhibited performance, depending on when the test was taken (morning or evening); the personality of the subject (introvert or extravert); and amount of practice (first or second day). That is, the efficacy of caffeine depended on the combination of all these variables (Revelle, Humphreys, Simon, & Gilliland, 1980). Immediate free recall of word lists by women was, in one case, impaired following a dose of caffeine (Erikson et al., 1985), and, in another study, enhanced (Arnold, Petros, Beckwith, Coons, & Gorman, 1987). Caffeine had little consistent effect on men in either study.

The arousal-producing aspects of stimulants are confounded by other effects these may have on memory. Any drug that has stimulating or depressing effects on the central nervous system affects neurotransmitter activity. For example, the drug lorazepam, which is used to reduce anxiety, both reduces central nervous system arousal and inhibits the action of some neurotransmitters. The effects of this drug were compared to those of a control drug that only decreased arousal but was not known to affect other brain chemicals related to learning. (The researchers used an antihistamine as the control drug, and you know what antihistamines can do to your level of alertness.) The lorazepam subjects remembered much less than did the antihistamine subjects in tests of word recall and recognition (Curran, Pooviboonsuk, Dalton, & Lader, 1998). That is, the antianxiety drug impaired memory whereas the antihistamine did not.

Stimulant drugs include those used to treat ADHD and other disorders. Do these drugs increase learning and memory when used by non-ADHD individuals? Although d-amphetamine (d-AMP, or Adderall) and methylphenidate (MPH) are used by students for the purpose of cognitive enhancement, it is not at all clear that these drugs can enhance learning. As noted with caffeine, well-done experiments show sometimes a benefit, and often no effect. One recent review found that drugs such as d-AMP do not increase initial learning of, for example, word lists, or immediate free recall. The drug may increase retention over delays of hours, days, or a week. There were also no consistently-found benefits in working memory or executive function. What seems like a logical possibility, once again, may not be supported by research findings.

Circadian Rhythms and Learning

Arousal varies during the course of the waking day. Do circadian variations influence learning ability? In one study of digit span, a measure of short-term memory, performance peaked at about 10:30 A.M. and declined thereafter into the early evening hours (Blake, 1967; see right panel of Figure 9.6). Immediate recall of specific facts from a 1,500-word science article peaked even earlier in the morning: Correct recall was maximal at 8 A.M. and steadily declined thereafter, with a slight bump back up after lunch (Folkard & Monk, 1980; left, Figure 9.6). (These studies both used British students. I would be surprised to see U.S. students peaking at that hour in the morning.)

One difficulty in linking arousal to circadian rhythms is the assumption that everyone has the same cycle. If people differ in their levels of alertness at different times of day (i.e., so-called morning "larks" and evening "owls"; Guthrie, Ash, & Bendapudi, 1995), there may be parallel

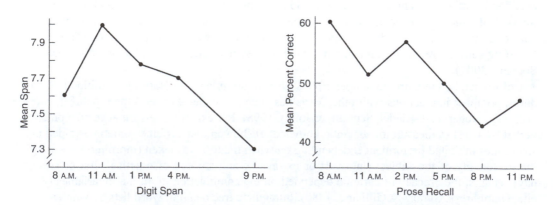

Figure 9.6 Digit-Span Recall (*left panel*) and Prose-Paragraph Recall (*right panel*) as a Function of Time of Day of Testing.

Source: Adapted from S. Folkard and T. H. Monk, "Circadian Rhythms in Human Memory," *British Journal of Psychology, 71,* pp. 295–307, 1980, published by The British Psychological Society. Reproduced with permission by John Wiley & Sons.

differences in recall at different times of day. Indeed, one study found that morning people were more accurate in paragraph recall when tested at 9 A.M. than at 8 P.M., whereas evening people did better at the later testing time (Petros, Beckwith, & Anderson, 1990).

Some Conclusions about Arousal

An implicit assumption of arousal theories is that an aroused brain simply works better at consolidating information into a stable memory. It is as if once the brain is cranked up, anything thrown in will be remembered better. Apart from any hypothesized neural effects, we need to consider the broader influence of arousal on cognition. Arousal affects what we attend to and what is ignored, what and how we encode, and how efficiently we retrieve. The source of arousal will also have different effects. Arousal elicited by a startling unknown sound will affect learning differently than arousal produced by loud but familiar background noise.

Emotions and Encoding

Are highly emotional events remembered better than neutral events? This question seems too easy and the answer seems too obvious. However, getting objective data to support our subjective impressions is not so easy. The two basic problems are determining whether what we recall is accurate and exactly how emotions influence remembering.

How Do Emotions Affect Memory?

First, emotional arousal will focus attention on certain aspects of a situation. Given our limited capacity to divide attention, this means that peripheral details may go unnoticed. In an experimental simulation of memory for an emotional event, a story was presented via a series of seven slides, and, simultaneously, the participants' eye movements were recorded. When one slide depicted an emotional outcome to the story (a child hit by a car), there were more fixations on the central details of the picture. These details were also recalled better than in the neutral condition, but peripheral details were not recalled as well in the emotional condition. Central detail memory was better for the emotional slide (Christianson, Loftus, Hoffman, & Loftus, 1991).

A second effect of emotion is to produce bodily arousal that could contribute to long-term memory formation. Epinephrine is released from the adrenal medulla during and after an emotional stressor, which leads (through a series of intermediate steps) to stimulation of the amygdala in the brain. The amygdala is active during the formation of long-term memory for emotional events (McGaugh, 1991; Thompson & Gluck, 1991).

Third, emotional events are distinctive. Often, they are not everyday experiences. Finally, emotional events are talked about and thought about, and so they are well rehearsed and elaborated in memory (Heuer & Reisberg, 1992). In the extreme example of posttraumatic stress disorder, the memories replay and intrude into thoughts and dreams.

Thus, emotions incorporate several themes from this chapter: attention, arousal, distinctiveness, and elaboration. (Emotions may also affect retrieval, either to facilitate or inhibit recall. These latter possibilities are discussed in the next chapter.)

Flashbulb Memories

One striking memory phenomenon that most of us have experienced is that of having a vivid memory for a surprising, emotional, and consequential event. The precipitant is particular to our own lives, for example, unexpected tragic news or unexpected good news. Some emotional events are shared by a community or a nation, such as the news of the attacks on September 11,

2001. Brown and Kulick (1977) used the term **flashbulb memories** to capture the essence of such memories. It is as if a photograph of the moment when we heard the news is encoded into memory. This image is assumed to be complete, detailed, and accurate. Brown and Kulick proposed the existence of a special memory mechanism, triggered by surprising and emotional events, that immediately creates a record of the contents of consciousness at that moment. These memories are immune to normal forgetting.

The method introduced by Brown and Kulick to study flashbulb memories was to ask people if they remembered when they first learned of a significant news event, such as the assassination of President John F. Kennedy or Martin Luther King, Jr. Even long afterwards people reported photolike memories. These included details of where they were when they heard the news, what they were doing at the time, from whom or how they heard the news, their immediate affective reactions, and what they did next.

Neisser (1982) criticized the Brown and Kulick procedure on several grounds. What people claim they remember is not necessarily true, no matter how vivid the memory seems. The developmental psychologist Jean Piaget distinctly remembered being kidnapped as a young child and often retold the story, although he later learned this had not happened (cited in Loftus & Ketcham, 1994). Neisser also argued that the memories might have formed, not in a flashbulb instant, but in the hours or days afterwards, when people tell and retell their story. Indeed, people's recollections do have a news-reporting quality to them: when, where, why, who, and what.

Researchers next moved to questioning people shortly after a traumatic experience, then retesting them months later. The first memory test is used to verify the accuracy of the delayed test (a method which presupposes people remembered accurately the first time). McClosky, Wible, and Cohen (1988) questioned people about flashbulb memories for the explosion of the space shuttle *Challenger* one week afterwards and again 9 months later. The participants evidenced remarkable consistency in their answers to specific questions about where they were, who told them, and so on. Over time, memories did become more general and contained fewer details. About 9 percent of the "facts" remembered 9 months later were inconsistent with the 1-week recollections, and about 6 percent of the facts were forgotten. One could be impressed by the robustness of the memories: These are very good memories. Or, one could focus on the forgetting: These memories were not perfect, unchanging, or immune to forgetting.

Are flashbulb memories remembered any better than everyday memories? Talarico and Rubin (2003) interviewed college students the day after the September 11, 2001 attack on the World Trade Center, asking them about where they were, how they heard, who was with them, and so on (the sorts of things we recall about flashbulb memories). The students were also asked the same questions about some everyday event that had occurred near that same day, which often turned out to be a school-related or social event. When the students were interviewed again 32 weeks later, they showed fairly consistent recall of the September 11th details, forgetting a few and adding some others. Their memories were rated as "vivid," which was as expected for flashbulb memories. Remarkably, the students' recall of the everyday events was no different. They recalled the same number of details that were consistent with their previous statements and the same number of details that were inconsistent. Their flashbulb and everyday memories did not differ. What did differ was that the students were more sure of the accuracy and veracity of their flashbulb memories.

Is there a separate flashbulb mechanism? Maybe instead we should view memory as a continuum, with different factors such as surprise, emotionality, consequentiality, or rehearsal acting to push memories toward one end point or the other.

Eyewitness Memory and Emotional Arousal

Eyewitness recall offers another source of data on the effect of emotional arousal on memory. Are witnesses to a crime or an accident, who have been exposed to an emotional event in a realistic situation, more or less likely to recall significant details? Once again, there is no simple answer, because recall is determined by a complex set of interacting variables. Emotional arousal may lead to focusing and retention of central details, but poorer retention for peripheral and unattended details. One example of this is labeled *weapons focus*: Victims or witnesses focus attention on a weapon, but possibly do not remember other details of the situation, such as the face of the perpetrator (Loftus, Loftus, & Messo, 1987). In one study of weapons focus, participants who thought they were waiting for an experiment heard an argument in the next room. Someone emerged from the room carrying either a pen or what appeared to be a bloody letter opener. The participants were then tested for face recognition of this person, which was the real purpose of the study. The perpetrator's picture was less often identified in the weapon condition than in the pen condition (cited in Loftus, 1979). An emotional witness and a nonemotional person might remember equal amounts of information, but different details of the situation.

A great deal of research has focused on memory for emotional versus peripheral details. Given a negative-emotion item against a neutral background (such as a picture of a snake in the forest) and a nonemotion item (a chipmunk in the forest), there is a trade-off in memory for the emotional detail versus the background. The emotional item is remembered better than a neutral item in the same location (that is, remember more snake and less chipmunk). Less of the background is remembered from the emotion pictures than the neutral pictures (remember less of the forest that had the snake, but remember more of the forest that had the chipmunk). This trade off, i.e., remembering more negative central detail and less peripheral detail, is enhanced by anxiety. Individuals who have greater anxiety showed a larger remember-negative effect (Waring, Payne, Schacter, & Kensinger, 2010).

A traumatic experience may also produce an amnesic effect, so that details are forgotten due to their temporal placement near to a startling event. Loftus and Burns (1982) showed a 2-minute video depicting a bank robbery, a film used by banks to instruct their employees on how to handle this kind of situation. Toward the end of one version of the film, a bank teller is shot, but this does not happen in the control version. Participants who viewed the first version of the film did not recall a critical fact shown just before the violent act: the number on a bystander's football jersey. Only 4 percent of those seeing the violent film remembered it, whereas 28 percent of the control participants did. Christianson and Nilsson (1984) found forgetting on the other side of the traumatic event. Their participants did not recall a critical detail that followed the arousing stimulus.

Conclusions about Emotions and Memory

Emotional arousal can facilitate encoding into memory. But knowing this fact will not tell us what details will be encoded. Remembering a suspect's face would be helpful to the police, but the victim's attention may have been focused on a weapon. Significant details that preceded or followed a startling moment may be forgotten. Rehearsal may elaborate some of the memories, but at the same time can introduce distortions. We are therefore limited in our ability to make broad statements about the effects of emotion on the accuracy of memory.

Schemas

Schemas are outlines of general knowledge that are stored in semantic memory. Schemas, also called scripts, are ways of organizing knowledge. Schemas have a hierarchical structure, with packets of information stored at each level. One often-cited example is the "restaurant script," as listed in Table 9.1. The restaurant schema has categories such as entering, ordering, eating, and exiting. In these categories is general knowledge about each step: Ordering involves reading the menu and telling the server what you want; exiting involves paying the bill and leaving a tip.

Table 9.2 Restaurant Schema

1. Entering
Customer enters
Looks for table
Sits down
2. Ordering
Looks at menu
Signals server
Orders food
3. Eating
Server brings food from kitchen
Food brought to table
Customer eats
4. Leaving
Server brings check
Customer leaves tip
Customer pays cashier

There are several ways a schema can influence what is learned in a given situation (Alba & Hasher, 1983).

1. *Selection.* Schemas guide selection of what is to be encoded, usually details that are relevant to the schema.
2. *Storage.* A schema can organize memory for events, providing an outline of where each new piece fits.
3. *Abstraction.* Common features across a number of similar experiences are abstracted and stored in the schema; specific details from any one event need not be retained.
4. *Retrieval.* A schema provides retrieval cues to guide and direct memory search.
5. *Normalization.* The schema may lead to memory distortion, in that we remember what usually happens, as recorded in the schema, rather than what actually happened.

There are some nice examples of schema influence in remembering the objects in a room. Rooms that have different purposes, say, an office or a dorm room, typically contain different items. Pezdek, Whetstone, Reynolds, Askari, and Dougherty (1989) showed their participants one of two rooms: a graduate student office and a preschool classroom. Each contained schema-consistent objects (books, a beer bottle, and a desk; or toys, games, and blocks); or schema-inconsistent objects (simply exchanging some things between the office and preschool room). The results of this study make several important points about what is and is not remembered. Items highly relevant to the schema are remembered, for example, books and a chair in an office. Unusual or unexpected items were recalled even better, for example, a toy truck in a graduate student's office. However, objects that are neither schema-relevant nor unexpected seem to get lost. There was a clock on the desk in the office. We might not expect it to be there, yet its presence is not surprising either. So it is forgotten. (I was once surprised to see a playpen in an associate dean's office. He had been babysitting his grandchild that day. This is a schema-inconsistent item and was thus memorable.)

Schemas unfortunately can lead to mis-encoding. When students in a speech-and-hearing course were shown a list of symptoms that led them to make a diagnosis of a specific hearing disorder, they later falsely recalled some symptoms that had not been presented but that were consistent with the diagnosis. They remembered what is typical for this disorder. On the other hand, making the diagnosis improved recall in one way: on a recognition test, the participants were able to correctly reject symptoms unrelated to the diagnosis that had not been seen before. There was a trade-off between the memory-improving and memory-distorting effects of the schema (Arkes & Harkness, 1980).

As memory for repeated events becomes schematized, specific details are lost. Linton (1982) kept a diary of personal events in her life over 6 years. She periodically tested herself by sampling items and trying to determine whether she really remembered the events. She reported forgetting specific details for repeated events. For example, Linton could recall details of the first meeting of a committee to which she was appointed. As more meetings accumulated, details of each became blurred, and, instead, a more generic memory (or schema) developed. Now, specific events that differentiated one meeting from another (where they had lunch one day or who missed a given meeting) were lost.

Strict adherence to a schema would allow recall of only those events that conform to the schema. However, exceptions to the rule are remembered, especially if they are unusual or surprising. And schemas can undergo change, as new examples are assimilated into the schema. The restaurant schema you first developed as a child, likely based on Happy Meals, is modified as you experience different types of eating establishments.

Metamemory

Metamemory refers to our knowledge about memory. It includes our estimates about the difficulty of learning certain materials, which strategies will be most effective, monitoring progress during learning, and beliefs about how our own memory differs from memory in general. (Metamemory also includes knowledge about retrieval, which will be discussed more in the next chapter.)

Metamemory is usually assessed by self-report questions, the scores on which can then be correlated with actual memory performance. For example, students can be asked to make ease-of-learning judgments, possibly using a 10-point scale, prior to actually attempting to learn material. U.S. students should predict that their learning the capitals of former Soviet republics will be more difficult than learning the county seats of a U.S. state. When students subsequently attempt to learn the facts, they actually spend more time on the items they had predicted would be more difficult (Nelson & Leonesio, 1988). Judgments of learning (JOL) are made after studying, when subjects rate how well they think they have learned the material. JOL estimates often predict how much of the material is recalled on an actual test.

What factors guide a student's decision that they have studied sufficiently or not? Judgments of learning are primarily affected by characteristics intrinsic to the material. In the case of remembering word lists, the factors of imagery, familiarity, or associations affect JOL ratings. The conditions of learning, such as increasing the number of repetitions or spacing the repetitions, do not increase JOL ratings. If students actually study under these conditions (such as spaced practice), the students remember more than they had predicted. Having studied under effective conditions did not increase the belief that more was learned (Koriat, 1997).

The disconnect between metamemory beliefs and actual recall is readily demonstrated (Kornell, Rhodes, Castel, & Tauber, 2011). In one study, words were presented one-at-a-time on the computer screen, and the subjects were asked to estimate how well they would remember the word. Some words were presented in large type (64 point) and others in smaller type (16 point). The subjects overwhelmingly predicted they would better remember the large font words. They did not. Type size has no effect. As the words were being presented, the students were also asked whether an additional presentation of the word would help them remember better. The students did not predict a second presentation would help memory. (They just saw the word. It seemed obvious to them the word would be recalled later.) But in fact, twice-presented words were recalled better. Here we see metamemory judgments were wrong on two counts: Students falsely believed that larger type contributed to retention, and the students did not believe that additional study was beneficial. The implication is that students will sometimes study using a method they think is effective (and it is not); and ignore a technique that is effective.

Metamemory perceptions show a developmental progression. Rehearsal increases as children age, as does their metamemory belief that rehearsal is beneficial. Five-year-olds realize that teenagers have better memories. Older children can predict better when they are ready to be tested (judgment of learning) than younger children (Kail, 1990). On the other hand, even very young children have accurate perceptions of when memory might fail. When asked how they could remember to bring something to school tomorrow, they offered reasonable strategies such as placing the object in their school bags or asking Mom to remind them (Kreutzer, Leonard, & Flavell, 1982).

People also know how good their own memories are. This is referred to as *memory self-efficacy*: judgments about how effectively we think our memory will function in a particular situation. Self-efficacy can be assessed through self-report inventories, such as that presented in Box 9.3.

Differences in self-efficacy beliefs can be seen in the comparison of younger and older adults (Ryan, 1992). Participants aged 25 to 85 rated self-perceived memory for such things as conversations or names, and the incidence of absentmindedness. Both older and younger participants believed that, in general, memory declines with aging. However, most people, young or old, did not think their memories are as bad as those of others their age. Personal self-efficacy was rated better than the perceived effectiveness of memory for an individual's own age group.

Box 9.3   Example Metamemory and Self-Efficacy Items From the *Motivated Strategies for Learning Questionnaire*

This is a self-report inventory illustrating aspects of metamemory. Retention is affected by the strategies we use, how well we regulate our learning, our beliefs in our own abilities, the importance of the subject matter, and test anxiety. Students were instructed to respond to these items using a 7-point scale (1 = not at all true of me, to 7 = very true of me).

Cognitive Strategy Use

- When I study, I put important ideas into my own words.
- When I study for a test, I practice saying the important facts over and over to myself.
- When reading, I try to connect the things I am reading about with what I already know.

Self-Regulation

- I ask myself questions to make sure I know the material I have been studying.
- I work on practice exercises and answer end-of chapter questions even when I don't have to.

Self-Efficacy

- I'm certain I can understand the ideas taught in this class.
- My study skills are excellent compared with other students in this class.
- Compared with other students in this class, I think I know a great deal about the subject.

Intrinsic Value

- It is important for me to learn what is being taught in this class.
- I prefer class work that is challenging so I can learn new things.
- I think I will be able to use what I learn in this class in other classes.

Test Anxiety

- I worry a great deal about tests.
- I have an uneasy, upset feeling when I take a test.
- When I take a test, I think about how poorly I am doing.

Each of these subscales correlated with academic performance: higher ratings were associated with higher test grades, with the exception of Test Anxiety, which corresponded with lower academic performance (Pintrich & DeGroot, 1990).

Source: Adapted from "Motivational and self-regulated learning components of classroom academic performance," P. R. Pintrich & E. V. DeGroot, (1990), *Journal of Educational Psychology, 82*, p. 40. Copyright American Psychological Association. Reprinted with permission.

The direction of cause and effect between self-efficacy beliefs and actual performance is debatable. Certainly, low expectations will limit effort devoted to trying to remember. I often hear students complain that they just cannot learn some type of material (foreign languages or statistics as examples). These beliefs can be as detrimental as any lack of ability. On the other hand, our self-perceptions may be accurate representations based on our actual experiences. If I constantly forget names, I should correctly believe that I have a name–memory problem.

Individual students differ in the ability to evaluate their own learning and performance. Unfortunately, it is sometimes the weakest students who have the least insight. Research on the "unskilled-and-unaware" phenomena (Kruger & Dunning, 1999) shows that those who scored the lowest on various tests (e.g., reading comprehension, grammar evaluation) believed their competence and test performance was comparable to the average of the class. Dunning and Kruger have shown this in studies using college students, across several domains (e.g., academic or social). For instance, after completing a course exam, students who scored in the 25th percentile (the lowest quarter of the class) rated their mastery of the material and their expected test score in the 60th percentile. (Dunning, Johnson, Ehrlinger, & Kruger, 2003). Overall, the bottom half of the class thought they were among the top 60–70 percent.

Conclusion

To understand how new learning occurs, we need to consider several factors: the material to be learned, the context in which learning occurs, the cognitive resources available, the task demands, the existing knowledge base of the subject, the strategies selected, and our beliefs about how learning occurs. The point of this lengthy list is to remind you, once again, of the complexity of obtaining a scientific understanding of the learning process.

Applications

The Future of Memory Encoding

The current chapter describes a number of cognitive methods to increase encoding into memory. The discussion of arousal and memory suggested that various stimulant drugs might increase learning ability. Students now use drugs normally prescribed for attention deficit disorder to increase alertness or increase study time. One report suggested that university faculty members who worry about productivity, tenure, and demanding intellectual workloads are sometimes using cognitive enhancers (Sahakian & Morein-Zamir, 2007).

The Yerkes-Dodson law suggests that stimulant drugs can only be effective under limited conditions. This principle says that a cognitive enhancer does not have single, simple effect. A given drug could increase performance by pushing arousal to the optimal level (the peak of the inverted-U curve). However, if arousal is already near peak the drug could raise arousal beyond the optimum and onto the down-sloping side of the curve. Yerkes-Dodson also says that different tasks require different optimal levels. A drug dose that is effective for one cognitive task might be too high or too low for others tasks (Cools & Robbins, 2004).

Cognition-enhancing drugs might have effects that are too widespread in the brain. A drug could produce opposite effects on various cognitive processes within the same individual. For instance, a drug that stimulates dopamine will increase dopamine throughout the brain. Some areas may benefit, but some will receive too much. The drug might increase working memory, but decrease cognitive flexibility and impulse control (Husain & Mehta, 2011). Effective drugs will have to be tailored to enhance specific areas of the nervous system while minimilizing side effects.

A developing field of neuroethics considers the moral and ethical issues involved with the use and potential misuse of memory-enhancing drugs. These questions are considered in more detail in Box 9.4.

Box 9.4   Neuroethics and Artificial Memory Enhancement

News reports in recent years have increasingly focused on athletes' use of performance-enhancing drugs. There is general acknowledgement among amateur athletic organizations and Olympic sports sponsors that such drugs should be banned. New developments in brain science will likely produce means of artificially enhancing memory. The ethical questions raised by drug enhancement of the mind will be the same as we now face in athletics.

It is already the case that stimulant drugs used to treat attention-deficit and hyperactivity disorders (ADHD) are being used on college campuses for the purpose of enhancing academic performance. Adderall is prescribed for the treatment of ADHD, yet non-ADHD students can readily obtain the drug. A survey of college students found that about 4 percent reported using Adderall or Ritalin in the previous year (McCabe, Knight, & Teter, 2005). The numbers were higher in schools that had more competitive admission standards. In parallel to the athletic advantage gained by the use of steroids, students in high school could obtain a drug-enhanced advantage over those who learned naturally: They could learn more and faster, increase their grades, and maybe their college admission test scores.

The hundreds of thousands of school-age children who were put on Ritalin and other drugs in the 1990s are now in college. A new generation sees stimulant drugs in school as normal (Jacobs, 2005).

The emerging field of neuroethics deals with moral, social, and scientific decisions that arise from developments in the brain sciences. Artificial remediation of memory is desirable for premature decline of memory, as in Alzheimer's, or due to brain injury earlier in life. Who could argue against restoring memory to those who have been cruelly deprived? But once the technology becomes available, will unimpaired individuals seek an advantage provided by a drug? The list of questions such advances provoke is long: Should people with normal memory have unrestricted access to the enhancing drugs? Should drugs be prescribed to counteract normal aging? Will younger adults be pressured to take the drugs just to stay competitive, in school or on the job? Can people realistically weigh the side effects and health risks versus the potential benefits? Will only the affluent have access to what will likely be expensive treatments? These are some of the questions that need societal discussion and answers.

In the future, drugs will be tailored to specific forms of memory loss. Well-known memory researchers, some cited in this textbook, have partnered in businesses to develop chemicals to restore or enhance memory. Companies with names like Memory Pharmaceuticals, Cortex Pharmaceuticals, and NeoTherapeutics are testing drugs with names like Neotrophin and Memantine, as reported in news sources such as Businessweek and the Neuro Investment newsletter (Arnst, 2003; Freundlich, 2001). These drugs will be developed to treat Alzheimer's, but off-label and black-market use will be virtually uncontrollable.

The reverse side of memory enhancement is *forgetting* enhancement. Drugs or other techniques might be used to prevent distressing or traumatic memories. Possibly the adverse aftereffects of a traumatic experience, such as posttraumatic stress disorder, could be prevented by the administration of a memory-blocking drug. This would seem to be a beneficial outcome. But should all unpleasant memories be blocked? We learn from adversity, and blocking memories of traumatic experiences might also block the knowledge that would prevent us from re-experiencing the trauma in the future. One could also argue that adversity sometimes produces great benefits. Some individuals may become better people after surviving a trauma, translating pain into masterpieces of music, art or literature, or new discoveries in science and technology (see *Beyond Therapy: Biotechnology and the Pursuit of Happiness*, The President's Council on Bioethics, 2003). The future sciences of learning and memory may be very different from the present ones.

Academic Learning and Encoding

Elaboration

Consider some student-learning techniques in light of elaborative processing. Underlining in textbooks, taking notes during lectures, and writing summaries are often used by students, but actually may contribute little to learning (Snowman, 1986). Although each could be done in a manner that promotes elaborative processing, students may instead become accomplished at passive underlining and transcribing. In one study, college students extensively practiced taking dictation while reading unrelated material simultaneously. The students became proficient at doing both tasks at once, with little cross-interference. This suggests that students might in fact be able to take lecture notes without really attending to the content of the lecture (Hirst, Spelke, Reaves, Caharack, & Neisser, 1980). Some studies have found that students who took notes recalled no more than did students who simply listened to the lecture (Kiewra et al., 1991).

Other student study techniques promote shallow processing. Students tend to underline too much when reading or include too much verbatim copying while summarizing, which in either case is a passive rather than active strategy. Both underlining and summarizing improve recall when students are limited in the amount of each: for example, only three lines of underlining per page or summaries restricted to three sentences (Kulhavy, Dyer, & Silver, 1975).

One means of getting students to think about facts they are asked to remember is to prompt them with a question: Why would this be so? These questions force elaboration of the to-be-learned material. In one demonstration of this method of *elaborative interrogation*, Canadian college students studied short paragraphs about universities. In the interrogation condition, they were asked why each fact might be true. A sample fact might be "McGill University stands on land donated by a fur trader." These students recalled more facts and correctly associated them to the universities than did control participants who simply read the paragraphs (Woloshyn, Willoughby, Wood, & Pressley, 1990). Elaborative interrogation forces subjects to integrate the given facts with existing knowledge.

Meaningfulness

Meaningfulness is enhanced in textbooks that use text adjuncts such as headings and titles to help organize and interpret the to-be-remembered information. Headings or titles can increase recall of prose passages by activating existing knowledge or schemas that can guide encoding and subsequent retrieval. Other text techniques are advance organizers and analogies. Advance organizers are longer introductory statements that act as a bridge between what the student knows and the new material. Analogies activate prior knowledge to facilitate the understanding of new material that is being presented. Each of these adjuncts can produce meaningful learning that increases retention over longer intervals (Royer, 1986).

Generation Effect

What are the educational implications of the generation effect? Suppose you are required to memorize a series of facts. (For example: Who was the first person to fly solo across the Atlantic? Answer: Charles Lindbergh.) The teacher could present a list of questions and answers for you to read. Or the questions could be followed by some clues for you to generate the correct answer. These clues could be, for instance, an anagram made up of the letters spelling the correct answer (Last Name: BNIREHGLD), or the answer with certain letters omitted (First Name: _H_R_E_). In either case, you must generate the correct answer. De Winstanley (1995) tested college students in the preceding manner, and found that the generate condition produced better recall of the answers. What was also notable was that this effect was present 2 days later, when the participants were given a surprise test on the answers to the questions.

In another case, teaching math facts, such as times tables ($8 \times 9 = 72$), can be facilitated by generation. The answers to the math problems are remembered if participants do the arithmetic themselves rather than simply reading the results (Crutcher & Healy, 1989).

Self-Efficacy

Teaching students a study strategy will not be of much benefit unless the students are convinced it will make a difference in their learning. In the standard intervention design, someone is first taught a mnemonic technique; the method is tested once to show it works; and then you hope the students will continue to use it. Pressley, Levin, and Ghatala (1988) added another step after teaching an imagery mnemonic for foreign-language acquisition. The students attempted to learn other vocabulary words using their own methods, whatever those were. The most beneficial training condition was one in which the participants learned better using the imagery mnemonic than with their own techniques. Those participants who had clearly seen the benefit of the imagery strategy continued to use it for subsequent trials in the study. Without the explicit comparison, students simply dropped the mnemonic when given the opportunity.

Circadian Rhythms

Does time of day affect academic learning and retention? Ebbinghaus conducted an early study for a school system and concluded that the early afternoon was the worst time for academic instruction. N. F. Skinner (1985) found that course grades among Canadian college students at his university were higher in afternoon and evening sections than in morning sections. Unfortunately, enrollment in morning and afternoon sections is a mix of voluntary and involuntary assignments. There are also individual differences in alertness at different times of day, the morning types, and the evening types. Students who rated themselves high on a "morningness" scale had higher grades in their 8 A.M. classes than later in the day, whereas low-morningness people had their lowest grades in 8:00 classes (Guthrie et al., 1995).

Summary

This chapter focused on variables that affect the encoding of information into memory. However, encoding cannot be isolated from storage and retrieval factors. Most laboratory studies of encoding use episodic learning tasks such as free recall or recognition.

Some Basic Variables in Encoding

Encoding is affected by rehearsal, imagery, and meaningfulness.

A distinction can be made between elaborative rehearsal, a form of deep processing in which the to-be-remembered material is related to other information, and maintenance rehearsal, a form of shallow processing in which information is passively repeated. Elaborative rehearsal promotes better retention through associations to existing knowledge, the formation of distinctive memories, and the effortful processing that it entails.

Elaboration can be enhanced by organization, imagery, and mnemonics. Student study tactics, such as underlining and note taking, are often passive and do not promote much elaboration. The technique of elaborative interrogation, asking "why" questions about the to-be-recalled material, increases retention.

Material that is more imagable, or concrete instead of abstract, is better remembered. Pictures and objects are remembered better than are words. This may be because of dual coding of both an image and a word.

Meaningful material is better remembered. Meaningfulness is defined by imagability, familiarity, and the number of associations to other items. Meaningful items have a high frequency of occurrence in language and are easily pronounceable. Basically, meaningful items are ones you are already have some knowledge of. Material can be encoded better if we can find some meaning to it, as in the case of finding a meaningful pattern in an otherwise random string of numbers or letters.

Presentation Variables

Encoding is also affected by the way material is presented. This section of the chapter included several "effects": the testing effect, the isolation effect, the spacing effect, and the generation effect.

The testing effect refers to the greater benefit of taking a preliminary or refresher test on recently studied material over additional study, as assessed on later retention of the studied material. The practice test mimics what the students are required to do on the final test, that is, retrieve the information from memory. The practice test may enhance retention of untested information, although retention is better if misrecall is corrected immediately.

An isolation effect occurs when an unusual item, embedded in an otherwise homogeneous list of items, is particularly well remembered. The isolation effect may be due to enhanced rehearsal or to the distinctive memory representation of the isolated item.

If a to-be-remembered item is presented two or more times, distributed repetitions produce better recall than do massed repetitions. This *spacing effect* may be due to the total amount of rehearsal that two widely separated items permit; the reduced attention to a closely spaced repeated item; or to different encodings of spaced repetitions.

The generation effect is increased recall of study material that is generated by the participant rather than provided by the experimenter. If the participant can be guided to produce the correct information during study rather than simply reading it, retention will be enhanced.

Learner Variables

A number of learner variables can influence encoding, including the intention to learn, incentives to learn, arousal, and emotion.

Retention is often more a function of how information is processed rather than of explicit attempts to remember. Incidental learning, or remembering without any deliberate intention to do so, is sometimes as effective as intentional remembering.

Explicit incentives to remember, such as money or points, usually do not improve recall in laboratory experiments. Given that our student participants will try their best to remember, incentives do not increase cognitive processing. However, trade-offs may occur if both high- and low-incentive items are presented, as the former are better rehearsed at the expense of the low-incentive items.

We expect arousal to facilitate learning, and generally it can. However, there are no simple effects of arousal on learning. Each statement about daily rhythms, stimulants, and so on, must be qualified by interactions with multiple other variables. According to the Yerkes-Dodson law, performance is usually better at an intermediate level of arousal and less efficient at both lower and higher arousal levels. The optimal level of arousal varies with task difficulty, such that more difficult cognitive tasks are more efficiently performed at lower levels of arousal than easier tasks.

Circadian rhythms affect arousal and thus indirectly learning. Some studies have shown better memory in the morning than later in the day. However, there are individual differences in circadian rhythms. Stimulant drugs such as caffeine can facilitate remembering, but again, the effects interact with other variables.

Emotional arousal enhances retention, first by focusing attention on certain aspects of the situation. The weapons focus of crime victims attests to their vivid memory for the central details of a situation and poor recollection of peripheral details. Second, emotion produces bodily arousal (e.g., epinephrine is secreted) that contributes to long-term memory formation. Third, emotional events are distinctive. They are talked about and thought about, and so they are well rehearsed and elaborated in memory.

A flashbulb memory is a particularly vivid memory for a surprising, emotional, and consequential event. It is as if a picture of that moment is encoded into memory. Some researchers have emphasized the persistence and apparent accuracy of flashbulb memories over time. Others have focused on misrecall and inaccuracy in these memories.

Eyewitness memory is affected by all the complexities involved in encoding, arousal, and emotion in memory. Because of their intense emotional arousal, one could expect witnesses to be good rememberers. Emotional arousal can facilitate encoding, but knowing this fact will not tell us which details are encoded.

Schemas

Encoding is affected by our extensive preexisting knowledge, often summarized in the form of schemas.

Schemas or scripts are ways of organizing general knowledge in semantic memory. New events are encoded into memory using the existing schema as an organizing guide. Schemas affect attention, selection, abstraction, and normalization. Schemas also influence retrieval, sometimes leading to the misrecall of schema-relevant events. Items that are consistent with a schema (what is expected) and items that are discrepant with a schema (what is surprising) can be well recalled, although for different reasons.

Metamemory

Metamemory refers to our knowledge about learning and remembering. How we learn is affected by knowledge of which encoding factors work, our beliefs that they will indeed work, and our monitoring of progress during learning. Self-efficacy, or how effective we believe our memory will be in a given situation, correlates with memory performance, but it is not clear whether poor memory in past situations lowers expectations, or low expectations reduce future memory performance.

10 Storage and Retrieval

Why does forgetting occur? One explanation is that memories decay. Decay corresponds to a commonsense intuition that memories spontaneously fade over time. As obvious as the idea sounds, a fundamental problem with this theory is its suggestion that the passage of time alone somehow "explains" forgetting. McGeoch (1932) offered the analogy that iron rusts over time, yet time is not the cause of rust. Similarly, time alone does not account for forgetting, but something that happens during that time.

In contemporary learning theory retrieval failure is the primary source of forgetting. What appears to be forgotten is still there, but it cannot be retrieved. Loftus and Loftus (1980) informally surveyed individuals with graduate training in psychology. Eighty-four percent agreed with the statement "everything we learn is permanently stored in the mind, although sometimes particular details are not accessible." This is the *permanent-memory hypothesis.*

The respondents offered several sorts of evidence for their belief in permanent memories. The most often cited finding was the claim that memories can be elicited through electrical stimulation of the brain. Wilder Penfield, a Canadian neurosurgeon, electrically stimulated areas of the cortex during surgery for the treatment of epilepsy. The patients were awake during this portion of the operation so that the surgeon could map out abnormal tissue that was the focus of the disorder. Stimulation of the temporal lobes apparently caused patients to reexperience events from their past. The patients said these seemed like long-lost memories that could have not be recalled by other means. For example, one 26-year-old woman reported: "Yes, I think I heard a mother calling her little boy somewhere. It seemed to be something that happened years ago." When stimulated in another location several minutes later she said, "Yes, I hear voices. It is late at night, around the carnival somewhere—some sort of traveling circus. I just saw lots of big wagons that they use to haul animals in." Penfield concluded that all of our memories are permanently stored, a fact acknowledged in the title of his paper, "A Permanent Record of the Stream of Consciousness" (1955/1967). Penfield's notions of memory can be cast into a modern analogy to a video recording: There is a complete and continuous record of our mental experiences stored in the cortex. We just need a means of replaying those memories.

Although Penfield's findings are widely known in psychology, their support for permanent memory can be challenged. First, the majority of stimulated patients did not recover memories. Second, the mental experiences might not be remembering, but instead could be instances of imagination, something created at the time of stimulation. Third, the validity of the memories can be questioned. Even the patients themselves sometimes did not recognize the "remembered" events (Squire, 1987).

Other evidence offered for the permanent-memory hypothesis is the supposed recovery of memories through hypnosis. Hypnotized crime victims or witnesses are said to be able to recall facts and details that were not reported before. However, hypnotized witnesses may be more willing to venture a guess about an uncertain memory, and they may be more susceptible to leading questions. Just as with the memories recovered by brain stimulation, how do we know these memories are of actual events?

The more pervasive difficulty with the evidence for permanent memory is the underlying logic: The successful recovery of *some* long-lost memories cannot prove that *all* of our life experiences are retained in memory.

This chapter will consider several factors that affect retrieval of information from memory. Although individual memories may or may not be permanent, retrieval conditions can be arranged to enhance recall. Our first consideration, however, will be the duration of memory. How long are memories stored and in what form are they stored?

Storage

We can begin with an apparent contradiction: the dual observations that we seemingly forget so quickly and remember so long. According to Ebbinghaus's curve of forgetting (shown in Figure 6.1 in Chapter 6), a great deal of forgetting occurs shortly after learning is completed. (The correctness of this principle is demonstrated if you have forgotten Ebbinghaus's curve.) Yet our everyday experience suggests that many memories are in fact long retained. Is Ebbinghaus's curve wrong, or are we wrong about our own memories?

The inability to recall does not necessarily mean a loss from memory but could instead reflect an inability to retrieve what is still there. What is of particular interest are controlled studies that quantify retention for naturalistically learned information. A number of modern studies do just that, assessing long-term retention of classmates, school-learned material, and even TV shows.

Long-Term Memory for Naturalistically Learned Material

Fifty Years of Memories for High School Classmates

Bahrick has studied retention of school-learned materials, ranging from high school Spanish vocabulary to the grades obtained in those classes. In a seminal study, Bahrick, Bahrick, and Wittlinger (1975) assessed memory for high school classmates by people who had graduated as long as 48 years earlier. Retention was tested in different ways: recalling names of classmates; recognition of their names from among a pool of distractor names; recognition of classmates' yearbook pictures from distractors; and name–face matching.

What practical difficulties are encountered in studying memory under these conditions? Primarily, there are individual differences among participants that may confound measures taken at different delays. For example, there are differences in exposure to classmates since graduation. Some people remain in their home town, return to class reunions, or take out the old yearbook to reminisce. Others have had little occasion to refresh their memories over the years. Bahrick's participants answered detailed questionnaires about such variables so that he could statistically control for some of the differences from one person to another.

The results of several types of retention tests are shown in Figure 10.1. In one test, the subjects were asked to name as many members of their graduating class as they could recall. The number

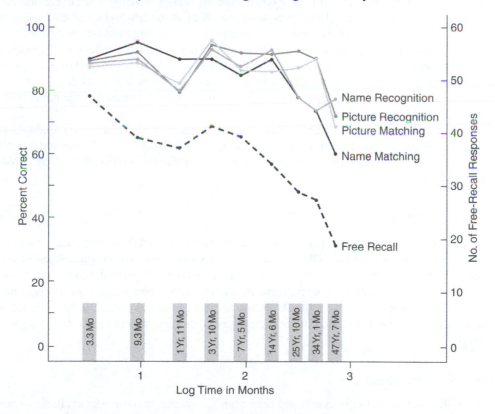

Figure 10.1 Memory for High School Classmates. The scale on the right shows the number of names in unaided recall; the scale on the left is for correct choices in name recognition, picture recognition, and name–picture matching. Recall was tested 33 months to over 47 years later in individuals from different graduating classes.

Source: From "Fifty Years of Memory for Names and Faces: A Cross-Sectional Approach," by H. P. Bahrick, P. O. Bahrick, and R. P. Wittlinger, 1975, *Journal of Experimental Psychology: General, 104*, pp. 54–75. Copyright © 1975 by the American Psychological Association. Reprinted with permission.

of names that could be free-recalled ranged from about 15 percent for recent graduates down to less than 7 percent for the oldest graduates. But measures such as name or face recognition and name–face matching show basically no loss of information out to 14 years postgraduation, and, in general, memory does not severely decline until 47 years after. Even among the oldest graduates, recognition scores are in the 70 to 80 percent range. This is far better than would be anticipated from laboratory studies of Ebbinghaus's curve.

Why is memory so good here? Bahrick notes two factors in particular: naturalistic learning of classmates involves repeated exposure, and spaced repetition of these exposures. For example, exposures are spaced across holiday breaks and summer vacations.

Remembering Knowledge Learned in School

In contrast to the rapid forgetting in Ebbinghaus's data, several reviews of the literature suggest that, in some cases, the amount lost is relatively small. Semb, Ellis, and Araujo (1993) assessed learning 4 and 11 months after completion of a child psychology course. In comparison to end-of-term test scores, grades only fell about 20 percent on the delayed tests. Multiple-choice tests produced higher scores than did recall tests, just as they often do in laboratory tests of memory using much shorter delay intervals.

How much will be remembered from a course like the one in which you are using this text? Conway, Cohen, and Stanhope (1991) compared groups of students who had taken a cognitive psychology course up to 12 years earlier. The largest portion of forgetting occurred within the first 3 to 4 years. After that, knowledge retention stabilized at above chance levels. The shape of Ebbinghaus's curve was present (i.e., rapid initial loss followed by more gradual forgetting), but the time frame is of a different order of magnitude: in this case years instead of days. Names, of theorists and researchers, were most likely to be forgotten, the same material we have trouble with outside the classroom as well.

Bahrick tested the retention of Spanish or algebra studied in high school. He found that the primary determinant of persistent retention is the initial level of acquisition. Those students who took higher-level courses in high school and earned higher grades retained more (Bahrick, 1984a; Bahrick & Hall, 1993).

Memory for TV Shows

Squire and Slater (1975) tested memory for TV shows that had aired for just one season and had not been repeated in syndication. (Okay, these were really bad shows.) A recognition test of titles of recent shows (those from a year or two earlier) averaged over 70 percent. Interestingly, show titles from 8 to 15 years earlier were still correctly identified 55 to 60 percent of the time. Control groups of junior high school students, who would not have been old enough to have seen these shows, and people who were living out of the country when these shows aired, scored at guessing levels.

Memory for Public Events

Information about newsworthy events and celebrities is assumed to have been available to most people living at the time. We can use tests of knowledge of public events from past years and even past decades to get an estimate of the pattern of forgetting across the lifespan. One example asks participants to identify faces of once famous individuals (Marslen-Wilson & Teuber, 1975). The people pictured were in the news during different decades. Older participants were good at identifying faces from the more recent decades and forgot more of the names from earlier decades.

Long-Term Retention in Animals

Most laboratory studies of animal memory assess retention over short intervals of minutes or days. There are anecdotal reports of learned responses that persisted for years in pigeons (Skinner) or dogs (Pavlov). However, Vaughn and Greene (1984) demonstrated long-term retention of visual information by pigeons. Their subjects were trained to discriminate between 160 nature photos that were cues for food availability and another 160 photos that signaled no food. That is, the pigeons were trained to key-peck during the positive pictures but not during the negative ones. The animals were still able to discriminate (i.e., remember) between the rewarded and non-rewarded slides after retention intervals ranging from 235 to 730 days.

This research has been extended with two pigeons trained on 1,600 or 1,800 pictures over three years. The pigeons pecked a key when each picture was presented, and the pigeon had to learn whether that picture was rewarded on either the left or right key. The animals achieved over 70 percent accuracy in associating pictures and the left/right key.

The Nature of Storage

How are memories stored in long-term memory? Models have been proposed on both the psychological and biological levels. Psychological models describe the organization of knowledge, and how facts are connected. Biological theories hypothesize changes in the activity at the synapses between neurons. Examples of each of these approaches are described in what follows.

Psychological Models of Semantic Memory

A number of network models have been proposed to illustrate the storage of general knowledge in semantic memory. **Semantic network** theories assume that items of knowledge are interconnected via associations, relationships, or pathways. These connections can vary in strength or, in some models, in the distance separating one item from another. Thus, the representations of TABLE and CHAIR share a stronger connection or they are stored closer together in memory than are TABLE and AARDVARK.

An example of a semantic network model is illustrated in Figure 10.2. Collins and Quillian (1969) hypothesized a hierarchical arrangement of superordinate to subordinate knowledge. For example, the higher-order unit ANIMALS has subordinate categories such as FISH and BIRDS. Knowledge that is general to the entire category is stored at a higher level in the hierarchy. Information that is restricted or limited is stored at the subordinate levels. Thus, the ANIMAL node includes information that is general to animals, such as that they breathe and they move. The BIRD node contains the facts that birds have wings and lay eggs. The OSTRICH node stores an exception to the generalization about birds—the fact that ostriches do not fly.

This hypothesized organization is tested by measuring True–False reaction times to statements that require accessing two elements in memory. Test items are selected to be at varying distances from one another in the hierarchy. For example, "BIRDS have WINGS" pairs two items from the same level; "OSTRICHES lay EGGS" pairs items that are a level apart. Faster responding to a statement indicates the two items are closer together, whereas slower responding suggests the two items are farther apart. For True statements, the farther apart the two items are in the network, the longer it took to verify. This suggests that memory search begins with one item and then trees up or down the hierarchy to the second item in order to verify the truth value of the statement.

Reaction times to the False statements presented an intriguing finding. Some False statements contrast two items that are farther apart than any pair of True statements. For example, "OSTRICHES have GILLS" has two items that are widely separated in the hierarchy. Such

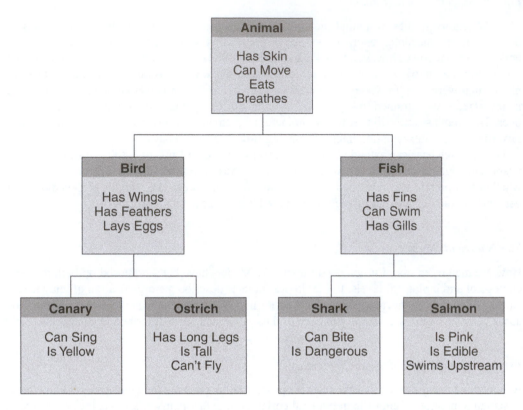

Figure 10.2 Semantic-Memory-Hierarchy Network Model.

Source: From "Retrieval Time from Semantic Memory," by A. M. Collins and M. R. Quillian, 1969, *Journal of Verbal Learning and Verbal Behavior*, *8*, pp. 240–247. Copyright © 1969 by Elsevier. Reprinted with permission.

statements took longer to reject than did the True statements, suggesting that the participants actually traced through the hierarchy from OSTRICH to GILLS before responding False. Other False statements, those obviously nonsensical, were quickly rejected, indicating that not every proposition gets thoroughly checked (e.g., "Statistics is a fun course").

In other models of semantic memory items are distanced depending on frequency and contiguity in experience, although these would certainly overlap with a hierarchical model. In depicting such a model, as in Figure 10.3, the distance between nodes reflects the strength of the connection between items in memory (Collins & Loftus, 1975). There are also overlapping associations: Red is linked to fire engines, other colors, and roses.

A common assumption among semantic memory models is that of **spreading activation**: Activation of one item in memory spreads to adjacent items, causing related knowledge to be activated. Spreading activation can be demonstrated by employing a *priming* manipulation in semantic memory judgments. The task is to rapidly decide whether a string of letters forms a word. Immediately before presenting the to-be-identified item, a related word is flashed on the screen to "prime" the target. For example, the word DOG is presented as a priming stimulus a fraction of a second before the test item COLLIE. Participants are then faster at identifying the string of letters COLLIE as being a word. Activation of DOG in semantic memory spread to related items, thus activating COLLIE before it was actually presented by the experimenter.

Other sorts of knowledge can be primed in semantic memory. Priming of gender stereotypes has been shown in a task that required naming the gender of target pronouns, for example, shown

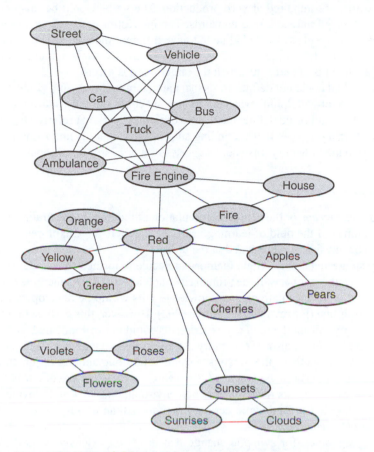

Figure 10.3 **An Alternative Network Model of Semantic Memory.** The strength of connections is illustrated by the distance between nodes.

Source: From "A Spreading Activation Theory of Semantic Processing," by A. M. Collins and E. F. Loftus, 1975, *Psychological Review, 82,* pp. 407–428. Copyright © 1975 by the American Psychological Association. Reprinted with permission.

HE, the participant's response should be "male," or given SHE, the participant responds "female" (Banaji & Hardin, 1996). The priming stimuli were gender-related nouns (DOCTOR, NURSE). Male pronouns were more quickly labeled when preceded by male-stereotyped primes (e.g., DOCTOR—HE), and female pronouns were quicker when preceded by female-stereotyped primes (e.g., NURSE—SHE).

There are two factors that limit the spread of activation. First, activation weakens as it diffuses across the network. Second, activation spreading from an item having many associations will be divided across those many connections, resulting in weaker activation of each of them. This is known as the *fan effect.* An item with fewer associations will have its activation less divided, and so connected items will be more strongly primed.

Neuropsychological Dissociations

The patterns of knowledge loss found with neurological injuries also say something about the organization of semantic memory. For example, semantic memory may have separate categories for different grammatical classes, such as nouns and verbs. Caramazza and Hillis (1991) studied two patients who were impaired at verb production. The verbs would be mispronounced, misspelled, misread, or go unrecognized as words. The interesting test was to present homonyms, two words that sound and are spelled alike but have different meanings. Thus, one patient could read "there was a CRACK in the mirror," in which the target word is a noun, but could not read "don't CRACK the nuts in here," in which the target word is a verb.

Another individual could not define words that named living things, but could define nonliving objects. When the word "dolphin" was read to him, he could not tell what it was. The man was otherwise articulate, and could define much more difficult words that referred to nonliving things (McCarthy & Warrington, 1988). This finding suggests that there is not a single vocabulary (or dictionary) in semantic memory. Instead, categories of words are stored separately.

Biological Substrates

The search for the *engram*, or the neural representation of memory in the brain, has been ongoing since the beginnings of the field of learning itself. Researchers have explored various ways that learning could be physically represented in the brain.

One theory suggested that a unique memory molecule is formed to encode each new experience. For example, the synthesis of the protein ribonucleic acid (RNA) increases during learning. For a while, there were speculations that knowledge pills would be developed, each containing the facts of a discipline (for reviews, see Rose, 1992). However, this early support for the memory-molecule theory fell apart and many experiments could not be replicated (see Rilling, 1996).

A more promising mechanism for memory storage is that change occurs at the synaptic connections. Neurons, the cells of the nervous system, adjoin one another at junctures called synapses. The number of synaptic connections between neurons is not fixed, but is affected by life experiences. For example, rats raised in enriched environments (toy- and playmate-filled cages) develop more synaptic connections in certain brain areas than do rats raised in pairs in empty laboratory cages (Greenough, 1985).

One model preparation for synaptic change that has been extensively studied is *long-term potentiation* in hippocampal cells (Lynch, Larson, Staubli, Ambros-Ingerson, & Granger, 1991). Repetitive stimulation of one cell or set of cells triggers activity in adjacent cells. Repeated experience allows activation of one cell by another to occur more readily. In a sense, something like spreading activation occurs from one cell to another. This corresponds with what we say occurs when one stimulus cues another, as exemplified in classical conditioning, paired-associate learning, or cued recall.

Eric Kandel and his research group have found evidence for two storage processes, a short-term and a long-term one (Kandel, 2001). Kandel started deciphering the synaptic changes that underlie learning in *Aplysia*, a marine snail with a simple nervous system (see Chapter 2). Later work has included long-term potentiation in the mouse hippocampus. Kandel has found similar molecular chemical processes that subserve learning in both species. An intense stimulus, the kind that will produce either sensitization in *Aplysia* or long-term potentiation in the mouse hippocampus, leads to transient chemical changes at the synapses that allow subsequent stimuli to trigger a nerve impulse. This is the short-term process that lasts for a few hours. Repeated intense stimulation leads to chemical changes in the synapse, coding in the nucleus of the cell, and the growth of additional connections (synapses) between the cells. It is these later changes that characterize consolidation and the formation of a durable long-term memory.

Consolidation Theory

Memory theorists often distinguish temporary and permanent memories. **Consolidation theory** theorizes that memories start off in a temporary form and that over time memories consolidate

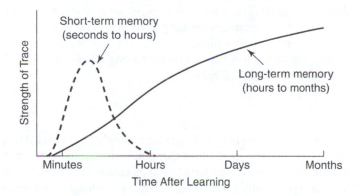

Figure 10.4 **Time After Learning.** Hypothetical strength of the memory trace over time in a prototypical model of consolidation. In different specific models the short-term memory ranges from second-to-minutes in duration; consolidation into long-term memory occurs over intervals ranging from minutes and hours, to days and months.

into a more permanent form. The short-term memories might be retained in the form of persisting activity of recently stimulated nerve cells. Hebb (1949) called this reverberation. These labile memories are susceptible to disruption which would then prevent their consolidation into permanent memory. Long-term memories might be encoded by structural changes that occur at the synapses. Consolidated memories are more resistant to loss, change, or interference. (See Lechner, Squire, & Byrne, 1999 and McGaugh, 2000 for historical and contemporary reviews of consolidation theory.)

When learning occurs it can be demonstrated immediately after the learning experience. However, this memory is in the short-term, unconsolidated state, which will decay and be lost unless consolidated into permanent memory. Experimental treatments given immediately after the learning experience can interfere with consolidation, so that on later tests what was initially remembered is no longer present. One such consolidation-blocking treatment is electroconvulsive shock. (See Box 7.1 of Chapter 7.) ECS given shortly after a learning trial prevents retention of that learning. Another consolidation blocking treatment is the administration of protein synthesis inhibitors, or drugs that inhibit metabolic activity in the brain, shortly after the learning trial. The normal chemical activities that would hypothetically have consolidated a fresh memory are blocked, and so a permanent memory does not form (Lewis, 1979).

Different versions of consolidation posit different details, for example, whether consolidation occurs over minutes and hours, or months and years. The remembering and forgetting curves for a generic model of consolidation are shown in Figure 10.4. There is the short-term memory for an experience, which is strong initially but decays quickly. Then there is the gradually forming long-term memory. The gradual consolidation suggests that chemical or structural changes take time to develop, and that there is an extended period during which their formation could be disrupted.

Preventing Storage

There are some things we would rather not remember. Some researchers are exploring the possibility of using drugs to prevent memories of traumatic events from forming. Experimental research on animals suggests that when drugs are used to reduce the emotional arousal normally experienced in fear, less fear conditioning occurs. In a study with humans, participants were recruited in the emergency room of a hospital because they had experienced a recent trauma (e.g., been in a motor vehicle accident). These individuals were susceptible to developing post-traumatic stress disorder (PTSD). These subjects were put on a 10-day regimen of the drug propranolol, which blocks the brain receptors normally activated in times of stress. In other words, the drug blocks emotional arousal. One month after having experienced the traumatic incident, 30 percent of the placebo patients met the criteria for having PTSD, but only 10 percent of the propranolol patients did (Pitman et al., 2002).

Retrieval

One explanation of forgetting is the idea that memories simply decay and disappear from storage. A recurring theme in this book is the idea that much more is available in memory than is typically recalled. Retrieval failure is an alternative explanation for forgetting. In most research on retrieval, subjects are specifically asked to recall some knowledge or a memory. We saw this in the long-term memory studies described in the section on Storage; and is used in the episodic memory studies in what follows. However, remembering also just happens, without intention, direction, or searching. These spontaneous memories can also teach us about the conditions for retrieval (See Box 10.1).

Box 10.1   Spontaneous Recall

Sometimes a memory just comes to mind with no intention to recall. We are likely thinking or doing something else entirely, when from out of nowhere comes a memory from childhood, or last year, or last week. Why did I just remember *that*? These *involuntary autobiographical memories* are memories of events and experiences from one's personal past. Research and theory has only recently begun to address uninvited remembering.

This chapter emphasizes the importance of retrieval cues to access memories. Involuntary memories are no different. It is probable that the current situation and our current thoughts act as the cue for the involuntary memory. Berntsen (2010) offers an example: A student notices the sound of wind and thunder outside the house, and then remembers an earlier event in which she calmed a young child who was afraid of thunder. The stimuli that cue involuntary remembering include context (time and place), internal feelings (affect or emotion), actions, thoughts, and associations. The specific combination of several dimensions might evoke a particular memory.

We can ask people about their involuntary memories in surveys, or we can ask them to track spontaneous memories in diary studies. Involuntary autobiographical memories occur at least several times a day (Berntsen, 1998), although this may be an underestimate. Spontaneous memories are often emotional: positive and pleasant, or negative and unpleasant. (As mentioned in Chapter 9, emotional events are encoded better, are distinctive, and possibly have more potential retrieval cues, than nonemotional events.) Negative emotional memories can be a sources of distress, as is the case of flashbacks in PTSD.

Spontaneous recall may be like the "free association" test psychologists once used. "What's the first thing that comes to mind when I say: TABLE? SCHOOL?" The associations that are produced are not really free and unconstrained. The word may prompt idiosyncratic associations; personal memories; or maybe ideas connected to the present context.

Kvavilashvili and Mandler (2004) studied another class of spontaneous memories: involuntary *semantic* memories. This can be a word, an image, or a tune that comes to mind, but it is not a memory of a personal experience. These semantic memories do not have the emotional feeling that autobiographical memories have. Semantic long-term memory represents our generalized knowledge, so an involuntary semantic memory might simply be the triggering of a bit of knowledge. The stimuli for involuntary semantic memories are sound-alikes cues (e.g., you recently heard a similar sounding word or tune); or semantic cues (e.g., hearing or seeing the word DOG might lead to an image of a COLLIE, or vice versa).

Semantic memories may be supplemented by priming effects. A word, image, or idea that was recently processed is "primed" and so is easily available in memory. Priming also occurs through spreading activation in a semantic memory network. A prime activates a network of words and ideas, which are primed and waiting to come to mind.

Another type of involuntary memory is the experience of having a song stuck in your head. An "earworm" or "brain bug" is usually a short fragment of music, and the tune or song is repetitive (it plays over and over). The triggers are similar to the cues for sponta-neous memories: Recent exposure, repeated exposure, and associations (sound, situation, or word) were most frequently reported (Williamson et al., 2011). Earworms occur with similar frequency to involuntary memories, that is, they occur frequently. *Too* frequently. (No one has reported how to get rid of the songs.)

An evolutionary perspective suggests that spontaneous memory can serve an adaptive purpose. Organisms live in a constantly changing environment and memory bridges the temporal intervals across changing events. Being frequently reminded of things in mem-ory gives us the opportunity to notice relationships that recur ("the same thing happened when. . .") or changed ("that didn't happen the last time. . .").

Spontaneous recall might also be beneficial for memory updating. Updating suggests replacing one memory with another (e.g., where I parked this morning replaces the mem-ory of where I parked yesterday). Hintzman (2011) says that a better strategy would be to keep both old and new memories in order to learn predictive relationships. One needs a record of successive memories to detect a pattern of changes: Remember what occurred last time. . . .and what happened this time. If this is true, then updating does not always mean replacing. Spontaneous memories may be the mind's way of checking whether an earlier memory is relevant to the present, and which might provoke an update.

Retrieval From Episodic Memory

What factors affect retrieval? As we will see, several variables are important, but three general factors can be offered: the distinctiveness of the memory, practice at retrieving the memory, and the presence of effective retrieval cues.

Distinctiveness

Events that are *distinctive*, or that stand out from a background of other events by being dif-ferent, are generally well remembered. Flashbulb memories are well recalled, even if not accurately, because they represent events that are so different from others in our lives. In the isolation effect an item that differs from the remaining items in a list is better recalled (see Chapter 9).

Why are distinctive events retrieved better? One explanation is that their retrieval cues uniquely target a single memory. When asked to recall where you were on September 11, 2001 (or 9/11), this request cues a very particular memory. By contrast, other retrieval cues might be too broad, potentially retrieving many items but not specifically one item (Roediger, 1973).

Testing Effects

Retrieval is facilitated by previous retrieval. For instance, taking a test shortly after studying greatly enhances the amount that can be recalled on a later retest. The general design of studies of **testing effects** is to give one or more practice tests shortly after learning, and then a final test sometime later. It is this later test that interests us. For example, the number of pictures recalled at the end of a 1-week delay nearly doubled when three other tests of memory had occurred, versus no other tests, immediately after studying the week before (Wheeler & Roediger, 1992). (Testing effects were described in Chapter 9.)

A phenomenon known as hypermnesia offers a dramatic demonstration of testing effects. **Hypermnesia** is remembering that actually improves over successive attempts at reproduction of the studied material, in contrast to the forgetting that we expect to occur over time. Erdelyi and Kleinbard (1978) presented a list of 60 object line drawings for study (DOG, CAT, TREE, etc.). The participants were then repeatedly tested for recall of the pictured objects. The list was presented just once for study, but in some cases memory was tested 20 times over the following week. During each test, the participants were asked to name as many objects as they could recall. The total number of different items recalled across repeated testing is shown in Figure 10.5. Whereas just over 26 items were recalled on the first test, 38 were recalled on the final tests. This hypermnesia is the opposite of forgetting, or amnesia.

Bahrick and Hall (1993) reported hypermnesia for other test materials, including recall of general information, foreign-language vocabulary, and names. From one test to another, some items are indeed forgotten. But the number of newly recovered items on successive tests exceeded the number lost, leaving hypermnesia as a net gain.

Why would people remember more and not less across successive tests? One factor is that during "free" recall, people prompt their memories with self-generated cues (Roediger & Thorpe, 1978). The participants are thinking of one thing or another to help remember. The self-prompting cues vary across successive tests as different things come to mind at different times. These later cues tap items that were not adequately cued on the earlier tests.

This capacity for additional recall of material across a series of tests has implications for eyewitness testimony. One assumption too often made is that the first recall is the most valid,

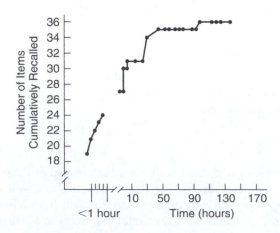

Figure 10.5 **Hypermnesia.** The number of different items recalled after a single presentation of the list. The list was tested more than 20 times over a period of a week.

Source: From "Has Ebbinghaus Decayed with Time? The Growth of Recall (Hypermnesia) over Days," by M. H. Erdelyi and J. Kleinbard, 1978, *Journal of Experimental Psychology: Human Learning and Memory, 4*, pp. 275–289. Copyright © 1978 by the American Psychological Association. Reprinted with permission.

and anything remembered later is suspect. Yet here we are asserting that additional accurate information can be elicited through repeated recall attempts. In a simulation study of witnessing, participants watched a film depicting a burglary. Memory recall was tested four times, and each time additional details were remembered without an increase in intrusions of incorrect facts (Scrivener & Safer, 1988).

In addition to distinctive memories and practice at retrieval, a third important factor in retrieval is to have effective retrieval cues. The consideration of such cues is taken up next.

What Makes a Good Retrieval Cue?

We will consider two answers here: cues that have strong preexisting associations to the target memory and cues that were encoded along with the to-be-recalled item when it entered into memory.

Associations

Effective retrieval cues are those that are connected to the target by strong associations. Given the word TABLE, you might retrieve CHAIR as the first association that comes to mind, but not AARDVARK. TABLE is a good retrieval cue for CHAIR but not for AARDVARK.

Memory is dramatically improved when effective cues are given. In a typical free recall experiment, students might be able to recall 15 out of 48 words presented in a single list. If a retrieval cue was presented for each word (e.g., was there an ANIMAL in the list? A FOOD? A PLANT?), the number of words remembered increases to around 36 (Tulving & Pearlstone, 1966).

In a dramatic demonstration of the effectiveness of retrieval cues, Mantyla (1986) attempted to improve recall of several hundred random words. As each word was presented, the subjects were asked to generate up to three properties that described the word. These self-generated (one-word) cues were presented during the test phase. When the test occurred immediately after list presentation, more than 90 percent of the cued words were recalled, and even after one week, 60 to 65 percent of the words could be recalled. If someone else's cues were used, only 20 percent of the words were remembered after a week. In one massive session, subjects studied *600* words and generated three cues for each, and then were tested for all 600 words. (The procedure took over 6 hours.) Again, 90 percent of the words could be retrieved from all three cues, and 60 percent from one cue.

Encoding Specificity

Cues that are effective in aiding retrieval are the cues that were also present at the time of encoding. If you forget where you left an object, you mentally go back to where you were when you last had it. If you want to recollect your childhood, go back to where you lived as a child. The cues that were present when the memory was encoded can aid retrieval later.

This idea of matching cues between encoding and retrieval has been made explicit in Tulving's **encoding specificity principle**: Retrieval is better when the cues present at encoding also occur at the time of retrieval. In one demonstration, Tulving and Thompson (1973) varied the cues present at the time of studying and at testing. Their college student participants studied target words that were paired with weakly associated words as study aids. Thus, the to-be-remembered word LIGHT is presented along with its weak associate HEAD. On the recognition test the target words were presented with the same cue words as before, or with cue words that had stronger associations to the target (e.g., DARK is presented as the cue). LIGHT was more often recognized in the context of the weak associate HEAD than when in the context of the strong associate DARK. This is because LIGHT had initially been encoded in the context of HEAD LIGHT rather

Table 10.1 Variations in the Encoding–Retrieval Paradigm

A.   Encoding-Specific (Tulving & Thompson, 1973, Table 1)

Study	Test	Percent of Words Recognized
head LIGHT	head LIGHT	65
	dark LIGHT	23

B.   Context-Specific (Godden & Baddeley, 1975)

Study Context	Test Context	Percent of Words Recalled
Land	Land	38
	Water	24
Water	Land	23
	Water	32

C.   (Drug-)State-Dependent (Eich, Weingartner, Stillman, & Gillin, 1975)

Study Drug State	Test Drug State	Number of Words Recalled
Placebo	Placebo	11.5
Placebo	Marijuana	9.9
Marijuana	Placebo	6.7
Marijuana	Marijuana	10.5

D.   Mood-Dependent Recall (Bower, 1981)

Mood at Study	Mood at Test	Percent Recall
Happy	Happy	78
Happy	Sad	46
Sad	Happy	46
Sad	Sad	81

than of DARK (see the results in Table 10.1). According to the encoding specificity principle, recognition occurred when the test reactivated the same meaning with which the target words had been encoded.

The experimental arrangement of manipulating the encoding conditions in combination with the retrieval conditions is referred to as the **encoding–retrieval paradigm** (Tulving, 1983). The basic manipulation is that the cues present during encoding can be arranged to be the same, or different, at the time of retrieval. The cues can be words, as in Tulving and Thompson's experiments. The cues can also be contextual cues of time and place; internal cues of emotional or drug-induced mental and physical states; or cognitive operations the participant performs with the target material. A sample of encoding–retrieval manipulations is shown in Box 10.2.

Box 10.2   Examples of the Encoding–Retrieval Paradigm

Music as Context Stimuli

Mozart or jazz served as background music while the participants tried to remember a word list. Recall 2 days later was better when the same music was repeated (Smith, 1985). Interestingly, no context-dependent "quiet" effect was found when no music prevailed at study and test.

Odor as a Contextual Stimulus

Recall of faces after a 2-day delay was better when the same odor was present during studying and testing (Cann & Ross, 1989).

Temperature

Rats were first made hypothermic and then trained to avoid shock. When retested later, retention was better among animals that were rechilled than those tested at different body temperatures (Richardson, Guanowsky, Ahlers, & Riccio, 1984).

Time-of-Day Dependency

Time-of-day effects have been found in animal conditioning studies. For example, rats performed better when they were tested at the same time of day at which they were first trained (Holloway, 1978). Some attempts to find time dependency in human memory have not been successful (Folkard & Monk, 1985).

Bodily Kinesthetic Context

Subjects studied a word list while standing up or lying down. Recall was better when tested in the same position than when positions were switched (Rand & Wapner, 1967). Finally, one football coach complained about the NCAA requirement that preseason workouts not be in full gear. "We teach them all their patterns and plays and as soon as they put on the shoulder pads they forget everything we taught them" (quoted by Green, 1991).

Ritalin and State Dependency

The drug Ritalin is sometimes used to treat hyperactivity in children. Swanson and Kinsbourne (1976) found state dependency in a sample of hyperactive children taking Ritalin, using a paired-associate learning task. However, in one other case, this effect only partially replicated (Shea, 1982).

Don't Phone in Your Answers

Canas and Nelson's (1986) participants studied a word list in the lab and were then dismissed. Those brought back to the lab a day later recalled more words than those tested by phone.

Pain-Dependent Learning

Subjects exposed to a list of words while experiencing experimentally induced pain (i.e., immersing their hands in ice water) later remembered more words when reexposed to the pain. Fewer words were remembered if the pain occurred only during list exposure or only during testing (Pearce et al., 1990).

State-Dependent Phobia

Spider phobics were given a single session of exposure therapy after consuming either caffeine or not. One week later the phobics were retested for their fear of spiders. Those who were desensitized and tested in the same drug state (caffeinated both times or decaf both occasions) had less fear on the test. The researchers suggested that fluctuations in caffeine use might lead to variations in the level of fear from week to week that are unrelated to therapeutic effectiveness (Mystkowski, Mineka, Vernon, & Zinbarg, 2003).

Contextual Learning

You have probably been given the advice to study in the same room you will take the test in. There is some validity, with limitations, to this claim. For example, Smith (1979) had students study a word list in a college classroom. The students were then tested either in the same room or in a different room. (Both rooms were made equally familiar in a preliminary phase.) More words were recalled when testing was in the same room in which the word list had been presented. Smith also found that the different-room deficit was reduced if the students were instructed to mentally "reinstate" the study room prior to testing. You don't actually have to be there; just imagine you are there! This idea has been applied to a witness interview technique that emphasizes reinstatement of a crime or accident scene as an aid to retrieval.

State-Dependent Learning

State-dependent learning refers to better recall when testing occurs in the same drug-influenced state as was present during learning. A variety of drugs, including alcohol and marijuana, can produce state dependency in humans and animals. A study by Eich et al. (1975) illustrates the case for marijuana. Participants studied word lists either while under the influence of marijuana or not and then were tested after exposure to marijuana or a placebo. (The use of controlled drugs for research purposes is highly regulated. Potential participants must be screened. They cannot be recruited from the Psych 101 subject pool for dope studies.)

The design of this study and the results are shown in Table 10.1. There was a drug state-dependency effect: Recall was better in the two groups in which the drug conditions at testing matched those present while studying. That is, recall was better in the group who studied and tested after placebos and in the group who studied and tested after the drug.

Mood-Dependent Recall

Bower (1981) theorized that internal stimuli arising from mood and emotional state can enter into associations just as do the external stimuli that experimental psychologists typically employ. Bower, Monteiro, and Gilligan (1978) demonstrated mood-dependent recall in an experiment in which happy or sad moods were induced in hypnotized college student participants. Recall of the to-be-remembered material was better when students were tested in the same mood state, whether this was happy or sad, as they were in when learning had occurred (see Table 10.1). This is sometimes referred to as *mood-congruent memory.*

Mood-specific recall has implications for depression and other affective disorders. Being depressed may lead to the retrieval of mostly sad memories, which only perpetuates the depressive mood. For example, if depressed individuals are given cue words and asked to recall any personal memory that comes to mind, they more often recall unpleasant experiences. In longitudinal research designs that tested the same individuals at different times, more unpleasant memories were recalled when the individuals were depressed, and the frequency of pleasant memories increased when they were less depressed (Clark & Teasdale, 1982; Fogarty & Helmsley, 1983).

The opposite of depression is the excited state of mania. In one study, a word-association test was administered to individuals currently in a manic state. On succeeding days, the manic individuals were asked to recall the associations generated in that previous free-association phase. Recall was better when the mood state matched that of when the list was first generated (Weingartner, Miller, & Murphy, 1977). According to one anecdotal report, a man in a manic state withdrew a large sum of money from his bank and hid it in his house. After his mania abated, he could not remember where he had put the money. Six months later, the man became manic once again and went to hide something else behind a picture, whereupon he found the lost money.

Although he still did not remember hiding the money, it is interesting that the same location seemed so sensible in the manic phase, but was not at all memorable in the normal state (Williams & Markar, 1991).

What do the several manipulations of context, drug-induced state, and mood have in common? One possibility is that they all reduce to mood-dependent memory. What is common when encoding and retrieval conditions are equated is "not *environmental* context dependent memory, but rather *experiential* context dependence, of the kind customarily associated with alterations of a person's affective, circadian, or pharmacological state" (Eich, 1985, p. 769, italics in the original). Eich (1995) found that matching the self-rated affect (i.e., feelings) between encoding and recall was more important than matching physical locations. That is, being in the same mood was more important than being in the same place.

Limitations of Encoding–Retrieval Paradigm Effects

We should not overemphasize the magnitude of the effect of matching encoding and retrieval cues on memory retrieval. State-dependent effects are more often found on recall tests but not on recognition tests. State-dependent effects are also obtained after minimal amounts learning. These facts suggest that retrieval cues are helpful when memory is weak and the participant therefore has few spontaneously produced retrieval cues to access the memory.

Also, not all contextual cues, moods, or drug-induced states necessarily become associated with the target. For instance, if cues in the classroom do not become associated with the lecture material in some manner, such as inspecting some element of the room while thinking about a lecture point, the room should have no special retrieval power (Smith & Vela, 2001).

Retrieval-Induced Forgetting

A good retrieval cue is not always a good retrieval cue. We have seen this in one instance already with Tulving's *encoding specificity principle*. The word JELLY might be a great reminder for the word JAM, unless you earlier had been thinking about TRAFFIC JAM.

The act of retrieving memories can itself cause forgetting of related items. In **retrieval-induced forgetting**, or RIF, practice at remembering one answer produces interference with retrieval of other viable answers (see e.g., Storm, 2011). There are many situations in which a cue retrieves multiple answers, and the goal is to recall/use just one. What is that medicine you take now, or what is your current class schedule? Competitor answers are your old medicines and last semester's classes. We have to inhibit recall of these answers in preference for newer answers. This inhibition of the now-wrong answers is learned. Simply put, we practice not giving the "old" answer.

For instance, right now you may remember your old password and the new password for a given website. But for the next several weeks you will be "practicing" the new password. If then asked for both passwords, you cannot recall the old one. This is not just normal forgetting or the passage of time. Other passwords you have not used for the last several weeks are still remembered. It is the act of recalling your new password that blocks recall of the old password. Just as you practiced remembering the new password, you practiced not recalling the old one. Inhibiting the old password is more than simple ignoring it or not using it. A stronger mental action was required: The old password needed to be suppressed.

There are other instances in which retrieval produced interference. In the tip-of-the-tongue phenomenon, a wrong word, name, or fact often comes to mind. You know it is not the right answer, yet repeated searching keeps pulling up this same wrong answer. The wrong answer is now active in memory, and its repeated recall keeps it the most accessible answer. The advice to "stop trying to remember" works here, allowing time for the activation of the primed item to fade.

Emotional Arousal and Retrieval

Emotional arousal can have opposing effects on memory. Emotions are stimuli that can become associated with other events in memory, and thus act as retrieval cues. And emotional arousal can impair our ability to retrieve memories.

High levels of an emotion, particularly fear or anxiety, can block retrieval of memories that otherwise would be recalled. In one particularly dramatic demonstration of emotional blocking, army recruits were tested in what they thought was a life-threatening situation. Prior to boarding a military aircraft, different groups of soldiers were given a sheet of emergency instructions to study. During the flight, the experimental treatment group was put under extreme emotional distress. One engine of the plane was stopped and the soldiers were told to prepare for an emergency ditching in the ocean. Then the soldiers were given a written test on the emergency procedures. Would life-threatening fear interfere with retrieval? Compared to nonfear control groups, the crash-fearing group recalled significantly less of the emergency procedures (Berkun, Bialek, Kern, & Yagi, 1962). (No doubt the soldiers recalled significantly more about this plane flight.)

Manipulating fear in this manner should provoke ethical concerns about the treatment of research participants. Yet the research addresses a significant question about whether emotional arousal interferes with the performance of critical duties. Individuals trained in emergency procedures might not be able to access the information under the stressful conditions of an emergency.

One study demonstrated a correlation between the level of stress hormones in the blood and remembering. Rats were first trained to swim to a submerged platform in the Morris water escape maze. The rats were then given electric shocks 2 minutes, 30 minutes, or 4 hours before being tested the next day. The shocks were used to induce emotional arousal. During Day 2 testing, the rats could not recall the platform location 30 minutes after the shocks, a time when stress hormones were highest in the blood. The rats could recall 2 minutes after the shocks, before hormone secretions peaked; and 4 hours after the shocks, when the hormone levels had subsided (deQuervain, Roozendaal, & McGaugh, 1998).

Among people exposed to the same unpleasant event, individuals may nevertheless experience different degrees of negative emotion. Does the experienced intensity of negative emotion affect memory? In some cases, greater unpleasantness provokes *less* remembering. Crying by children would be a good indicator of negative emotional arousal. In one case, children aged 2 through 6 underwent a catheterization procedure, during which some of them cried. (Only *some* cried?) Six months later, the children who had cried recalled less information and with less accuracy, even when given memory prompts (Salmon, Price, & Pereira, 2002).

What if the emotional state is relieved? Will the forgotten material then return? In several older experiments, participants first studied a number of word lists and recall was tested. The subjects were then given feedback designed to induce concern over their performance. They might be told they had not done well on the task, or a personality test indicated abnormal traits. After this, recall of the studied material was tested again. Participants given upsetting feedback did not recall as many items as did those given neutral feedback. The important manipulation, from our perspective, is what happened after the emotional stress was relieved. The experimenters disclosed their deception, the distress was eliminated, and the supposedly forgotten information was recalled (Holmes, 1992).

In a student's life test anxiety can interfere with retrieval. Benjamin, McKeachie, Lin, and Holinger (1981) found that highly test-anxious college students performed poorly on essay and short-answer questions, which make heavy demands on retrieval of information. These students performed better on multiple-choice tests, which are less demanding on retrieval. Other research confirmed that some anxious students benefited from training to calm themselves in the test-taking situation, and their grades actually increased the following semester (Naveh-Benjamin, 1991).

Remembering to Remember

One of the lessons learned from memory experts is that they plan for retrieval at the time of encoding (see Chapter 11). That is, while they are rehearsing, elaborating, imaging, and all the other things people do when they try to remember, the experts are also devising strategies to retrieve the encoded material later.

Planning for retrieval is particularly important in **prospective memory**, or remembering to perform future actions. For instance, say I have to remember to pick up dinner on the way home. A prospective memory failure would be forgetting to recall at the correct time or place on the drive home. I remember to get dinner; I just don't remember until I get home.

External cues and electronic devices can reduce our dependence on memory. Professional bartenders use external cues when they set out each type of glass needed to fill an order. A programmed alert tells you when to act.

In other instances prospective memory depends on internal cues, or "remembering to remember." Remembering to take something out of the oven, to stop at the store on the way home, and to call someone later that day are examples. Recall can depend on an internal prompt to remember at the correct time. Prospective remembering is simulated in laboratory studies using dual-task procedures. The research participant engages in a primary task that engages attention, while the secondary task is to remember to push a response button. The button has to be pushed every so many minutes, and it is up to the participant to keep track of when to respond. Just as in the real world, forgetting occurs in the laboratory prospective memory task (Einstein, McDaniel, Richardson, Guynn, & Cunfer, 1995).

Do laboratory tests and real-world estimates of prospective memory failure correspond? Mantyla (2003) tested multiple prospective tasks, some in the lab and some outside. People were asked, for instance, to remember to tell the experimenter something before leaving, or to call back in a week. Those who complained of memory problems, either retrospective (e.g., forgetting names) or prospective (e.g., forgetting appointments), did poorly on the prospective measures. In general, poor prospective memory correlated with reports of all kinds of everyday memory failure. Mantyla suggested that prospective tests might be more sensitive measures of memory impairment than some of the standard retrospective tasks, such as recalling a list of words.

Metamemory and Partial Retrieval

Metamemory, our knowledge about memory, applies to retrieval. We know how to search memory, for example, by using active strategies to facilitate recall (see the section on Applications). We also know what is stored in our memories (or at least, we think we know what's there). This latter form of knowing has been studied in the two related phenomena of feeling of knowing and tip-of-the-tongue.

Feeling of Knowing

Each of us has probably had the experience of not being able to remember something but we are sure that we know it. This **feeling of knowing** (FOK) is characterized by an "irritating mixture of surety and bafflement. The individual is convinced he knows but is frustrated by the inability to demonstrate his knowing" (Reed, 1979, p. 9). FOK is related to *tip-of-the-tongue* (TOT). This is a more intense feeling that not only do we know the sought-after word, but we are so close to recalling it. In Brown and McNeil's (1966) classic study, tip-of-the-tongue "states" (as the authors labeled them) were elicited by reading definitions of unusual words to their college students. In the TOT state, often the participants could accurately report the first letters of the unrecalled word, the number of syllables it contained, and the stress pronunciation pattern across syllables. For example, an unrecalled street name in Boston led to recall of similar names that were rejected: CONGRESS, CORINTH, and CONCORD. The actual street name was CORNISH. What is interesting about FOK or TOT is how confident we are that we know, even though the item cannot be recalled to verify our feelings. (The tip-of-the-tongue experience seems to be universal, although the linguistic expression for it varies. Schwartz found evidence in 45 languages that referred to the tongue: On top of my tongue, lost on my tongue, or the Korean "sparkling at the end of the tongue" [Schwartz, 1999].)

These partial recalls are also interesting because we can readily reject wrong answers. As William James said, "Suppose we try to recall a forgotten name. . . . There is a gap therein; but no mere gap. It is a gap that is intensely active. . . . If wrong names are proposed to us, this singularly definite gap acts immediately to negate them. They do not fit into its mold. And the gap of one word does not feel like the gap of another, all empty of content as both might seem . . . when described as gaps" (1890, p. 251).

How do we know our feelings of knowing are correct if we cannot recall the item? Hart (1965) introduced a three-step procedure to assess FOK accuracy. The participants are first tested with some general information questions. For example, "Which planet is the largest in the solar system?" Second, for the unanswered questions, the participants rate their confidence that they really do know the answer. These are the FOK ratings. Third, a multiple-choice test is given to see whether the unrecalled items are selected. For the example question given here, the alternatives might be "Pluto, Venus, Saturn, and Jupiter." Items that received high FOK scores are more likely to be answered correctly in multiple-choice tests, showing that the initial failure was indeed one of retrieval.

High FOK ratings might suggest that people can assess the strength of unrecalled knowledge. People know what they know. However, respondents often use other information to *infer* whether they should know the answer. The recall of related facts or familiarity with the topic may mislead you into thinking you will know the answer. In these cases, the participant makes an educated guess that the answer is indeed known (Nelson & Gerler, 1984).

It is also the case that high FOK ratings sometimes correspond to flat-out wrong answers. People give a high FOK rating to a particular question; select the wrong answer on the multiple choice; and are highly confident in the correctness of their (wrong) choice.

False Retrieval

False Memory

A different sort of retrieval failure is the mistaken recall of some stimulus or event that had not actually occurred. False recall and **false memory** are used to label mistaken recollection. Deese (1959) demonstrated false recall by presenting lists in which the words were associated with a target word that was not included in the list. For example, the list might include BED, REST, AWAKE, SNOOZE, SLUMBER, and SNORE. When subsequently tested, many participants believed that the word SLEEP had been on the list. It was not. Deese found that intrusions of the target (e.g., the word SLEEP) occurred 30 to 40 percent of the time, and Roediger and McDermott (1995) found intrusions in as many as 50 percent of their participants. (This task is now referred to as the Deese-Roediger-McDermott procedure, or the DRM, in the research literature.)

The false memory effect is extremely robust. For instance, warning subjects about it only minimally decreases false recall (and by making participants cautious, decreases correct recall of the actual list items.) Falsely remembered items are forgotten over time at about the same rate as the presented words. In one study, the associated words were recalled and recognized more so than were actual list words on tests given two days, two weeks, or two months later (Seamon et al., 2002). About the only factor that reduces false recall is to present the list items as pictures (i.e., line drawings). During testing, there is more certainty in recall of the specific images (Israel & Schacter, 1997; see review by Roediger & McDermott, 2000).

Why does false recall occur? According to the notion of spreading activation discussed earlier, activation spreads from the representations of each list item in memory to associated items in memory, including the nonpresented word. The cumulative effect of activation from several cues is stronger activation of the related word. The more associates there are in the list, the more likely false retrieval becomes (Robinson & Roediger, 1997).

The DRM procedure draws on associations that most people share. However, the procedure can also be illustrated among specialist groups or experts who have unique associations to words in their fields. A study of undergraduate business students found that they could recall more investment-related words (such as *P-E ratio, IPO, day trade*, and *midcap*) than could nonbusiness students, although both groups recalled equal numbers of noninvestment-related words. This result was as expected, given that these words were familiar to the business students. However, the business students also falsely recalled more business-related words that had not been on the list but were associated with the list words (Baird, 2003).

An important question in explaining false recall is when do they appear in memory: at encoding or at retrieval? One could imagine that during list presentation the associated target words become activated in memory. Alternatively, maybe the target first appears later during testing, as the subject uses some remembered words to retrieve a few more. One way to test for presence of the target words during study is to have the subjects rehearse out loud while they are listening to and encoding the list words. In one case, the associated targets were frequently said aloud by the subjects during the study phase and became "part of the lists" (Goodwin, Meissner, & Ericsson, 2001).

In some ways, the falsely recalled words are as real in the brain as are the actually presented words. If event-related potentials are recorded, a form of EEG recorded from electrodes placed on the scalp, the reaction to falsely recognized words (e.g., SLEEP) is no different from that to correctly identified words (e.g., SLUMBER), and differs from distractors presented during testing (e.g., DOG) (Johnson et al., 1997). Thus, calling this phenomenon "false retrieval" may be a misnomer. From the perspective of the neural reaction, the recognition of actually presented and associatively activated words does not differ.

Generality of False Memory in the DRM procedure

The DRM procedure has been tested in many experimental variations and in several types of subject populations. Generally, some degree of false recall of the lures occurs no matter what the variation. Some examples follow.

AMNESICS SHOW FALSE RECALL

Not surprisingly, amnesic individuals remember fewer of the actual list words, and they remember fewer of the associated lures that were not presented. But they do misremember more lures than expected by chance or guessing. It may be that remembering actual words from the list might be necessary to induce misremembering of the associated words (Schacter, Verfaellie, & Pradere, 1996).

CHILDREN ARE SUSCEPTIBLE TO FALSE RECALL

Children remember fewer of the actual list words than do adults, and so remember fewer lures than do adults. Comparisons of children across ages 6 to 11 show increasing likelihood of false recall. Getting older and remembering more of the actual words is accompanied by more misremembering (Brainerd, Forrest, Karibian, & Reyna, 2006). This finding has implications for the reliability of younger children as eyewitnesses. The increased general knowledge possessed by older children might make them more susceptible to false recall.

FALSE-RECALL CROSSES LANGUAGES

Bilingual participants can be presented with word lists in one language (e.g., French or English), and a recognition test in the other language. False recognition of the lures still occurs (Cabeza & Lennartson, 2005). Possibly there is a common lexical representation that is activated by the words of either language.

Source Memory

False memory has parallels in other false retrieval phenomenon. Have you ever been unable to remember whether you actually said something or had only intended to say it? This distinction is one of **source memory**: distinguishing between an actually experienced event and one that was imagined, thought of, heard about, or even dreamed (e.g., Johnson & Raye, 1981). A memory's origin can be external in the words we spoke, actions we performed, or objects we perceived, or the memory's origin could be internal in words thought of, actions planned, and objects imagined.

We distinguish between externally and internally derived memories by making a judgment about the qualitative aspects of the memory: What does the memory feel like? Johnson and Raye (1981) hypothesize that we look for certain attributes that indicate whether the memory seems to have originated externally or internally. Actual memories are richer in sensory attributes: there are stronger traces of sight, sound, or texture. The memory is more firmly set in time and place, as events preceding or following the target are also remembered. In contrast, imagined memories are more schematic and lacking in sensory detail. There is less recall of what came before and after the remembered event. A decision on the likely origin of any given memory is based on the number of internal and external attributes. Some memories will be judged probably internal or external, and some memories we are just not sure of.

Mistaking the source of a memory could lead to the false belief that the event really occurred. (Remember Piaget's vivid memory of having been kidnapped as a young child, when in fact he was only told that he had been kidnapped.) Loftus and Pickrell (1995) were able to implant childhood memories in both children and adults by getting family members to talk about fabricated events as if they had really happened. In one case, a 14-year-old boy was told how he had been temporarily lost in a shopping mall several years prior. Other family members corroborated the story, adding details. After two days the boy really believed that he had been lost, "remembering" more details, his feelings while lost, and even the man who eventually rescued him. (I suspect we now have a generation of young adults who vividly "remember" events from childhood, when in fact what they are remembering are the videos of themselves that they saw later.)

Whose Memory Is It?

A new form of source memory has been identified: a memory whose origin is claimed by two people. For example, one person claims to remember some long-ago event, such as being sent home from school, but someone else, maybe a sibling, claims ownership of the memory and the experience. In studying a sample of same-sex twins, Sheen, Kemp, and Rubin (2001) found that about two thirds had a disputed memory. (It is possible that neither twin actually experienced the incident and both are falsely remembering.)

Imagination Inflation

Memories that originate internally can seem more real if they are they are thought about often. In **imagination inflation,** frequently imagining or thinking about some event or action leads to an increase in the belief that the action or event actually happened. Goff and Roediger (1998) had their subjects perform some simple actions, such as knocking on the table or breaking a toothpick, and imagine performing other actions. Some imaginings were repeated. During a later session the subjects had to recall whether they had performed or imagined the action. The more frequently an action had been imagined, the more likely it was remembered as an actual memory.

Are some people more prone to imagination inflation? Inflation correlates with hypnotic suggestibility, the capacity to respond to hypnotic instructions (Heaps & Nash, 1999). Some psychotherapies for trauma combine hypnosis and imaginal exposure (thinking about the distressing event). The phenomenon of imagination inflation suggests these are the same conditions that convert something imagined into a memory for an actual event.

The Effect of Postevent Information

One of the more provocative issues in memory research today is the effect of postevent information on recall. After some to-be-remembered event occurs, other contradicting information is presented. Will the postevent alter the target memory? One example of this are experiments on the effect of misleading postevent questions. These experiments had three steps. First, the participants watched a short video depicting a minor car accident. Next, they were asked a misleading question. They were asked about a traffic sign that was *not* present in the film. ("How fast was the car going when it passed the stop sign?") Finally, the participants were tested on their memory of the video. Here the participants "recalled" seeing the sign in the film (Loftus, Miller, & Burns, 1978). The outcome is referred to as the **misinformation effect:** remembering incorrect information that is presented instead of remembering the previously studied correct information.

The misinformation effect can occur for several reasons. One possibility is that the original memory is no longer there. Maybe the first event memory has been forgotten, and so the postevent fact is all that is available for the subject to recall. Another possibility is that the subject remembers both memories at the time of testing, but only reports the postevent information because the experimental procedure seems to suggest that is the correct response.

Witnesses certainly can be led to misrecall events by misleading questions. Some of this may be due to acquiescence with the questioner's suggestions or an assumption that the questioner must be right about what appears (to the participant) to be an unimportant detail. The critical question concerns the fate of the original memory. Is it still there, but rendered less accessible to retrieval by the postevent information? Or has the misinformation actually changed the memory? Obviously, this distinction is important to evaluating eyewitness memory.

Attempts to correct misinformation can actually backfire. So your professor tells you that such-and-such a theory actually was proven wrong, but all you remember at the time of the test is that the professor talked about such-and-such theory. It must be a right answer! An example of this sort of misremembering occurred in a study that tried to correct medical misinformation. Skurnik, Yoon, Park, and Schwarz (2005) presented a number of hypothetical medical "facts," some with the disclaimer that they were not true. On later testing, most of the facts were recognized as having been presented earlier by the experimenter. However, errors were made in remembering which had been labeled false. Misremembering was worse when the facts had been presented three times (and labeled false each time).

Questions about postevent information are related to interference theories of forgetting. A persisting concern in laboratory experiments is whether remembering one event retroactively interferes with retrieval of the earlier memory or whether it actually alters the earlier memory.

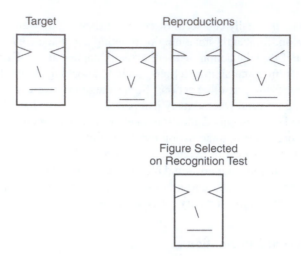

Figure 10.6 In Zangwill's (1937) study, the participants first studied figures like those labeled TARGET (on the left); the participant then made several attempts to reproduce the target from memory, leading to successive distortions in their reproductions; finally, the participants were given a multiple-choice recognition test. The participants chose correctly even though the distractors were more like the participant's own reproductions.

Source: From "Processes of Memory Loss, Recovery, and Distortion," by W. K. Estes, 1997, *Psychological Review, 104*, p. 159. Copyright © 1997 by the American Psychological Association. Reprinted with permission.

Estes (1997) argues that some of both occur. In an early study by Zangwill (1937), participants were shown a drawing, say, of an irregular figure and then produced a series of reproductions (see Figure 10.6). Systematic distortion appeared across the successive drawings, which became less like the original. However, when a recognition test was given afterwards, the original figure was more often correctly chosen and not some figure closer to the participant's own most recent reproductions. Memory for the original object was still there even after much potentially distorting interference.

Reconsolidation

Memories can be altered. Misinformation effects and false memory show this occurs. But how can this happen if the original memory produced a fixed, structural change in the brain, as consolidation theory suggests. The permanent memory should be resistant to modification.

It now appears that the activation or retrieval of a consolidated memory can make *it* susceptible to modification or disruption. The **reconsolidation** hypothesis asserts that, when a memory is retrieved, it returns to a short-term memory state. If undisturbed, the memory would normally undergo consolidation again, or reconsolidate back into long-term memory. However, the memory is susceptible to change and alteration at this time. Since the reactivated memory is in the labile state, reconsolidation can be blocked using the same means that block consolidation: administer electroconvulsive shock or protein inhibitors. If you remember the description of consolidation theory earlier in this chapter, I noted that an ECS treatment given after a training trial could block permanent memory formation. Similarly, after a reminder of the initial learning, ECS can block reconsolidation of the memory (Alberini, 2005).

Reconsolidation is analogous to updating a document on your computer. The document is retrieved from storage on the hard drive. Then, while it is active on your desktop you can make modifications. When you hit "save," the new document replaces the old one on the hard drive. This

Table 10.2 **Outline of Reconsolidation-Blocking Studies.** After fear-conditioning at Time 1, the rats are given a reminder of this at Time 2, as well as a treatment to disrupt the reactivated memory: ECS or a protein inhibitor.

Time 1 (Learning)	Time 2 (Reminder/ Reconsolidation)	Time 3 (Test)
Reconsolidation Controls		
Tone–Shock	Tone	Tone → fear
Or		
Tone–Shock	Shock	Tone → fear
Reconsolidation Blocked		
Tone–Shock	Tone–ECS	Tone → no/less fear
Or		
Tone–Shock	Shock–Protein Inhibitor	Tone → no/less fear

is the idea of reconsolidation as an updating mechanism. The one difference between reconsolidation and the computer analogy is that if you lose the RAM version of your document—power goes out or the computer freezes—the old copy is still on the hard drive. With reconsolidation, however, the only copy of the memory is in RAM memory on the desktop. If that memory is disrupted, then that memory is lost.

The design of two animal experiments to demonstrate reconsolidation blocking are shown in Table 10.2. At Time 1, all the rats received tone-shock pairings. At Time 2, usually the next day, the animals are given a reminder treatment. Either the tone alone or the shock alone reminds the rat of the previous day's conditioning treatment. (Control groups show the rats remember the fear from Day 1.) One of the reconsolidation blocking groups gets ECS after the reminder test. When tested again at Time 3, the control subjects are still fearful. However, the ECS subjects, which initially remembered the shock at Time 2, apparently do not remember it at Time 3. The reconsolidation of the memory was blocked (e.g., Misanin, Miller, & Lewis, 1968).

Another group gets a different treatment at Time 2. In this case, a protein-synthesis inhibiting drug is injected into the brain. This also prevents reconsolidation, and so memory of the tone-shock association, learned at time 1, is disrupted. Testing at Time 3 show the fear has been lost (Nadar, Schafe, & LeDoux, 2000).

Reactivation of a memory at Time 2 makes it susceptible to change. An alternative manipulation to weaken the memory at this time is to give extinction training. Extinction given after a reminder reduces the fear, more so than extinction given without the reminder (Schiller et al., 2010). The original memory might also be strengthened by manipulations during the reconsolidation time period. For instance, the presentation of an emotional stimulus after the reminder increases the original memory (Finn & Roediger, 2011).

We noted above that reconsolidation is like *updating*. Updating is an important adaptive function of memory. For an animal, a place that was once safe is now dangerous. Where food was once found, none is present later. When the remembered does not match the present, this should set the condition for altering memory.

Recovered Memory

Can memories of childhood abuse be repressed? Can memories of repeated and extended trauma remain hidden and unrecalled? Such questions place research psychologists in the middle of a controversy. On one hand there is research showing that emotional events are well remembered, that false recollection occurs in laboratory tasks, and that misleading information or suggestion can lead to misrecall. On the other hand there is clinical experience showing that the sudden recovery of repressed memory is a genuine psychological process. To deny these recovered memories on the grounds of "insufficient" scientific evidence is tantamount to condoning the abuse of women or children.

The debate over "repressed" memories or "false" memories (depending on which side of the controversy you take) is a public one. (In an effort to be neutral some psychologists use the term "recovered" memory.) The conflict pits psychological experts against one another, frequently in court settings. Recovered memories of abuse can lead to accusations that a parent or relative is the abuser, and to countercharges that suggestions made by therapists are the source of the memories.

There can be repercussions against psychologists who even suggest the memories might be false. Susan Clancy studied women who reported recovered memories of abuse, testing their memories in innocuous laboratory tasks. When this became too sensitive, she turned to studying individuals who believed they had been abducted by aliens. The idea of studying "false" memories of alien abduction seemed like a safe choice. As it turned out, Alien Abduction Syndrome (there is a label for this) had supporters in high places, jeopardizing Clancy's academic career (Grierson, 2003).

Arrigo and Pezdek (1997) tried to defuse the controversy surrounding recovered memories of childhood abuse by reminding us that amnesia occurs after other sorts of traumas. These include forgetting of accidents, natural disasters, combat, suicide attempts, or violent crimes. Unfortunately, as scientific evidence, claims for repression and subsequent recovery of memory for these traumas are often as weak as claims for recovery of childhood abuse memories. Many times we cannot independently verify the facts or events now being recalled.

L. M. Williams (1994) confronted two problems frequently noted in repression research: Did abuse actually occur in the past, and did the victim forget that the trauma occurred? Williams first identified documented cases of childhood abuse that had occurred 17 years previously (on average). She then interviewed the (now) adult women for their recollections of the event. Williams found 49 women (or about 38 percent of her sample) who did not remember the abuse. The present "forgetting" was not a reluctance to discuss something painful or embarrassing, because the women were willing to relate intimate details about other events. This study offers strong evidence that, indeed, forgetting of a traumatic experience can occur.

By what mechanisms could memories be unremembered yet still be in storage for later recall? Brewin and Andrews (1998) considered several. One explanation is in terms of repression: the mind suppresses recall of a painful memory. This could be an unconscious defense against the psychological distress produced by the trauma, or the repression could be conscious and deliberate. Alternatively, the traumatic memory might involve the implicit memory systems of the brain rather than the explicit systems. By definition, an implicit memory is less available for conscious recall. For instance, fear could be classically conditioned to a stimulus or cue without conscious awareness of that association. Finally, memory may not be accessible because adequate retrieval cues are not present. A memory formed during the intense emotional state of a traumatic experience could remain unrecalled as long as this strong and unique emotional state does not recur.

Retrieval Versus Reconstruction

One misconception about memory is that it consists of static memory traces. This might be called a copy theory of memory. Our casual description of flashbulb memories fits the copy theory. We believe these memories persist unchanged over the years, almost like a photographic image. (In Chapter 9, we considered the evidence for accuracy of flashbulb memories.) An alternative conception of remembering emphasizes less the retention of detailed memory images and more the *reconstructive* process of retrieval. **Reconstructive memory** describes retrieval as being more like a reconstruction of what happened on the basis of some stored fragments of information, cues, and knowledge we have about similar events. Neisser offered an analogy to the work of a paleontologist who reconstructs the appearance of a dinosaur from some fossil fragments (Neisser, 1967).

In 1932, Sir Frederick Bartlett reported some now well-remembered experiments demonstrating memory distortion. His subjects listened to a Native American folk tale entitled "The War of the Ghosts" and then attempted to reproduce the story several times later. The story had many unfamiliar elements, or at least they were unfamiliar to Bartlett's subjects, who were British and probably college students. The story simply was not organized the way familiar fairy tales are, containing a sequence of characters, a danger, and a (usually) happy resolution. The subjects' retellings of the story were marked by omissions and distortions, attempts to make the flow more consequential, and the use of English paraphrasing. The then-unfamiliar word *canoe* was replaced by *boat*, and *hunting seals* became *fishing*. Also, the man who survived the attack was apparently "feeling none the worse for his experience." Bartlett said the listeners were trying to make sense of the story. Bartlett introduced the word *schema* to memory theory, suggesting that the students formed a schema in memory, or a general outline of the story, which was influenced by their knowledge, beliefs, and expectancies.

This study was key in demonstrating that remembering is not simply the passive recoding of events. Rather, the rememberer is active in the construction of a memory and in the reconstruction at retrieval. In some circles today, Sir Frederick Bartlett (who was ultimately knighted for his contributions to psychology) is ranked with Ebbinghaus as a pioneer in the field of memory.

Familiar and repetitive events, such as going to the movies or taking a trip, are represented in memory by schemas (or schemata, an alternative plural spelling) (Alba & Hasher, 1983). The use of a schema during retrieval of a specific event can lead to recall of what typically occurs (and is thus stored in the schema) rather than what actually occurred in a specific instance (e.g., Hudson, 1990; Linton, 1982). For example, you believe you bought popcorn on your last visit to the movies, when in fact you arrived late and so did not buy any snacks. Memory reconstructed according to the schema is not accurate in this instance.

Instead of an either–or position of memory reproduction versus memory reconstruction, we could treat these alternatives as end points on a continuum. Consider remembering a conversation you heard. Occasionally, the exact wording is later recalled: a particular phrase or the wording of a joke. More often, we retain the general meaning of the conversation and paraphrase when recounting it. Finally, when the conversation is reconstructed later, inferences or interpretations are added to the memory.

Applications

Strategies for Searching Memory

What strategies are used in everyday life to aid retrieval? Two frequently reported techniques are retracing one's steps (mentally or physically) to retrieve mislaid objects or forgotten intentions; and alphabetical searching when names or words cannot be recalled (Harris, 1978).

The search strategies that people use can be uncovered using a thinking-out-loud protocol. Participants are given general prompts and are asked to think out loud as they attempt to recollect a specific instance (Reiser, Black, & Kalamarides, 1986). The strategies employed tend to direct and narrow the scope of the search. To recall, as examples, a chance meeting with someone or the date of the first exam this semester, you might ask yourself questions like: Where was I? What was I doing when this happened? Who was with me? What preceded or followed the event? Why would I have been doing that? Temporal landmarks are used to cue relevant information: At that time, where did I live, or go to school, or work?

Some cues better than others. If you tried to recall last year's class schedule, what sorts of cues would be most effective in helping you? Wittman and Healy (1995) tested their college students' recall of course schedules: each course name, who the instructor was, where the course met, and at what time. Each of these details was used as a prompt for the remaining information. For example, "Last fall semester, you had a 9:30 class on Tuesday. What course was it, who taught it, and where did it meet?" The best prompt was the *where* cue: Given a map of the campus with an unlabeled building circled, students could reconstruct over 80 percent of the remaining items about that class. The other cues were only effective in recounting about 60 percent of the course information.

Another retrieval strategy is to change your perspective about the to-be-recalled material. After searching memory fruitlessly, we sometimes realize we were simply thinking of the lost item in the wrong manner. Changing perspective is illustrated in a study in which students read a paragraph-long description of a house. For some readers, the story was titled "Buying a House," and for others, the same story was titled "Burglary." Either version led to about the same number of recalled details. However, if the participants were asked to think about the story from the perspective of the alternate title, additional details were recalled on a second test (in comparison to a second test without a changed title) (Anderson & Pichert, 1978). The alternate perspective lead to some different retrieval cues that evoked otherwise unrecalled information.

Studies of brain-injured individuals show that controlled or strategic search of memory is associated with the frontal lobes of the brain. The recollective process can be thought of as an example of active problem solving, in which the participant selects plausible retrieval cues and evaluates the information each evokes. Frontal-lobe-injured individuals have trouble searching memory. Memories are haphazardly recalled, being accurately remembered on one occasion but not on another. There is difficulty generating specific personal memories from cues, such as recalling an event involving a DOG. The frontal-injured patients might not evaluate the plausibility of what they do remember. For instance, one patient recollected that he had two brothers named Martin (Baddeley & Wilson, 1986).

The notions of state-dependency and search strategies are also relevant to understanding the effect of alcohol on memory. This is discussed in Box 10.3.

Box 10.3   Alcohol and Memory

As noted in this chapter, alcohol intoxication can produce state-dependent learning effects. However, alcohol affects memory in other ways. These effects can be organized in terms of the stage model of memory: encoding, storage, and retrieval.

Alcohol can inhibit memory encoding. Participants, usually volunteer college students, learn less well when they are intoxicated than when they are sober. For example, recall of just-presented word lists was impaired in intoxicated participants (Weingartner, Adefris, Eich, & Murphy, 1976). By using an immediate test, the participants are still in the same drug state during input and output, so the forgetting was not a state-dependency effect.

This encoding deficit raises a question with respect to alcoholic amnesias for criminal actions. The notion of state dependency suggests that reentering the alcohol state could reinstate the forgotten memory. One attempt to do so did not lead to memory recall (Wolf, 1980). Thus, the memories may not have been encoded in the first place.

Alcohol seems to be less detrimental to retrieval than to encoding. Introducing intoxication after studying did not significantly reduce recall of previously studied word lists (e.g., Birnbaum, Parker, Hartley, & Noble, 1978). However, retrieval from semantic memory is impaired, as assessed by reaction-time measures. Alcohol slowed comparisons between words (e.g., are these two words from the same category: DOG–CAT).

Alcohol can impair the maintenance of stored memories, at least in extreme cases. Korsakoff's syndrome is a neurological degenerative disorder associated with prolonged (i.e., decades-long) alcohol abuse. A characteristic of Korsakoff's patients is that memories that were clearly present in storage earlier are later lost. In one case study, a distinguished scientist had completed his autobiography shortly before the onset of Korsakoff's. Test questions were constructed about his professional life (papers written, conferences attended, developments in his field) to quantify his memory loss. The scientist had profound loss of memories, going back decades, for what had once been known (Butters & Cermak, 1986).

Among non-Korsakoff's, there is impaired learning and remembering as a function of the amount of alcohol consumption: a dose-impairment continuum ranging from social drinkers to alcoholics. The cessation of drinking may lead to recovery of normal cognitive abilities within a few weeks, particularly for nonelderly individuals (Goldman, 1983). The cognitive loss in Korsakoff's, however, is not reversible.

The adverse effects of alcohol on memory seem to occur at several stages, making it difficult to isolate alcohol's effects to any one stage. One review of the literature suggests that alcohol has such a pervasive effect on information processing in general that a deficit at any stage of memory is bound to be found (Maylor & Rabbit, 1993).

Context-Specific Learning

The possibility that learning is context-specific has important implications for training programs. If people are trained in one context, will they remember when tested elsewhere? As a specific instance, Baddeley noted that scuba diving students are taught emergency procedures in the classroom that might well be unrecallable under water during an emergency (a change in both context and emotional arousal). Godden and Baddeley (1975) assessed this possibility by having diving students study word lists on land or under water. Memory testing then occurred in the same or the opposite location. Their results, summarized earlier in Table 10.1, showed context specific retrieval. More words were recalled when study and testing both occurred on the dock or under water. The implication is that training might be more profitably accomplished if done in the same location, or under the same conditions, as expected testing may occur.

How significant are context effects for classroom learning? Should you worry about forgetting everything you learned in this course when you leave the room? As we noted earlier, context effects are often subtle, and occur with minimally learned material. An extensive series of studies was carried out on 5,000 college students enrolled in five different kinds of courses. The students were told earlier in the semester that some would be taking their final exams in other rooms to relieve overcrowding and facilitate monitoring of finals. As it turned out, there were no significant effects of context change on final exam grades (Saufley, Otaka, & Bavaresco, 1985). Average grades of those students who took their finals in the course classroom did not differ from those who took their finals elsewhere.

Prospective Memory

Research on prospective memory, or remembering to do things in the future, suggests the importance of reminder cues (Harris, 1984). The cue needs to be active, like an alarm, and not passive, like a note in your pocket. Also, the cue needs to be timely, to remind you at the right time. A morning reminder about an afternoon meeting is not a timely signal for when to leave for the meeting. Finally, the cue needs to be specific. The proverbial "string tied around your finger" does not remind you what it is you need to remember.

Reconsolidation

Methods of fear desensitization have been considered in several places in this book. For example, exposure therapy and desensitization are used to reduce phobic fear. The research on reconsolidation suggests there may be ways to enhance such therapies. Recall that in the reconsolidation procedure, the subject is reminded about a previous learning experience. At this time, as the reactivated memory is about to be reconsolidated, a new outcome could be introduced that will become the new permanent memory.

For example, maybe fear could be reduced if extinction treatments are presented while a reactivated memory has instigated reconsolidation. Schiller et al. (2010) first conditioned human subjects to associate a colored square with shock. The next day, the subjects are given extinction training: The colored square is presented alone without the shock. We should remember that extinction is not all that effective in reducing fear. However, in this case the subjects were given a reminder of the previous conditioning just before extinction. The idea was to provoke the reconsolidation phase. In this case, what gets reconsolidated is the extinction experience, which was timed to occur just after the reminder. When extinction was given 10 minutes after the reminder, fear reduction was effective. Skin conductance measured a day later showed no reaction to the stimulus that once signaled shock. Extinction that began 6 hours after the reminder, when the reconsolidation period had passed, was not effective and was not different from an unreminded control group (Schiller et al., 2010).

Propranolol is a drug that suppresses the fear response. Kindt, Soeter, and Vervliet (2009) used the drug to facilitate extinction. They first conditioned a fear response in human participants. On a second day the subjects in the experimental group were reminded of the first day's fear learning and given propranolol, a fear blocker. When tested on a third day, the measures showed no fear reactions from the propranolol subjects. Propranolol with memory activation had weakened the fear response, and so what was reconsolidated overnight between Days 2 and 3 was a lesser level of fear.

Summary

Long-Term Memory

According to the permanent-memory hypothesis, everything we learn is permanently stored in the brain. Forgetting is due to the inability to retrieve some things. Often-cited support for this hypothesis comes from Penfield's use of electrical stimulation of the temporal lobes during surgery to elicit supposedly long-lost memories, and memories recovered through hypnosis or free association. However, these mental experiences are not necessarily memories, nor are they necessarily valid.

Although Ebbinghaus's curve of forgetting seems to suggest rapid loss, a number of studies of naturalistic memory show substantial retention after delays of years and even decades. These include memory for names and faces of high school classmates, high school and college courses, one-season TV shows, and public events.

The Nature of Storage

How are memories organized in long-term memory? Semantic network theories assume that items of knowledge are interconnected in memory. Collins and Quillian used reaction-time measures to verify the hierarchical arrangement of knowledge organization. Statements that related more distantly separated facts took longer to verify than comparisons involving more proximal facts.

Activation of one item in memory spreads to other connected items. An item in memory is identified more readily when it has been primed shortly before by a related item. This spreading activation is diluted if there are many connections from the activated item.

Case studies from neuropsychology illustrate the organization of memory, when whole categories of words (e.g., nouns or "living things") are lost following brain injury. The possible biological mechanisms of memory include protein changes, synaptic change, and long-term potentiation.

Forgetting is increasingly being construed as a failure of retrieval of memories that are potentially available, rather than attributing forgetting to either decay or interference.

Retrieval From Episodic Memory

Three general factors affect retrieval: the distinctiveness of the memory, the presence of effective retrieval cues, and prior practice at retrieving that memory. Distinctive memories are retrievable because they stand out against a background on otherwise similar memories.

Testing benefits memory more than does additional study. Hypermnesia is an increase in recall across successive tests in the absence of additional study and is the opposite of forgetting (or amnesia).

What makes a good retrieval cue? One theory identifies cues that are strongly associated to the target. Thus, TABLE would be a good cue for CHAIR. Alternatively, the encoding specificity principle states the best retrieval cues are those that were also present and encoded with the target. Recall is facilitated when encoding and retrieval conditions are matched, as shown by studies of context-specific (or place-specific) retention; drug-state-dependent learning; and mood-dependent memory. However, context-specific memory is not always found. Contextual cues are sometimes overshadowed by more explicit retrieval cues, and interaction of the context with the to-be-remembered items may be required.

Retrieval can be impaired by high levels of emotional arousal, as is the case with test anxiety and momentary forgetting.

Metamemory

Metamemory judgments include the feeling of knowing, the belief that we know something that cannot be recalled now; and the tip-of-the-tongue experience, an even more urgent feeling of knowing a word or name even though it cannot be recalled. The accuracy of our unrecalled knowledge can be verified by recognition tests. However, our intuitions are sometimes based on educated guesses about what we think we should know, and sometimes our intuitions are incorrect.

Prospective memory, or remembering to do something in the future, requires the establishment of retrieval cues that will prompt the desired behavior at the appropriate time. Prospective memory can be externally cued by reminders such as alarms or a list of instructions, or internally cued by intentions to remember.

False Retrieval

Mistakenly remembering something that did not actually occur is referred to as false recall or false memory. Deese, and Roediger and McDermott, elicited false recall of a target word, such as SLEEP, by presenting a list of associates of the target. Source memory refers to distinguishing between actually experienced events and those events that were imagined, thought of, heard about, or even dreamed of. External- and internal-originating memories are discriminated partly on the basis of memory attributes and partly on the basis of judgment. Similarly, one could forget the source of information, but correctly remember the information itself. False memories of childhood experience could be produced through combined failures of reality monitoring and source forgetting.

Witnesses can be led to misrecall an event after exposure to misleading postevent information. Although such effects readily occur, their interpretation is still uncertain. Does postevent information block access to the original memory? Or does postevent misinformation replace the original memory?

Finally, in some cases, memory retrieval is a reconstruction based on some fragments of memory and schematic knowledge.

Applications

Retrieval can be a directed process, in which we employ strategies to direct the scope of memory search. One search strategy is to change your perspective or way of thinking about the to-be-recalled material. Neuropsychological studies suggest the frontal lobes are critical for initiating, directing, and evaluating retrieval.

If people are trained in one context, will they remember when tested elsewhere? An experiment using scuba diving students showed context specificity of retrieval, suggesting that training should occur in the same location, or under the same conditions, in which testing will occur. However, studies on college students who took final exams in other rooms showed no significant effects of room change on exam grades.

11 Spatial, Motor-Skill, and Implicit Learning

Current psychological theories distinguish among different forms of long-term memory. One distinction is between declarative and procedural knowledge. **Declarative knowledge** refers to memory for verbalizable knowledge. It includes semantic memory and episodic memory. **Procedural knowledge** underlies skilled behavior and the ability to quickly perform various cognitive, perceptual, and motor operations. Whereas declarative knowledge is shown by recall of information, procedural knowledge is demonstrated by facilitated performance of behavior.

This chapter includes several forms of learning that correspond, in a general fashion, to the procedural description: spatial learning, or knowing how to get from place to place in an environment; motor-skill learning, knowing how to perform coordinated bodily movements quickly and accurately; implicit learning, knowing the underlying rules that govern complex sequences of behaviors; and expertise, or expert performance in a specific domain. All of these refer to fluent, quick, and skilled performance, whether running a maze or reading an MRI scan. To anticipate what follows in this chapter, consider the following questions: Is spatial information remembered in the form of a route or a map? What is the role of feedback in learning skilled movements? Is the knowledge underlying skilled behavior accessible to conscious description, or is it outside of awareness? Is the expertise due to talent or to practice?

Interest in procedural learning can be traced to the convergence of several influences. For instance, amnesic individuals can learn motor skills and strategies for problem solving, even though they have no recollection of having practiced the tests before. In people with normal memory, learning can be detected in habits, attitudes, or the ease with which behavior and cognition occurs, in the absence of explicit recollection of prior experience.

Procedural learning is often referred to as a form of implicit learning. Explicit and implicit refer to the awareness and conscious accessibility of the knowledge learned. In some cases of procedural learning, we can perform but we cannot articulate how we do it. Some theorists have suggested that procedural learning is indeed unconscious, because it evolved earlier than conscious forms of knowledge representation (Reber, 1993). One important question we will consider is whether procedural learning is implicit or whether there is instead some explicit knowledge that can indeed be reported.

Spatial Learning

Spatial ability in our everyday lives is often taken for granted until we become lost. On leaving a movie theater, you forget whether to turn left or right. You exit the mall at a different place from which you entered. You forget where you parked the car earlier. (On a really good day, you forget all three.) What sorts of experiences are necessary for acquiring spatial knowledge, and what exactly do we learn?

Rats, Mazes, and Psychology

The rat and the maze are two stereotypes that are inextricably linked to psychology's image. The use of rats as subjects began early in American psychology laboratories. Willard S. Small at Clark University first studied rats in mazes in 1900, capitalizing on the animals' burrowing and tunneling behavior. John Watson began research at the University of Chicago on the sensory cues used by rats in maze learning. At both schools biologists were studying rat anatomy and physiology, so it was natural for biologically oriented psychologists to start studying rat behavior.

Routes Versus Cognitive Maps

An organism moving within a complex environment needs to develop a representation of that environment. There are two broad conceptions of how spatial knowledge might be represented. **Route knowledge** is knowledge of a series of routes, directions, or paths through a spatial environment. For instance, we could describe maze learning as the memorization of a sequence of left and right turns in the maze. When you ask directions to an unfamiliar location, the response is likely to be in the form of a route: a sequence of distances and turns, with maybe an occasional landmark ("go straight 2 miles, turn left at the light, then the next right"). In its extreme, a route is characterized by knowledge of sequential locations but not of general interrelationships. By contrast, a **cognitive map** is a more abstract representation of an environment, placing specific routes in context with the surrounding area. The phrase *cognitive map* implies that a schematic image is represented internally (Cohen, 1989). Route maps might have a first person perspective, representing the view you saw as you traveled. Cognitive maps might have a third person perspective, as if you were viewing the area from above. Table 11.1 list some other contrasting descriptors of route maps and cognitive maps.

Route and cognitive maps should be considered as endpoints along a continuum rather than as separate categories of representation. In practice, a route has some elements of a map. Repeated experience navigating a specific environment can lead to the development of more map-like representations. Landmarks would be part of a route description, indicating locations along the route, or where to make a turn. Yet landmarks would also be part of a cognitive map, serving as boundaries, or as orienting stimuli from which to compute direction or location.

Given these two possibilities, route versus cognitive map, which form of representation does spatial knowledge take?

Table 11.1 Terms Used to Characterize Cognitive Map and Route Knowledge of Spatial Information

Cognitive Map	Route Knowledge
Paths in context	List of directions
Global	Local
Semantic	Episodic
Bird's eye	Ground-based
Schematic	Concrete
Third-person perspective	First-person perspective
Flexible	Habitual

Place Versus Response Studies

According to one tradition in psychology, rats learn to make specific turns in mazes. Hull (1949) theorized that the stimuli at each choice point in a maze became associated with a certain *response*, a left or right turn, for example. Tolman (1948) hypothesized instead that the rats acquired a cognitive map of the maze and the surrounding environment. The rat learned the *place* where food was located in the maze, and importantly also within the room. The two views can be illustrated by reference to learning in a simple T maze (see Figure 11.1, left). Rats start at point A and are trained to turn right at the choice point to get to the goal box (Y). What have the rats learned? Hull said they learned the response of turning right. Tolman said they learned a cognitive map of the maze, and the *place* where food was in the maze. Each theory describes what the animal learns to do. How can the two hypotheses be separated?

Tolman proposed an experimental test to distinguish learning of responses from cognitive maps (Tolman, Ritchie, & Kalish, 1946, 1947). He simply rotated the maze 180 degrees, so that now the rat would be starting from a new location in the room (point B in Figure 11.1, right). Which direction would the rats turn according to the two theories? Hull's theory predicts that the rats will make a right turn as they have been trained to do, and now go away from the food to point X in the diagram. Tolman's theory predicts the rats will check their cognitive map for the location of the maze within the room, make a left turn to compensate for the change in starting location, and arrive at point Y. The design of the place versus response experiment nicely contrasts route versus cognitive map descriptions of learning and the differing predictions of the two theories.

What did the rats actually do? Most students guess that the rats turned left (after all, rats are pretty smart). It would be nice to say the data turned out clearly in favor of one theory or another. In fact, in some experiments the rats turned right as Hull predicted; in other studies, they went left as Tolman predicted. Stating the results in this manner does not seem to be helpful (and also leaves you wondering what will be the correct answer on the exam).

This simple and elegant experimental manipulation did not, in fact, resolve the controversy. Instead, the results told us something about the stimuli used in spatial learning. For example, in the studies done by Hull and his followers, the maze arms had walls, and the maze itself was surrounded by curtains. There were no prominent cues for the rat to orient itself within the room. This lack of external cues (or "landmarks") encouraged response learning. In the experiments by Tolman and his students, the mazes were flat boards with no walls, and were elevated several feet off the floor. Distinctive features in the room were clearly visible from the maze. This procedure encouraged cognitive map learning. The place versus response controversy taught us that either specific responses or cognitive maps can be learned: Rats, and people, are flexible in their use of whatever cues are available (Restle, 1957).

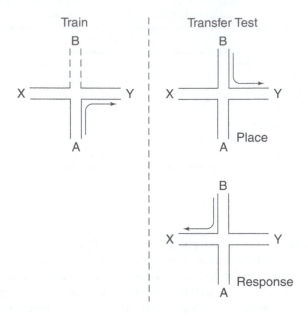

Figure 11.1 Maze Arrangements for Testing Place Versus Response Learning.

Source: From "Mazes, Maps, and Memory," by D. S. Olton, 1978, *American Psychologist, 34*, p. 590. Copyright © 1978 by the American Psychological Association. Reprinted with permission.

The Radial Maze

Cognitive mapping is demonstrated by performance in the *radial maze*. The prototype of this maze has eight arms radiating out from a central platform, as shown in Figure 11.2. The maze is usually elevated, often without walls. Food is placed in recessed food cups at the end of each arm. The rat is allowed to enter any and all arms. The optimal strategy for a foraging animal is to retrieve all the pieces of food without repeating an arm entry. Rats quickly learn this, achieving an accuracy level of entering 7.6 different maze arms among the first 8 choices after only 15 trials of practice (Olton & Samuelson, 1976).

During each trial the rat must keep track of which arms it has entered and which ones remain. The rat could do this with a cognitive map. But there are simpler alternative explanations. A rat could use odor stimuli, either from its own previous perambulations or from the smell of food, to determine which arms have been entered and which not. Scents can be ruled out by several manipulations, ranging from surgically making the rats anosmic to dousing the maze in Old Spice aftershave to mask any scents. Correct choices are relatively unaffected by such manipulations (Olton & Samuelson, 1976; Zoladek & Roberts, 1978).

Rats instead use cues outside of the maze, or *extramaze cues*, to keep track of entered and unentered maze arms. One means of demonstrating this is by rotating the maze within the room between maze-arm choices. The subject is allowed to make four arm entries and then is removed from the maze temporarily while the maze is rotated slightly. The animal is then returned to the maze and allowed to complete its selection of arms. The rat mistakenly reenters previously chosen arms that are in the direction not yet visited and will avoid an arm that is in the direction previously visited. The animal is responding to locations within the room and not to cues (such as smells) within the maze (Olton, Collison, & Werz, 1977). If these extramaze cues are blocked, for example, by surrounding the maze with curtains, the accuracy of choosing different maze arms declines.

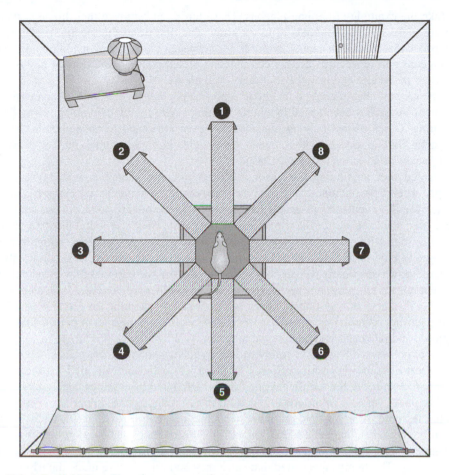

Figure 11.2 **A Radial Maze.** Note the presence of extramaze cues.

Source: Adapted from "Spatial Memory," by D. S. Olton, 1977, *Scientific American, 236.*

If external cues are not available, rats can use internal, kinesthetic cues to help navigate the maze. Even in total darkness, the rats can learn to choose at better than chance levels (Brown & Moore, 1997). There are multiple types of cues available to navigate spatially. This is especially the case in long-distance navigation (see Box 11.1).

Box 11.1   Long-Distance Travel by Animals

A small dog named Sam was left behind in Colorado when his family moved to California. The dog showed up at their new home 10 weeks later, after apparently having traveled 840 miles across plains, deserts, and mountains of four states ("Dog Roams," 1983). The dog, tired and dirty from his trek, was also described as being nervous and suspicious. "He follows us everywhere," his owners say. (Hey, no kidding!) How does a dog find its way from Colorado to California?

Many feats of animal migration require extraordinary spatial abilities. Studies of animal way-finding indicate that there are several components to spatial ability: some means of determining direction, sensitivity to different kinds of stimuli, and possibly a cognitive map.

Take the example of homing pigeons. These birds can return to their home nests after having been released hundreds of miles away. The first thing the pigeon needs to do is determine direction. You cannot fly north, for instance, without knowing which way north is. Pigeons and other birds use the combination of sun position and time of day (i.e., the sun rises in the east and is in the southern sky at noon).

Pigeons may also possess a magnetic sense, as if possessing a built-in compass. This magnetic sense has been tested in natural homing situations by using magnets to disrupt orienting. Cases of lost homing pigeons have been attributed to anomalies in the local magnetic fields associated with mountains, iron fields, sun spots, and so on, that disrupt the birds' sense of direction (Walcott, 1989).

Granted direction finding, the pigeons also need to know where home is. Maybe pigeons simply observe the outbound route, and can then retrace it when released. However, pigeons home even if prevented from seeing the route taken to the release point. (In one study, they were even anesthetized for the trip to the release point. They still found their way home!) Pigeons fitted with opaque eye cups, which allowed in light but not clear vision, were able to home to the general vicinity of their roost. Once there, the birds circled aimlessly and fluttered down anywhere. Apparently, visual landmarks are important for proximal homing, but not for long-distance travel. (Homing mechanisms are reviewed in Pearce, 1997).

Other instances of way-finding have been attributed to an ability to perceive and follow subtle sensory stimuli. For example, a "nuisance" wolf living near an airport in Alaska was captured and relocated several hundred miles away. When the wolf returned to the airport, it was hypothesized that it had followed low-frequency sounds from planes, which carry over great distances in Arctic regions. The proof was a second relocated wolf that found its way to an airport, but a different one from which it had been relocated (Rogers, 1989).

The place- versus response-learning controversy taught us an important lesson about spatial learning. Animals (and presumably people, too) can learn to use different kinds of stimuli: landmarks, magnetic sense, sun and star positions, olfactory stimuli, and so on.

Okay, so how did Sam find his family? I really don't think the dog could smell them 800 miles away. The family speculated that since they had once before made the trip with the dog, Sam "remembered" the route and retraced it. This is a little far-fetched. I think the Colorado people who took in Sam got tired of him, drove overnight to California, and left the dog on his owner's porch. That's my theory.

Morris Water Maze

Another widely-used test of spatial navigation is the Morris water maze (Morris, 1981). A rat or mouse is placed in a small swimming pool in which the water is clouded by the addition of powdered milk. (Rats are very good swimmers.) There is a hidden platform just under the surface of the water, and the goal is to learn the location of this platform. From trial to trial, the starting location in the pool is varied, so the animal learns the platform location on the basis of cues in the room. On the first trials, the animals spend considerable time searching for the platform. Over trials, the animals become faster and follow more direct paths in going to the platform.

Virtual water mazes have been developed in which human subjects "move" through a computer-presented maze. A Morris maze simulation has distinctive cues, such as patterned and colored walls, outside the maze to provide orientation information. The mazes have a progressively changing image, as if one were "swimming" (well, maybe wading) through the pool. The time to find the hidden platform, and the directness of the route from different starting points, can be recorded just as with mice and rats. In these virtual mazes, men typically perform better than women, although the males are usually more experienced with computer games (Astur, Ortiz, & Sutherland, 1998). In one case, college students were tested in a series of progressively more difficult virtual mazes, and were compared to mice trained in actual mazes. Not surprisingly, the humans learned faster than did the mice. But males of both species performed better than did females (Shore, Stanford, MacInnes, Klein, & Brown, 2001).

Maze Learning and the Brain

The radial maze and the water maze are particularly useful for testing theories about the anatomical basis of spatial memory. The radial-maze task differs from the mazes used earlier by psychologists, in which both food locations and the route through the mazes remained fixed over trials. The flexible use of working memory in the radial maze has been contrasted with habit learning by training animals with different rules in the radial maze. McDonald and White (1993) produced a double dissociation among tasks and brain areas. Rats who received hippocampal lesions were impaired in learning the regular radial-maze task, which requires choosing all different arms in a trial. Rats with hippocampal lesions reenter already visited arms. A second task was a form of association learning, in which the rats were taught that only lighted maze arms contained food. (The lighted arm varied from trial to trial.) Lesions of the amygdala impaired learning of this stimulus–reinforcer association. In each case, the alternative lesion did not inhibit learning or performance. The pattern between lesions and impairments is summarized in Table 11.2.

As you may recall from Chapter 7, damage to the hippocampus produces amnesia (Squire, 1992). In humans the left hemisphere exerts more control over verbal memory, whereas the right hemisphere exerts more influence over spatial memory. People with right hippocampus injury are more impaired on spatial learning and memory. This includes tests of maze learning, remembering the location of objects, and learning to tap a series of blocks in sequence (Kolb & Whishaw, 1985). Patients with left hippocampus damage had less difficulty on these tasks (Kesner, Hopkins, & Chiba, 1992).

The role of the hippocampus is clearly shown by H. M., the amnesic individual profiled in Chapter 7. To refresh your memory, H. M. had most of the hippocampus on both sides of his brain removed in an experimental treatment for his epilepsy. H. M. was severely impaired on spatial tasks, as shown in the following passage reported by the researchers working with him:

> His limitations . . . are illustrated by the manner in which he attempted to guide us to his house, in June, 1966, when we were driving him back from Boston. After leaving the main highway, we asked him for help in locating his house. He promptly and courteously indicated to us several turns, until we arrived at a street which he said was quite familiar to him. At the same time, he admitted that we were not at the right address. A phone call to his mother revealed that we were on the street where he used to live before his operation.
>
> (Milner, Corkin, & Teuber, 1968, as cited in Kolb & Whishaw, 1985, p. 482)

This was 8 years after he had moved away from that address.

Table 11.2 Dissociation of Two Learning Tasks Conducted in a Radial Maze After Lesions of Different Brain Regions

Maze Tasks	Choose Different Arms	Choose Lighted Arm
Impairing lesion	Hippocampus	Amygdala
Unaffecting lesion	Amygdala	Hippocampus

Source: McDonald and White (1993).

One widely cited study shows vividly the importance of the hippocampus for spatial naviga-tion. London taxi drivers were found to have more development and greater volume in their hip-pocampi (the plural of hippocampus) than did matched control subjects (Maguire et al., 2000). This study used magnetic resonance imaging to obtain graphic images of the brain for compari-son purposes. The researchers believe that the extensive use of spatial navigation skills led to the increased development in the hippocampus. (The alternative possibility is that those who become taxi drivers had better spatial skills and larger hippocampi to begin with. If you cannot find your way around, you likely won't last long as a cabbie.)

Landmarks

There are distinctive elements in an environment that by virtue of their features (e.g., size or shape) or their meaning (e.g., historical or social) stand out from other elements. Because such elements are literally outstanding, these *landmarks* will be readily perceived, remembered, and used as reference points. When we give someone directions, or when asked where we live, we often start with some nearby landmark and describe a route from there. The cues used by rats in place learning or the radial maze, such as a door, window, or light fixture, can be consid-ered landmarks. According to some theories of spatial knowledge, we first learn landmarks, then routes around them, and finally we develop cognitive maps. Although spatial memory declines with aging, elderly participants can still recognize landmarks after traveling through an unfamil-iar hospital building, even if they cannot reconstruct the route. College-aged participants could remember both routes and landmarks (Wilkins, Jones, Koral, Gold, & Manning, 1997).

Schemas in Spatial Memory

Schemas are ways of abstracting, organizing, and storing general knowledge (see Chapter 9). Spatial knowledge can be organized hierarchically. We may know the basic geography of the United States, and subsumed under that is the local geography of our home states, then towns, and below that the layout of our homes and workplaces. Some of this knowledge was learned through direct experience with places; some knowledge was learned indirectly through study; and some knowledge is inferential: We guess this must be so.

Schemas have two prominent effects on spatial memory: They facilitate organization and they can distort recall.

Distortion in Cognitive Maps

Spatial schemas distort recall due to the averaging, normalizing, or rounding off that occurs when a generalized map is acquired. For example, we tend to encode all turns as being 90 degrees, or right angles. Byrne (1979) asked people to draw some familiar road intersections. The intersec-tions actually deviated from right angles by at least 20 degrees, yet the angles drawn averaged close to 90 degrees. This means that if a series of left turns are consistently greater than 90 degrees, going "around the block" will not return us to our starting point as we might predict from a schematic memory.

Distortion in spatial schemas is also seen in comparisons involving geographic locations. For example, which U.S. city is farther to the west, San Diego or Reno? We assume the correct answer is San Diego because California is farther west than Nevada. Which city named Portland is far-ther north, the Portland in Maine or the one in Oregon? Since Maine is the northernmost state on the east coast, then its Portland must also be farther north. In fact, Reno and Oregon's Portland are the correct answers. Our wrong guesses derive from the schematic spatial knowledge. The locations of the states are used to infer the relative locations of cities (Stevens & Coupe, 1978).

Spatial schemas seem to have a preferred perspective. Much like a physical map, the picture-like image of a spatial environment has a top, or a "specific orientation" (Sholl, 1987). Aligning the image with the environment facilitates using the cognitive map as a guide. (Have you ever consulted a map and found yourself turning either the map, or yourself, to line up with nearby landmarks?) Judgments are easier and more accurate if forward in the environment corresponds to upward in the cognitive map (just as it is with a physical map). For example, we could ask college students to point in the direction of various unseen campus locations. The students could more quickly identify locations in front of them than locations behind them. When the students were asked to turn around, locations now in front were more quickly identified than were locations behind (Sholl, 1987).

Organization in Spatial Memory

The recall of verbal material is often marked by organization. Spatial memory also shows organization during output. Menzel (1973) showed that chimps will organize their food searching route to be more efficient and direct. Juvenile chimps were used as participants in a study. As one researcher carried the chimp around a 1-acre enclosed field, the second researcher would show the placement of pieces of banana or lettuce. The experimenters criss-crossed the field distributing 18 pieces of food in a random fashion. (This probably mimics your class schedule: one class here, the next one is across campus, and so on.) When later released to retrieve the food, the chimps did not retrieve the food in the same sequence in which the pieces had been hidden. Instead, the chimps employed a principle of least distance in going from one piece to the next nearest piece (Menzel, 1973). (Incidentally, the animals remembered an average of 12.5 pieces per trial. Control animals that had not seen the placements but were simply allowed to search averaged less than one piece.) Locations were further organized by type of food. The chimps first retrieved the fruit pieces, and then went back for the vegetables. They would even pass by a vegetable on the way to the next piece of fruit!

The Development of Spatial Memory in Children

The distinction between learning routes and maps has been demonstrated in the development of spatial knowledge in children. Cornell and Heth (1979) arranged a learning task analogous to the place-versus-response procedure of Tolman and Hull. Infants ranging in age from 4 to 12 months old were seated in their mothers' laps. Small projection screens were placed on either side. Random shapes were projected to one side every 10 seconds and a constant checkerboard pattern appeared simultaneously on the opposite side. Infants orient to novel stimuli and look less at repetitive stimuli (Chapter 2), and so the infants learned to turn and look in the direction of the changing patterns. To test whether the infants had learned turn responses or a cognitive map, the mothers turned their chairs around to face in the opposite direction. Just as the starting location was rotated 180 degrees in Tolman's studies, the orientation with respect to the novel images was rotated. On these test trials, the youngest infants continued to turn in the same direction as before, which indicates response learning. The oldest infants correctly compensated for change of orientation within the room and now turned in the opposite direction.

Children have been tested in a human-sized radial-arm maze constructed outdoors (Overman, Pate, Moore, & Peuster, 1996). The eight arms were about 8 feet long and were enclosed by plastic mesh walls. Optimal performance in the radial maze requires entry into each arm without repetition. Children as young as 20 months were somewhat able to do this, with 40 to 50 percent accuracy in selecting different arms over the first eight choices. By 5 years of age, the children were as good as the adults, who achieved 97 percent accuracy. In parallel to the rat experiments, the provision of distinctive cues for each arm improved performance, and a delay interval between choices led to forgetting of the previously visited arms.

Motor-Skill Learning

Spatial knowledge is one component of performance in a spatial task. There is also the contribution of skilled movements. A well-trained rat, running through a maze at 4 feet per second, "generally look(s) like a piece of well-oiled machinery, moving smoothly through the maze with no hesitation or jerkiness, rounding off all corners, banking off the centrifugal walls, and generally moving at full tilt throughout" (Olton, 1979, p. 584). Maze times decrease over trials because the animal learns the way, and because it also knows how to run the maze efficiently. To cite a human example, downhill skiers know the path and have learned precise movements to traverse the route efficiently.

Motor-skills learning can be defined as the acquisition of precisely adjusted movements in which the amount, direction, and duration of responding corresponds to variations in the regulating stimuli (Adams, 1987). The skill of playing tennis, for example, involves precise and accurate movements in response to momentary changes in stimulus conditions, often in anticipation of stimulus changes. A motor skill has perceptual, cognitive, and motor components, the relative contributions of which vary from skill to skill. For instance, eye-to-hand coordination is required in typing, but the cognitive component is important in reading in advance of what is currently being typed (Inhoff & Gordon, 1997).

The combination of perceptual with motor skills is central in tasks such as the pursuit rotor and mirror drawing (see Figure 11.3). The goal of the pursuit rotor is to keep a stylus on a fixed

Figure 11.3 Pursuit Rotor and Mirror-Tracing Apparatus.

Source: Courtesy of Lafayette Instrument Company, Lafayette, Indiana.

point on a rotating disk (the latter being like a phonograph turntable). The speed can be increased over trials to increase difficulty, and time on target is measured. In mirror drawing, the subject attempts to follow the outline of an object, say, a star, with a pencil or stylus, but visual guidance is through a mirror. Eye–hand coordination must compensate for the difference in actual direction of hand movements from their perceived direction. The time taken to outline an object or the number of deviations from the outline can be taken as a measure of accuracy. Each of these tasks requires eye–hand coordination, or perceptual (and) motor skill.

Is motor-skill learning procedural knowledge or is it declarative knowledge? Motor habits are sometimes implicit: We know how to do something, but we cannot describe what we know. Try to verbally relay the steps involved in programming your cell phone or performing a computer routine. Even manipulations intended to increase conscious control in mirror drawing, such as studying written instructions or having the experimenter verbally guide your drawing, do not improve tracking performance (Borresen & Klingsporn, 1992). On the other hand, motor learning does possess aspects of declarative learning. Conscious intention to learn, verbal self-guidance, and knowledge of the goal are indicative of declarative knowledge.

The separation of motor-skill learning and declarative learning is demonstrated by comparing people with various neurological disorders. For example, mirror tracing occurs at a normal rate among Alzheimer's dementia individuals, even though they are grossly impaired in declarative memory tasks such as the recall of word lists (Gabrieli, Corkin, Mickel, & Growdon, 1993). An opposite pattern can be seen in some individuals with movement diseases of the basal ganglia, such as Huntington's or Parkinson's diseases. These subjects are impaired at pursuit rotor learning but not (always) in recall of word-lists (Harrington, Haaland, Yeo, & Marder, 1990; Heindel, Butters, & Salmon, 1988).

Although the emphasis in this portion of the chapter is on the motor skill, these tasks also have a memory component that improves with training. Fendrich, Healy, and Bourne (1991) had participants enter random-number strings into one of two keyboards that had different placements of the numbers 1–9. On one touch pad the numbers ran from 1 to 9, top to bottom; on a different keyboard the numbers ran from 9 to 1. Learning was tested 1 week later by having the participants copy old versus new number strings, using the same or different keypads. Old number strings were typed faster than new strings, indicating memory for the old sequences. Typing old strings on the original keyboard was faster still, indicating memory for the motor movements originally used.

Decades of research on motor-skill learning has emphasized two important controlling factors: practice and feedback.

Practice

Amount of Practice

Motor skills improve with repetition. The relationship between practice and one measure of skilled behavior, the speed of performance, is well described by the *power curve*. The idea of the power curve is much like that of the learning curve, a concept we have seen before (Chapter 1). Basically, responses become faster with additional practice, but not in a one-to-one fashion with the number of practice trials. Rather, the idea behind a power function is that ever greater amounts of practice are required to produce comparable increments in performance. That is, whereas the first 10 trials might produce a certain increment in speed, the next increment of that size may require 100 additional trials. Thus, the first point on the learning curve represents x number of practice trials, the next point is x^2 number of trials, and then x^3 number of trials. Plotting speed over the log number of trials produces a nice, straight-line increase in speed over trials.

This is essentially what we said about learning curves at the beginning of this book. Increments may be rapid at the start of training, but performance improves much more slowly as proficiency increases. You may have noticed something like this in learning a video game or a new sport. At some point, improvements in playing seem to have diminished. Frustration or discouragement may prevent the additional (and extensive) practice needed to further improve performance.

Schedules of Practice

A general principle of learning is that spaced repetitions lead to faster learning than do massed repetitions. The spaced-practice advantage also applies to motor-skill learning. For example, mirror star tracing accuracy improves more quickly with one trial per day than with 10 trials—that is, if one counts trials, not days (Hovland, 1951).

Bourne and Archer (1956) compared different spacings between practice trials in the pursuit rotor task. Each trial lasted 30 seconds. Different conditions had different intervals of down time between practice trials. As shown in Figure 11.4, there was greater improvement when there were longer intervals between trials (30 or 60 seconds) than when the trials were massed one-after-another (0 second interval).

Baddeley and Longman (1978) studied the spacing of practice sessions on learning to type. The participants, British postal workers, were divided into four groups who received either one or two training sessions per day, with each session being 1 or 2 hours in length. The most dramatic results come from the two extreme conditions, one group that practiced one hour a day, and another group that received two, 2-hour sessions each day (see Table 11.3). After 60 hours of practice, members of the group that received the most distributed practice, a single 1-hour session per day, were the best typists. The group that had the most concentrated training conditions, two 2-hour sessions daily, had the poorest performance.

Specifically, Baddeley and Longman (1978) found that the 1-hour daily group required fewer hours to learn the keyboard than did the 4-hour daily group. The 1-hour group was typing faster

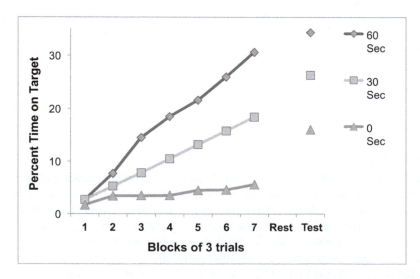

Figure 11.4 **Effect of trial spacing on pursuit rotor time-on-target.** Trials were separated by 0, 30, or 60 seconds. After 21 trials, a 5-minute rest interval was given, and then three test trials were given.

Source: Adapted from "Time continuously on target as a function of distribution of practice," by L. E. Bourne and E. J. Archer, 1956, *Journal of Experimental Psychology, 51*, p. 27. Copyright American Psychological Association. Reprinted with permission.

Table 11.3 Learning to type as a function of the distribution of practice

Groups	1 x 1	1 x 2	2 x 1	2 x 2
	1 hr/day	1 hr/2x day	2 hr/1x day	2 hr/2x day
Hours to learn	35	42	43	50
Letters/min	79	73	71	65
Errors	1.1	1.1	1.4	2.0

Groups received one-hour or two-hour practice sessions; and one or two sessions each day.

Source: From "The Influence of Length and Frequency of Training Sessions on the Rate of Learning to Type," by A. D. Baddeley and D. J. A. Longman, 1978, *Ergonomics, 21*, p. 630. Copyright © 1978 by Taylor & Francis, Inc. Reprinted with permission.

by the end of training. And the 1-hour group made half as many errors as the 4-hour group. (The latter group was given twenty additional hours of training to catch up.) The advantage for spacing persisted on tests given 1, 3, and 9 months later.

Although spaced training produced better performance, training extended over many more days than it did in the massed conditions. The 1 × 1 group, training 5 days a week, took 12 weeks to complete the standard 60 hours of training, whereas the 2 × 2 group finished in 3 weeks. (I'll let you check the math.) The postal workers were surveyed for their reactions to the training regimen. Surprisingly, the spaced groups were less satisfied and said they would not choose to train under those conditions. The extended number of training days did not appeal to them. As Baddeley and Longman note, if left to the participants, people would choose to train under the conditions that produced the slowest learning and the poorest retention.

Another means of spacing trials is to intermix training of different skills within a session. Given several skills to learn, one could block trials on one skill at a time (massed practice on each) or alternate trials among the skills (spaced trials). Goettl, Yadrick, Connolly-Gomez, and Regian (1996) compared a schedule of massed practice versus alternating blocks of practice on the acquisition of three very different tasks: "Space Fortress," an attention-demanding, spatial- and motor-skills video game; "Phoenix," a flight-simulator video game but using the keyboard instead of a joystick; and algebra problems, a cognitively demanding task that is not quite as much fun as the other two. Participants either practiced one task in a single day, or alternated tasks within each day. Both schedules provided the same total amount of practice on each task over the several days of the experiment. The alternating schedule enhanced performance on two of the tasks, Space Fortress and algebra, and was no worse on the flight simulator. This is an especially nice demonstration, because the results have implications for organizational training. Organizations usually want to schedule training sessions over a day or two, especially if the employees need to be brought in from the field. Companies cannot afford to conduct training across days spaced weeks apart. The alternating module schedule might offer the benefits of distributed practice but in the same 2 or 3 days a company might otherwise devote to massed practice.

Massed presentation of practice trials can actually inhibit performance. Massing a large number of trials can lead to fatigue, loss of motivation, or attentional lapses that lower performance. Spaced trials allow time for recovery from the "work decrement," as it was called by Hovland (1951). This is our learning-versus-performance distinction again. Performance after a series of massed trials sometimes improves immediately if the next trial is delayed, presumably allowing opportunity for fatigue or other inhibiting factors to dissipate (Kientzle, 1949).

The Bourne and Archer (1956) data shown earlier in Figure 11.4 shows the effects of allowing some recovery from work decrement. At the end of training, all subjects received a 5-minute rest interval, and then additional practice trials commenced. As can be seen in the figure, each condition showed an *increase* in performance after the rest interval. The massed practice subjects had the greatest increase. Their performance during the previous practice trials did not indicate how much they had actually learned. This group would have had the most fatigue, work decrement, or inhibition and so would have benefitted the most from a rest interval.

Practice-Independent Learning

Earlier research found that skill learning improved if the learning session was followed by a period of uninterrupted sleep (see Sleep Learning, Chapter 9). New research indicates that there are indeed two contributors to motor-skill learning. The first is *practice-dependent learning*, which is the improvement in skill that comes with (duh?) practice. In addition, there is the improvement in skill that comes with sleep after training, which is *practice-independent learning*. This is a relatively permanent change in behavioral repertoire (per the definition of *learning* from Chapter 1), but it occurs without additional practice.

For example, one study looked at the speed of typing a sequence of numbers repetitively (e.g., 4-1-3-2-4). Students could type this sequence about 22 times in 30 seconds after a single training session. Retesting after 12 hours of wakefulness only raised the score to about 24 times in 30 seconds. A more dramatic effect was observed in testing 12 hours later, during which time sleep had occurred, when performance increased to about 27 times in 30 seconds. The time spent sleeping was more effective than the time spent awake in improving performance. In another experiment, sleep was found to be as effective as a second training session (Walker et al., 2003). Practice? Or sleep? There's a difficult choice.

The idea is that sleep—or specifically, certain phases of sleep—is important for the long-term consolidation of recently acquired skills and habits. This is the practice-independent component of learning.

Knowledge of Results

Repeated practice will be of little benefit unless you know how well you are performing. Thorndike (1931) conducted a study in which students attempted to draw 4-inch lines. Actually, they drew 3,000 lines over 12 sessions. The student-participants were not given any feedback about how well they were doing, and having their eyes closed, the students could not see the lines they drew. At the end, they were no more accurate at drawing 4-inch lines than when they began.

Knowledge of results (KR) is feedback concerning the success or accuracy of a response that is given to the participant after study or practice. This information serves as a basis for corrections on the next trial. Following in the Thorndike tradition, learning theorists long considered KR to be analogous to reinforcement in instrumental learning, and therefore was manipulated in ways that paralleled reinforcement variations. For example, one could vary (1) the frequency with which feedback was given, in parallel to continuous versus partial reinforcement schedules; or (2) the immediacy of feedback, in parallel to delay of reinforcement. The commonsense expectation is that more frequent and more immediate knowledge of results should enhance learning. Practice trials without KR are either neutral or detrimental to learning.

Imagine learning to hit a golf ball. Without feedback after each stroke, how can you know whether you hit the ball well or not? If feedback is delayed, will you remember the exact movements you made that led to a good or poor shot? A long history of research clearly indicates that frequent, immediate, and detailed feedback leads to faster learning of motor responses (see Adams, 1987).

However, some researchers have questioned the benefits of using too much feedback during training (e.g., Schmidt & Bjork, 1992). Granted that immediate and consistent feedback leads to superior performance (e.g., greater speed or accuracy) of a skill that is trained during a single session in the laboratory. However, will this skill still be better remembered if testing is delayed? Do these variables lead to better transfer when the skills demanded are altered slightly? Many studies indicate a "no" answer to both of these questions. We can cite examples involving both the frequency of feedback and the delay of feedback.

In one study, the participants learned a tracking response, basically using one finger to follow a curve projected on a screen that changes in speed and direction. Feedback was given after each trial or in summary form after every fifth or fifteenth trial. The group that received the most consistent feedback made smaller errors throughout the acquisition phase of the experiment. However, after only a 10-minute delay interval before retesting, the difference disappeared; all three frequencies of feedback conditions were then equivalent. Even more interesting was the fact that on a test given 2 days later, the leanest feedback schedule (that given every fifteenth trial) had the best performance (Schmidt, Young, Swinnen, & Shapiro, 1989). Although consistent feedback produced better performance during initial acquisition of the skill, a partial feedback schedule led to better performance on delayed retention tests of the skill.

Why would less frequent KR lead to performance as good as or better than more frequent KR? One explanation is the *self-guidance hypothesis*. Feedback has beneficial effects in that it guides the learner toward the correct movements. But consistent feedback may block the participants' learning to detect their own errors. As the participants become dependent on external KR, they are less likely to attend to their own bodily kinesthetic feedback, and do not learn to recognize good and poor performance. Skilled athletes know immediately whether a movement (e.g., a pitch or a hit in softball) was good or not, before seeing the actual outcome. Thus, frequent KR has both positive and negative effects. Optimal performance requires a balance between the two.

Is there a way to combine the beneficial effect of consistent KR on initial learning with the beneficial effect of partial KR on delayed retention? Wulf and Schmidt (1989) did so by initially providing feedback on each trial and then fading (or gradually reducing) feedback to a 50 percent schedule. In this case, acquisition was as rapid as it was for a continuous-feedback group, and the 50 percent KR group performed better on tests of novel versions of the required movements.

Delayed KR

In studies similar to those varying frequency of feedback, knowledge of results is given immediately or is delayed. There is good reason to expect that immediate feedback would benefit learning. However, just as with the partial schedules of feedback, delaying feedback allows the participants to develop their own error-detection capabilities. In comparison to participants given immediate feedback, participants for whom feedback was delayed for 3 seconds after each movement learned just as well during an initial training session. The delayed-feedback group actually did better on the second day, and this superiority persisted on a test given 2 days after that (Swinnen, Schmidt, Nicholson, & Shapiro, 1990).

What is happening during the delay-until-feedback interval? During the delay interval, participants may be "rehearsing" the response they just made (although this rehearsal need not be verbal) and making a judgment about how accurate their response was. If this delay interval is filled by some distractor activity, then learning with delayed feedback is impaired (Swinnen, 1990).

Metacognition in Motor Skills

In addition to objective measures of the speed or accuracy of motor skills, we can also question participants about how well they think they are performing. Actual skill and perceived skill may be different things (much like your friend's dancing skill). *Metacognition* deals with beliefs and self-knowledge about what we have learned. Simon and Bjork (2001) had their subjects practice a keypad skill: typing out three numbers in a specific sequence and timing pattern (e.g., 2–7–5, or 4–6–9). Subjects who practiced one pattern at a time (massed trials on one pattern, then the second pattern, then the third), performed better than subjects who practiced the three patterns intermixed. So far, this is an objective measure of performance. The participants were brought back to be tested the next day. Given what you have read so far in this chapter, you know how delayed testing will turn out: The intermixed practice condition will do better than the massed practice condition. However, before being tested, the students were asked how well they thought they would do on the keypad patterns. The massed practice subjects judged they would do better; their superior performance during massed trials the day before misled them into thinking they really did know the skill better than they did. Instead, they actually did far worse: They were badly off in reproducing the timing between keypunches in the sequences. The lesson might be that if it seems too easy, maybe it is.

Some Concluding Comments on Learning Motor Skills

The effects of some variables on motor-skills learning are the same as in other learning situations. Thus, spaced practice can be better than massed practice, just as it is in learning paired associates. More will be said about skill learning in two other contexts: the relationship of motor learning to implicit learning and the development of expertise with extended practice.

Implicit Learning

Another form of "learning how to" is implicit learning. **Implicit learning** is knowledge of cognitive, motor, or perceptual skills that develops with training, independent of conscious awareness of specific details of the tasks. Implicit learning is exemplified in learning our first language. We learn the rules of word order, word endings, pronunciation, and stress patterns, even though we cannot articulate the rules. Similarly, in laboratory simulations of implicit learning, participants are exposed to cognitive tasks governed by abstract sets of rules. Skilled performance develops as a function of practice, and in such a way that the knowledge is difficult to express verbally. Learning is therefore said to be implicit.

Some Implicit-Learning Tasks

Many implicit-learning tasks are rule-based tasks. One well-studied example is that of learning an artificial grammar. Human languages are guided by a set of rules, or the grammar. For example, the usual word order in English is subject–verb–object (e.g., dog bites man). We readily reject ungrammatical strings of words (dog man bites). Reber (1967) devised an artificial grammar involving a set of letters instead of words, such as P, S, T, V, and X. The grammar determines which letters can follow which other letters. Allowable sequences are shown in Figure 11.5. For instance, the first letter would be T or P and the last letter would be S or V. The arrows show the permissible transitions from letter to letter; recursive loops allow letters to be repeated. TSXS is a grammatical string; PSXS is not.

Participants first memorize short sets of letter strings. The strings derive from the grammar, although the participants are typically not told there is an underlying set of rules. For instance, a set of three strings of letters is presented, and recall tested, until the participants can repeat them back. Then another set of letter strings would be learned. If the rules that govern grammatical string formation are learned over trials, learning should become easier with practice. Indeed, participants who memorized grammatical strings made fewer errors than did participants who studied letter strings that did not correspond to the grammar.

A direct means of determining whether the grammatical rules have been learned is to ask the participants to classify novel strings of letters as being grammatical or not. Participants who

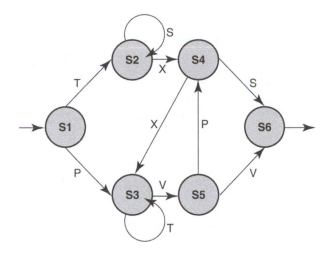

Figure 11.5 **Artificial Grammar.** Each "state" (S) represents a random choice: a certain proportion of the time the transition is in one direction (from S1 to S2, producing the letter T) or the other (from S1 to S3, producing the letter P).

Source: Adapted from "Implicit Learning and Tacit Knowledge" by A. S. Reber, (1989), *Journal of Experimental Psychology: General, 118,* p. 220. Copyright by the American Psychological Association. Reprinted with permission.

studied grammatical letter strings were about 60 to 65 percent accurate in classification, significantly better than a chance level of 50 percent.

The grammar learning is said to be implicit because it occurs incidentally, not deliberately. The regularities of the letter strings are abstracted across memorized sets. Deliberate intention to discover and learn those rules can actually impede learning. Informing the participants that there are rules leads to more errors during set memorization and more mistakes in later classifying grammatical and ungrammatical strings (Reber, 1976).

Another example of an implicit-learning task is the serial-reaction-time procedure. A sequence of items is presented and the participant's task is to respond to each as it occurs. For instance, a light appears at one of four locations on a video screen and the participant pushes a corresponding key for each location. The sequence is seemingly random, although in fact it actually repeats. Sequence learning is indicated by reaction times that become faster over practice trials. The results from a representative study are shown in Figure 11.6 (Nissen & Bullemer, 1987), in which the sequence is repeated after every 10 lights. Key-pressing reactions become faster across 80 trials, even for those participants who said they were unaware that the sequence repeated. Are people faster because they have learned something about the sequence, or have they just become practiced at more general aspects of the task? A control condition received the lights in a random sequence, and their speed of reaction improved little over trials.

Some implicit tasks produce learning only for the specific items studied, whereas other tasks teach a more general skill. Both specific and general learning effects are found in learning to read transformed text. The letters in words are mirror-reversed (left-right) or inverted (rotated upside down). Moscovitch, Winocur, and McLachlan (1986) recorded the time to read word triplets composed of inverted letters. One group of their subjects were older, community-dwelling, but memory-impaired individuals. Another group of subjects were age-matched controls. Both groups became faster at reading transformed words with practice. This shows learning of the general skill. What is interesting is that this skill was retained when the subjects were tested 2 hours and 2 weeks later. As can be seen in Figure 11.7, reading times continued to decrease from the

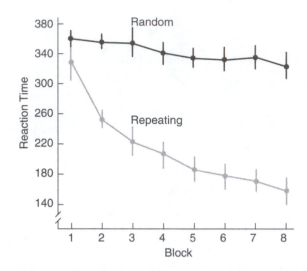

Figure 11.6 Mean reaction times in milliseconds to repeating versus random sequences of locations.

Source: From "Attentional Requirements of Learning: Evidence from Performance Measures," by M. J. Nissen and P. Bullemer, 1987, *Cognitive Psychology, 19*, p. 8. Copyright © 1987 by Elsevier. Reprinted with permission.

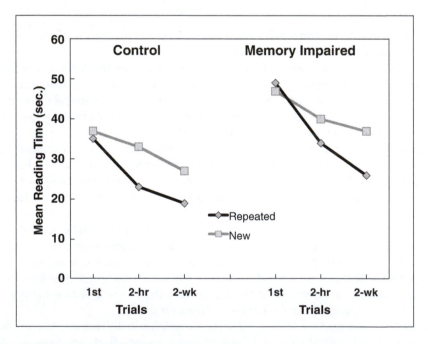

Figure 11.7 Mean Times to Read Inverted-Letter Text.

Source: Adapted from "Memory as assessed by recognition and reading time in normal and memory-impaired people with Alzheimer's disease and other neurological disorders," by M. Moscovith, G. Winocur, and D. McLachlan, 1986, *Journal of Experimental Psychology: General, 115*, p. 335. Copyright by the American Psychological Society. Reprinted with permission.

first practice session through the two delayed tests. Although the memory impaired read slower than the matched control subjects, the impaired still showed faster reading with practice. Some of the words from the first session were repeated on the 2 hour and 2 day tests, and some words were new words. The repeated words were read faster than new words, indicating some memory for the repeated words.

The subjects were also given explicit tests of memory. Words were presented and the subjects judged whether the words were old (had been seen before) or new. The memory-impaired were consistent with their label: They not able to distinguish the old and new words on the delayed tests. Yet, they read old (repeated) words faster than they read new words, even when those words had last occurred two weeks earlier. This shows they "implicitly" remembered words they had read earlier. But they were not able to explicitly recognize the words they had practiced.

Is Implicit Learning Unaware Learning?

The difficulty in answering this question is in determining whether the knowledge is actually unconscious. One means is to show a dissociation between a measure of performance and direct verbal report. For instance, maybe the participants can perform the implicit task but they cannot articulate the rules (Dienes & Berry, 1997).

One example of this strategy is research on the *Iowa Gambling Task* (or IGT) (Bechara, Damasio, Tranel, & Damasio, 1997). (The researchers were at the University of Iowa Medical School at the time.) In the IGT, participants make a succession of choices from four decks of cards. Cards in two decks produce large winnings (e.g., $100), but also large and more frequent losses. In the long run, these decks produce net losses. Cards in the other two decks produce smaller winnings ($50) and less frequent losses. After sufficient training, the subjects learn to choose from the decks with the modest payoffs. This is explicit knowledge. Early in training, the subjects cannot yet describe these contingencies. Yet measurement of the skin conductance response, an indicator of emotional arousal, shows that the participants react more strongly as they choose the next card from the "bad" decks. The reaction occurs before the outcome—gain or loss—is revealed. Before participants consciously know which are good or bad decks, the subjects are unconsciously aware which ones could produce large losses. The science writer Malcolm Gladwell (2005) describes this as a gut-level feeling; just a premonition that this is not the best choice. What is the basis for this intuition? Antonio Damasio says that implicit knowledge produces emotional reactions in the body. Participants do not know which deck is better. Instead they feel it.

This dissociation of implicit and explicit learning is based on the comparison of bodily (SCR) reactions to the subjects' self reports. Verbal reports are not always accurate. Maia and McClelland (2004) found that their participants knew a lot more, and much earlier in their experiment, than Damasio found. Using an extensive set of questions, they found that participants' verbal answers revealed they knew relatively early in the sequence. In fact, subjects knew which sets produced more advantageous outcomes even though their choices did not.

Even if the subject has explicit knowledge of the rules, when was this learned? Awareness could develop before implicit learning occurs; after implicit learning; or coordinately with the implicit learning. Thus, the degree and influence of explicit knowledge on performance of an implicit learning task is still unknown (Frensch & Runger, 2003).

Dissociating Categories of Implicit Learning

Priming is another form of implicit-memory, in which the identification of a stimulus is facilitated by prior exposure to that stimulus. In a priming experiment, a list of words is first presented as part of some incidental task. In a second phase, the words are presented in the form of word fragments. A priming effect occurs if the fragments are completed with the previously shown words.

In our theories, priming, implicit learning, and procedural learning are often categorized together as one form of memory (Squire, 1987; Tulving & Schacter, 1990; see Chapter 7). However, priming and procedural learning are separable (Schwartz & Hashtroudi, 1991). Priming and motor-skill learning have been dissociated in comparisons among individuals with various neurological disorders. Huntington's disease is a neurological disorder characterized by involuntary movements of the body and by progressive cognitive dementia. Average age of onset is in the 30s and 40s. Alzheimer's disease is evidenced by primarily cognitive deficits and has a later age of onset. Individuals with these diseases have been compared in learning a motor skill, such as the pursuit rotor. The goal in this task is to keep a stylus on a fixed spot on a rotating turntable. The starting speed is adjusted so that everyone starts with the same time on target. Alzheimer's individuals improve across blocks of trials; that is, they become more skilled. Huntington's disease participants do not (Heindel et al., 1988). The reverse pattern is found on a priming task: The Huntington's patients completed more word fragments with the primed words than did the Alzheimer's participants (Shimamura, Salmon, Squire, & Butters, 1987). Note that the Alzheimer's participants were cognitively capable of completing word fragments; they just completed them with other words.

There is other neurological evidence that word priming and skill tasks are dissociable. Behaviors having a motor component, such as mirror tracing and pursuit rotor performance, involve an area of the brain called the basal ganglia. Damage here, as occurs in Huntington's and Parkinson's diseases, impairs skill learning but leaves word priming intact (Saint-Cyr & Taylor, 1992).

Expertise

Expertise can be developed in many domains of knowledge or skill. One can become skilled at playing video games, programming a computer, speaking a foreign language, or reading brain scans. Where does expertise come from? What is it that differentiates chess masters from lesser players, or world-class musicians from others? One assumption is that expertise requires an inherent talent. A particular ability is inherited that allows performance at an expert level, and not everyone has this talent. This inherent-ability conception is a popular stereotype about child prodigies, and "savants" who display an exceptional talent in music, art, or math. (See Chapter 12 for further discussion of memory in savants.)

The notion of inborn talent has been challenged by Anders Ericsson (see particularly Ericsson & Charness, 1994), who argues that what separates the expert from the also-rans is the sheer amount of practice devoted to their skill. The difference between most participants in some activity and those who attain expert status is the amount of deliberate training and instruction. Individuals on their way to expert status maintain schedules of intense and prolonged practice, in some cases essentially engaging in the activity full time. For example, college students were trained to develop digit spans of 80 to 100 numerals (Ericsson, Chase, & Faloon, 1980). The students did this through extended practice, learning various coding schemes and becoming adept at rapidly encoding number strings into long-term memory. In chapter 6, we mentioned Joshua Foer, who spent a year learning to become a memory expert (partly by studying with Ericsson), and won a Memory Championship. Maybe child prodigies get an early start at practicing; savants have often spent years perfecting their talents.

Other researchers argue that expertise is determined by a combination of factors (Oerter, 2003). Genetics may contribute to a number of individual skills, not just a single talent. For example, musical expertise might require absolute pitch, memory for music, and performance skills. Such individual skills (and their underlying genes) would be distributed throughout the population, but some individuals would fortuitously inherit the combination of genes for exceptional musical ability. In addition, certain advantageous environments might foster its development. A child's aptitudes may be recognized and encouraged by her parents, or the precocious child seeks out experiences that enhance his skill. Moreover, differences in the brain's structure, functioning, or biochemical makeup might underlie exceptional performance. Such brain differences may be present from birth, or result from the early childhood use of musical abilities. (As an analogy, earlier in this chapter I mentioned that London taxi drivers have larger hippocampi. But is this the result of practice at navigating, or does having a larger hippocampus allow one to become a good navigator?) Finally, the influence of practice is undeniable.

Hambrick and Meinz (2011) found evidence for talent *and* practice. They studied the ability to sight-read music as a function of practice and working memory (the latter their proxy for talent or ability.) The results showed independent effects for both factors: reading music was better among those with better working memory, and those who had more total practice. The best performance was by those with both good memory and lots of experience.

Talent and practice may contribute at different stages of becoming expert. Intelligence, semantic memory, or motor skills may be more important in the beginning. Being smarter or faster may compensate for other limitations. After sufficient practice, knowledge moves from declarative to procedural. Skilled performance requires more than just declarative knowledge. Here practice can circumvent the limits of ability. For instance, memory experts are not limited by the small spans of short-term memory or working memory.

How much practice is necessary to attain expertise? Ericsson, Krampe, and Tesch-Romer (1993) concluded that it takes about 10 years of full-time preparation, which corresponds to several thousand hours of practice or study. This 10-year rule applies to many domains of expertise, such as sports, chess, or music. For the most talented in the arts and sciences, more than 10 years may be required. Ericsson et al.'s (1993) review showed that those who attained the highest levels of expertise had begun practicing 2 to 5 years before less accomplished experts and spent more time on deliberate practice. Top violinists at age 20 had spent more than 10,000 hours in practice, twice as much as that by those at lower levels of accomplishment (who were still experts themselves).

Is 10,000 hours necessary? In a study of chess masters, the mean number of self-reported hours of deliberate practice was about 11,000 (Gobet & Campitelli, 2007). However, the range was great, plus-or-minus 6,000 hours. So, a few (the number is not reported) achieved master status with far-less than 10,000 hours. Is 10,000 hours sufficient? Players who had not achieved master status practiced an average of 8,000 hours, and many as much as 16,000 hours (and one individual with 20,000 hours of practice and nonmaster status). So, in general something like the 10,000 hour rule holds. And there are exceptions: Some become expert after fewer hours, and some do not attain expertise with considerably more hours (Campitelli & Gobet, 2011).

We might argue in response that without sufficient innate intelligence or athletic ability, no amount of practice could turn each of us into a Bobby Fischer or an Arthur Ashe. The point Ericsson wants to make is that when we look at the lives of experts, we see they have devoted an enormous number of hours to their craft. Ten thousand hours of training can account for a substantial amount of talent. Ericsson does allow a possible hereditary factor, but it is not a specifically inherited talent. What may be inherited is motivation: the drive and perseverance necessary to practice.

From Declarative to Procedural

In several points in this chapter, we considered the role of conscious and unconscious factors in the skilled behaviors. Recent theories of skill learning have incorporated both by breaking down skill learning into a series of steps or stages. First, factual knowledge is acquired: learning the nature of the task, the rules of the game, and so on. With additional practice, less conscious guidance is required. And after extensive practice, a skill is performed seemingly automatically. This succession of steps marks the transition from declarative knowledge to procedural knowledge.

Anderson's adaptive control of thought (ACT*) theory (1983) is designed specifically to describe this transition. The major variable that accounts for skill development is practice: plain old repetition. Anderson proposes a two-stage model of skill acquisition, with a transitional step between stages. During the *declarative stage* of skill learning, information is learned. This stage involves conscious processing and attention, so there is heavy reliance on working memory. For example, you need to learn the different pieces in chess, their range of moves, and some strategies. During the initial phase of skill learning, we verbally encode and rehearse information or give ourselves feedback and guidance. The declarative stage is followed by a transition phase in which knowledge application starts to become proceduralized. During this transition, groups of rules or operations that are frequently used together are chunked, or compiled, which increases efficiency. This transitional state is known as *knowledge compilation*. An analogy can be made to playing a complex piece of music. With practice, individual notes become combined into chunks that are stored in long-term memory. Playing then becomes the activation of groups of notes, rather than playing note by note. Performance now depends less on conscious control and more on long-term retrieval, thus freeing up working memory. The final stage, or *procedural stage*, is marked by skill refinement. Continued practice leads to further strengthening of the procedures. The procedural skills are refined as a result of generalization and discrimination. With generalization, the procedures are applied to new situations. Discrimination restricts the range of the procedures to only appropriate situations.

Applications

Implicit Learning

Professionals in the field of cognitive rehabilitation help individuals who have amnesia cope with everyday life in the face of memory deficits. If amnesic individuals are, by definition, memory-impaired, how can they learn new skills? Because implicit-learning and procedural abilities are usually spared in amnesia, these can be used instead of explicit-learning methods in remediation.

Glisky and Schacter (e.g., 1989) used implicit learning to teach a woman with anterograde (or ongoing) amnesia to use a computer. She was first taught technical definitions using a "vanishing-cue" method. A word and its definition were first presented, and across repeated trials, a letter, then more letters, were omitted from the target word (e.g., DISK DRIVE, then D_ _K DR_ _ _E, then D_ _ _ D_ _ _ _). Eventually, the letter cues were omitted as the woman learned to name the word given the definition. Similar "vanishing instructions" were used to teach the steps involved in operating the computer. Gradually, each line of instructions became abbreviated by omitting words, then whole steps were eliminated. This woman eventually learned enough to perform a data-entry job and was able to return to work with her former company. She eventually learned over 250 codes, symbols, and abbreviations. Through all this, her explicit memory remained impaired.

Why is implicit-memory training successful? One explanation is that implicit methods minimize retrieval of the wrong information, which might later be mistakenly recalled as the correct answer. The vanishing-cue method is easy enough at first to elicit just correct responses. If errors were made, they, and not the correct words, might be recalled in future trials (Baddeley, 1992b).

The errorless learning interpretation was tested in a word-stem completion task using 16 patients with severe memory problems (Wilson, 1992). In the error*less* condition, participants were shown a stem (e.g., BR_ _ _) and told what the correct word was (BREAD). In the error condition, the participants were first allowed to guess at a word that completed the stem (e.g., they might guess BREAK) and were then told the word for which the researcher was looking. When the participants were later tested with just the stems, more of the correct words were produced after the errorless study condition. In the error condition, more of the previous wrong guesses persisted.

Spatial Memory

Sense of Direction

Surveys of real-world memory often turn up a statistical factor associated with way finding, or, conversely, the ease of getting lost (Ryan, 1992). Individuals will readily volunteer self-estimates about their own sense of direction, and interestingly, these estimates are accurate. Kozlowski and Bryant (1977) had students rate their sense of direction on a simple 7-point scale. These estimates were significantly correlated with the accuracy in pointing to (unseen) campus buildings, judging the distance between pairs of buildings, and pointing in the direction of nearby cities. After being led back and forth through an underground utility tunnel on campus, students who rated themselves as having a good sense of direction showed improved accuracy in pointing to the end point, whereas students with a poor sense of direction showed no improvement whatsoever.

It is easy to get lost when we travel. After finding your way there, the problem is then remembering how to get back. The psychologist Colin Ellard (2010) offers a number of ways to find your way back. Some of his suggestions include:

1. When going forward, occasionally look back. That's the view you will need to recognize on the way home.
2. In visiting a new area, choose one location as a home base. This will aid in forming a cognitive map. Learn the relationship of other locations to this starting point.
3. Make up a story to link together locations or landmarks you pass. This elaboration makes for a better memory, and the story will be helpful in retracing the outbound route.
4. Don't get upset: Emotional arousal interferes with retrieval. Whether it is fear or anger over being lost, the results will be poor recall of what you do have in memory.
5. Keep track of time. Sometimes the novel outbound trip seemed to take so long. Overestimating time (and distance) on the way back can lead to missed landmarks or turns that occur too early.

A related issue is whether sense of direction might be affected by the use of electronic way-finding devices, such as GPSs. Just as our memory for phone numbers seems to have disappeared, maybe our way finding abilities will become extinct also. This topic is considered in Box 11.2.

Box 11.2   GPS and Spatial Knowledge

Physical maps have been replaced by ground positioning devices (GPSs), turn-by-turn directions, and location detectors. Is our learning of routes and directions different from what we would have acquired by using a map? Following directions with a GPS might be easier than using a printed map. However, a map and a GPS differ in several ways. The GPS (often) shows only a portion of the route at a time; or you might be listening to turn-by-turn directions with no map image at all. The GPS continuously displays the user's location, whereas someone using a printed map needs to update their position on the map as they travel. Researchers in cognitive science wonder whether less effortful cognitive processing—or at least, different processing—will lead to a decline in spatial cognition, as more of us off-load wayfinding to electronic devices. Just as we have stopped memorizing phone numbers—the cell phone does that for us—we might not remember spatial directions.

Studies have compared memory after the use of a GPS or a printed map to travel through an unfamiliar city. In one case, Japanese college students traveled several such routes. After reaching the end point of each route, the students who followed GPS directions drew less accurate maps of the route, and made larger errors in estimating the direction back to the starting location. Interestingly, the GPS students traveled longer distances (Ishikawa, Fujiwara, Imai, & Okabe, 2008). Maybe the map users found shorter and faster routes to the goal on their maps?

In another case, American college students traveled two routes, one with a map and one with a GPS. Again students produced more detailed and accurate sketches of the routes when they used a map. The researchers also noted that two kinds of knowledge are acquired while traversing a given route: the spatial information of distance, direction, and turns; and semantic or verbal information, such as the names of buildings or roads. Semantic knowledge was not so different between the map and GPS conditions. Items could be equally named and arranged sequentially along the route (e.g., a store near the railroad crossing). The differences seemed to be more in the actual overall spatial arrangement that was less-well known in the GPS conditions (Wessel, Ziemkiewicz, Chang, & Sauda, 2010).

Inuit

The native Inuit populations of northern North America have long had their own way-finding methods to navigate their barren terrains (or, what seem to be barren to the rest of us). The Inuit use wind direction, patterns of snowdrifts on land, direction of currents in the water, and celestial patterns in the sky as navigational aids. It takes many years to learn to navigate by physical environmental cues and to build mental knowledge of the area. However, this method of wayfinding is changing as the younger Inuit generations began using GPS units. Their elders are concerned that traditional lore and skills will be lost. Parallel concerns have echoed throughout history: that printed books would replace the need to remember information; that photographs would replace artists' renderings; and, among the Inuit, that snowmobiles would replace dog sleds (Aporta & Higgs, 2005).

The GPS has advantages over traditional environmental navigation cues. It provides a margin of safety for the inexperienced, or when fog and snowstorms distort environmental cues. Even the traditional hunters will use the GPS in certain circumstances. Interestingly, experienced hunters who used the GPS knew when *not* to follow its advice. The GPS points in straight lines but does not indicate obstacles (chasms or ice) that block the direct path.

Navigating with environmental stimuli requires a high degree of engagement with the environment: paying attention to the cues associated with distance and direction. Learning to navigate with environmental stimuli also requires a long period of apprenticeship. The GPS can be learned quickly. It is yet unclear whether the GPS will replace, or simply supplant, traditional Inuit techniques for wayfinding. In the end, the GPS may follow the same route as the snowmobile, by becoming an accepted part of Inuit life.

Improved Building Design

The principles of spatial learning can be applied to improving everyday navigation. Hospitals, large public buildings, shopping malls, some university buildings, and residential complexes for the elderly all tax user-orientation skills. These are difficult environments to get to know because of size, infrequent exposure, or lack of external frames of reference.

One aid to negotiating large buildings is to use a color-coding scheme to distinguish different sections. Evans, Fellows, Zorn, and Doty (1980) took advantage of the repainting of a large university building. Students in the "before" condition toured the four-story building when the interior was painted a monochromatic beige. They were then taken to a central point and asked to find their way back to a specific location (e.g., go to the chem lab). The interior walls on each floor were subsequently painted with different colors. The "after" group, who took the same tour and way-finding test, were faster in finding target locations and made fewer errors along the way.

"You-are-here" maps are another aid to orientation. However, careful placement and alignment with the environment is necessary for these to be effective. Judging direction from a cognitive map is faster and more accurate if the user is facing the same direction as the mental map (Levine, Marchon, & Hanley, 1984). You-are-here maps are sometimes simply placed on a convenient wall, and so are reversed or inverted with respect to the surrounding environment. A survey of one city's maps found they were correctly aligned only 25 percent of the time. One mall had the same map mounted on all four sides of a square column, which meant that only one was correctly oriented (Montello, 2010). This forces the user to make some cognitive rearrangements and leads to a greater number of direction errors. Planners should choose the map location first and then design the map, and different sites may require different versions of the map.

Long-Term Retention of Skills

All too often, a student's goal is to learn something "just long enough": long enough to get past the exam tomorrow morning. Another goal of education is long-term retention. Performance in a job or occupation often depends on skills and knowledge that are used infrequently. To take one extreme example, for many of us, certain emergency procedures are not needed every day, yet will need to be quickly recalled when an emergency does arise.

A research team at the University of Colorado at Boulder has been especially interested in long-term retention of skills (see, e.g., Healy & Bourne, 1995; Healy et al., 1993). They studied skills ranging from detecting single letters to remembering math facts and foreign-language vocabulary, to performing in an army tank simulator (which is like the most awesome video game ever!). These researchers verified several guidelines that promote long-term retention. (*Note*: We are emphasizing long-term remembering, not ease of acquisition.) Their recommendations are summarized in Table 11.4. Some examples are cited in what follows.

Table 11.4 Guidelines for Optimizing Long-Term Retention of Knowledge and Skills

Guidelines
1. Optimize conditions of training.   Examples: Use spaced practice   Intermix training of several components   Encourage generation during practice
2. Optimize learning strategy used.   Example: Mnemonics as mediators
3. Achieve automaticity.   Example: Remembering rather than computing arithmetic answers
4. Optimize retention conditions.   Example: Refresher and practice tests

Source: Healy et al. (1993).

Optimize the Conditions of Training

There are many factors that facilitate encoding (see Chapter 9). Two examples may be mentioned here: spacing and generation effects. If several arithmetic or vocabulary items are to be learned, it is better to intermix them within the study sequence rather than to mass study trials on each. This mixing schedule will likely slow acquisition of the information at first, as compared to massed practice, but it leads to better retention in the long run.

The generation effect refers to getting the participants to generate to-be-remembered answers rather than simply having the experimenter provide the correct answers. In applying the generation effect to learning multiplication answers (e.g., $13 \times 8 = ?$), one should attempt to produce the correct answer rather than simply read it. One potential problem, as noted with errorless learning by amnesics, is that your previous wrong answers may be recalled later instead of the correct one. Prompts or cues might be provided to ensure the correct answers are generated, and thus remembered, rather than incorrect answers ($13 \times 8 = 104$).

Optimize Learning Strategies

Healy et al. (1993) used the keyword mnemonic to teach language vocabulary in a series of studies. Each foreign word was paired with a similar sounding English word, which in turn could be connected to the English translation. For example, the Spanish DORONICO and LEOPARD might be linked by a similar-sounding word DOOR. The keyword mnemonic facilitated acquisition and produced better long-term retention.

Train Until Retrieval Is Automatic

Linking mnemonics facilitate learning, but retrieval is indirect and slow: One must chain through the links. Practice should continue until retrieval becomes direct: DORONICO comes to elicit LEOPARD directly, leading to faster response times and better long-term retention.

In solving novel arithmetic problems, students often will employ an algorithm, or shortcut. The multiplication problem 13×8 might be solved as 10×8 plus 3×8, each of which has already known solutions. However, these computations take time. Extensive practice of problems like 13 x 8 will make retrieval of the correct answer automatic and the computations will no longer be necessary. These overlearned answers will be better retained.

Optimize Retention Conditions

This may be accomplished with refresher trials or practice quizzes. As we noted in the previous chapters, practice at retrieval can be just as important as additional study. In one applied example, soldiers were first trained to disassemble and reassemble an M60 machine gun. One group was tested 8 weeks later, and they showed substantial forgetting. A second group received some refresher training midway through the retention interval. On the 8-week test, the second group showed significantly better performance (Schendel & Hagman, 1982).

Developing Memory Skill

The study of memory experts offers some learnable skills that will enhance our own memories. Individuals who are expert at remembering various types of material—numbers, maps, or scripts as examples—share a number of remembering techniques.

Skilled memory theory was developed to characterize the skill of those individuals who learned to remember long strings of random numbers (Chase & Ericsson, 1981). Three central features are postulated. First, during encoding, existing knowledge is used to organize and make target items meaningful. For instance, random numbers might be encoded as running times. Second, experts have well-developed retrieval routines. They can recall the cues (e.g., a fast mile, or 3:55). Third, with practice, both encoding and retrieval processes become faster.

Good map learners use several strategies during encoding. First, they partition the map into smaller sections and focus attention on one area at a time. This is comparable to grouping a string of numbers into smaller chunks. Good learners use visual imagery to encode patterns and spatial relationships. Poor learners use more verbal rehearsal and naming of components. Finally, the good learners engage in more self-testing to assess whether they know the map yet (Thorndyke & Stasz, 1980).

Acting and Memory. If there is one group of people who should have skilled memorizing ability it would be actors. They obviously need to remember dialogue, but also actions and emotions. Studies by Noice and Noice (1997, 2006) show that actors do not learn lines by brute memorization. Instead they use many strategies to encode material, such as distinctiveness, mood congruency, self-generation, and imaginal elaboration. The lines in a speech would be organized into the successive reasons for the lines (to flatter, to warn, to reassure). Maybe most importantly, the actors tried to mean what they were expressing. Emotions, movements, expressions, and dialogue would be integrated into a meaningful unit. The behavior might be best described as less acting and more meaning. Students could be taught this general idea, which Noice and Noice call "active experiencing." Undergraduates with no acting experience but trained in active experiencing were able to remember more than students simply given instructions to memorize.

Summary

Spatial Learning

Two types of spatial representation are considered. Route knowledge is knowledge of a series of routes, directions, or paths in a spatial environment. By contrast, a cognitive map is a more abstract representation of an environment, placing specific locations in context with the surrounding area.

Place versus response-learning experiments attempted to distinguish whether rats learned cognitive maps (Tolman) or specific turns (Hull) in mazes. The results were inconclusive with respect to the theories. Depending on which sorts of cues are available, most organisms can learn about local cues to guide specific turns (i.e., routes); and global cues to guide general orientation (i.e., cognitive maps).

Cognitive mapping is shown by performance in the radial maze and the water maze. In the radial maze, the participant must enter each goal arm once without repetition. In the water maze, the subject learns the location of an unseen platform. In both mazes, subjects rely on cues outside of the maze—room cues—to orient themselves with respect to the goal location. Lesions of the hippocampus impair radial-maze and water-maze performance, just as hippocampal damage also impairs human declarative and spatial memory.

Landmarks are elements in an environment that by virtue of their distinctive design or meaning stand out. Landmarks are central to either route or survey maps. Landmark memory seems to be neurologically separable from route learning and cognitive mapping.

Spatial schemas can lead to distortion during recall due to the averaging and normalizing that occurs when spatial knowledge becomes general. Errors in distance estimation, road-intersection angles, and relative proximity of geographic locations result from incorrect inferences from schematic spatial knowledge. Spatial information is organized, just as is verbal information. For example, chimpanzees organized a search route to retrieve food efficiently.

Cognitive mapping shows a developmental progression. Human infants learn turn responses before place responses, and radial-maze performance increases from age 2 to nearly adult levels of accuracy by age 5.

Motor-Skills Learning

Motor-skill learning is the acquisition of control over the amount, direction, and duration of responding in response to the regulating stimuli. Pursuit rotor and mirror tracing are exemplars of laboratory motor tasks.

One important determinant of skill is the amount of practice. The power law describes the relationship between practice and the speed of performance. There is a linear increase in speed when the data is plotted as a function of the log of the number of practice trials. That is, greater amounts of practice are required to produce successive increments in performance. As with verbal learning, spacing practice produces better learning than does massing trials.

A second factor affecting skill learning is knowledge of results. Outcome information or feedback on the success or accuracy of the response can be externally provided to the participant. Consistent feedback (given after each trial) and immediate feedback generally produce faster acquisition. However, partial-feedback schedules and delayed feedback can produce better long-term retention and better transfer to novel motor responses. According to the guidance hypothesis, occasional omitted or delayed feedback promotes attention to internal kinesthetic feedback, and thus learning to recognize good and poor performance.

Implicit Learning

Procedural knowledge is "knowing how" to perform a motor, perceptual, or cognitive act, rather than the factual "knowing that" of declarative learning. Procedural learning is often measured by an implicit test of learning. Implicit learning is the improvement in performance of cognitive, motor, or perceptual skills that develops with training. Knowledge of a complex skill is acquired largely independent of conscious awareness of specific components of that skill. Artificial grammar, sequence learning, and the Iowa Gambling Task, are examples of implicit-learning tasks. Different forms of implicit learning, such as priming and skill learning, can be dissociated in certain neurological conditions such as Alzheimer's or Huntington's disease.

Expertise

Although popular conception asserts that innate talent underlies exceptional ability, an alternative theory emphasizes the role of extensive practice. Expertise in many domains comes after years of deliberate and intensive training. The 10,000 hour rule is one reliable guideline for acquiring expertise.

The acquisition of procedural skill is marked by a series of stages: acquiring factual knowledge during the declarative stage; knowledge compilation, in which procedures are grouped into units; and proceduralization, in which operations become speeded and automatic.

Applications

Implicit training has been applied to teaching skills to amnesics, persons who otherwise could not acquire information explicitly. The vanishing-cue technique is one example of implicit training.

Knowledge of spatial learning can used to understand our sense of direction, and improving the design of buildings. Long-term retention can be improved by applying several guidelines: optimize training conditions and strategies; train until retrieval is automatic; and optimize retention conditions.

Memory skills can be improved by partitioning material into smaller units, establishing retrieval cues at the time of encoding, and self-testing to ensure that learning has occurred.

12 Individual Differences in Learning and Memory

One of the goals of a scientific psychology is to describe general laws. This textbook, which includes the word *principles* in its title, attempts to specify some general, maybe even universal, principles of learning and memory. There are exceptions to the principles, and individual differences are one source of variation. The combination of genes, physical constitution, environment, and life experiences causes each of us to react somewhat differently to what are seemingly the same situations. The remarkable thing, then, is that there are any general principles at all!

It would be impossible to describe the laws for each and every individual. Instead, researchers focus on broad categories of differences. How are children and adults alike or different in their remembering? Are there gender or personality differences that interact with the principles of learning?

Two distinctive approaches to research in psychology are the experimental approach and the correlational approach (Cronbach, 1957). The *experimental approach* focuses on those variables that can be actively manipulated by researchers, in order to demonstrate what effects these variables have on learning. The experimental approach seeks the general principles that transcend individual differences. The *correlational approach* focuses on variables that experimenters cannot control, such as gender, personality, or age, but that nevertheless may be important deter-minants of learning in individuals. The correlational approach notes the limiting conditions of the general principles. A complete theory of learning should provide two kinds of knowledge: the general principles, and the contributions of individual differences.

In some ways, what we are offering is a comparative psychology. As Robert Yerkes said, "Comparative psychology in its completeness necessarily deals with the materials of the psy-chology of the infant, child, adult, whether the being be human or infra-human; of animal or plant (!)—of normal and abnormal individuals; of social groups and of civilizations" (cited by Cronbach, 1957).

The Nature of Nurture: The Genetics of Learning Ability

The ability to learn (or the effect of *nurture*) is affected by the genetic makeup (or *nature*) of the individual. Genetic factors could directly affect learning, for example, by affecting the struc-ture or functioning of the nervous system. Genetic influences also can indirectly affect learning, because people differ in their sensitivity to various stimuli, their intensity of reaction, or their level of emotionality, all factors that can influence learning and retention.

Animal Studies

The classic experiment on the genetics of learning ability was Tryon's breeding of rats for maze learning (e.g., Tryon, 1940). Tryon used the method of *selective breeding*, in which animals of similar learning ability were bred together over several generations. This is the same method used by animal breeders to produce specific physical traits. Tryon first trained a large number of generic laboratory rats in a 17-turn maze. Some animals learned quickly; some learned slowly. Even among rats, there are sizable individual differences. Tryon selected the best maze learners and paired them for breeding. He also selected the worst learners and allowed them to breed. This selection and breeding continued for several generations.

After 18 generations of selective breeding, the two lines of descendants had diverged into the Maze Bright (MB) and Maze Dull (MD) rats. There was almost no overlap in maze performance between the MB and MD lines of rats. The MB were all good maze learners. The MD were uni-formly poor learners.

Rats, mice, and fruit flies can be bred for differences in specific learning abilities. For instance, genetic mutations in fruit flies can be induced by exposure to certain chemicals. Tim Tully tested mutated flies in a shock-avoidance learning procedure (Tully, 1996). The flies were trained in a T-maze made of Plexiglas tubes. An odor is introduced into one arm of the T; after the flies enter that arm, they receive a mild electric shock. (Mild! This is not a bug zapper.) A different odor in the other arm of the T-maze is not shocked. Tulley found, and subsequently bred, flies that could not learn this odor discrimination (so-called Dunce flies). He also found flies that could learn but quickly forget (Amnesic flies).

Another method that derives from molecular genetics is to introduce altered DNA into fertil-ized cells. Tang et al. (1999) produced strains of transgenic mice. The inserted DNA altered cells in the hippocampus, an area we have frequently noted is involved in learning. This particular strain of mice, labeled Doogie (after Doogie Howser, MD, the character on TV who was a preco-cious child), did indeed learn better than normal mice. What was especially nice about this study is that the researchers used a battery of learning tests, not just one task. The transgenic mice were better at detecting novel objects added to their environment; were better at learning the placement of the hidden platform in the Morris water maze; and were faster in acquisition and extinction of classical conditioning. This enhancement of general learning ability is important in ruling out genes that simply increased attention, emotionality, or activity levels.

To say that genes affect learning seems to imply that genetic makeup predetermines later ability. In actuality, heredity combines with environment, so that the outcome is better described as an interaction of genes and environment. For example, maze learning by MB and MD rats is affected by the quality of social and environmental stimulation the animal experiences. Cooper and Zubek (1958) compared MB and MD rats raised in three different environments. In the restricted condition, the rats were housed individually in small cages. In the stimulating environment, several rats were housed together in a multilevel cage filled with toys and objects to manipulate (like a hamster habitat). The "normal" environment was something in between: a few rats living together, but with no toys. The animals were later trained in the maze. The MB rats from the so-called normal living conditions were superior to the MD from the normal environment (see Figure 12.1). This is what Tryon found. Rats reared in the deprived environment were very poor learners, regardless of genetic background (i.e., MB or MD). Rats reared in the stimulating environment were very good learners, again regardless of genetic background. Thus, a bad environment could make all rats "dull"; a good environment could make all rats "bright."

The Biological Costs of Learning Ability

If learning conveys such an adaptive advantage, then why haven't animals (including humans) become incredibly smarter than they are? The experiments on selective breeding and gene transplants have shown that smarter rats and mice can be created. (Just what the world needs: smarter

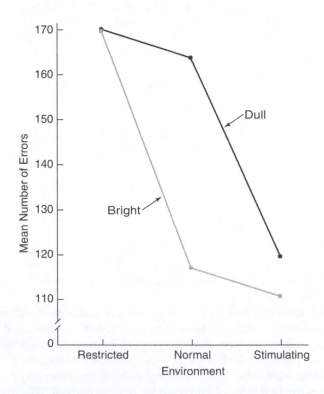

Figure 12.1 Number of maze errors made by Maze Bright and Maze Dull rats as a function of the rearing environment: restricted, normal, or enriched (stimulating).

Source: Adapted from "Effects of Enriched and Restricted Early Environments on the Learning Ability of Bright and Dull Rats," by R. M. Cooper and J. P. Zubek, 1958, *Canadian Journal of Psychology, 12*, pp. 159–164. Copyright © 1958 by the Canadian Psychological Association. Reprinted with permission.

rodents.) The Flynn Effect refers to the observation that human intelligence test scores have been rising throughout the twentieth century (Flynn, 2012). These sorts of findings show that there is room for improvement. So why hasn't evolution already produced better learners?

The answer may be that there are metabolic costs associated with superior learning ability. It takes energy to form new neural connections and to retain memories in the brain. What evolution may have arrived at is an optimal balance among several metabolic-intensive activities, such as learning, food seeking, predator avoidance, disease resistance, etc. (Mery & Kawecki, 2004). Kawecki (2010) demonstrated this trade-off by selectively breeding fruit flies to be better learners. Flies were subjected to taste aversion learning. A novel flavor, either pineapple or orange, was paired with bitter tasting quinine (bitter even to flies). Flies that learned the flavor-quinine association aversion best were bred. The flies were selectively bred across 15 generations to produce better learners. However, superior learning came at a cost. The flies had fewer offspring that survived to maturity; were less successful in competition for scarce food resources; and lived shorter lives (Burger, Kolss, Pont, & Kawecki, 2008). In a parallel study, flies were bred to live longer, but when tested in the taste aversion paradigm, they were not as smart. That last point is interesting: so far, flies have been bred to be better learners or to live longer, but not both.

Human Studies

Looking for genetic differences in learning among humans is more difficult than in animals. Breeding history and environment are not experimentally controllable. However, genetic influences are inferred from the results of methods such as the comparison of twins.

The *twins method* measures the similarity of identical twins (or monozygotic twins, referring to the production of two individuals from a single fertilized ovum) and the similarity of (same-sex) fraternal twins (or dizygotic twins, referring to two fertilized ova). Basically, we are asking whether identical twins are more alike in learning or memory than are fraternal twins. For example, in one study of 10-year-old twins, the identical pairs were more alike in the number of names and pictures recalled (the correlation was .43) than were fraternal pairs (the correlation was .31; Thompson, Detterman, & Plomin, 1991). At the other end of the age spectrum, elderly identical twins (mean age of 67 years) were more similar in the number of word lists they could recall and in memory for abstract figures (Finkel & McGue, 1993). Results such as these are taken to suggest that memory has a hereditary component.

The statistical estimates of the heritability of memory are often relatively small. This may be because memory is treated as a single ability, as opposed to partitioning it into different types of memory, such as short term versus long term. A better approach is to compare identical twins and fraternal twins on a variety of memory tests (Thapar, Petrill, & Thompson, 1994). The identical twins were more similar on tests of associative memory, such as learning names and faces. Identical twins were no more alike than were fraternals on tests requiring brief retention, such as the digit span. Similarly, a twin study of episodic and semantic memory suggested that each had a genetic component, yet episodic and semantic were independent of one another (Volk, McDermott, Roediger, & Todd, 2006). Thus, rather than concluding that memory, broadly speaking, is heritable, these results suggest there are genetic influences on certain kinds of learning or remembering.

Even among genetically identical individuals, a given gene will not make a difference unless it is *expressed*. The environment determines whether or when genes turn off or turn on. Gene expression was demonstrated in a study in which mice were reared in enriched or deprived environments like that described earlier. The researchers determined that the enriched environment enhanced the expression of 100 genes (Rampon et al., 2000). We do not yet know what function each of those genes control. The enriched mice and deprived mice were nearly genetically alike, yet they developed differently because of how the environments affected their genes. This suggests that people, even identical twins, could be different because the environment stimulates their genes differently.

Age Differences in Learning and Memory

Changes in learning and memory across the lifetime have been studied experimentally using the same basic methods otherwise described in this text. Learning, the acquisition of information, has been studied using classical and instrumental conditioning procedures. Memory, the retention of learned information, has been studied using episodic procedures such as recognition and recall methods.

Conditioning

Conditioning techniques have been applied across the age spectrum, from (literally) prenatal to elderly subject groups. As a general principle, the very young and the very old do not condition as well as the age groups in between.

Prenatal Learning

The general procedure for studying prenatal learning is to expose the fetus to some experience before birth, and then test after birth to see whether prenatal learning had occurred. For instance, in a taste-aversion learning study, fetal rats were exposed in utero to apple juice paired with an illness-inducing agent. When the rat pups were tested after birth, they showed an aversion that is specific to the taste of apple juice (Smotherman, 1982). Human classical conditioning also occurs before birth. In one study of pregnant women, music was used as the CS and the mothers were trained in deep muscle relaxation as the US. After 24 pairings of music and relaxation during the thirtieth to thirty-seventh weeks of gestation, the activity level of the fetuses decreased when the music was again played. This calming effect persisted as a reaction to the music even after birth (Feijoo, as cited in Hepper, 1989).

A stimulus experienced *before* birth can function as a positive reinforcer *after* birth in instrumental conditioning. (Recall that instrumental conditioning is reinforcement or reward conditioning.) DeCasper and Fifer (1980) studied learning by 1-to-4-day-old infants. Sucking on a pacifier was the instrumental response, which was reinforced by presentation of a recording of their mothers' voice. The infants increased sucking when the mother's voice occurred as the positive reinforcer, but not when a stranger's voice was used. DeCasper says that these newborns did not have sufficient experience with the mother's voice after birth to have learned it then. In a later study, mothers-to-be read a specific story out loud during the last 6 weeks of the pregnancy. When the infants were later tested, they increased sucking to hear the particular story exposed during pregnancy rather than a different story read by their mother (DeCasper & Spence, 1986). (In these studies, the infants did not differentiate between their father's voice and another male's voice.)

Conditioning in Infants

Research with human infants has demonstrated conditioning of a number of responses such as eye-blink, head-turn, and sucking responses (Fitzgerald & Brackbill, 1976; Marquis, 1941). Eye-blink conditioning, in which a tone CS is followed by an airpuff US, occurs in human infants as young as 10 days old (Little, Lipsitt, & Rovee-Collier, 1984). Newborns seem to quickly learn "scents" associated with their mothers. Such learning is important in helping to maintain mother–infant contact in any species, not just humans, and particularly for neonates, whose auditory and visual systems function poorly at birth. In one study of newborn infants, a neutral odor was accompanied with stroking their torsos (Sullivan, Taborsky-Barbar, Mendoza, Ition, & Leon, 1991). The experimental design included a number of control conditions missing in earlier investigations. Thus, other groups of newborns were exposed to just the odor, just the stroking, or the two unpaired. Those infants who had received pairings of the odor with bodily contact turned their heads more often in the direction of the odor and were more active when the odor was presented. These infants did not respond to a different odor, one not previously presented.

Aging and Conditioning

At the other end of the age spectrum, classical conditioning begins a decline with increased age. Solomon and Pendlebury (1992) studied eyeblink conditioning in both rabbits and humans, in each case pairing a tone and an airpuff. The rabbits ranged in age from 6 months to 4 years; the humans, 25 years to over 70. The younger subjects in each species reached a higher level of responding to the CS, between 65 and 80 percent, whereas the oldest subjects responded to only about 20 to 30 percent of the CSs. Human conditioning, in general, begins to show a decline after the age of 40 or so.

Memory Development in Children

The capacity to remember develops from infancy, through childhood and adolescence, and into young adulthood. The interest for us here is not that children seem to remember less than adults, but why? As Flavel (1971) posed the question: "What is memory development the development of?" Several answers have been proposed, ranging from hypotheses that children have lesser short-term memory capacities to their having less knowledge of how memory works. What we find is that much develops in children's memory.

Assessing Memory in Infants

Episodic memory—remembering specific events or experiences—is most often assessed using verbal reports available in older children and adults. When adults are asked about specific events from their first years of life, such as the birth of a sibling, episodic memories are conspicuously absent. Adults' earliest childhood memories are typically from age 3 or so, occasionally a memory from before; often, our first memories appear later (Eacott & Crawley, 1998). Is it really possible that the experiences of our first years are not remembered? This phenomenon of *childhood amnesia* has been of interest since at least the time of Freud and is the subject of many theories. One explanation is that key areas of the brain, particularly the hippocampus, have not yet matured in infants and so episodic memories are not formed (Nelson, 1995). Other explanations are that younger and older children differ in encoding, memory span, existing knowledge, use of learning strategies, and metamemory.

Encoding Differences

Episodic memory is memory that we can access consciously and (usually) report verbally. The difficulty with testing preverbal children is that memories might be acquired but the children cannot tell us about them.

If memories are there, maybe episodic recall in infants can be tested by nonverbal means, rather than waiting a few years for the children to become old enough to question. Bauer (e.g., 1996) has developed an elegant set of procedures in which children as young as 11 months can demonstrate remembering by imitating activities they have observed the experimenter performing.

The procedure is called *elicited imitation.* The experimenter demonstrates an activity for the child, such as putting a teddy bear into a small bed, pulling the covers up, and reading the bear a bedtime story. The child is then encouraged to repeat the sequence. The number of target actions that the child reproduces and their sequence can be recorded, giving a measure of immediate memory. Even 11-month-olds correctly imitate two action sequences, and children of 24 to 30 months can repeat events of five to eight actions. After a delay ranging from a week to, in some cases, 8 months, the child was shown the props used initially. Retention was demonstrated when these children spontaneously imitated the previous sequences. Apparently, quite a bit can be remembered during the early years of development.

If episodic memory does begin so early, then the explanation of childhood amnesia is still a mystery. Older children and adults do not recall episodes from this early in life. Bauer suggests one reason is that the memory storage process, or consolidation, has not yet developed. Episodic memories can be learned, or encoded, but the neural bases for permanent storage have not yet matured. Bauer has shown that when younger infants are given sufficient repetitions of the task to be able to reproduce it, the sequence is forgotten after a brief delay. Six-month-old infants remember a sequence for one day; 9-month-olds remember for three months; 20-month-olds remember for a year (Bauer, 2006).

Another factor contributing to childhood amnesia may be that the episodic memory is not encoding verbally. It is not accessible to the verbal recall procedures we use with older children and adults. Maybe memories in infants are encoded based more on sensory and movement dimensions, rather than verbally, and these former modes of encoding become inaccessible to retrieval when the child does become verbal. As we become more verbal with age, and particularly as schooling shapes the ways we think, we come to categorize the world differently. Adult schemata are different from those we had as infants. So, new retrieval or search cues simply do not work in retrieving nonverbally encoded memories (Neisser, 1967). An analogy would be a new software program that cannot access or open files written in older software.

Simcock and Hayne (2002) tested this possibility that, as children age, they can remember what they had seen but cannot put those memories into words. If the vocabulary was not present when the memory was formed, it is not used later when the memory is retrieved. In their study, 27-month-old children were shown five actions performed with a variety of target objects. (e.g., a toy is placed in a Magic Shrinking Box, a crank is turned, a door is opened, and a smaller version of the toy is revealed). The children's expressive vocabulary does contain the words to name and describe these actions and objects. The children were tested one year later, after their vocabulary had developed sufficiently so that they could have described the event. The children could recognize pictures of the objects that were used, and discriminate them from similar objects; the children could re-enact the sequence, the delayed imitation measure. Clearly the children remembered. However, when the children were asked to "describe the game we played. . ." they children did not use their later-developed vocabulary to describe the event.

Capacity

Another explanation for what differentiates younger from older children is the capacity of their immediate memories. That is, maybe the short-term memory span or working-memory capacity is smaller in younger children. Processing in sort-term memory is restricted and therefore limits what can be entered into long-term memory.

Memory span, the number of items that can be retained after a single presentation, is less in younger children. For example, children in first grade (about 6 to 7 years old) retained 3 or 4 digits; sixth graders had a span of 5 to 6 digits; and adults had a span of 7 ± 2 items (Engle & Marshall, 1983). Working-memory capacity, as assessed by requiring simultaneous performance of two tasks, also increases with age.

Knowledge

A general rule is that the more you know, the more new you can remember. Maybe older children can remember more than younger children and infants because of the amount of preexisting knowledge they have.

This hypothesis predicts that younger children might do as well as, or even better, than older individuals if the younger children are more knowledgeable about the to-be-remembered material. This was nicely demonstrated by Chi (1978), who had 10-year-olds and adults remember arrangements of 20 chess pieces on a board and random strings of numbers. As expected, the adults had a longer span for digits. These particular children were chosen for the study because they were more knowledgeable about chess than were the adults. So, memory spans completely reversed for chess memory. Here, the children remembered the correct positions of more chess pieces than did the adults.

Strategies

Retention increases with the use of various mnemonic strategies: rehearsing the to-be-recalled material, forming mental images, grouping and organizing the items for later recall, and so on. Younger children do not use these strategies, and therefore do not recall as well as older children.

In simple memory tasks, children of different ages are asked to remember a series of picture triplets. Four- and five-year-olds tend not to rehearse spontaneously, whereas older children, usually by age 8 or so, do rehearse. (We know this from watching their mouth movements; Locke & Fehr, 1971.) Teaching the younger children to rehearse helps them to remember more (Keeney, Cannizzo, & Flavell, 1967). With still longer lists and somewhat older children, more efficient rehearsal strategies develop. Younger children repeat one item at a time, whereas older children intermix rehearsal of several items, a pattern that increases recall (Ornstein, Naus, & Liberty, 1975; Ornstein, Naus, & Stone, 1977).

Metamemory

Knowledge of memory in younger and older children differs, both about their own memories and how memory in general works. Metamemory, or knowledge about memory, is important in deciding what types of learning tasks will be difficult or when learning strategies should be used. For example, children were asked how they would remember to bring something to school with them tomorrow (Kreutzer, Leonard, & Flavell, 1975). This question asks children to tell something of what they know about memory. The children were very aware that they might forget, so they suggested using reminders, such as placing the item near the front door or in their backpack, or writing themselves a note (or just asking mom to remind them). As age increased from kindergarten to fifth grade, the children suggested more and more sophisticated solutions.

Although children are knowledgeable about memory in general, this knowledge is inaccurate in detail. When asked how many items of a given kind they could recall, children of most ages (including college students) overestimate. Practicing a memory test does not eliminate these overestimates. Pressley and Ghatala (1989), in a study spanning grades 1 to 8, asked students for three estimates of their performance on a vocabulary test: first, how well they thought they would do on a test; then, after taking the test, how well they thought they did; and, finally, how well they thought they would do on another test. Figure 12.2 shows the percentage of children who overestimated their performance. Before the quiz, 60 to 90 percent of the kids predicted they would do better than they actually did. The older children were most inaccurate in their predictions. After the quiz, the kids still thought they had done pretty well (though, on average, they only got 15 out of 30 items correct). The older children benefited most from their poor first test performance

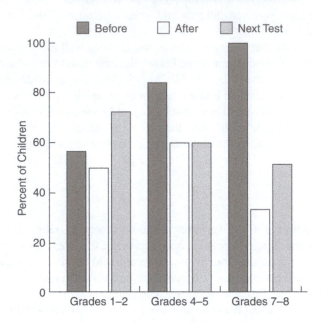

Figure 12.2 Percentages of children who overestimate performance before taking a difficult vocabulary
quiz, estimating performance on the quiz they just took, and predicting how they will do on
another quiz.

Source: Adapted from "Metacognitive Benefits of Taking a Test for Children and Young Adolescents," by M. Pressley
and E. S. Ghatala, 1989, *Journal of Experimental Child Psychology, 47*, Table 3. Copyright © 1989, with permission
from Elsevier.

and were best able to lower their estimates of future performance, adjusting their predictions so
that fewer eighth graders overestimated performance.

Autobiographical Memory

Infants and children can form and retain memories at an early age but adults recall very little from this period. One more answer to the question "what develops?" is *autobiographical
memory*. Autobiographical memory is related to the development of a sense of self, or self-
recognition. We cannot say definitively when a child develops a sense of self (and thus also personal memory). Self-recognition is sometimes tested by the mirror test: Does a child recognize
himself or herself in the mirror? If an ink mark is surreptitiously placed on the child's forehead,
will he or she notice the spot in the mirror and rub it? At age 2, children usually do not realize
that the spot they see in the mirror is in fact on them, whereas by age 4, children do realize this
(Howe, 2000).

Another factor in the development of autobiographical memory is *language*, which provides
both words and schemas to organize memories for later retrieval. Language also allows social
interaction with parents and others to elaborate memories. Talking about the past teaches children the narrative structure we employ in remembering our life stories. That is, parents' discussion of the day's events suggest to the child the "who, what, where, when" format (Fivush &
Nelson, 2004).

Finally, children need to develop a sense of the past and to learn labels for different times in the past. As children develop, broad time markers, such as SUMMER, are supplemented by more precise markers, such as LAST WEEK.

So What Is It That Develops?

There does not seem to be any one reason why memory improves from infancy to adulthood. Several factors, including encoding differences, memory strategies, knowledge, memory span, and metamemory, contribute. As we will see later (i.e., cross-cultural comparisons), age alone is not the only determiner of memory. Schooling influences both metamemory and the use of rehearsal strategies, two factors that affect recall independently of age.

Aging and Memory

Memory in older adults, typically referring to those over age 60, is not as good as in younger adults. In parallel to our question about what develops in children, Perlmutter (1978) asked: "What is memory aging the aging of?" The explanations for memory decline are similar to those offered for the poorer memory found in young children. Thus, reduced memory capacity and metamemory failures are two hypotheses considered, as well as encoding and/or retrieval difficulties.

Capacity

Tests of working memory show a decline with aging. For instance, there is an increased difficulty in doing two tasks at once, such as adding successively presented pairs of numbers and remembering the sums. This could indicate that the capacity of memory has been reduced (Charness, 1987; Light & Anderson, 1985). Others have suggested that there is a general cognitive slowing that accompanies aging (Salthouse, 1994). This slowing would be manifested at each step in performing a working-memory task: more time to encode the numbers, add the numbers, rehearse the accumulating sums, and then recall them. Thus, even if memory capacity was unchanged in the older adult, working memory still could be overtaxed by cognitive slowing.

Metamemory

Older adults might have poorer memories because they have different or inaccurate beliefs about memory. Having been out of school for a while, they have forgotten all those strategies they used when they were students. Maybe the elderly have unrealistic expectations about what can be remembered. Explanations such as these are not often supported by survey results. Perlmutter (1978) did not find any age effects in reported use of memory strategies, whether these were external aids such as lists and reminder notes, or internal methods such as relating to-be-remembered information to already known information. Knowledge about how memory works (e.g., memory is better for organized, concrete, or interrelated material) also did not vary with age.

However, the belief that memory declines with age could influence performance. In one demonstration of this age stereotype, both young and elderly female subjects read vignettes (case examples) of everyday forgetting by people. The cases were accompanied by a picture of the person, which could be of an older or younger person, as a way of introducing age into the manipulation. The participants were asked to explain why forgetting had occurred. Participants from both age groups attributed the memory failures in the older person vignettes to declining memory ability. Memory failures in younger person examples were attributed to a lack of effort: They could have remembered well, but they just didn't try (Erber & Rothberg, 1991).

Noncognitive Sources of Decline

Recall the distinction between learning versus performance. Performance could be poor even though the underlying learning or memory is not impaired. Aging is associated with a number of variables that could affect *performance* on a test of memory. Older individuals may suffer poorer health, take more medications that affect cognition, or experience mood impairments due to depression, grief, or life-style changes. Maybe the decline in memory is attributable to other factors associated with aging, but not necessarily to a decline in memory itself.

It is certainly the case that memory is impaired by many of these factors. Depression leads to poorer memory performance (Niederehe, 1991), and the side effects of combining many medicines is well recognized (e.g., Cammen, Simpson, Fraser, Preker, & Exton-Smith, 1987). One survey found that general health problems were good predictors of everyday memory problems (Cutler & Grams, 1988). By contrast, being healthier, educated, and intellectually active all predicted better memory performance (Arbuckle, Gold, Andres, Schwartzman, & Chaikelson, 1992). However, even when the elderly participants selected for research purposes are uniformly healthy, the major factor in describing memory decline is age (West, Crook, & Barron, 1992). Holding other factors constant still left a deficit that correlated with aging.

Summary of Age and Memory

Memory in young children and in aging adults is affected by many of the same factors, such as encoding, strategy use, or metamemory knowledge. A summary of these factors is presented in Table 12.1. In some cases, a factor has opposite effects. For instance, toddlers do not have sufficient knowledge to make information meaningful. Older adults may have knowledge and schemas which interferes with remembering new experiences.

Table 12.1 Sources of Memory Change With Age

	Improves as Children Age	*Declines as Adult Age*
Encoding	• use of strategies (rehearsal) develops • switch to verbal and imagery coding	• less use of strategies • slower processing; need more time to encode
Capacity	• short-term memory span increases	• working memory capacity decreases • multi-tasking declines
Knowledge	• semantic memory increases • schemas are acquired	• existing knowledge causes interference • schematic mis-recall
Meta-memory	• inaccurate knowledge about memory	• self-efficacy decreases • aging stereotypes
Neuro-	• hippocampus still developing	• hippocampus starts to decline

Intellectual Deficits

Developmental disability describes a condition of lowered intellectual ability. The causes are many; genetic disorders and birth defects, head injury, anoxia, malnutrition, and exposure of toxic substances are just a few. In some cases, the specific cause is unknown. A developmental disability is defined by the level of intellectual functioning. Levels significantly below average of same-age children are used to define categories from moderate to profound developmental disability.

The field of learning has made several contributions to research on developmental disabilities. One application is the behavior modification techniques used to teach developmentally disabled individuals (Chapters 4 and 5). A second contribution is the application of principles of memory to enhance learning, such as training in the use of rehearsal, imagery, or elaboration. We will consider here another contribution, that of describing individual differences in learning and memory. As examples, we can cite research on two exemplar forms of learning, classical conditioning and free recall.

Conditioning

Developmentally disabled individuals learn through classical conditioning and, in some cases, perform at about the same level as nondisabled participants. In a study of eyeblink conditioning, institutionalized, developmentally disabled young adults (mean age of 25) and a sample of college students each required about 25 CS–US pairings to condition. There was no difference during acquisition of conditioning. Where the developmentally disabled and nondisabled diverged was during extinction: The disabled individuals continued to respond after the control subjects had ceased (Lobb & Hardwick, 1976).

An important research tool is the study of learning and cognition associated with certain genetic disorders. Down syndrome (DS) is a genetic disorder in which an extra chromosome appears. Intellectual impairment varies widely in DS children and adults, from mild to profound. Down syndrome is of particular interest because the brain pathology that develops in older DS individuals (in this case, over age 35) is similar to that which develops in Alzheimer's disease.

Down syndrome individuals were participants in a study of eyeblink conditioning (Woodruff-Pak, Papka, & Simon, 1994), in which a tone was paired with an airpuff. The researchers had a portable computer control system that allowed them to take their laboratory with them. The participants could therefore participate within a familiar environment. The results of one study are shown in Figure 12.3, which shows the percentage of eyeblink CRs from the final block of 16 trials. We can note three interesting findings in these data. First, the overall level of conditioning in each DS group was lower than in age-matched control groups (under or over age 35). Second, the younger DS subjects (under age 35) responded more frequently than did the older DS participants. And third, conditioning in the older DS individuals did not differ statistically from that of elderly Alzheimer's individuals.

How General Is the Learning Deficit?

Is poor conditioning due to an overall intellectual impairment, or are there specific deficits, such as verbal versus spatial? Some research suggests that Down syndrome has a particular impact on spatial-learning ability. In designs that parallel the cognitive map-learning experiments discussed in Chapter 11, some DS infants (16 to 30 months of age) learned the location of a toy that was hidden in a familiar room. In one condition, the infants started from different locations within the room from trial to trial, but the toy remained in the same location. This is analogous to place learning or learning the platform location in the Morris water maze. The infant must

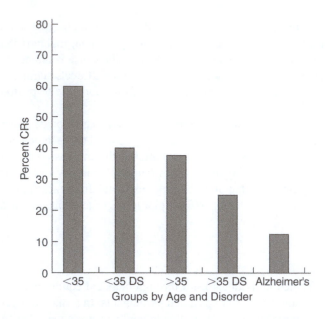

Figure 12.3 **Mean Percent Conditioned Eyeblink Responses at the End of Training.** Graph shows results for young adults (under age 35), young adult Down syndrome, older adult and older adult Down syndrome (both over age 35), and Alzheimer's patients.

Source: Based on "Eyeblink classical conditioning in Down's syndrome, fragile X syndrome, and normal adults over and under age 35," by D. S. Woodruff-Pak, M. Papka, & E. W. Simon, E. 1994, *Neuropsychology, 8,* p. 20. Copyright American Psychological Association. Reprinted with permission.

learn a cognitive map of the goal in relation to multiple environmental cues within the room. DS children were particularly impaired at this task in comparison to non-Down children of a similar age (Uecker, Mangan, Obrzut, & Nadel, 1993).

The profile of abilities and disabilities also differs among genetic disorders. Williams syndrome (WS) is a rare genetic disorder that produces mild to moderate developmental disabilities. In common with Down syndrome, Williams syndrome individuals are typically impaired on visual-spatial tasks, such as reproducing geometric designs with blocks. However, in contrast to DS, WS children are more articulate, fluent, and grammatical in their use of language. On verbal tests, such as word recall or digit span, WS children perform significantly better than DS children. During word recall, WS children cluster similar items. This indicates an awareness of the categorical nature of the lists (Bellugi, Wang, & Jernigan, 1994).

Memory

Other research has investigated the roles of working-memory capacity, memory strategies, and metamemory in the developmentally disabled. One prevailing theme across chapters in this text is that strategies play a major role in remembering. Children with developmental disabilities are less likely to use rehearsal during encoding or to self-prompt at retrieval. This suggests a lack of awareness of the effectiveness of memory strategies (see review by Kail, 1990).

Recall can be substantially increased by instruction in rehearsal. For example, adolescents with developmental disabilities were trained to rehearse to remember short strings of object names. The same items often recurred across lists over the 10 days of training, so the task required keeping track of the most recently presented items. As can be seen in Figure 12.4, children given rehearsal training remembered the list items better; those without such training remembered only

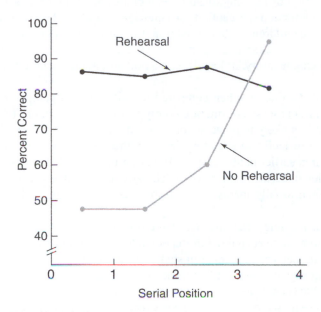

Figure 12.4 **Effects of Rehearsal Training on Short-Term Retention in Developmentally Disabled Adolescents.** Without rehearsal training, only the final item in the list is well recalled.

Source: Brown et al. (1973, p. 126).

the final items well (a recency effect). An interesting companion experiment used the same procedure with children without developmental disabilities. One group received no formal instructions and they recalled nearly 90 percent of the items, presumably because they were rehearsing. When rehearsal was disrupted in a second group, their recall fell to less than 50 percent. This study shows that by manipulating rehearsal, the developmentally disabled and nondisabled individuals could achieve comparable levels of either good or poor performance (Brown, Campione, Bray, & Wilcox, 1973).

If strategies such as rehearsal can be taught, will use of the strategy generalize beyond a particular experiment? Research on the transfer of strategies can be summarized on two levels (Kramer, Nagle, & Engle, 1980). On one level, the use of strategies does not spontaneously transfer to the learning of different types of materials. This is unfortunately characteristic of mnemonic training in children in general, whether they are developmentally disabled or not (Pressley & Dennis-Rounds, 1980). On a broader level, developmentally disabled individuals have difficulty with a number of metamemory skills, including estimating their memory spans, making judgments of learning, apportioning study time, self-testing, or searching memory.

The previously reviewed findings suggest that memory performance by the developmentally disabled can be improved. There is a caveat (or caution) here. Tactics such as rehearsal or metamemory training do not eliminate the gap between the developmentally disabled and the nondisabled, although such instruction can increase the adaptive functioning of both.

Learning Disabilities

A learning disability is an impairment of a specific cognitive ability. Learning-disabled individuals show a discrepancy between their poor performance in one area and better performance in other areas. The disability could be in reading (such as dyslexia), mathematics, or language.

A full consideration of learning disabilities includes much more than just learning. There may be deficits in attention, perception, or language that affect learning. However, research on learning-disabled children has benefited from the various component approaches described in previous chapters. For example, we can ask whether learning disabilities are accompanied by deficits in working memory, or localized to a problem in the encoding stage or the retrieval stage.

Learning-disabled children, when compared to children with comparable intelligence test scores, were found to process information poorly in short-term memory (Swanson & Cooney, 1991). They were less likely to rehearse, or if they did rehearse they less often used organization or elaboration to facilitate encoding. We saw these same factors in comparing younger versus older children earlier in this chapter. The question is whether the failure to use effective rehearsal strategies underlies poorer recall. The answer is that instructing learning-disabled children in rehearsal usually increases recall, but does not eliminate the difference from the control group.

Students with a learning disability may have difficulties at any stage of processing, from attending to information, to encoding information into long-term memory, to retrieving information from long-term memory. A number of studies have found particular difficulty with retrieval from *semantic memory*, or so-called fact retrieval (e.g., remembering arithmetic facts). McNamara and Wong (2003) compared fifth graders with and without learning disabilities on a series of laboratory tests (e.g., sentence memory) and everyday learning tests (e.g., recalling details of everyday objects). Given free-recall instructions (e.g., "Recall the sentence" or "List the features of a penny"), the learning-disabled students consistently remembered fewer details, items, and facts. However, when recall was prompted, the disabled and control subjects were different on only a few tasks. Thus, in recalling the procedure for checking out a book from the library, asking specific questions about the steps involved elicited more recall from the learning-disabled students. Similarly, when given a list of the features of a penny, these students could properly locate them on a penny. The success on these prompting tests showed a role for retrieval difficulties by learning-disabled students.

Children with reading and language disabilities have a particular problem with verbal memory. Dyslexic children were tested on both verbal and nonverbal memory tasks, such as reproducing abstract designs or remembering the sequence of a series of designs. Dyslexia is characterized by reading impairments, and so one could expect poor verbal memory performance. Actually, the dyslexic children had lower scores on both forms of memory than did the control children. However, not all dyslexics were equivalently affected. Neither verbal memory nor memory for designs correlated very strongly with reading ability (Fein, Davenport, Yingling, & Galin, 1988).

Similarly, Swanson (1993) tested 10-year-olds with a math or a reading learning disability on a battery of working-memory tests. Each test required the child to remember a series of items (e.g., a story or the location of X's in a matrix) and also to answer a question about the material. Thus, this dual-task procedure exemplifies Baddeley's definition of working memory as simultaneously holding information while performing mental operations. The math-disabled and the reading-disabled students had lower working-memory scores on both verbal and visual-spatial tests than did their nondisabled classmates. These results are surprising: The learning disability was specific (either math or reading) whereas the working memory deficit was general. The studies by Fein et al. (1988) and Swanson (1993) suggest that children with different disabilities, such as mathematics versus reading disabilities, have a generalized working-memory impairment that is not specific to verbal versus visual-spatial information processing.

Although cognitive approaches offer one means to describe what aspects of learning or remembering are disabled, it will not be a complete explanation. Learning-disabled children (and adults) experience social and emotional difficulties that interact with their learning disabilities.

Exceptional Memory: The Mnemonists

The psychology literature contains examples of individuals with truly exceptional memory abilities, some showing talents for remembering numbers or languages, others for memorizing the Bible, the Koran, or the *Iliad*. Many such remarkable claims cannot be supported by documentation and so they fall in the category of anecdotes: interesting stories but ones that cannot be accepted unquestioningly. However, other cases include testing under controlled conditions, and here we can ask how good can memory be, and what causes it to be exceptional?

One of the most remarkable cases of memory is a man referred to as *S*, studied by the Russian neuropsychologist Luria (1968). *S* could remember extraordinary amounts of verbal material. Long lists of names, numbers, and words could be recalled even years later. As examples, *S* memorized from a single presentation lines from Dante's *Divine Comedy* in its original Italian, a language with which *S* was unfamiliar. He also memorized the following meaningless mathematical formula:

$$N \cdot \sqrt{d^2 \times \frac{85}{vx}} \cdot \sqrt{\frac{276^2 \times 86x}{n^2 v \pi 264}} n^2 b = sv \frac{1624}{32^2} \cdot r^2 s$$

When given a surprise test 15 years later (that's right, 15 *years*), *S* was able to reproduce both the Italian verse and the formula. *S* worked as a mnemonist in clubs, doing several shows a night memorizing lists of words provided by the audiences. (*Mnemonist* is one name for people with exceptional memories. "Memorist" has been offered as an alternative label.) If *S* had any problem with his memory, it was that he remembered too much (you should have that problem!). *S* would occasionally make mistakes in recalling a given list, but this was because he was misrecalling lists from an earlier performance that evening. *S* eventually learned how to forget these earlier-learned lists by "erasing" them from his mental blackboard.

How did *S* remember so much? One factor for him was he actually experienced stimuli in multiple sensory modalities. This is called synesthesia, a condition of cross-modal perception. Spoken words would evoke visual images, smells, tastes, and tactile feelings. It is an inborn condition of the brain (Cytowic & Wood, 1982) and so may not be a trait that is learnable. If exceptional memory is biologically determined, of what benefit is there to the rest of us in studying memorists? One lesson is that remembering is better for items presented in multiple sensory modalities. Another lesson is that even mnemonists use strategies to aid retention. For example, *S* would encode to-be-remembered words and numbers into images to be retained. *S* also used the method of loci, or locations (Chapter 6). To remember a list, he would mentally place each object at some location during his mental walk down an imagined street.

Are there differences between the brains of exceptional memorists and others? A neuroimaging study explored the differences between exceptional and regular rememberers (Maguire, Valentine, Wilding, & Kapur, 2003). The memorists and the controls were matched for general intellectual levels. The memorists were bright but not exceptionally so. The memorists had, however, competed at the top level of the World Memory Championships, which requires players to memorize 57-line poems, columns of 25 unrelated words, and strings of 40 random digits. All of the subjects performed memory tests while their brains were scanned to detect the regions of most activity, a procedure known as *functional brain imaging*. The memorists were better than the controls at remembering strings of numbers in sequence but not at recalling faces or images of individual snowflakes. (Snowflakes are difficult to encode verbally.) Thus, the memorists were good at remembering verbal material, which was related to their memory competition skill, but they were not significantly better at remembering other things. So, they did not have a general memory expertise.

Interestingly, the more active brain areas were those usually involved in spatial and navigation tasks and not particularly those involved in verbal memory. Most of the memorists reported they had used the method of loci mnemonic (just like *S*, described above), in which to-be-recalled items are pictured at points along a mental route. Thus, their world-class memories were attributed to the use of a specific strategy, not to physical differences in their brains or to innate general memory ability.

Highly Superior Autobiographical Memory

History and biography record cases of individuals who said that they could remember every day, or nearly so, of their lives (Neisser, 1982). A Reverend Dr. Phelps claimed he could recall something specific about any day for the preceding 60 years of his life. If given the date March 6, 1879, "In a few moments he will state the day of the week. Then he will give you the weather for that day, and describe some particular thing that happened" (Neisser, 1982, p. 413).

Contemporary examples of such individuals are subject to scientific verification. A woman with exceptional personal or autobiographical memory approached three memory psychologists, who studied her over a 5-year period (Parker, Cahill, & McGaugh, 2006). A.J., in her 30s when the research began, can apparently remember every day of her life since age 11. Give her a date, and she can tell you what she did that day. When asked to recollect Easter Sundays, which fall on different dates each year, within a few minutes she had produced a list of the past 24 years, listing the date and some personal recollection of the day. Two years later, she repeated this feat, noting the same personal events for each year as noted in the first test. The memories are automatic, and not retrieved by specific search or reconstructive strategies. Her recollections are personal: what happened to her, what she did, what she felt. The external events of the day, such as newsworthy events, are recollected only if the event related to her life story.

On formal memory tests, A.J. scored well above average on some tests. Yet some of her other memory capacities were below average, such as remembering word lists, nonsense drawings, and recognizing faces she had seen earlier.

Not all aspects of A.J.'s ability were welcome. Her initial desire to contact the psychologists was partly due to the distress experienced by constantly remembering her past. She describes herself as being a prisoner of her memories. One memory leads to another, then another, and so on, as if she cannot stop chaining through these linked memories.

This exceptional memory ability has been labeled *Highly Superior Autobiographical Memory*, or HSAM. Since A.J., McGaugh and his colleagues have identified several more individuals who have these same detailed memories of their lives. In one study, they compared 11 HSAM individuals to matched control subjects, and gave everyone a battery of memory tests (LePort et al., 2012). The HSAM were clearly better than the normal memory controls in personal memory, memory for public events, and details of what happened on specific dates. Public events are tied to dates (e.g., national elections, natural disasters, or sporting events) and so the personal and the public interrelate. This is basically what defines HSAM. However, the HSAM subjects were mostly average on other memory measures: digit span, learning paired associates, and free recall. Their superior memory ability was domain specific.

In addition, the HSAM subjects were given structural MRI scans. The HSAM and the controls showed a number of differences. One difference was, roughly speaking, in the parietal lobe of the brain. This area is believed to be involved in integrating information across sensory modalities. (The same area that might underlie the synesthesia of the mnemonist *S*.) This area is also involved in binding or joining elements of episodic memory (context, perception, emotion, etc).

A summary of some comparisons of HSAM and world memory champions on the one hand, with matching controls is shown in Table 12.2. The memory experts do not have superior memories overall. Memory champs remember things that use their practiced skills, such as recalling strings of

Table 12.2 Standard Memory Tests in Which Memory Experts Remembered More Than Matched Controls, or Remembered as Well as Controls

Memory experts exceed controls	Memory experts same as controls
Digit Span HSAM and WMC	Sequence (of names, faces) WMC
Story Recall HSAM and WMC	Verbal Paired Associates HSAM
Recall Name-to-Face HSAM	Recognizing Faces WMC
Autobiographical Memory HSAM	Visual Memory (snowflakes, abstract design) HSAM and WMC

HSAM = Highly Superior Autobiographical Memory; WMC = World Memory Championship participants.

numbers or names matched to faces. But they are unexceptional with memory for other types of information, such as recognizing whether a face was seen earlier, or the sequence in which faces were shown.

The Case of Savants

Savants are individuals with an exceptional cognitive ability in the presence of otherwise low intelligence. Savants (formerly called idiot savants, indicating the contradictory nature of the abilities) can be calendar calculators (they can tell you what day of the week any date occurred on) or math whizzes. Some savants have exceptional mnemonic talents. The film *Rain Man* often defines the public stereotype of a savant: an individual who can memorize local phonebooks. But how good is memory in savants?

O'Conner and Hermelin (1989) studied savants who excelled at remembering bus schedules, such as routes, bus numbers, stops along the itinerary, and so on. Six savants were compared to six other autistic individuals of the same age and overall intelligence level, which was 23 years old and having an IQ of about 80. The savants were able to learn paired-associate lists of numbers (actually, London bus numbers) significantly faster than did the controls, thus showing the savants indeed did have better memory for bus-related information. Do savants have a better memory in general than do the controls? O'Conner and Hermelin gave both groups 10 tests, including both verbal and non-verbal memory measures (e.g., paired-associate learning of fruit and vegetable words). The savants and their IQ-matched controls did not differ overall, or on any of the single tests.

Two important points can be made. First, savants may have exceptional memories, but sometimes it is exceptional only in comparison to other areas of their intellectual performance. Second, savants often have had years of practice with material within a certain domain, such as bus routes or songs. Treffert (1989) noted that parents may notice a talent in their child early in life, and heavily reinforce this talent thereafter. These individuals may come to possess prodigious skills, but due to years of practice.

Gender and Cognitive Abilities

Do men and women differ in their memory abilities? Most research has focused more broadly on cognitive ability rather than specifically on memory. As examples, verbal ability is often defined by performance on a specific test, such as the verbal SAT; spatial ability is often measured as spatial perception or mental imagery, such as a test of mental rotation of objects (see Figure 12.5). At one time, the prevailing view was that men performed better on spatial tests and women on verbal tests. However, the differences in language and mathematics test scores have been decreasing for several decades (e.g., Feingold, 1988).

What about other measures of spatial cognition? In a study of actual way-finding, male and female college students were individually led through a wooded area by two researchers. Men were more accurate in identifying the direction of the starting location; and men took shorter paths back (Silverman et al., 2000). In responding to questionnaires, more women reported having difficulties than did men in way-finding, and the women expressed higher levels of anxiety about spatial situations. For example, women described more nervousness about finding their way back after making a wrong turn, and finding their way out of a complex office building (Lawton, 1994).

Differences in performance on spatial tasks do not necessarily mean differences in underlying ability. Women's anxiety about getting lost (Lawton, 1994) could impair actual spatial performance. Self-fulfilling expectancies come into play when the instructions for a task emphasize its "spatial" nature. In one case, women did more poorly than did men on the mental rotation test task (shown in Figure 12.5), when the usual spatial instructions were given (i.e., "this is a test of your spatial abilities"). However, when nonspatial instructions were given, men and women did not differ (Sharps, Welton, & Price, 1993).

Other studies have compared men and women on verbal memory. One study was able to control for a number of incidental variables by using a large and representative sample of subjects (Herlitz, Nilsson, & Backman, 1997). The 1,000 subjects were randomly selected from the population of a region in Sweden, sampling ages from 35 to 80 years old. Education, intelligence, and general health were assessed to statistically control for these factors. A battery of verbal episodic memory tests was administered, including tests of recall and recognition of word lists, sentences, new factual information, and names and faces. There were also measures of short-term memory and semantic memory (i.e., general knowledge and vocabulary). The women performed better, on the average, than men at word recall and recognition, learning new facts, and recognizing newly learned names and faces. These are all tests of episodic memory, and mostly verbal memory. Men and women did not differ in semantic memory or in short-term memory.

In some cases, gender differences in memory are due to differential familiarity with the to-be-learned material. If the target material is more familiar to one gender, performance may be better. Davies and Robertson (1993) found that males were better at recognizing pictures of cars they had been shown earlier, and females were better at recognizing faces. This difference appeared as early as ages 9 to 11. Gender differences may even appear if one *thinks* he or she knows more. When college students listened to a vaguely worded prose passage titled either "Building a Workbench" or "Making a Shirt," male students remembered more when given the workbench title, but female students remembered more when given the shirt title (Herrmann, Crawford, & Holdsworth, 1992). Yet everyone had heard the same passage.

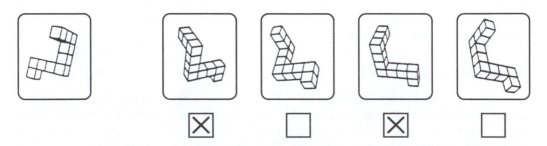

Figure 12.5 **Mental Rotation Test for Spatial Cognitive Ability.** A sample three-dimensional drawing of an object is given on the left. The task is to identify which two objects from the right are rotated version of the sample object.

Source: From R. N. Shepard & J. Metzler, 1988, "Mental Rotation: Effects of dimensionality of objects and type of task," *Journal of Experimental Psychology: Human Perception and Performance, 14*, 3–11. Copyright American Psychological Association, and reprinted with permission.

Gender differences also arise from expectations or stereotypes about how one should perform. Ceci and Bronfenbrenner (1985) conducted a study of prospective remembering in which children had to remember to perform some action 30 minutes later. Boys remembered better to check a battery charger (a stereotypically "guy" thing) and girls remembered better to check the oven. These effects were larger among the 14-year-olds than among the 10-year-olds.

There can be a number of explanations for gender differences in learning and memory. A social-cultural explanation posits there may be differences in life experiences, education, expectations, and/or stereotypes between boys and girls (and men and women). Such differences could begin early in life.

Alternatively, men and women might differ in memory capabilities because of inherent biological differences. One source of such differences may be hormones. There are reports that memory is related to changes in estrogen levels. For instance, adult women showed fluctuations across the menstrual cycle on tests of spatial ability (Hampson & Kimura, 1988). This study did not show that women performed *worse* than men, only that the performance of women varied across their cycle. In another study, women who received estrogen-replacement therapy following a hysterectomy maintained their preoperative levels of performance on prose-paragraph recall and in paired-associate learning (Sherwin, 1994). It should be noted that estrogen did not cause an increase in memory but rather prevented a decline. Research with female mice and rats (which can be experimentally treated) showed an interesting pattern of results. Ovarian hormones (versus the absence of such hormones) benefitted performance on tasks of working memory, such as the radial arm maze and the Morris water maze (see Chapter 11). Hormones had little effect on long-term conditioning tasks (Dohanich, 2003).

Corresponding research has been conducted using the male hormone testosterone. Typically, men with higher levels of testosterone (occurring either naturally or through supplementation) showed better spatial cognition. However, most of the benefits seemed to be among older men, in which the level of testosterone is decreasing. So, taking a hormone supplement could increase verbal memory in older women or spatial memory in older men (Hogervorst, DeJager, Budge, & Smith, 2004; Janowsky, Oviatt, & Orwoll, 1994).

As we have seen before, gender differences can be addressed by theories ranging from hormones to socialization, and from interest levels to self-handicapping. The point of mentioning these alternatives is to show the uncertainty that underlies explanations of gender differences.

Personality and Learning

Personality can be defined as an individual's characteristic mode of thinking, feeling, and acting. Personality is often described in terms of relatively stable and enduring traits, such as the degree of extraversion, emotional stability, openness to new experience, impulsiveness, or conscientiousness (McCrae & Costa, 1986). Personality becomes relevant to learning if variations in one or another trait are associated with different behaviors or cognitions that affect learning. For instance, a combination of traits, which includes higher levels of extraversion and conscientiousness and a lower level of anxiety, does correlate with academic success (Roberts, Kuncel, Shiner, Caspi, & Goldberg, 2007). Two individual traits in particular that are important for learning are self-control and anxiety.

Self-Control

The classic demonstration of self-control in children is the "marshmallow" experiment conducted by Walter Mischel and his students (see Mischel, Shoda, & Rodriguez, 1989). Two- to four-year-old children were given a choice between receiving one marshmallow now or a few marshmallows later. Self-control was shown if the child waited for the better reward. Older children typically can delay gratification, and a number of other positive benefits accrued to these children. Years later, Mischel decided to follow-up on some of the children from the initial studies. He wondered whether this early self-control, or lack thereof, was related to later development. The researchers found that those who had earlier shown better self-control had fewer behavior problems in school, and higher SAT scores (Mischel, Shoda, & Peake, 1988).

Duckworth and Seligman (2005) conducted a year-long study of self-discipline among eighth graders. Self-control in this case was measured by self-report questionnaires, and parent- and teacher-reports. Self-control was a better predictor of final grades that year than was intelligence. Self-control also correlated with study habits, time spent on homework, and (less) time watching television.

Research from a number of disciplines suggests that **self-control**, and related concepts such as self-discipline, conscientiousness, persistence, and the ability to delay gratification, are important predictors of educational attainment, income, and even longevity (Roberts et al., 2007). A major community study followed 1,000 children in New Zealand from birth to age 32. Measures of self-control that were obtained between the ages of 3 and 11 had significant correlations with adult measures of health (such as the absence of various diseases; substance abuse); wealth (income; socioeconomic status; financial difficulties); positive social outcomes (higher levels of education); and fewer negative social outcomes (e.g., criminal convictions; Moffitt et al., 2011).

The importance of self-control is now gaining substantial currency among researchers, social scientists, and educators. The topic of one book, *How Children Succeed* (Tough, 2012) is persistence. A measure of self-discipline is the Grit scale (Duckworth & Quinn, 2009). Where the IQ score was once believed to be the best predictor of academic success, we may now grant at least equal validity to self-control or self-discipline (Roberts et al., 2007).

Anxiety

The debilitating effects of test anxiety are all too familiar to many students. As the exam is distributed, your heart starts to race; as you scan the first few questions, you read but without comprehending; you try to calm yourself, only to realize you have used up valuable exam time. In such cases, the obvious effect of anxiety has been to impair performance.

Anxiety can be temporary and situational, as is the anxiety on the day of the SAT or GRE exam. Anxiety can also refer to a relatively stable personality trait. *Trait* anxiety can be thought of as a continuum, and someone is chronically more or less nervous. This trait of anxiousness affects memory in several ways: by increasing arousal, limiting the available capacity of working memory, and influencing attention.

In some cases, additional arousal of the nervous system is beneficial for encoding. The extra arousal coming from being anxious sometimes improves performance, just as some caffeine might. However, too much anxiety, in combination with a difficult task, most likely will impair new learning or impair retrieval of previously learned material (Eysenck, 1981).

A second hypothesis states that anxiety reduces the capacity of working memory (Eysenck, 1979; Hasher & Zacks, 1988). Anxiety is accompanied by worry about how you are doing. Task-irrelevant self-talk co-opts some of the capacity of working memory. Working memory, therefore, is divided between the cognitive task and worrying. An anxious individual can compensate for some divided attention if the task is easy enough. However, with a difficult task, there may not be sufficient spare capacity to maintain accurate performance (see Chapter 8).

A third hypothesis is that anxiety biases how events are perceived and interpreted, and thus remembered. Anxiety could bias attention towards negative information, leading to enhanced recall of it. Young and Martin (1981) presented anxious and nonanxious subjects with fictitious personality descriptions. They used a very convincing procedure in which the subjects first completed some personality inventories and a little later were read a series of adjectives that were ostensibly the results of the tests. Actually, everyone heard the same list of descriptors, which contained both positive and negative traits. The participants were later asked to recall as many of the trait adjectives as possible. The high-anxious subjects recalled many more negative words (that supposedly applied to themselves) and fewer positive words; the less anxious subjects recalled more positive and fewer negative words. Note that the high and low-anxious participants recalled the same total number of words. The difference was in what was remembered.

Does anxiety predict everyday memory problems? Several studies have found correlations between anxiety and scores on the Cognitive Failures Questionnaire (Martin & Jones, 1984). Anxious people report more instances of forgetting, habit slips of doing the wrong thing, misperceiving stimuli, forgetting what they just read, and so on. In addition, people working in high-stress jobs (i.e., critical care nurses) also had high Cognitive Failures scores.

Learning can be seriously impaired in other psychological disorders. Research on two, post-traumatic stress disorder and schizophrenia, are discussed in Box 12.1.

Box 12.1 Learning and Psychopathology

The field of psychopathology, or abnormal psychology, deals with behavioral and psychological disorders. Some researchers in this field seek to determine whether and how cognitive processes such as learning and remembering are impaired in mental illnesses. Learning and memory are directly involved in certain psychological disorders, such as psychogenic amnesias; and indirectly involved in others, possibly as a side effect of brain or biochemical abnormalities.

Schizophrenia is a severe psychological disorder characterized by emotional and social impairments, and in more serious cases, by hallucinations and delusions (false, irrational beliefs). Neurological research has implicated a number of brain regions and processes in this disease. Schizophrenia may involve frontal-lobe dysfunction, as evidenced by increased distractibility. The central executive of working memory is impaired in schizophrenic individuals, consistent with similar impairments found with frontal lobe injuries (Park, Holzman, & Goldman-Rakic, 1995). Those who are researching the genetic basis for schizophrenia have found similar working-memory deficits among close relatives of schizophrenic individuals, relatives who are themselves free of the disorder. The hippocampus has also been found to be smaller in schizophrenics. As you should know by now, the hippocampus is important in both explicit memory recall and in spatial memory.

Posttraumatic stress disorder (PTSD) is a disorder that has altered memory functioning as a central symptom. PTSD, which results from a traumatic experience, is characterized by repetitive and intrusive memories of the initiating event. The memories can be ongoing and ruminative, appear in dreams and nightmares, or be triggered by stimuli in the environment. Does PTSD affect other memory forms of learning? One reaction that is manifested is increased startle reaction to sudden stimuli, and sometimes a failure to habituate to those stimuli when they are repeated. Classical conditioning may also be affected, especially aversive conditioning. In one study, individuals diagnosed with PTSD (war veterans, fire-fighters, or assault victims) were compared with controls who experienced similar traumas but did not develop PTSD. Classical conditioning consisted of discrimination training between pairings of a colored disk (e.g., yellow) with shock and a different color (e.g., blue) without shock. The PTSD group (1) had higher reaction levels to the stimuli at baseline before conditioning began; (2) showed more fear conditioning to the stimulus paired with shock; and (3) showed more persistence of conditioned responding during extinction, when the non-PTSD subjects had ceased reacting to the stimulus (Orr et al., 2000). These several findings suggest that individuals with PTSD do not habituate to neutral stimuli, and learn more fear to aversive stimuli. The researchers questioned whether this higher level of fear is an aftereffect of the trauma, or whether the emotionality existed before the trauma and predisposed these individuals to develop PTSD.

PTSD patients also show deficits on standard measures of memory (Bremner et al., 1993). Vietnam War veterans were impaired at word-list learning, remembering a paragraph of information, and reproducing visual designs. These materials are not trauma related, so the findings suggest that trauma victims suffer a generalized deficit in new learning and remembering. Traumatic experiences affect numerous functions in the nervous system, from neurotransmitter levels to hormone secretions to cell death and loss. We can only speculate which are most relevant to the learning deficits shown in PTSD. One suggestion is that trauma-induced arousal of the amygdala strengthens or consolidates emotional, unconscious, and implicit memories (such as conditioned fear responses), while correspondingly, overarousal of the hippocampus makes it *less able* to preserve the declarative and conscious aspects of memory (van der Kolk, 1994).

Learning Styles

A topic of continuing interest in the field of education is that of learning styles. The phrase **learning style** is used in many ways, but it generally refers to a way of categorizing individual differences in how people learn. For instance, style is used in reference to those who are said to be left brain thinkers versus right brain. An advertisement for a new car will present a table of facts for the left brain (the verbal and analytic half) and a picture of a hot car for the right brain (the visual and emotional half). Much of the prose on learning styles has generated more heat than light. Although theories and inventories of style have been developed, there is little empirical work to validate the idea that people of different styles learn differently. A few typologies, however, have generated some empirical support.

The Visualizer–Verbalizer Dimension

One style dichotomy that is mentioned frequently is a preference for *verbal learning* (via words, books, lectures) versus *visual learning* (via pictures, illustration, or videos). Mayer and Massa (2003) gave college students a battery of tests that were selected to measure both style (i.e., preference) and ability. Mayer and Massa indeed found that visualizers tended to score higher on spatial ability than did verbalizers, as measured by tests similar to the mental-rotation test (shown earlier in Figure 12.5). Visualizers also had a preference for the visual versus verbal presentation of information. In a computer-learning exercise on cloud and lightning formation, for example, visualizers preferred the "help" screens that elaborated on the material with drawings (maybe water vapor rising to the sky), whereas the verbalizers preferred "help" screens that provided textual descriptions. As another example, I would guess that visualizers would prefer maps and verbalizers would prefer a set of directions.

Kolb

Another conception of learning style is a two-dimensional organization offered by Kolb (1984). One dimension describes a preference for learning from *concrete* experiences (such as hands-on activities) versus a preference for learning in the *abstract* (such as principles taught by lecture or text). The second dimension expresses a preference for deriving knowledge through *reflection*

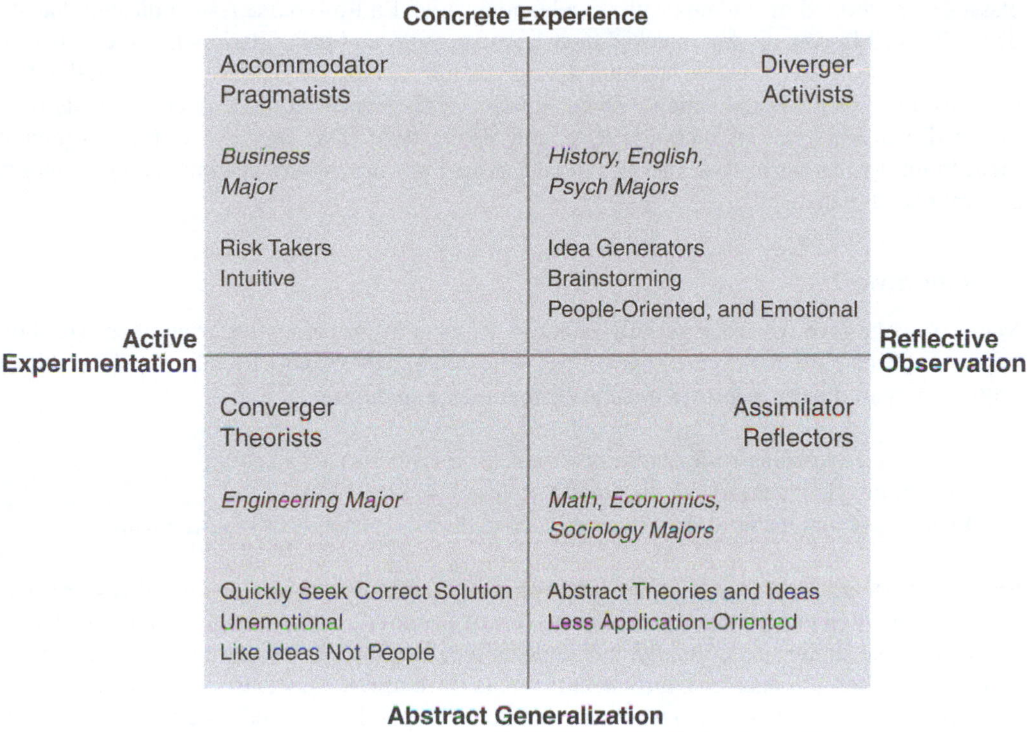

Concrete Experience

Accommodator Pragmatists *Business Major* Risk Takers Intuitive	Diverger Activists *History, English, Psych Majors* Idea Generators Brainstorming People-Oriented, and Emotional
Converger Theorists *Engineering Major* Quickly Seek Correct Solution Unemotional Like Ideas Not People	Assimilator Reflectors *Math, Economics, Sociology Majors* Abstract Theories and Ideas Less Application-Oriented

Active Experimentation (left)   **Reflective Observation** (right)

Abstract Generalization

Figure 12.6 Kolb's Learning Styles.
Source: Derived from Kolb (1984).

(thinking as a source of generalizations) versus active *experimentation* (trying out newly derived principles). As shown in Figure 12.6, an individual's learning style depends on his or her location in this two-dimensional space (based on Claxton & Murrell, 1987). Placement in the grid is determined by answers to a self-report inventory. However, there is little data to show that these individuals indeed learn differently. One difficulty in testing this hypothesis is that a given student's preferred style of learning may conflict with the style enforced by a given teacher. Some educators who write on learning styles suggest that teachers and students should be matched by style or that instructors should use different styles over the course of a semester to accommodate different student styles (Claxton & Murrell, 1987).

Sternberg

One ambitious attempt to match student and instructional style has been reported by Sternberg and Grigorenko (1997; Grigorenko & Sternberg, 1997). Students taking a summer general psychology course were first tested to determine which of three cognitive styles they possessed: analytical, creative, or practical thinking. As examples, analytic teaching involves asking students to compare and contrast, evaluate, or critique an idea. The creative style asks students to invent or answer "imagine/what if?" types of questions. Practical thinking is taught by asking students to demonstrate how something could apply in the real world. The students were then assigned to course sections that were taught using analytical, creative, or practical styles. Thus, students could be in a course that matched their preferred mode (e.g., creative students in a section emphasizing creative thinking) or were explicitly mismatched. In addition, some mixed classes were formed of students with each learning style. End-of-course tests indicated that students did well in courses that matched their learning styles and particularly when the tests were of that same style (i.e., creative students were given tests asking for creative answers rather than analysis and practical application). Thus, superior performance required three elements to be matched: student style, instructional style, and testing style. This suggests a practical impediment to implementing of style theories to educational settings, where such matching cannot be accomplished realistically.

Learning Styles?

Many of us believe we are especially effective learners in one modality or another. Are those perceptions accurate and do they correspond with actual performance? Kratzig and Arbuthnott (2006) compared three measures obtained from college students:

> Self-labeled learning style (auditory, visual, or kinesthetic)
> Learning style inventory results (auditory, visual, or kinesthetic)
> Learning actual material that was presented auditorily, visually, or kinesthetically

Students first labeled themselves as being primarily auditory, visual, or kinesthetic learners. The students then completed a standardized test of learning styles to obtain a numerical score for these same dimensions. Finally, the students took actual tests of auditory, visual, and kinesthetic learning. For example, the students would have to remember lists of words they heard (auditory) or saw (visual). The results showed no correspondence among the several measures. Fewer than half of the participants' self-reported dominant learning style corresponded with the inventory's determination of the dominant style; and the inventory's assignment of style did not correspond to actual numbers of items remembered from tasks involving verbal, drawn, and handled objects.

Social and Cultural Differences

Different cultures emphasize different aspects of remembering. Verbal transmission of knowledge is more important in some societies, whereas spatial or visual memory is more useful to others. Is memory enhanced in societies that value remembering? To what extent do schooling and education change the way we learn and use memory? These are questions that cross-cultural studies of learning and memory can address. By studying other cultures, we may discern universal aspects of memory and, conversely, how our own conceptions of memory are shaped by the culture and society we live in.

Epic Memories

Back in high school you probably learned about the Greek poet Homer, and his epic tales the *Iliad* and the *Odyssey*. Maybe you were stunned to hear that these stories were repeated from memory, without a written version to consult. How do poets and performers do this?

Earlier in the last century, anthropologists began to study cultures whose literature was primarily oral rather than written. For example, the Gola people of Liberia in Africa remember extensive genealogical histories (D'Azevedo, 1962). These family histories were repeated at formal ceremonies or to settle disputes, giving the new generation opportunities to learn their family tree. The elders who knew the lineages were respected individuals. The outsiders who studied the Gola did not know the genealogies and so could not verify their accuracy.

Lord (1960) began in the 1930s to study the performance of poets who sang folk tales in areas of Yugoslavia where this oral tradition existed. These songs sometimes ran to thousands of lines and would take hours to perform. Experienced singers claimed to know 30 or more of these epics. New tales were learned by listening to other performers, and some singers claimed they could learn a new song after hearing it once. Such claims reinforced a popular belief that memory is especially well developed in nonliterate societies. But had these accomplished performers really memorized these poems?

Lord found that the singers had a very different skill than what we are daily exposed to in Western societies. Our singers do indeed memorize the words to relatively short songs. The singers in the oral tradition, however, remembered the outline of the story and some facts, but otherwise essentially recomposed the story for each performance. The singers knew formulas, fillers, and different ways of phrasing the same idea. They would then select an appropriate expression to fit the rhyme or meter. The same story might be related, yet each performance would be somewhat different. Although the performers claimed to remember "word for word" this phrase has no correspondence in a culture without writing; that is, what is a word? Instead, the performers were referring to the veracity of their recall. To suggest that these folk performers do not remember the tales verbatim in no way diminishes their abilities. Instead, we now perceive that their talent is of a different sort: They create anew each time that they perform.

This reconstructive aspect of memory is in accord with some current conceptions of memory retrieval. Some theorists argue that remembering is not so much the activation of a static trace stored in memory but instead is the reconstruction of the earlier experience.

Goody (1998) made the paradoxical observation that it is literate cultures that most emphasize the word-for-word recall of written texts. Homer's epic tales and the Bible have existed in written form for over 2,000 years and the Quran for over 1,000. It was only when the texts were written that they became guides to verbatim memorization.

Experimental Studies

Experimental studies in countries other than the United States, and in cultures other than Western European, shed important light on universal versus specific factors of learning and memory. Our theories assume there are certain features of memory, for example, separate short-term and long-term memory systems. We have also described memory strategies, such as organization or imagery. Are these universal features of memory, or are they due to the effects of schooling, television, or other constants of Western societies? Comparisons with other cultures may help answer such questions.

A modern classic in cross-cultural research is D. Wagner's "Memories of Morocco" (1978). One of his research goals was to see whether certain memory capacities were universal, such as short-term memory. If so, then children with widely differing life experiences should still be similar. A second goal was to determine whether certain memory capacities were culturally influenced. If so, the use of strategies such as rehearsal might differ among same-aged children as a function of schooling or urbanization.

Wagner tested short-term memory for a sequence of seven cards, each having an animal drawn on it. The cards were shown one at a time for 2 seconds each before being turned upside down and placed in a row before the participant. A test card was then shown, and the child had to indicate where that picture had occurred in the list. Several samples of children ranging in age from 6 to 19 were obtained: children from an urban and a rural area of Morocco, and within each of these areas, children who attended school or were unschooled. The recall of the test card's location improved with age. This is not surprising, given what we reviewed earlier about the development of memory. What was new was the finding that schooled children, particularly adolescents and older, remembered more than did unschooled children. This was especially so when the probe assessed memory for the first cards in the list. Schooling was associated with a primacy effect, which most likely reflects the development of rehearsal. Wagner's results suggest that the use of intentional learning strategies, like rehearsal, are due to experiences in school, such as the demands placed on new learning.

These results are supported by another series of studies, this time done in the Yucatan Peninsula of Mexico (Sharp, Cole, & Lave, 1979). In a free-recall experiment, children and adults were read a list of 20 common nouns from several categories (e.g., animals, clothing). Separate subject groups differed in age, education, and ethnic background. Adults and adolescents with schooling recalled more of the words. But more importantly, the educated adults (but not the uneducated ones) categorized the items during recall. They clustered semantically similar items at output. Sharp and colleagues' study shows that this strategy of organization can be a function of schooling and not just of age.

What about a popular notion that other cultures may excel at different forms of memory? We earlier reviewed Lord's observations of oral poetry in Yugoslavia. Another study assessed a hypothesis derived from evolutionary psychology, that people living in hunter-gatherer societies have better-developed visual or spatial memories, necessary for survival in the environments they occupy, than people from industrialized societies. Kearins (1981) tested this idea by measuring object location memory in Australian Aborigines and in Australians of European descent. The participants were all school children, aged 12 to 16 years. The stimuli were objects placed within a grid and shown briefly to the subjects. Each array contained between 12 and 20 items, either all man-made (e.g., thimble, eraser) or all natural objects (rock, leaf). After 30 seconds of viewing the array, the experimenter heaped all the objects in a pile, and the children then had to replace each item back in its original location. Previous research on the Aborigines had shown that they performed poorly on standard cognitive tests, even after attempts to make the tests culture-fair. However, in this case of location memory, the Aboriginal children excelled. In every test (natural and man-made objects, all the same category or all different), the Aboriginal children did better than the children of European descent. One striking finding was the number of times that the Aboriginal kids had perfect scores: 75 percent were perfect on at least one of four trials and 41 percent on two trials, whereas only 18 percent of the European children were perfect on one trial and none on two.

Contemporary Cultural Psychology

The initial goals of cross-cultural research were to seek cognitive universals and specific adaptations, such as the effects of schooling on rehearsal or location memory in aboriginal populations. We now realize that we cannot measure universal memory ability in tasks that are unrelated to everyday experience. How we test memory influences how well memory appears to function. If we ask people to display memory in a way that resembles what they do in school (e.g., remembering lists of items in the sequence the experimenter presented them), then people with schooling do better. The current trend in research is toward investigating cognitive skills as they relate to everyday behavior within a culture, rather than as universal traits that are culture-free. Indeed, this trend is represented by a change from the label "cross-cultural" psychology to simply "cultural" psychology (Rogoff & Chavajay, 1995).

Summary

The experimental approach to learning focuses on those variables that can be manipulated by researchers, in order to determine the effects of such variables on learning. A correlational approach focuses on variables that experimenters cannot control, such as gender, personality, or age, but that nevertheless are important determinants of learning and memory.

The Genetics of Learning Ability

Learning ability is affected by genetic predispositions. Tryon's classic experiments used the method of selective breeding to produce two strains of rats, Maze Bright and Maze Dull, that differed in maze-learning ability. Genetic differences in learning have also been demonstrated by inducing genetic mutations in fruit flies, and transplanting genes between mice. Environment still plays an important role even where there are genetic differences: The extremes of either deprived or enriched rearing conditions equated the bright and dull rats in maze learning.

In human studies, identical twins are more alike for some kinds of memory than are fraternal twins. Even among genetically identical individuals, a given gene will not make a difference unless the environment causes the gene to be expressed.

Age Differences in Learning and Memory

Both learning and memory show developmental trends, from infancy to old age. Prenatal learning of the mother's voice occurs, and taste-aversion conditioning in prenatal rats. Newborns show olfactory conditioning.

Episodic memory develops with age in children. The childhood amnesia of adults may indicate an absence of memories from the first years of life, possibly due to neural maturation, or simply an inability for adults to recollect those years. However, the method of elicited imitation shows that infants as young as 11 months old can reproduce specific sequences of activities.

What develops as children age? Children and adults differ in the capacity of short-term or working memory. Young children have a smaller knowledge base that limits new learning. Younger children do not use strategies, such as rehearsal and elaboration, as much as older children. Knowledge about the functioning of memory develops early in children's lives, but metamemory judgments are neither accurate nor sophisticated.

Similarly, some aspects of memory decline with aging. Again we can ask what changes. The capacity of working memory decreases, although this may be due to slowing of mental processing rather than a reduction in the amount that can be retained. Metamemory knowledge about how memory works is unchanged in the elderly. However, expectancies and stereotypes may affect the belief that one's own memory is less competent. Memory performance may decline because of other factors associated with aging, such as illness, depression, or the side effects of medications.

Intellectual Deficits

Principles of learning have been used to teach and train individuals with developmental disabilities. Even though possessing a neurological disability, disabled individuals typically learn through classical conditioning at about the same rate as nondisabled. Down's syndrome, a genetic abnormality, impairs conditioning to a similar extent as does aging. Down syndrome infants also have poorer spatial learning.

Other research has investigated the roles of working-memory capacity, memory strategies such as rehearsal, and metamemory. Failure to use memory strategies contributes to the poor memory performance of developmentally disabled individuals. Training in rehearsal increases recall, but there is little tendency to generalize beyond the immediately given task. Cognitive-skills training usually does not eliminate the difference between the developmentally disabled and age-matched comparison participants.

A learning disability is a specific cognitive impairment, such as difficulty reading or doing arithmetic. Usually other abilities are normal. The learning disabled may have both verbal and nonverbal working-memory deficits, which does not correlate with the type of disability (reading, math, language). Individuals with learning disabilities are less likely to rehearse or to use organization or elaboration to facilitate encoding if they do rehearse.

Exceptional Memory

The history of psychology is replete with examples of mnemonists, people with exceptional memories. Luria's friend S employed strategies such as imagery, and mnemonics such as the method of locations. His sensory experience was cross-modal, cutting across sensory modalities, a property called synesthesia. Other mnemonists sometimes use verbal elaboration, mentally coding new information into meaningful items.

Recent research has found cases of exceptional memory by individuals who can remember nearly every day of their lives. People with Highly Superior Autobiographical Memory do have exceptional personal, or autobiographical memory. Their other forms of memory are often unremarkable when assessed by standard tests of short-term, episodic, or semantic memory.

Savants, individuals having an exceptional ability but who otherwise have average or below average intelligence, may excel in memory within a specific content area or domain.

Gender and Cognitive Abilities

The truism is that men are better at spatial and women at verbal tasks. Even when performance does differ by gender, this does not necessarily indicate that this is due to inherent biological differences between the sexes. Gender differences have been shown to occur when there are differences in knowledge or experience, self-handicapping, or gender expectancies or stereotypes about how one should perform.

Personality and Learning

Some personality traits interact with learning and remembering. Research from a number of disciplines suggests that self-control, and related traits of self-discipline, conscientiousness, or persistence, are important predictors of educational success. Walter Mischel conducted follow-up studies on some of the children from his initial "marshmallow" experiments. He found that better self-control was associated with fewer behavior problems later in school, and higher SAT scores.

Other measures of childhood self-control correlate with adult measures of health, wealth, educational attainment, and (negatively) with criminal convictions.

High levels of anxiety affect memory by increasing arousal, directing attention to threatening or negative information, and limiting the capacity of working memory. Worry and irrelevant thoughts co-opt memory capacity. Anxious participants recall negative self-referent information, whereas nonanxious subjects recall more positive information. High levels of anxiety correlate with self-reported everyday memory problems.

Learning Styles

Several theories of learning styles have been developed, but there is little empirical work to validate that, in fact, people of different styles learn differently. Well-developed style theories include Kolb's two dimensions of concrete versus abstract learning, and reflective versus active application of knowledge. Sternberg and Grigorenko describe analytic, creative, and practical styles. They say that students' style should be matched to corresponding teaching and evaluation styles.

Social and Cultural Differences

Cross-cultural studies of learning and memory can address questions about universal features of memory; different demands placed on memory by different environments; or specific effects of social changes such as schooling. Older descriptions of memory in nonliterate societies, while impressive, do not often produce verifiable data. Newer research provides better control and more nuanced findings. Singers in an oral tradition, for example, remember the outline and general features of an epic story, but otherwise recompose the story during each performance. Experiments in Morocco and Mexico show that recall increases with age, but that schooling enhances memory even more so through the development of strategies such as rehearsal.

Glossary

accessible memory information that can be remembered. Not all memories are accessible, even if they are present (*available*).

acquisition learning or encoding; acquiring knowledge or new behaviors. Acquisition is usually measured as a function of study, practice or learning trials.

amnesia forgetting due to an impairment in the retention or retrieval of memories that once were available; or in the formation of memories which normally would have been encoded.

amnesic syndrome a type of amnesia characterized by the inability to form or encode new episodic and semantic long-term memory. Short-term memory, implicit memory, and procedural learning are usually not affected. Amnesic syndrome is caused by damage to certain brain areas (the hippocampus and possibly others).

anterograde amnesia the inability to form new memories or acquire new knowledge. If a person is amnesic for events since the onset of the amnesia, this is anterograde. Anterograde amnesia is not remembering events that have occurred since the onset of the amnesia. Not remembering events that occurred before the onset of amnesia is retrograde.

applied research the application of principles of learning and memory to solving a practical problem. Applied research is often conducted in field settings using ecologically realistic tasks, situations, and subject populations.

approach–avoidance conflict behavioral vacillation and uncertainty in an avoidance learning situation when a response has both positive and negative consequences, such as food and shock.

arousal a state of heightened mental or physiological attention, readiness, or emotion. Arousal can refer to a psychological state of alertness; to physiological arousal as assessed by measures of heart rate or the skin conductance response (SCR); or to a trait, such as anxiousness or impulsivity.

available memory information that is present in memory, although this does not mean it can be retrieved. Contrast this with *accessible memory*, which can actually be recalled.

avoidance learning an experimental contingency, or rule, stating that performance of an instrumental response prevents the occurrence of the aversive consequence. Avoidance is also called *negative reinforcement*: "negative" because the response removes or prevents the aversive outcome; "reinforcement" because the instrumental response increases in frequency.

basic research has as its purpose an understanding of the fundamental processes of learning and memory. In order to demonstrate cause-and-effect relationships between key variables, basic research uses simplified tasks and situations, in which extraneous variables are eliminated or controlled.

behavior modification applies the principles of operant learning to changing behaviors in a variety of applied settings. Also known simply as behavior mod.

behavioral approach   describes learning in terms of the relationship among antecedent stimuli that precede behavior, the behavior itself, and the consequences that follow behavior. The behavioral approach emphasizes observable stimuli, responses, and outcomes.

blocking effect   conditioning to one CS is prevented because another CS already signals the US. In the blocking procedure, the new CS (e.g., CS_X) is presented simultaneously with an already-trained CS (CS_A), and the compound is followed by the US (that is, $CS_{A+X} \rightarrow US$). The trained-CS_A blocks conditioning to the new CS_X.

Brown–Peterson distractor task   used to test short-term memory. The to-be-remembered item (often three letters or three words) is presented; a distracting task such as counting backwards is performed for up to 30 seconds to block rehearsal; and then recall is attempted.

central executive   the working memory component that roughly corresponds with conscious attention. The central executive focuses, allocates, and distributes attention across the other memory stores and across multiple tasks.

chaining   training the organism to perform a sequence of separate instrumental responses, with reinforcement occurring at the end of the chain.

classical conditioning   a method developed by Pavlov for establishing an association between two (or more) stimuli. A neutral stimulus (the conditioned stimulus) is paired with a significant stimulus (the unconditioned stimulus.) The development of a conditioned response to the conditioned stimulus indicates that an association has been learned.

cognitive approach   knowledge is encoded, transformed, stored, and retrieved in the mind and/or brain. The cognitive approach focuses on the internal representations of knowledge and memory.

cognitive map   the mental representation of a spatial environment, analogous to a map, placing specific objects, places, and routes in context with the surrounding area (see *route learning*).

compensatory response   when certain drugs are used as unconditioned stimuli, the conditioned response may be the opposite of the unconditioned response. The learned bodily response compensates for, or balances out, the effect of the drug.

compound CS   two or more conditioned stimuli are presented simultaneously or in close succession. For example a tone and a light are presented together, followed by the US (e.g., tone + light → food).

conditioned inhibition   a type of classical conditioning which occurs when a CS is presented without the US, in a context in which the US otherwise occurs. The inhibitory CS reliably signals the absence of the US (in contrast to an excitatory CS which reliably signals the presence of the US.)

conditioned response (CR)   the response to the conditioned stimulus that is learned during classical conditioning.

conditioned stimulus (CS)   or to-be-conditioned stimulus, that is paired with the unconditioned stimulus. The CS is usually a neutral stimulus (such as a tone).

connectionist models   mathematical and computer simulations of memory as a network of hypothetical neurons. Connectionist models statistically model the changes in learning and memory that occur over trials or over time. Also called neural network models.

consolidation theory   the theory that memory is initially stored in a temporary form in the brain (a biological short-term memory), and that over time the memory consolidates into a more permanent form (a biological long-term memory).

contiguity   the principle which says that two events become associated when they occur close together in time, place, or thought.

contingency   one event is dependent on the occurrence of another. In instrumental learning, the reinforcer is contingent upon the occurrence of the instrumental response. In classical conditioning, the unconditioned stimulus is contingent on the occurrence of the conditioned stimulus.

contrast effect   the effectiveness of a given reinforcer is influenced by experience with other rewards that differ in amount or quality. A change to a larger or better reward leads to enhanced responding, or positive contrast. A change to a lesser reward leads to reduced performance, or negative contrast.

cued recall   a cue or prompt is presented to aid recall of a specific item from memory.

curve of forgetting   the course of forgetting over time. In Ebbinghaus's experiments, a great deal of forgetting occured shortly after learning; forgetting continues to occur over longer retention intervals, but at a slower rate.

declarative memory, declarative knowledge   memory or knowledge that can be consciously recalled and reported. Declarative includes semantic memory and episodic memory. Also known as explicit memory, because memory is explicitly questioned. Declarative knowledge contrasts with procedural memory's facilitated performance of skilled behavior.

delay of reinforcement (delayed reward)   a reinforcement schedule in which the instrumental response is not reinforced immediately, but reinforcement is given after a delay interval.

depth of processing   the theory that remembering depends on the amount of cognitive elaboration, or processing depth. Shallow processing leads to poor retention, whereas deep processing that involves meaningful analysis and comprehension produces better retention.

discrimination   (a) in classical conditioning, one CS (the CS+) is paired with the US while another CS (the CS−) is presented without the US. Discrimination learning occurs when there is more responding to the CS+ than to the CS−. (b) In instrumental conditioning, the instrumental response is reinforced in the presence of the discriminative stimulus (S^D). This response is not reinforced in the absence of the discriminative stimulus, or in the presence of S^Δ (S-delta), a stimulus signaling that reinforcement is not available. Discrimination learning occurs when there is more responding during the S^D than during the S^Δ.

discriminative stimulus (SD)   in instrumental learning, a stimulus that signals the availability of reinforcement. Responses during the discriminative stimulus are reinforced. Responses in the absence of the S^D are not reinforced.

dishabituation   reinstatement of orienting to a habituated stimulus by presentation of a different stimulus, e.g., after habituating the OR to a tone, a light stimulus could reinstate the response to the tone.

dissociation   a research technique used to demonstrate that a treatment variable has opposite effects on different memory systems, tasks, or measures. Dissociation is used to differentiate among memory systems.

drive   a motivational need or desire to obtain a given reinforcer (such as food) or to terminate an aversive reinforcer (such as shock).

drive reduction   a theory which states that stimuli are reinforcing because they reduce primary biological drives, such as hunger or pain.

dual coding   an item is encoded into memory in two modalities or forms, e.g., an object may be remembered both as an image and as the verbal name for the object.

dual-process theory   two processes, habituation, and sensitization occur concurrently. The magnitude of the orienting response is a combination of these two opposing tendencies.

elaborative rehearsal   type of processing in which there is active cognitive interaction with, reflection on, or use of the to-be-remembered information. Corresponds to deep processing in depth-of-processing approach.

electroconvulsive therapy (ECT)   electroconvulsive shock, sometimes used as a psychiatric therapy, often produces amnesic side effects and so is of interest to memory researchers.

empiricism   the philosophical belief that the origin of knowledge is through experience.

encoding   the acquisition of information, or the formation of a memory trace. In the stage approach to describing memory, encoding is the first stage, followed by storage and retrieval.

encoding specificity information is encoded into memory in the presence of specific cues, either environmental or mental. Retrieval information is best when that these cues also occur at the time of retrieval.

encoding–retrieval paradigm an experimental manipulation that varies the encoding conditions in combination with the retrieval conditions, e.g., encoding- and retrieval-conditions can match (studying and testing occur in the same room) or the conditions can differ (testing occurs in a different room). Examples include mood-dependent remembering and drug state-dependent learning.

episodic buffer the component of working memory that integrates information across (a) the phonological and visual stores, and (b) information entry and retrieval from long-term memory.

episodic memory our own, individual, personal memories. Episodic memories contain temporal and contextual information about when and where the events occurred. Some of our autobiographical memories are episodic (but some are semantic.) Episodic can be characterized as remembering, as in "I remember . . ."

epistemology the field of philosophy that studies how we come to have knowledge.

evaluative conditioning an affectively neutral stimulus, often a word or a picture, is paired with another word or picture that evokes a positive or negative emotional reaction. The emotional tone of the neutral stimulus becomes positive or negative as a function of this conditioning experience.

evolution the biological change in organisms over generations in order to better adapt to the environment to which they are exposed.

explicit memory task a test of memory that contains a direct request to recall something from episodic or semantic memory.

exposure therapy psychotherapy treatment that uses repeated or prolonged exposure to fear-inducing stimuli as a means of reducing the fear. Stimulus exposure might reduce fear through, for example, habituation or extinction.

extinction in classical conditioning, the previously-conditioned CS is presented alone without the US; in instrumental conditioning, the previously-reinforced instrumental response is no longer followed by reinforcement. In either case, the learned response diminishes, or extinguishes across extinction trials.

false memory the mistaken recall of some item, stimulus, or event that did not actually occur. Also can refer specifically to the Deese-Roediger-McDermott procedure for producing false recall, in which lists of highly associated words are presented, and the subject misrecalls an associated word that was not on the list.

feeling of knowing unable to recall a specific item or fact now (such as a name or a word), but subjectively feeling sure the information is known and is present in memory. Related to the tip-of-the-tongue phenomenon.

flashbulb memory a particularly vivid memory for a surprising, emotional, and consequential event. It is as-if a picture of a moment in time is stored in memory.

free recall a method for studying learning and memory for lists of items. The items can be recalled in any order, so recall is free or unconstrained (in contrast with serial recall).

functional approach learning and memory are ways of adapting to the changes and inconstancies in their environment. Learning is considered in light of survival, adaptation, and evolution.

generalization (a) after classical conditioning to one CS, the conditioned response is made to stimuli that are similar to the trained CS (i.e., conditioning generalizes to similar stimuli). (b) In instrumental conditioning, the instrumental response occurs in the presence of stimuli similar to the initially trained discriminative stimulus (i.e., responding generalizes to other discriminative stimuli.)

generation effect   memory is enhanced if the participant can be guided to produce (generate) the correct information during study, rather than simply being given the correct information to study.

habit   a highly trained response or behavior that can be performed without conscious intention or conscious direction. The response is elicited by stimuli with which it is associated, often without conscious awareness.

habit slip: the intrusion of a habit when an alternative behavior had been intended; or the performance of a habitual behavior in the absence of intention to do so. Also called action slip.

habituation   the decrease in orienting (and other) reactions to a stimulus that is repeatedly presented, in the absence of any consequent stimuli. Habituation is sometimes used to refer to the procedure (frequent presentation of a stimulus) or to its effect (decrease in responding).

hypermnesia   enhanced remembering. Remembering increases over time, in contrast to the forgetting that we expect to occur over time. Hypermnesia is usually demonstrated when more is recalled across successive attempts at reproduction of the studied material.

imagination inflation   frequently imagining or thinking about some event or action leads to an increase in the belief that the action or event actually happened.

implicit learning   improvement in the performance of cognitive, motor, or perceptual skill that develops with training, independent of conscious awareness of specific details of the tasks.

implicit memory task   a test to assesses the effects of prior experience indirectly, by measuring performance on some task that does not require explicit recall. For example, responding more quickly to a word that has been primed in memory.

incentive motivation   a theory that states that stimuli are reinforcing because they excite a drive, need, or desire for the reinforcer.

incidental learning   learning occurs without intention to remember, but incidental to other processing of the information.

instrumental conditioning   an experimental contingency, or rule, stating that performance of a designated instrumental response leads to the occurrence of a particular consequence. Also known as goal-directed behavior, operant learning, and trial-and-error learning. Instrumental conditioning includes positive reinforcement (or reward learning); negative reinforcement (or avoidance learning); and punishment.

instrumental response   in instrumental conditioning, the behavior that is being trained or conditioned; it is instrumental in producing reinforcement.

isolation effect   an unusual item or an item presented in a distinctive manner is especially remembered. Also known as the von Restorff effect.

knowledge of results   feedback concerning the success or accuracy of a response that is given to the participant after study or practice. This term usually occurs in the context of motor skill learning.

Korsakoff's syndrome   a form of amnesia that is associated with prolonged alcohol abuse and thiamine vitamin deficiency. Forgetting can be both retrograde (loss of previously recalled memories) and anterograde (impaired encoding of new memories).

latent learning   knowledge or behavior that is not displayed in performance. Learning occurred but the knowledge is hidden unless prompted by the right circumstances.

learned helplessness   produced by an experimental contingency, or rule, in which there is an explicit lack of contingency between response and an aversive outcome. There is not an instrumental response that produces punishment, nor is there a response that avoids it.

learning   a relatively permanent change in behavior or behavioral repertoire that occurs as a result of experience. Learning refers to the acquisition of knowledge or behavior.

learning curve   a graph showing the acquisition of learning, plotting practice or repetitions along the X axis, and size or frequency of a response along the Y axis.

learning style   categorizing individual differences in how people learn. This can refer to the dominant sensory dimensions (visual, verbal, or tactile learning); or cognitive style (left brain learner-rational and verbal, versus right brain learner-more visual and intuitive).

long-term memory   a memory storage system that retains information indefinitely, has a virtually unlimited capacity, and stores information across various modalities (verbal, spatial, emotional, etc).

maintenance rehearsal   type of processing characterized by passive repetition or recycling of information in order to keep it available in short-term memory. Corresponds to shallow processing in depth-of-processing approach.

massed practice (massed repetition)   when to-be-remembered material is repeated, the second presentation occurs immediately after the first presentation (or shortly after), rather than after a longer interval between the repetition.

meaningfulness   to-be-remembered information can vary in how well known, familiar, significant, or relevant it is. Meaningfulness is experimentally defined by imagery, familiarity, number of associations, or frequency of occurrence.

memory   (a) the representation of information from past experiences; (b) learning refers to the acquisition of knowledge or behavior, whereas memory refers to retention and recall of knowledge or behavior.

memory span   the capacity of short-term memory is defined as the longest string of items that can be immediately recalled, in correct order. The digit span is often used to measure the capacity of STM.

mere exposure effect   the development of a preference for a stimulus that occurs through exposure to the stimulus, in the absence of rewards, problems, or other tasks that engage active processing.

metamemory   knowledge about learning and remembering in general, as opposed to the specific knowledge and memories we have. Metamemory includes beliefs about how learning and memory generally work, and our own self-knowledge and expectations about encoding, storage, and retrieval in specific circumstances.

misinformation effect   the presentation of incorrect information is remembered instead of the previously studied correct information. In a misinformation design, correct information is first presented, and then the misinformation is presented.

mnemonics   techniques or strategies used to aid encoding and retrieval in everyday memory. Mnemonics can range from simple devices, such as using an acronym to cue the first letters of the to-be-remembered items; to elaborate coding systems used to memorize large sets of information.

motor-skill learning   acquisition of precisely adjusted movements in which the amount, direction, and duration of responding corresponds to variations in the regulating stimuli.

n-back task   used to assess working memory and executive functioning. A sequence of items (e.g., letters, numbers) is presented. As each item occurs the subject must decide whether that item matches the one presented n-steps earlier, e.g., if n = 2, does the current letter match the one two-letters before.

nativism   the belief that some knowledge or ability is innate.

neophobia   "fear of the new," is often used to label the avoidance of new tastes or foods.

neuroscience approach   seeks to understand the underlying biological basis for learning and memory; the changes that occur in the nervous system during learning and remembering.

omission   an experimental contingency, or rule, stating that performance of an instrumental response will prevent a positive reinforcer from occurring. Omission of reward should decrease the frequency of the response. An omission contingency usually implies that some other response does lead to positive reinforcement.

operant learning   B. F. Skinner's term for instrumental learning. The organism's response (such as a rat's bar press) operates on the environment to produce a certain outcome (such as food).

organization   grouping together items that are similar, related, or associated to facilitate recall.

orienting response (OR)   reactions to a novel stimulus. The OR is a composite of several physiological and behavioral responses, including startle, arousal, and sense receptor focusing.

paired-associate learning   a method in which pairs of items are presented for study, labeled stimulus and response (abbreviated S and R). The task is to learn the response item that is paired with each stimulus.

partial reinforcement   a reinforcement schedule in which the instrumental response is reinforced some of the time, not every time.

partial reinforcement extinction effect   extinction of an instrumental response is slower if the response was originally conditioned with a partial reinforcement schedule rather than with continuous reinforcement.

perceptual learning   learning to perceive differences among stimuli that develop with repeated exposure to the stimuli.

performance   measures of behavior or memory that are used to indicate whether learning has occurred. The organism's actual behavior may not always be a reliable indicator of what has been learned.

persistence   the continued performance of a given instrumental response even though the outcome is aversive (such as no reward, reduced reward, or punishment).

phobia   a strong and excessive fear of a specific object or situation, e.g., fear of snakes and spiders, heights, or speaking in public.

phonological loop   working memory's verbal short-term store that is used in rehearsal, verbal problem solving, and language processing.

positive reinforcement   an experimental contingency, or rule, stating that performance of an instrumental response will lead to the occurrence of a particular consequence. "Positive" means the response produces an outcome, and "reinforcement" means the response increases in frequency. A positive reinforcer is usually a desirable consequence, leading to an increase in the frequency of the response.

potentiated startle   the startle response elicited by a stimulus is magnified by arousal from other sources, such as fear or nervousness.

Premack principle   a principle of reinforcement that says a higher-probability activity will reinforce a lower-probability activity; or a more-preferred activity will reinforce a less-preferred activity.

prepared learning   some types of learning occur easily, rapidly, and early in life, such as taste aversions, phobias, and language. Evolutionary psychology suggests that evolution has prepared organisms to readily acquire knowledge that is essential to survival.

primacy effect   enhanced recall of the first items in a list relative to the middle items. A subcomponent of the serial-position effect.

priming   a stimulus that has been recently experienced, or has been recently activated in memory by an associated cue. A *priming effect* is a facilitated response to the primed stimulus.

proactive interference   items studied or presented earlier interfere with recall of the current or more-recently presented items.

procedural learning (procedural memory)   our store of knowledge of how to do things. This includes perceptual, motor, and cognitive skills. Procedural knowledge can be characterized as "knowing how to."

propositional learning   the relationships among events (stimuli, responses, consequences) can be stated as a series of facts or propositions. Propositional learning is the acquisition of these facts through exposure to and interaction with events.

prospective memory   remembering to perform future actions, or remembering at the appropriate time in the future.

psychogenic amnesia (functional amnesia) a type of amnesia associated with psychological trauma. Psychogenic amnesia is retrograde: there is forgetting for the past, or some part of the past, that preceded or coincided with the traumatic event.

punishment an experimental contingency, or rule, stating that performance of an instrumental response is followed by an aversive consequence. This contingency should decrease the frequency of the response. In the sense used here, punishment is more than just withholding reward (which is called omission) but is instead the application of an aversive consequence.

recall test a test of learning or memory that requires the recall or reproduction or studied information or items.

recency effect enhanced recall of the last items in a list relative to the middle items. A subcomponent of the serial-position effect.

recognition test a test of learning or memory that presents previously studied items along with distractors, to see if the studied items can be identified.

reconsolidation retrieving a memory returns it to a short-term memory state. At this time, the memory can be altered or modified, after which the changed memory reconsolidates back to long-term memory. See *consolidation theory*.

reconstructive memory the view that remembering is the reconstruction of an event on the basis of memory fragments, cues, and present knowledge. Memory reconstruction contrasts with the view that remembering is simply recalling a static, stored representation of the actual event.

recovered memory remembering something that was previously forgotten or unrecalled. Often used in the context of unremembered trauma.

rehearsal repeating or recycling to-be-remembered items, either vocally or mentally.

reinstatement a classical conditioning procedure that restores an extinguished response. Following extinction of the conditioned response, presentation of the unconditioned stimulus alone can reinstate the extinguished response.

relearning test a test of learning or memory in which previously studied material is re-studied. The amount of savings or ease of relearning is taken as a measure of memory for the original learning before relearning began.

remembering versus knowing judgments about whether an item is clearly remembered as having been experienced before, versus an item that seems familiar but produces no specific memory.

remote associations in learning a list of items, associations may develop among items that are not adjacent (i.e., not contiguous).

renewal a classical conditioning procedure that restores an extinguished response. Following extinction of the conditioned response, exposure to the context in which conditioning occurred can lead to recovery of the extinguished response.

Rescorla-Wagner model a theory of classical conditioning. The amount of conditioning to a CS depends on the degree to which the US is surprising, or unexpected. The theory describes the changes in conditioning to individual CSs that occur when multiple CSs are presented.

resistance to extinction a given response may persist during extinction even though it is no longer rewarded. Certain reinforcement conditions during training enhance resistance to extinction, such as partial reinforcement.

response–reinforcer learning theory an explanation of instrumental learning that asserts learning is the formation of a connection between the instrumental response and the reinforcer.

retrieval recalling, remembering, or reactivating a stored memory. In the stage approach to describing memory, retrieval is the final stage, preceded by encoding and storage.

retrieval-induced forgetting practice at remembering one item (i.e., retrieval) produces interference with remembering other related items, such as previously studied material or formerly correct items.

retroactive interference   current or recently-presented items interfere with recall of items studied or presented earlier.

retrograde amnesia   forgetting of events that occurred before the onset of the disorder. Memories that were once available, or that otherwise would have been remembered, are forgotten. Retrograde amnesia is forgetting events that occurred before the onset of amnesia. Not remembering events that occur after the onset of amnesia is anterograde.

route learning, route knowledge   knowing a sequence of routes, directions, or paths through a spatial environment. In contrast to a cognitive map, the representation of route knowledge is sequential, point-to-point, and habit-like (see *cognitive map*).

schedule of reinforcement   the specific rule that relates the delivery of reward to the timing or frequency of instrumental responding. In general terms, reinforcement can be given after a certain number of instrumental responses (ratio schedule) or a response that occurs after some specified amount of time (interval schedule).

schema (schemas)   outlines of general knowledge that are stored in semantic memory. Schemas guide the perception, organization, and later recall of familiar events. Also called scripts.

second-order conditioning   in first-order conditioning, a CS is paired with a US. In second-order conditioning, a second CS is paired with the first CS. Second-order conditioning is demonstrated when the second CS evokes the conditioned response.

secondary reinforcer   a neutral stimulus that has been paired with a primary reinforcer acquires the capacity to reinforce on its own, e.g., a clicker that has been followed by food can become a secondary reinforcer.

seductive detail effect   an interesting but tangential fact is used to maintain the learner's attention, but which paradoxically actually interferes with memory for the main facts of the lecture or text.

self-control   the capacity to inhibit an immediate response for reward, in preference for a better reward at a later time.

semantic memory   our store of general knowledge; generic knowledge that most of us share. Semantic memory is like dictionary or encyclopedic knowledge. Semantic can be characterized as knowledge, as in "I know that. . . ."

semantic network   the theory that knowledge is stored in semantic memory as a network of interconnected associations, relationships, or pathways. These connections vary in strength or distance that separate one item from another.

sensitization   an increase in responsiveness due to repeated stimulus presentation, and thus the opposite of habituation. Sensitization is likely to occur with intense stimuli and may reflect heightened arousal of the nervous system.

serial learning   a method for studying learning and memory in which a list of items is learned and reproduced in the same sequence in which the items were presented.

serial-position effect   in recalling a list of items, the first items are well remembered (primacy) and the last items are well remembered (recency), relative to relatively poorer recall of the middle items.

shaping   to condition a behavior that is not currently in the organism's repertoire, one can reinforce a series of successive approximations to the desired response. Shaping is used to train novel behaviors, or sequences of behaviors.

short-term memory (STM)   memory storage that is limited both in its duration and its capacity. As assessed in laboratory tests, STM retains on the order of five to seven items, for several seconds to less than a minute in the absence of rehearsal. Working memory is a later extended version of STM.

skin conductance response (SCR)   changes in electrical conductivity in the skin that are associated with arousal or emotionality. SCRs are measured by electrodes placed on the skin (the wrist or palm, for example).

Skinner box   an operant conditioning chamber. A controlled environment designed for the presentation of stimuli such as a tone or light; recording responses, such as bar pressing; and the administration of reinforcers such as food or shock.

social learning   learning through observation or imitation of other's experiences or through verbal communication, rather than through direct personal experience. Also referred to as vicarious learning.

social reinforcement   praise, attention, facial expressions, or physical contact given by parents, peers, or others that act as reinforcers to enhance or decrease instrumental behavior.

source memory   remembering the true origin of a memory. Source memory is usually used in reference to a failure to distinguish between what was actually experienced and what was imagined, thought of, or heard about.

spaced practice (spaced repetition)   when to-be-remembered material is repeated, the second presentation occurs after a delay rather than immediately after the first presentation. Also called distributed repetition.

spacing effect (spaced repetition)   when to-be-remembered material is repeated, learning is better when there is greater separation between the first and second presentations, than when repetitions are massed.

spatial learning, spatial memory   the acquisition, retention, and internal representation of spatial information. Spatial can vary along a number of dimensions, e.g., episodic, semantic or procedural; short-term or long-term; implicit or explicit.

spontaneous recovery   the return of a response that had diminished or ceased. Following either habituation or extinction of a stimulus, the response may spontaneously recover after a period of time without stimulus presentations.

spreading activation   activation of a memory spreads to associated or connected items in memory, allowing related knowledge to become activated. Usually used in the context of semantic networks and priming.

statistical learning   associations, rules, or algorithms are acquired through extensive experience, that reflect actual consistent patterns experienced in the world.

stimulus control   learned responding is brought under the control of conditioned stimuli (in classical conditioning) or discriminative stimuli (in instrumental conditioning.)

stimulus–response learning theory   an explanation of instrumental learning that asserts learning is the formation of a connection between the discriminative stimulus and the instrumental response.

storage   In the stage approach to describing memory, storage is the second stage, preceded by encoding and followed by retrieval. Once something has been encoded into memory, it needs to be retained, maintained, or *stored* in long-term memory.

systematic desensitization   a psychotherapy for phobias that is based on classical conditioning. The phobic stimulus is paired with a response that is incompatible with fear (e.g., pairing images of snakes with instructions to relax). The goal is to recondition the phobic stimulus to elicit a less-fearful reaction.

taste-aversion learning   a taste is used as the conditioned stimulus that is paired with an unconditioned stimulus that induces illness. The conditioned response is the development of aversion or avoidance of the taste.

testing effect   the benefit to learning of taking a preliminary test on recently studied material rather than engaging in additional study.

trial-and-error learning   solving a problem by trying various responses until one produces the desired outcome. Trial-and-error was the term used by Edward Lee Thorndike for what later became known as instrumental conditioning and goal directed learning.

two-process theory   a theory that avoidance learning is governed by classical and instrumental conditioning. The first process conditions fear to the warning signal via classical conditioning. In the second process, escape from the warning signal is reinforced with fear reduction via instrumental conditioning. Also known as the Watson–Mowrer theory.

unconditioned response (UR) the response to the unconditioned stimulus. This response is sometimes reflexive.

unconditioned stimulus (US) a stimulus that is significant prior to the onset of conditioning (such as food or shock), and which usually elicits a substantial response or emotion (the unconditioned response).

verbal learning (a) methods used to study variables that affect acquisition, retention, and recall of verbal items (usually words). These methods include serial learning, paired associate learning, and free recall. (b) The verbal learning approach that assumed human learning was analogous to conditioning, and followed similar principles of associative learning.

visual-spatial sketchpad (or *visuo*spatial sketchpad) working memory's visual and spatial short-term memory store. The visual-spatial sketchpad is used for the brief retention or manipulation of visual images and spatial information.

von Restorff effect an unusual item or an item presented in a distinctive manner is especially remembered. See *isolation effect*.

working memory (WM) a system of short-term memory that allows for both retention and manipulation of information. Alan Baddeley proposed four components of WM. Temporary storage occurs in either the *phonological store* or the *visual-spatial* memory. The *central executive* allocates attention. The *episodic memory buffer* connects working memory to long-term memory.

Yerkes-Dodson law the effect of arousal on performance follows an inverted U-shaped curve. Peak performance occurs at a moderate or intermediate level of arousal; performance is poorer when arousal is too low or too high.

References

Aarons, L. (1976). Sleep-assisted instruction. *Psychological Bulletin, 83,* 1–40.

Adam, N. (1979). Disruption of memory functions associated with general anesthetics. In J. F. Kihlstrom & F. J. Evans (Eds.), *Functional disorders of memory* (pp. 219–238). Hillsdale, NJ: Erlbaum.

Adams, C. D. (1982). Variations in the sensitivity of instrumental responding to reinforcer devaluation. *Quarterly Journal of Experimental Psychology, 34B,* 77–98.

Adams, J. A. (1987). Historical review and appraisal of research on the learning, retention, and transfer of human motor skills. *Psychological Bulletin, 101,* 41–74.

Ader, R., & Cohen, N. (1975). Behaviorally conditioned immuno suppression. *Psychosomatic Medicine, 37,* 333–340.

Ader, R., & Cohen, N. (1982). Behaviorally conditioned immunosuppression and murine systemic lupus erythematosus. *Science, 215,* 1534–1536.

Ader, R., & Cohen, N. (1993). Psychoneuroimmunology: Conditioning and stress. *Annual Review of Psychology, 44,* 53–85.

Alba, J. W., & Hasher, L. (1983). Is memory schematic? *Psychological Bulletin, 93,* 203–231.

Alberini, C. M. (2005). Mechanisms of memory stabilization: Are consolidation and reconsolidation similar or distinct processes? *Trends in Neurosciences, 28,* 51–56.

Alessandri, S. M., Sullivan, M. W., & Lewis, M. (1990). Violation of expectancy and frustration in early infancy. *Developmental Psychology, 26,* 738–744.

Amsel, A. (1962). Frustrative nonreward in partial reinforcement and discrimination learning: Some recent history and a theoretical extension. *Psychological Review, 69,* 306–328.

Anderson, J. R. (1983). *The architecture of cognition.* Cambridge: Harvard University Press.

Anderson, M. C., & Green, C. (2001). Suppressing unwanted memories by executive control. *Nature, 410,* 366–369.

Anderson, M. C., & Levy, B. J. (2009). Suppressing unwanted memories. *Current Directions in Psychological Science, 18,* 189–194.

Anderson, R. C., & Pichert, J. W. (1978). Recall of previously unrecallable information following a shift in perspective. *Journal of Verbal Learning and Verbal Behavior, 17,* 1–12.

Andrade, J. (1995). Learning during anaesthesia: A review. *British Journal of Psychology, 86,* 479–507.

Aporta, C., & Higgs, E. (2005). Satellite culture: Global positioning systems, Inuit wayfinding, and the need for a new account of technology. *Current Anthropology, 46,* 729–753.

Arbuckle, T. Y., Gold, D. P., Andres, D., Schwartzman, A., & Chaikelson, J. (1992). The role of psycho social context, age, and intelligence in memory performance of older men. *Psychology and Aging, 7,* 25–36.

Arkes, H. R., & Harkness, A. R. (1980). Effect of making a diagnosis on subsequent recognition of symptoms. *Journal of Experimental Psychology: Human Learning and Memory, 6,* 568–575.

Arnold, M. E., Petros, T. V., Beckwith, B. E., Coons, G., & Gorman, N. (1987). The effects of caffeine, impulsivity, and sex on memory for word lists. *Physiology and Behavior, 41,* 25–30.

Arnst, C. (2003, August 21). I can't remember. *Businessweek,* pp. 42–44.

Arrigo, J. M., & Pezdek, K. (1997). Lessons from the study of psychogenic amnesia. *Current Directions in Psychological Science, 6,* 148–152.

Ash, D. W., & Holding, D. H. (1990). Backward versus forward chaining in the acquisition of a keyboard skill. *Human Factors, 32,* 139–146.

Ashcraft, M. H., & Krause, J. A. (2007). Working memory, math performance, and math anxiety. *Psychonomic Bulletin & Review, 14*, 243–248.

Aspinwall, L. G., & Taylor, S. E. (1992). Modeling cognitive adaptation: A longitudinal investigation of the impact of individual differences and coping on college adjustment and performance. *Journal of Personality and Social Psychology, 63*, 989–1003.

Astur, R. S., Ortiz, M. L., & Sutherland, R. J. (1998). A characterization of performance by men and women in a virtual Morris water task: A large and reliable sex difference. *Behavioural Brain Research, 93*, 185–190.

Atkinson, R. C., & Raugh, M. R. (1975). An application of the mnemonic keywords method to the acquisition of Russian vocabulary. *Journal of Experimental Psychology: Human Learning and Memory, 1*, 126–133.

Atkinson, R. C., & Shiffrin, R. M. (1968). Human memory: A proposed system and its control procedures. In K. W. Spence & J. T. Spence (Eds.), *The psychology of learning and motivation* (Vol. 2, pp. 80–195). New York: Academic Press.

Atkinson, R. C., & Shiffrin, R. M. (1971, August). The control of short-term memory. *Scientific American*, pp. 152–161.

Averill, J. R., & Rosenn, M. (1972). Vigilant and nonvigilant coping strategies and psychophysiological stress reactions during anticipation of electric shock. *Journal of Personality and Social Psychology, 23*, 128–141.

Ayduk, O., & Kross, E. (2008). Enhancing the pace of recovery: Self-distanced analysis of negative experiences reduces blood pressure reactivity. *Psychological Science, 19*, 229–231.

Ayllon, T. (1963). Intensive treatment of psychotic behavior by stimulus satiation and food reinforcement. *Behavior Research and Therapy, 1*, 53–61.

Ayllon, T., & Azrin, N. H. (1964). Reinforcement and instructions with mental patients. *Journal of the Experimental Analysis of Behavior, 7*, 327–331.

Ayllon, T., & Azrin, N. H. (1968). Reinforcer sampling: A technique for increasing the behavior of mental patients. *Journal of Applied Behavior Analysis, 1* 13–20.

Baddeley, A. D. (1966). Short-term memory for word sequences as a function of acoustic, semantic, and formal similarity. *Quarterly Journal of Experimental Psychology, 18*, 362–365.

Baddeley, A. D. (1978). The trouble with levels: A reexamination of Craik and Lockhart's framework for memory research. *Psychological Review, 85*, 139–152.

Baddeley, A. D. (1992a). Working memory. *Science, 255*, 556–559.

Baddeley, A. D. (1992b). Implicit memory and errorless learning. In L. R. Squire & N. Butters (Eds.), *Neuropsychology of memory* (2nd ed., pp. 309–314). New York: Guilford Press.

Baddeley, A. D. (2000). The episodic buffer: A new component of working memory? *Trends in Cognitive Sciences, 4*, 417–423.

Baddeley, A. D. (2001). Is working memory still working? *American Psychologist, 56*, 851–864.

Baddeley, A. D., & Hitch, G. (1974). Working memory. In G. H. Bower (Ed.), *The psychology of learning and motivation* (Vol. 8, pp. 47–89). New York: Academic Press.

Baddeley, A. D., & Longman, D. J. A. (1978). The influence of length and frequency of training session on the rate of learning to type. *Ergonomics, 21*, 627–635.

Baddeley, A. D., Thomson, N., & Buchanan, M. (1975). Word length and the structure of short-term memory. *Journal of Verbal Learning and Verbal Behavior, 14*, 575–589.

Baddeley, A. D., & Wilson, B. (1986). Amnesia, autobiographical memory, and confabulation. In D. C. Rubin (Ed.), *Autobiographical memory* (pp. 225–252). New York: Cambridge University Press.

Badia, P. (1990). Memories in sleep: Old and new. In R. R. Bootzin, J. F. Kihlstrom, & D. L. Schacter (Eds.), *Sleep and cognition* (pp. 67–76). Washington, DC: American Psychological Association.

Baeyens, F., Eelen, P., & Crombez, G. (1995). Pavlovian associations are forever: On classical conditioning and extinction. *Journal of Psychophysiology, 9*, 127–141.

Bahrick, H. P. (1979). Maintenance of knowledge: Questions about memory we forgot to ask. *Journal of Experimental Psychology: General, 108*, 296–308.

Bahrick, H. P. (1984a). Semantic memory content in permastore: Fifty years of memory for Spanish learned in school. *Journal of Experimental Psychology: General, 113*, 1–29.

Bahrick, H. P. (1984b). Memory for people. In J. E. Harris & P. E. Morris (Eds.), *Everyday memory, actions, and absentmindedness* (pp. 19–34). New York: Academic Press.

Bahrick, H. P., Bahrick, P. O., & Wittlinger, R. P. (1975). Fifty years of memory for names and faces: A cross-sectional approach. *Journal of Experimental Psychology: General, 104*, 54–75.

Bahrick, H. P., & Hall, L. K. (1993). Long intervals between tests can yield hypermnesia: Comments on Wheeler and Roediger. *Psychological Science, 4*, 206–208.

Bahrick, L. E., Parker, J. F., Fivush, R., & Levitt, M. (1998). The effects of stress on young children's memory for a natural disaster. *Journal of Experimental Psychology: Applied, 4*, 308–331.

Baird, R. B. (2003). Experts sometimes show more false recall than novices: A cost of knowing too much. *Learning and Individual Differences, 13*, 349–355.

Ball, G. F., & Hulse, S. H. (1998). Birdsong. *American Psychologist, 53*, 37–58.

Balota, D. A., Duchek, J. M., & Paullin, R. (1989). Agerelated differences in the impact of spacing, lag, and retention interval. *Psychology and Aging, 4*, 3–9.

Balter, M. (2010). Did working memory spark creative culture? *Science, 32*, 160–163.

Banaji, M. R., & Crowder, R. G. (1989). The bankruptcy of everyday memory. *American Psychologist, 44*, 1185–1193.

Banaji, M. R., & Hardin, C. D. (1996). Automatic stereotyping. *Psychological Science, 7*, 136–141.

Banbury, S. P., & Berry, D. C. (1997). Habituation and dishabituation to speech and office noise. *Journal of Experimental Psychology: Applied, 3*, 181–195.

Banbury, S. P., Macken, W. J., Tremblay, S., & Jones, D. M. (2001). Auditory distraction and short-term memory: Phenomena and practical implications. *Human Factors, 43*, 12–29.

Bandura, A. (1965). Influence of models' reinforcement contingencies on the acquisition of imitative responses. *Journal of Personality and Social Psychology, 1*, 589–595.

Barlow, D. H. (2000). *Anxiety and its disorders: The nature and treatment of anxiety and panic.* New York: Guilford Press.

Bartlett, F. C. (1932, reprinted 1995). *Remembering: A study in experimental and social psychology.* New York: Cambridge University Press.

Bauer, P. J. (1996). What do infants recall of their lives? Memory for specific events by one- to two-year olds. *American Psychologist, 51*, 29–41.

Bauer, P. J. (2006). Constructing a past in infancy: A neuro-developmental account. *Trends in Cognitive Sciences, 10*, 175–181.

Bechara, A., Damasio, H., Tranel, D., & Damasio, A. R. (1997). Deciding advantageously before knowing the advantageous strategy. *Science, 275*, 1293–1295.

Bechara, A., Tranel, D., Damasio, H., Adolphs, R., Rockland, C., & Damasio, A. R. (1995). Double dissociation of conditioning and declarative knowledge relative to the amygdala and hippocampus in humans. *Science, 269*, 1115–1118.

Beck, H. P., Levinson, S., & Irons, G. (2009). Finding little Albert. *American Psychologist, 64*, 605–614.

Beilock, S. L., Rydell, R. J., & McConnell, A. R. (2007). Stereotype threat and working memory: Mechanisms, alleviation, and spillover. *Journal of Experimental Psychology: General, 136*, 256–276.

Beitz, J. M. (1997). Unleashing the power of memory. *Nurse Educator, 22*, 25–29.

Bellugi, U., Klima, E. S., & Siple, P. (1974–1975). Remembering in signs. *Cognition, 3*, 93–125.

Bellugi, U., Wang, P. P., & Jernigan, T. L. (1994). Williams Syndrome: An unusual neuropsychological profile. In S. H. Broman & J. Grafman (Eds.), *Atypical cognitive deficits in developmental disorders* (pp. 23–56). Hillsdale, NJ: Erlbaum.

Benjamin, M., McKeachie, W. J., Lin, Y.-G., & Holinger, D. P. (1981). Test anxiety: Deficits in information processing. *Journal of Educational Psychology, 73*, 816–824.

Benjet, C., & Kazdin, A. E. (2003). Spanking children: The controversies, findings, and new directions. *Clinical Psychology Review, 23*, 197–224.

Berkun, M. M., Bialek, H. M., Kern, R. P., & Yagi, K. (1962). Experimental studies of psychological stress in man. *Psychological Monographs: General and Applied, 76* (15, Whole No. 534).

Bernstein, I. L. (1991). Aversion conditioning in response to cancer and cancer treatment. *Clinical Psychology Review, 11*, 185–191.

Bernstein, I. L., & Webster, M. M. (1980). Learned taste aversions in humans. *Physiology and Behavior, 25*, 363–366.

Bernstein, J. (1993, October). In many tongues. *The Atlantic Monthly*, pp. 92–102.

Berntsen, D. (1998). Voluntary and involuntary access to autobiographical memory. *Memory, 6*, 113–141.

Berntsen, D. (2010). The unbidden past: Involuntary autobiographical memories as a basic more of remembering. *Current Directions in Psychological Science, 19,* 138–143.

Berrios, G. E., Markova, I. S., & Girala, N. (2000). Functional memory complaints: Hypochondria and disorganization. In G. E. Berrios & J. R. Hodges (Eds.), *Memory disorders in psychiatric practice* (pp. 384–399). Cambridge, UK: Cambridge University Press.

Bevan, W., & Steger, J. A. (1971). Free recall and abstractness of stimuli. *Science, 172,* 597–599.

Birch, L. L., Gunder, L., Grimm-Thomas, K., & Laing, D. G. (1998). Infants' consumption of a new food enhances acceptance of similar foods. *Appetite, 30,* 283–295.

Birch, L. L., & Marlin, D. W. (1982). I don't like it, I never tried it: Effects of exposure on two-year-old children's food preferences. *Appetite, 3,* 353–360.

Birnbaum, I. M., Parker, E. S., Hartley, J. T., & Noble, E. P. (1978). Alcohol and memory: Retrieval processes. *Journal of Verbal Learning and Verbal Behavior, 17,* 325–335.

Blake, M. J. (1967). Time of day effects on performance in a range of tasks. *Psychonomic Science, 9,* 349–350.

Bloom, L. C., & Mudd, S. A. (1991). Depth of processing approach to face recognition: A test of two theories. *Journal of Experimental Psychology: Learning, Memory, and Cognition, 17,* 556–565.

Bolles, R. C. (1970). Species-specific defense reactions and avoidance learning. *Psychological Review, 77,* 32–48.

Bolles, R. C. (1972). Reinforcement, expectancy, and learning. *Psychological Review, 79,* 394–409.

Boorstin, D. J. (1983). *The discoverers.* New York: Random House.

Booth, D. (1990). Learned role of tastes in eating motivation. In E. D. Capaldi & T. L. Powley (Eds.), *Taste, experience, and feeding* (pp. 179–194). Washington, DC: American Psychological Association.

Bornstein, M. H., Kessen, W., & Weiskopf, S. (1976). Color vision and hue categorization in young human infants. *Journal of Experimental Psychology: Human Perception and Perfomance, 2,* 112–129.

Borresen, C. R., & Klingsporn, M. J. (1992). Some perceptual and cognitive factors in mirror tracing: Their limits. *Journal of General Psychology, 119,* 365–384.

Bourne, L. E., & Archer, E. J. (1956). Time continuously on target as a function of distribution of practice. *Journal of Experimental Psychology, 51,* 25–33.

Bouton, M. E., Westbrook, R. F., Corcoran, K. A., & Maren, S. (2006). Contextual and temporal modulation of extinction: Behavioral and biological mechanisms. *Biological Psychiatry, 60,* 352–360.

Bovjberg, D. H., Redd, W. H., Maier, L. A., Holland, J. C., Lesko, L., Niedzwiecki, D., . . . Hawkes, T. (1990). Anticipatory immune suppression in women receiving cyclic chemotherapy for ovarian cancer. *Journal of Consulting and Clinical Psychology, 58,* 153–157.

Bower, G. H. (1970). Analysis of a mnemonic device. *American Scientist, 58,* 496–510.

Bower, G. H. (1981). Mood and memory. *American Psychologist, 36,* 129–148.

Bower, G. H., & Clark, M. C. (1969). Narrative stories as mediators for serial learning. *Psychonomic Science, 14,* 181–182.

Bower, G. H., Clark, M. C., Lesgold, A. M., & Winzenz, D. (1969). Hierarchical retrieval schemes in recall of categorized word lists. *Journal of Verbal Learning and Verbal Behavior, 8,* 323–343.

Bower, G. H., & Hilgard, E. R. (1981). *Theories of learning* (5th ed.). Englewood Cliffs, NJ: Prentice Hall.

Bower, G. H., & Karlin, M. B. (1974). Depth of processing pictures of faces and recognition memory. *Journal of Experimental Psychology, 103,* 751–757.

Bower, G. H., Monteiro, K. P., & Gilligan, S. G. (1978). Emotional mood as a context of learning and recall. *Journal of Verbal Learning and Verbal Behavior, 17,* 573–585.

Bowers, J. S., & Schacter, D. L. (1990). Implicit memory and test awareness. *Journal of Experimental Psychology: Learning, Memory, and Cognition, 16,* 404–416.

Brainerd, C. J., Forrest, T. J., Karibian, D., & Reyna, V. F. (2006). Development of the false-memory illusion. *Developmental Psychology, 42,* 962–979.

Bransford, J. D., & Johnson, M. K. (1973). Considerations of some problems of comprehension. In W. G. Chase (Ed.), *Visual information processing* (pp. 383–438). New York: Academic Press.

Bransford, J. D., Nitsch, K. E., & Franks, J. J. (1977). Schooling and the facilitation of knowing. In R. C. Anderson, R. J. Spiro, & W. E. Montague (Eds.), *Schooling and the acquisition of knowledge* (pp. 31–55). Hillsdale, NJ: Erlbaum.

Breen, N., Caine, D., Colthart, M., Hendy, J., & Roberts, C. (2000). Towards an understanding of delusions of misidentification: Four case studies. *Mind & Language, 15,* 74–100.

Breland, K., & Breland, M. (1961). The misbehavior of organisms. *American Psychologist, 61*, 681–684.

Bremner, J. D., Krystal, J. H., Southwick, S. M., & Charney, D. S. (1995). Functional neuroanatomical correlates of the effects of stress on memory. *Journal of Traumatic Stress, 8*, 527–553.

Bremner, J. D., Scott, T. M., Delaney, R. C., Southwick, S. M., Mason, J. W., Johnson, D. R., Innis, R. B., McCarthy, G., & Charney, D. S. (1993). Deficits in short-term memory in postraumatic stress disorder. *American Journal of Psychiatry, 150*, 1015–1019.

Brewer, J. B., Zhao, Z., Desmond, J. E., Glover, G. H., & Gabrieli, J. D. E. (1998). Making memories: Brain activity that predicts how well visual experience will be remembered. *Science, 281*, 1185–1187.

Brewin, C. R., & Andrews, B. (1998). Recovered memories of trauma: Phenomenology and cognitive mechanisms. *Clinical Psychology Review, 18*, 949–970.

Broadhurst, P. L. (1963). *The science of animal behavior*. Baltimore: Penguin.

Brooks, B. M. (1994). A comparison of serial position effects in implicit and explicit word-stem completion. *Psychonomic Bulletin and Review, 1*, 264–268.

Brooks, J. O., & Watkins, M. J. (1990). Further evidence of the intricity of the memory span. *Journal of Experimental Psychology: Learning, Memory, and Cognition, 16*, 1134–1141.

Brown, A. L., Campione, J. C., Bray, N. W., & Wilcox, B. L. (1973). Keeping track of changing variables: Effects of rehearsal training and rehearsal prevention in normal and retarded adolescents. *Journal of Experimental Psychology, 101*, 123–131.

Brown, A. S. (2003). A review of the déjà vu experience. *Psychological Bulletin, 129*, 394–413.

Brown, A. S., & Murphy, D. R. (1989). Cryptoamnesia: Delineating inadvertant plagiarism. *Journal of Experimental Psychology: Learning, Memory, and Cognition, 15*, 432–442.

Brown, A. S., & Rahhal, T. A. (1994). Hiding valuables: A questionnaire study of mnemonically risky behavior. *Applied Cognitive Psychology, 8*, 141–154.

Brown, J. S. (1958). Some tests of the decay theory of immediate memory. *Quarterly Journal of Experimental Psychology, 10*, 12–21.

Brown, J. S. (1969). Factors affecting self-punitive locomotor behavior. In B. A. Campbell & R. M. Church (Eds.), *Punishment and aversive behavior* (pp. 467–514). New York: Appleton, Century, Crofts.

Brown, M. F., & Moore, J. A. (1997). In the dark II: Spatial choice when access to extrinsic spatial cues is eliminated. *Animal Learning & Behavior, 25*, 335–346.

Brown, R. T., & Kulick, J. (1977). Flashbulb memories. *Cognition, 5*, 73–99.

Brown, R. T., & McNeil, D. (1966). The "tip of the tongue" phenomenon. *Journal of Verbal Learning and Verbal Behavior, 5*, 325–337.

Bruer, J. T. (1997). Education and the brain: A bridge too far. *Educational Researcher, 26*(8), 4–16.

Burger, J. M., Kolss, M., Pont, J., & Kawecki, T. J. (2008). Learning ability and longevity: A symmetrical evolutionary trade-off in *Drosophila. Evolution, 62*, 1294–1304.

Burgess, P. W. (2000). Strategy application disorder: The role of the frontal lobes in human multitasking. *Psychological Research, 63*, 279–288.

Burns, D. J. (1990). The generation effect: A test between single- and multifactor theories. *Journal of Experimental Psychology: Learning, Memory, and Cognition, 16*, 1060–1067.

Bushman, B. J., & Baumeister, R. F. (1998). Threatened egotism, narcissism, self-esteem, and direct and displaced aggression: Does self-love or self-hate lead to violence? *Journal of Personality and Social Psychology, 75*, 219–239.

Butler, A. C., & Roediger, H. L. III. (2008). Feedback enhances the positive effects and reduces the negative consequences of multiple choice testing. *Memory & Cognition, 36*, 604–616.

Butters, N., & Cermak, L. S. (1986). A case study of the forgetting of autobiographical knowledge: Implications for the study of retrograde amnesia. In D. C. Rubin (Ed.), *Autobiographical memory* (pp. 253–272). New York: Cambridge University Press.

Byrne, R. (1979). Memory for urban geography. *Quarterly Journal of Experimental Psychology, 31*, 147–154.

Cabeza, R., & Lennartson, E. R. (2005). False memory across languages: Implicit associative response vs fuzzy trace views. *Memory, 13*, 1–5.

Cameron, C. L., Cella, D., Herndon, J. E. 2nd, Kornblith, A. B., Zuckerman, E., Henderson, E., . . . Holland, J. C. (2001). Persistent symptoms among survivors of Hodgkin's disease: An explanatory model based on classical conditioning. *Health Psychology, 20*, 71–75.

Cammen, T. J., Simpson, J. M., Fraser, R. M., Preker, A. S., & Exton-Smith, A. N. (1987). The memory clinic: A new approach to the detection of dementia. *British Journal of Psychiatry, 150*, 359–364.

Campitelli, G., & Gobet, F. (2011). Deliberate practice: Necessary but not sufficient. *Current Directions in Psychological Science, 20*, 280–285.

Canas, J. J., & Nelson, D. L. (1986). Recognition and environmental context: The effect of testing by phone. *Bulletin of the Psychonomic Society, 24*, 407–409.

Candland, D. K. (1993). *Feral children and clever animals*. New York: Oxford University Press.

Cann, A., & Ross, D. A. (1989). Olfactory stimuli as context cues in human memory. *American Journal of Psychology, 102*, 91–102.

Capaldi, E. J. (1971). Memory and learning: A sequential viewpoint. In W. K. Honig & P. H. R. James (Eds.), *Animal memory* (pp. 112–154). New York: Academic Press.

Capretta, P. J., & Berkun, M. M. (1962). Validity and reliability of certain measures of psychological stress. *Psychological Reports, 10*, 875–878.

Caramazza, A., & Hillis, A. E. (1991). Lexical organization of nouns and verbs in the brain. *Nature, 349*, 788–790.

Carey, M. P., & Burish, T. G. (1988). Etiology and treatment of the psychological side effects associated with cancer chemotherapy: A critical review and discussion. *Psychological Bulletin, 104*, 307–325.

Ceci, J. S., & Bronfenbrenner, U. (1985). "Don't forget to take the cupcakes out of the oven": Prospective memory, strategic time-monitoring, and context. *Child Development, 56*, 152–164.

Cepeda, N. J., Pashler, H., Vul, E., Wixted, J. T., & Rohrer, D. (2006). Distributed practice in verbal recall tasks: A review and quantitative synthesis. *Psychological Bulletin, 132*, 354–380.

Chan, J. C. K., McDermott, K. B., & Roediger, H. L., III. (2006). Retrieval-induced facilitation: Initially nontested material can benefit from prior testing of related material. *Journal of Experimental Psychology: General, 135*, 553–571.

Chance, P. (1992, November). The rewards of learning. *Phi Delta Kappan*, pp. 200–207.

Chapman, G. B. (1991). Trial order affects cue interaction in contingency judgement. *Journal of Experimental Psychology: Learning, Memory, and Cognition, 17*, 837–854.

Charness, N. (1987). Component processes in bridge bidding and novel problem-solving tasks. *Canadian Journal of Psychology, 41*, 223–243.

Chase, W. G., & Ericsson, K. A. (1981). Skilled memory. In J. R. Anderson (Ed.), *Cognitive skills and their acquisition* (pp. 141–180). Hillsdale, NJ: Erlbaum.

Chen, M. K., Lakshminarayanan, V., & Santos, L. R. (2006). How basic are behavioral biases? Evidence from capuchin monkey trading behavior. *Journal of Political Economy, 114*, 517–537.

Cheyne, J. A., Goyeche, J. R. M., & Walters, R. H. (1969). Attention, anxiety, and rules in resistance to extinction in children. *Journal of Experimental Child Psychology, 7*, 231–244.

Chi, M. T. H. (1978). Knowledge structures and memory development. In R. Siegler (Ed.), *Children's thinking: What develops?* (pp. 73–96). Hillsdale, NJ: Erlbaum.

Chorover, S. L., & Schiller, P. H. (1965). Short-term retrograde amnesia in rats. *Journal of Comparative and Physiological Psychology, 59*, 73–78.

Choy, Y., Fyer, A. J., & Lipsitz, J. D. (2007). Treatment of specific phobia in adults. *Clinical Psychology Review, 27*, 266–286.

Christianson, S.-A., Loftus, E. F., Hoffman, H., & Loftus, G. R. (1991). Eye fixations and memory for emotional events. *Journal of Experimental Psychology: Learning, Memory, and Cognition, 17*, 693–701.

Christianson, S.-A., & Nilsson, L.-G. (1984). Functional amnesia as induced by a psychological trauma. *Memory & Cognition, 12*, 142–155.

Clark, D. M., & Teasdale, J. D. (1982). Diurnal variation in clinical depression and accessibility of positive and negative experiences. *Journal of Abnormal Psychology, 91*, 87–95.

Claxton, C. S., & Murrell, P. H. (1987). *Learning styles: Implications for improving education*. Washington, DC: Association for the Study of Higher Education.

Cohen, G. (1989). *Memory in the real world*. Hillsdale, NJ: Erlbaum.

Cohen, G., & Conway, M. A. (2008). *Memory in the real world*. East Sussex, UK: Psychology Press.

Cohen, G., & Faulkner, D. (1986). Memory for proper names: Age differences in retrieval. *British Journal of Developmental Psychology, 4*, 187–197.

Coleman, S. R. (1975). Consequences of responsecontingent change in US intensity upon the rabbit nictitating membrane response. *Journal of Comparative and Physiological Psychology, 88*, 591–595.

Collins, A. M., & Loftus, E. F. (1975). A spreading activation theory of semantic processing. *Psychological Review, 82*, 407–428.

Collins, A. M., & Quillian, M. R. (1969). Retrieval time from semantic memory. *Journal of Verbal Learning and Verbal Behavior, 8*, 240–247.

Conrad, R. (1958). Accuracy of recall using key set and telephone dial, and the effect of a prefix digit. *Journal of Applied Psychology, 42*, 285–288.

Conrad, R. (1964). Acoustic confusions in immediate memory. *British Journal of Psychology, 55*, 75–83.

Conrad, R. (1970). Short-term memory processes in the deaf. *British Journal of Psychology, 61*, 179–195.

Conway, M. A., Cohen, G., & Stanhope, N. (1991). On the very long-term retention of knowledge acquired through formal education: Twelve years of cognitive psychology. *Journal of Experimental Psychology: General, 120*, 395–409.

Conway, M. A., Gardiner, J. M., Perfect, T. J., Anderson, S. J., & Cohen, G. (1997). Changes in memory awareness during learning: The acquisition of knowledge by psychology undergraduates. *Journal of Experimental Psychology: General, 126*, 393–413.

Cook, M., & Mineka, S. (1990). Selective associations in the observational conditioning of fear in rhesus monkeys. *Journal of Experimental Psychology: Animal Behavior Processes, 16*, 372–389.

Coolidge, F. L., & Wynn, T. (2009). *The rise of homo sapiens: The evolution of modern thinking*. Chichester, UK: Wiley-Blackwell.

Cools, R., & Robbins, T. W. (2004). Chemistry of the adaptive mind. *Philosophical Transactions of the Royal Society London A, 362*, 2871–2888.

Cooney, J. B., & Swanson, H. L. (1990). Individual differences in memory for mathematical story problems: Memory span and problem perception. *Journal of Educational Psychology, 82*, 570–577.

Cooper, R. M., & Zubek, J. P. (1958). Effects of enriched and restricted early environments on the learning ability of bright and dull rats. *Canadian Journal of Psychology, 12*, 159–164.

Coren, S. (1994). *The intelligence of dogs*. New York: The Free Press.

Corkin, S. (2002). What's new with the patient H. M.? *Nature Reviews: Neuroscience, 3*, 153–160.

Corkin, S. (2013). *Permanent present tense: The unforgettable life of the amnesic patient, H. M.* New York: Basic Books.

Cornell, E. H., & Heth, C. D. (1979). Response versus place learning by human infants. *Journal of Experimental Psychology: Human Learning and Memory, 5*, 188–196.

Cornell, E. H., Heth, C. D., Kneubuhler, Y., & Sehgal, S. (1996). Serial position effects in children's route reversal errors: Implications for police search operations. *Applied Cognitive Psychology, 10*, 301–326.

Cowan, N. (2001). The magical number 4 in short-term memory: A reconsideration of mental storage capacity. *Behavioral and Brain Sciences, 24*, 87–114.

Cowan, N. (2010). The magical mystery four: How is working memory capacity limited, and why? *Current Directions in Psychological Science, 19*, 51–57.

Craik, F. I. M., & Lockhart, R. S. (1972). Levels of processing: A framework for memory research. *Journal of Verbal Learning and Verbal Behavior, 11*, 671–684.

Craik, F. I. M., & Tulving, E. (1975). Depth of processing and the retention of words in episodic memory. *Journal of Experimental Psychology: General, 104*, 268–294.

Crespi, L. P. (1942). Quantitative variation in incentive and performance in the white rat. *American Journal of Psychology, 55*, 467–517.

Cronbach, L. J. (1957). The two disciplines of scientific psychology. *American Psychologist, 12*, 671–684.

Crook, T. H., & Larabee, G. L. (1990). A self-rating scale for evaluating memory in everyday life. *Psychology and Aging, 5*, 48–57.

Crowder, R. G. (1972). Visual and auditory memory. In J. F. Kavanagh & I. G. Mattingly (Eds.), *Language by ear and by eye* (pp. 251–275). Cambridge, MA: The MIT Press.

Crowder, R. G. (1993). Short-term memory: Where do we stand? *Memory & Cognition, 21*, 142–145.

Crutcher, R. J., & Healy, A. F. (1989). Cognitive operations and the generation effect. *Journal of Experimental Psychology: Learning, Memory, and Cognition, 15*, 669–675.

Cuddy, L. J., & Jacoby, L. L. (1982). When forgetting helps memory: An analysis of repetition effects. *Journal of Verbal Learning and Verbal Behavior, 21*, 451–467.

Curran, H. V., Pooviboonsuk, P., Dalton, J. A., & Lader, M. V. (1998). Differentiating the effects of centrally acting drugs on arousal and memory: An event-related potential study of scopolamine, lorazepam, and diphenhydramine. *Psychopharmacology, 135*, 27–36.

Cutler, S. J., & Grams, A. E. (1988). Correlates of selfreported everyday memory problems. *Journal of Gerontology: Social Sciences*, *43*, S82–S90.

Cytowic, R. E., & Wood, F. B. (1982). Synesthesia 1: A review of major theories and their brain basis. *Brain and Cognition*, *1*, 23–35.

Dadds, M. R., Bovbjerg, D. H., Redd, W. H., & Cutmore, T. R. H. (1997). Imagery in human classical conditioning. *Psychological Bulletin*, *122*, 89–103.

Dallal, N. L., & Meck, W. H. (1990). Hierarchical structures: Chunking by food type facilitates spatial memory. *Journal of Experimental Psychology: Animal Behavior Processes*, *16*, 69–84.

Daneman, M., & Carpenter, P. A. (1980). Individual differences in working memory and reading. *Journal of Verbal Learning and Verbal Behavior*, *19*, 450–466.

Daneman, M., & Merikle, P. M. (1996). Working memory and language comprehension: A meta-analysis. *Psychonomic Bulletin & Review*, *3*, 422–433.

Dark, V. J., & Benbow, C. P. (1990). Enhanced problem solving translation and short-term memory: Components of mathematical skill. *Journal of Educational Psychology*, *82*, 420–429.

Dark, V. J., & Benbow, C. P. (1991). Differential enhancement of working memory with mathematical versus verbal precocity. *Journal of Educational Psychology*, *83*, 48–60.

Darwin, C. (1859). *On the origin of species by means of natural selection, or the preservation of favoured races in the struggle for life*. London: John Murray (New York: Modern Library, 1967).

Daum, I., Channon, S., & Canavan, A. G. M. (1989). Classical conditioning in patients with severe memory problems. *Journal of Neurology, Neurosurgery, and Psychiatry*, *52*, 47–51.

Daum, I., & Schugens, M. M. (1996). On the cerebellum and classical conditioning. *Current Directions in Psychological Science*, *2*, 58–61.

Daum, I., Schugens, M. M., Ackerman, H., Lutzenberger, W., Dichgans, J., & Birbaumer, N. (1993). Classical conditioning after cerebellar lesions in humans. *Behavioral Neuroscience*, *107*, 748–756.

Davey, G. C. L. (1995). Preparedness and phobias: Specific evolved associations or a generalized expectancy bias? *Behavioral and Brain Sciences*, *18*, 289–325.

Davey, G. C. L., & Matchett, G. (1994). Unconditioned stimulus rehearsal and the retention and enhancement of differential "fear" conditioning: Effects of trait and state anxiety. *Journal of Abnormal Psychology*, *103*, 708–718.

Davies, G., & Robertson, N. (1993). Recognition memory for automobiles: A developmental study. *Bulletin of the Psychonomic Society*, *31*, 103–106.

Davis, H. P., & Bernstein, P. A. (1992). Age related changes in explicit and implicit memory. In L. Squire & N. Butters (Eds.), *The neuropsychology of memory* (2nd ed., pp. 249–261). New York: Guilford Press.

Davis, M. (1974). Sensitization of the rat startle response by noise. *Journal of Comparative and Physiological Psychology*, *87*, 571–581.

Davis, M. (2006). Neural systems involved in fear and anxiety measured with fear-potentiated startle. *American Psychologist*, *61*, 741–756.

Dawson, M. E., & Schell, A. M. (1987). Human autonomic and skeletal classical conditioning: The role of conscious cognitive factors. In G. C. L. Davey (Ed.), *Cognitive processes and Pavlovian conditioning in humans* (pp. 27–55). Chichester, UK: Wiley.

Dawson, M. E., Schell, A. M., & Banis, H. T. (1986). Greater resistance to extinction of electrodermal responses conditioned to potentially phobic CSs: A noncognitive process? *Psychophysiology*, *23*, 552–561.

D'Azevedo, W. L. (1962). Uses of the past in Gola discourse. *Journal of African History*, *3*, 11–34.

DeCasper, A. J., & Fifer, W. P. (1980). Of human bonding: Newborns prefer their mother's voices. *Science*, *208*, 1174–1176.

DeCasper, A. J., & Spence, M. J. (1986). Prenatal maternal speech influences newborns' perception of speech sounds. *Infant Behavior and Development*, *9*, 133–150.

Deese, J. (1959). On the prediction of occurrence of particular verbal intrusions in immediate memory. *Journal of Experimental Psychology*, *58*, 17–22.

DeHouwere, J., Baeyens, F., & Field, A. P. (2005). Associative learning of likes and dislikes: Some current controversies and possible ways forward. *Cognition and Emotion*, *19*, 161–174.

Dekker, E., Pelser, H., & Groen, J. (1957). Conditioning as a cause of asthmatic attacks: A laboratory study. *Journal of Psychosomatic Research*, *2*, 97–108.

Delgado, M. R., Jou, R. L., LeDoux, J. E., & Phelps, E. A. (2009). Avoiding negative outcomes: Tracking the mechanisms of avoidance learning in humans during fear conditioning. *Frontiers in Behavioral Neuroscience, 3*, 1–9.

Delis, D. C., Kramer, J. H., Kaplan, E., & Ober, B. A. (1987). *California verbal learning test* (manual). San Antonio, TX: Psychological Corporation.

Dempster, F. N. (1988). The spacing effect: A case study in the failure to apply the results of psychological research. *American Psychologist, 43*, 627–634.

Dempster, F. N. (1996). Distributing and managing the conditions of encoding and practice. In E. L. Bjork & R. A. Bjork (Eds.), *Memory* (pp. 317–344). New York: Academic Press.

deQuervain, D. J., Roozendaal, B., & McGaugh, J. L. (1998). Stress and glucocorticoids impair retrieval of long-term spatial memory. *Nature, 394*, 787–790.

Descartes, R. (1641/1960). *Discourse on methods and meditations*. Indianapolis, IN: Bobbs-Merrill.

Desimone, R. (1996). Neural mechanisms for visual memory and their role in attention. *Proceedings of the National Academy of Sciences, 93*, 13494–13499.

Dess, N. K., & Chapman, C. D. (1998). "Humans and animals"? On saying what we mean. *Psychological Science, 9*, 156–157.

Detterman, D. K. (1975). The von Restorff effect and induced amnesia: Production by manipulation of sound intensity. *Journal of Experimental Psychology: Human Learning and Memory, 1*, 614–628.

de Wijk, R. A., Schab, F. R., & Cain, W. S. (1995). Odor identification. In F. R. Schab & R. G. Crowder (Eds.), *Memory for odors* (pp. 21–37). Hillsdale, NJ: Erlbaum.

de Winstanley, P. A. (1995). A generation effect can be found during naturalistic learning. *Psychonomic Bulletin & Review, 2*, 538–541.

Diamond, A., & Lee, K. (2011). Interventions shown to aid executive function development in children 4 to 12 years old. *Science, 333*, 959–964.

Diamond, B. (1969, September). Interview regarding Sirhan Sirhan. *Psychology Today*, pp. 48–55.

Dickinson, A. (1980). *Contemporary animal learning theory*. Cambridge: Cambridge University Press.

DiClemente, D. F., & Hantula, D. A. (2003). Applied behavioral economics and consumer choice. *Journal of Economic Psychology, 24*, 589–602.

Dienes, Z., & Berry, D. (1997). Implicit learning: Below the subjective threshold. *Psychonomic Bulletin & Review, 4*, 3–23.

Dog roams 840 miles, finds family after move. (1983, March 27). *Charlotte Observer*, p. 12A.

Dohanich, G. (2003). Ovarian steroids and cognitive function. *Current Directions in Psychological Science, 12*, 57–61.

Dollard, J., & Miller, N. E. (1950). *Personality and psychotherapy*. New York: McGraw-Hill.

Domjan, M. (1976). Determinants of the enhancement of flavored-water intake by prior exposure. *Journal of Experimental Psychology: Animal Behavior Processes, 2*, 17–27.

Domjan, M., & Purdy, J. E. (1995). Animal research in psychology: More than meets the eye of the general psychology student. *American Psychologist, 50*, 496–503.

Duckworth, A. L., & Quinn, P. D. (2009). Development and validation of the Short Grit Scale (Grit-S). *Journal of Personality Assessment, 91*, 166–174.

Duckworth, A. L., & Seligman, M. E. P. (2005). Self-discipline outdoes IQ in predicting academic performance of adolescence. *Psychological Science, 16*, 939–944.

Dulany, D. E. (1968). Awareness, rules, and propositional control: A confrontation with S—R behavior theory. In T. R. Dixon & D. H. Horton (Eds.), *Verbal behavior and general behavior theory* (pp. 340–385). Englewood Cliffs, NJ: Prentice Hall.

Dunlosky, J., Rawson, K. A., March E. J., Nathan, M. J., & Willingham, D. T. (2013). Improving students' learning with effective learning techniques: Promising directions from cognitive and educational psychology. *Psychological Science in the Public Interest, 14*, 4–58.

Dunning, D., Johnson, K., Ehrlinger, J., & Kruger, J. (2003). Why people fail to recognize their own incompetence. *Current Directions in Psychological Science, 12*, 83–87.

Dweck, C. S. (1975). The role of expectations and attributions in the alleviation of learned helplessness. *Journal of Personality and Social Psychology, 31*, 674–685.

Dweck, C. S., & Reppucci, N. D. (1973). Learned helplessness and reinforcement responsibility in children. *Journal of Personality and Social Psychology, 25*, 109–116.

Dweck, C. S., & Wagner, A. R. (1970). Situational cues and correlation between CS and US as determinants of the conditioned emotional response. *Psychonomic Science, 18*, 145–147.

Dwyer, D. M., Mundy, M. E., & Honey, R. C. (2011). The role of stimulus comparison in human perceptual learning: Effects of distractor placement. *Journal of Experimental Psychology: Animal Behavior Processes, 37*, 300–307.

Eacott, M. J., & Crawley, R. A. (1998). The offset of childhood amnesia: Memory for events that occurred before age 3. *Journal of Experimental Psychology: General, 127*, 22–33.

Ebbinghaus, H. (1964). *Memory: A contribution to experimental psychology* (H. A. Ruger & C. E. Bussenius, Trans.). New York: Dover. (Original work published 1885).

Eich, E. (1985). Context, memory, and integrated item/context imagery. *Journal of Experimental Psychology: Learning, Memory, and Cognition, 11*, 764–770.

Eich, E. (1995). Mood as a mediator of place dependent memory. *Journal of Experimental Psychology: General, 124*, 293–308.

Eich, J. W., Weingartner, H., Stillman, R. C., & Gillin, J. C. (1975). State dependent accessibility of retrieval cues in the retention of a categorized list. *Journal of Verbal Learning and Verbal Behavior, 14*, 408–417.

Eikelboom, R., & Stewart, J. (1982). Conditioning of drug-induced physiological responses. *Psychological Review, 89*, 507–528.

Einstein, G. O., McDaniel, M. A., & Lackey, S. (1989). Bizarre imagery, inteference, and distinctiveness. *Journal of Experimental Psychology: Learning, Memory, and Cognition, 15*, 137–146.

Einstein, G. O., McDaniel, M. A., Richardson, S. L., Guynn, M. J., & Cunfer, A. R. (1995). Normal aging and prospective memory: Examining the influences of self-initiated retrieval. *Journal of Experimental Psychology: Learning, Memory, and Cognition, 20*, 996–1007.

Eisenberger, R., & Cameron, J. (1996). Detrimental effects of reward: Reality or myth. *American Psychologist, 51*, 1153–1166.

Eisenberger, R., Heerdt, W. A., Hamdin, M., Zimet, S., & Bruckmeir, G. (1979). Transfer of persistence across behaviors. *Journal of Experimental Psychology: Human Learning and Memory, 5*, 522–530.

Ellard, C. (2010). *You are here: Why we can find our way to the moon, but get lost in the mall*. New York: Doubleday.

Ellis, N. C., & Hennelly, R. A. (1980). A bilingual word-length effect: Implications for intelligence testing and the relative ease of mental calculation in Welsh and English. *British Journal of Psychology, 71*, 43–52.

Ellis, N. R., Detterman, D. K., Runcie, D., McCarver, R. B., & Craig, E. M. (1971). Amnesic effects in short-term memory. *Journal of Experimental Psychology, 89*, 357–361.

Emmons, W. H., & Simon, C. W. (1956). The non-recall of material presented during sleep. *American Journal of Psychology, 69*, 76–81.

Engen, T., Kuisma, J. E., & Eimas, P. D. (1973). Short-term memory of odors. *Journal of Experimental Psychology, 99*, 222–225.

Engle, R. W., & Marshall, K. (1983). Do developmental changes in digit span result from acquisition strategies? *Journal of Experimental Child Psychology, 36*, 429–436.

Engle, R. W., Tuholski, S. W., Laughlin, J. E., & Conway, A. R. A. (1999). Working memory, short-term memory, and general fluid intelligence. *Journal of Experimental Psychology: General, 128*, 309–331.

Erber, J. T., & Rothberg, S. T. (1991). Here's looking at you: The relative effects of age and attractiveness on judgements about memory failure. *Journal of Gerontology, 46*, P116–P123.

Erdelyi, M. H., & Kleinbard, J. (1978). Has Ebbinghaus decayed with time? The growth of recall (hypermnesia) over days. *Journal of Experimental Psychology: Human Learning and Memory, 4*, 275–289.

Ericsson, K. A., & Charness, N. (1994). Expert performance: Its structure and acquisition. *American Psychologist, 49*, 725–747.

Ericsson, K. A., Chase, W. G., & Faloon, S. (1980). Acquisition of a memory skill. *Science, 208*, 1181–1182.

Ericsson, K. A., Krampe, R. T., & Tesch-Romer, C. (1993). The role of deliberate practice in the acquisition of expert performance. *Psychological Review, 100*, 363–406.

Erikson, G. C., Hager, L. B., Houseworth, C., Dungan, J., Petros, T., & Beckwith, B. E. (1985). The effects of caffeine on memory for word lists. *Physiology and Behavior, 35*, 47–51.

Essman, W. B. (1983). *Clinical pharmacology of learning and memory*. New York: Spectrum Publications.

Estes, W. K. (1944). An experimental study of punishment. *Psychological Monographs, 57* (3, No. 263), 1–40.

Estes, W. K. (1972). An associative basis for coding and organization in memory. In A. W. Melton & E. Martin (Eds.), *Coding processes in human memory* (pp. 161–190). Washington, DC: V. H. Winston.

Evans, G. W., Fellows, J., Zorn, M., & Doty, K. (1980). Cognitive mapping and architecture. *Journal of Applied Psychology, 65*, 474–478.

Evans, G. W., & Johnson, D. (2000). Stress and open-office noise. *Journal of Applied Psychology, 85*, 779–783.

Evans, H. (2004). *They made America*. New York: Back Bay Books.

Eysenck, H. J. (1981). *A model for personality*. Berlin: Springer.

Eysenck, M. W. (1979). Anxiety, learning, and memory: A reconceptualization. *Journal of Research in Personality, 13*, 363–385.

Eysenck, M. W., & Eysenck, M. C. (1979). Processing depth, elaboration of encoding, memory stores, and expended processing capacity. *Journal of Experimental Psychology: Human Learning and Memory, 5*, 472–484.

Fabiani, M., & Donchin, E. (1995). Encoding processes and memory organization: A model of the von Restorff effect. *Journal of Experimental Psychology: Learning, Memory, and Cognition, 21*, 224–240.

Fagan, J. W., Ohr, P. S., Flechenstein, L. K., & Ribner, D. R. (1985). The effect of crying on long-term memory in infancy. *Child Development, 56*, 1584–1592.

Fein, G., Davenport, L., Yingling, C. D., & Galin, D. (1988). Verbal and nonverbal memory deficits in pure dyslexia. *Developmental Neuropsychology, 4*, 181–197.

Feingold, A. (1988). Cognitive gender differences are disappearing. *American Psychologist, 43*, 95–103.

Fendrich, D. W., Healy, A. F., & Bourne, L. E. (1991). Long-term repetition effects for motoric and perceptual procedures. *Journal of Experimental Psychology: Learning, Memory, and Cognition, 17*, 137–151.

Ferster, C. B., & Skinner, B. F. (1957). *Schedules of reinforcement*. New York: Appleton, Century, Crofts.

Finkel, D., & McGue, M. (1993). The origins of individual differences in memory among the elderly: A behavior genetic analysis. *Psychology and Aging, 8*, 527–537.

Finn, B., & Roediger, H. L. III. (2011). Enhancing retention through reconsolidation: Negative emotional arousal following retrieval enhances later recall. *Psychological Science, 22*, 781–786.

Fitzgerald, H. E., & Brackbill, Y. (1976). Classical conditioning in infancy: Development and constraints. *Psychological Bulletin, 83*, 353–376.

Fivush, R., & Nelson, K. (2004). Culture and language in the emergence of autobiographical memory. *Psychological Science, 15*, 573–577.

Flavel, J. H. (1971). First discussant's comments: What is memory development the development of? *Human Development, 14*, 272–278.

Flynn, J. R. (2012). *Are we getting smarter? Rising IQ in the twenty-first century*. New York: Cambridge University Press.

Foa, E. B., Gillihan, S. J., & Bryant, R. A. (2013). Challenges and successes in dissemination of evidence-based treatments for posttraumatic stress: Lessons learned from prolonged exposure therapy for PTSD. *Psychological Science in the Public Interest, 14*, 65–111.

Foa, E. B., Steketee, G., Grayson, J. B., Turner, R. M., & Latimer, P. R. (1984). Deliberate exposure and blocking of obsessive-compulsive rituals: Immediate and long-term effects. *Behavior Therapy, 15*, 450–472.

Foer, J. (2011). *Moonwalking with Einstein*. New York: Penguin Books.

Fogarty, S. J., & Helmsley, D. R. (1983). Depression and the accessibility of memories—a longitudinal study. *British Journal of Psychiatry, 142*, 232–237.

Folkard, S., & Monk, T. H. (1980). Circadian rhythms in human memory. *British Journal of Psychology, 71*, 295–307.

Folkard, S., & Monk, T. H. (1985). *Hours of work: Temporal factors in work scheduling*. New York: Wiley.

Folkman, S., & Lazarus, R. S. (1985). If it changes it must be a process: Study of emotion and coping during three stages of a college examination. *Journal of Personality and Social Psychology, 48*, 150–170.

Freedman, D. G. (1958). Constitutional and environmental interactions in rearing of four breeds of dogs. *Science, 127*, 585–586.

Frensch, P. A., & Runger, D. (2003). Implicit learning. *Current Directions in Psychological Science, 12*, 13–18.

Freud, S. (1901/1960). *The psychopathology of everyday life*. New York: Norton.

Freundlich, N. (2001, June 11). Arresting Alzheimer's. *Business Week*, 94.

Gabrieli, J. D. E., Corkin, S., Mickel, S. F., & Growdon, J. H. (1993). Intact acquisition and long-term retention of mirror-tracing skill in Alzheimer's disease and global amnesia. *Behavioral Neuroscience, 107*, 899–910.

Gallistel, C. R., Fairhurst, S., & Balsam, P. (2004). The learning curve: Implications of a quantitative analysis. *Proceedings of the National Academy of Science, 101*, 13124–13131.

Garcia, J., & Koelling, R. A. (1966). Relation of cue to consequence in avoidance learning. *Psychonomic Science, 4*, 123–124.

Gardiner, J. M., Gawlik, B., & Richardson-Klavehn, J. (1994). Maintenance rehearsal affects knowing, not remembering; elaborative rehearsal affects remembering, not knowing. *Psychonomic Bulletin & Review, 1*, 107–110.

Gartman, L., & Johnson, N. F. (1972). Massed versus distributed repetition of homographs: A test of the differential-encoding hypothesis. *Journal of Verbal Learning and Verbal Behavior, 11*, 801–808.

Gatchel, R. J. (1975). Effects of interstimulus interval length on short-term and long-term habituation of autonomic components of the orienting response. *Physiological Psychology, 3*, 133–136.

Gathercole, S. E. (1994). The nature and uses of working memory. In P. E. Morris & M. Gruneberg (Eds.), *Theoretical aspects of memory* (pp. 50–78). London: Routledge.

Gesell, A., & Thompson, H. (1929). Learning and growth in identical twins: An experimental study by the method of co-twin control. *Genetic Psychology Monographs, 6*, 1–23.

Gibson, E. J. (1969). *Principles of perceptual learning and development*. New York: Appleton, Century, Crofts.

Gibson, E. J., & Walk, R. D. (1956). The effect of prolonged exposure to visually presented patterns on learning to discriminate them. *Journal of Comparative and Physiological Psychology, 49*, 239–242.

Gibson, J. J., & Gibson, E. J. (1955). Perceptual learning: Differentiation or enrichment? *Psychological Review, 62*, 32–41.

Gilliland, K., & Andress, D. (1981). Ad lib caffeine consumption, symptoms of caffeinism, and academic performance. *American Journal of Psychiatry, 138*, 512–514.

Gladwell, M. (2005). *Blink*. New York: Little, Brown and Company.

Glanzer, M. (1972). Storage mechanisms in recall. In G. H. Bower (Ed.), *The psychology of learning and motivation* (Vol. 5, pp. 129–193). New York: Academic Press.

Glanzer, M., & Cunitz, A. R. (1966). Two storage mechanisms in free recall. *Journal of Verbal Learning and Verbal Behavior, 5*, 351–360.

Glass, D. C., & Singer, J. E. (1972). *Urban stress: Experiments in noise and social stressors*. New York: Academic Press.

Glisky, E. L., & Schacter, D. A. (1989). Extending the limits of complex learning in organic amnesia: Computer training in a vocational domain. *Neuropsychologia, 27*, 107–120.

Gobet, F., & Campitelli, G. (2007). The role of domain-specific practice, handedness, and starting age in chess. *Developmental Psychology, 43*, 159–172.

Gobet, F., & Simon, H. A. (1996). Recall of rapidly presented chess positions is a function of skill. *Psychonomic Bulletin & Review, 3*, 159–163.

Godden, D. R., & Baddeley, A. D. (1975). Context dependent memory in two natural environments: On land and underwater. *British Journal of Psychology, 66*, 325–331.

Goettl, B. P., Yadrick, R. M., Connolly-Gomez, C., Regian, W., & Shebilske, W. L. (1996). Alternating task modules in isochronal distributed training of complex tasks. *Human Factors, 38*, 330–346.

Goff, L. M., & Roediger, H. L. (1998). Imagination inflation for action events: Repeated imaginings lead to illusory recollections. *Memory & Cognition, 26*, 20–33.

Goldman, M. S. (1983). Cognitive impairment in chronic alcoholics. *American Psychologist, 38*, 1045–1054.

Goldman-Rakic, P. (1996). Regional and cellular fractionation of working memory. *Proceedings of the National Academy of Sciences, 93*, 13473–13480.

Goldstone, R. L. (1998). Perceptual learning. *Annual Review of Psychology, 49*, 585–612.

Goodwin, K. A., Meissner, C. A., & Ericsson, K. A. (2001). Toward a model of false recall: Experimental manipulation of encoding context and the collection of verbal reports. *Memory & Cognition, 29*, 806–819.

Goody, J. (1998). Memory in the oral tradition. In P. Fara & K. Patteson (Eds.), *Memory* (pp. 73–94). Cambridge, UK: Cambridge University Press.

Gormezano, I. (1966). Classical conditioning. In J. B. Sidowski (Ed.), *Experimental methods and instrumentation in psychology* (pp. 385–420). New York: McGraw-Hill.

Gormezano, I., & Kehoe, E. (1975). Classical conditioning: Some methodological—conceptual issues. In W. K. Estes (Ed.), *Handbook of learning and cognitive processes* (Vol. 2, pp. 143–179). Hillsdale, NJ: Erlbaum.

Gorn, G. J. (1982, Winter). The effects of music in advertising on choice behavior: A classical conditioning approach. *Journal of Marketing, 46*, 94–101.

Graf, P., & Schacter, D. L. (1989). Unitization and grouping mediate dissociations in memory for new associations. *Journal of Experimental Psychology: Learning, Memory, and Cognition, 15*, 930–940.

Graf, P., Squire, L., & Mandler, G. (1984). The information that amnesic patients do not forget. *Journal of Experimental Psychology: Learning, Memory, and Cognition, 10*, 164–178.

Grant, L., & Evans, A. (1994). *Principles of behavior analysis.* New York: HarperCollins.

Green, R. (1991, August 18). Woods: Shorten shorts days. *Charlotte Observer*, p. 14C.

Greene, R. L. (1986). Sources of recency effects in free recall. *Psychological Bulletin, 99*, 221–228.

Greenough, W. T. (1985). The possible role of experience dependent synaptogenesis, or synapses on demand, in the memory process. In N. M. Weinberger, J. L. McGaugh, & G. Lynch (Eds.), *Memory systems of the brain* (pp. 77–103). New York: Guilford.

Greenspoon, J. (1955). The reinforcing effect of two spoken sounds on the frequency of two responses. *American Journal of Psychology, 68*, 409–416.

Grierson, B. (2003, July 27). A bad trip down memory lane. *New York Times Magazine*, pp. 36, 38–39.

Grigorenko, E. L., & Sternberg, R. J. (1997). Styles of thinking, abilities, and academic performance. *Exceptional Children, 63*, 295–312.

Grillon, C. (2002). Startle reactivity and anxiety disorders: Aversive conditioning, context, and neurobiology. *Biological Psychiatry, 52*, 958–975.

Groninger, L. D., Groninger, D. H., & Stiens, J. (1995). Learning the names of people: The role of image mediators. *Memory, 3*, 147–167.

Groves, P. M., & Thompson, R. F. (1970). Habituation: A dual-process theory. *Psychological Review, 77*, 419–450.

Gudjonsson, G. H. (1979). The use of electrodermal response in a case of amnesia. *Medicine, Science and the Law, 19*, 138–140.

Gulya, M., Galluccio, L., Wilk, A., & Rovee-Collier, C. (2001). Infants' long-term memory for a serial list: Recognition and reactivation. *Developmental Psychobiology, 38*, 174–185.

Gunter, B., Berry, C., & Clifford, B. R. (1981). Proactive interference effects with television news items: Further evidence. *Journal of Experimental Psychology: Human Learning and Memory, 7*, 480–487.

Gunther, L. M., Miller, R. R., & Matute, H. (1997). CSs and USs: What's the difference? *Journal of Experimental Psychology: Animal Behavior Processes, 23*, 15–30.

Gustavson, C. R. (1977). Comparative and field aspects of learned food aversions. In L. M. Barker, M. R. Best, & M. Domjan (Eds.), *Learning mechanisms in food selection* (pp. 23–44). Waco, TX: Baylor University Press.

Gustavson, C. R., & Garcia, J. (1974, August). Pulling a gag on the wily coyote. *Psychology Today, 8*(3), 68–72.

Guthrie, J. P., Ash, R. A., & Bendapudi, V. (1995). Additional validity evidence for a measure of morningness. *Journal of Applied Psychology, 80*, 186–190.

Hall, G. (1994). Pavlovian conditioning: Laws of association. In N. J. Mackintosh (Ed.), *Animal learning and cognition* (pp. 15–43). San Diego, CA: Academic Press.

Hamann, S. B., Squire, L. R., & Schacter, D. L. (1995). Perceptual thresholds and priming in amnesia. *Neuropsychology, 9*, 3–15.

Hambrick, D. Z., & Meinz, E. J. (2011). Limits on the predictive power of domain-specific experience and knowledge in skilled performance. *Current Directions in Psychological Science, 20*, 275–279.

Hammerl, M., Bloch, M., & Silverthorne, C. P. (1997). Effects of US-alone presentations on human evaluative conditioning. *Learning and Motivation, 28*, 491–509.

Hammond, D., Fong, G. T., Borland, R., Cummings, K. M., McNeill, A., & Driezen, P. (2007). Text and graphic warnings on cigarette packages: Findings from International tobacco control four country study. *American Journal of Preventive Medicine, 32*, 210–217.

Hampson, E., & Kimura, D. (1988). Reciprocal effects of hormonal fluctuations of human motor and perceptual-spatial skills. *Behavioral Neuroscience, 102*, 456–459.

Hanley-Dunn, P., & McIntosh, J. L. (1984). Meaningfulness and recall of names by young and old adults. *Journal of Gerontology, 39*, 583–585.

Harlow, H. F. (1959). Love in infant monkeys. *Scientific American, 200*(6), 68–74.

Harp, S. F., & Mayer, R. E. (1998). How seductive details do their damage: A theory of cognitive interest in science learning. *Journal of Educational Psychology, 90*, 414–434.

Harrington, D. L., Haaland, K. Y., Yeo, R. A., & Marder, E. (1990). Procedural memory in Parkinson's disease: Impaired motor but not visuoperceptual learning. *Journal of Clinical and Experimental Neuropsychology, 12*, 323–339.

Harris, B. (1979). Whatever happened to Little Albert? *American Psychologist, 34*, 151–160.

Harris, J. E. (1978). External memory aids. In M. M. Gruneberg, P. E. Morris, & R. N. Sykes (Eds.), *Practical aspects of memory* (pp. 172–179). London: Academic Press.

Harris, J. E. (1980). Memory aids people use: Two interview studies. *Memory & Cognition, 8*, 31–38.

Harris, J. E. (1984). Remembering to do things: A forgotten topic. In J. E. Harris & P. E. Morris (Eds.), *Everyday memory, actions and absentmindedness* (pp. 71–92). New York: Academic Press.

Hart, J. T. (1965). Memory and the feeling-of-knowing experience. *Journal of Educational Psychology, 56*, 208–216.

Hasher, L., & Zacks, R. T. (1988). Working memory, comprehension, and aging: A review and a new view. *The Psychology of Learning and Motivation, 22*, 193–225.

Hastie, R., & Kumar, P. A. (1979). Person memory: Personality traits as organizing principles in memory for behaviors. *Journal of Personality and Social Psychology, 37*, 25–38.

Hawkins, R. D., Cohen, T. E., Greene, W., & Kandel, E. R. (1998). Relationships between dishabituation, sensitization, and inhibition of the gill- and siphon-withdrawal reflex in *Aplysia californica:* Effects of response measure, test time, and training stimulus. *Behavioral Neuroscience, 112*, 24–38.

Healy, A. F., & Bourne, L. E. (1995). *Learning and memory of knowledge and skills*. Thousand Oaks, CA: Sage.

Healy, A. F., Clawson, D. M., McNamara, D. S., Marmie, W. R., Schneider, V. I., Rickard, T. C., Crutcher, R. J., King, C. L., Ericsson, K. A., & Bourne, L. E. (1993). The long-term retention of knowledge and skills. *The Psychology of Learning and Motivation, 30*, 135–164.

Healy, A. F., & McNamara, D. S. (1996). Verbal learning and memory: Does the modal model still work? *Annual Review of Psychology, 47*, 143–172.

Heaps, C., & Nash, M. (1999). Individual differences in imagination inflation. *Psychonomic Bulletin & Review, 6*, 313–318.

Hearst, E., & Jenkins, H. M. (1974). *Sign tracking: The stimulus-reinforcer relation and directed action*. Austin, TX: Psychonomic Society.

Hebb, D. O. (1949). *Organization of behavior*. New York: Wiley.

Hebb, D. O. (1955). Drives and the C. N. S. (conceptual nervous system). *Psychological Review, 62*, 243–254.

Heindel, W. C., Butters, N., & Salmon, D. P. (1988). Impaired learning of a motor skill in patients with Huntington's disease. *Behavioral Neuroscience, 102*, 141–147.

Hepper, P. G. (1989). Foetal learning: Implications for psychiatry? *British Journal of Psychiatry, 155*, 289–293.

Herlitz, A., Nilsson, L. G., & Backman, L. (1997). Gender differences in episodic memory. *Memory & Cognition, 25*, 801–811.

Hermans, D., Craske, M. G., Mineka, S., & Lovibond, P. F. (2006). Extinction in human fear conditioning. *Biological Psychiatry, 60*, 361–368.

Herrmann, D. J. (1987). Task appropriateness of mnemonic techniques. *Perceptual and Motor Skills, 64*, 171–178.

Herrmann, D. J., Crawford, M., & Holdsworth, M. (1992). Gender-linked differences in everyday memory performance. *British Journal of Psychology, 83*, 221–231.

Heth, C. D. (1976). Simultaneous and backward fear conditioning as a function of number of CS-UCS pairings. *Journal of Experimental Psychology: Animal Behavior Processes, 2*, 117–129.

Heuer, F., & Reisberg, D. (1992). Emotion, arousal, and memory for detail. In S.-A. Christianson (Ed.), *The handbook of emotion and memory* (pp. 151–180). Hillsdale, NJ: Erlbaum.

Hiby, E. F., Rooney, N. J., & Bradshaw, J. W. (2004). Dog training methods: Their use, effectiveness, and interaction with behavior and welfare. *Animal Welfare, 13,* 63–69.

Hicks-Pass, S. (2009). Corporal punishment in America today: Spare the rod, spoil the child? A systematic review of the literature. *Best Practices in Mental Health: An International Journal, 5,* 71–88.

Hill, W. F. (1978). Effects of mere exposure on preferences in nonhuman animals. *Psychological Bulletin, 85,* 1177–1198.

Hillner, K. P. (1978). *Psychology of learning: A conceptual analysis.* New York: Pergamon Press.

Hintzman, D. L. (1990). Human learning and memory: Connections and dissociations. *Annual Review of Psychology, 41,* 109–139.

Hintzman, D. L. (2011). Research strategy in the study of memory: Fads, fallacies, and the search for the "coordinates of truth". *Perspectives on Psychological Science, 6,* 253–271.

Hintzman, D. L., Block, R. A., & Summers, J. J. (1973). Modality tags and memory for repetitions: Locus of the spacing effect. *Journal of Verbal Learning and Verbal Behavior, 12,* 229–238.

Hiroto, D. S. (1974). Locus of control and learned helplessness. *Journal of Experimental Psychology, 102,* 187–193.

Hirst, W., Spelke, E., Reaves, C. C., Caharack, G., & Neisser, U. (1980). Dividing attention without alternation or automaticity. *Journal of Experimental Psychology: General, 109,* 98–117.

Hogervorst, E., DeJager, C., Budge, M., & Smith, A. D. (2004). Serum levels of estradiol and testosterone and performance in different cognitive domains in healthy elderly men and women. *Psychoneuroendocrinology, 29,* 405–421.

Hogervorst, E., Riedel, W. J., Schmitt, J. A. J., & Jolles, J. (1998). Caffeine improves memory performance during distraction in middle-aged, but not in young or old subjects. *Human Psychopharmacology, 13,* 277–284.

Hollis, K. L. (1997). Contemporary research on Pavlovian conditioning: A new "functional" analysis. *American Psychologist, 52,* 956–965.

Holloway, F. A. (1978). State dependent retrieval based on time of day. In B. Ho, D. Richards, & D. Chute (Eds.), *Drug discrimination and state dependent learning* (pp. 319–344). New York: Academic Press.

Holmes, D. S. (1992). The evidence for repression: An examination of sixty years of research. In J. L. Singer (Ed.), *Repression and dissociation* (pp. 85–102). Chicago: University of Chicago Press.

Horton, D. L., & Mills, C. B. (1984). Human learning and memory. *Annual Review of Psychology, 35,* 361–394.

Hostetler, A. J. (1988, January). If you said it once, you'll say it again. *APA Monitor,* p. 9.

Houston, J. P. (1983). Psychology: A closed system of self-evident information? *Psychological Reports, 52,* 203–208.

Hovland, C. I. (1938). Experimental studies in rote learning theory: III. Distribution of practice with varying speeds of syllable presentation. *Journal of Experimental Psychology, 23,* 172–190.

Hovland, C. I. (1951). Human learning and retention. In S. S. Stevens (Ed.), *Handbook of experimental psychology* (pp. 613–688). New York: Wiley.

Howe, M. L. (2000). *The fate of early memories: Developmental science and the retention of early childhood experiences.* Washington, DC: American Psychological Association.

Hudson, J. A. (1990). The emergence of autobiographical memory in mother-child conversation. In R. Fivush & J. A. Hudson (Eds.), *Knowing and remembering in young children* (pp. 166–196). New York: Cambridge University Press.

Hull, C. L. (1943). *Principles of behavior.* New York: Appleton, Century, Crofts.

Hull, C. L. (1949). Behavior postulates and corollaries—1949. *Psychological Review, 57,* 173–180.

Hulme, C., & Mackenzie, S. (1992). *Working memory and severe learning difficulties.* Mahwah, NJ: Erlbaum.

Hunt, R. R. (1995). The subtlety of distinctiveness: What von Restorff really did. *Psychonomic Bulletin & Review, 2,* 105–112.

Hunt, R. R., & Elliott, J. M. (1980). The role of nonsemantic information in memory: Orthographic distinctiveness effects on retention. *Journal of Experimental Psychology: General, 109,* 49–74.

Husain, M., & Mehta, M. A. (2011). Cognitive enhancement by drugs in health and disease. *Trends in Cognitive Sciences, 15,* 28–36.

Huston, J. P., Mondadori, C., & Waser, P. G. (1974). Facilitation of learning by reward of post-trial memory processes. *Experientia, 30,* 1038–1040.

Hyde, T. S., & Jenkins, J. J. (1969). Differential effects of incidental tasks on the organization of recall of a list of highly associated words. *Journal of Experimental Psychology, 82,* 472–481.

Hydén, H., & Egyhazi, E. (1963). Glial RNA changes during a learning experiment with rats. *Proceedings of the National Academy of Sciences, 49,* 618–624.

Ince, L. P., Brucker, B. S., & Alba, A. (1978). Reflex conditioning of a spinal man. *Journal of Comparative and Physiological Psychology, 92,* 796–802.

Inhoff, A. W., & Gordon, A. M. (1997). Eye movements and eye-hand coordination during typing. *Current Directions in Psychological Science, 6,* 153–157.

Inoue, S., & Matsuzawa, T. (2007). Working memory of numerals in chimpanzees. *Current Biology, 17,* 1004–1005.

Ishikawa, T., Fujiwara, H., Imai, O., & Okabe, A. (2008). Wayfinding with a GPS-based mobile navigation system: A comparison with maps and direct experience. *Journal of Environmental Psychology, 28,* 74–82.

Israel, L., & Schacter, D. L. (1997). Pictorial encoding reduces false recognition of semantic associates. *Psychonomic Bulletin & Review, 4,* 577–581.

Jacobs, A. (2005, July 31). The Adderall advantage. *New York Times,* p. ED16.

Jacoby, L. L., Woloshyn, V., & Kelley, C. M. (1989). Becoming famous without being recognized: Unconscious influences of memory produced by divided attention. *Journal of Experimental Psychology: General, 118,* 115–125.

James, W. (1890). *The principles of psychology* (2 vols.). New York: Henry Holt. (Dover reprint edition, 1950).

Janet, P. (1907). *The major symptoms of hysteria.* New York: Macmillan.

Janis, I. L., & Astrachan, M. (1951). The effects of electroconvulsive treatments on memory efficiency. *Journal of Abnormal and Social Psychology, 46,* 501–511.

Janowsky, J. S., Oviatt, S. K., & Orwoll, E. S. (1994). Testosterone influences spatial cognition in older men. *Behavioral Neuroscience, 108,* 325–332.

Jauhar, S. (2002, May 5). Jolts of anxiety. *New York Times Magazine,* pp. 16, 18, 22, 24.

Jenkins, H. M., & Moore, B. R. (1973). The form of the autoshaped response with food or water reinforcers. *Journal of the Experimental Analysis of Behavior, 20,* 163–181.

Jenkins, J. G., & Dallenbach, K. M. (1924). Obliviscence during sleep and waking. *American Journal of Psychology, 35,* 605–612.

Jenkins, J. J., & Russell, W. A. (1952). Associative clustering during recall. *Journal of Abnormal and Social Psychology, 47,* 818–821.

Jensen, A. R. (1962). Temporal and spatial effects of serial position. *American Journal of Psychology, 75,* 390–400.

Johnson, M. K., Nolde, S. F., Mather, M., Kounios, J., Schacter, D. L., & Curran, T. (1997). The similarity of brain activity associated with true and false recognition memory depends on test format. *Psychological Science, 8,* 250–257.

Johnson, M. K., & Raye, C. L. (1981). Reality monitoring. *Psychological Review, 88,* 67–85.

Jones, B. F., & Hall, J. W. (1982). School applications of the mnemonic keyword method as a study strategy by eighth graders. *Journal of Educational Psychology, 74,* 230–237.

Jones, M. C. (1924). The elimination of children's fears. *Journal of Experimental Psychology, 7,* 382–390.

Jones, W. T. (1952). *A history of Western philosophy.* New York: Harcourt, Brace & World.

Kagan, J. (2011). Three lessons learned. *Perspectives on Psychological Science, 6,* 102–113.

Kail, R. (1990). *The development of memory in children* (3rd ed.). New York: Freeman.

Kalish, H. I. (1958). The relationship between discriminability and generalization: A re-evaluation. *Journal of Experimental Psychology, 55,* 637–644.

Kamin, L. J. (1956). The effects of termination of the CS and avoidance of the US on avoidance learning. *Journal of Comparative and Physiological Psychology, 49,* 420–424.

Kamin, L. J. (1969). Predictability, surprise, attention, and conditioning. In B. A. Campbell & R. M. Church (Eds.), *Punishment* (pp. 279–296). New York: Appleton, Century, Crofts.

Kaminski, J., Call, J., & Fischer, J. (2004). Word learning in the domestic dog: Evidence for "fast mapping". *Science, 304,* 1682–1683.

Kandel, E. R. (2001). The molecular biology of memory storage: A dialogue between genes and synapses. *Science, 294*, 1030–1038.

Kandel, E. R. (2006). *In search of memory*. New York: Norton.

Kang, S. H. K., McDermott, K. B., & Roediger, H. L., III. (2007). Test format and corrective feedback modify the effect of testing on long-term retention. *European Journal of Cognitive Psychology, 19*, 528–558.

Karni, A., Tanne, D., Rubenstein, B. S., Askenasy, J. M., & Sagi, D. (1994). Dependence on REM sleep of overnight improvement of a perceptual skill. *Science, 265*, 679–682.

Karpicke, J. D., & Roediger, H. L., III. (2007). Repeated retrieval during learning is the key to long-term retention. *Journal of Memory and Language, 57*, 151–162.

Kassam, K. S., Gilbert, D. T., Swencionis, J. K., & Wilson, T. D. (2009). Misconceptions of memory: The Scooter Libby effect. *Psychological Science, 20*, 551–553.

Kausler, D. H., Wiley, J. G., & Lieberwitz, K. J. (1992). Adult age differences in short-term memory and subsequent long-term memory for actions. *Psychology and Aging, 7*, 309–316.

Kawecki, T. J. (2010). Evolutionary ecology of learning: Insights from fruit lies. *Population Ecology, 52*, 15–25.

Kazdin, A. E. (1994*). Behavior modification in applied settings* (5th ed.). Pacific Grove, CA: Brooks/Cole.

Kearins, J. M. (1981). Visual spatial memory in Australian aboriginal children of desert regions. *Cognitive Psychology, 13*, 434–460.

Keenan, J., McWhinney, B., & Mayhew, D. (1977). Pragmatics in memory: A study of natural conversation. *Journal of Verbal Learning and Verbal Behavior, 17*, 549–560.

Keeney, T. J., Cannizzo, S. R., & Flavell, J. H. (1967). Spontaneous and induced rehearsal in a recall task. *Child Development, 38*, 953–966.

Kempermann, G., Kuhn, H. G., & Gage, F. H. (1997). More hippocampal neurons in adult mice living in an enriched environment. *Nature, 386*, 493–495.

Kenny, L. M., Bryant, R. A., Silove, D., Creamer, M., O'Donnell, M., & McFarlane, A. C. (2009). Distant memories: A prospective study of vantage point of trauma memories. *Psychological Science, 20*, 1049–1052.

Keppel, G. (1964). Facilitation in short- and long-term retention of paired associates following distributed practice in learning. *Journal of Verbal Learning and Verbal Behavior, 3*, 91–111.

Kesner, R. P., Hopkins, R. O., & Chiba, A. A. (1992). Learning and memory in humans, with an emphasis on the role of the hippocampus. In L. R. Squire & N. Butters (Eds.), *Neuropsychology of memory* (pp. 106–121). New York: Guilford Press.

Kientzle, M. J. (1949). Ability patterns under distributed practice. *Journal of Experimental Psychology, 39*, 532–537.

Kiewra, K. A., DuBois, N. F., Christian, D., McShane, A., Meyerhoffer, M., & Roskelley, D. (1991). Notetaking functions and techniques. *Journal of Educational Psychology, 83*, 240–245.

Kihlstrom, J. F. (1987). The cognitive unconscious. *Science, 237*, 1445–1452.

Kihlstrom, J. F., Schacter, D. L., Cork, R. C., Hurt, C. A., & Behr, S. E. (1990). Implicit and explicit memory following surgical anesthesia. *Psychological Science, 1*, 303–306.

Kim, J., Allen, C. T., & Kardes, F. R. (1996). An investigation of the mediational mechanisms underlying attitudinal conditioning. *Journal of Marketing Research, 33*, 318.

Kimble, G. A. (1967). The definition of learning and some useful distinctions. In G. A. Kimble (Ed.), *Foundations of conditioning and learning* (pp. 82–99). New York: Appleton, Century, Crofts.

Kindt, M., Soeter, M., & Vervliet, B. (2009). Beyond extinction: Erasing fear responses and preventing the return of fear. *Nature Neuroscience, 12*, 256–258.

Kirby, F. D., & Shields, F. (1972). Modification of arithmetic response rate and attending behavior in a seventh-grade student. *Journal of Applied Behavior Analysis, 5*, 79–84.

Kivetz, R., Urminsky, O., & Zheng, Y. (2006, February). The goal-gradient hypothesis resurrected: Purchase acceleration, illusory goal progress, and customer retention. *Journal of Marketing Research, 43*, 39–58.

Klatzky, R. L. (1984). *Memory and awareness: An information-processing perspective*. New York: Freeman.

Klein, D. C., & Seligman, M. E. P. (1976). Reversal of performance deficits and perceptual deficits in learned helplessness and depression. *Journal of Abnormal Psychology, 85*, 11–26.

Klingberg, T. (2009). *The overflowing brain*. Oxford, UK: Oxford University Press.

Knowlton, B., McGowan, M., Olton, D. S., & Gamzu, E. (1985). Hippocampal stimulation disrupts spatial working memory even 8h after acquisition. *Behavioral & Neural Biology, 44*, 325–337.

Kobre, K. R., & Lipsitt, L. P. (1972). A negative contrast effect in newborns. *Journal of Experimental Child Psychology, 14*, 81–91.

Kohn, A. (1993). *Punished by rewards: The trouble with gold stars, incentive plans, A's, praise, and other bribes*. Boston: Houghton Mifflin.

Kolb, B., & Whishaw, I. Q. (1985). *Fundamentals of human neuropsychology* (2nd ed.). New York: Freeman.

Kolb, D. A. (1984). *Experiential learning: Experience as the source of learning and development*. Englewood Cliffs, NJ: Prentice Hall.

Kopelman, M. D. (1987). Amnesia: Organic and psychogenic. *British Journal of Psychiatry, 150*, 428–442.

Kopelman, M. D. (1994). Working memory in the amnesic syndrome and degenerative dementia. *Neuropsychology, 8*, 555–562.

Koriat, A. (1997). Monitoring one's own knowledge during study: A cue-utilization approach to judgments of learning. *Journal of Experimental Psychology: General, 126*, 349–370.

Kornell, N., Rhodes, M. G., Castel, A. D., & Tauber, S. K. (2011). The ease-of-processing heuristic and the stability bias: Dissociating memory, memory beliefs, and memory judgments. *Psychological Science, 22*, 787–794.

Koulack, D., & Goodenough, D. R. (1976). Dream recall and dream recall failure: An arousal-retrieval model. *Psychological Bulletin, 83*, 975–984.

Kozlowski, L. T., & Bryant, K. J. (1977). Sense of direction, spatial orientation, and cognitive maps. *Journal of Experimental Psychology: Human Perception and Performance, 3*, 590–598.

Kraiger, K., Ford, J. K., & Salas, E. (1993). Application of cognitive, skill-based, and affective theories of learning outcomes to new methods of training evaluation. *Journal of Applied Psychology, 78*, 311–328.

Kramer, J. J., Nagle, R. J., & Engle, R. W. (1980). Recent advances in mnemonic strategy training with mentally retarded persons: Implications for educational practice. *American Journal of Mental Deficiency, 85*, 306–314.

Kratzig, G., Arbuthnott, K. (2006). Perceptual learning style and proficiency: A test of the hypothesis. *Journal of Educational Psychology, 98*, 238–246.

Kreutzer, M. A., Leonard, C., & Flavell, J. H. (1975). An interview study about children's knowledge about memory. *Monographs of the Society for Research in Child Development, 40* (1, Serial No. 159).

Kreutzer, M. A., Leonard, C., & Flavell, J. H. (1982). Prospective remembering in children. In U. Neisser (Ed.), *Memory observed* (pp. 343–348). San Francisco: Freeman.

Krug, D., Davis, T. B., & Glover, J. A. (1990). Massed versus distributed repeated reading: A case of forgetting helping recall? *Journal of Educational Psychology, 82*, 366–371.

Kruger, J., & Dunning, D. (1999). Unskilled and unaware of it: How difficulties in recognizing one's own incompetence lead to inflated self-assessments. *Journal of Personality and Social Psychology, 77*, 1121–1134.

Kuhara-Kojima, K., & Hatano, G. (1991). Contribution of content knowledge and learning ability to the learning of facts. *Journal of Educational Psychology, 83*, 253–263.

Kulhavy, R. W., Dyer, H. W., & Silver, L. (1975). The effects of notetaking and test expectancy on the learning of text material. *Journal of Educational Research, 68*, 363–365.

Kulhavy, R. W., Schwartz, N. H., & Peterson, S. (1986). Working memory: The encoding process. In G. D. Phye & T. Andre (Eds.), *Cognitive classroom learning* (pp. 115–140). New York: Academic Press.

Kunst-Wilson, W. R., & Zajonc, R. B. (1980). Affective discrimination of stimuli that cannot be recognized. *Science, 207*, 557–558.

Kurbat, M. A., Shevell, S. K., & Rips, L. J. (1998). A year's memories: The calendar effect in autobiographical memory. *Memory & Cognition, 26*, 532–552.

Kurtz-Costes, B., Schneider, W., & Rupp, S. (1995). Is there evidence for intraindividual consistency in performance across memory tasks? New evidence on an old question. In F. E. Weinert & W. Schneider (Eds.), *Memory performance and competencies: Issues in growth and development* (pp. 245–262). Hillsdale, NJ: Erlbaum.

Kvavilashvili, L. (1992). Remembering intentions: A critical review of existing experimental paradigms. *Applied Cognitive Psychology*, *6*, 507–524.

Kvavilashvili, L., & Mandler, G. (2004). Out of one's mind: A study of involuntary semantic memories. *Cognitive Psychology*, *48*, 47–94.

Kyllonen, P. C., Tirre, W. C., & Christal, R. E. (1991). Knowledge and processing speed as determinants of associative learning. *Journal of Experimental Psychology: General*, *120*, 57–79.

Landauer, T. K. (1969). Reinforcement as consolidation. *Psychological Review*, *76*, 82–96.

Landauer, T. K., & Bjork, B. J. (1978). Optimum rehearsal patterns and name learning. In M. M. Gruneberg, P. E. Morris, & R. N. Sykes (Eds.), *Practical aspects of memory* (pp. 625–632). New York: Academic Press.

Landers, S. (1988, June). Skinner joins aversives debate. *APA Monitor*, p. 22.

Lashley, K. S. (1917). The effect of strychnine and caffeine upon rate of learning. *Psychobiology*, *1*, 141–170.

Lashley, K. S. (1929). *Brain mechanisms and intelligence*. Chicago: University of Chicago Press. (Dover reprint, 1963).

Lashley, K. S. (1951). The problem of serial order in behavior. In L. A. Jeffress (Ed.), *Cerebral mechanisms in behavior* (pp. 112–136). New York: Wiley.

Lawton, C. A. (1994). Gender differences in way-finding strategies: Relationship to spatial ability and spatial anxiety. *Sex Roles*, *30*, 765–779.

Lechner, H. A., Squire, L. R., & Byrne, J. H. (1999, March/April). 100 years of consolidation: Remembering Muller and Pilzecker. *Learning & Memory*, *6*, 77–87.

LeDoux, J. E. (2000). Emotion circuits in the brain. *Annual Review of Neuroscience*, *23*, 155–184.

Lee, C. L., & Estes, W. K. (1977). Order and position in primary memory for letter strings. *Journal of Verbal Learning and Verbal Behavior*, *16*, 395–416.

Lemonick, M. D. (1995, July 24). Einstein strikes again. *Time*, p. 55.

Lenehan, M. (1986, April). Four ways to walk a dog. *The Atlantic Monthly*, pp. 35–48, 89–99.

Lenneberg, E. H. (1967). *Biological foundations of language*. New York: Wiley.

LePort, A. K. R., Matfield, A. T., Dickinson-Anson, H., Fallon, J. H., Stark, C. E. L., Kruggel, F., Cahill, L., & McGaugh, J. L. (2012). Behavioral and neuroanatomical investigation of Highly Superior Autobiographical memory (HSAM). *Neurobiology of Learning and Memory*, *98*, 78–92.

Lepper, M. R., Greene, D., & Nisbett, R. E. (1973). Undermining children's intrinsic interest with extrinsic rewards: A test of the overjustification hypothesis. *Journal of Personality and Social Psychology*, *28*, 129–137.

Levin, I. P., & Hinrichs, J. V. (1995). *Experimental psychology: Contemporary methods and applications*. Madison, WI: WCB Brown & Benchmark.

Levine, M., Marchon, I., & Hanley, G. L. (1984). The placement and misplacement of you-are-here maps. *Environment and Behavior*, *16*, 139–157.

Lewis, D. J. (1979). Psychobiology of active and inactive memory. *Psychological Bulletin*, *86*, 1054–1083.

Lewis, D. J., & Duncan, C. P. (1958). Expectation and resistance to extinction of a lever-pulling response as a function of percentage of reinforcement and number of acquisition trials. *Journal of Experimental Psychology*, *55*, 121–128.

Lieberman, D. A., McIntosh, D. C., & Thomas, G. V. (1979). Learning when reward is delayed: A marking hypothesis. *Journal of Experimental Psychology: Animal Behavior Processes*, *5*, 224–242.

Light, L. L., & Anderson, P. A. (1985). Working memory capacity, age, and memory for discourse. *Journal of Gerontology*, *40*, 737–747.

Linscheid, T. R., Iwata, B. A., Ricketts, R. W., Williams, D. E., & Griffin, J. C. (1990). Clinical evaluation of the self-injurious behavior inhibiting system (SIBIS). *Journal of Applied Behavior Analysis*, *23*, 53–78.

Linton, M. (1982). Transformations of memory in everyday life. In U. Neisser (Ed.), *Memory Observed* (pp. 77–91). San Francisco: Freeman.

Little, A. H., Lipsitt, L. P., & Rovee-Collier, C. K. (1984). Classical conditioning and retention of the infant's eyelid response: Effects of age and inter-stimulus interval. *Journal of Experimental Child Psychology*, *37*, 512–524.

Lobb, H., & Hardwick, C. (1976). Eyelid conditioning and intellectual level: Effects of repeated acquisition and extinction. *American Journal of Mental Deficiency*, *80*, 423–430.

Locke, J. L. (1690/1956). *An essay concerning human understanding.* Chicago: Geteway Edition, Henry Regnery.

Locke, J. L., & Fehr, F. S. (1971). Young children's use of the speech code in a recall task. *Journal of Experimental Child Psychology, 10,* 367–373.

Lockhead, G. R., & Crist, W. B. (1980). Making letters distinctive. *Journal of Educational Psychology, 72,* 483–493.

Loftus, E. F. (1979). *Eyewitness testimony.* Cambridge: Harvard University Press.

Loftus, E. F., & Burns, T. E. (1982). Mental shock can produce retrograde amnesia. *Memory & Cognition, 10,* 318–323.

Loftus, E. F., & Ketcham, K. (1994). *The myth of repressed memory.* New York: St. Martin's Press.

Loftus, E. F., & Loftus, G. R. (1980). On the permanence of stored information in the brain. *American Psychologist, 35,* 409–420.

Loftus, E. F., Loftus, G. R., & Messo, J. (1987). Some facts about "weapon focus". *Law and Human Behavior, 11,* 55–62.

Loftus, E. F., Miller, D. G., & Burns, H. J. (1978). Semantic integration of verbal information into a visual memory. *Journal of Experimental Psychology: Human Learning and Memory, 4,* 19–31.

Loftus, E. F., & Pickrell, J. E. (1995). The formation of false memories. *Psychiatric Annals, 25,* 720–725.

Logan, F. A., & Wagner, A. R. (1962). Direction of change in CS in eyelid conditioning. *Journal of Experimental Psychology, 64,* 325–326.

Logue, A. W., Forzano, L. B., & Ackerman, K. T. (1996). Self-control in children: Age, preference for reinforcer amount and delay, and language ability. *Learning and Motivation, 27,* 269–277.

Lord, A. B. (1960). *The singer of tales.* Cambridge: Harvard University Press.

Lubow, R. E. (1973). Latent inhibition. *Psychological Bulletin, 79,* 398–407.

Lukowiak, K., & Jacklet, J. W. (1972). Habituation and dishabituation: Interactions between peripheral and central nervous systems in Aplysia. *Science, 178,* 1306–1308.

Luria, A. R. (1968). *The mind of a mnemonist.* New York: Basic Books.

Lynch, G., Larson, J., Staubli, U., Ambros-Ingerson, J., & Granger, R. (1991). Long-term potentiation and memory operations in cortical networks. In R. G. Wister & H. J. Weingartner (Eds.), *Perspectives on cognitive neuroscience* (pp. 110–131). New York: Oxford University Press.

Lynch, S., & Yarnell, P. R. (1973). Retrograde amnesia: Delayed forgetting after concussion. *American Journal of Psychology, 86,* 643–645.

Lyubomirsky, S., Kasri, F., & Zehm, K. (2003). Dysphoric rumination impairs concentration on academic tasks. *Cognitive Therapy and Research, 27,* 309–330.

MacFadyen, J. T. (1986, October). Educated monkeys help the disabled to help themselves. *Smithsonian, 17,* 125–132.

Mackay, D. G., Shafto, M., Taylor, J. K., Marian, D. E., Abrams, L., & Dyer, J. R. (2004). Relations between emotion, memory, and attention: Evidence from taboo Stroop, lexical decision, and immediate memory tasks. *Memory & Cognition 2004, 32,* 474–488.

Mackintosh, N. J. (1974). *The psychology of animal learning.* New York: Academic Press.

Mackintosh, N. J. (1983). *Conditioning and associative learning.* New York: Oxford University Press.

Madigan, S., & O'Hara, R. (1992). Short-term memory at the turn of the century: Mary Whiton Calkins's memory research. *American Psychologist, 47,* 170–174.

Magnussen, S. Andersson, J., Cornoldi, C., De Beni, R., Endestad, T, Goodman, G.S., . . . Zimmer H. (2006). What people believe about memory. *Memory, 14,* 595–613.

Maguire, E. A., Gadian, D. G., Johnsrude, I. S., Good, C. D., Ashburner, J., Frackowiak, R. S., & Frith, C. D. (2000). Navigation-related structural change in the hippocampi of taxi drivers. *Proceedings of the National Academy of Science, 97*(8), 4398–4403.

Maguire, E. A., Valentine, E. R., Wilding, J. M., & Kapur, N. (2003). Routes to remembering: The brains behind superior memory. *Nature Neuroscience, 6,* 90–95.

Maia, T. V., & Cleeremans, A. (2005). Consciousness: Converging insights from connectionist modeling and neuroscience. *Trends in Cognitive Sciences, 9,* 397–404.

Maia, T. V., & McClelland, J. L. (2004). A reexamination of the evidence for the somatic marker hypothesis: What participants really know in the Iowa gambling task. *Proceedings of the National Academy of Sciences, 101,* 16075–16080.

Maier, N. R. F., & Schneirla, T. C. (1935). *Principles of animal psychology*. New York: McGraw-Hill.

Maier, S. F., Seligman, M. E. P., & Solomon, R. L. (1969). Pavlovian fear conditioning and learned helplessness: Effects on escape and avoidance behavior of (a) the CS-US contingency and (b) the independence of the US and voluntary responding. In B. A. Campbell & R. M. Church (Eds.), *Punishment and aversive behavior* (pp. 299–342). New York: Appleton, Century, Crofts.

Mammes, M. E., & Terry, W. S. (2013). *Misplacing electronic files: A survey*. Washington, DC: Association for Psychological Science.

Mandler, G. (1967). Organization and memory. In G. H. Bower (Ed.), *The psychology of learning and motivation* (Vol. 1, pp. 327–372). New York: Academic Press.

Mantyla, T. (1986). Optimizing cue effectiveness: Recall of 500 and 600 incidentally learned words. *Journal of Experimental Psychology, Learning, Memory, and Cognition, 12*, 66–71.

Mantyla, T. (2003). Assessing absentmindedness: Prospective memory complaint and impairment in middle-aged adults. *Memory and Cognition, 31*, 15–25.

Marks, I. (1977). Phobias and obsessions: Clinical phenomena in search of a laboratory model. In J. D. Maser & M. E. P. Seligman (Eds.), *Psychopathology: Experimental models* (pp. 174–213). San Francisco: Freeman.

Marler, P. (1970). A comparative approach to vocal learning: Song development in white-crowned sparrows. *Journal of Comparative and Physiological Psychology, 71*, 1–25.

Marquis, D. P. (1941). Learning in the neonate: The modification of behavior under three feeding schedules. *Journal of Experimental Psychology, 29*, 263–282.

Marslen-Wilson, W. D., & Teuber, H. L. (1975). Memory for remote events in anterograde amnesia: Recognition of public figures in news photographs. *Neuropsychologia, 13*, 347–352.

Martin, E. (1975). Generation-recognition theory and the encoding specificity principle. *Psychological Review, 82*, 150–153.

Martin, I., & Levey, A. B. (1987). Learning what will happen next: Conditioning, evaluation, and cognitive processes. In G. Davey (Ed.), *Cognitive processes and Pavlovian conditioning in humans* (pp. 57–81). Chichester, UK: Wiley.

Martin, M., & Jones, G. V. (1984). Cognitive failures in everyday life. In J. E. Harris & P. E. Morris (Eds.), *Everyday memory, actions and absentmindedness* (pp. 173–190). New York: Academic Press.

Maslow, A. H. (1937). The influence of familiarization on preferences. *Journal of Experimental Psychology, 21*, 162–180.

Masserman, J. (1943). *Behavior and neurosis: An experimental psychoanalytic approach to psychobiologic principles*. Chicago: University of Chicago Press.

Mayer, R. E., & Massa, L. J. (2003). Three facets of visual and verbal learners: Cognitive ability, cognitive style, and learning preference. *Journal of Educational Psychology, 95*, 833–846.

Maylor, E. A., & Rabbitt, P. M. A. (1993). Alcohol, reaction time, and memory: A meta-analysis. *British Journal of Psychology, 84*, 301–317.

McCabe, S. E., Knight, J. R., & Teter, C. J. (2005). Non-medical use of prescription stimulants among US college students: Prevalence and correlates from a national survey. *Addiction, 100*, 96–106.

McCarthy, R. A., & Warrington, E. K. (1988). Evidence for modality-specific meaning systems in the brain. *Nature, 334*, 428–430.

McCarthy, R. A., & Warrington, E. K. (1990). *Cognitive neuropsychology: A clinical introduction*. New York: Academic Press.

McClosky, M., Wible, C. G., & Cohen, N. J. (1988). Is there a special flashbulb memory mechanism? *Journal of Experimental Psychology: General, 117*, 171–181.

McCrae, R. R., & Costa, P. T. (1986). Clinical assessment can benefit from recent advances in personality psychology. *American Psychologist, 41*, 1001–1003.

McDonald, R. J., & White, N. M. (1993). A triple dissociation of memory systems: Hippocampus, amygdala, and dorsal striatum. *Behavioral Neuroscience, 107*, 3–22.

McGaugh, J. L. (1974). ECS: Effects on learning and memory in animals. In M. Fink, S. Kety, J. McGaugh, & T. Williams (Eds.), *Psychobiology of convulsive therapy* (pp. 85–97). New York: Wiley.

McGaugh, J. L. (1991). Neuromodulation and the storage of information: Involvement of the amygdaloid complex. In R. G. Wister & H. J. Weingartner (Eds.), *Perspectives on cognitive neuroscience* (pp. 279–299). New York: Oxford University Press.

McGaugh, J. L. (2000). Memory—a century of consolidation. *Science, 287,* 248–251.

McGeoch, J. A. (1932). Forgetting and the law of disguise. *Psychological Review, 39,* 352–370.

McGuire, W. J. (1961). A multiprocess model for paired associate learning. *Journal of Experimental Psychology, 62,* 335–347.

McIsaac, H. K., & Eich, E. (2004). Vantage point in traumatic memory. *Psychological Science, 15,* 248–253.

McKeithan, K. B., Reitman, J. S., Rueter, H. H., & Hirtle, S. C. (1981). Knowledge organization and skill differences in computer programmers. *Cognitive Psychology, 13,* 307–325.

McNally, R. J. (1987). Preparedness and phobias: A review. *Psychological Bulletin, 101,* 283–303.

McNamara, J. K., & Wong, B. (2003). Memory for everyday information in students with learning disabilities. *Journal of Learning Disabilities, 36,* 394–406.

McNaughton, B. L., & Smolensky, P. (1991). Connectionist and neural modeling: Converging in the hippocampus. In R. G. Wister & H. J. Weingartner (Eds.), *Perspectives on cognitive neuroscience* (pp. 93–109). New York: Oxford University Press.

McWeeny, K. H., Young, A. W., Hay, D. C., & Ellis, A. W. (1987). Putting names to faces. *British Journal of Psychology, 78,* 143–149.

Melby-Verlag, M., & Hulme, C. (2013). Is working memory training effective: A meta-analytic review. *Developmental Psychology, 49,* 270–291.

Melcher, J. M., & Schooler, J. W. (1996). The misremembrance of wines past: Verbal and perceptual expertise differentially mediate verbal overshadowing of taste memory. *Journal of Memory and Language, 35,* 231–245.

Melton, A. W. (1963). Implications of short-term memory for a general theory of memory. *Journal of Verbal Learning and Verbal Behavior, 2,* 1–21.

Menzel, E. W. (1973). Chimpanzee spatial memory organization. *Science, 182,* 943–945.

Mery, F., & Kawecki, T. J. (2004). An operating cost of learning in Drosophila melanogaster. *Animal Behavior, 68,* 589–598.

Merzenich, M. M., Jenkins, W. M., William, M., Johnston, P., Schreiner, C., Miller, S. L., & Tallal, P. (1996). Temporal processing deficits of language-learning impaired children ameliorated by training. *Science, 271,* 77–81.

Midkiff, E. E., & Bernstein, I. L. (1985). Targets of learned food aversions in humans. *Physiology and Behavior, 34,* 839–841.

Miller, G. A. (1956). The magical number seven plus-or- minus two: Some limits of our capacity for processing information. *Psychological Review, 63,* 81–97.

Miller, L. C., Barrett, C. L., & Hampe, E. (1974). Phobias of childhood in a prescientific era. In A. Davis (Ed.), *Child personality and psychopathology: Current topics* (pp. 89–134). New York: Wiley.

Miller, M. E., Adesso, V. J., Fleming, J. P., Gino, A., & Lauerman, R. (1978). Effects of alcohol on the storage and retrieval processes of heavy social drinkers. *Journal of Experimental Psychology: Human Learning and Memory, 4,* 246–255.

Miller, N. E. (1948). Theory and experiment relating psychoanalytic displacement to stimulus-response generalization. *Journal of Abnormal and Social Psychology, 43,* 155–178.

Miller, N. E. (1959). Liberalization of basic S-R concepts: Extensions to conflict behavior, motivation, and social learning. In S. Koch (Ed.), *Psychology: A study of a science* (Vol. 2, pp. 196–292). New York: McGraw-Hill.

Miller, N. E. (1985). The value of behavioral research on animals. *American Psychologist, 40,* 423–440.

Miller, N. E., & Dollard, J. (1941). *Social learning and imitation.* New Haven, CT: Yale University Press.

Miller, R. R., Barnet, R. C., & Grahame, N. J. (1995). Assessment of the Rescorla-Wagner model. *Psychological Bulletin, 117,* 363–386.

Miller, R. R., & Springer, A. D. (1973). Amnesia, consolidation, and retrieval. *Psychological Review, 80,* 69–79.

Milton, F., Muhlert, N., Pindus, D. M., Butler, C. R., Kapur, N., Graham, K. S., & Zeman, A. (2010). Remote memory deficits in transient epileptic amnesia. *Brain, 133,* 1368–1379.

Mineka, S. (1979). The role of fear in theories of avoidance learning, flooding, and extinction. *Psychological Bulletin, 86,* 985–1010.

Mineka, S., & Zinbarg, R. (2006). A contemporary learning theory perspective on the etiology of anxiety disorders. *American Psychologist, 61,* 10–26.

Misanin, J. R., Miller, R. R., & Lewis, D. J. (1968). Retrograde amnesia produced by reactivation of a consolidated memory trace. *Science*, *160*, 203–204.

Mischel, W., Shoda, Y., & Peake, P. (1988). The nature of adolescent competencies predicted by preschool delay of gratification. *Journal of Personality and Social Psychology*, *54*, 687–696.

Mischel, W., Shoda, Y., & Rodriguez, M. L. (1989). Delay of gratification in children. *Science*, *244*, 933–938.

Mishkin, M., & Appenzeller, T. (1987, June). The anatomy of memory. *Scientific American*, *256*(6), 80–89.

Modigliani, V., & Hedges, D. G. (1987). Distributed rehearsals and the primacy effect in single-trial free recall. *Journal of Experimental Psychology: Learning, Memory, and Cognition*, *13*, 426–436.

Moffitt, T. E., Arseneault, L., Belsky, D., Dickson, N., Hancox, R. J.Harrington, H., . . . Caspi, A. (2011). A gradient of childhood self-control predicts health, wealth, and public safety. *Proceedings of the National Academy of Science*, *108*, 2693–2698.

Montello, D. R. (2010). You are where? The function and frustration of you-are-here (YAH) maps. *Spatial Cognition & Computation*, *10*, 94–104.

Moore, T.E. (1982). Subliminal advertising: What you see is what you get. *Journal of Marketing*, *46*, 38–47.

Morris, P. E., & Fritz, C. O. (2000). The name game: Using retrieval practice to improve the learning of names. *Journal of Experimental Psychology: Applied*, *6*, 124–129.

Morris, R. G. M. (1981). Spatial localization does not require the presence of local cues. *Learning and Motivation*, *12*, 239–260.

Morrison, A. B., & Chein, J. M. (2011). Does working memory training work? The promise and challenges of enhancing cognition by training working memory. *Psychonomic Bulletin and Review*, *18*, 46–60.

Moscovitch, M., Winocur, G., & McLachlan, D. (1986). Memory as assessed by recognition and reading time in normal and memory-impaired people with Alzheimer's Disease and other neurological disorders. *Journal of Experimental Psychology: General*, *115*, 331–347.

Mowrer, H. O. (1947). On the dual nature of learning—a reinterpretation of "conditioning" and "problem solving". *Harvard Educational Review*, *17*, 102–148.

Muller, G. E., & Pilzecker, A. (1900). Experimentalle Beitrage zur Lehre vom Gedachtnis. *Zeitschrift fur Psychologie*, *1*, 1–300.

Mynatt, C. R., & Doherty, M. E. (1999). *Understanding human behavior*. Boston: Allyn & Bacon.

Mystkowski, J. L., Mineka, S., Vernon, L. L., & Zinbarg, R. E. (2003). Changes in caffeine state enhance return of fear in spider phobia. *Journal of Consulting and Clinical Psychology*, *71*, 243–250.

Nadar, K., Schafe, G. E., & LeDoux, J. E. (2000). Fear memories require protein synthesis in the amygdala for reconsolidation after retrieval. *Nature*, *406*, 722–726.

Naveh-Benjamin, M. (1991). A comparison of training programs intended for different types of test-anxious students: Further support for an information processing model. *Journal of Educational Psychology*, *83*, 134–139.

Naveh-Benjamin, M., & Ayres, T. J. (1986). Digit span, reading rate, and linguistic relativity. *Quarterly Journal of Experimental Psychology: Human Experimental Psychology*, *38A*, 739–751.

Neisser, U. (1967). *Cognitive psychology*. New York: Appleton, Century, Crofts.

Neisser, U. (1978). Memory: What are the important questions. In M. M. Gruneberg, P. E. Morris, & R. N. Sykes (Eds.), *Practical aspects of memory* (pp. 3–24). New York: Academic Press. (Reprinted in Neisser, 1982).

Neisser, U. (1982). Snapshots or benchmarks. In U. Neisser (Ed.), *Memory observed* (pp. 43–48). San Francisco: Freeman.

Nelson, C. A. (1995). The ontogeny of human memory: A cognitive neuroscience approach. *Developmental Psychology*, *31*, 723–738.

Nelson, D. L., & Schreiber, T. A. (1992). Word concreteness and word structure as independent determinants of recall. *Journal of Memory and Language*, *31*, 237–260.

Nelson, T. O. (1976). Reinforcement and human memory. In W. K. Estes (Ed.), *Handbook of learning and cognitive processes* (Vol. 3, pp. 207–246). Hillsdale, NJ: Erlbaum.

Nelson, T. O. (1978). Detecting small amounts of information in memory: Savings for nonrecognized items. *Journal of Experimental Psychology: Human Learning and Memory*, *4*, 453–468.

Nelson, T. O., & Gerler, D. (1984). Accuracy of feeling-of-knowing judgments for predicting perceptual identification and relearning. *Journal of Experimental Psychology: General*, *113*, 282–300.

Nelson, T. O., & Leonesio, R. J. (1988). Allocation of self-paced study time and the "labor-in-vain effect". *Journal of Experimental Psychology: Learning, Memory, and Cognition, 14*, 676–686.

Nemiah, J. C. (1979). Dissociative amnesia. In J. H. Kihlstom & F. J. Evans (Eds.), *Functional disorders of memory* (pp. 303–323). Hillsdale, NJ: Erlbaum.

Neumann, D. L., Lipp, O. V., & Siddle, D. A. T. (1997). Conditioned inhibition of autonomic Pavlovian conditioning in humans. *Biological Psychology, 46*, 223–233.

Neuringer, A., Kornell, N., & Olaf, M. (2001). Stability and variability in extinction. *Journal of Experimental Psychology: Animal Behavior Processes, 27*, 79–94.

Newell, A., & Rosenbloom., P. S. (1981). Mechanisms of skill acquisition and the law of practice. In J. R. Anderson (Ed.), *Cognitive skills and their acquisition* (pp. 1–55). Hillsdale, NJ: Erlbaum.

Nickerson, R. S., & Adams, M. J. (1979). Long-term memory for a common object. *Cognitive Psychology, 11*, 287–307.

Niederehe, G. (1991). Depression and memory impairment in the aged. In L. Poon (Ed.), *Handbook for clinical memory assessment of older adults* (pp. 226–237). Washington, DC: American Psychological Association.

Nigro, G., & Neisser, U. (1983). Point of view in personal memories. *Cognitive Psychology, 15*, 467–482.

Nilsson, L. (1987). Motivated forgetting: Dissociation between performance data and subjective reports. *Psychological Research, 49*, 183–188.

Nissen, M. J., & Bullemer, P. (1987). Attentional requirements of learning: Evidence from performance measures. *Cognitive Psychology, 19*, 1–32.

Noice, H., & Noice, T. (1997). *The nature of expertise in professional acting: A cognitive view*. Mahwah, NJ: Erlbaum.

Noice, H., & Noice, T. (2006). What studies of actors and acting can tell us about memory and cognitive functioning. *Current Directions in Psychological Science, 15*, 14–18.

Norman, D. A. (1981). The categorization of action slips. *Psychological Review, 88*, 1–15.

Norman, G. R., Brooks, L. R., & Allen, S. W. (1989). Recall by expert medical practioners and novices as a record of processing attention. *Journal of Experimental Psychology: Learning, Memory, and Cognition, 15*, 1166–1174.

Nyberg, L., Cabeza, R., & Tulving, E. (1996). PET studies of encoding and retrieval: The HERA model. *Psychonomic Bulletin & Review, 3*, 135–148.

O'Conner, N., & Hermelin, B. (1989). The memory structure of autistic idiot-savant mnemonists. *British Journal of Psychology, 80*, 97–111.

Oerter, R. (2003). Biological and psychological correlates of exceptional performance and development. *Annals of the New York Academy of Sciences, 999*, 451–460.

Ogden, J. A., & Corkin, S. (1991). Memories of H. M. In W. C. Abraham, M. C. Corballis, & K. G. White (Eds.), *Memory mechanisms* (pp. 195–215). Hillsdale, NJ: Erlbaum.

Ohman, A., Fredrikson, M., Hugdahl, K., & Rimmo, P. (1976). The premise of equipotentiality in human classical conditioning: Conditioned electrodermal responses to potentially phobic stimuli. *Journal of Experimental Psychology: General, 105*, 313–337.

Ohman, A., & Mineka, S. (2001). Fears, phobias, and preparedness: Toward an evolved module of fear and fear learning. *Psychological Review, 108*, 483–522.

Olds, J., & Milner, P. (1954). Positive reinforcement produced by electrical stimulation of septal area and other regions of rat brain. *Journal of Comparative and Physiological Psychology, 47*, 419–427.

Olson, G. M. (1976). An information-processing analysis of visual memory and habituation in infants. In T. J. Tighe & R. N. Leaton (Eds.), *Habituation: Perspectives from child development, animal behavior, and neurophysiology* (pp. 239–277). Hillsdale, NJ: Erlbaum.

Olsson, A., & Phelps, E. A. (2004). Learned fear of unseen faces after Pavlovian, observational, and instructed fear. *Psychological Science, 15*, 822–828.

Olsson, A., & Phelps, E. A. (2007). Social learning of fear. *Nature Neuroscience, 10*, 1095–1102.

Olton, D. S. (1977, June). Spatial memory. *Scientific American, 236*, 82–98.

Olton, D. S. (1979). Mazes, maps, and memory. *American Psychologist, 34*, 583–596.

Olton, D. S., Collison, C., & Werz, M. A. (1977). Spatial memory and radial arm maze performance in rats. *Learning and Motivation, 8*, 289–314.

Olton, D. S., & Samuelson, R. J. (1976). Remembrance of places passed: Spatial memory in rats. *Journal of Experimental Psychology: Animal Behavior Processes, 2*, 97–116.

Ornstein, P. A., Naus, M. J., & Liberty, C. (1975). Rehearsal and organizational processes in children's memory. *Child Development, 46*, 818–830.

Ornstein, P. A., Naus, M. J., & Stone, B. P. (1977). Rehearsal training and developmental differences in memory. *Developmental Psychology, 13*, 15–24.

Orr, S. P., Metzger, L. J., Lasko, N. B., Macklin, M. L., Peri, T., & Pitman, R. K. (2000). De novo conditioning in trauma-exposed individuals with and without posttraumatic stress disorder. *Journal of Abnormal Psychology, 109*, 290–298.

Osgood, C. E. (1953). *Method and theory in experimental psychology*. New York: Oxford University Press.

Overman, W. H., Pate, B. J., Moore, K., & Peuster, A. (1996). Ontogeny of place learning in children as measured in the radial arm maze, Morris search task, and the open field task. *Behavioral Neuroscience, 110*, 1205–1228.

Paivio, A. (1969). Mental imagery in associative learning and memory. *Psychological Review, 76*, 241–262.

Papka, M., Ivy, R. B., & Woodruff-Pak, D. S. (1997). Eyeblink classical conditioning and awareness revisited. *Psychological Science, 8*, 404–408.

Park, D. C., Smith, A. D., & Cavanaugh, J. C. (1990). Metamemories of memory researchers. *Memory and Cognition, 18*, 321–327.

Park, S., Holzman, P. S., & Goldman-Rakic, P. S. (1995). Spatial working memory deficits in the relatives of schizophrenic patients. *Archives of General Psychiatry, 52*, 821–828.

Parker, E. S., Cahill, L., & McGaugh, J. L. (2006). A case of unusual autobiographical memory. *Neurocase, 12*, 35–49.

Parkin, A. J., & Streete, S. (1988). Implicit and explicit memory in young children and adults. *British Journal of Psychology, 79*, 361–369.

Pashler, H., Rohrer, D., Cepeda, N. J., & Carpenter, S. K. (2007). Enhancing learning and retarding forgetting: Choices and consequences. *Psychonomic Bulletin & Review, 14*, 187–193.

Paul, G. L. (1967). Insight vs. desensitization in psychotherapy two years after termination. *Journal of Consulting Psychology, 31*, 333–348.

Pavlov, I. P. (1927/1960). *Conditioned reflexes* (G. V. Anrep, Trans.) (Dover reprint, 1960). New York: Dover.

Pearce, J. M. (1997). *Animal learning and cognition: An introduction* (2nd ed.). East Sussex, UK: Psychology Press.

Pearce, S. A., Isherwood, S., Hrouda, D., Richardson, P. H., Erskine, A., & Skinner, J. (1990). Memory and pain: Tests of mood congruity and state dependent learning in experimentally induced and clinical pain. *Pain, 43*, 187–193.

Peckstein, L. A., & Brown, F. D. (1939). An experimental analysis of the alleged criteria of insight learning. *Journal of Educational Psychology, 30*, 38–52.

Penfield, W. (1955). The permanent record of the stream of consciousness: Proceedings of the 14th international congress of psychologists. *Acta Psychologica, 11*, 46–69. (Reprinted in T. K. Landauer, *Readings in physiological psychology*. New York: McGraw-Hill, 1967).

Penfield, W., & Jasper, H. (1954). *Epilepsy and the functional anatomy of the human brain*. Boston: Little, Brown.

Penfield, W., & Rasmussen, T. (1950). *The cerebral cortex of man*. New York: Macmillan.

Perfetti, C. A., & Lesgold, A. M. (1979). Coding and comprehension in skilled reading and implications for reading instruction. In L. B Resnick & P. A. Weaver (Eds.), *Theory and practice of early reading* (pp. 57–84). Hillsdale, NJ: Erlbaum.

Perkins, C. C. (1968). An analysis of the concept of reinforcement. *Psychological Review, 75*, 155–172.

Perlmutter, M. (1978). What is memory aging the aging of? *Developmental Psychology, 14*, 330–345.

Peterson, L. R., & Peterson, M. J. (1959). Short-term retention of individual items. *Journal of Experimental Psychology, 58*, 193–198.

Petri, H. L., & Mishkin, M. (1994). Behaviorism, cognitivism and the neurpsychology of memory. *American Scientist, 82*, 30–37.

Petros, T. V., Beckwith, B. E., & Anderson, M. (1990). Individual differences in the effects of time of day and passage difficulty on prose memory in adults. *British Journal of Psychology, 81*, 63–72.

Pezdek, K., Whetstone, T., Reynolds, K., Askari, N., & Dougherty, T. (1989). Memory for real-world scenes: The role of consistency with schema expectation. *Journal of Experimental Psychology: Learning, Memory, and Cognition, 15*, 587–595.

Pillemer, D. B., Goldsmith, L. R., Panter, A. T., & White, S. H. (1988). Very long-term memories of the first year in college. *Journal of Experimental Psychology: Learning, Memory, and Cognition, 14*, 709–715.

Pilley, J. W., & Reid, A. K. (2011). Border collie comprehends object names as verbal referents. *Behavioural Processes, 86*, 184–195.

Pillsbury, W. B., & Sylvester, A. (1940). Retroactive and proactive inhibition in immediate memory. *Journal of Experimental Psychology, 27*, 532–545.

Pinker, S. (1994). *The language instinct*. New York: Morrow.

Pintrich, P. R., & DeGroot, E. V. (1990). Motivational and self-regulated learning components of classroom academic performance. *Journal of Educational Psychology, 82*, 33–40.

Pitman, R. K., Sanders, K. M., Zusman, R. M., Healy, A. R., Lasko, N. B., Cahill, L., & Orr, S. P. (2002). Pilot study of secondary prevention of posttraumatic stress disorder with propranolol. *Biological Psychiatry, 51*, 189–192.

Pliner, O. (1982). The effects of mere exposure on liking for edible substances. *Appetite, 3*, 283–290.

Plous, S. (1996). Attitudes toward the use of animals in psychological research and education: Results from a national survey of psychology majors. *Psychological Science, 7*, 352–358.

Polsky, R. (2000). Can aggression in dogs be elicited through the use of electronic pet containment systems? *Journal of Applied Animal Welfare Science, 3*, 345–357.

Powers, R. B. (2006). *The echo maker*. New York: Farrar, Straus & Giroux.

Powers, R. B., & Osborne, J. G. (1976). *Fundamentals of behavior*. St. Paul, MN: West Publishing.

Premack, D. (1962). Reversibility of the reinforcement relation. *Science, 136*, 235–237.

Premack, D. (1965). Reinforcement theory. In D. Levine (Ed.), *Nebraska symposium on motivation* (pp. 123–180). Lincoln: University of Nebraska Press.

Pressley, M., & Dennis-Rounds, J. (1980). Transfer of a mnemonic keyword strategy at two age levels. *Journal of Educational Psychology, 72*, 575–582.

Pressley, M., & Ghatala, E. S. (1989). Metacognitive benefits of taking a test for children and young adolescents. *Journal of Experimental Child Psychology, 47*, 430–450.

Pressley, M., Levin, J. R., & Ghatala, E. S. (1988). Strategy comparison opportunities promote long-term strategy use. *Contemporary Educational Psychology, 13*, 157–168.

Pressley, M., Levin, J. R., Hall, J. W., Miller, G. E., & Berry, J. K. (1980). The keyword method and foreign word acquisition. *Journal of Experimental Psychology: Human Learning and Memory, 6*, 163–173.

Pressley, M., McDaniel, M. A., Turnure, J. E., Wood, E., & Ahmad, M. (1987). Generation and precision of elaboration: Effects on intentional and incidental learning. *Journal of Experimental Psychology: Learning, Memory, and Cognition, 13*, 291–300.

Rachman, S., & Lopatka, C. (1988). Return of fear: Underlearning and overlearning. *Behaviour Research and Therapy, 26*, 99–104.

Rahhal, T. A., Hasher, L., & Colcombe, S. J. (2001). Instructional manipulations and age differences in memory: Now you see them and now you don't. *Psychology and Aging, 16*, 697–706.

Raichle, M. E. (1994). Images of the mind: Studies with modern imaging techniques. *Annual Review of Psychology, 45*, 333–356.

Rajaram, S., & Roediger, H. L. (1993). Direct comparison of four implicit memory tests. *Journal of Experimental Psychology: Learning, Memory, and Cognition, 19*, 765–776.

Rampon, C., Jiang, C. H., Dong, H., Tang, Y-P., Lockhart, D., Schultz, P., Tsien, J. Z., & Hu, Y. (2000). Effects of environmental enrichment on gene expression in the brain. *Proceedings of the National Academies of Science, 97*, 12880–12884.

Rampon, C., Tang, Y.-P., Goodhouse, J., Shimizu, E., Kyin, M., & Tsien, J. Z. (2000). Enrichment induces structural changes and recovery from nonspatial memory deficits in CA1 NMDAR1-knockout mice. *Nature Neuroscience, 3*, 238–244.

Rand, G., & Wapner, S. (1967). Postural states as a factor in memory. *Journal of Verbal Learning and Verbal Behavior, 6*, 268–271.

Rauscher, F. H., Shaw, G. L., & Ky, K. N. (1993). Music and spatial task performance. *Nature, 365*, 611.

Reason, J. T. (1990). *Human error*. Cambridge: Cambridge University Press.

Reason, J. T. (1993). Self-report questionnaires in cognitive psychology: Have they delivered the goods? In A. Baddeley & L. Weiskrantz (Eds.), *Attention: Selection, awareness, and control: A tribute to Donald Broadbent* (pp. 406–423). Oxford: Clarendon Press.

Reason, J. T., & Lucas, D. (1984). Using cognitive diaries to investigate naturally occurring memory blocks. In J. E. Harris & P. E. Morris (Eds.), *Everyday memory, actions and absent-mindedness* (pp. 53–70). New York: Academic Press.

Reber, A. S. (1967). Implicit learning of artificial grammar. *Journal of Verbal Learning and Verbal Behavior, 6*, 855–863.

Reber, A. S. (1976). Implicit learning of synthetic languages: The role of instructional set. *Journal of Experimental Psychology: Human Learning and Memory, 2*, 88–94.

Reber, A. S. (1993). *Implicit learning and tacit knowledge: An essay on the cognitive unconscious*. New York: Oxford University Press.

Reber, R., Winkielmanm, P., & Schwartz, N. (1998). Effects of perceptual fluency on affective judgements. *Psychological Science, 9*, 45–48.

Reed, G. (1979). Everyday anomalies of recall and recognition. In J. F. Kihlstrom & F. J. Evans (Eds.), *Functional disorders of memory* (pp. 1–28). Hillsdale, NJ: Erlbaum.

Reed, P. (2001). Human response rates and causality judgments on schedules of reinforcement. *Learning and Motivation, 32*, 332–348.

Reeves, R. R., & Bullen, J. A. (1995). Mnemonics for ten DSM-IV disorders. *Journal of Nervous and Mental Disease, 183*, 550–551.

Reiser, B. J., Black, J. B., & Kalamarides, P. (1986). Strategic memory search processes. In D. C. Rubin (Ed.), *Autobiographical memory* (pp. 100–121). Cambridge: Cambridge University Press.

Rescorla, R. A. (1967). Pavlovian conditioning and its proper control procedures. *Psychological Review, 74*, 71–80.

Rescorla, R. A. (1987). A Pavlovian analysis of goal directed behavior. *American Psychologist, 42*, 119–129.

Rescorla, R. A. (1988). Pavlovian conditioning: It's not what you think it is. *American Psychologist, 43*, 151–161.

Rescorla, R. A., & Wagner, A. R. (1972). A theory of Pavlovian conditioning: Variations in the effectiveness of reinforcement and nonreinforcement. In A. H. Black & W. F. Prokasy (Eds.), *Classical conditioning II* (pp. 64–99). New York: Appleton, Century, Crofts.

Restle, F. (1957). Discrimination of cues in mazes: A resolution of the "place-vs.-response" question. *Psychological Review, 64*, 217–228.

Revelle, W., Humphreys, M. S., Simon, L., & Gilliland, K. (1980). The interactive effect of personality, time of day, and caffeine: A test of the arousal model. *Journal of Experimental Psychology: General, 109*, 1–31.

Revusky, S., Coombes, S., & Pohl, R. W. (1982). US pre-exposure: Effects on flavor aversions produced by pairing a poisoned partner with ingestion. *Animal Learning & Behavior, 10*, 83–90.

Richardson, R., Guanowsky, V., Ahlers, S. T., & Riccio, D. D. (1984). Role of body temperature in the onset of, and recovery from, hypothermia-induced anterograde amnesia. *Physiological Psychology, 12*, 125–132.

Rilling, M. (1996). The mystery of the vanished citations. *American Psychologist, 51*, 589–598.

Rivlin, G. (2004, May 9). Bet on it. *New York Times Magazine*, pp. 42–47, 74, 80, 81.

Roberts, B. W., Kuncel, N. R., Shiner, R., Caspi, A., & Goldberg, L. R. (2007). The power of personality: The comparative validity of personality traits, socioeconomic status, and cognitive ability for predicting important life outcomes. *Perspectives on Psychological Science, 2*, 313–345.

Robinson, K. J., & Roediger, H. L. III. (1997). Associative processes in false recall and false recognition. *Psychological Science, 8*, 231–237.

Roediger, H. L., III. (1973). Inhibition in recall from cueing with recall targets. *Journal of Verbal Learning and Verbal Behavior, 12*, 644–657.

Roediger, H. L., III. (1980). The effectiveness of four mnemonics in ordering recall. *Journal of Experimental Psychology: Human Learning and Memory, 6*, 558–568.

Roediger, H. L., III. (1990). Implicit memory: Retention without remembering. *American Psychologist, 45*, 1043–1056.

Roediger, H. L., III, & Karpicke, J. D. (2006). Test-enhanced learning. *Psychological Science, 17*, 249–255.

Roediger, H. L., III, & McDermott, K. B. (1995). Creating false memories: Remembering words not presented in lists. *Journal of Experimental Psychology: Learning, Memory, and Cognition, 21*, 803–814.

Roediger, H. L., III, & McDermott, K. B. (2000). Tricks of memory. *Current Directions in Psychological Science, 9*, 123–127.

Roediger, H. L., III, & Thorpe, L. A. (1978). The role of recall time in producing hypermnesia. *Memory & Cognition, 6*, 296–305.

Rogers, L. (1989, September). Home, sweet-smelling home. *Natural History*, pp. 61–66.

Rogoff, B., & Chavajay, P. (1995). What's become of research on the cultural basis of cognitive development. *American Psychologist, 50*, 859–877.

Roitblat, H. L., Penner, R. H., & Nachtigall, P. E. (1990). Matching-to-sample by an echolocating dolphin. *Journal of Experimental Psychology: Animal Behavior Processes, 16*, 85–95.

Rolls, B. J. (1990). The role of sensory-specific satiety in food intake and selection. In E. D. Capaldi & T. L. Powley (Eds.), *Taste, experience, and feeding* (pp. 197–209). Washington, DC: American Psychological Association.

Rose, S. (1992). *The making of memory*. New York: Doubleday.

Rosenbaum, R. S., Kohler, S., Schacter, D. L., Moscovitvh, M., Westmacott, R., Black, S. E., Gao, F., & Tulving, E. (2005). The case of K. C.: Contributions of a memory-impaired person to memory theory. *Neuropsychologia, 43*, 989–1021. Hillsdale, NJ: Erlbaum.

Roth, S., & Cohen, L. J. (1986). Approach, avoidance, and coping with stress. *American Psychologist, 41*, 813–819.

Rothbaum, B. O., Anderson, P., Zimand, E., Hodges, L., Lang, D., & Wilson, J. (2006). Virtual reality exposure therapy and standard (in vivo) exposure therapy in the treatment of fear of flying. *Behavior Therapy, 37*, 80–90.

Rovee, C. K., & Rovee, D. T. (1969). Conjugate reinforcement of infant exploratory behavior. *Journal of Experimental Child Psychology, 8*, 33–39.

Rovee-Collier, C. K., Sullivan, M. W., Enright, M., Lucas, D., & Fagan, J. W. (1980). Reactivation of infant memory. *Science, 208*, 1159–1162.

Royer, J. M. (1986). Designing instruction to produce understanding. In G. D. Phye & T. Andre (Eds.), *Cognitive classroom learning* (pp. 83–113). New York: Academic Press.

Rozin, P., & Kalat, J. W. (1971). Specific hungers and poison avoidance as adaptive specializations of learning. *Psychological Review, 78*, 459–486.

Rubin, D. C. (1977). Very long-term memory for prose and verse. *Journal of Verbal Learning and Verbal Behavior, 16*, 611–621.

Rubin, D. G., & Friendly, M. (1986). Predicting which words get recalled: Measures of free recall, availability, goodness, emotionality, and pronounciability for 925 nouns. *Memory & Cognition, 14*, 79–94.

Rundus, D. (1971). Analysis of rehearsal processes in free recall. *Journal of Experimental Psychology, 89*, 63–77.

Ryan, E. B. (1992). Beliefs about memory changes across the adult life span. *Journal of Gerontology: Psychological Sciences, 47*, 41–46.

Ryan, J. D., Althoff, R. R., Whitlow, S., & Cohen, N. J. (2000). Amnesia is a deficit in relational memory. *Psychological Science, 11*, 454–461.

Sachs, J. S. (1967). Recognition memory for syntactic and semantic aspects of connected discourse. *Perception & Psychophysics, 2*, 437–442.

Sacks, O. (1985). *The man who mistook his wife for a hat*. New York: Summit Books.

Saffran, J. R. (2009). What can statistical learning tell about infant learning? In A. Woodward (Ed.), *Learning and the infant mind* (pp. 29–46). New York: Oxford University Press.

Saffran, J. R., Aslin, R. N., & Newport, E. L. (1996). Statistical learning by 8-month-old infants. *Science, 274*, 1926–1928.

Sahakian, B., & Morein-Zamir, S. (2007). Professor's little helper. *Nature, 450*, 1157–1159.

Saint-Cyr, J. A., & Taylor, A. E. (1992). The mobilization of procedural learning: The "key signature" of the basal ganglia. In L. R. Squire & N. Butter (Eds.), *Neuropsychology of memory* (2nd ed., pp. 188–202). New York: Guilford Press.

Salmon, K., Price, M., & Pereira, J. K. (2002). Factors associated with young children's long-term recall of an invasive medical procedure: A preliminary investigation. *Journal of Developmental and Behavioral Pediatrics, 23*, 347–352.

Salthouse, T. A. (1994). The aging of working memory. *Neuropsychology, 8*, 535–543.

Saufley, W. H., Otaka, S. R., & Bavaresco, J. L. (1985). Context effects: Classroom tests and context independence. *Memory & Cognition, 13*, 522–528.

Schacter, D. L. (1983). Amnesia observed: Remembering and forgetting in a natural environment. *Journal of Abnormal Psychology, 92*, 236–242.

Schacter, D. L., Verfaellie, M., & Pradere, D. (1996). The neuropsychology of memory illusions: False recall and recognition in amnesic patients. *Journal of Memory and Language, 35*, 319–334.

Schacter, D. L., Wang, P. L., Tulving, E., & Freedman, M. (1982). Functional retrograde amnesia: A quantitative case study. *Neuropsychologia, 20*, 523–532.

Scheier, M. F., & Carver, C. S. (1993). On the power of positive thinking: The benefits of being optimistic. *Current Directions in Psychological Science, 2*, 26–30.

Schendel, J. D., & Hagman, J. D. (1982). On sustaining procedural skills over a prolonged retention interval. *Journal of Applied Psychology, 67*, 605–610.

Schiller, D., Monfils, M.-H., Raio, C. M., Johnson, D. C., LeDoux, J. E., & Phelps, E. A. (2010). Preventing the return of fear in humans using reconsolidation update mechanisms. *Nature, 463*, 49–53.

Schilling, R. F., & Weaver, G. E. (1983). Effects of extraneous verbal information on memory for telephone numbers. *Journal of Applied Psychology, 68*, 559–564.

Schmidt, R. A., & Bjork, R. A. (1992). New conceptualizations of practice: Common principles in three paradigms suggest new concepts for training. *Psychological Science, 3*, 207–217.

Schmidt, R. A., Young, D. E., Swinnen, S., & Shapiro, D. C. (1989). Summary knowledge of results for skill acquisition: Support for the guidance hypothesis. *Journal of Experimental Psychology: Learning, Memory, and Cognition, 15*, 352–359.

Schneider, V. I., Healy, A. F., & Bourne, L. E., Jr. (2002). What is learned under difficult conditions is hard to forget: Contextual interference effects in foreign vocabulary acquisition, retention, and transfer. *Journal of Memory and Language, 46*, 419–440.

Schneiderman, N., Fuentes, I., & Gormezano, I. (1962). Acquisition and extinction of the classically conditioned eyelid response in the albino rabbit. *Science, 136*, 650–652.

Schooler, J. W., Ryan, R. S., & Reder, L. (1996). The costs and benefits of verbally rehearsing memory for faces. In D. Herrmann, C. McEvoy, C. Hertzog, P. Hertel, & M. K. Johnson (Eds.), *Basic and applied memory research* (Vol. 2., pp. 51–65). Mahwan, NJ: Erlbaum.

Schultz, D. P., & Schultz, S. E. (1996). *A history of modern psychology* (6th ed.). Fort Worth, TX: Harcourt Brace & Company.

Schwartz, B. L. (1999). Sparkling at the end of the tongue: The etiology of tip-of-the-tongue phenomenology. *Psychonomic Bulletin & Review, 6*, 379–393.

Schwartz, B. L., & Hashtroudi, S. (1991). Priming is independent of skill learning. *Journal of Experimental Psychology: Learning, Memory, and Cognition, 17*, 1177–1187.

Schwartz, B. N. (1978). *Psychology of learning and behavior*. New York: Norton.

Scoville, W. B., & Milner, B. (1957). Loss of recent memory after bilateral hippocampal lesions. *Journal of Neurology, Neurosurgery and Psychiatry, 20*, 11–19.

Scrivener, E., & Safer, M. A. (1988). Eyewitnesses show hyperamnesia for details about a violent event. *Journal of Applied Psychology, 73*, 371–377.

Seamon, J. G., Luo, C. R., Kopecky, J. J., Price, C. A., Rothschild, L., Fung, N. S., & Schwartz, M. A. (2002). Are false memories more difficult to forget than accurate memories? The effect of retention interval on recall and recognition. *Memory and Cognition, 30*, 1054–1064.

Sears, S. F., Jr., Kovacs, A. H., Azzarello, L., Larsen, K., & Conti, J. B. (2004). Innovations in health psychology: The psychosocial care of adults with implantable cardioverter defibrillators. *Professional Psychology: Research and Practice, 35*, 520–526.

Sehulster, J. R. (1989). Content and temporal structure of autobiographical knowledge: Remembering twenty-five seasons of the Metropolitan Opera. *Memory & Cognition, 17*, 590–606.

Seligman, M. E. P. (1970). On the generality of the laws of learning. *Psychological Review, 77*, 406–418.

Seligman, M. E. P. (1972). Phobias and preparedness. In M. E. P. Seligman & J. L. Hager (Eds.), *Biological boundaries of learning* (pp. 451–462). New York: Appleton, Century, Crofts.

Seligman, M. E. P. (1975). *Helplessness: On depression, development, and death*. San Francisco: Freeman.

Seligman, M. E. P., & Johnson, J. C. (1973). A cognitive theory of avoidance learning. In F. J. McGuigan & D. B. Lumsden (Eds.), *Contemporary approaches to conditioning and learning* (pp. 69–110). Washington, DC: Winston.

Seligman, M. E. P., Maier, S. F., & Geer, J. H. (1968). Alleviation of learned helplessness in the dog. *Journal of Abnormal Psychology, 73*, 256–262.

Semb, G. B., Ellis, J. A., & Araujo, J. (1993). Long-term memory for knowledge learned in school. *Journal of Educational Psychology, 85*, 305–316.

Seymour, B., Singer, T., & Dolan, R. (2007). The neurobiology of punishment. *Nature reviews: Neuroscience, 8*, 300–311.

Shah, P., & Miyake, A. (1996). The separability of working memory resources for spatial thinking and language processing: An individual differences approach. *Journal of Experimental Psychology: General, 125*, 4–27.

Shallice, T. (1988). *From neuropsychology to mental structure*. Cambridge: Cambridge University Press.

Shallice, T., & Burgess, P. (1991). Deficits in strategy application following frontal lobe damage in man. *Brain, 114*, 727–741.

Shallice, T., & Warrington, E. K. (1970). Independent functioning of verbal memory stores: A neuropsychological study. *Quarterly Journal of Experimental Psychology, 22*, 261–273.

Shand, M. A., & Klima, E. S. (1981). Nonauditory suffix effects in congenitally deaf signers of American Sign Language. *Journal of Experimental Psychology: Human Learning and Memory, 6*, 464–474.

Shanks, D. R. (1993). Human instrumental learning: A critical review. *British Journal of Psychology, 84*, 319–354.

Shanks, D. R. (1995). *The psychology of associative learning*. Cambridge: Cambridge University Press.

Shanks, D. R. (2010). Learning: From association to cognition. *Annual Review of Psychology, 61*, 273–301.

Shanks, D. R., & Dickinson, A. (1991). Instrumental judgment and performance under variations in action-outcome contingency and contiguity. *Memory & Cognition, 19*, 353, 360.

Sharp, D., Cole, M., & Lave, C. (1979). Education and cognitive development: The evidence from experimental research. *Monographs of the Society for Research in Child Development, 44* (1–2, Serial No. 178).

Sharps, M. J., Welton, A. L., & Price, J. L. (1993). Gender and task in the determination of spatial cognitive performance. *Psychology of Women Quarterly, 17*, 71–83.

Shaughnessy, J. J., Zimmerman, J., & Underwood, B. J. (1972). Further evidence on the MP-DP effect in free-recall learning. *Journal of Verbal Learning and Verbal Behavior, 11*, 1–12.

Shea, V. T. (1982). State-dependent learning in children receiving methylphenidate. *Psychopharmacology, 78*, 266–270.

Sheen, M., Kemp, S., & Rubin, D. (2001). Twins dispute memory ownership: A new false memory phenomenon. *Memory and Cognition, 29*, 779–788.

Sheffield, F. D., & Roby, T. B. (1950). Reward value of a non-nutritive sweet taste. *Journal of Comparative and Physiological Psychology, 43*, 471–481.

Sherry, D. F., & Schacter, D. L. (1987). The evolution of multiple memory systems. *Psychological Review, 94*, 439–454.

Sherwin, B. B. (1994). Estrogenic effects on memory in women. *Annals of the New York Academy of Science, 743*, 213–231.

Shettleworth, S. (1975). Reinforcement and the organization of behavior in golden hamsters: Hunger, environment, and food reinforcement. *Journal of Experimental Psychology: Animal Behavior Processes, 1*, 56–87.

Shimamura, A. P., Salmon, D. P., Squire, L. R., & Butters, N. (1987). Memory dysfunction and word priming in amnesia. *Behavioral Neuroscience, 101*, 347–351.

Shimp, T., Stuart, E. W., & Engle, R. W. (1991). A program of classical conditioning experiments testing variations in the CS and context. *Journal of Consumer Research, 18*, 1–12.

Sholl, M. J. (1987). Cognitive maps as orienting schemata. *Journal of Experimental Psychology: Learning, Memory, and Cognition, 13*, 615–628.

Shore, D. I., Stanford, L., MacInnes, J. W., Klein, R. M., & Brown, R. E. (2001). Of mice and men: Virtual Hebb-Williams mazes permit comparisons across species. *Cognitive, Affective, & Behavioral Neuroscience, 1*, 83–89.

Siddle, D. A. T. (1985). Effects of stimulus omission and stimulus change on dishabituation of the skin conductance response. *Journal of Experimental Psychology: Learning, Memory, and Cognition, 11,* 206–216.

Siddle, D. A. T., Kuiack, M., & Kroese, B. S. (1983). The orienting reflex. In A. Gale & J. A. Edwards (Eds.), *Physiological correlates of human behavior* (pp. 149–170). London: Academic Press.

Siddle, D. A. T., & Lipp, O. V. (1997). Orienting, habituation, and information processing: The effects of omission, the role of expectancy, and the problem of dishabituation. In P. J. Lang, R. F. Simons, & M. T. Balaban (Eds.), *Attention and orienting: Sensory and motivational processes* (pp. 23–40). Mahwah, NJ: Erlbaum.

Siegel, S. (1974). Flavor preexposure and "learned safety". *Journal of Comparative and Physiological Psychology, 87,* 1073–1082.

Siegel, S. (1982). Pharmacological habituation and learning. In M. L. Commons, R. J. Herrnstein, & A. R. Wagner (Eds.), *Quantitative analyses of behavior* (Vol. 3, pp. 195–217). Cambridge, MA: Ballinger.

Siegel, S. (1984). Pavlovian conditioning and heroin overdose: Reports by overdose victims. *Bulletin of the Psychonomic Society, 22,* 428–430.

Siegel, S. (1991). Feedforward processes in drug tolerance and dependence. In R. G. Lister & H. J. Weingartner (Eds.), *Perspectives on cognitive neuroscience* (pp. 405–416). New York: Oxford University Press.

Siegel, S., Hinson, R. E., Krank, M. D., & McCully, J. (1982). Heroin "overdose" death: Contribution of drug-associated environmental cues. *Science, 216,* 436–437.

Silverman, I., Choi, J., Mackewn, A., Fisher, M., Moro, J., & Olshansky, E. (2000). Evolved mechanisms underlying wayfinding: Further studies on the hunter-gatherer theory of spatial sex differences. *Evolution and Human Behavior, 21,* 210–213.

Silverman, I., & Eals, M. (1992). Sex differences in spatial abilities: Evolutionary theory and data. In J. H. Barkow, L. Cosmides, & J. Tooby (Eds.), *The adapted mind: Evolutionary psychology and the generation of culture* (pp. 533–549). New York: Oxford University Press.

Simcock, G., & Hayne, H. (2002). Breaking the barrier? Children fail to translate their preverbal memories into language. *Psychological Science, 13,* 225–231.

Simon, D., & Bjork, R. A. (2001). Metacognition in motor learning. *Journal of Experimental Psychology: Learning, Memory, and Cognition, 27,* 907–912.

Simons, D. J., & Chabris, C. F. (2011). What people believe about how memory works: A representative survey of the U. S. population. *Plos One, 6*(8), e22757.

Singh, D. (1970). Preference for bar pressing to obtain reward over freeloading in rats and children. *Journal of Comparative and Physiological Psychology, 73,* 320–327.

Skinner, B. F. (1938). *The behavior of organisms.* New York: Appleton, Century, Crofts.

Skinner, B. F. (1953). *Science and human behavior.* New York: Macmillan.

Skinner, B. F. (1956). A case history in scientific method. *American Psychologist, 11,* 221–233. (Reprinted in S. Koch (Ed.), *Psychology: A study of a science* [Vol. 2, pp. 359–379]. New York: McGraw-Hill).

Skinner, B. F. (1971). *Beyond freedom and dignity.* New York: Knopf.

Skinner, B. F. (1988, June). A statement on punishment. *APA Monitor,* p. 22.

Skinner, N. F. (1985). University grades and time of day of instruction. *Bulletin of the Psychonomic Society, 23,* 67.

Skurnik, I., Yoon, C., Park, D. C., & Schwarz, N. (2005). How warnings about false claims become recommendations. *Journal of Consumer Research, 31,* 713–724.

Slamecka, N. J., & Graf, P. (1978). The generation effect: Delineation of a phenomenon. *Journal of Experimental Psychology: Human Learning and Memory, 4,* 592–604.

Slater, L. (2003, November 2). The cruelest cure. *New York Times Magazine,* pp. 34–37.

Smeets, T., Otgaar, H., Candel, I., & Wolf, O. T. (2008). True or false? Memory is differentially affected by stress-induced cortisol elevations and sympathetic activity at consolidation and retrieval. *Psychoneuroendocrinology, 33,* 1378–1386.

Smith, S. M. (1979). Remembering in and out of context. *Journal of Experimental Psychology: Human Learning and Memory, 5,* 460–471.

Smith, S. M. (1985). Background music and context-dependent memory. *American Journal of Psychology, 98,* 591–603.

Smith, S. M., & Vela, E. (2001). Environmental context-dependent memory: A review and meta-analysis. *Psychonomic Bulletin & Review, 8*, 203–220.

Smotherman, W. P. (1982). Odor aversion learning by the rat fetus. *Physiology and Behavior, 29*, 769–771.

Snowman, J. (1986). Learning tactics and strategies. In G. D. Phye & T. Andre (Eds.), *Cognitive classroom learning* (pp. 243–275). New York: Academic Press.

Snyder, J., Schrepferman, L., & St. Peter, C. (1997). Origins of antisocial behavior. *Behavior Modification, 21*, 187–215.

Sokolov, Y. N. (1963). *Perception and the conditioned reflex*. London: Pergamon Press.

Solomon, P. R., & Pendlebury, W. W. (1992). Aging and memory: A model systems approach. In L. R. Squire & N. Butters (Eds.), *Neuropsychology of memory* (2nd ed., pp. 262–276). New York: Guilford Press.

Solomon, R. L., Turner, L. H., & Lessac, M. S. (1968). Some effects of delay of punishment on resistance to temptation in dogs. *Journal of Personality and Social Psychology, 8*, 233–238.

Spear, N. E., & Riccio, D. C. (1994). *Memory: Phenomenon and principles*. Boston: Allyn & Bacon.

Spence, K. W. (1956). *Behavior theory and conditioning*. New Haven, CT: Yale University Press.

Spiegler, M., & Guevremont, D. (1993). *Contemporary behavior therapy* (2nd ed.). Pacific Grove, CA: Brooks/Cole.

Sporer, S. L. (1991). Deep-deeper-deepest? Encoding strategies and the recognition of human faces. *Journal of Experimental Psychology: Learning, Memory, and Cognition, 17*, 323–333.

Squire, L. R. (1981). Two forms of human amnesia: An analysis of forgetting. *Journal of Neuroscience, 1*, 635–640.

Squire, L. R. (1987). *Memory and brain*. New York: Oxford University Press.

Squire, L. R. (1992). Memory and the hippocampus: A synthesis from findings with rats, monkeys, and humans. *Psychological Review, 99*, 195–231.

Squire, L. R., & Cohen, N. J. (1984). Human memory and amnesia. In J. L. McGaugh, G. Lynch, & N. Weinberger (Eds.), *Neurobiology of learning and memory* (pp. 3–64). New York: Guilford Press.

Squire, L. R., Knowlton, B., & Musen, G. (1993). The structure and organization of memory. *Annual Review of Psychology, 44*, 453–495.

Squire, L. R., & Slater, P. C. (1975). Forgetting in very long-term memory as assessed by an improved questionnaire technique. *Journal of Experimental Psychology: Human Learning and Memory, 1*, 50–54.

Squire, L. R., Slater, P. C., & Miller, P. L. (1981). Retrograde amnesia and bilateral electroconvulsive therapy. *Archives of General Psychiatry, 38*, 89–95.

Staddon, J. (1995, February). On responsibility and punishment. *The Atlantic Monthly*, pp. 88–94.

Standing, L., Conezio, J., & Haber, R. N. (1970). Perception and memory for pictures: Single trial learning of 2560 visual stimuli. *Psychonomic Science, 19*, 73–74.

Steele, K. M., Bass, K. E., & Crook, M. D. (1999). The mystery of the Mozart effect: Failure to replicate. *Psychological Science, 10*, 366–369.

Sternberg, R. J., & Grigorenko, E. L. (1997). Are cognitive styles still in style? *American Psychologist, 52*, 700–712.

Stevens, A., & Coupe, P. (1978). Distortions in judged spatial relations. *Cognitive Psychology, 13*, 422–437.

Stevenson, H. W., & Zigler, E. F. (1958). Probability learning in children. *Journal of Experimental Psychology, 56*, 185–192.

Stickgold, R., Hobson, J. A., & Fosse, M. (2001). Sleep, learning, and dreams: Off-line memory reprocessing. *Science, 294*, 1052–1057.

Stigler, J. W., Lee, S. Y., & Stevenson, H. W. (1986). Digit memory in Chinese and English: Evidence for a temporally limited store. *Cognition, 23*, 1–20.

Stoltz, S. B., & Lott, D. F. (1964). Establishment in rats of a persistent response producing a net loss of reinforcement. *Journal of Comparative and Physiological Psychology, 57*, 147–149.

Storm, B. C. (2011). Retrieval-induced forgetting and the resolution of competition. In A. S. Benjamin (Ed.), *Successful remembering and successful forgetting* (pp. 89–106). New York: Taylor and Francis.

Strayer, D., & Drews, F. (2007). Cell-phone-induced driver distraction. *Current Directions in Psychological Science, 16*, 128–131.

Sullivan, R. M., Taborsky-Barbar, S., Mendoza, R., Ition, A., & Leon, M. (1991). Olfactory classical conditioning in neonates. *Pediatrics, 87*, 511–518.

Sutherland, A. (2006). *Kicked, bitten and scratched*. New York: Viking/Penguin.

Swanson, H. L. (1993). Working memory in learning disability subgroups. *Journal of Experimental Child Psychology, 56*, 87–114.

Swanson, H. L., & Cooney, J. B. (1991). Learning disabilities and memory. In B. Y. L. Wong (Ed.), *Learning about learning disabilities* (pp. 103–127). New York: Academic Press.

Swanson, J., & Kinsbourne, M. (1976). Stimulant-related state-dependent learning in hyperactive children. *Science, 192*, 1354–1357.

Swartz, K. B., Chen, S., & Terrace, H. S. (1991). Serial learning by Rhesus monkeys: I. Acquisition and retention of multiple four-item lists. *Journal of Experimental Psychology: Animal behavior Processes, 17*, 396–410.

Swinnen, S. P. (1990). Interpolated activities during the knowledge-of-results delay and post-knowledge-of-results interval: Effects on performance and learning. *Journal of Experimental Psychology: Learning, Memory, and Cognition, 16*, 692–705.

Swinnen, S. P., Schmidt, R. A., Nicholson, D. E., & Shapiro, D. C. (1990). Information feedback for skill acquisition: Instantaneous knowledge of results degrades learning. *Journal of Experimental Psychology: Learning, Memory, and Cognition, 16*, 706–716.

Talarico, J. M., & Rubin, D. C. (2003). Confidence, not consistency, characterizes flashbulb memories. *Psychological Science, 14*, 455–461.

Talland, G. A. (1968). *Disorders of memory and learning*. Middlesex, UK: Penguin.

Talwar, S. K., Xu, S., Hawley, E. S., Weiss, S. A., Moxon, K. A., & Chapin, J. K. (2002, May 2). Rat navigation by remote control. *Nature, 417*, 37–38.

Tang, Y.-P., Shimizu, E., Dube, G., Rampon, C., Kerchner, G., Zhuo, M., Liu, G., & Tsien, J. (1999). Genetic enhancement of learning and memory in mice. *Nature, 401*, 63–69.

Tenenbaum, G., Tehan, G., Stewart G., & Christensen, S. (1999). Recalling a floor routine: The effects of skill and age on memory for order. *Applied Cognitive Psychology, 13*, 101–123.

Terrace, H. S. (1974). On the nature of non-responding in discrimination with and without errors. *Journal of the Experimental Analysis of Behavior, 22*, 151–159.

Terry, W. S. (1983). Effects of food primes on instrumental acquisition and performance. *Learning and Motivation, 14*, 107–122.

Terry, W. S. (1987). Everyday forgetting: Data from a diary study. *Psychological Reports, 62*, 299–303.

Terry, W. S. (1995). When proper names are not forgotten: Recall of eponymous medical disorders. *Perceptual and Motor Skills, 81*, 923–928.

Terry, W. S. (1996). Retroactive interference effects of surprising reward omission on serial spatial memory. *Journal of Experimental Psychology: Animal Behavior Processes, 22*, 472–479.

Terry, W. S., & Anthony, S. G. (1980). Arousal and short-term memory: Effects of caffeine and trial spacing on delayed alternation performance. *Animal Learning and Behavior, 8*, 368–374.

Thapar, A., Petrill, S. A., & Thompson, L. A. (1994). The heritability of memory in the Western Reserve Twin Project. *Behavior Genetics, 24*, 155–160.

Thompson, L. A., Detterman, D. K., & Plomin, R. (1991). Associations between cognitive abilities and scholastic achievement: Genetic overlap but environmental differences. *Psychological Science, 2*, 158–165.

Thompson, R. F. (2005). In search of memory traces. *Annual Review of Psychology, 56*, 1–23.

Thompson, R. F., & Gluck, M. A. (1991). Brain substrates of basic associative learning and memory. In R. G. Wister & H. J. Weingartner (Eds.), *Perspectives on cognitive neuroscience* (pp. 24–45). New York: Oxford University Press.

Thompson, R. F., & Spencer, W. A. (1966). Habituation: A model phenomenon for the study of neuronal substrates of behavior. *Psychological Review, 73*, 16–43.

Thorndike, E. L. (1898). Animal intelligence: An experimental study of the associative processes in animals. *Psychological Review Monograph Supplements, 2* (Whole No. 8, i–109).

Thorndike, E. L. (1911). *Animal intelligence: Experimental studies*. New York: Macmillan.

Thorndike, E. L. (1931). *Human learning*. New York: Century. (Cambridge, MA: The MIT Press, 1966).

Thorndyke, P. W., & Stasz, C. (1980). Individual differences in procedures for knowledge acquisition from maps. *Cognitive Psychology, 12*, 137–175.

Timberlake, W., & Allison, J. (1974). Response deprivation: An empirical approach to instrumental performance. *Psychological Review, 81*, 146–164.

Tinklepaugh, O. L. (1928). An experimental study of representative factors in monkeys. *Journal of Comparative Psychology*, *8*, 197–236.

Tolman, E. C. (1933). Sign-gestalt or conditioned reflex? *Psychological Review*, *40*, 391–411.

Tolman, E. C. (1948). Cognitive maps in rats and men. *Psychological Review*, *55*, 189–208.

Tolman, E. C., & Honzik, C. H. (1930). Introduction and removal of reward, and maze performance in rats. *University of California Publications in Psychology*, *4*, 257–275.

Tolman, E. C., Ritchie, B. F., & Kalish, D. (1946). Studies in spatial learning: II. Place learning versus response learning. *Journal of Experimental Psychology*, *36*, 221–229.

Tolman, E. C., Ritchie, B. F., & Kalish, D. (1947). Studies in spatial learning: IV. The transfer of place learning to other starting points. *Journal of Experimental Psychology*, *37*, 39–47.

Tough, P. (2012). *How children succeed*. Boston: Houghton Mifflin Harcourt.

Treffert, D. A. (1989). *Extraordinary people: Understanding "idiot savants"*. New York: Harper & Row.

Tryon, R. C. (1940). Genetic differences in maze learning in rats. *Yearbook of the National Society for the Study of Education*, *39*, 111–119.

Tuber, D. S., Hothersall, D., & Voith, V. L. (1974). Animal clinical psychology: A modest proposal. *American Psychologist*, *29*, 762–766.

Tuber, D. S., Miller, D. D., Caris, K. A., Halter, R., Linden, F., & Hennessy, M. B. (1999). Dogs in animal shelters: Problems, suggestions, and needed expertise. *Psychological Science*, *10*, 379–386.

Tully, T. (1996). Discovery of genes involved with learning and memory: An experimental synthesis of Hirschian and Benzerian perspectives. *Proceedings of the National Academy of Sciences*, *93*, 13460–13467.

Tulving, E. (1962). Subjective organization in free recall of "unrelated" words. *Psychological Review*, *69*, 344–354.

Tulving, E. (1969). Retrograde amnesia effect in free recall. *Science*, *64*, 88–90.

Tulving, E. (1983). *Elements of episodic memory*. Oxford, UK: Clarendon Press.

Tulving, E. (1985). How many memory systems are there? *American Psychologist*, *40*, 385–398.

Tulving, E. (1989). Remembering and knowing the past. *American Scientist*, *77*, 361–367.

Tulving, E., & Pearlstone, Z. (1966). Availability versus accessibility of information in memory for words. *Journal of Verbal Learning and Verbal Behavior*, *5*, 381–391.

Tulving, E., & Schacter, D. L. (1990). Priming and human memory systems. *Science*, *247*, 301–306.

Tulving, E., Schacter, D. L., & Stark, H. A. (1982). Priming effects in word-fragment completion are independent of recognition memory. *Journal of Experimental Psychology: Learning, Memory, and Cognition*, *8*, 336–342.

Tulving, E., & Thompson, D. M. (1973). Encoding specificity and retrieval processes in episodic memory. *Psychological Review*, *80*, 352–373.

Tulving, E., & Watkins, M. J. (1975). Structure of memory traces. *Psychological Review*, *82*, 261–275.

Uecker, A., Mangan, P. A., Obrzut, J. E., & Nadel, L. (1993). Down syndrome in neurobiological perspective: An emphasis in spatial cognition. *Journal of Clinical Child Psychology*, *22*, 266–276.

Underwood, B. J. (1964). The representativeness of rote verbal learning. In A. W. Melton (Ed.), *Categories of human learning* (pp. 47–56). New York: Academic Press.

Underwood, B. J. (1983). *Attributes of memory*. Glenview, IL: Scott, Foresman.

Underwood, B. J., Boruch, R. F., & Malmi, R. A. (1978). Composition of episodic memory. *Journal of Experimental Psychology: General*, *107*, 393–419.

Unsworth, N., & Engle, R. W. (2007). On the division of short-term and working memory: An examination of simple and complex span and their relation to higher order abilities. *Psychological Bulletin*, *133*, 1038–1066.

van der Kolk, B. A. (1994). The body keeps the score: Memory and the evolving psychobiology of posttraumatic stress. *Harvard Review of Psychiatry*, *1*, 253–265.

van der Kolk, B. A., & Fisler, R. (1995). Dissociation and the fragmentary nature of traumatic memories: Overview and exploratory study. *Journal of Traumatic Stress*, *8*, 505–525.

Vaughn, W., & Greene, S. L. (1984). Pigeon visual memory capacity. *Journal of Experimental Psychology: Animal Behavior Processes*, *10*, 256–271.

Verplanken, B., & Wood, W. (2006). Interventions to break and create consumer habits. *Journal of Public Policy & Marketing*, *25*, 90–103.

Volk, H. E., McDermott, K. B., Roediger, H. L., & Todd, R. D. (2006). Genetic influences on free and cued recall in long-term memory tasks. *Twins Research and Human Genetics, 9*, 623–631.

Waddill, P. J., & McDaniel, M. A. (1998). Distinctiveness effects in recall: Differential processing or privileged retrieval? *Memory & Cognition, 26*, 108–120.

Wagner, A. D., Schacter, D. L., Rotte, M., Koutstaal, W., Maril, A., Dale, A. M., Rosen, B. R., & Buckner, R. L. (1998). Building memories: Remembering and forgetting of verbal experiences as predicted by brain activity. *Science, 281*, 1188–1191.

Wagner, A. R. (1969). Frustrative nonreward: A variety of punishment? In B. A. Campbell & R. M. Church (Eds.), *Punishment and aversive behavior* (pp. 157–181). New York: Appleton, Century, Crofts.

Wagner, A. R. (1976). Priming in STM: An information processing mechanism for self-generated or retrieval-generated depression in performance. In T. J. Tighe & R. N. Leaton (Eds.), *Habituation: Perspectives from child development, animal behavior, and neurophysiology* (pp. 95–128). Hillsdale, NJ: Erlbaum.

Wagner, A. R., & Brandon, S. E. (1989). Evolution of a structured connectionist model of Pavlovian conditioning (AESOP). In S. B. Klein & R. B. Mowrer (Eds.), *Contemporary learning theories: Pavlovian conditioning and the status of traditional learning theory* (pp. 149–189). Hillside, NJ: Erlbaum.

Wagner, A. R., & Rescorla, R. A. (1972). Inhibition in Pavlovian conditioning: Application of a theory. In R. A. Boakes & M. S. Halliday (Eds.), *Inhibition and learning* (pp. 301–336). London: Academic Press.

Wagner, A. R., Siegel, S., Thomas, E., & Ellison, G. D. (1964). Reinforcement history and the extinction of a conditioned salivary response. *Journal of Comparative and Physiological Psychology, 58*, 354–358.

Wagner, A. R., & Terry, W. S. (1975). Backward conditioning to a CS following an expected vs. a surprising UCS. *Animal Learning & Behavior, 3*, 370–374.

Wagner, D. A. (1978). Memories of Morocco: The influence of age, schooling, and environment on memory. *Cognitive Psychology, 10*, 1–28.

Walcott, C. (1989, November). Show me the way to go home. *Natural History*, pp. 40–46.

Walker, M. P., Brakefield, T., Seidman, J., Morgan, A., Hobson, J. A., & Stickgold, R. (2003). Sleep and the time course of motor skill learning. *Learning and Memory, 10*, 275–284.

Walker, S. (1987). *Animal learning: An introduction*. London: Routledge & Kegan Paul.

Walls, R. T., Zane, T., & Ellis, T. (1981). Forward and backward chaining, and whole task methods: Training assembly tasks in vocational rehabilitation. *Behavior Modification, 5*, 61–74.

Waring, J. D., Payne, J. D., Schacter, D. L., & Kensinger, E. A. (2010). Impact of individual differences upon emotion-induced memory trade-offs. *Cognition and Emotion, 24*, 150–167.

Warrington, E. K., & Weiskrantz, L. (1968a). A new method of testing long-term retention with special reference to amnesic patients. *Nature, 217*, 972–974.

Warrington, E. K., & Weiskrantz, L. (1968b). A study of learning and retention in amnesic patients. *Neuropsychologia, 6*, 283–291.

Wasserman, E. A., Dorner, W. W., & Kao, S. F. (1990). Contributions of specific cell information to judgments of interevent contingency. *Journal of Experimental Psychology: Learning, Memory, and Cognition, 16*, 509–521.

Watson, J. B. (1936). Autobiography. In C. Murchison (Ed.), *A history of psychology in autobiography* (Vol. 3, pp. 271–281). Worcester, MA: Clark University Press.

Watson, J. B., & Rayner, R. (1920). Conditioned emotional reactions. *Journal of Experimental Psychology, 3*, 1–20.

Watson, J. M., & Strayer, D. L. (2010). Supertaskers: Profiles in extraordinary multitasking ability. *Psychonomic Bulletin and Review, 17*, 479–485.

Waugh, N. C., & Norman, D. A. (1965). Primary memory. *Psychological Review, 72*, 89–104.

Weingartner, H., Adefris, W., Eich, J. E., & Murphy, D. L. (1976). Encoding-imagery specificity in alcohol state-dependent learning. *Journal of Experimental Psychology: Human Learning and Memory, 2*, 83–87.

Weingartner, H., Miller, H., & Murphy, D. L. (1977). Mood-dependent retrieval of verbal associations. *Journal of Abnormal Psychology, 86*, 276–284.

Weinstock, S. (1954). Resistance to extinction of a running response following partial reinforcement under widely spaced trials. *Journal of Comparative and Physiological Psychology, 48*, 318–322.

Weiss, J. M. (1977). Psychosomatic disorders. In J. D. Maser & M. E. P. Seligman (Eds.), *Psychopathology: Experimental models* (pp. 232–269). San Francisco: Freeman.

Weldon, M. S., & Roediger, H. L. (1987). Altering retrieval demands reverses the picture superiority effect. *Memory & Cognition, 15*, 269–280.

Werker, J. F. (1989, January–February). Becoming a native listener. *American Scientist, 77*, 54–59.

West, R. L., Crook, T. H., & Barron, K. L. (1992). Everyday memory performance across the life span: Effects of age and noncognitive individual differences. *Psychology and Aging, 7*, 72–82.

Westbrook, J. I., Woods, A., Rob, I., Dunsmuir, W. T. M., & Day, R. O. (2010). Association of interruptions with an increased risk and severity of medication administration errors. *Archives of Internal Medicine, 170*, 683–690.

Wetherington, C. L. (1982). Is adjunctive behavior a third class of behavior? *Neuroscience & Biobehavioral Reviews, 6*, 329–350.

Wheeler, M. A., & Roediger, H. L. (1992). Disparate effects of repeated testing: Reconciling Ballard's (1914) and Bartlett's (1932) results. *Psychological Science, 3*, 240–245.

White, N. H., & Milner, P. M. (1992). The psychobiology of reinforcers. *Annual Review of Psychology, 43*, 443–471.

Whitlow, J. W., & Wagner, A. R. (1984). Memory and habituation. In H. V. S. Peeke & L. Petrinovich (Eds.), *Habituation, sensitization, and behavior* (pp. 103–153). New York: Academic Press.

Whitten, W. B., & Leonard, J. M. (1981). Directed search through autobiographical memory. *Memory & Cognition, 9*, 566–579.

Wickelgren, I. (1997). Getting a grasp on working memory. *Science, 275*, 1580–1582.

Wickelgren, W. A. (1970). Multitrace strength theory. In D. A. Norman (Ed.), *Models of human memory* (pp. 65–100). New York: Academic Press.

Wickens, D. D., Dalezman, R. E., & Eggemeier, F. T. (1976). Multiple encoding of word attributes in memory. *Memory & Cognition, 4*, 307–310.

Wiggs, C. L. (1993). Aging and memory for frequency of occurrence of novel, visual stimuli: Direct and indirect measures. *Psychology and Aging, 8*, 400–410.

Wightman, D. C., & Sistrunk, F. (1987). Part-task training strategies in simulated carrier landing final-approach training. *Human Factors, 29*, 245–254.

Wilensky, A. E., Schafe, G. E., Kristensen, M. P., & LeDoux, J. E. (2006). Rethinking the fear circuit: The central nucleus of the amygdala is required for the acquisition, consolidation, and expression of Pavlovian fear conditioning. *Journal of Neuroscience, 26*, 12387–12396.

Wilkins, S. M., Jones, M. G., Koral, D. L., Gold, P. E., & Manning, C. A. (1997). Age-related differences in an ecologically based study of route learning. *Psychology and Aging, 12*, 372–375.

Williams, B. A. (1994). Conditioned reinforcement: Neglected or outmoded explanatory concept? *Psychonomic Bulletin & Review, 1*, 457–475.

Williams, J. M. G., & Markar, H. R. (1991). Money hidden and rediscovered in subsequent manic phases: A case of action dependent on mood state. *British Journal of Psychiatry, 159*, 579–581.

Williams, L. M. (1994). Recall of childhood trauma: A prospective study of women's memories of childhood sexual abuse. *Journal of Consulting and Clinical Psychology, 62*, 1167–1176.

Williamson, V. J., Jilka, S. R., Fry, J., Finkel, S., Mullensiefen, D., & Stewart, L. (2011). How do "earworms" start? Classifying the everyday circumstances of involuntary musical imagery. *Psychology of Music, 40*, 259–284.

Wilson, B. A. (1987). *Rehabilitation of memory*. New York: Guilford Press.

Wilson, B. A. (1992). Rehabilitation and memory disorders. In L. R. Squire & N. Butters (Eds.), *Neuropsychology of memory* (2nd ed., pp. 315–321). New York: Guilford Press.

Wilson, M. A., & McNaughton, B. L. (1994). Reactivation of hippocampal ensemble memories during sleep. *Science, 265*, 676–679.

Winograd, E. (1981). Elaboration and distinctiveness in memory for faces. *Journal of Experimental Psychology: Human Learning and Memory, 7*, 181–190.

Winograd, E., & Soloway, R. M. (1986). On forgetting the locations of things stored in special places. *Journal of Experimental Psychology: General, 115*, 366–372.

Wirtz, P. W., & Harrell, A. V. (1987). Effects of postassault exposure to attack-similar stimuli on longterm recovery of victims. *Journal of Consulting and Clinical Psychology, 55*, 10–16.

Wittman, W. T., & Healy, A. F. (1995). A long-term retention advantage for spatial information learned naturally and in the laboratory. In A. F. Healy & L. E. Bourne (Eds.), *Learning and memory of knowledge and skills* (pp. 170–205). Thousand Oaks, CA: Sage.

Wixted, J. T. (1991). The conditions and consequences of maintenance rehearsal. *Journal of Experimental Psychology: Learning, Memory, and Cognition, 17*, 963–973.

Wolf, A. S. (1980). Homicide and blackout in Alaskan natives. *Journal of Studies on Alcohol, 41*, 456–462.

Wolf, M. M., Giles, D. K., & Hall, R. V. (1968). Experiments with token reinforcement in a remedial classroom. *Behavior Research and Therapy, 6*, 51–54.

Woloshyn, V. E., Willoughby, T., Wood, E., & Pressley, M. (1990). Elaborative interrogation facilitates adult learning of factual paragraphs. *Journal of Educational Psychology, 82*, 513–524.

Wolpe, J. (1969). *The practice of behavior therapy.* New York: Pergamon Press.

Wood, W., Tam, L., & Witt, M. G. (2005). Changing circumstances, disrupting habits. *Journal of Personality and Social Psychology, 88*, 918–933.

Woodruff-Pak, D. S., Papka, M., & Simon, E. W. (1994). Eyeblink classical conditioning in Down's syndrome, fragile X syndrome, and normal adults over and under age 35. *Neuropsychology, 8*, 14–24.

Wright, A. A., Cook, R. G., Rivera, J. J., Shyan, M. R., Neiworth, J. J., & Jitsumori, M. (1990). Naming, rehearsal, and interstimulus interval effects in memory processing. *Journal of Experimental Psychology: Learning, Memory, and Cognition, 6*, 1043–1059.

Wright, A. A., Santiago, H. C., Sands, S. F., Kendrick, D. F., & Cook, R. G. (1985). Memory processing of serial lists by pigeons, monkeys and people. *Science, 229*, 287–289.

Wulf, G., & Schmidt, R. A. (1989). The learning of generalized motor programs: Reducing the relative frequency of knowledge of results enhances memory. *Journal of Experimental Psychology: Learning, Memory, and Cognition, 15*, 748–757.

Wynn, K. (1992). Addition and subtraction by human infants. *Nature, 358*, 749–750.

Wynn, K. (1995). Infants possess a system of numerical knowledge. *Current Directions in Psychological Science, 4*, 172–177.

Yates, F. A. (1966). *The art of memory.* Chicago: University of Chicago Press.

Yerkes, R. M., & Dodson, J. D. (1908). The relation of strength of stimulus to rapidity of habit-formation. *Journal of Comparative Neurology of Psychology, 18*, 459–482.

Young, A. W., Hay, D. C., & Ellis, A. W. (1985). The faces that launched a thousand slips: Everyday difficulties and errors in recognising people. *British Journal of Psychology, 76*, 495–523.

Young, G. C. D., & Martin, M. (1981). Processing of information about self by neurotics. *British Journal of Clinical Psychology, 20*, 205–212.

Young, M. E. (1995). On the origin of personal causality theories. *Psychonomic Bulletin & Review, 2*, 83–104.

Young, R. J., & Cipreste, C. F. (2004). Applying animal learning theory: Training captive animals to comply with veterinary and husbandry procedures. *Animal Welfare, 13*, 225–232.

Zajonc, R. B. (1968). Attitudinal effects of mere exposure. *Journal of Personality and Social Psychology Monograph, 9* (Part 2), 1–28.

Zangwill, O. L. (1937). An investigation of the relation between the processes of reproducing and recognizing simple figures, with special reference to Koffka's trace theory. *British Journal of Psychology, 27*, 250–276.

Zeeuws, I., & Soetens, E. (2007). Verbal memory performance improves via an acute administration of D-amphetamine. *Human Psychopharmacology: Clinical and Experimental, 22*, 279–287.

Zhao, X. (1997, October). Clutter and serial order redefined and retested. *Journal of Advertising Research, 37*(5), 57–73.

Zoladek, L., & Roberts, W. A. (1978). The sensory bases of spatial memory in the rat. *Animal Learning & Behavior, 6*, 77–81.

Zola-Morgan, S., & Squire, L. R. (1993). Neuroanatomy of memory. *Annual Review of Neuroscience, 16*, 547–563.

Author Index

Subject Index

Page numbers in italics indicate figures and page numbers in bold indicate tables.